The Lives of Roger Casement

Roger Casement at about thirty years of age. Courtesy of the National Library of Ireland.

The Lives of

Roger Casement

B. L. Reid

New Haven and London , Yale University Press

International standard book number: 0-300-01801-0

Designed by John O. C. McCrillis
and set in Janson type.
Printed in the United States of America by
The Murray Printing Co., ForgeVillage, Massachusetts.

Published in Great Britain, Europe, and Africa by
Yale University Press, Ltd., London.
Distributed in Latin America by Kaiman & Polon,
Inc., New York City; in Australasia by Book & Film
Services, Artarmon, N.S.W., Australia;
in Japan by John Weatherhill, Inc., Tokyo.

"A Good Man—Has Had Fever: Casement in the Congo"
was first published in the *Sewanee Review* 82 (Summer
1974). Copyright 1974 by the University of the South.
Reprinted by permission of the editor.

To certain good friends:
   Lois and Jess Cusick
   Barbara and Geoffrey Whatmore

I made awful mistakes, and did heaps of things wrong, confused much and failed at much—but I *very near* came to doing some big things. . . . It was only a shadow they tried on June 26; the real man was gone.

Casement to Richard Morten, 28 July 1916

CONTENTS

Illustrations

MAPS

Preface

ANYONE who does any work on Irish affairs of this century soon encounters, in one or another melodramatic situation, the mysterious figure of Roger Casement. These scenes strike the mind's eye with a certain characteristic strangeness: the vaguest thing in them is the central figure; there is a great deal of bright light around the edges but the light on Casement himself is flickering and lurid. One can make out a dim handsome figure, doing and suffering remarkable things, but the man himself as a real person, a nature, a character, never comes clear. The figure seems defined only in outlines, without depth and without content: what Gulley Jimson calls a figment. One began to wonder if Casement was ever there, if he existed. Perhaps he had always been only the ghost that W. B. Yeats heard "beating on the door" in 1937, more than twenty years after the recorded death, when this "most gallant gentleman" was said to have been "in quicklime laid." There had been a great deal of talk and writing about Casement, even several "lives," but it was nearly all about his public life, the big things that he did or that were done to him; none of it made any real penetration of the man, or made him seem any more knowable or even credible.

This "Casement" did not add up, did not make sense; he was a set of contradictions, an incoherency. Was he indeed a most gallant gentleman, or was the phrase ritual Irish persiflage? How is one to understand a man who to the public view of one country is a corrupt and despicable person, at best a fool, and to the public view of a neighboring country is a great man, a hero and a sort of lay saint? Ireland put Roger Casement in her secular pantheon; Madame Tussaud put his effigy in her Chamber of Horrors. Does the difference lie altogether in point of view or is some of the conflict real and organic, built into the nature of the man himself?

I began to feel that Casement was one of those men who embody the dilemma of a culture and present a general problem: that, excessively strange as he seemed in what he was and in what happened to him, he was still not only "one of us" but signally so, in fact symptomatic, a representative modern figure, not a freak but an archetype. Indeed Casement's very strangeness, his complex dualities, set inside the melodramatic order of circumstances that life offered him or that he reached out and seized (what Yeats would have called his Body of Fate), join to create his representativeness, his racial familiarity.

Feeling that all of this called for a better grounded understanding than was available in the printed record, I resolved to try to study the Casement materials more patiently and seriously and objectively than they had been studied before, seeking not the White Knight or the Black Beast but the actual man who did all those strange things. When I went to work in London and Dublin in the summer of 1971, I soon found that able people had anticipated me and that I was galling the kibe of David Rudkin, who was writing a BBC play about Casement, and of Brian Inglis, who was well along with a full-scale biography. There was one day of comedy when the three of us were trying to read the same Casement diary at the same time in the same guarded room in the Public Record Office in London. Mr. Rudkin and Mr. Inglis treated me kindly, and I had resolved to persevere in any case, feeling that my personal obligation to the problem of Casement had not diminished and suspecting that the problem was complex and significant enough to accommodate us all. Mr. Rudkin's and Mr. Inglis's works are out now and I am happy to say that they are excellent and that the Casement record is therefore no longer in its old shabby state.

For one thing, the issue of Casement's ambiguous sexuality has at last received intelligent and dispassionate attention. I do not think the matter has much to do with what I wish to call character: the stature, the moral tilt and size of the man; but it has a great deal to do with personality, the shape and tonality of the man. It must interest one who wishes to know everything that is knowable about his subject; and one who accepts Casement's "black" diaries as authentic (as I do for reasons I explain in Appendix B) must take them very seriously as evidence of personality and must accept the idea that (in conjunction with other evidence) they demonstrate that Casement was an active homosexual. What *weight* to give the fact, is another and difficult question. I do not think it makes Casement a worse or better man: it merely makes him a special kind of man. It seems to me chiefly to dramatize the fact of tension, stress, dividedness in his nature, an indwelling mysteriousness that one ought neither to deny nor to simplify.

In a generally brilliant review-article treating Brian Inglis's biography, the Ulster-born playwright David Rudkin, after saluting fairly the excellences of Inglis's book, goes on to propose an alternative way of putting Casement together as an "essential continuum": by assigning a definitive function to his homosexuality, situated within a Freudian frame of "emancipated anality."[1] Mr. Rudkin argues that as a successful practicing sodomist, generally a receiving partner, "violently" enjoying his own anus, "in absolute sensual harmony with his own backside,"[2] Casement found his own extraordinary unity: his special freedom to function independently, even rebelliously, within the "anti-anal" value-system of Western culture and politics, and to do so with a peculiar grace and serenity.

In the crudeness of summary I am doing poor justice to Rudkin's ingenious, carefully qualified argument. I do not mean to scorn it; I think there is a good deal in it: that Casement was indeed basically at ease with his anus (though the Western ethic kept warning him to be uneasy with his ease) and that the fact gave him the only deep serenity he knew, fitful and hedged with danger as it must have been. But Rudkin's complex analysis seems to me to lead finally to too much simplicity. I do not believe that Casement's emancipated anality was a defining condition in his life as a whole, in which I find pitifully little ease of spirit or wholeness of mind. Like the rest of us Rudkin has wished to straighten Casement out, to make sense of him. But one must make the right sense, the sense that is visible in the evidence, and accept the leading of the evidence to the possibility that Casement's Body of Fate was indeed a kilt upon which his coloring altered bewilderingly, chameleon-wise. Inglis may very well have been right in his reticent decision to leave Casement "as fragmented and elusive as ever." For he was fragmented, and he was elusive: he was defined not by coherency but by complex tensions barely contained.

Both Rudkin and Inglis have rightly emphasized Casement's Irish representativeness, what Rudkin calls "the full rich meaning of

Casement's example in modern schismatic Ireland."[3] No one who goes into the story at all can fail to be haunted by the way in which Casement's history incarnates not only the motives of 1916 but the same passions deadly and alive today. And I am haunted still more by the feeling alluded to earlier, that the man's deep dividedness expresses a condition even more general in the culture of us all. The elusiveness of the Casement persona to the spectator was its own elusiveness; his was a divided spirit pursuing wholeness: in a very strange way his nobility was a function of that sundering.

I have tried to examine all the available evidence, with special attention to Casement's intimate writings, his diaries and letters, in order to find the daily Casement who was to me the primary mystery. It has seemed important to do justice to the well-known public actions: the investigations in the Congo and the Putumayo, the mission to Germany, the dramatic return to Ireland, the trial and execution for high treason; also to the unresolved cruxes: the political partisanship, the morality of motives, the homosexuality, the Black Diaries, and the charge of forgery. But mindful of the primary mystery, I have sought mainly to lay out the evidence for an induction about the character of the man behind the famous events.

In the course of this book I find myself reprimanding, in a way that both will think unbecoming, the English and the Irish for their treatment of Casement and the issue he raises. My argument is that the most general and audible response in both countries has been wrong in emphasis and in tone, a set of defensive passions not well based on fact. Of course there have been honorable exceptions, but those voices speaking more gently have been harder to hear. I hope that readers in England and Ireland will believe that my heavy-father chiding arises from admiration and good will: one who loves both the English and the Irish must wish them to love each other, to behave more rationally, with less wrong swollen partisan feeling, on the issues that divide them. I hope this book will make it easier to think and talk about Casement from a point beyond ignorance and if possible beyond petulance.

Acknowledgments

THE last and keenest pleasure in preparing such a book as this is the satisfaction of naming the many persons and institutions who have offered kindness and generous assistance.

At the beginning of my work Brigadier R. F. Parry, Mrs. Elspeth Parry, and the late Major J. O. Parry gave me their blessing, their hospitality, and much practical help. So did their neighbors Mrs. Guy Bloxam and H. Montgomery Hyde. Brian Inglis and David Rudkin, rivals of my watch, offered good will and a friendly helpfulness, as did Jon Stallworthy, John L. Nevinson, W. C. Allison, J. P. Smith, Manus Nunan, and Miss Joan Cambridge—all of these in England. My friend Geoffrey Whatmore was of immense help in obtaining illustrative material. My friend and former student Cornelia Clark Cook put in some hard work for me at Oxford.

My Irish obligations are still more numerous. I should pay tribute especially to Mrs. Florence Patterson of Crawfordsburn, County Down, sister of Bulmer Hobson and herself a friend of Casement, for her generous interest and general usefulness. Seamus Clarke of Ballycastle, County Antrim, helped me to understand that important local scene. Jack and Maire Sweeney gave hospitality and information in County Clare.

In and about Dublin I accumulated much pleasant indebtedness. Professors Roger McHugh and Nessa Doran of University College, Dublin, offered special knowledge and good will. Michael and Grainne Yeats gave me their typical hospitable kindness. Dr. John de Courcy Ireland provided a fascinating re-creation of the seagoing side of the Easter Rising. Liam Redmond and Barbara MacDonagh Redmond spoke to me particularly of the personalities associated with Casement and the Rising. (I should also thank the nameless countryman who hauled me back two miles on the pilion of his motorcycle, my briefcase flapping in the rain, after I had got lost searching for the Redmonds' house in Chapelizod.) John and Nuala Creagh gave me not only family recollections but a view of the memorial art inspired by Casement and his legend. Colm Gavan Duffy talked to me of the parts played by his father and by Serjeant Sullivan in the legal defense of Casement. M. G. O'Beirn told me of Casement's friendship with his doctor father and other Tawin Islanders. My friends Richard and Sigrid Weber smoothed my way in Dublin and helped with details of my quest. My thanks go also to Gordon Standing of the *Irish Times*, to P. M. Bottomley of the Public Record Office of Northern Ireland, to Mrs. Seamus McCall, and to Frank Columb, Eoin O'Maille, William Glynn, Michael J. Murphy, and the Reverend P. O'Gallachair.

My heaviest obligations, conferred with great lightness of spirit, are owed to staff members of the repositories that hold the two principal Casement archives: the Public Record Office in London and the National Library of Ireland in Dublin. In London I wish especially to name J. L. Walford, C. D. Chalmers, N. G. Cox, and P. A. Penfold; in Dublin, Padraic Henchy, Noel Kissane, Desmond Kennedy, Jerry Nash, and Michael Hewson of the Library staff, and my fellow researcher Robert Henry West. All of these men treated me with the handsomest courtesy, a helpfulness far beyond the call of duty. I am obliged as well to staff members of the National Museum and the National Gallery of Ireland.

In South Hadley, Joan Regan helped me a great deal with details of research, working with energy and common sense as well as imagination. My colleagues Eugenio Suárez-Galbán and Emmanuel Atolagbe advised me on certain exotic problems of translation. Michael Feinstein helped me greatly with photographic illustrations.

Professor James Ellis of Mount Holyoke College and Professor David Greene of New York University read my long manuscript with discriminating sympathy and offered suggestions which I have valued and adopted. My wife, Jane Davidson Reid, and my son, Colin Way Reid, not only read the manuscript but supported me in many ways culminating in the last big task, the making of an index. I also wish to thank George Core of the *Sewanee Review* for his kind continuing interest in my work.

To Chester Kerr, Ellen Graham, Nancy Ahlstrom, and John O. C. McCrillis of Yale University Press, and most particularly to

Whitney Blake, my former editor there, I am grateful for the good will, the good judgment, and the hard work they have devoted to the long process of making my manuscript into a book. It was Mr. Blake who turned up at a late stage a valuable group of letters from Roger Casement to Poultney Bigelow in the collection of Princess Simon Sidamon-Eristoff and the Honorable Constantine Sidamon-Eristoff—to whom, and to whose archivist, Dr. R. E. Allen, I return thanks for making the letters available to me.

A Senior Fellowship from the National Endowment for the Humanities made the whole thing possible, and I wish to thank that organization, especially in the persons of Wallace B. Edgerton and Guinivere L. Griest. It is a pleasure, too, to acknowledge the steady support of President David B. Truman and the Trustees of Mount Holyoke College.

Abbreviations Used in Citations

NLI   National Library of Ireland (Dublin)
NYPL   New York Public Library
PRO FO   Public Record Office (London), Foreign Office
PRO HO   Public Record Office (London), Home Office

I A Touch of Conquistador

WHEN Roger David Casement was born, on the first day of September 1864 at Doyle's Cottage, Lawson Terrace, in the Sandycove suburb of Dublin, his family was already long and fairly illustrious in the land. When in his later days of intensified Irishry he congratulated himself on carrying "scarce a drop of English blood" in his veins,[1] however, he must have been thinking only of his paternal line, since his mother's people had been English yeomanry. In the deep past Casements had arrived among the Norse invaders of the Isle of Man and Roger Casement pictured them with pride as "Manx Gaelic speakers all."[a] The Irish branch of the family stemmed from Hugh Casement, who crossed from Ramsay in the Isle of Man early in the eighteenth century and married the daughter of the rector of Ballinderry in County Antrim, the northeastern tip of Ireland. Thenceforward the Casements were mainly rural gentry, persons of land and means in the beautiful Antrim glen and seacoast country of Ballymena and Ballycastle. Four uncles of Casement's father, for example, held 8,387 acres with a rentroll in 1891 of £5,300. But Casements also became doctors, lawyers, Church of Ireland clergymen, colonial administrators, and officers of the British army and navy. The tradition of ease, however, had little to do with Roger Casement, who was hard up all his life and contrived to be a generous and charitable person on a limited income of his own earning.

[a]To Mrs. A. W. Hutton, 26 November 1904. NLI 8602. Originally the name had been Asmund and MacAsmund, with the last letter of the prefix eventually attaching itself to the root name and the whole anglicized as Casement in the seventeenth century. This was Roger Casement's own understanding of his paternal lineage. Another tradition held that the family was originally French: Caissement. So far as I can see, the account of the family in Burke's *Landed Gentry of Ireland* wipes out the line of the senior Roger Casement altogether.

1

Casement's maternal line, the Jephsons, stemmed from Hampshire and Leicestershire but were established in Ireland by the middle of the seventeenth century. The Jephsons, too, produced persons of some eminence: several baronets, a Chief Justice of the King's Bench, a Postmaster General of Ireland. Casement's mother, Anne Jephson, was the daughter of James Jephson and Anne Ball. Her sister Grace, "wee Auntie," married Edward Bannister of Liverpool and Africa and founded a home and a family that were to matter a great deal to Roger Casement.

Casement's father, also named Roger, was born in 1819 and as a young Cornet in the Third Dragoon Guards went in 1839 to India, where a cousin, Major-General Sir William Casement, was a member of the Supreme Council. Virtually all his military service was spent in India, but he told his family one tale of romantic adventure in Europe that became an enduring heroic legend to his son. The story has appeared in so many forms and sounds so improbable that one is inclined to dismiss it altogether as myth; but the skeptical reader can find it confirmed in the memoirs of the Hungarian patriot Ludwig Kossuth. Roger Casement resigned his commission in India late in the summer of 1848. What he did for the next year is unknown, but in September 1849 he abruptly appeared in Widdin, in Turkish territory on the Danube, and announced that he had "come from India in order to fight for Hungarian freedom." Defeated in the struggle for Hungarian independence, Kossuth had taken refuge in Widdin with about 5,000 men, the remnant of his army. He was expecting momentarily that the Turks would be forced to give in to Austrian pressure to yield up the rebels, and everyone agreed that England was the only power capable of protecting them from vengeance. As Kossuth was racking his brain to find a way to get a message through safely and swiftly to the British Prime Minister, there suddenly appeared "the typical Englishman, tired and dusty, top hat at the back of his neck, his huge umbrella under his arm."[b] Having remarked that he had evidently arrived too late to fight for Hungarian freedom, the man sat down, wiped his brow, placed his umbrella between his legs, and began to clean his fingernails. A friend whispered to Kossuth that here was the man they needed, the messenger to Palmerston. They explained the case to the visitor: the lives of the patriots hung on the chance of their finding a courier who

[b]The account is taken from Ludwig Kossuth's *Meine Schriften aus der Emigration*, III: 342–46. (My translation.)

would ride non-stop to London, never resting until he had placed the letter in Palmerston's hands. "The Englishman" stuffed the letter into his knapsack, pulled his hat over his eyes, put his umbrella under his arm, and said good-bye. In a few minutes they heard the clatter of his horse in the street, and the next noise they heard was that of the sensation created in England and on the Continent by Palmerston's publication of Kossuth's letter. The patriots had not even learned their messenger's name.

But the story was not finished. Having been freed by British intervention, Kossuth was traveling in America a year or so later. En route to Niagara Falls his train stopped in a station to allow another train to pass and an assembled crowd called the famous man to appear at the window of his coach. At this moment, "the arm of a man extends from the window of the train passing and gives me a calling card. I take it. On it was printed: 'Mr. Roger Casement' and under this the words in pencil: 'I gave Palmerston the letter from Widdin'." Only thus did Kossuth learn the name of "this brave man," and he never heard of him again; but he called down "God's abundant blessing . . . on his ways." Ironically, Kossuth told the whole story to illustrate "the English character"—the Englishman's "wonderful energy and imperturbable tenacity"—not realizing that his prize exhibit was an Irishman.

An American travel journal of forty pages, kept by Roger Casement, Senior, confirms that he was in New York in October 1850. A few other odd bits of writing from his pen have survived—enough to authenticate the eccentric aspects of character visible in the Kossuth episode: a long essay on "spiritual" phenomena, especially in India; a letter, dated 26 October 1870, offering a scheme for the defense of Paris by means of a herd of 10,000 horses which were to bring in supplies and then remain to be eaten; a letter of 28 June 1872 on the keeping of captive birds, written by Roger Casement as an amateur of forty years' experience.[2] The Irishman was not so un-English after all.

The senior Roger Casement was invalided out of the army in 1854 as a Captain on half pay. Thus he was officially an invalid and fifteen years her senior when he married Anne Jephson, born in 1834. The marriage produced four children: Agnes, always called Nina, in 1856; Charles in 1861; Thomas in 1863; Roger in 1864. The rootlessness that became a defining fact of Casement's life began for him at birth. The father was a man in pursuit of health, and the family moved restlessly about with him, spending intervals in France, Italy or various parts of England, and once staying several years near St. Heliers in the island of Jersey. Nina recalled her father's habit of swimming out into the sea there with one or another son on this back, then tossing him off.[3] Young Roger learned to swim before either Charlie or Tom and was an eager and powerful swimmer all his life.

The Casements were a tall, good-looking couple and they produced handsome children. The general conformation was one of height, strength and grace of movement, dark coloring in hair and skin, and grey eyes—though in his first years Roger Casement showed blue eyes and blond curls about a well-shaped head. He was to mature into one of the handsomest men in Europe, and he was a beautiful child with a gay, humorous, confiding way about him. According to Nina, Charlie and Tom as "the Terrors" tended to league together against their elder sister, and when they grew too outrageous young Roger would come to her defense with swinging fists and butting head.[4]

Though neither unloving nor unloved, Captain Casement was a stern parent, and the real center of warmth and affection in the family was his gentle, graceful wife. Anne Casement died, however, in September 1873 and her husband followed in May 1877. After the death of his mother, Roger Casement turned more and more grave and inward. By the time he became a full orphan at less than thirteen, he was a tall, dark, slender lad with a look of serious and troubled spirituality. Captain Casement had used up his patrimony, and when he died there was little left for his children, who became wards in Chancery with small expectations and no hope of genteel education or professional training. In effect the four orphans were dependent upon the charity of relations and the strength of their own powers.

Roger Casement, Senior, was a member of the Church of Ireland. Anne Casement was a convert to the Catholic Church who subdued her preference in submission to her husband and allowed her children to be reared as Protestants. But in a gesture that was to bear consequences at the end of Roger Casement's life, when on a holiday in north Wales apart from her husband, on 5 August 1868, she secretly accomplished the baptism of her three sons in the Catholic Church of St. Mary's in Rhyl. Roger was a church chorister as a small boy, and Nina remembered him at seven fleeing his first performance in his surplice because he thought he would be required to sing "all by himself" as he had seen others do.[5] Though he never developed a musical taste of any sophistication, he liked to sing and sang well such traditional things as Schubert's "Serenade" and Moore's Melodies, often to Nina's accompaniment. In mature life his speaking voice was a part of the charm to which many attested, a pleasantly modulated baritone, peculiarly persuasive, his accent that of a cultivated Englishman with a lingering bit of Irish tuning.[c]

The Casement orphans were often separated from each other in the care of relations in Ulster or Liverpool. Nina and Roger lived much with their mother's sister in Stanley, a pleasant park-like suburb of Liverpool with little city feeling about it. Their uncle Edward Bannister was a West African agent of the big Liverpool trading company of Hatton and Cookson and later a British Vice-Consul at Loanda and Boma in the Congo, and he was absent from home for what seemed years at a time. It struck young Roger as a poor sort of life; but it was one he was to emulate almost helplessly. There were three young Bannister cousins, Gertrude or "Gee," Elizabeth, and Eddie. "Wee Auntie" did her best to mother the orphans and looked on Roger particularly as a second son. Nina, much the eldest of the five cousins, stood somewhat apart. She was becoming a difficult person, jealous, easily injured, bitter tongued.

Roger, or Roddie, with his dark good looks, was a romantic figure to the younger Bannister girls, especially to Gertrude, exactly nine years younger than he. Fifty years later both Elizabeth and Gertrude remembered being at play in their back garden when Roddie dashed past them and sailed over a high fence. He was given to demonstrations of that kind. Nina told of his vaulting a farmyard fence in a game of hare and hounds and sinking to his armpits in a pile of dung. At sixteen he had nearly reached his full adult height of six feet and two inches and had the frame and movement of an athlete. He was a graceful dancer and played tennis and football, but best of all he liked swimming off the rocks in the bays of Antrim or taking long walks in the mountain glens. The landscape entered his blood. In Pentonville Prison under sentence of death he said to Gertrude: "When they

[c]A hostile colleague of Casement's during later years in the Consular Service, Ernest Hambloch, admitted the seductiveness of Casement's speech: "His greatest charm was his voice, which was very musical . . . yet I think he was quite unconscious of the charm of his voice. A cultured American at Rio once said to me, 'Casement has not kissed the Blarney Stone for nothing.' An Englishman put it another way. 'Casement doesn't talk to you,' he said. 'He purrs at you.' " *British Consul*, p. 71.

have done with me, don't let me lie in this dreadful place—take me back to Murlough and let me lie there."[6]

He also fell into the more standard and statuesque romantic postures of adolescence. On 20 May 1881 he was confirmed at the Anglican Church of St. Anne's in Stanley, and Gertrude described the event later: "I can remember him in dark clothes, very tall, very slim, and very handsome . . . I think he went off by himself for a long walk afterward." He began to write poetry, very copious, very bad, in the manner of the English Romantics. And he had begun to brood much on what James Joyce was to call the sorrowful legend of Ireland. He fell often into reverie, his deep-set grey eyes far fixed; when offered the traditional penny for his thoughts he usually answered: "I was thinking of Ireland." In a school play he was cast as a girl because of his almost feminine good looks, and at the same period he fell in love with the "principal boy" in a Liverpool pantomime, played by a girl: "Her name was Millie Hylton, and she was very pretty," wrote Gertrude. Roger's part in the affair was limited to repeated visits to the play and gifts of candy and flowers sent to the stage door.[7]

Casement's formal education was completed at Ballymena Academy, a diocesan school headed by Robert King whose seven sons were among the students and whose wife saw to the physical welfare of the boys. It was a sound establishment and Casement acquired gook grounding in Greek, Latin, and French, in the English poets, and in classical and English history. He won prizes in classical studies, formed his taste for Keats and Shelley and Tennyson, and did a good deal of scribbling of his own. History was his great love, and he deeply resented the fact that the curriculum, on the English model, paid little attention to Irish history. The Irish language received no attention whatever, of course, although both Dr. King and Dr. Reeves, another master, were graduates of Trinity College, Dublin, and could speak Irish. One evening Casement chanced to hear Dr. King carrying on a long conversation in fluent Irish with an old beggar-man who came to the door, and the episode moved him strangely: it had never occurred to him before that Ireland possessed a tongue that belonged to her alone and that to some Irishmen it was still a living thing.

In a later letter to his great friend E. D. Morel the African reformer, in which he laments the fact that both of them are hampered as advocates of dear causes by being "so confoundedly poor," Casement sets at fifteen and a half the age at which, left penniless by his father's extravagance, he "went off into the world straight from my old schoolmaster's house."[8] The year, then, must have been 1880. After that, as Casement went on to say, justly, it was "entirely off my own bat I got every step in life." His movements for the next dozen years were striking and significant, but it is not easy to follow them fully or confidently.

What he did first was to settle in Liverpool with the Bannisters and take up a post as clerk in the shipping line of the Elder Dempster Company who were active in the West African trade and whose head, Alfred Jones (later Sir Alfred), was a friend of the Bannister family. Later, with good reason, Casement came to despise the man,[d] but for the moment Jones made a pet of him and invited him often to his house. Casement had taken his post to "learn something about Africa." But his body and his spirit chafed under the office regimen, and though he stuck it out for nearly four years, he lay on watch for a chance to escape, feeling that "I must have an open-air life or I will die."[9] Both his older brothers, likewise "detesting the notion of a stool and pen,"[10] had already sought freer horizons, Charlie in Australia, Tom in South Africa. Finally, still only nineteen, Roger Casement was offered a post as purser on the *Bonny*, an Elder Dempster ship bound for Boma, near the mouth of the Congo, and he accepted it eagerly. Captain Harrison of the *Bonny* had seen him reported (in 1916) as "a noisy, talkative character," but in his own experience (intermittently over thirty years) he had found him quiet and intense, speaking little but with a tendency to "denounce England" when he did speak.[11]

Casement's first taste of Africa had been seductive enough to draw him back the following year (1884) to stay, as it happened, for nearly twenty years. Yet his work there remains, like the huge continent itself, fundamentally mysterious and only the late portions of it can be followed with fair clarity and coherence. He himself wrote

---

[d]In the letter to Morel, for example, he called Jones a "low cad" and an "unspeakable snob." He earned Casement's contempt as a tool of Leopold II of Belgium and an interested apologist for his regime on the Congo. Nina, whose account is prone to extravagance and must be read skeptically, wrote that in Casement's early years as a Consul Jones offered him a bribe of £3,000 to promote an installation for Jones's company upon a West Coast station, a proposition that Casement angrily refused.

vaguely, for example, in an autobiographical sketch provided for his
lawyers at his trial for high treason, that he spent the years from 1884
to 1889 in the Congo "in varied employments."[12] What is certain is
that his African experience, long, active, and varied, gave him a
knowledge of the southern half of the continent equaled by very few
men. When the enthusiastic Morel, writing on 12 April 1911, to W.
H. Lever, who intended to undertake commercial ventures in West
Africa on a large scale, advised Lever to meet "my friend Mr. Roger
Casement, who knows more about the Congo than any man living
and is one of the finest men that God ever made,"[13] his language was
extravagant but it was more than persiflage: Morel was an old African hand and he knew both Africa and Casement very well. But precisely what Casement was *doing* in Africa, especially in the first eight
years, is still not easy to say.

Something of the flavor, at least, of Casement's early African years
can be apprehended from a reminiscing letter he sent from the Eden
Hotel in Berlin on 10 May 1915 to the author of an article in the
Deutsche Revue of that month.[14] He knew the area of Vivi[e] well, he
wrote, and had been there in 1885 and again in 1886 when the German explorer Wissmann had passed through with his party and
given Casement his greyhound well-named Guerra: "she bit every
hand, including that of her master."[f] His first five years, he went on,
he had spent "travelling over much of the country, and learning to
love and pity the natives." It was this early knowledge of the blacks
and of the ways in which they were being betrayed and undone "that
enabled me to look for light in 1903 when I visited the upper Congo
as a public 'avenger.' "

Still brooding backward in his German exile, Casement reflected
that he was probably the only white man living "who ever swam the
Nkisi River . . . the biggest river between Manyanga and the Pool
[Stanley Pool]. I used to swim all those rivers, plein des crocodiles,
Kwilu, Lukungu, Inpozo, Lunzadi:—but the greatest of these was
the Nkisi, about 100 metres broad, and swift at canoe crossing,

---

[e]One of the haunting relics of Casement's trial is an unsigned note apparently handed in at
the time: "Can you get a message through to the one of whom we are all thinking? It is only
this: 'I saw a dead man win a fight,/And I think that man was I . . . ' Perhaps you have not
forgotten Masala at Vivi in 1886." NLI 13089.

[f]NLI 5459. Hermann von Wissmann (1853–1905) headed a large expedition sent out by
Leopold II of Belgium to establish trading stations in the Congo in 1884–85; he proved the fact
that the Kasai River was navigable by boat.

because the great fall of the Nkisi was not far below."[g] He had happened to be at this crossing of the Nkisi in 1887, Casement remembered, when Henry Stanley came up river with his expedition to "relieve" Emin Pacha. A cable from Sir Francis de Winton in London had invited Casement to join the expedition, but though the idea was flattering and appealed to "a very young and very adventurous Irishman," he declined because his "instinct" told him that the real motive of the enterprise was not the relief of Emin but "the capture of Emin & his ivory & the district he controlled for the Br. Empire."[h] Twenty-eight years later he was still convinced he had been right.

Still, just what was Casement doing there, in the heart of darkness? Most of the time, apparently, he was restlessly on the move, on foot or by canoe or river steamer, with a dog or two dogs and a few native bearers: a "surveyor," an explorer, an outrider of commercial interests of several countries under the loose ingestive mantle of King Leopold's Congo International Association. Europeans had been pecking at the edges of Africa for hundreds of years, but the immense interior was still virtually unknown and certainly untamed, and it drew adventurous idealists and buccaneering spirits from all over the world.[i] When Casement joined an earlier surveying party of Stan-

[g]Ibid. Compare an entry in Joseph Conrad's Congo diary under the date of 28 July 1890: "Inkisi River very rapid; is about 100 yards broad. Passage in canoes. Banks wooded very densely, and valley of the river rather deep, but very narrow."

[h]Ibid. Emin Pacha was a German named Eduard Schnitzer who became an Egyptian general and governor of the Equatorial province of Egypt, controlling trade in the southern Sudan. He was cut off by the Mahdi revolt of 1882 and was thought to be beleaguered by Dervish troops in the region of Lake Albert. Stanley's "relief" expedition of 1887–89, sponsored by the British East Africa Company, was his last venture in Africa. When Stanley finally reached him in April 1888 he found Emin quite reluctant to be rescued: he had collected a large horde of ivory and was happily pursuing his avocation of amateur botanizing. A year later Emin did make his way back to the east coast.

[i]Several of Casement's bold young African friends have spoken of the attraction of the mystery of the place. E. J. Glave recalled: "A great map of the 'Dark Continent' hung on the walls of my classroom; the tentative way in which the geographers of that day had marked down localities in almost unknown equatorial regions seemed to me delightful and mysterious. There were rivers with great estuaries, which were traced on the chart for a few miles into the interior and then dribbled away in lines of hesitating dots; lakes with one border firmly inked in and the other left in vaguest outline; mountain ranges to whose very name was appended a doubtful query; and territories of whose extent and characteristics, ignorance was openly confessed by vast unnamed blank spaces." *Six Years of Adventure in Congo-Land*, p. 16. Joseph Conrad was drawn by the same attraction.

Portuguese explorers had found the Atlantic estuary of the Congo near the end of the fifteenth century, but no European had penetrated more than a few miles into the basin of the river until Stanley followed its entire course from the opposite direction in his great journey of

ley's, probably as an unpaid volunteer, at the age of twenty in 1884, it was less than six years after the "rescuer" of Livingstone had completed the first traversing of the basin of the Congo from Zanzibar on the Indian Ocean to its mouth on the Atlantic: it had taken Stanley nearly three years and he was the only white survivor of those who had set out.

In later years Casement always placed himself among the adventurous idealists in Africa, and the image is crudely accurate. Writing to E. D. Morel on 27 June 1904, for example, he denied that he had ever been "a trader": that is, he had "neither bought nor sold produce at any time."[15] His tone was defensive because he was under attack from interests damaged by his famous Congo Report of 1904. In 1886 Casement joined the "exploring expedition" of the American General Henry Shelton Sanford, another crony of Leopold's. The motives of the expedition were certainly ultimately commercial and its records show Casement drawing for over a year in 1886–87 sums that have the look of commission fees.[16] He left the Sanford expedition in 1888, he wrote Morel, "to go elephant-shooting"— presumably for ivory. In his Congo diary for 24 June 1890 Joseph

---

1874–77. Meanwhile the travels of such men as Livingstone, Speke, and Burton had aroused much interest in the commercial possibilities of Central Africa, and in 1876 King Leopold II of Belgium had called an international conference of geographers which led to the formation of an International Association for the Exploration and Civilization of Africa, with national headquarters in various countries. After Stanley had failed to enlist British merchants in the development of the region, Leopold snapped him up in the fall of 1878 and engaged him as the agent of a new committee of the International Association: the *Comité d'études du Haut Congo*. He was to cut a forest road past the unnavigable cataract region above Boma, to make agreements with native chiefs, and to establish a chain of stations along the course of the river. The rivalry of European powers with an interest in the region led to the calling of the Berlin Conference in 1884–85, which agreed to the establishment of the International Association as a sovereign state and stipulated that it was to be a region of free trade, that the Congo and its affluents were to be open to navigation, that trade monopolies were forbidden, that the slave trade was to be suppressed, and that protection was to be offered to missionaries, scientists, and explorers. By action of April 1885 the Belgian Chamber named Leopold the chief of the new state and declared that the union between Belgium and the new state, the *État Indépendant du Congo*, was to be "exclusively personal": vested in the king. Leopold thus became master of a rough rectangle of largely unexplored territory covering nearly a million square miles, an area one-third the size of the United States and eighty times as large as Belgium, debouching on the Atlantic by a narrow mouth at the southwest corner, where it was compressed between French possessions on the north and Portuguese possessions on the south. Leopold did not deny that his purposes would be in part commercial, but he represented commerce as the agent of the superior purpose of "civilization": he would develop the resources of the country with the aid of the blacks, to the mutual benefit of blacks and whites. His philanthropic vision and energy were praised throughout the world.

Conrad recorded that he had just seen his new acquaintance, Roger Casement, off on the short trek from Matadi down to Boma at the Congo mouth "with a large lot of ivory." If Casement "neither bought nor sold produce," he was clearly involved, if only intermittently, in its acquisition and transport. For some months in 1888–89, for example, he "commanded" the advance surveying expedition of the Congo Railway Company which was trying to create a rail link from Matadi to Kinchasa to bypass the unnavigable stretches of the lower Congo.[17]

Casement had been in Africa long enough to meet and impress a great many men, a number of whom remained friends of his as long as they lived: explorers and traders such as Edward Glave, Herbert Ward, Major W. G. Parminter and his nephew Alfred Parminter, missionaries such as T. H. Hoste and Lawson Forfeitt. That they liked him is clear, and several of them have left testimonials showing that they admired Casement as a valuable and exceptional person. We shall see Conrad's striking "conquistador" image of Casement in his letter of 1903 to Cunninghame Graham. Herbert Ward saluted him as a "comrade," a good man to have near in Africa where situations were always in one way or another critical, and described his distinction of appearance and temperament: "A tall, handsome man of fine bearing: thin, mere muscle and bone, a sun-tanned face, blue eyes and black curly hair. A pure Irishman he is, with a captivating voice and a singular charm of manner. A man of distinction and great refinement, high-minded and courteous, impulsive and poetical."[18] In his *African Drums* of 1930, Casement's fellow adventurer Fred Puleston (called "Puli") spoke of the same qualities but emphasized his strong sense of honor and of loyalty, particularly his "tender and sympathetic" nature in relations with people or with animals. Puleston told of Casement hovering and weeping "like a girl" as Puleston and Glave practiced frontier surgery on his little fox terrier who had been disemboweled by a wild hog. Citing Casement's native names, "Swami Casement" and "Monafuma Casement," ("Woman's God" and "Son of a King"), Puleston felt that he "deserved both, for a more charming, lovable man never lived."[19] He called Casement "my dearest friend" and joined his name with that of Stanley in the dedication of his book.

After about five years of the African life, a hiatus occurred when Casement went home in the summer of 1889 as "a complete free lance" of twenty-five. "I found myself," as he put the case to Morel, "still a very young man, with all the love of Africa still upon me, with no wish to continue what was clearly becoming a Belgian enterprise."[20] Casement's hatred of Leopold and his rule in the Congo was an affair of slow growth, however, and on 23 October 1889, "spending a night here in the old place" (Portglenone), and about to set out for Ballycastle, he wrote Gertrude Bannister that he was negotiating with people in Brussels for further work in West Africa: "they want me to go out . . . for some special work and I am going to Brussels to see if it is good enough to accept."[21] Apparently the matter hung fire for several months, for it was not till 6 May 1890 that he wrote Gertrude that he was leaving for Brussels the next day, to sail from Antwerp on the *Kinsembo*.[22] At the urging of Major Parminter he was returning to organize transport on the Lower Congo for Belgian authorities. A few days earlier in company with his sister Nina he had heard a lecture by Henry Stanley in St. James's Hall in London, with the future Edward VII presiding and his beautiful Princess Alexandra and their three daughters in the front row. On the way out of the hall Casement's gold watch was neatly lifted by a thief who cut the chain across his waistcoat.

The most circumstantial account of these early years from Casement's own pen appears in a letter of 4 September 1890 to Gertrude, three days past their common birthday, when Casement turned twenty-six and his cousin seventeen. He wrote from a hundred miles up the Congo in the native village of Luvituku, which he assured her was "not a jolly place" and not a place where "a wee girl" would enjoy being alone.[j] As he wrote, his bulldog Patrick (also called Paddy or Patsie or the O'Patrick) was snoring by his side and thought to be dreaming of superior "chop" in the cook's quarters at Ballycastle. Casement was missing the company of two other dogs, Denis and Biddy, who had had to be left tied up at the English "factory" at Nkalakala near Matadi, almost a hundred miles down stream: only the distance prevented him from going to fetch them, he said.

He calculated the distances covered in his major journeys since 2 July: 75–80 miles from Matadi to Kimpese, 65 from Kimpese to Manyanga, 50 from Manyanga to Bwende and back, 65 from Manyanga to Kimpese, and 25 from Kimpese to Luvituku where he was

---

[j]NLI 13074. He often addressed Gertrude as "wee Gee" or "Geelet." She was short and slight of frame and suffered from a lame leg that caused a hitch in her gait.

writing—"not counting of course the numbers of miles walked between on days I have not been actually on the march. These 280 miles represent 17–18 days real walking—the rest of the time I have been squatting somewhere or other." On the fourth the squatting had taken the form of interviews with several chiefs of the area, and there was to be a similar, larger gathering on the coming Sunday. In the next few days he will be tramping the region in search of a satisfactory spot for building, and when that is settled on "I move out my whole brigade and we commence running up grass houses": presumably a new trading station.

This year, 1890, happens also to be Joseph Conrad's Congo year, an interval disastrous for his career as seaman but seminal for his career as artist. Pursuing a vivid boyhood dream of exploring one day "the very middle of the then white heart of Africa,"[k] and proceeding, like Casement, after interviews in Brussels, Conrad had reached Matadi on 13 June. Roger Casement was virtually the first person he met in Africa: "Made the acquaintance of Mr. Roger Casement, which I should consider as a great pleasure under any circumstances and now it becomes a positive piece of luck. Thinks, speaks well, most intelligent and very sympathetic."[23] From Conrad this is high praise; and indeed Casement seems to have been almost the only amiable and admirable person he came across in the disturbing year in Africa which simmered in his mind for nearly ten years before finding a vent in 1899 as his classic novella *Heart of Darkness*.

One ought to resist the temptation to make too much, too confidently, of Casement's part in the conception of the story. The obsessed tale of Conrad's talkative narrator-hero Marlow is provably based on events and impressions of the writer's own Congo year: the story is the product of his own imagination at work on his own experience. But the point is that Casement was a vital element in that experience, and one is haunted by the feeling that Casement as well as Conrad stands somewhere near the heart of *Heart of Darkness*. The association of the two was brief but intense and it was significant to both. They met as Conrad stepped ashore on the continent, as it were, and they were thrown together with peculiar intimacy, sharing a room for "three weeks" at Matadi and making short trips to-

[k]"Geography and Some Explorers," *Last Essays*, p. 17. In nineteenth century maps of Africa the unknown interior was often left blank or white.

gether to arrange with village chiefs for porters for caravans to Leopoldville and Kinchasa.[1] It is clear that Conrad "met Africa" through the eyes of Casement—as corrected by his own powerful vision.

Exactly what they talked about we cannot know, but that Casement's accounts of six years' life in Africa formed much of the subject matter comes perfectly clear in a letter of 26 December 1903 in which Conrad was trying to enlist R. B. Cunninghame Graham on Casement's behalf in the cause of Congo reform:

> He is a Protestant Irishman, pious too. But so was Pizarro. For the rest I can assure you that he is a limpid personality. There is a touch of conquistador in him too; for I have seen him start off into an unspeakable wilderness swinging a crookhandled stick for all weapon, with two bull-dogs, Paddy (white) and Biddy (brindle) at his heels and a Loanda boy carrying a bundle for all company. A few months afterwards it so happened that I saw him come out again, a little leaner, a little browner, with his stick, dogs, and Loanda boy, and quietly serene as though he had been for a stroll in the park. . . . I always thought some part of Las Casas' soul had found refuge in his indomitable body. . . . He could tell you things! Things I have tried to forget, things I never did know. He has had as many years of Africa as I had months—almost.[24]

Casement's talk surely entered into *Heart of Darkness*. What is more haunting is the feeling that his own personality had something to do with the mysterious themes and airs of the story, its strange hallucinatory atmosphere, and with Marlow's search for a moral center in Africa and in himself. Conrad's "things I have tried to forget, things I never did know," derived from Casement, must surely be related to the dreadful opening of the fetid emptiness at the center of the hollow man Kurtz and "the horror" that he stares upon as he nears death. One supposes that an apprehension of the character of Casement himself was in Conrad's mind as he thought about Marlow as well as Kurtz.

[1]Conrad to John Quinn, 24 May 1916. NYPL. Quinn collection. The Congo diary shows that they were continuously together for only fifteen days, from 13 June to 28 June when Conrad "parted from Casement in a very friendly manner"; but they met again in an almost hallucinatory fashion "a few months afterwards": see the letter of 26 December 1903 to Cunninghame Graham above.

Now it is illuminating, and perhaps necessary and not unfair, to look ahead twenty-six years to Conrad's last view of Casement, much more complex, heavily qualified, as compared to his early praise, by time and intervening events:

> He was a good companion; but already in Africa I judged that he was a man, properly speaking, of no mind at all. I don't mean stupid. I mean that he was all emotion. By emotional force (Congo report, Putumayo, etc.) he made his way, and sheer temperament—a truly tragic personality: all but the greatness of which he had not a trace. Only vanity. But in the Congo it was not visible yet.[25]

The cold-douche effect of such a statement is probably salutary at this early stage. In any case it must be reckoned with as the report of a knowing observer—though one must remember in reading it that Conrad now wrote as a passionate partisan of an opposed cause, as a Polish Englishman with a dear son fighting in France, and that Casement was facing trial on the capital charge of high treason, having put love of Ireland above loyalty to the Allied cause that was the current breath of life to Conrad.

It is already clear that the young Casement was fortunately endowed and possessed many winning and even impressive qualities: good looks, grace and charm of manner, ready but modest address, energy and strength of body, a sympathetic and affectionate nature, an almost unthinking personal courage. It all added up to distinction, and it seemed to Gertrude Bannister that when her cousin entered a room, quietly and with no flourishes of any kind, everybody else there turned "commonplace."[26] The power of his mind and his ruling moral motives had not yet defined themselves; and it is on those that Conrad's later judgment casts doubt. His statement was cold and it was perhaps over-emphatic; but it was shrewd and it moved toward essential truths. Perhaps no more penetrating observation of Casement was ever made. But the earlier and the later judgments must be set side by side, and neither must be forgotten.

2   A Desperate Shop

LETTERS that have only recently come to light clarify the hitherto vague story that Casement carried out a "lecturing tour" in the United States sometime in 1890. What actually happened was that he was in America from December 1889 to March 1890, as a companion to Herbert Ward, who was lecturing on life in the Congo in a tour arranged by the J. B. Pond Lyceum Bureau.[a] His next distinct surfacing occurred in 1892 at a point considerably north of the Congo on the West African coast, in Nigeria on the great Gulf of Guinea. He had been back in Ireland in the winter and early spring of 1892. From Old Calabar on 28 July he wrote Gertrude that he had "left home" in April and that he had traveled on eleven different vessels since leaving Antwerp on 6 April.[1] He went on to urge his young cousin to persevere in her training as a pupil teacher so as to qualify for financial independence—a great good.[b] Casement is feeling lonely, as he writes, because he has no dog,[c] and he is convalescing from a fit of

[a]Casement to Poultney Bigelow, 11 September 1913. Papers of Poultney Bigelow, Esq., private collection in the possession of Mr. Bigelow's niece, Princess Simon Sidamon-Eristoff; used by kind permission of Princess Eristoff and the Hon. Constantine Sidamon-Eristoff.

[b]"It is glorious to be independent," he had told her, and she wrote it down in her exercise book along with the injunction: "WORK, for R's sake," which she came across years later. NLI 5588. Maloney papers.

[c]Apparently it was sometime in this period that he lost the redoubtable Patrick. Casement and his dog had been put on board a German steamer, both ill with fever. When Casement came round, he discovered that the cook had closed Patrick up in a cubbyhole and then forgotten him for several days, and the animal had died. When Casement visited the Bannisters in Liverpool with Patrick, he would throw down an old coat as he left the house and Patrick would lie on it until he anticipated Casement's return, then he would descend to the front door and lie on the mat with his huge head on his paws. If he sensed his master's approach he would stand up, his stump tail wagging, ready for a tumultuous reunion. The next move was to go for a walk, when Patrick would race madly ahead and every thirty or forty yards tuck his head under and turn a complete somersault. Parry, "Early Recollections." NLI 5588. Maloney papers.

16

illness: "I have been having a queer time of it up on the Kroo Coast roughing it among the naked savages of that region—until I got quite ill from bad food and exposure to cold and damp through sleeping on the earthen floors of the native houses." Now, after one more change of steamer, he expects to "settle down for a year or two of good hard work."

Casement's new appointment in the Niger (Oil Rivers) Protectorate was his first under the British crown, his employer for the rest of his working life. His base was at Old Calabar[d] in the armpit of the Gulf of Guinea. The precise nature of his duties is still hard to define. He said later that he functioned as "travelling Commissioner and in other capacities for the Govt."[2] and his official task was certainly that of exploring and mapping routes for trade and potential military purposes; but there is little doubt that in the intricate and jealous African political situation he observed and reported upon the trafficking on the coast and in the interior of commercial and quasi-military agents of Britain's jostling rivals: French, German, Belgian, Portuguese. By October of 1892 Casement was signing himself "Acting Director-General of Customs"—though his first official consular appointment did not come until 1895.

In the fall of 1893 Casement was back in Britain and ill again. On 6 November he wrote Gertrude from Chiswick that he had been released from the hospital the preceding day:[3] he was too delicate minded to say that what had put him there was a case of *fistula in ano* on which Dr. F. C. P. Dean had operated.[e] Now he was leaving for Brussels for a month's visit with the Heyn family, old friends from early African days, to sail again on 6 December and reach Africa in mid-January after a stopover of two weeks in Grand Canary.

On 6 June and 4 July 1894 Casement reported to his chief Sir Claude MacDonald on recent explorations,[f] the latter account a lengthy description of a hard journey on foot through flooded coun-

---

[d]Following my request for information about Casement printed in the *Times Literary Supplement* of 3 December 1971, two correspondents wrote to testify to the fact that Casement's ghost still inhabits the District Officer's house, the old Consulate in Calabar. Mr. Manus Nunan wrote on 10 January 1972 that the District Officer in 1954 told him of its frequent appearance. Mr. J. P. Smith wrote on 4 January 1972 that he had seen the ghost himself in 1952, and knew of others who had seen it, too: "The apparition was always said to be of a kindly nature." Mr. Nunan also affirmed Casement's surviving reputation as "a true Christian gentleman" whose conduct was "above reproach" while at Old Calabar.

[e]Casement suffered intermittently from rectal troubles for the rest of his life.

[f]MacDonald was the Chief Officer of the Protectorate, a figure of eminence in the Foreign Service and a continuing admirer of Casement.

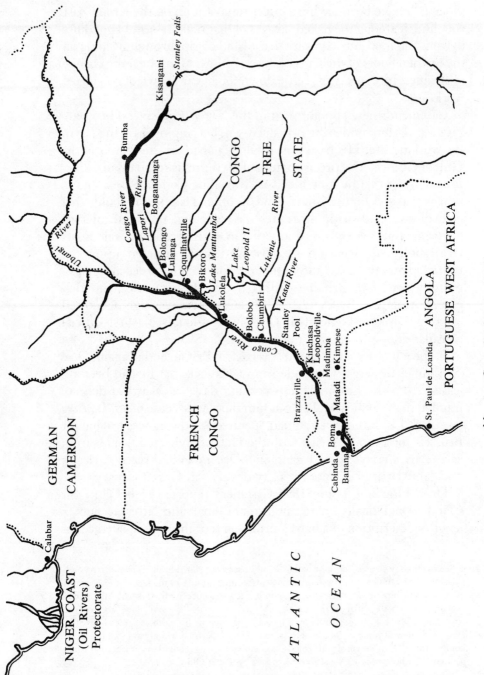

Map 1. Central Africa in 1900

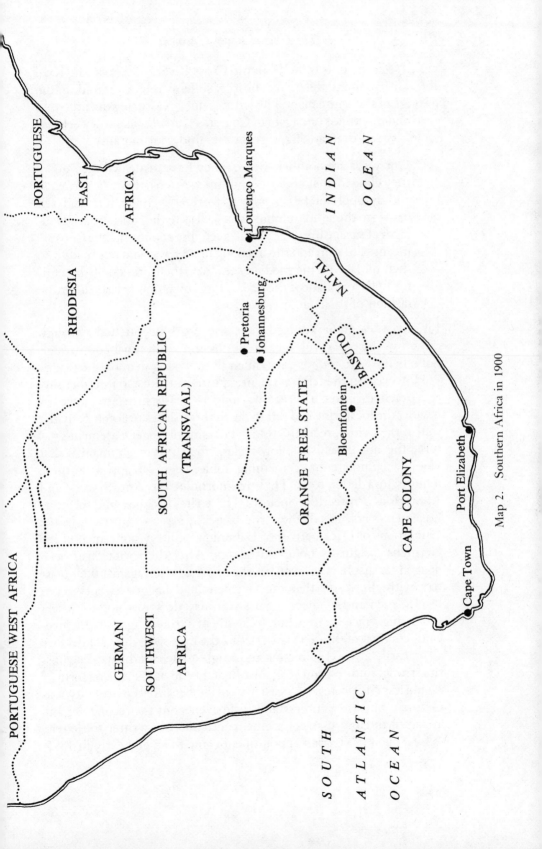

Map 2. Southern Africa in 1900

try to seek the best route from the Cross River to Eket on the Kwo Ibo. He had found the natives hostile, sullenly reluctant to admit the passage of the white man. The letter is not a reassuring document to read and it reminds one again of Conrad's Kurtz by its showy eclectic style, its self-dramatizing urgency, its undercut morality:

> Our ways are not their ways. They have made evil their good; they cling to their cruelties and superstitions, their *idion* crowns, and symbols of fetish power, to their right to buy and sell man—to the simple emblems as well as to the substantial advantages of savage life. . . . To all such, the coming of "the Consul" means "red ruin and the breaking up of laws" and our roads into their midst, and the good we seek to do them are equally hateful, for both foreshadow the end of their own power to do after the fashion of their fathers.[4]

Finally Casement advised that the road be pushed through anyhow—by peaceful means if possible, but pushed through nonetheless. He sounds very much like a young man on the make.

However, in the fall Casement reported a failure to interdict savage practices: after a direct warning to cease such atrocious behavior, the local tribe had put to death three slaves to accompany the soul of their chief, recently dead.[5] This side of Roger Casement's nature, the hot unselfish fellow-feeling for suffering humanity that would accumulate into something noble, begins to appear in these months in a letter to R. H. Fox-Bourne of the Anti-Slavery and Aborigines Protection Society. He writes in plea and protest, Casement says, to tell the "true facts" of a recent uprising in the Cameroons of black natives of Dahomey, military policemen of the Germans, originally bought as slaves. After their wives had been flogged for disobeying an order, the men had risen against their masters with the result that the Germans had hanged twenty-seven blacks, men and women. "I trust you may do something to raise a protesting voice in England," Casement wrote, "against the atrocious conduct of the Germans. Altho' the men were their soldiers we all on earth have a commission and a right to defend the weak against the strong, and to protest against brutality in any shape or form."[6] Doubtless the protest was easier to make because the brutality was German; but the rightness and inclusiveness of the feeling are still apparent and impressive. Casement need not have written the letter.

Casement's Nigerian appointment came to an end early in 1895.

He made his way south along the coast back to the mouth of the Congo, to the mission station of T. H. Hoste, with the vague intention of passing time there while looking about for something new. He had known Hoste for a number of years and he said later that Hoste "had a great influence over me at that time."[g] Finding the missionary on the point of departure for England, he decided to return with him, "with absolutely nothing to do";[7] and, as usual when he was in Ireland, he made his home with his uncle John Casement of Magherintemple near Ballycastle. He loafed and swam and walked and scribbled and began to think seriously of putting together a volume of verse.[h]

What had looked like an end of the African career turned out to be merely another breathing space. In June a telegram from Lord Kimberley, Under Secretary of State for Foreign Affairs, arrived offering an appointment as Consul at Lourenço Marques on Delagoa Bay in Portuguese East Africa, quite across the continent from Casement's familiar West Coast. At that time, as he wrote later, he scarcely knew "what a Consul was or what his functions were."[8] He did not feel qualified for the post and said as much to his aunt; but she encouraged him strongly, he telegraphed his acceptance, and the appointment was confirmed on the last day of June 1895. A month later he was on his way back to Africa.[9]

Though the situation at Delagoa Bay offered few charms it was a position of some delicacy and importance, and it meant that Casement at thirty had finally achieved a title and a confirmed bureaucratic status—by virtue of experience and reputation, without passing through the mill of Civil Service qualification. Lourenço Marques was the main seaport of Portuguese East Africa and it was the chief means of access to the Boer Republics for the rest of the world.[i] With trouble generally and chronically imminent in Africa, and trouble

[g]Brief to Counsel. NLI 13088. Hoste was an intimate of the family of the Duke of Hamilton and later introduced Casement into their circle where he was made welcome. Hoste was undoubtedly the addressee of Casement's poem, "To T. H." NLI 13082.

[h]He had made what was probably his first appearance in print, publishing "A Song of Tyrconell" in the *New York Ledger*. On 26 June the paper sent him a copy of the issue containing the lines and gave him permission to reprint. NLI 13073.

[i]Hollanders under the Dutch East India Company had settled the southern tip of Africa in the middle of the seventeenth century and had gradually extended the area of the Cape Colony by subduing the native Bantu tribes. England took possession of the colony in the political settlements at the end of the Napoleonic Wars and in 1820 the first contingent of 5,000 British immigrants arrived. The independent, conservative, slave-holding Boers ("farmers") chafed

with the Boers visibly impending, Casement was supposed to stay
alert for materials of war passing through the port that might be destined for the Boers in the interior via the linking railways to Swazi-
land and the Transvaal. In his routine consular duties, though he
found them trivial and boring, Casement showed himself a conscien-
tious and efficient public servant. "Writing, writing, writing all day
& every day in my office" left him with a poor appetite for friendly
correspondence, he told Gertrude in apologizing for the infrequency
of his letters home.[10]

The inefficiency of the port under Portuguese control seemed to
Casement so grotesque that it was hard to take the military threat
seriously. In a report of 12 March 1896 to the Marquess of Salisbury,
his new chief in the Foreign Office, he suggested that anybody shipping through Delagoa Bay would be well advised to claim loss of his
cargo as soon as it was landed—the condition of the port was so hopeless. Casement hated untidiness in any form and he went on to describe a heroic case of it with a sense of personal disgust: the harbor
bed heavily silted, lighters few and small, laborers scarce and
drunken, hardly any covered storage space or any principle of order
in storage, inadequate means for transshipping. The whole area with
its two thousand blacks and two thousand whites sat in a virtual
swamp of sewage and stink, and the air was so unhealthy that the
place had achieved a disease of its own: "Delagoa Bay fever."[11] In
the fall he wrote to Gertrude that, with the weather worsening and

---

under British domination and in 1836 the Voortrekkers undertook the Great Trek to the north
and east that led to the establishment of two new Boer republics, the Transvaal in 1852 and the
Orange Free State in 1854. Tension continued; in 1877 Britain annexed the Transvaal but was
forced to restore its independence after being defeated by forces led by President Paul Kruger
in the First Boer War. When gold was discovered in the Transvaal in 1886, so many miners,
mostly British, poured into the country that they came to outnumber the Boers. Kruger resisted strong British pressure to enfranchise these Uitlanders and began to accept German
influence in the form of arms and military instructors. A conference in May-June 1899 involving Kruger, President Martinus Steyn of the Orange Free State, and Lord Milner, British
High Commissioner in South Africa, produced no accommodation and war broke out after
Britain rejected Kruger's ultimatum of 10 October 1899 which demanded the withdrawal of
British troops from the frontiers and the recall of reinforcements. The Boers under General
Piet Joubert invaded Natal and for two years thereafter their guerilla-style armies, who never
numbered as many as 100,000 men altogether, gave a half-million British troops under Lord
Roberts and Lord Kitchener an embarrassingly hard time. Finally the Boer republics accepted
terms of peace on 31 March 1902 and became colonies of Britain, and in 1910 they became
provinces of the Union of South Africa. Afrikaner nationalism in the form of "Krugerism" and
"apartheid," of course, continued and eventually won the day, making a mockery of the military settlement.

the fever increasing, the white women were clearing out to the high veldt: "6,000 feet above the sea, where the fever can't climb."[12] In the previous spring Casement had suffered an attack himself and had taken sick leave to Cape Town from early April to early May.[13]

The local Portuguese were showing not only inefficiency but arrogance and violence of temper so pointless and indiscriminate that it was hard to interpret it politically. The German Consul, Count Pfeil, and his French counterpart had been assaulted and beaten in the railway station by the station master and a group of policemen; Casement's own bedroom window was broken by a stone late one night. His spy reports were remarkably vague. On 6 June 1896 he wrote the Foreign Office that, whereas he felt sure that considerable quantities of arms had recently entered the Transvaal through Delagoa Bay and Cape ports, it was hard to be precise in the matter as such materials were always landed under the label of "Government Goods." Certainly "large stores" of war materials were in Boer hands. On the other hand he felt fairly sure that the German officers and time-expired soldiers who were coming in were destined for the police force rather than the army.[14] Ten days later he was able to report some exact figures at last: 104 cases of Maxim guns, 65 cases of rifles, 4,000,000 cartridges had passed through to the Transvaal since 11 March.[15] Within another ten days General Joubert had announced that 30,000 burghers had been armed with modern rifles and the whole of South Africa was alarmed at the Boers' readiness for hostility.[16]

The African climate, so deadly to invading Europeans, kept giving Casement trouble and he went home in March 1897 and again the following winter, reaching England on 6 January 1898 with three months' leave. On 16 February, Dr. P. M. Laffan of Dublin sent the Foreign Office a certificate citing "effects of recent malarial fever, Neurasthenia, Haemmorhage & weak circulation."[17] Casement's leave was extended for three months on 1 March and for a further six weeks on 28 May. By no means all of this time was necessary for convalescence. The Foreign Office was deciding what to do with him next, and Casement was dividing a relaxed interval in long visits to his uncle in Ballycastle, to the Bannisters in Liverpool, and to Richard Morten at "The Savoy"—in Denham, Buckinghamshire, a half-hour's train ride from Marylebone Station. On 17 May, for example, Casement wrote Morten that he would be back in England by the end of the month; meanwhile a sort of reunion of "the Clan

Casement" was taking place at Magherintemple: "We are a big party at my uncle's."[18] Richard Morten, whom he had met some years earlier in Africa, was becoming Casement's closest friend in England and his comfortable house a welcome haven for a homeless Irishman. Casement often stayed with the Mortens for weeks at a time and the heading "The Savoy, Denham, Bucks" becomes a familiar feature of his letters. The Morten family had been resident squires for 250 years. Though it had gradually shrunk with time, the manor farm had originally occupied thousands of acres along the river Colne. The house of warm red brick and stucco is an architectural classic, one of the oldest surviving English manor houses, dating back to about 1100.[j]

The new appointment came through on 29 July 1898: Casement was to return to West Africa, as Consul "for the Portuguese possessions in West Africa south of the Gulf of Guinea, to reside at Loanda." Supplementary letters of the same day assigned him the further consular responsibility "for the Independent State of the Congo, and for the Gaboon."[k] But the actual congé for Africa was slow in coming. When he wrote Dick Morten from Ballycastle on 19 September, Casement said he had not heard from his superiors "for months," but distaste for the workings of the Foreign Office was still temperate: "It's a desperate shop that—beats any West End tailor for patience and delay." Meanwhile he was greatly enjoying this extended holiday (he had been home for nearly a year), the good weather, and the company of Nina, now Mrs. George Newman.[l] He luxuriated especially in the swimming in the bay at Ballycastle:

> I bath, too, in the deep blue sea off rocks, two or three times daily—glorious dives of over 20 feet into the deepest sea imaginable—blue & sparkling and painted red, green & white, by the weed (rack we call it here) & sands of varying depths. I

[j]After the death of Richard Morten the house was owned for a time by Sir Oswald Mosley, the British fascist. The present owner, Mr. Cakebread, kindly showed me over the house, including the big airy bedroom that was reserved for Casement's use. Years ago Mrs. Morten showed Mr. Cakebread a small enclosed loft chamber where she said Casement "hid out" in 1909. But this was romancing or bad memory. Casement's only hiding in England occurred in search of privacy to work; and in 1909 he was in good odor and had no need to hide from anybody.

[k]Sao Paolo de Loanda, in Angola, was situated about 200 miles south of Boma. His pay would be relatively good: salary of £1,000, office allowance of £300, outfit allowance of £220. PRO FO 63.1352.

[l]She parted swiftly from her husband but kept her married name all her life.

always think looking at our bit of sand coast between two great headlands of Tennyson's—"like a blue sea shading into green"—which by the way applied to a lady's shot-silk dress.[m]

A few weeks later Casement was back in West Africa and his official reports, over-long and over-resonant compared to their real content, began again to flow into the Foreign Office. A ragged little notebook containing jottings of the period from 1899 to 1901, which has survived in the National Library in Dublin, offers more interesting glimpses of his life at this time. On 29 January 1899, for example, he took a six-mile walk round Langosta Point, saw fresh fish for sale, recalled the plight of four young Englishmen at the submarine cable station whose mess lately had been limited mainly to a dish they call "Famine Onion," bought soles for them, and on the way back by train composed burlesque verses to accompany his gift.[n] A few days later he composed eighteen lines of fragments of a poem "On Youth" which he annotated as follows: "after watching some fine young Portuguese naval sailors with old Don Antonio López hauling at seining net on the sands towards Kakuako"; and signed, on 4 February 1899: "His heart was ever tutor to his hand. R. C."[19] Casement's habit of admiring the muscular bodies of young men grows more visibly ominous as time passes.

In the context of Roger Casement's political convictions as they subsequently developed, radically Irish nationalist and bitterly anti-British, some of his words and actions over the next months appear odd, even grotesque. In a fragment of a letter from Loanda, undated but evidently written shortly before the outbreak of the Boer War on 9 October 1899, Casement spoke to a straightforward British patriot, his friend, Richard Morten, in the voice of a wholly persuaded servant of the Raj:

> We—well we have the ships, the men, and the money—and the grievance—and I say have it out once and for all with the Boers & S. Africa generally. Send Kruger an ultimatum and if he

[m]To Richard Morten, 19 September 1898. NLI. MS. unclassified. The Tennyson reference is doubtless a recollection of the following from "Geraint and Enid" (lines 685-688): "one among his gentlewomen / Displayed a splendid silk of foreign loom, / Where like a shoaling sea the lovely blue / Played into green."

[n]NLI 12116. The notebook even supplies his laundry list for 13 May 1899 at Loanda: 28 pieces ranging from "1 Shirt with Collar" and "2 DO without Collars" to "2 Singlets" and 1 pr Socks (grey)."

doesn't come to straight forward terms, then make him—That means war, of course—and it's better than give up South Africa to Kruger.[20]

It was paraphrased classic Jingoism of a kind that in a few years Casement would recall with amazement and shame.[21] His brother Tom was already in service with British troops in South Africa and Casement wanted to take a more active part himself. He took leave and made his way to Cape Town as a guest of the captain of a man-of-war, and then, after a telegram from Lord Salisbury to Lord Milner, the British High Commissioner, he was ordered to go once more to Delagoa Bay.[22] Military authorities were convinced that the Portuguese, under the guise of neutrality, were again conniving in the shipment of arms to the Transvaal.

Casement reached Lourenço Marques on 8 January 1900 under what he felt was the transparent cover of a civil officer on holiday revisiting an old post. In strategic quarters he offered a reward of £500 for information as to the smuggling of arms and stood on watch himself during January and February; but the most dangerous packages he could discover were a case of saddles and two cases of bridles that turned out to be consigned to a bona fide Arab merchant. Against the insistent suspicions of the British military men, Casement succeeded in absolving both the Portuguese and the British Consul Ross, who had been attacked as incompetent, and earned lasting gratitude in both quarters.[23]

But he still chafed for real action and in a cypher telegram of 5 February 1900 he proposed to the Foreign Office a more dramatic scheme: the real way to stop the movement of contraband arms, if it was occurring, was to "seize and to hold or else destroy" the key bridge on the Netherlands Railway joining Lourenço Marques and Pretoria. Casement stood ready "to give personal assistance and to bring several useful helpers from Lourenço Marques."[24] He saw himself as leading a small guerrilla band of scouts and sappers attached to a military expedition of some size. Ordered to send further details by cypher he declined to do so, being convinced that at least one of the British codes had been penetrated by the Boers.[25] Instead he telegraphed again on 24 February expressing confidence in his plan "if strictly carried through" and asking permission to go to Cape Town to lay his scheme before the military leaders: he noted that he was doing little good where he was.[26] Permission came by wire next day and Casement left on the *Racoon* on the last day of the month to make his case for "the easiest as well as the manliest" line of behavior.

In Cape Town he put his proposal into a memorandum suggesting a force of some five hundred mounted men with artillery to proceed through Zululand to Komantipoert where they would destroy the railroad bridge and hold the line against counterattack. Lords Kitchener, Roberts, and Milner approved the plan in April and the operation was mounted—with no great energy. Strathcona's Horse, some 540 men, embarked from Cape Town at the end of May, one contingent bound for Durban, and another, under Captain Steele and accompanied by Casement, for Kosi Bay. But the affair ended ingloriously when Lord Milner recalled the expedition before it even approached its objective. Casement set down all these matters in a long mournful report to Lord Salisbury on 5 July 1900, trying to explain the "causes of possible non-success" as he awkwardly put it. In the Foreign Office his letter was annotated dyspeptically:

> If the bridge had been blown up, it would have been repaired in a fortnight. Smuggling by road would not have been stopped. There was another question from the very beginning. The small destroying force could not have held Komantipoert had the Boers sent a large force there. The utility of the destruction would then have been measured by the time it would have taken to repair the bridge.[27]

Casement's involvements in enterprises of such kind, now and later, and the disorderly course they tended to run, keep revealing a strange amateurishness in British conduct of public affairs in late Victorian and Edwardian times—full of whim and happenstance and flaccid wisdom by hindsight.

For the time being Casement remained somewhat sullenly in South Africa, officially at the disposal of Lord Milner but with little real occupation. His feelings about Africa, indeed about the shape of his life generally, were growing complicated if not downright confused. But he continued to practice a kind of ritual or somnambular allegiance to British political motives as he understood them. Considering the later movements of his own life, his air of shock and outrage at the news of the formation of an Irish Brigade within the Boer army must strike one with an effect of comic irony.[o] Casement's letter to Lord Salisbury of 3 August 1900 applauded recent British

---

[o]PRO FO 2.368. Casement was later to admire one of the leaders of the Brigade, Major John MacBride, and take instruction from him.

successes and went on to advocate rigorous treatment of enemy prisoners.[28] Such opinions were not surprising in a man defining himself
at the moment simply as a loyal British civil servant, but they were
really dutiful talk, not deeply examined, and carried little energy of
personal conviction: the talk of a man soon to suffer profound
changes of mind.

By midsummer of 1900 Casement was home again on leave, reaching London on 26 July and taking lodgings at 12 Aubrey Walk in
Kensington. He suffered an attack of jaundice in London and on 7
August applied for sick leave of two months, offering testimony of
Dr. Dean that his hemorrhoids needed an operation and that he was
too run-down generally to return to the tropics immediately.[29] The
two months were granted, as well as another four weeks from 26 September.[p] His ailments were genuine but minor and they did not keep
him from traveling about a good deal, including a trip to Paris in
early September for a visit with Herbert Ward, his old friend from
the Sanford Expedition who had married a well-to-do American girl
and set up in Paris as a sculptor specializing in bronzes.[q] But the great
city left him jaded and restless.

Much of Casement's leave was spent as usual at Magherintemple
where he always had free bed and board and could walk and swim,
read and tinker with his poems. He thought a good deal, indecisively, about the logic of his life. At thirty-five, he felt, it was time to
begin to find some shape and coherence. For a man long orphaned,
long homeless, half-educated, his siblings scattered, a bachelor of
problematical sexuality,[r] a Protestant in a Catholic country that was

[p]Sir Martin Gosselin to Casement, 26 September 1900. PRO FO 63.1357. On 12 September
1900, Casement submitted an expense account of £385 for his special missions in the winter,
figured at £2 per day, twice the normal allowance—as he was reminded by the Foreign Office
who grumbled but paid up. PRO FO 2.336.

[q]Ward was a year older than Casement, having been born in London in 1863. He left home at
fifteen and traveled widely, working as a seaman, a herdsman, an amateur soldier, and so on.
When he went to Africa at twenty-one in 1884 he had already been around the world three
times. He commanded Stanley's rear guard in the Emin Pacha expedition and was the only
white survivor of his contingent. When he left Africa, he carried with him a very large and
valuable collection of African art and artifacts. He married Sarita Sanford (no relation of the
general's) in 1890 and worked as a sculptor in London before moving on to Paris. Several of his
works were bought for the Luxembourg Palace collection. See below, pp. 417, 434, 437, 463
for the end of the story.

[r]Consider, for example, Casement's note at the end of two pages of penciled drafts of incoherent verses of unhappy love: "Casaldo's friend—R. C. / Naples, 3 September 1900 /
Written going to lunch at Naval & Military / on Saturday, Sept. 22 / 1900—Oh Sad! Oh!
grief stricken." NLI 13082.

less a nation than an irritated appendage of arrogant England, an outlander, an Irish civil servant in an awkward minor branch of a
haughty inbred government department, sent by them to a chaotic
tropical continent where he was expected to brawl with rival whites
for rights of exploitation: it was not easy to know who he was, or
why. But he wished to find a role and begin to play it.

Casement had always kept up his reading in Irish history and
legend, but his early nationalist fervor had gone to sleep with the
death of Parnell in 1891 and the ensuing collapse of Irish influence in
Parliament. By the end of 1900, as he later claimed, his views on African affairs had already veered round to the point where he called
himself "Pro-Boer."[30] The early notebook contains a draft of a poem
of sixteen lines headed "Briton to Boer at Stillenbosch early May
1900 when walking up the lovely [one word illegible] with 'Scottie,'
to the blue grim walls of the Jonkersboek mountains." The poem begins: "Come, brother, come: this was not of our seeking./ We each
have stood from each too far apart,/ And listening each to hostile
prompters speaking/ Neither hath heard the beating of his heart."
His Irishry was unconsciously rousing again in this sort of
generalized subterranean sympathy for troubled folk, white or black;
but in 1900 he thought of himself less as "Irish" or "Anti-English"
than as "African"—which was to say a citizen not of a nation but of
an exotic atmosphere and a formless but dynamic way of life.

This was not to say, either—though in later troubled times Africa
would always return to his mind as an image of youth and purity and
naturalness—that Casement now "loved Africa" uncritically. His
life there had often failed to satisfy—had bored or offended him. The
mood of a letter to Morten, undated but evidently written in the fall
of 1899, sounded indeed fatally disenchanted:

> I've come to the conclusion that I'd like to conclude Africa—I'm
> sick of the place—it isn't the Early Paradise I once felt it—or
> rather I'm no longer the bird of that Paradise. I've grown old and
> grey—and now I want peace and music—and nice people round
> me—and old friends—and not any more truculent savages—
> and dirty bad servants—and worse food—and no single
> civilized distraction in life. I shall try for some nice healthy post
> when I get home from this . . . and shake the dust & chiggers of
> Africa off my feet for ever I hope—save perhaps an occasional
> winter in Egypt or somewhere up there.[31]

That was the wishful cultivated Briton speaking in Casement and no doubt a valid part of him. Yet Paris bored him when he got home. But he was not free to indulge his moods and his most significant African experience, with plenty of dust, chiggers, and savages, lay still ahead.

Casement returned to West Africa in the middle of December 1900. But before returning he made a second trip to the continent and on October 10, when he called on Constantine Phipps, the British envoy in Brussels, he learned that he had been invited to "breakfast" with King Leopold that day at one o'clock. Casement's reputation in Africa had extended beyond official British quarters, and Leopold evidently considered him a person worth cultivating. At the palace he found a company that included the King, the Queen, Princess Clementine, the Duke of Aosta, and Prince Victor Napoleon. After a polite chat Leopold invited Casement to return the next day. During this meeting he got down to business, doing most of the talking in a conversation lasting an hour and a half. Leopold's tone was at once defensive and placatory. He admitted that bad things were going on in the Congo as well as elsewhere in Africa and that Belgian agents were among the guilty; but he attributed that to unlucky choices of men and the general corrupting influence of the African atmosphere.[8] The motives of his administration remained high and pure, he affirmed, and he intended to carry out the trust of the Independent State of the Congo for the benefit of the natives as well as of international trade; he wished to honor England's interests in Africa and to stand well in her regard. "I trusted I should always be found trying to facilitate good relations between my countrymen and His Majesty," Casement told him solemnly.

---

[8]During the 1890s Leopold's administration of the Congo Free State had grown rapidly more greedy and overbearing, particularly as the potential wealth of the region in ivory and rubber came to be realized. The State government had gone far in the suppression of cannibalism, had controlled the demoralizing liquor trade, and had broken the power of the Arabs who had dominated the slave trade in the interior for centuries. But at the same time it had placed virtually monopolistic control on land and trade: a native could not even leave his village without special permission; the State could demand his labor and it required him to sell his produce to State agents for absurd kinds of compensation. Any show of malingering or defiance was likely to be dealt with brutally. Protests against the trade monopoly led to the formation of "concession" companies in 1891; but in all of these the State held a significant financial interest. Under the screen of a *Fondation* Leopold had set up by a secret decree of 1896 a private *Domaine de la Couronne*, reserving to himself an area of more than 100,000 square miles between the Kasai and Ruki rivers, and in this richest rubber region of all the treatment of the blacks was said to be notably oppressive and cruel.

The whole occasion had a rather Swiftian air, at least as recorded in Casement's confidential memorandum to Lord Salisbury on October 14: one recalls court scenes in *Gulliver's Travels*. In the Foreign Office his report was annotated unemphatically:"We might thank Mr. Casement for what seems a very good account of his conversations."[t]

Casement was to spend three more years in Africa, years of increasingly exacting and significant work culminating in his crucial Congo Report delivered in December 1903, itself the culmination of a chorus of voices protesting the brutalities of Leopold's Congo regime. He did not really want to be there at all, or so he told himself, but he did not know where else to go: he had to earn a living and he saw no other way open to him. In low moods he cursed the place, writing to Gertrude Bannister on 28 August 1901, for example: "I shall be awfully glad to get away from the Congo—it is a Horrid Hole.[32] On 21 May 1901 he sent Lord Lansdowne a labored sarcastic account of his financial situation as a British civil servant, creating the occasion by enclosing a newspaper clipping telling of the theft of furniture and plate to the value of £1,000 from the house of M. van der Hoeven, Secretary to the Transvaal Legation in Brussels. He recalled that in 1895 he had hired van der Hoeven as a clerk at Lourenço Marques at £10 per month. He had found the man a good worker and an accomplished linguist and he had advised him to take a post in the Transvaal public service when it was offered. "Today," he reflected bitterly, "he is in a position to be quite comfortably robbed of £1,000 worth of 'plate and furniture' while I, his once employer would find the attempt *clanam Herculi extorquere* easier than to realize £50 upon all the furniture I possess. As for 'plate'—this in my case consists of some pieces of crockery of the material termed delf—the whole contained in a travelling luncheon case, or to give them their local habitation and its name—a Congo 'chop box.' "[33] But alternatives were few and unclear and he had, after all, more than fifteen years of African experience of almost unique variousness

[t]14 October 1900. PRO FO 2.336. Casement's close friend Bulmer Hobson told René Mac-Coll many years later that Leopold offered Casement an actual blank-check bribe to turn a blind eye to Belgian malfeasance in the Congo. Like MacColl, I have found no evidence to support this story and I am inclined to place it among the Casement myths. It would have been out of character for him to keep generally quiet about it or to fail to record it among his papers. Hobson probably misinterpreted some part of Casement's oral account several years after the event. Casement and Hobson met in the summer of 1904, shortly after Casement's Congo Report. See MacColl, *Roger Casement*, p. 26, n.1.

that ought to have been capable of being brought to some sort of justifying account. He had, too, a deep physical and emotional involvement in Africa. In high moods he still felt a kind of glory in the
life: the endless strangeness and beauty of the country, the very
barbarousness of its demands upon the body and the spirit.
Moreover, a rage at the pitiful lot of the native blacks had got into his
blood now and he was obsessed by the need to do something to restore to their lives the freedom and dignity "the system" was taking
from them.

Whenever he could get free from routine consular duties, Casement moved restlessly about in the interior, in the basin of the great
river and its tributaries. His numerous formal reports from Loanda
and Boma and Kinchasa increasingly turned into attacks upon the
iniquities of the Congo administration; the general theme, though
not the characteristic tone, of his reports is suggested by a relatively
brief and temperate statement to Lord Lansdowne from Boma on 28
June 1901:

> The only hope for the Congo, should it continue to be governed
> by Belgium, is that its governor should be subject to a European
> authority responsible to public opinion, and not to the unques-
> tioned rule of an autocrat whose chief preoccupation is that au-
> tocracy should be profitable.[34]

In London on leave again in the fall, essaying an alternative to Africa or at least a relief from it, Casement tidied up and put together all
of his poems that he considered finished and came to a tentative arrangement with T. Fisher Unwin to bring out a privately printed
volume. He called the collection "The Dream of the Celt" and arranged it in three divisions: a first group of fourteen poems on Irish
subjects, headed by the long Ossianic title poem, a second group of
fourteen generally African in inspiration, and a final group of a dozen
poems on themes of love.

When Unwin and his readers got into the poems, they were unen-
thusiastic. Sending the author an estimate of costs on 19 November,
Unwin cautioned him carefully:

> We have been reading your MS and I think I ought to say at once
> that I do not look forward to a remunerative sale; it is seldom we
> can make volumes of poetry sell or even to cover expenses; in-
> deed as a rule we sell very few copies, unless the author's friends

take it up; so I do not ask you to spend much money in advertising.

He went on to say that many poems needed radical revision and tightening and offered to send criticisms and suggestions. "I write somewhat frankly," Unwin summed up.[35] He then sent on four pages of his reader's notes directed mainly at the title poem, calling attention particularly to involved grammar, conventional imagery, and "bluggy" expression and applying such phrases as "minor poet" and "of the earth most earthy." Reading the notes Casement suffered an almost hysterical attack of wounded vanity and sat down and wrote out three tortured ripostes,[u] each of which he then scored out heavily with his pen before coming to his senses and writing: "I am grateful to this man, whoever he is, for his kindness in going thro' my verses with such attention & care."[36]

After further sullen reflection, Casement abandoned the idea of publishing his poems for the moment. But he never really abandoned the secret image of himself as a potential "writer": it was always one of the things he was about to become. Even his quotidian prose, as in letters and reports, tended to be "literary," meant to be heard as the language of a writer who would one day declare himself. He was a case of the artist *manqué*. Casement's papers contain many schemes of literary projects, some of them, such as planned accounts of his experiences in Africa and South America, thoroughly feasible and promising, others visibly stillborn.[v] A biographer must be thankful when his subject is a paper-generating and paper-saving animal, as Casement was, but one has no obligation to praise bad writing spread out with such stunning prolixity, and it is better to admit the fact at once: Casement was a very bad writer.

His poems offer lines that are tolerable; but mainly they show a dead ear for sound and rhythm and vague inspiration never realized,

---

[u](1) "I wrote 'The Dream of the Celt' in two sittings—when in a certain mood. I am aware of its faults but I would sooner walk in these muddy boots, 'of the earth earthy' than have them, if I can't clean them myself, polished at the hands of a shoeblack." (2) "It is evident that one may be a minor poet without knowing it just as one may be a major critic without anyone else knowing it." (3) "At any rate the minor poets have all the hope of attaining their majority; and the major critics may reasonably hope, some day, for shares in the Cloaca Maxima. The filtered stream will run on to that heroic river—to whom all men pray—the remaining dirt constitutes an enjoyable diet for the unhealthy excavators in the forum of letters." NLI 13073. If Casement had a forte as a writer, it was not irony.

[v]For example the plan jotted in his 1903 diary for a novel to be called " 'The Far from Maddening Crowd' by R. McAsmunde"—a "Gaelic" form of his name. PRO HO 161.

never brought to full clarity or point: influences half-understood
and unassimilated, stilted and irrelevant structural and grammatical
forms, all overlaid with a lather of loose feeling. His prose was that of
a failed poet: wordy, awkward, inflated. Both prose and verse attracted clichés like magnetized dust, and he seems to have been quite
unconscious of the fact. Casement's public and private writings show
a poverty of culture that would be easier to forgive if he showed more
awareness of his need. After his student years Casement read comparatively little and most of his reading was pointed at one or another
passing pragmatic purpose; he showed little interest in music or
theatre or art and made small use of the cultural resources spread before him in London or Paris or Dublin; he made little serious effort to
learn the language of the strange places of his life or to penetrate those
ancient and exotic cultures to any depth: he was satisfied to bring
home specimens and curios.

One has to fight through Casement's writings to the finer man. He
had a ready flux of words not really grounded in knowledge, hence
he was verbal but not fundamentally articulate. He wrote in mere-
tricious forms of true feelings. What was great in Casement, or more
properly what was noble, has to be sought in the less audible quality
of his presence and his actions: a quality moved by energies and
principles not so much intellectual as instinctive and spiritual. It was
some such apprehension that led Conrad to call him a man "of no
mind at all," a creature of "sheer temperament," "all emotion." Quite
coincidentally, Casement also had the looks to embody grand or
romantic attitudes convincingly. He could be infuriating and he
could be a bore. If the dominant impression was romantic, he could
impress a skeptical or humorous eye as Cervantic, a sardonic eye as
Hudibrastic. Still, at the center of him was a quality too deep to be
caught by any of those epithets and tough enough to outlast even the
hectic theatricals of his final months.

3 Infamous, Shameful System

I N the spring of 1902 Casement was back in West Africa pursuing
his slow quest of the Beast Leopold, known by his high dome, his
great white shovel beard, and the gleam of cruelty and avarice in his
eyes. With consular responsibility for the French, Portuguese, and
Belgian areas of the Congo, Casement felt his official base in Portuguese Loanda was too peripheral and he persuaded the Foreign Office, at some cost in salary and prestige to himself, to send another
Consul to Loanda and to allow him to move to Boma near the Congo
mouth. His official behavior continued in the main successfully formal and loyally British. On 8 March Lord Lansdowne's secretary
wrote to thank him for forwarding the sum of £48.4.0 "contributed
towards the National Monument to her late Majesty Queen Victoria
by British subjects of Matadi" and for "the expressions of loyalty
which accompanied it."[a] In London in the winter Casement submitted to the Foreign Office a long formal indictment of the iniquities of
the Free State regime. It was printed for study by the staff and generally praised, although some readers felt they detected a tendency to
intemperate language and extravagant assertion.[1]

Because a diary has survived with jotted entries covering most of
1903 and the first few days of 1904, it is possible to follow Casement's
movements more closely at this time than ever before. The pages for
1 January to 13 February of 1903 are torn out of the book and Brian
Inglis supposes, probably accurately, that these were "torn out in
1916, so that they could be shown to journalists as proof of his

---

[a]PRO FO 2.626. Among the contributors were many "natives of His Majesty's colonies":
Casement had called a meeting of the local blacks under British authority and proposed that
they join in a common donation.

homosexual activities."[2] The entries for the third week in February
show Casement lodging again in Aubrey Walk and being socially and
officially busy in anticipation of yet another return to Africa, with a
first stop in Madeira. On 15 February, for example, his sister Nina is
in town and so are quite a crowd of old African hands: the Mortens,
the Wards, the Cuibonos ("Cui and Mrs. Cui"), T. H. Hoste the
missionary, and Baron Nisco the judge of the Boma court. Casement
bustles about the city in beautiful frosty winter weather: sees the
Mortens off for Denham, takes supper at the Carlton with the
Cuibonos. Next day he shops for Congo supplies, goes out to the
Mortens' for an overnight, and falls asleep after dinner. In the city he
keeps an eye out for sexual partners, rating them by age and genital
promise: "saw enormous—youthful";[3] takes Nina to a pantomime,
"Aladdin" ("awfully stupid piece"); takes a crowd to dinner at the
Grand Central and then to *La Bohème* (no comment).

At noon on 20 February he is seen off at Euston by Nina and a
crowd of friends. He reaches Liverpool in the late afternoon and calls
at once on the Bannisters, finding "Auntie [and] . . . Lizzie & G."
(Gertrude) all well. En route to his lodgings he stops off at the Sailors'
Home for what appears a homosexual episode that costs him 11/
6: "H. Abrahams from Demerara, 'Arthur' 11/6 . . . Medium—but
mu nua ami monene monene beh! beh!" Mrs. Bannister and
Elizabeth join him for breakfast next morning and then he is off on
the *Jebba* for Madeira before noon: "good cabin, beastly ship."

In following Casement from England to Africa closely for the first
time one discovers with an illogical effect of surprise that the process
has for him a sort of stylization: after all, Casement has covered the
route a couple of dozen times. Things keep happening that have happened before and he even marks anniversaries. At sea he knows
winds and distances, the ships and their officers, and some of the
sailors and serving staff, even the menus. The trip is the beginning or
ending of holiday and on sea or land he treats it as such: sleeping,
lounging, strolling, reading a little, writing letters, chatting, gam-
bling mildly, drinking a bit, smoking too much, giving vent to his
sexual feelings. In each port of call there is a resident society that he
knows—innkeepers, servants, business people, officials, night
people; and everywhere there is a transient society of persons like
himself, travelers of some station and some degree of elegance. But
he is also peculiar in all of this, with his dark good looks, his dark
African experience, and his dark secret, social death to reveal.

When the ship docks in Funchal after seven days of bad weather, the first person Casement meets is one Perestrello, who runs what appears to be a trade in off-color photographs and with whom he has dealt in other years: "Perestrello as in September 1897, on 'Scott' with photos. Grown tall, eyes beautiful, down on lip, curls."[4] On shore he goes to the Careno with the hotel proprietor Reid; lunches with friends and sees them off on the *Jebba;* walks in the Alameda and sees "types, dark, distressful"; listens to the band in the public gardens; loses a single milreis in a weak flutter at the casino; after a bad dinner at the hotel he walks out "to Old Town, same place as in Feb. 1885!!! 18 years ago—then to square. Two offers, one doubtful, the other got cigarettes." An Edwardian day.

The next days essentially repeat the first. He meets Lady Wilton, Lady Edgecumbe, and the young Duke of Montrose and finds them good company. A Mrs. Somerset gives him a hymn book. He strolls about a good deal with a Miss Rolland but his glance keeps straying toward what he calls "types"—handsome young men with an air of availability. He sizes up passing youths as most men inspect women: when Casement says "Delightful, beautiful creature coming down by stream at tramlines," or "Many beauties there, exquisite eyes," one can be sure he is not talking about women. Most of his compulsive sexuality, apparently, is merely ocular and wishful: he looks and longs. A consummation, or even a contact, is exceptional. He treats with a young "clubfoot," gives him cigarettes, makes an appointment that is not kept, and concludes: "Clubfoot a traitor"; gives money to Alvaro, a "poor boy" of nineteen; pursues fruitlessly for several days a young "beauty" named, approximately, Veirra de Machicos (he never can decide how to spell the name); Agostinho, "about 17½," allows himself to be "kissed several times" for a fee of four dollars.[5]

En route to Grand Canary Casement is troubled by "vile Germans" on board the *Teneriffe*, "the worst ship I've been on yet."[6] Las Palmas where he lands on the twentieth is a familiar and favorite haunt, and he spends his time essentially as at Funchal, though his sexual adventures are still more frequent and apparently more decisive. He learns that his big basket of official papers has been misplaced somewhere during his passage from England and starts writing about trying to trace it. He has been worrying for several weeks about a certain George Brown in New York and is relieved to hear from him now, even though Brown asks for money.[b] He re-

[b]He is probably the "G. B. of 6 File" of Casement's entry of 17 February.

ceives two letters from Nina and three from his brother Tom in South Africa, in deep trouble with his wife: "Wretched story of deception and misery again unfolding."[7] He retrieves his bulldog John from people who have been boarding him since he passed through from Africa in October. Casement is not feeling well, "very seedy," sleeping badly, and at night on 24 March suffers an attack of what he calls "near dysentery" and makes eleven trips to the toilet: "feeling very ill, lots of blood passing." Meanwhile John is barking most of the night. Next day he feels a little better and decides, against his doctor's orders, to sail for Africa on the *Anversville* on 26 March as scheduled.

The voyage to Cabinda with stops along the coast takes over a fortnight. Casement is still feeling "very seedy indeed" and "bleeding badly aft as in Santa Cruz"; but he gradually recovers his tone. He sleeps a great deal and reads romances in his bunk, including several in French. In his diary entry for 6 April he makes a typically elliptical record of a homosexual episode, in this case probably a consummated one and necessarily hurried and furtive as the ship is nearing Banana; "X X X 'Accra' enormous . . . . Monrovian . . . . Down and oh! oh! quick—about 18." At Banana and Boma and Loanda Casement steps on shore to visit with friends or invites them to the ship for a meal and a chat. His consular deputy Arthur Nightingale joins him at Loanda and they travel on together to Cabinda. Casement arranges with Nightingale to send £20 via Lisbon to New York for George Brown. Cabinda is reached on 12 April and Casement has been nearly two months en route from England.

Only a few days after Casement's return, H.M.S. *Odin* arrived with shocking news of Sir Hector Macdonald, a brave and much-decorated Scots soldier.[c] Following exposure for homosexual practices in Ceylon Macdonald had been brought back to London, denounced, and ordered to return to Ceylon to undergo a court-martial. On the way back he took his own life in a hotel in Paris. In his diary Casement handled the matter in this way:

> . . . news of Sir Hector Macdonald's suicide in Paris! The reasons given are pitiably sad. The most distressing case this

---

[c]Macdonald had served in the army for over thirty years in India and South Africa during which he had risen from Private to Major-General, and had been made Honorary Aide-de-camp to both Queen Victoria and King Edward VII.

surely of its kind and one that may awake the national mind to saner methods of curing a terrible disease than by criminal legislation.

He then went on about his business: "The commander of 'Odin' on shore with his 1st Lieut. Turned in early. Wrote S[ierra] Leone men about estates."[8]

If the response had been that of an ordinary person of the day, one would have been struck by its letter-to-the-editor style ("awake the national mind to saner methods") and its advanced humane sympathy. In fact it is the relative impersonality of the statement that surprises, knowing, or suspecting, what one does of Casement's sexual habits. For surely he faced the threat of the same exposure, the same disgrace, perhaps the same deadly way out. Casement's apologists have argued, reasonably, that no homosexual person would have reacted in this way to such a signal episode: the response is that of a normal heterosexual man of enlightened sympathies, not deeply involved emotionally in the issue.

It is a specious reading and finally an unsound one. One must bear in mind, first of all, the general laconic form of such a diary: quick jottings, unreflective, only an aide-memoire for later thought and possible development. Expressions of feeling are fairly rare in Casement's journals and almost never deep. In fact this entry is an uncommonly passionate one, in its way—a way that is undeniably curious. Whatever the motive of the comment, the quality of feeling is not that of a disinterested observer. It expresses, at a minimum, deep pity and frustration at the irony of Macdonald's hard lot.

Interested or disinterested, it is impressive to see an Edwardian civil servant of genteel provenance calling Macdonald's pathology not a sin or a crime but a "terrible disease"—though of course that remains one of the traditional ways of judging the sexual tilt that tortured both Macdonald and Casement. And indeed one reads the sympathy in the statement as disinterested for the moment and quite genuinely high-minded. And surely what is most significant of all in the comment is this very detachment. Casement seems hardly to recognize that it is his own pathology he is talking about—his own habit, his own danger. It is as if he really has not told his left hand what his right hand is doing; or as if his imagination has persuaded his body that it does not run the risks of ordinary men. That dividedness, that self-persuaded immunity to the realities of the world, suggests another order of pathology altogether. For the same man wrote, only four days earlier in the same journal: "This day last year I arrived at Lisbon, and curls and green in Avenida."[9] If he were describing a woman, it would all be simple enough, and it is easy to see why those who need to hold Casement flawless would say that the same man could not have written this note and that on Sir Hector Macdonald, that only the Macdonald statement is genuine and expresses the real Casement: notes such as this anniversary savoring of a curled youth in green must be malevolent forgeries.

But what is really significant is that the same man did write both notes and feel both emotions: that both express aspects of his history and of his way of thinking. If we are to deal aright with Casement, behaving even more sanely than he asks, we must begin by forgiving his kind of sexuality, if it requires forgiving, and pitying it only because it drove him into pitiable straits. And we must understand his own way of thinking and acting as a sign of a total complex symptomatology: to give it a clinical name, he was a schizoid personality, hazardously rooted in the real world. His treatment of his own sexuality was only one of the signs of that.[d]

With Casement back at his post and his diary of the period to hand, it is possible at last to answer some questions about the daily life of a British Consul on the West Coast of Africa in Edwardian times. It is a busy life but hardly laborious, surprisingly varied, and at once exotic and homelike. The spectator senses a sort of working transplanted domesticity, partly a property of the place, partly a property of the person and therefore portable; one possesses a social cluster, or a chain of small clusters, of people and animals; one's dog is an entertainment and a trial, as at home: John gets sick from drinking salt water; John routs Jack and Snap but gets his eyes bunged up. Much time is taken up with correspondence, official and personal: ship schedules are carefully watched because ships fetch and carry mail. Weather is a problem: days are too hot and often the nights; it rains a great deal. Mosquitoes are numerous and active and their old touch

[d]It is important to note that Casement did not drop the Macdonald tragedy after a single reference. The diary shows that it lay on his mind some time. An entry on 19 April suggests that he knew the man slightly, or at least had heard him talked about in innocent contexts: "Very sorry at Hector Macdonald's terrible end. Poor old Mrs. Young with her love for him." (Mrs. Young may be the "Mrs. Jimmie" of Nina's and Gertrude's reminiscences: an old family friend in Ballymena with whom Casement often spent time when a student.) On 30 April, tortured by sandflies during a sleepless night in a wretched hotel room in Banana, he thinks again: "Hector Macdonald's death very sad."

lingers: "Fever on me all thro' night. First attack since I came out! Took 16 grains quinine and lay down till 3 P.M." An occasional strange creature terrifies: "No sleep on account of centipede last night. A huge thing all over mosquito curtain and then it disappeared and I lay in dread."[10]

Other homely kinds of things are going on, equally typical of Casement and his life. He keeps in touch by mail with his scattered family. On 20 April he writes Gertrude to thank her for her present of the *Reminiscences of an Irish R.M.*, the delightful account by Somerville and Ross of the disorderly courses of housekeeping, fox hunting, and rural justice among the Anglo-Irish squirearchy in Victorian southern Ireland: "This I found at Loanda and read *all* last night from 2 A.M. 'till dawn today by candle under my mosquito curtain with a healthy crop of large mosquitoes also under it, and 'John' my bulldog giggling to himself under all as I laughed at each page."[e]

The youngest and probably the most perilously balanced of an unstable group of siblings, Roger Casement continued to be required to offer audience and support for his sister and his two brothers. The Portuguese mail of 2 May, for example, brought letters from Charlie, Tom, and Blanche (Balharry), Tom's wife: "All three affairs more and more complicated." Blanche acknowledged Casement's gift of £20 in January. On 11 May his diary note runs: "Wrote Charlie sent £15. Wrote Tom and Blanche—hopeless affair that is. I see no possible outlook. Wrote Nina all about the Balharry question." By no means all of Casement's sympathies lay with his brother. When the mail of 20 June brought a letter from Blanche and "many" from Tom, he reflected: "It is a sad sad business for her, poor thing."[f]

In Africa and in England Congo affairs were concentrating toward a crisis that would involve Casement in the effort that formed the grand finale of his African service and made him a public figure. English official disenchantment with Leopold and his "system" had been long and slow in collecting, but its intensification now and its concentration upon Casement were swift, and visible in his own notes. On 14 May he wrote: "Two wires from F.O. [Foreign Office]

---

[e]NLI 13074. This letter offers one of many opportunities to check the authenticity of Casement's diaries. The diary records of 20 April: "I had a very bad night with Morginton [unexplained] and heat and sand flies. Reading Gertrude's present of the *'Reminiscences of an Irish R.M.'*. They are delicious." PRO HO 161.

[f]The affair proved hopeless indeed and Tom and Blanche were eventually divorced. He later remarried and lived happily with his Katje, aside from his chronic incapacity to earn a living.

important. At last they are taking action." Next day: "The F.O. wires I got y'day will cause me a lot of trouble I fear." On 20 May: "Congo going strong in papers."[g] On 2 June at Matadi, Casement learned that three telegrams from the Foreign Office awaited him at Boma. He sent a boat down for them and when it returned on 4 June he found two of the wires in garbled code and unintelligible; but the third was clear enough: he was commanded "to go to interior as soon as possible, and to send reports soon. The debate in Commons has been terrible attack on Congo States."[11] England was making "Congo misgovernment" a national cause and naming Casement her official investigator. Next morning at 7:00 A.M. he was on his way.

Whereas Casement saw the Upper Congo as his true field of inspection, and though he was delayed at Leopoldville for about three weeks after only two days' march, he still thought of himself as officially on watch from the moment he left Matadi on 5 June. He took as his natural standard of comparison his last systematic traversing of the entire area, sixteen years before in 1887, as a junior member of the Sanford Expedition. As he put the case in his report to Lord Lansdowne on 11 December: "I was thus able to institute a comparison between a state of affairs I had myself seen when the natives lived their own savage lives in anarchic and disorderly communities, uncontrolled by Europeans, and that created by more than a decade of very energetic European intervention." It came as no surprise to him to report formally that the blacks had found cause to fear and hate the white man and that their developed instinct was now to run and hide whenever they saw him approaching.

Moving with a file of Congo porters, whom he preferred to the men of the coast, Casement began at once to set down notes as an official investigator. "The country a desert," he noted at Kimpese, "no natives left."[12] Next day his march ran from Timeba "across Nkisi and to Kisantu and to Madimba, then down the Nsele valley to Ndolo and Kinchasa and Leo[poldville]. No signs of improvement," he found, "save a few broader paths to the water where we swam of old."

---

[g]It was on this day that Herbert Samuel, the future Home Secretary, presented a motion in the House of Commons calling for a reconvening of representatives of the countries who had signed the Berlin Agreement in 1885, to take steps to deal with "the evils prevalent in the State."

Wherever he went, Casement enjoyed reunions with old acquaintances from earlier visits. It was an international society, Europe in scattered transplantation: such names appear as Fuchs, van der Most, Swerts, Hortner, Dupont, Van Damme, McKay, Berckmann, Forfeitt, Blom, Fluviales, Wayleffe, Sandiki, Gohr,[h] all overlaid upon the fabric of strange and sometimes illegible names of persons and places. John accompanies Casement everywhere and excites interest and admiration, though his habit of fastening his great jaws on everything he can catch causes bother and sometimes needs radical response. In one day he captures in succession a pig, a goat, and a child. On 7 June Casement notes: "John out with a pig or goat—a bat"; on 14 June: "John caught Fataki's goat by the forearm—choked him off."

In the three weeks he spent in the towns on the southern edge of Stanley Pool, Casement was attending chiefly to local matters: investigating disputes sometimes involving Europeans or Arabs, sometimes "palavers" among the blacks alone, or between blacks and whites, which he was expected to adjudicate. But he was already collecting items that appeared in his formal report: three dilapidated mud huts, two of them roofless, called a native "hospital"; seventeen blacks far gone with sleeping sickness lying in filth inside or outside in the common pathway; a woman victim of the disease who had already been burned, lying with her head almost in the fire: when he tried to speak to her she turned about and upset a pot of scalding water over her shoulder; nearby a State workshop for fitting and repairing the fleet of forty-eight river steamers: busy, orderly, efficient. Above all he began to chronicle the appalling decline of the native population: whole tribes and villages scattered or simply wiped out by disease and the white man's terror.[i]

It was 2 July when Casement started up river for Chumbiri in the *P. Brugmann* whose captain had offered him a free passage, and, perhaps feeling some solemnity at setting out for the interior on an errand of state, Casement described the scene about him in some detail—a rare event in his diaries:

[h]And Brandel, "Père Supérieur," Jennings, Sparrow, Jones, Koffee, Kyffin, Villa, Vitta, Simms, Mayo, Weber, Meyer, Delhaie, Raji Ibadam, Sjöblom, Deshardes, Cuthbert Malet.

[i]Conditions across the Pool in French territory seemed better. Casement wrote on 24 June, for example: "I like B'zville [Brazzaville]. It is the beginning of a town: not as at Leo., only a great Govt factory."

Went lunch with Villa and at 2:30 P.M. got off by B. round French bank. Beautiful Dover cliffs, lovely view. Camped in island in Pool at 6:30 about. Hippo downstream. Saw three pelicans feeding, close to us. Also saw a beautiful Egyptian ibis, black body, white wings; a lovely fellow in full flight over us for his Home in the woods below Dover cliffs.

On the fourth they passed a "black river" mouth that Casement remembered: "where Rabinek died, 1st Sept. 1901, the day I left Congo for Loanda, I thought the last time!j A couple of hours later they passed a French post where he recalled playing snooker in 1887. At noon on the sixth they reached Chumbiri, sufficiently desolate: "State telegraphy post in midst of old Chumbiri village—gone all, alas."

At Chumbiri Casement was waiting for the steam launch *Henry Reed* to take him to Bolobo where he hoped to charter her for the longer voyage ahead. He had taken on as cook and general handyman a mysterious person named Hairy Bill, who was "an excellent chap and a good worker" but an unimaginative chef, offering an unvarying menu of chicken, custard, and something called boiled sugar. Casement was finally driven to phrase it in pidgin: "Chicken, chicken, custard, custard, every day—come Sunday, Goddam."[13] Hairy Bill has had troubles that Casement leaves unclarified: "Poor old Hairy Bill. A queer life." Some of his troubles involve women. When the *Henry Reed* was ready on 10 July, a final delay threw Casement into a passion of mixed figures: "Delayed in starting by the infallible cause of all delay and every miscarriage since Eve first upset Adam's applecart—woman."k On ship the diet does not improve: "We had boiled sugar again for change, also custard." At Chumbiri Casement was delayed for another week while the *Henry Reed* was being scrapped down and repainted.

At Impoko on 21 July he interviewed Bazengeli people "and heard the dreadful story of their illtreatment." Late in 1900 when the villagers had been slow in producing their levy of food, they had been disciplined by a white officer at the head of black soldiers who had killed sixteen people including three women and a boy of five years,

---

jGustave-Marie Rabinek was an Austrian trader who was arrested by the Congo State for working in the Southern Congo although that was a free trade region. He died mysteriously, possibly poisoned, after smuggling out a letter predicting that he would never reach Boma alive. See Inglis, *Roger Casement*, p. 60 and *passim*.

kCasement first wrote "slew" in place of "upset."

seized 48 goats and 225 fowls, and pillaged and leveled a number of houses. It became a familiar kind of story. At Bolobo on 22 and 23 July Casement talked long with the famous Baptist missionary George Grenfell,[1] "fire at our feet to keep mosquitoes off." In an area that had once held some forty thousand blacks, keen hunters and traders, only some eight thousand listless survivors lingered, and Grenfell blamed the sleeping sickness for only a minor part of the decimation. At Lukolela the Reverend John Whitehead gave Casement copies of detailed indictments of cruelties that he later appended verbatim to his report. Almost worse than the specific atrocities was the working assumption that the blacks were the white man's chattels to command and to exploit with only derisory compensation or none at all. Casement gave the Congo State credit for putting a stop to the old frank trade in black bodies: the State's way was to take possession of the very lives of the blacks—by forced labor and ruinous exactions of food to make them slaves in all but name. At Lukolela a native population of 5,000 in 1887 had shrunk to 600.

At Irebu above Lukolela the party entered Lake Mantumba in the late afternoon of 28 July: "Passed last big point and struck across lake into vague unknown." In more than a fortnight while a new crew was being collected for the trip further inland, Casement wrote letters and interim reports and collected local testimony; on 3 August, for example, he "interviewed Frank Eteva and drew a long story from him of recent 'indecents' of State." On 6 August in a canoe with twelve paddlers he followed Nkaka Creek for a dozen miles inland and spent the day taking depositions from natives: "took copious notes from natives—all they say points to great mal-administration. They are cruelly flogged for being late with their baskets [of rubber] for Bikoro." The stories are those of savage reprisals—looting, burning, imprisonment, flogging, mutilation, death—for failure or delay in meeting the State's arbitrary exactions of food and rubber. Some-

---

[1]Grenfell (1849–1906) was one of the most notable of the extraordinary group of men who were the Victorian missionary-explorers. Born in Cornwall of Anglican stock he joined the Baptists and, influenced particularly by the example of Livingstone, he trained to be a missionary. The loss of the sight of one eye in boyhood apparently did not handicap him at all. In 1875 he went to the Cameroons and in 1878 to the Congo. In both areas, in addition to establishing and conducting mission stations, he traveled widely and systematically and made meticulous observations that added immensely to knowledge of the country, especially of the Congo and its affluents. After 1882 a familiar sight on the rivers was a little steamer the *Peace*, built to his design at Chiswick to draw only eighteen inches with a load of six tons and made in seven watertight compartments that could be taken apart and reassembled when the vessel was stopped by a cataract. He became a severe critic of Leopold's regime in his last years.

times the punitive parties of black soldiers or "sentries" were led by white men, but often they were sent out unaccompanied and ordered to bring back evidence of success. The customary token was a severed right hand but genitals were also accepted. Casement heard stories of canoes full of returning soldiers with baskets of hands or strings of hands dangling from sticks. Some of the stories, he wrote, were "unfit for repetition."

He did not accept all the tales he heard as true. There was a sameness about them that might be read either as collusive or as evidence of a gross general brutality. If one in fifty were true, he thought, the facts were bad enough. On a round of visits to shore villages on 8 August he saw for himself the effect of unexpected white faces: "People everywhere fled from us until we cried out [phrase illegible] finding us mission folk and not the Govt. they returned." At Ikoko on Lake Mantumba on 12 August, he wrote: "Declarations of some few of the Mission girls as to how they became orphans and entered the Mission. Dreadful. . . . Writing busily and took depositions . . . as to murder of their parents." There they were, after all, visible orphans. Next day he received a message that five people from the Bikoro region had come to show him that their hands had been cut off; he sent a canoe to fetch them but they had left already, having been told that he had set out while they were camped at Nyanga.

Casement was "not at all well," dosing with quinine and snatching rest when he could get it. The signs of the decay of native life left him sad and sick. At Ikenge he noted on 15 August:

> State post now—a few huts showing. In 1887 when I passed up a fine big town. Everywhere the same tale. . . . All the long lines of villages, once extending from Ikenge up have gone— only scattered houses here and there, and wastes of forest or patches of thicker later bush to show where once the clearings stretched.

He kept remembering places in relation to old friends now gone who seemed a purer race: "Walked to Balingi native village. Wangata Island in midstream—poor old Glave with all his memories round here. His people these."[m] Next day again: "Back in canoe. Botolo

---

[m] 16 August 1903. PRO HO 161. Edward Glave (born 1862) was one of the best known of the Congo explorers and a friend of Casement's on the Sanford expedition. He died in 1893 attempting to recreate Stanley's traversing of the Congo from east to west, leaving papers that formed a telling indictment of "the system." Casement composed a memorial poem.

and others paddling—past down old Ted's [Glave's] beach—ah! in Sep. 1887—what a change."

On 18 and 19 August the *Henry Reed* steamed slowly upriver to Coquilhatville and Lulanga, pausing often to cut or buy wood for the boilers. Casement bought souvenirs, paying for them in the queer derisory currency of the region, brass rods: a leopard skin for 350 rods, 16 black-dyed Bangola women's dresses for 160 rods, 8 white undyed dresses for 65 rods. The ordinary value of the rods paid for the dresses came to eleven francs all told, he estimated. Occasionally as they passed along a shore they would hear drums beating "to warn someone or tell of our passing."[15] In free time Casement was reading Captain Guy Burrows' recent book *The Curse of Central Africa and the Belgian Administration* and finding it "horribly true."[n]

On 27 August at Lulanga the launch turned up the Lapori, running due east and roughly parallel to the Congo, and there on 1 September Casement observed his thirty-ninth birthday, "in the heart of Africa indeed." At Bongandanga on 29 August he found the A.B.I.R. or Abir[o] chief agent "a gentlemanly man" presiding over something far from gentle:

> . . . saw rubber "Market"—nothing but guns—about 20 armed men—some with Albinis, most with cap guns. The people 242 men with rubber all guarded like convicts. To call this "trade" is the height of lying.

Next day he saw sixteen men, women, and children all tied up in the town. When he protested, the men were put in the local prison and the women and children released. "Infamous! Infamous!" Casement exclaimed in his diary: "Infamous, shameful system." On 2 September he heard "many complaints" and himself observed sixteen women being seized by the black sentries and taken off to prison "on account of the meat"—apparently a failure to deliver the exacted food tax.

On 3 September Casement turned downstream to begin his return trip. That night, sleepless with mosquitoes, he began drafting a long letter of protest to the Governor General about the A.B.I.R. exac-

---

[n]25 August 1903. PRO HO 161. After leaving the British Army, Captain Burrows served in the Force Publique of the Free State and as a Commissioner before publishing his denunciation of the Congo administration.

[o]The Anglo-Belgian Indian Rubber Corporation: one of the "private" licensed companies in which the Congo State maintained a dominant interest.

tions and continued it next day. The *Henry Reed* made nearly twice as good speed downstream, and Casement raised his consular flag and put on something he called a "patrol jacket." He felt a lightening of mood but his labors were by no means ended. On the fifth they met the *Ville de Paris* and Casement received his collected mail up to 23 July. "Hurrah!" he exulted. "Cypher from F.O.—good things are moving. Admiralty interested."

At Banginda "Bompoli came with wounded boy—hand off. . . . Awful story."[16] On the strength of this fresh and ocular evidence Casement decided to make a side trip to Ekanza to look into the workings of the La Lulanga Company with headquarters at Mampoko. "Then they poured in," he wrote on the seventh. "See depositions. . . . Fearful state of affairs." On the previous day he had written formal protests to the Foreign Office and to the Vice-Governor General of the Congo State against the work of the A.B.I.R. To Lord Lansdowne he wrote that the natives had been "handed over hand and foot to a gang of unscrupulous plunderers and are reduced to a condition of servitude and unhappiness in the interest of these privileged scoundrels I could not have believed possible had I not seen it with my own eyes." The spectacle left him "sick at heart for the lot of these people and ashamed of my own skin and colour, where to be a whiteman means to be a greedy and pitiless oppressor."[17] He heard a series of stories of horrifying similarity and senselessness. One party brought him a group of four victims: two men and a boy of six or seven who had been wantonly wounded by gunfire and a small boy whose right hand had been cut off. This was the work of the savage "sentries" or "forest guards" quartered in the villages or loosed to raid and "discipline." Casement heard of whole villages ordered to uproot and resettle closer to the factory, of fifty women carried off by force to work there. When he asked one of the chiefs why he did not complain to higher authorities the man opened his mouth and showed him a dangling tooth, a relic of his complaint four days previously.

The brutality sounded pointless, and perhaps incredible—except that there were the bullet holes and the maimed limbs, quite real. And one day the parts fell together to form a complete episode. After crossing the Lulanga by canoe and walking for several miles through a flooded forest, Casement was led to a lad of fifteen whose arm was wrapped up in a dirty rag. He removed it and saw that the hand had been hacked off at the wrist and there was a bullet hole in the forearm. Furthermore, the boy said, the sentry of the La Lulanga Company who had mutilated him was still in the town. Accompanied by the victim and a crowd of villagers, Casement marched through the town to confront the man, who lounged out carrying his rifle. The boy accused him and was corroborated by his friends. The sentry brazened it out and insisted that the crime must have been the work of his predecessor, known to be given to bad habits of that kind. Casement told him, and told the crowd, that he would charge him formally and would try to see that he was punished. He took the boy with him to Coquilhatville where charges were lodged with the Commandant; later he learned with satisfaction that the sentry had at least been arrested.

At Bolongo as Casement proceeded downstream "the poor people put off in canoe to implore my help." The drums had carried good news of him: apparently he was the first white man they had seen in a long time who brought some promise of effectual relief. At Wangata an official denounced the sentries for their crimes: Casement in response "denounced the system which permitted armed savages to go about the country."[18]

Casement now determined to head directly for Stanley Pool. On 14 September, he drafted a letter to the Governor General "on atrocious system." At Leopoldville again on the fifteenth he "wrote F. O. all night." At Brazzaville next day he heard evidence, not news to him, that the Belgians and their black soldiers did not stand alone in guilt: "Shocking stories of the mutilation and illtreatment of natives in French Congo." He was feeling "very tired and used up over excitement of last few days," but he spent the seventeenth at Brazzaville "all day writing." His teeth ached, his eyes troubled him, even his hearing was affected. The "fearful hiding" he gave John in Kinchasa on the twenty-first, breaking his stick over him, was untypical behavior and showed nervous exhaustion. On the twenty-fourth he paid off his crew, "all good lads," and left for Matadi next day, arriving on the twenty-sixth.[p] He spent two days working over his long letter to the Governor General on the lamentable condition of native life in the interior, sent it off by messenger as he passed through Boma on 29 September, and next day wrote out a fair copy

---

[p]Here he found a lover again: "Richard Coffee took letter at 9 P.M. and returned with answer and then we talked and he said 'Yes—true Massa, a big one and I swear God Sir'—and so to bed at last!" 26 September 1903. PRO HO 161.

to go to the Foreign Office. On 3 October Casement was back "home" in Loanda, having spent exactly three months on his investigation.

The ensuing month was a quiet time. Casement saw much of his friends, especially Dorbritz the German Consul, played some tennis, dined out often, and attended to local affairs and to his copious correspondence. He still had not met E. D. Morel[q] the most persistent and effective Leopold-hunter in England, but he received several letters from him at this time, and he wrote in form to Morel, to his friend the American journalist Poultney Bigelow,[r] and to Joseph Conrad describing what he had just seen on the Upper Congo. He wanted an active and informed public audience for the cause of the wretched blacks that would be less cool and policy-bound than a government bureau. When the *Heron* came in on 24 October, Casement saw that the British note to the Berlin Act powers had been published and had referred to him as a "Consul of extensive experience." He reflected: "Well, we'll see." On 4 November a wire from the Foreign Office instructed him to return to London to prepare his formal report. Two days later he boarded the *Zaire* with John.

[q]Morel was a major influence in Casement's career. He was born Georges Edmond Dene Morel-de-Ville in Paris in 1873 of a French father and an English Quaker mother. After schooling in England he worked for a time in a bank in Paris; then he became a clerk in the office of Elder Dempster and Co. in Liverpool where (like Casement) he became interested in Africa. After ten years of general journalism, chiefly for the *Daily Chronicle*, he founded in 1903 the *African Mail* to espouse the cause of native rights. He attacked Leopold's regime in a series of polemical books of which *King Leopold's Rule in Africa* (1904) and *Red Rubber* (1906) were especially influential. In 1914 he resigned his candidacy for Parliament on grounds of pacifism and personal political conviction, then helped to form the Union of Democratic Control which argued that guilt for the war was "distributed," and preached the spread of democracy and international cooperation. He suffered heavily for his unpopular views: according to H. W. Nevinson, "no one in this country was so madly hated and so shamefully vilified." (Letter to the *Manchester Guardian*, November 1914, quoted in *The Nation* (119), p. 718). In 1917 he was sentenced to six months in prison for the crime of causing one of his pamphlets to be sent to Switzerland (to Romain Rolland) without a permit. After the war he was elected Labour M.P. for Dundee. In the year of his death (1924) he was one of the nominees for the Nobel Peace Prize.

[r]Bigelow (1855–1944) was the son of John Bigelow, an American Minister to France. He was a Yale graduate and a qualified lawyer but made his career as a traveler and journalist and semi-professional historian. Casement evidently came to know him in the area of Delagoa Bay in the late 1890s. See below, pp. 53, 206*n*, 207, 370, 389 for later developments.

4   A Gang of Stupidities

T HE troubled interval of nearly three years that now ensued was a crucial one in Casement's life. It looked aimless and often felt so to him, yet it dictated directions and emphases for the future. It was a period of veering moods and fortunes: illness and health, trial and vindication, success and failure and success. Above all it was the period in which Casement "rediscovered" Ireland, as he put it later,[1] though "discovered" might be a more accurate word: in any case a revelation laden with passion, with beauty, and with potential pain.

On the first day of December 1903 with a bad cold coming on Casement reported in at the Foreign Office and spoke with many men there. Immediately he felt the ominous deflation and impatient irritation that always attacked him at the headquarters of his service: "They are a gang of stupidities in many ways." In the next days things improved and his mood lifted and grew more energetic. On the second he had a long talk with Lord Percy ("Think I gave him some eye openers") and next day Lord Lansdowne asked him to Lansdowne House for a long oral report. Casement found him "very nice" and his response to the "dire tale" solidly satisfactory. "Proof of the most painfully convincing kind, Mr. Casement," said his Lordship resonantly.

As always when he reached a large city where he could hope to move with anonymity, Casement resumed his restless and reckless prowling of the night streets in search of sexual partners or at least of visual gratification. On 6 December, he noted: "Dined at Comedy Restaurant alone. First time there in life. Porter good, excellent dinner, French chef. Then walked. Dusky depredator—Huge. Saw 7 in all—Two beauties." On the seventh: "Dick, West End—biggest and cleanest—mu nua ami."

By day he was getting well started with his formal report of the Congo journey, dictating to a "typer" or "typewriter," a stenographer from an agency: "a good boy named Jordan." Working through the weekend he had done 15,000 words by Monday, 7 December. The Congo was the vivid subject of the day and Reuters and other reporters came to him for interviews. On the seventh he noted: "Papers full of my Congo journey." The Reverend Grattan Guinness, founder of the Regions Beyond Missionary Society, called on the afternoon of the tenth; then later in the same day Casement met for the first time, with great satisfaction, the fiery Morel, a handsome man with prematurely white hair and moustache and burning dark eyes. The two men took to each other at once. They talked for several hours, went out to a late dinner at the Comedy Restaurant, and came back to Casement's rooms for further talk until 2:00 A.M.; Morel finally slept the balance of the night on a couch in the study. "The man is honest as day," Casement concluded at once.[2]

In the morning Morel left after breakfast and Casement spent that day and the next winding up and revising his report which he finally handed in to Harry Farnall of the Foreign Office on 12 December. But Brussels despatches sent him by messenger from the Foreign Office the same day showed that Leopold and his men had begun "their anti-Casement campaign." Two days later a letter from Morel quoted a dark statement in the Congo apologist paper *African World* to the effect that it had procured "curious particulars of Mr. R. Casement's tour which it proposes publishing after his report is issued." Casement's note on this message is itself enigmatic: "This is poor boy child Askill Hardwick at my breakfast at Loanda."[3] In October he had seen a good deal of young Hardwick, a clerk in a trading post in Loanda, but in seemingly innocent contexts.[a] The evidence does not show why, but Casement evidently sensed danger now in Hardwick or in their relationship. But in fact his anxiety was general.

Casement's diary gives the impression that for the time being he took the prospect of personal attacks calmly, though he did send off a refutation of one of the Foreign Office papers: "wrote reply to Cow-

---

[a]On 9 October Hardwick was "drunk and smiling." On the tenth Casement gave Hardwick breakfast and listened to him talk: "Only a boy—but rather a decent boy—who told me all about himself and his plans." On the thirteenth Hardwick sent him a present of a guinea fowl and a franklin. PRO HO 161.

elici mendacious note to Grattan Guinness."[4] And a long letter of the same day to Poultney Bigelow took a much more serious and dramatic view of his risks. Once he had determined to make a full investigation, he said, he had felt certain that he must endure "bitter days, much keen regret . . .and in the end perhaps ruin—*if I told the truth*." Now he had seen "some revolting things" and meant "to speak the truth straight out from the heart" and he foresaw "Hades," a "fearful row." He went on: "The easiest way to refute the truth of my observations or diminish their significance is to—vilify the individual; and the Congolese authorities are past masters in the art of innuendo and the basest forms of *tu quoque*." He quoted a Yoruba proverb: "A man doesn't go among thorns unless a snake's after him—or he's after a snake," in direct application: "I'm after a snake and please God I'll scotch it." Casement was in full flow of that passion and that rhetorical journalese which he shared with Morel and which perhaps even showed a residue of Morel's visit:

> If I go under in the tide of abuse I shall not sink in vain—for I feel an undying certainty that truth will win in this campaign and that the freedom and happiness which may yet come to the poor, persecuted beings I saw on the Upper Congo will in some measure—in no small measure—be due to me.[5]

Off and on up to 19 December he worked with "typewriter Jordan" at revisions and appendices of his Congo report. He was anxious to get home to Ireland for Christmas and he had promised a visit to the Mortens in Denham, so he found himself too pressed to accept a winning invitation from Joseph Conrad to visit him at Pent Farm near Hythe in Sussex. "If you are the man I knew in Africa," Conrad wrote, "you shall not shirk coming all the way here to see a more or less lame friend." Since they had last met, he said, he had married, "got a boy," and acquired gout. He had always "had a high opinion" of Casement's courage and so dared propose he come for a whole weekend, promising "no more ceremony than if we asked you to step under a tent on the road to Kinchassa." Conrad had been pleased to receive Casement's praise of *Heart of Darkness* but now dismissed the story as "an awful fudge."[6] After a dull weekend with the Mortens, Casement crossed to Dublin by the night boat on 21 December and next day found a lover again, apparently a familiar one: "At Harcourt Place, J. B. grown greatly in all ways. . . . £1.8/—came, handled, and also came."[b] After a day's stopover in Belfast he reached Ballycastle on a gloomy Christmas Eve and evidently wondered why he had been so anxious to come: "train late. . . . No one to meet me. Cold and black. I will not go there again."

It must have been in Ballycastle that Casement received Joseph Conrad's handsome letter of 21 December. Casement had sought Conrad's formal support in what he now thought of as his cause, his and Morel's; but Conrad felt himself too busy, too poor, too harried, too ill to involve himself in a public campaign. So he passed Casement on, with his blessing, to people like Cunninghame Graham that he thought better fitted and more influential. But he saw the cause as both large and critical and Casement's part in it as admirable. The letter bears the tone of elicited statement and Casement marked extended portions for probable quotation. But the fact does not diminish its sincerity and the letter requires quotation as a whole:

> My dear Casement
>
> You cannot doubt that I form the warmest wishes for your success. A king, wealthy and unscrupulous, is certainly no mean adversary; for if the personality in this case be a rather discredited one, the wealth, alas, has never a bad odour—or this wealth in particular would tell its own suffocating tale.
>
> It is an extraordinary thing that the conscience of Europe which seventy years ago has put down the slave trade on humanitarian grounds tolerates the Congo State today. It is as if the moral clock had been put back many hours. And yet nowadays if I were to overwork my horse so as to destroy its happiness of physical wellbeing I should be hailed before a magistrate. It seems to me that the black man—say, of Upoto— is deserving of as much humanitarian regard as any animal since

---

[b]22 December 1903. PRO HO 161. Another opportunity to check the authenticity of the diaries appears here, this time in what I take to be a clearly homosexual context. Immediately before the "J.B." item appears the entry: "Went Bray. Francis Naughton not there—back to Westland Row." (Casement apparently failed to find one lover, then found another.) On a loose notebook page in the National Library is the following entry: "Francis Naughton/Station Hotel/Bray/Co. Wicklow/Home address Cavan House/Bundoran/ He gets £20 a year & his keep/ at the Station/ Hotel in Bray Is/ a Catholic/ & has both parents/ living at Bundoran/ Has been only 9 months in Dublin." (NLI MS. unclassified.) Notes on the back of the sheet mention 1901 and 1902 but seem to refer to past events. The sheet strikes me as a sort of file-card on an actual or prospective partner. One should recall George Brown "of 6 File at New York" (17 February 1903) to whom Casement sent £15 on 30 March and £20 on 11 April.

he has nerves, feels pain, can be made physically miserable. But as a matter of fact his happiness and misery are much more complex than the misery or happiness of animals and deserving of greater regard. He shares with us the consciousness of the universe in which we live—no small burden. Barbarism per se is no crime deserving of a heavy visitation; and the Belgians are worse than the seven plagues of Egypt insomuch that in that case it was a punishment sent for a definite transgression; but in this the Upoto man is not aware of any transgression, and therefore can see no end to the infliction. It must appear to him very awful and mysterious; and I confess that it appears so to me too. The amenities of the "middle passage" in the old days were as nothing to it. The slave trade has been abolished—and the Congo State exists today. This is very remarkable.

What makes it more remarkable is this: the slave trade was an old established form of commercial activity; it was not the monopoly of one small country established to the disadvantage of the rest of the civilized world in defiance of international treaties and in brazen disregard of humanitarian declarations. But the Congo State created yesterday is all that and yet it exists. This is very mysterious.

One is tempted to exclaim (as poor Thiers did in 1871) "Il n'y a plus d'Europe." But as a matter of fact in the old days England had in her keeping the conscience of Europe. The initiative came from here. But now I suppose we are busy with other things; too much involved in great affairs to take up cudgels for humanity, decency and justice. But what about our commercial interests? They suffer greatly as Morel has very clearly demonstrated in his book. There can be no serious attempt to controvert his facts. It is impossible to controvert them for the hardest of lying won't do it. That precious pair of African witch-men seem to have cast a spell upon the world of whites—I mean Leopold and Thys of course. This is very funny.

And the fact remains that in 1903, seventy-five years or so after the abolition of the slave trade (because it was cruel) there exists in Africa a Congo State, created by the act of European powers where systematic cruelty towards the blacks is the basis of administration, and bad faith towards all the other states the basis of commercial policy.

I do hope we shall meet before you leave. Once more my best

wishes go with you in your crusade. Of course you may make any use you like of what I write to you.

Cordially yours,
Joseph Conrad.[7]

Also waiting for him at Ballycastle Casement found a copy of his report with some supplementary papers suggested for addition by Harry Farnall of the Foreign Office. On Christmas day and for three days thereafter he worked at revisions incorporating the new matter, sending it all off by registered post on the twenty-eighth. Farnall had written that the report was excellent: "could not be better, admirable both in style and substance." On that Casement commented briefly: "Good."[8] He began to feel some hope that the Congo apologists and persons he vaguely classified as his "enemies" might fail to clap a lid on the stench he was opening.

His cold was worse and he felt bored and stifled at his uncle's house, though he went about a bit with his Casement cousins Roger and Kitsie, and the weather was good and the natural scene lovely as ever: "Glorious light on Cantyre in sunshine." "Miserable" was the word he kept repeating in his diary. On the twenty-eighth he left thankfully for Portrush, farther west along the northern coast, where Nina was staying. There with Nina, or "Numkins" as he also called her, in a better mood he saw out the few days left of the year, walking about paying visits and listening to Ulster cottage entertainment: " 'Wee Donegal' sang a song and McAllister recited a lot of things, 'Paddy in the Butter' the best."[9] On the last day of 1903 he traveled by Ballymena, where he called on Mrs. King, widow of his old schoolmaster, to Larne where he took the *Princess May* to Stranraer in Scotland, thence by train to London. He traveled all the way by third class and he slept little in the bitter cold.

Casement's diary covers the first eight days of 1904 then breaks off abruptly except for a few scattered notes and addresses. It shows him very busy, in and out of London. Again he saw many old Africa friends and "yarned Congo," as he put it, for hours at a time. He prepared two long new memos and was in and out of the Foreign Office constantly, seeing Farnall, Francis Villiers, and Gerald Spicer and enjoying "many compliments" on his draft report. Just how the document was to be used had not been determined, but Casement was promised that he would have a major voice in deciding. Reluctantly, all had concluded that the names of persons he had indicted and, for fear of reprisals, the names of witnesses and even of their villages, would have to be suppressed in the printing, and on 8 January Casement was at work on what he fervently hoped would be his last revision.

Joseph Conrad had written again on 29 December to urge Casement to meet Cunninghame Graham,[c] who had also asked for the meeting, and Casement did see him and felt he had made a useful ally. Conrad closed his year's-end letter with strong good wishes: "God bless you and your work in the New Year and in long years to come."[10] On 3 January 1904 Casement at last went down for a "delightful day" with the Conrads at Pent Farm in Sussex and on the fifth he took the train to Liverpool to see the Morels at home. He liked Mrs. Morel, "a good woman," and the two men talked "all night nearly."

On 8 January 1904 when Casement's diary breaks off, his chronically unlucky brother Tom was writing him from Johannesburg. Tom's lame knees were better but otherwise times were hard as usual: he was out of work and had had to give up his room and move in with another man where he slept on a "stretcher" on the floor and breakfasted on a glass of milk and a biscuit. But he was as indomitable as he was unlucky and he agreed with Roger that it was a genetic trait: "As you say we are a cheerful family."[11]

Casement was now on leave and he used much of the remainder of the winter in driving on the personal crusade in behalf of the Congo natives, a labor of love now shared with E. D. Morel and about to take public form in the Congo Reform Association. As a public servant and one intimately involved officially in the issue, Casement had to be wary of playing an obviously partisan public role, or so he felt, and Morel became the ostensible originator as well as the prime mover in the organization. But privately Casement let it be known

---

[c]Robert Bontine Cunninghame Graham (1852–1936) was a flamboyant and engaging figure. By descent from Robert II he was considered by many to be the "uncrowned king of Scots." His maternal grandmother was Spanish and he himself came to know Spain, Morocco, and Spanish America intimately. He was a famous rider and breeder of horses, a friend of *gauchos* and of "Buffalo Bill" Cody. He became a disciple of William Morris and an ardent socialist, was elected to Parliament as a Liberal in 1886 and was sent to prison in the next year for his part in the Trafalgar Square riots, in which he was severely beaten. He was an accomplished writer and produced many volumes of poems, stories, biography, and history.

that the idea for the Association had been his and he had passed it on to Morel—in whose purposes he cordially joined, of course.[12] Casement worked hard to enlist influential supporters, among them two Irish peers of his own generation, Lord Ennismore and Lord ffrench whom he had first met in early African days. The same search for useful influence led Casement to write for the first time on 24 April to a scholarly Irish-born writing lady, "the widow Green": Alice Stopford Green, widow of the famous English historian J. R. Green.[d] It was a letter full of consequences for both correspondents; but by the time he wrote it Casement was well caught in the major passion of his life: his love for Ireland and his identification, progressive and obsessive, of his own destiny with Ireland's troubled cause.

Casement's frame of mind at this time was complex indeed. In his fortieth year he still did not really know what he wanted to do with himself. He had to earn a living, not only for himself: he was now paying Nina a regular allowance of £100 a year and he knew he must expect periodical calls from Tom and Charlie; and more and more good causes, especially African and Irish, appealed to his susceptible generosity. Although his Congo report had brought him warm personal and official praise and a measure of fame, he still felt that his dozen years invested in the consular service would not yield a roundly satisfying professional and financial status, one equal to his capacities, his obligations, and his dream of the future, particularly his Irish future.

Furthermore he was more and more morbidly obsessed by the feeling that he had performed too well for his own good: that his very integrity was raising up enemies against him not only abroad but at home and that by corrupt and obscure processes he was being victimized in the Foreign Office, left exposed and unsupported in his honorable attack upon the Free State regime to suffer the consequences of an unworthy power game of politics that had little to do with the humane issues. Even his own Report turned to dust and ashes when it appeared in printed form on 15 February. The Foreign Office editors had put into his own mouth statements made to him years earlier by others, and the effect, as he noted, was both inaccu-

---

[d]Mrs. Green (1847–1929) was the daughter of the Archdeacon of Meath (Church of Ireland). One of the most scholarly women of her day, she helped her husband with his work and continued it after his death in 1883. Her half-dozen volumes on early Irish history did much to make clear the richness of a native culture antedating the influence of the English presence.

rate and mendacious. And for names of actual persons and places they had used an obscurative code of capital letters. The idea sounded reasonable but in practice the effect was curiously reductive, almost comic.[e]

Still he saw no ready means of escape from the consular service; if he were to stay a Consul, he wished it might yet be in the Congo where he loved the people, and even the land, in its benign intervals. But he did not see how he could hope ever to serve again usefully, with an air of impartiality, where Leopold's writ ran, after the things he had said about the regime. So, he said, reluctantly he would accept the post at Lisbon, when it was offered, upon the retirement of Consul Cowper. To these effects Casement wrote in a personal letter on 21 March to Sir Eric Barrington, whom he numbered among his enemies at the Foreign Office and upon whom he was soon to pronounce Edwardian anathema as a "fierce cad."[13] He anticipated, he said, an attack upon his report from the Congo Government that must exact from him a defense that could only make him more fatally unwelcome in Africa. But it hurt him to think of abandoning the cause of "the people out there," and he had even come to think sorely that perhaps he ought to resign from the service—in the blacks' interest or in the public interest.[14] The appointment to Lisbon, a healthier post in a civilized European capital, had been intended as a promotion and a reward for Casement and everyone had assumed he would so regard it. Barrington read his letter, evidently, with irritated astonishment and replied briefly and tartly on 27 March:

> Nobody wants you to resign. I never heard of such a thing. As to your temporary return to the Congo I think it is very unlikely, but it has always been intended to appoint you to Lisbon when the time came. The present incumbent will go I am assured, at any moment.[15]

In truth, however, Casement was less preoccupied with his career in the consular service at this time than one might suppose. What he was dreaming of, really, was finding a way to earn a living in Ireland—no easy problem for a landless Protestant of genteel tastes and no professional training. He was in the grip of an intense new excitement: the cause of Ireland herself as a nation and a culture.

---

[e]For example: "I, R.R., came from N.N. . . . N.N. and R. fought, and they killed several R. people and one R. man. O.O.O. took a man and sent him to L.L.L."

Twelve years later in Brixton Jail, poring over old copies of his poems, Casement annotated his lines on "The Irish Language": "Written up Glenshesk in the spring . . . when I had found Ireland again & the Gaelic League."[16] Two weeks before he wrote to Barrington about the long and short future he was writing to Gertrude Bannister from County Antrim: "I hope . . . not to be again in London for many a long day. I should like to stay in this beloved country till I die—I like it better every day—and I cannot think of England!!!"[17] With a void inside him waiting to be filled Casement had "found Ireland" and installed it.

Casement himself later attributed his Pauline conversion to Irish nationalism mainly to the influence of the Honorable Louise Farquharson, a "Scots Gael,"[18] and it was probably in the course of a round of visits to country houses in Antrim and south in Cork that he met her in February. But she was by no means a solitary voice. She spoke out of a new chorus of national fervor inspired particularly by the Gaelic League, and it was the League's ideals that she voiced: the recovery of Irish as the popular and official tongue, resurrection of distinctively Irish literature and history, preservation of native forms in all the arts and crafts, promotion of native industry and agriculture. All of this was designed to upheave and supplant the mortmain of English forms and power and restore life to traditional culture and polity. It is significant that Casement is not to be found staying at Magherintemple at this time, even when he is in Ballycastle. For it was Irish Ireland he was discovering, not English Ireland, and he would have met little sympathy for his new passion among the entrenched Ulster Casements.

It was typical of Casement's volatile and enthusiastic character that once exposed he was caught and once caught he was committed. But this time he had found the master passion of his life. As the Congo had brought him Morel, the new cause also brought him firm new friends: Bulmer Hobson, a struggling young Belfast journalist, a Quaker; Francis Joseph Bigger, a well-to-do Belfast solicitor and antiquarian; and Alice Stopford Green. The four made common cause within the common cause of Irish nationalism though not yet in a form radical and separatist. All were polemical in their way: Hobson with a special penchant for economic theory, Bigger sedentary and the least political, Mrs. Green the most learned and professional, Casement the poetical and chivalric figure.

It dawned on Casement that though he called himself an Irishman he had hardly set eye or foot on the country apart from the northeastern coastal areas from Dublin around to Portrush. So in April he made time for a fairly intensive tour of the Irish-speaking settlements on the west coast, in the beautiful and impoverished counties of Donegal and Galway. He made the acquaintance of Douglas Hyde, the energetic leader of the movement and learned in its lore, and visited the language training school at Cloghaneely, resolving that he would come again when he could do the thing right. The effort of the country folk to hold onto their old language, when merely to live at all needed a bitter struggle, warmed and stirred him.

Casement had never spent a busier or happier leave. He gave many days simply to walking the glens; and he set to work to learn what he now felt was his natural language, Irish, a part of a patrimony cruelly withheld. "I am busy in Ireland learning Irish and helping on the movement there," he wrote Gertrude Bannister on 2 May. "It is a delightful study."[19] He had acquiesced completely in the mystique of Douglas Hyde and others who were making the propagation of the old language the keystone in rebuilding an indigenous culture. As usual Casement spread his enthusiasm abroad in long letters to potential converts. Such a man as John Hughes, whom he had only met in passing through Madeira, because he was thought to have influence with the weekly *Irish News* received a half-dozen pages arguing that "if Ireland is to remain Irish in thought, in hopes, in generous emotions—in all, in fact, that we are accustomed to associate with our race at its best, then the Irish language must be kept a living tongue."[f] Not all his correspondents agreed with him. "My dear Roddie," wrote Lord Ennismore on 27 April: "Your eloquence on the subject of the Irish language is lost on me. If you want to improve this people, preach temperance, not two tongues. Drink is the curse of this country, & the publicans wax fat."[20]

Casement adopted as his own special cause the hard lot of the citizens of little Tawin Island at the head of Galway Bay. Here were fourteen families, all Irish speaking, with thirty children who had had no teacher since September 1903 when the school had been closed, partly because the building was ruinous and partly because

[f]6 March 1904. *Dublin Sunday Press*, 6 February 1972. On 28 April J. C. O'Boyce of Portsalon, Co. Donegal, thanked Casement for his offer to present books in Irish to the best Irish scholars in his school. He noted that Casement had been to Sligo recently and met "the celebrated Dr. Douglas Hyde." NLI 13073.

the teacher could not meet the parents' demand for instruction in Irish. It was now proposed to build a simple new structure where instruction would be bilingual. The Commissioners were willing to put up two-thirds of the needed £244 and Casement undertook to raise the balance. He composed a three-page pamphlet stating the case and sent it to likely donors.[g] He sent Hyde a copy and urged him to see to the opening of a subscription list in the newspapers. Casement offered £20 to start things off.[h] Hyde obliged with a gift of £2 and letters to the Irish papers speaking of Casement's moving account of "what met his eye in his recent tour through the West—of the pitiable Anglicisation of Kilronan and the coast south of Galway, and of the one little unaided community which he found struggling for their nationality against such tremendous odds."[21]

Already, in the first days of March, Casement had been drawn into a group who were planning a new-Gaelic "Feis [Festival] of the Glens" on the Antrim coast, seeking to awaken and to celebrate the drowsing spirit of ancient Ulster, the county most glorious in Irish legend. The planning took place in Cushendall, seat of its great proprietors, the MacNeill family. Ada MacNeill,[i] who had been in love with "Roddie" for years and had by no means abandoned hope of marrying him, was secretary of the committee. The umbrella of the Gaelic League was able to cover for the moment factions that would soon be bitterly divided: Unionists, Home Rulers, and Sinn Feiners now joined to proclaim the common Irish heritage of the coastal towns and the nine glens radiating back into the hills between Ballycastle and Carnlough. The affair was to occupy several days in late June. Sir Horace Plunkett, leader of the agricultural cooperative movement, was to come from London to deliver the opening address and there were to be shows and competitions in traditional arts, crafts, and games, spinning, weaving of tweed and flannel; the culture of eggs and fowls, of vegetables and flowers; story-telling in Irish, dancing, piping, solo and choral singing; a hurling match.

It happened that Tom Casement of South Africa was home in Ire-

---

[g]He signed himself "Roger Casement, H. M. Consul." NLI 8612.

[h]Casement's check stub survives: £20 for "my contribution to Tawin" on 28 November 1904. The following October he sent another £10 for the Tawin fund to Dr. Seamus O'Beirn. (NLI 15138.) He had made friends with Dr. O'Beirn and his mother, had stayed at their house on Tawin, and had greatly enjoyed a performance of Dr. O'Beirn's little comic play about the trials of a doctor in a bilingual peasant community. (Courtesy of Mr. M. G. O'Beirn.)

[i]Also called in the Irish form Ide, pronounced, roughly, Eedya.

land that summer for the first time in many years. Roger had gone to
meet his brother, an invalid on crutches, in London in May and had
taken him for treatment there and later in Belfast, where a "little Belfast doctor" cured the lameness that had baffled the London
specialists. By mid-summer Tom was getting about nimbly and
adding his attractive gaiety and energy to the Feis.

Roger Casement was especially anxious that the Rathlin Islanders,
a Gaelic enclave in Ballycastle harbor, take part in the Feis and he
begged the loan of a small steamer belonging to a local squire, Hugh
MacEldowney; but the owner refused to lend his craft to carry
Papists. So Casement went sixty-five miles to Belfast and chartered a
little steam tug which he and Tom took to Rathlin at 3:30 A.M. to
bring forty men and women across the bay in time for the opening.
During the morning Sir Hugh Smyly arrived from Belfast in his
yacht and entertained Sir Horace Plunkett, F.J. Bigger, the Casement brothers, and a crowd of reporters at luncheon on board. The
weather was sunny and fine and two thousand people had a glorious
time at the Feis. It pleased Casement that Rathlin men took first
prizes in the war pipes and solo dancing. The Irish writer Stephen
Gwynn has left a vivid impression of Casement's look to the eye on
21 June 1904:

> . . . what remains chiefly in my mind is the impression of his
> personal charm and beauty. It was a superb day in June and
> most of us were staying at the hotel in that attractive little village
> by the tideway of the river: he was lodged elsewhere and came
> strolling down after dinner, in evening clothes, but with a loose
> coat of Irish frieze thrown over them, and a straw hat crowning
> his dark, handsome face with its pointed black beard. Figure
> and face, he seemed to me one of the finest-looking creatures I
> had ever seen; and his countenance had charm and distinction
> and a high chivalry. Knight errant he was.[22]

By now Casement had been an entire half year without active
employment by the Foreign Office. Whereas he would have preferred to remain in Ireland, and though he remained deeply concerned with the Congo cause, the time had come when he must do
something about the Lisbon post—no other option inside or outside
the consular service having manifested itself. His tenure at Lisbon
was mysteriously abortive, however. Francis Cowper had in effect
been waiting there for Casement to relieve him so that he could retire

from the service, and Casement did go to Lisbon about the beginning of July 1904, but he seems hardly to have assumed office at all. The clearest evidence of the dates immediately involved appears in his letter of 8 September 1904 from London to Arthur Nightingale, his successor at Boma, in which Casement said he had returned, ill, on 4 September after "two months in Lisbon."[23] What he did during these two months is far from clear. That he was unwell is certain, but it also appears that he was rather sullenly reluctant to resume his British service in general and service in Lisbon in particular: he resolved not to like Lisbon and succeeded. He wrote Gertrude on 25 August in this strain:

> I have been somewhat seriously unwell and fear I shall not get better here, so have decided to go home. . . . I shall stay a day or two in Liverpool before going off to Ireland probably. I may have to go to Hospital—I don't know yet until my own doctor (in London) overhauls me. I *do not like Lisbon* at all and am not sorry to be leaving it—even for such a cause![24]

An undated note to Cowper, who was still held on the scene, must have been written a few days later: "I want to be ready tonight in case the 'Oravia' comes in as I shall go by her. I have not been at all fit since I saw you—Saturday night worst of all."[25] Poor Cowper was still trying to resign in December 1904 and Casement was still "unable" to take over. By that time it was evidently mutually agreed that Casement would never be installed at Lisbon.[j]

The whole episode was strange and unsatisfactory to all parties. Even though Casement's claim of ill health was demonstrably bona fide up to a point, his dragging out of the affair through the latter half of the year, his general reluctance to take up his work, coupled with his earlier threatened resignation in the spring of 1904 and his generally surly and defensive attitude toward some of his masters in the Foreign Office, must have tried their patience and it clearly compromised his future. No doubt, too, there were plenty of persons about such an office whose envy of the public successes of an upstart Irishman would feed gladly upon the proofs he gave of being an uncomfortable sort of employee.

---

[j]Honorius Grant of Oporto was put in as *locum* pending the appointment of a "new" consul. Sir Martin Gosselin to Francis H. Cowper, 13 December 1904. PRO FO 179.393. In the summary of Casement's career prepared by the Foreign Office at the time of his trial no mention whatever is made of service at Lisbon, and Casement made no effort to correct the record.

Following the appearance of Casement's Congo report in February 1904, King Leopold and his interested allies counterattacked
skillfully, impugning his evidence and his motives, hoping the thing
would flutter and die and let them get on with business as usual. But
his report was only the most formal and official of the pieces of
evidence against the Congo regime, and one of Casement's major
grievances against the Foreign Office was their failure to come to his
public defense by citation of the other evidence in their files. Why
they had not done so was in fact the question asked by Alfred Emmott, M.P., in a major debate in the House of Commons on 9 June.
By that time, however, Leopold was under heavy pressure from all
sides; the Foreign Office had asked him to allow a new inquiry by an
international group and he had had to submit. Casement's letter of
six pages to Arthur Nightingale on 8 September 1904, previously
mentioned, was composed almost entirely of dark assumptions about
the sinister implications, for himself and for an honorable situation in
the Congo, of the "independent" Commission of Inquiry Leopold
had at last agreed to appoint. The Commission about to set out for
Boma was made up of Baron Nisco, an Italian lawyer who was
Senior Judge of the Congo Court of Appeal; Dr. Edmund de
Schumacher, a Swiss jurist; and Emile Janssens of the Belgian Court
of Appeals, chairman. Casement was quite convinced that the
Commission was merely part of a preconcerted scheme to whitewash
the Free State, repudiate himself and his findings, and open an avenue by which the British Foreign Office could retreat quietly from a
position too radical and embarrassing.

So Casement wrote in a "very confidential" sense to Nightingale: "It is a duty I owe the cause of the Congo people to put you on
your guard." The "investigation," he felt, was a plot cooked up by
Leopold, Sir Constantine Phipps, the British Ambassador to Brussels, and Francis Villiers at the head of the Free State clique in the
Foreign Office, and it would all end with a "touching reconciliation
between Leopold and Lansdowne—who will kiss again with tears."
Casement denounced the Foreign Office cabal and indeed Balfour's
whole ministry as a "wretched set of incompetent noodles." He admitted that there was little Nightingale could do in the matter except
to "watch carefully" the Commission's way of conducting itself,
especially its mode of questioning and of handling the interpretation
of native testimony.[26]

The working of the Commission far away in Africa over the next
months could only add to Casement's complex anxieties. His letters

to Morel, and even to others only marginally concerned, recurred obsessively to the dark betrayal being prepared for him in high places. There was truth in his reading of the scheme behind the Commission and of the motives of Phipps and Villiers. But there was a disturbing paranoiac inclination in his assumption that the object of it all was to undermine his own character and his career. In the same way there was both truth and an unbecoming grandiosity in his image of himself as a beleaguered figure of peculiar integrity, an Irish knight standing gracefully on grounds of high principle, carrying on a brave lonely fight against the powers of greed and cynicism. Casement did tend to romanticize himself that way. Yet this chivalric character was real and an imposing thing to observe. His authentic distinction would have seemed profounder had he left more of the dramatizing to others. In this matter of the Congo report one wishes to see him resting more quietly and resolutely content with having done a hard thing well, better satisfied with the mere integrity of his work, and with having collected twenty years of random African experience into a humane and useful instrument.

5   Toward Santos

THE year 1904 wore to an end with Casement in a generally anx-ious frame of mind. Appeals from his brothers continued. Tom had extended his convalescence in Ireland through the summer.[a] On 3 December, he wrote from Johannesburg to refuse a gift or loan of £100 that Roger had offered: "I really cannot accept it. I owe you quite enough at present."[1] But a few weeks later he wrote that a gold mining venture had come to nothing and enclosed a small account from home he had "forgot to settle": "Will you settle it for me old man."[2] Charlie's situation in Melbourne was more dramatic. He wrote on 20 December to say that he and his wife Bea were going to "proclaim" their marriage "on its anniversary." Now that they were to be publicly married and to have a place of their own he hoped to have their two daughters with them. The place would need furniture and Charlie was counting on Roger for that. "I often have won-dered," he speculated comfortably, "is it because you have such a lot of poor relations that you are helping that you never got married yourself." Charlie had seen Tom's estranged wife Blanche several times in Melbourne and she had said bitterly that she had no inten-tion of divorcing Tom. He included a filip for Roger: I am told that you are well known in England by the title of 'Congo Casement.' "[3]

When Casement wrote to Cowper in the middle of September 1904 to apologize again for failing to relieve him at Lisbon, he said he had been "overhauled" by his London doctor and judged to need two relatively minor operations: for a fistula and for a chronically inflamed appendix that had caused his abdominal pain in July and

[a]Testified by a check stub of Roger Casement's dated 3 August: "Tom. Present to Bally-castle. He asked for it. £20.0.0." NLI 15138.

August: "I am in for some months of cutting up, recovery & convalescence," he said with a characteristic effect of inflation.[4] For some reason the surgery was delayed until after the turn of the year and then performed not in London but in Belfast. In a letter to Gertrude Bannister postmarked 5 January 1905 Casement wrote: "the surgeon has me in his clutches, and after tomorrow I am laid up. . . . This address will find me for one month."[b] The address was "Ardrigh," on the Antrim Road in Belfast, where Francis Joseph Bigger lived in comfortable bachelor state with his mother and his much loved housekeeper Bridget, or Biddy, and where Casement was henceforth a welcome guest as long as he lived, often for days or weeks at a stretch.

In 1904 Casement had managed to collect a year's pay for which his only formal service was the bootless two months in Lisbon in the late summer. He had exhausted the possibilities for paid leave and now must either return to his job or "go off the books" of the Foreign Office, as he expressed it to Cowper.[5] The latter occurred: he was "seconded" without pay for the whole of 1905—and in fact for the first half of 1906 as well. This was to say that he had not resigned or been discharged but had gone into a sort of officially suspended animation, in which he was not an active candidate for a post but was free to become so, and in which the Foreign Office was free to ignore him or to seek him out. During 1905, then, Casement lived like Thackeray's Rawdon Crawleys on nothing a year. It is hard to say just how he survived and one sees signs that he did not find it easy. What he accepted as obligations to his family and to the Irish and Congo causes did not diminish and he did not ignore them. He got by, apparently, on his savings though they could hardly have been large, on a few loans, on the hospitality of his friends, and by further simplifying his manner of living. Casement had always lived modestly and now he was driven to real frugality. His very rootlessness in keeping no establishment and living out of his suitcase, in the long run saved him money especially when combined with the expansive hospitality of such loyal friends as F. J. Bigger in Ireland and Richard Morten in England. Bigger kept him throughout January while he was convalescing, and his doctor gave him a clean bill on 1 February.

On 21 February Tom Casement sent another pitiful bulletin, this

---

[b]NLI 13074. Old check stubs show that Casement paid a hospital bill of £16.14.0 on 6 February and Dr. Kirke's bill for surgery of £21 on 11 March. NLI 15138.

time from Zantspanberg. "I am down in this God forsaken fever trap
trying to do something," he wrote. He was now prospecting for cin-
nabar, or mercury, but without his old outfit of wagon and mules.
He had got lost the day before, with a bad leg and with no coat, no
gun, and no food, finally finding his camp again in the evening.
Roger Casement wrote two notes at the top of the letter: "Poor old
chap"; and "The winding sheet in my bedroom candle was 27th
Feb., or 28th—a very marked & dreadful one."[c] Apparently he related the gloomy portent to Tom's situation.

The year was certainly an unsatisfactory one for Casement,
though perhaps less hectic emotionally than 1904 had been. He was
jobless, payless, and homeless, though by no means at a loss for ways
to pass the time. He pursued his master passions of Ireland and the
Congo, did a good deal of desultory writing, kept up with a large correspondence, and cast about for a career outside the Foreign Office.
His letter to Gertrude ("My dear wee Gee, alias Gougane Barra") of
15 March showed a typical mélange of motives. He and Nina were
"cowering before the March equinoctial gales" but "hoping for April
sun." He lamented that the *United Irishman* had spoiled his "Dream
of the Celt" (his long poem) with misprints, as had also occurred with
his unsigned polemic on Redistribution, which Gertrude had spotted as his. These things, he assured her, were "nothing to what I am
up to!" What he was up to was a program of verbal attacks on the
British rule of Ireland. He was sending her Arthur Griffith's pamphlet, "The Resurrection of Hungary," drawing out the lesson for
Ireland in Hungary's struggle. So he continued: "There is a spirit of
enlightened conviction swelling the Irish heart—and please God this
ancient people shall not go down to the grave."[6]

Again one thinks, how true and how false: how true the case and
the feeling, how false the language and the self-reference. Or were
they separable: mutually ennobling, or mutually corrupting? It was
the old and new enigma of Ireland, the enforced pathology. In his
inflated mood Casement dreamed happily of turning the newest Irish
crisis into an engine that would upend the Ministry: "Balfour is a
dirty soap bubble and please God we Irishmen will blow him into
suds. He won't wash clothes—and there's some dirty Cabinet linen
needs washing badly." He had been after Gertrude for some time to

[c]NLI 13076. "Winding sheet" refers to an old superstition as to the morbid significance of
the shapes of the melting wax.

join his attempt to "learn Irish seriously": "I believe it will be a joy to you yet. It is a lovely, a glorious language."[7] In fact Casement never learned enough Irish to judge it as a language and Gertrude learned a good deal more.

Finally he reported surprising and gratifying news from the Congo where Nightingale had written that the Commission of Inquiry, "convinced against their wills," were going to find themselves forced to substantiate the findings of his report. With that assurance in hand, Casement could afford to dismiss with amused contempt a new attack upon himself in the February issue of the Free State organ *New Africa*. The fact that it was "conceived in the taste of the guttersnipe" he now considered "very cheering indeed—for it is the voice of malice found out!"[8] All in all it was a rattling, energetic, vainglorious letter.

"What a queer fight this is," E. D. Morel had written Casement in the spring,[9] thinking of the struggle to secure justice for the Congo blacks and at the same time somehow to earn a living for oneself and one's family. When the Congo Reform Association was broached, Casement had sent Morel £100 to work with, at a time when that sum represented a third part of his annual pay on extended leave; and he kept in close correspondence with Morel and saw him whenever he could, in Liverpool or London. In their letters Morel and Casement were calling each other "Bulldog" and "Tiger" respectively—as metaphors of their chosen roles in the queer fight. On the first of February in a letter that Casement gratefully annotated "Offers Home Dear Soul," Morel joined him in contempt for Sir Constantine Phipps, recalled his generous gift, and went on to invite his friend in his needy state to come and make a home with the Morels in Liverpool, taking general potluck.[10] Now in April Morel was wondering what the future was to hold for himself and his family. He was thirty-two and journalists were supposed to be finished at forty, and he could not see that he was laying up any treasures on earth. Casement could do nothing at the moment, but he inwardly marked and later in slightly better times he took the Morels' future in hand.

On 3 July Casement learned with total surprise and with feelings otherwise profoundly mixed that he had been named a C.M.G. in the King's Birthday Honors List: A Companion of the Most Distinguished Order of Saint Michael and St. George—the order traditionally reserved for persons who had performed with high merit in the foreign service of Great Britain. The notice came in a letter of 30

June from the Duke of Argyll, Chancellor of the order, and Casement received it at Cushendall in County Antrim where he was
spending a day at the shore with Bulmer Hobson and his Casement
cousin, an Admiral. It was recognition of a sort far from trivial, it
came unsolicited from the Service upon which he had been heaping
contempt for many months, and it pointed specifically at the Congo
work to which, as he had just been writing Lady Margaret Jenkins,[d]
the Foreign Office had accorded "not one word of thanks, not a finger
lifted, or an official voice raised to affirm their knowledge of the absolute truth of my dealings."[11] Presumably Casement felt some
twinges of shame, though he also found the public testimonial rather
tardy: it would have served his spirit better a year earlier. But his
feelings were further complicated. He had received one previous
British decoration of a minor sort, the Queen's South African Medal
for his Boer War "service"—but he had asked for that one himself.[12]
His manner of receiving the new unsolicited honor shows the sharp
shift that had occurred in his system of values in the past three or four
years.

When the news came to the party at the shore, Casement was
greatly agitated and said at once that he would not accept the award.
Both Hobson and his cousin tried to reason him into acquiescence,
but he appeared resolved. Hobson argued that to refuse the honor
amounted to public repudiation of the foreign service—bridges
burned, in effect his own resignation. After walking the sands for an
hour in troubled thought, Casement agreed that he must accept his
C.M.G.[e] His reluctance was evidently quite genuine. His grounds
emerged in a letter of copiously qualified gratitude he sent on 20 July
to his friend Edward Clarke in the Foreign Office, a letter that Clarke
must have found both interesting and irritating. Casement was assuming that he owed his honor largely to Clarke's friendly influence,
and he explained why he reprobated the intervention while thanking
him sincerely for his kindness. He would have thought himself safely
defended in the first place, he said, by his habit of talking against this
sort of thing in the Foreign Office and elsewhere: by "my oft uttered
contempt (that's a nasty word—but I fear it expresses literally my

[d]A daughter of the Third Earl of Norbury. Casement knew the whole family and often visited their seat at Carlton Park, Market Harborough.

[e]MacColl, *Roger Casement*, p. 52. Bulmer Hobson's sister Mrs. Florence Patterson confirmed
this account in conversation with me on 11 March 1972.

feeling) for distinctions and honours and principalities and powers."
He confirmed again: "I dislike these things profoundly"—and hence
while grateful for Clarke's "kind thoughts," he would have felt "far
happier to have been spared."[13]

Casement now came out openly with his special embarrassment: the illogic and indignity he felt, as an Irishman and a
Nationalist, in accepting a British decoration. "You know I am a
confirmed Home Ruler, and various other things," he said, "and I
shall now be regarded askance in every respectable quarter of Ireland." He had his own notion of respectable quarters. What stuck
most painfully in his craw was to be helplessly enrolled in the company of the "Orange 'Loyalists,'" the Irish Sassenachs of the
North: "a positively awful punishment." Casement wondered if he
must now anticipate a Star of the Congo from King Leopold or a
Sevres dinner service from Sir Constantine Phipps. He argued in all
seriousness that persons in danger of honors ought to be warned in
advance and given a chance to show cause "why they should *not* be
decorated." Instead he now found himself forced to write of his
gratitude to Lord Lansdowne for a distinction he deplored. "To you,
my dear Clarke," he ended gracefully, "I reserve the full and unre-
served thanks of one who is not a formalist, but your very sincere and
grateful friend."[14]

By the time he wrote to Clarke, in fact, Casement was well into a
comedy of vacillation and evasion by means of which he escaped receiving the actual thing, the physical insignia of the C.M.G., from
the hands of the British King. On 6 July, Sir W. Baillie-Hamilton,
Officer of Arms of the order, sent the invitation to the presentation at
Buckingham Palace on 24 July. Casement answered from Richhill in
County Armagh on the twelfth that he was unable to appear, giving
no reason. On 25 November Baillie-Hamilton offered him a second
chance on 18 December. On 2 December Casement wrote that "as a
favourable opinion is now given of my hand" (unexplained) he expected to appear on the eighteenth. But on the eighth he demurred
again, on grounds of unspecified ill health. On 14 December
Baillie-Hamilton inquired whether, as the next investiture after the
eighteenth would probably not occur until July, he would prefer to
have the appointment conferred at once, by post. Though Casement
was now actually in London and perhaps even planning to attend at
the palace, he suddenly developed the perfect symbolic ailment: a
lame knee that prevented him from kneeling to the King. So, pur-

suant to his request of 16 December, the ensigns of the C.M.G. were finally sent to him by post, under seal.[15]

Clearly the whole matter of the honor had created a genuine emotional crisis for Casement; and clearly he was determined, consciously or unconsciously, that whereas he could not refuse the King's nomination, he need not accept it in the flesh. Now perhaps he could tell himself that he had accepted the honor but never received it—or put it the other way round? In fact when Casement's decorations were demanded of him for confiscation at the time of his trial the C.M.G. package was found among his effects with its seals unbroken: he had never opened it, never looked upon his decoration. Like many episodes in his life the whole affair was both absurd and impressive.

Had Casement trusted more calmly to the integrity of his own work in his Congo report the vindication he received from the Commission of Inquiry would have seemed more satisfying and less anticlimactic. For the report of the Commission in November 1905 was a triumph for Casement and indeed for the whole movement for reform in the Congo. Poor Phipps in Brussels had to transmit the report to his own government, his mouth full of humble pie: he certainly owned up in a manly way. The Commissioners' report, he allowed, pronounced "strong criticism," "severe condemnation," "the most scathing criticism" of the "coercive" policies of the Congo State: "In short, the entire report proves the administration . . . to be a system of hardly restricted savagery."[16] The Commissioners said, then, precisely what Casement had said, and Casement, Phipps, and Leopold must have been about equally astonished if not equally gratified. Leopold hung naked; Casement needed fear no further serious attack upon a document that was also a justification of twenty years of life.

At the same time, Casement was trying to puzzle out a genuine Irish function for himself and for men like himself, a class role of public service such as the English had developed over centuries and which in Ireland they had succeeded in denying a national consciousness. "This country," he wrote Hobson, "needs men of leisure, who would love her for herself, and who would give to her service what the English aristocracy are trained to give to English public life. All our men of leisure, with scarcely an exception, are English at heart, or by training." The Irish Party in Parliament, he felt, were merely "bartering the national mind and consciousness": getting caught up in intramural power games and playing for parliamentary advantages "which, in the end, only draw Ireland closer into the embrace of England."[17] Instead of such frittering and debilitating maneuvering, Casement preferred to envision a sort of Irish political Academy or Shadow Cabinet, wholly patriotic and national, Irish in every word and thought. Though he spoke always generally, he was apparently making wistful self-reference, trying to imagine a national role for himself if ever he should be free to play it.

But Casement was far from free. He might dream of being a man of cultivated leisure exercising a grave and reflective patriotic influence, an Irish senator of sorts, or even of being a new Parnell; but his circumstances did not allow elegant courses: in fact he was distinctly hard up. At the end of June, for example, his London bankers wrote to remind him that a quarterly installment of £25 was due on Nina's allowance and there was only £3.5.8 in his account: they might agree to an overdraft, they hazarded, if he would describe certain "security" he had mentioned.[18] In September Casement's banking processes collided with his enthusiasm for the Irish language when an official of the Northern Banking Co. Ltd., in Ballycastle wrote to him: "We would not undertake to deal with a correspondence in Irish."[19] The bank pointed out, for one thing, the danger of forgery in such peculiar script; but it seemed clear that nobody at the bank could read Irish and they saw no reason to trouble themselves with such a luxurious antiquarianism. Casement was soon convinced that he must return to the consular service. He had looked for jobs in London but had found nothing satisfactory. He found to his aggravated disgust that his new C.M.G. was actually a handicap in approaching City men: they did not want a C.M.G. in a junior position and they seemed disinclined to offer him a senior position.

As the year wore on, it appeared that not even a Foreign Office position was going to be easily forthcoming. At the beginning of September Casement wrote Lord Lansdowne that his health was reestablished and he wished to go back to work before the end of the year. This letter brought no action and on 12 December he wrote again to Sir Edward Grey, the new Under-Secretary of State for Foreign Affairs, to remind him that he would soon have been seconded for a full year and that he was ready to receive offers.[20] Again nothing happened: it seemed clear that the Lisbon fiasco was still rankling at headquarters.

Casement's situation continued muddled and indecisive through more than half of 1906.[f] He went on looking for a way to return to Africa outside British official service, and always in one corner of his mind was the thought of making a career with his pen, a graceful living that might still be serviceable to the Congo and to Ireland. But when he asked the advice of his friend the journalist and poet H. W. Nevinson, the reply was disenchanting: "One's best and most valuable work is shamefully treated. Nearly all my Russian letters were cut to bits & it is always very discouraging."[21] Nevinson advised him to go and see Sir Edward Grey personally and find out how things really stood for him at the Foreign Office. Just how vague was Casement's situation at this time is shown by his statement to Gertrude on 10 March: "I don't know how long I shall be in England—or where I shall go to from this—my plans are not of my own making and my movements do not altogether depend on my own wishes."[22] This he wrote from Morten's house in Denham and he was still there a month later.

He went on to encourage Gertrude to "stir all your Congo friends up—the more row made the better." He judged that the "present incumbents—or Incumbrances" at the Foreign Office needed a great deal of prodding: "These Liberals will want just as much stirring up over Ireland and Congo as Balfour & Co. . . . Once they get in to power all the delights of office & power overcome the longings and promises of Opposition."[23] If Casement had enemies in the Foreign Office, he certainly had loyal friends as well, and the most engaging and influential of these was Sir William Tyrrell, whom he called "Billie" and with whom he had enjoyed a confidential relationship for several years.[g] Tyrrell always spoke up for him at headquarters and he kept trying to placate Casement himself and to persuade him to reasonable behavior. He assured Casement he was wrong, for example, in supposing that Sir Eric Barrington wished him ill and

[f] In early January Casement borrowed £150 from his old African missionary friend T. H. Hoste. A check stub of 28 October 1907 for £20 is marked: "Interest (over 10%) on the £150 lent me." NLI 15138.

[g] Sir William Tyrrell (later Baron Tyrrell) was born of English parents (he also had oriental blood) in India in 1866. His early schooling was in Germany and he knew the country well. He entered the Foreign Office in 1889 after leaving Oxford. Sir Edward Grey made him his precis-writer in 1905 and his principal private secretary two years later and Tyrrell's influence was great. He was a man of fine grain and first rate intelligence and he became one of the best known and most respected of English diplomatists. He lived on to 1947, his middle and late years saddened by the loss of both his sons in World War I.

worked against him, and he arranged a meeting of the two. But the results were poor. After Casement had made his points, Barrington still wrote on 4 April in a strain that appeared to support all of Casement's suspicions:

> I am afraid from what I hear that the Secy. of State will not be able to offer you one of the present vacancies in the Consular Service, though he recognises your claim to re-employment when a suitable opportunity presents itself.
>
> It was in my opinion must unfortunate that you shd. have so hastily resigned Lisbon which is one of the nicest posts in the Service & was given you in recognition of your work in Africa.[24]

There indeed one seemed to hear the bagpipe voice of officialdom: growl, purr, and drone.

Next day, lying in bed with a lame leg and with Barrington's letter at hand and their interview a sore memory, Casement sent off a letter of fourteen octavo pages to Tyrrell reviewing the whole state of affairs as he saw them. Barrington, he said, had "misunderstood" him, or had affected to do so—"but there was no misunderstanding him." He had been "most discourteous" and Casement had left "wondering whether I had been a public servant of this country or a domestic servant of Barrington's." The great man had suggested that he had turned down Lisbon because he was "dissatisfied with it and wanted to choose a better post; and that a 'beggar who wanted to be a chooser' (his exact words) must take what he could get." Barrington insisted on misreading his motives, and fearing that he would misrepresent them in higher quarters Casement labored to explain himself to Tyrrell. When at the end of 1904 he had resigned the Congo consulate that was still technically his, refused Lisbon, and asked to be seconded for a year, he had proceeded on the assumption that he was unlikely ever to return to the consular service. Apart from his poor health at the time, he had felt honor-bound to make himself a free agent, at liberty to take up whatever position he chose on the Congo issue. Had he accepted the Lisbon position, and then resigned, he pointed out, he would have been given a transfer allowance and other emoluments that he had not earned.[h] Acting as he did, only he had suffered: the Foreign Office had easily found a good man for Lis-

---

[h]His argument seems to make it clear that Casement never actually took office in Lisbon.

bon. In calling him a choosy beggar Barrington had ignored the fact that he was dealing with a C.M.G. For Barrington's opinion of him, Casement said he did not "care a fig," and he himself made no play of his honor in justifying his claim to decent consideration: "I am no grumbling, dissatisfied office seeker . . . but one who has honestly and fearlessly done his duty"; and he had no intention of standing "as a species of lacquey who is to owe post and promotion to 'favour' and the fortunate disposal of appointments which are to be considered as 'gifts' and not public offices."

When at long last, near the end of July, the Foreign Office began to make overtures, Casement rather promptly acquiesced even though they were not very seductive. Emmott wrote on 26 July that he had heard from Grey that Casement was about to be offered a post "which is not all they would wish, but may lead to better things." Emmott advised him to take whatever was offered.[25] Actually Louis Mallet had written Casement the day before that the Consul at Bilbao in Spain had died and the position was his if he wanted it, at a salary of £650 a year and an office allowance of £350. The proposal was inglorious but pleasantly phrased: Sir Edward, according to Mallet, "would like very much to see you back in the Service & hopes that his offer will be agreeable to you."[26] Following Casement's acceptance, Mallet wrote on 30 July: "Sir Edward is glad to hear that you have decided to return to the fold & that the F.O. will have the benefit of your assistance," but he went on to propose the alternative of Santos in Brazil, which Casement's small knowledge of Portuguese might make attractive.[1] Tyrrell wrote on 3 August to say he was pleased that Casement was to be " 'one of us' again" and then on the ninth to stipulate that Santos paid £600 a year plus £200 rent allowance and £500 office allowance. The £300 difference in income carried the day and Tyrrell wrote on 15 August: "We are proceeding with your appointment to Santos."[27]

Casement promised to visit the Bannisters in Liverpool for a few days before sailing on 13 September, but he wrote Gertrude from London on 25 August to say that he had been overcome by a wish to spend his birthday (on 1 September) "in the 'old land' " and so would not be able to come.[28] The job hunt had kept him in England during much of the first half of the year, but the real brooding of his mind

---

[1]Casement noted on Mallet's letter that Cowper had told him Santos was "a hideous hole and very expensive." NLI 13073.

was upon Ireland. At the end of May he had been lamenting the recent death of Michael Davitt as the loss of "one of the last of the chivalrous sons who dreamed of an *independent* Ireland and did not fear to work for it by all manly means." The Sinn Fein movement, he felt, had thrown up no true leader and could have used a man like Davitt.[29] From Ballycastle where he had returned for another Feis, he had written Gertrude on 14 July that her letter had reached him on the twelfth "when the Orange drums were beating and the 'Loyalists' parading their sham of shams through the countryside." The Loyalist landlord Francis Turnley had tried to disrupt the Feis by threatening to "boycott" his tenant who had lent the Committee a field for their Gaelic sports, and some "evil dispoged persons" (including Casement no doubt) had retaliated by printing and circulating a ballad ridiculing Turnley.[30]

Writing, with rare economy and point, to Alice Stopford Green from Ballycastle on 8 September, Casement attacked the English "Devolution"[j] scheme for Ireland as one that would only

> create a new "Castle" and class dependent on it. In God's name what Ireland wants is Responsibility. Until the public here feel that they *must* tackle the state of their own country and abide by their own acts there can be no real improvement. We have to create a governing mind again after 106 years of abstraction of all mind from this outraged land. . . . England destroyed our Constitution, juggled our mind out of our body into hers, and left us only a "corpse on the dissecting table."[31]

At the top of a note he sent Mrs. Green from Cherbourg en route to Santos on 21 September Casement jotted: "Remember my address is Consulate of Great Britain and *Ireland*, Santos—not British Consulate!!"[k] Just before leaving Southampton on the *Nile* on the same day he had sent Gertrude Bannister a color postcard of the Euston Hotel in London on which he had blacked out the Union Jack in ink.[32]

From Vigo on 23 September he wrote Gertrude more at length, still saturated with Irish affections and sore irony at his British employment. He asked her to watch for Irish and Congo news and

---

[j]"Devolution" was a proposal of the Irish Reform Association in 1904, part of a general attempt by moderates in England and Ireland to conciliate Irish grievances by gradual means. The scheme was to place certain strictly Irish affairs in the hands of an elected Council which would have controlled the spending of six million pounds annually on national services.

[k]He had special stationery so imprinted.

send him cuttings: in Santos he was ordering only the weekly *Sinn Fein*, no English papers at all. "I am a queer sort of British Consul, alanna," he mused, one who "ought really to be in jail instead of under the Lion & Unicorn." He went on: "I must say, Gee, I *can't* [thrice underscored] stand Anglo-Saxons—or Imperialists." Of that taint he absolved the Bannister sisters and their mother (now dead), his aunt who was, of course, pure Irish: "You and Lizzerbuth [Elizabeth] are not Anglo-Saxons at all—that drop has been entirely forced out of yr. systems by the dear wee woman's big warm heart—for if ever there was an Irsishwoman in modern times it was she. I have that dear little photo of her in the bonnet—and like it so much." He had just been deeply stirred by reading an account of the "Manchester Martyrs" of 1867 by A.M. Sullivan in *New Ireland*: "God bless them—I read it last night—and it made my heart on fire."[1] Quite clearly he was moving toward that violent pitch of passion which would direct the melodramatic last movements of his life.

[1] NLI 13074. Parry papers. Michael Larkin, Michael O'Brien, and William Philip Allen were hanged after a raid on a prison van that freed two Fenian officers in Manchester in September 1867. In the melee a police officer was killed by a pistol shot intended to break open the lock of the van.

6   A Consul Malgré Moi

ON the long voyage to Santos Casement was "very seedy" for a time with an attack of fever. Arriving on 9 October he found letters of welcome awaiting from Mrs. Green and Gertrude. If he spoke literally in his reply to Gertrude, he had been in Santos exactly an hour when he sat down to write; yet he was already convinced that he would be "a failure in this environment," that the place was intolerable and he must get out. The Foreign Office had told him he need not stay in Santos if he did not like it and he was ready to hold them to their bargain.[1]

He had tried to suppress Francis Cowper's description of Santos as "a hideous hole and very expensive," but now he found it all too accurate. His consular office turned out to be a bare whitewashed room in a coffee warehouse, its doors standing open to casual strollers and the dirt and din of the street. The £90 a year he was to pay for this accommodation would have hired a comfortable home in England or Ireland, Casement noted. Living in a hotel several miles outside the city and commuting by mule-tram, as he would have to do, would cost another £2 a day. He saw how he had been deceived by the attractive sound of the Santos salary: he calculated that his pounds would be worth only seven shillings at the current rate of exchange. Later he learned that speculation in milreis was a national mania: values fluctuated throughout the day and banks received hourly reports by telegraph from Rio de Janeiro. Furthermore, Casement did not like the look of the people: "Everyone looks a half-caste or a hybrid." His letter, he admitted, was "one long, steady, persistent wail O! cousing dear," but he was still resolved to "get away from this and early, too." He ended with another rush of his old sentiments: "Send me news of Congo and Ireland—nothing else counts—Ireland 'first and ever'—and poor old Congo too for the sake of the dark skins and all they have suffered and all the brave, indomitable Morel has done to free them."[2]

In the same generally sad set of tones the year wore away. When Casement took up his duties, he found they only added to his sense of the futility of life in Santos. The port was a busy one, shipping £15,000,000 worth of coffee in a year, but with that the British Consul had little to do. In fact his work was trifling and seemed to consist mainly in trying to deal with derelict British seamen. "The men get drunk & come ashore & desert in shoals & the place is a pandemonium," he wrote to his friend Mrs. A. W. Hutton of Belfast.[3] He took to calling the drunken sailors "the Wonders of the Deep" and he decided that what Santos required was not a Consul but a "bar keeper's chucker out."[4] By Christmas time he had concluded that Brazil was "the least interesting country in the world" and Santos the absolute of "all the futile and absurd posts" he had "ever heard of, or read of, or dreamed of."[5] He had found a friend to share a house on the coast eight miles from town and daily bathing in the sea gave him almost his only pleasure in life—that, and talking with a boy from Kerry he had taken on as a clerk: "Patrick by name & a real Pat by nature too. . . . altho' only a poor boy I find I can talk to him on any subject."[a] To T. P. Gill, M.P. and Gaelic Leaguer, Casement wrote at the end of the year that he had found "some patriotic Irishmen" and would soon be sending in "some big subscriptions" for the Irish language movement.[6] But in Brazil he was in neither country of his heart: "Africa is the place for me—if it can't be Ireland."[7]

Sir Edward Grey had incautiously invited Casement to let him know what he thought of Santos and he did so on 4 March—not intimating that he had resolved within his first hour there not to stay, but presenting the judgment of five months' tenure. The letter is another example of Casement's steady willingness to speak his mind to his superiors. "Santos is not a nice place," he wrote, "indeed it is quite the nastiest place I've ever been in." He developed at great length his objections to the triviality of his work, to the ruinous expensiveness of life, and to the Brazilian people themselves. Casement's particular racial prejudice took the form of disgust for "hybrid" races. His respect and affection for "the dark skins," for African blacks and later for South American red men, held the senti-

---

[a]It sounded a bit like Gulliver at the end of his travels, conversing with his horses.

mental condescending paternalism of his class, but it was still not false. But something about the mixture of black with red, or of either with white, moved him to a fastidious distaste not always fastidiously expressed: "Brazil and the Brazilians are vile," he wrote Gertrude on 1 April; "I can't bear them—mud-coloured swine!" To Grey he wrote that whereas he had found the Africans "a happy-hearted, bright-faced people" in spite of their sufferings, the Brazilians were a bustling main-chance commercial race who never smiled: smiling might suggest to others that they were not serious in their pretentious assault upon the heaven of "Paris"—their ideal of "Parisian" finesse in business and society. Casement especially despised their habitual glossy formal European clothing: if they had gone naked, he suggested, they might have been happier and able to smile. But natural was the one thing Brazilians were resolved never to be. Of Santos, then, Casement could only say: "I don't like it *at all* at all."[8]

To help live with his situation as a British Consul in a place he loathed, Casement hugged to himself the thought that he was not really "one of them." He was an Irishman, unhappily and he hoped only temporarily, trapped in the service of Britain. "I, worse luck to it, am a Consul *malgré moi*," he wrote Alice Stopford Green on 20 April.[9] Whenever he had to identify himself in Brazil, he said he was "an Irishman": this he called, prophetically, "sowing seeds of 'Treason.' "[10] Mrs. Green had written to caution him that he was putting his own career at risk by his espousal of Alfred Parminter who had been fired by the Foreign Office for "incompetence." Casement had known Parminter well since 1885 in Africa and was godfather to his young son Reggie. He believed the man to be able and honorable and attributed his troubles to a single slanderous letter which his superiors refused to produce; and he defended Parminter stubbornly in representations to the Foreign Office. Now he offered his friend a haven in Santos for as long as he needed it and soon got him a managerial post on a big Brazilian coffee estate.

Casement used Mrs. Green's warning as an occasion for sending her a long analysis of his own history as leading to the tensions of his present situation. "It is a mistake for an Irishman to mix himself up with the English," he wrote her on 20 April.[11] If he does so, and if he "remains Irish," he will be driven "to the wall"; otherwise he must "become an Englishman himself." Casement had almost "become one"—at the time of the Boer War. Having been away from Ireland for years, "out of touch with everything native to my heart & mind," he had found that every bit of performance of his duty was pushing him closer in spirit to the "ideal of the Englishman." He had accepted the Imperialist program, meaning that "British rule was to be extended at *all* costs, because it was the best for everyone under the sun, & those who opposed . . . ought rightly to be smashed." He reflected in amazed retrospection: "I was on the high road to being a regular Imperialist Jingo." Yet his Irishness had dozed on "underneath all & unsuspected almost by myself."[12] When he "found" the Gaelic League early in 1904, "all the old hopes and longings" of his boyhood had "sprung to life again." The "fight" in Ireland, as he saw it, was a struggle to preserve, or rather to resurrect, "the continuity of our national character," so that Irishmen might not "cease to be Irish." Ireland must recover not only her language but all the values of the heart "filched" from her by years of exposure to English materialism: England valued nothing but "success in marketable terms."

To Mrs. Green's brother E. A. Stopford, addressing him as "the descendant of a Cromwellian invader," Casement wrote on 27 June of his faith that "this ancient Irish mind and character will conquer" and presented his mystique of "the Protean Irish resistance":

> Weak, ineffective, disorganized, seemingly purposeless, constantly obscured and submerged yet it has been there all the time, and the almost unconscious purpose of this thrice-conquered, wholly devastated and seemingly utterly lost people will, in the end, I believe outlive and triumph over the power and pride of the exploiter.[13]

Blessed with leave until 19 September 1907 Casement reached London on 22 July and settled briefly into his now customary rooms with Miss Cox at 110 Philbeach Gardens, Earls Court. Within a couple of weeks he had moved on to Ireland and on 14 August he was writing in a savage mood to Gertrude Bannister from Ballycastle, following an incident in Belfast involving striking workers and 4,000 British troops in which three persons had been killed and many hurt: "I go up there tomorrow and please God I'll take a gun & if it comes to shooting I know who I'll shoot."[14] Evidently he changed his mind overnight about the gun or at least about shooting it. On 22 August he left for three weeks in Donegal and the Irish College at Cloghaneely to pursue his Irish studies—which had never advanced far; "I don't know as much Irish as I do French," he confessed to Gertrude.[15]

The early stages of Casement's leave were lightened by signs that he had made his point about Santos with sufficient force and the Foreign Office had faced its obligations to him with enough candor to offer him a decent appointment at last. On 23 August he was told that he could replace A. S. Vansittart as Consul-General at Port-au-Prince, Haiti, when Vansittart retired at the end of December. Meanwhile there was no need to return to Santos and he was invited to apply for two months' extension of leave from 20 September.[16] Casement was quite set up by his prospects: the climate was good, living conditions pleasant, the salary relatively generous, and the cost of things low enough so that he could hope to save a fair sum for family obligations and Irish causes.[b]

Meanwhile Frank Gritton of the Foreign Office had written that C. B. Rhind, Consul at Pará (now generally called Belem) at the mouth of the Amazon on the Atlantic coast, was ill on leave in London and wondered if Casement might like to exchange Santos for Pará. Rhind would be glad of a chance to sit somnolent in Santos and he thought Casement might enjoy the more active options of Pará such as looking into still unexplored areas of the great strange river: "You see he has heard of your adventurous tastes and wants to make you happy."[17] Secure in the promise of Haiti, Casement paid little heed to the suggestion. But suddenly the Foreign Office began to mumble and turn evasive again, and it developed that they had now decided they needed Haiti for a Consul who had been wounded in the Boer War and was partially disabled, Murray of Warsaw. Finally the matter was put to Casement in such terms that he was made to feel that he must renounce Haiti or do a selfish unkindness to a man who was unwell.

On 19 November he saw his friend Tyrrell at the Foreign Office and agreed to make the sacrifice in favor of Murray. But he was disappointed and sore and he went home and wrote Tyrrell a bitter

[b]A minute in Casement's hand lists "Receipts to 1 October '07" of £1,440.13.1 and disbursements of £1,358.13.6, leaving a balance of just under £82. From other evidence it appears that the period covered is about thirteen months. Among other items he notes gifts of £5 to Charles Casement and "Nina (Extra)" and "Charlie—Suit of Clothes" £3.5.0. "Payments to Irish Causes in 1907" apparently came to £85.10.0 and included £15 to "Republic," £5 to the Consumption Crusade, £5 to Bulmer Hobson ("B.H."), £17 to Canon McFadden, £5 to the Belfast Dungannon Club, £5.4.0 to Sinn Fein, £11 to Cloghaneely College, £7 to Rathlin School, £3 to Irish schools in Ring and Munster, £5 to the North Leitrim Election Fund, and £2 for a prize at the Feis of the Glens. In May 1908 he notes another £25 to Cloghaneely College and in June £5 to the Rathlin [Irish] Teacher Fund. NLI 15138.

letter—which he never sent—to say that he could not stomach the thought of Santos or of São Paulo which had also been proposed: perhaps a small vice-consulate could be found for him somewhere that would give him time to look about for a job outside the consular service.[18] Next day Casement talked things over with Lord Dufferin who agreed that the Foreign Office now owed him something big and new in the way of decent treatment. Casement left London and went back to Ballycastle. But the Pará scheme began to be bruited again, and in early December Lord Dufferin wrote in much harder terms than he had used in London: it was Pará or nothing.

A former Consul at Pará, W. A. Churchill, sent Casement a description of what awaited him. Pará was a city of 120,000 souls which offered "nearly all modern conveniences" and the consular duties there were "not overwhelming." But the rainy season lasted from January to June and it was very disagreeable. In Churchill's day the best hotel had been "a superior sort of cow-shed called the Grand Hotel da Paz." The general cost of living was very high: for example most people wore dark clothes because washing was so expensive. To live decently in a house of his own had cost him £200 a year over his income, Churchill estimated. "I fully agree with you," he wrote, "about this being the most idiotic branch of the public service."[19] Certainly the Haiti fiasco and the crudely forced return to Brazil had killed off for Casement any lingering respect or affection for the Foreign Office as an employer or an institution.

In the weeks that remained before sailing Casement moved about in Ireland as much as he could before a long final visit to the Mortens in Denham. The last two weeks of December and the first days of January he passed happily with Nina in the Spa Hotel in Lucan on the coast north of Dublin, with the Dublin Hills "shining to the South."[20] From Lucan on 19 December he sent Hobson his bond for £100 to support his application for the job of manager of the Cooperative in Cushendall, a local function of the Gaelic League. Casement spoke vaguely of "the sacrifice of a good deal of money— now and to come" since October.[21] The reference is unexplained, but the sacrifice is pretty sure to have been made on behalf of Nina or one of their two brothers. "I'm leaving Ireland—for *bad*," he wrote Gertrude on 6 January, and passing through London two days earlier he had written her wretchedly: "I feel a foreigner at heart here."[22]

Finally occupying his office in Pará on 4 March, Casement spent a

fair portion of his first day in composing an eleven-page bill of complaint to Lord Dufferin. As at Santos his first look had convinced him
that the situation was hopeless. "I shall not be able to stay at Pará," he
wrote: he intended to leave as soon as he could get ready and could
find somebody to stand in for him, and when he got home he would
resign from the Consular Service. Again his deadliest objection was
to the cost of living as compared to the pay offered him. "You people
at home have no conception of the cost of life in Brazil," he said
bluntly.[23] He was sure he would be going into a hole from the very
outset: the cost of the office alone he estimated at more than £700 a
year. And all of this money was to go to sustain a life of "absolute
dreariness and futility." None of the Consul's duties in Pará were "of
the slightest interest or importance." The bottle of Pará beer and the
tin of Pará biscuits that would have made "excellent pigeon food," off
which he was lunching as he wrote, had cost him six shillings. At his
"impossible" hotel a cup of tea or a glass of stout cost two shillings,
and noise and mosquitoes had kept him virtually sleepless for ten
days. The Pará whores frequented the place by day for meals and by
night for amusement and custom and sometimes made the dining
room so crowded and uproarious that he could not sit down to eat.
Yet the simplest sort of private housekeeping would cost him £1,000
a year, and the alternative, a crowded indiscriminate boarding house
for clerks, seemed unsuited to the supposed status of H.M. Consul.
Between the demands of his office and the claims of his small dignity,
Casement estimated, he was worse off than the rawest local clerk
earning £500 a year.

Perhaps what rankled worst of all was the fact that he was being
asked to pay this price to live in a mongrel society that kept his
stomach churning: "These people are disgusting boors—rude, un-
couth and arrogant. They treat me with open rudeness and have far
less manner or courtesy than an African savage." Again it was the
mixing of bloods that Casement found peculiarly offensive:

> They are nearly all hideous cross-breeds—of Negro-Portuguese
> with, up here in the Amazon, a very large admixture of native
> Indian blood. Altogether the resultant human compost is the
> nastiest form of black-pudding you have ever sat down to. The
> native African is a decent, friendly, courteous soul—the Indian,
> too, I daresay is a hardy savage *chez lui*—but the "Brazilian" is
> the most arrogant, insolent and pig-headed brute in the world I
> should think.[24]

He was resolved to return to the black purities of Africa, by some means. He reminded Lord Dufferin that he had refused an offer to be Inspector of Finance for the Mozambique Company in the preceding July when he had been promised Haiti. He had heard that the place was still open and he would try for it again—if necessary at half what the Foreign Office "nominally" paid him at Pará. In the more passionate and intimate terms that he always used in writing to Gertrude, Casement reviewed the "penance" that was his life at Pará and the whole discouraging state of the career in which his thirteen years had been "utterly wasted and misplaced." The consular service had turned out to be "no Service at all—but only jobbery and corruption"; not a public service but "the domestic scullery of the F.O. officials—to be portioned out among menials and bottlewashers."[25]

Ever since landing in Pará at the end of February Casement had felt not only unhappy but unwell, "seedy." Early in June he fell truly sick and took to his bed under the care of a local Austrian doctor. His ailment was mysterious and not a mere recurrence of his old Congolese malaria. At first it was called "a sort of blood poisoning," but eventually it was diagnosed as acute gastritis. After three weeks on his back in Pará without significant improvement, he was ordered by his doctor to Barbados, 1,200 miles to the north, to "convalesce." When he was carried on board the *Cearense* on 25 July he was "a loathsome sight—blotches and sores and eruptions."[26] It was some comfort to realize that he could travel to Barbados, lie up there under medical care, and return to Pará for far less than it would have cost him in Pará merely to lie still without eating or drinking. At the end of the three weeks in Barbados that were supposed to bring him round he felt no better. He wrote to Bulmer Hobson on 20 August: "I have shrunk to a shadow & neither eat, sleep nor walk but lie on my back all day." He felt "like a badly ordered nightmare."[27] His illness was stubborn and in fact he remained two full months in Barbados with a succession of five doctors before he was able to return to Pará at the end of September.

On leave and still feeling shaky, Casement stopped in Lisbon for a week's pure rest to "recover from Pará" before reaching home on 4 December 1908, proceeding from Liverpool to Richhill with no gesture of any kind toward London or the Foreign Office. By 7 December he had moved on to Dublin where he passed the remaining days of the year. Casement's renewed application to the Mozambique Company came to nothing: the offer of July 1907 was not repeated. Now when the Foreign Office offered the post of Consul-

General at Rio de Janeiro he accepted at once, even though he had vowed several times never to consider it. The appointment was confirmed on 1 December and announced in the papers, so that the Foreign Office stood committed at last to Roger Casement's promotion to be chief consular officer in a major capital. Evidently feeling that if he must return to Brazil he could at least go slowly, he visited the Mortens in January and again in early February after a return to Dublin, and he spent the second week of February with the Wards in Paris before moving on to Lisbon for several weeks, finally taking the R.M.S. *Amazon* on 9 February for a pleasant voyage that unhappily ended at Rio. "I hate Brazil," he wrote again flatly to Gertrude on 31 March, a week after landing.[28]

He had fallen ill on his first day with a bout of his Congo fever, with a temperature of 106 degrees and violent nausea; but the sharp attack was also brief and in a day or two he was all right: "Fierce come soon go," he phrased a cheerful motto for his Congolese attacks.[29] Brazil did not improve on longer acquaintance and Casement put first impressions of his new situation in inclusive negatives: "No home; no privacy; no comfort; no friends; no social life or pleasant friendly intercourse." The resonance of his new title was not matched by the quality of daily life. His official quarters were "a hot stuffy office in a noisy tropical street" and he had to travel three miles by tram to and from his little hotel bedroom: "Such is life in this accursed country."[30]

In such circumstances, Casement's major consolation, as well as his continued frustration, lay in passionate thoughts of Ireland. Ireland still filled his mind and emptied his pocket. From Paris on 2 February he had sent Bulmer Hobson his proxy in affairs of the *Irish Nation*, W.P. Ryan's socialist paper in which Casement owned eighty £1 shares.[31] Such "investments" were really donations and were tacitly understood as such. This kind of gesture gave Casement a quite false reputation in Ireland as a man of wealth.[c] On 7 April, still looking for a graceful way to provide his friend with a bit of pock-

[c]Under the date of 10 November 1909 William O'Brien's diary records that Casement had happened to overhear in the *Irish Nation* office a conversation about the paper's serious financial straits: he wrote out a check for £70 on the spot. It is not clear whether O'Brien mistook the sum or Casement took another ten "shares" at another time. NLI 16274. Among his check stubs is also one dated 26 January 1909 for 60 shares at £1 in the Irish Ireland Printing and Publishing Co. Another dated 14 April 1909 shows payment of £25 to Arthur Griffith "for shares in Sinn Fein"—the paper of that name. A stub of 25 August 1909 for £5 is marked: "Remaining five shares in daily 'Sinn Fein'—completes £50." NLI 15138.

et money, he suggested that Hobson act as his commission agent in place of the London firm, W. J. Allison and Company, that he had dealt with since Congo days.[d] Hobson could take the London five percent commission but deal with Dublin or Belfast firms, and so the whole arrangement could remain Irish: "Sinn Fein" ("Ourselves"). Three weeks later he ordered through Hobson subscriptions to John Devoy's New York *Gaelic American* to be addressed to his name in its Irish form: "Ruari MacAsmund, P.O. Box 160, Rio de Janeiro." At the same time he promised an order for stationery to be procured from Dollards on the Dublin quays. He warned Hobson to take care not to lose the little die of the Royal Arms of Great Britain *and* Ireland that he had had cut in London at a cost of thirty-five shillings: he intended to use it regularly to imprint his official stationery.[32]

With an income of £1,600 and a wider range of options for economy, Casement's fiscal situation was somewhat improved in Rio. But it was still perilous even though he lived as always on a very modest scale. He really could not afford the kind of *beau geste* to which he was addicted and which had come to be expected of him. When he was home in the winter he had been forced to borrow largely from several friends.[e] Of Casement's hard-won surplus, what was not claimed by Irish causes was regularly required by his needy family. He had increased his allowance to Nina to £35 per quarter. A check stub of 11 December 1908 for a round £20 to "E. Peacock tailor" is marked "Tom's a/c."[33] The ebullient and unlucky Tom was now trying his hand at a farm in South Africa and Casement foresaw early calls for help. In early May came a wire from his elder brother Charlie in Melbourne imploring him to send £100 "at all costs" and it cost £106 to get the money together and wire it back.[34] It appears that Casement had to dip into office funds to meet this demand. Check stubs of 3 May and 12 May, each for £40, are marked respectively: "Part of money due to office at Consulate (*Charlie*)" and "Office expenditure (Charlie's a/c)."[35]

---

[d]Mr. W. C. Allison, who entered his father's firm in 1905 as a boy of fifteen and who is still in business in Farringdon Road in Holborn, recalls seeing Casement often about the premises when he was in London. A chain smoker, Casement had to be reprimanded for smoking in the Allison warehouse while sorting out his belongings in trunks and boxes stored there.

[e]On 9 February while in Paris he sent Alfred Emmott £100 in "Repayment of a December loan" and paid Herbert Ward £50 borrowed in December, leaving £50 still due from an earlier loan. NLI 15138. On 3 August from Rio he sent Richard Morten £20 in notes in partial payment of an old loan on which he had also paid £50 in 1908. NLI MS unclassified.

Irish notes flowed copiously from South America throughout the year. In August Casement was in a state of rage because Lieutenant Shackleton, a Home Rule Irishman whose family had resisted British domination for a hundred years, was being proclaimed an "English" hero in the British press.[f] "If he had cut a cow's tail off," Casement wrote Gertrude, "instead of gone near the South Pole of course he would have been an Irishman right enough." He blamed Shackleton himself for submitting to English adulation. On accomplishment of his feat he should have gone straight home to Dublin rather than to London: "I'd have sent the polite reply that after I had completed my visits in my own country I should be very happy to address foreign gatherings etc. etc."[36] To Gertrude and others Casement continued his attack on the Irish Party as "now the chief danger to our country." The Party and its leaders, John Redmond, John Dillon, and T. P. ("Tay Pay") O'Connor, had "abandoned every principle of Irish nationality and sacrificed our birthright not for a mess of pottage but for a promise of a chance to lick the plates in the scullery of John Bull's basement."[37]

Casement "presumed" that Tay Pay and the "three Johns"—Redmond, Dillon, and even Bull—"meant well" to Ireland, but under their leadership "the poor woman" (Shan Van Vocht: The Poor Old Woman) was "failing fast."[38] Writing to Hobson as one patriotic Protestant Irishman to another, Casement spent most of a twelve-page letter in railing at the Catholic clergy and at the Irish people's subservience to the Catholic hierarchy. The Bishops, he supposed, also "meant well" to Ireland, but their eye was not on the nation but on the Church: they were obsessed with keeping intact the acquiescent "discipline" of priest and parish. The result was yet further displacement and erosion of the national political will, which dissipated itself in religious beatitude or in the ritual rants of "our hoarse-throated patriots." Meanwhile, always hoping, he had sent Arthur Griffith £50 for the daily *Sinn Fein*—though he felt no great

[f]Sir Ernest Henry Shackleton (1874–1922) was one of the greatest of early Antarctic explorers. He was born in County Kildare of mixed English Quaker and Irish stock. After an early career as a seaman he performed heroically in the National Antarctic Expedition of 1901–02 as junior officer under Commander R. F. Scott. Shackleton's own expedition of 1907–08 reached the South Pole itself and added enormously to knowledge of the geography of the whole region. He was lionized on return to England. A still larger expedition of 1914–16 was defeated by the elements, but Shackleton's management of the affair was again masterly and courageous. He died of heart failure on a fourth expedition in January 1922 and his memorial service in St. Paul's Cathedral was attended by King George V and Queen Mary.

faith in Griffith as a national leader, thinking him too narrow and inflexible in mind, and he had somehow to find another £50 to make up the £80 he had pledged for the Hall at Cloghaneely College.[39]

In the latter half of 1909 Casement did at last begin to show some forms of energy and of interest in Brazil that were not hopelessly negative. As always he was happier when he was busy and peripatetic and he felt invigorated when duty required a journey of 360 miles to Victoria, "an Indian place up north."[40] He liked the purer racial forms and the more primitive quality of life there, as a relief from the sham Parisianism of citified Brazilians, and he stayed on for the full month of July—his satisfaction increased by finding two congenial Irishmen one of whom, Brian Barry, turned out to be a Ballymena schoolmate from thirty years back. Casement had also come alive to the physical beauty of the immense country, which he now called "a paradise," "beautiful beyond words."[41] The unappreciated beauty and richness of the land served to intensify his irritation at the people, but it also provided him with the exhilaration of a new political *bête noire*, the United States, to share obloquy with England, and with a new political idol, Germany: America was throttling South America, Germany was needed to set her free.

When Casement sent his "Birthday diatribe" to Gertrude on 1 September, he was staying in Petropolis, the haven of the diplomatic community, and spending four and a half hours daily in commuting the thirty miles to Rio, taking the railway 2,700 feet up and down the mountain and a steamer back and forth across the bay. The carriages of the "Leopoldina Railway"—English, of course—were wretched little trucks with no room for his handbag or his long legs. His basic opinion of Brazil remained contemptuous: where dress was "religion" and vanity "High Priest," life continued "perverted, comfortless and dreary." It was a nation of eighty-five percent illiteracy but endless self-praise: "My Heavens how they talk—of Brazil—its glories, its power, its magnificence, their excellent qualities, their intellect, their courage, their beauty, their 'good hearts' . . . They make me ill." What they really needed was "the great descending birch rod of some stronghanded Power to teach them to be men and women"; and what stood between them and salutary discipline was arrogant America and "that abominable Monroe Doctrine." "Someday," Casement hoped, Europe would "challenge this pretence of the U.S.A. and put it to the arbitrament of battle," and in that day he wished for a German triumph and the installation of "a great German state with honest clean laws and institutions here under the Southern Cross."[42]

Now, as later, Casement's cant praise of Germany was based less on positive knowledge than on negative prejudice. He knew little of Germany and he admired her because England hated her, because she stood poised at the throat of Ireland's ancient enemy. All of this was loose and dangerous talk, of Brazil and England and Ireland and Germany, by an Irishman earning a living in Brazil as a public servant of Britain, and Casement knew it was well that he was only talking in private to a confidential friend. "You must not quote your Cousin Scodge!" he warned Gertrude. If he were overheard in Rio, he imagined, his consulate would be stoned and he himself "expelled [from] the country with a howling mob of these piebald half-castes pelting me from the quays."[43]

In November having made the trip of 360 miles, sixty of them on foot, to Espirito Santo in Victoria, Casement found relief again in the natives who were "rather nice simple beings" with little thought of diamonds, frock coats, or Paris hats. He was staying in a house on a "wee hill" above the sea where he could run out to bathe every day and enjoying the company of his friend Brian Barry, a "very warm hearted and generous" man but one completely out of touch with Ireland. Brought up in Ulster as "a Protestant priest hater," Barry had never got beyond the traditional Loyalist view that "Ireland was a dependency of John Bull's waistband and could not live except tied to that old gentleman's paunch."[44]

Friends in Africa: Edward Glave, W. G. Parminter, Herbert Ward, Roger Casement. From Herbert Ward, *A Voice from the Congo, Comprising Stories, Anecdotes, and Descriptive Notes* (London: Wm. Heineman, 1910).

Casement with Juan Tizon on the Putumayo, 1910. From *The Sketch* (London), 2 December 1914.

7   Toward Uttermost Parts

AS Casement's jotted diary covering all but a few days of 1910 has survived, one can follow him fairly closely again. In fact his crucial action of the year, the investigation of atrocities in the rubber trade in the Putumayo basin of Peru, survives in five distinct forms.[a] They provide considerable detail, some of it uninteresting or unlovely. The first entry in the jotted diary, for example, that for 13 January 1910 in Rio, suggests that Casement's homosexual career had been going on actively during the long periods in which one has been unable to spy upon him:

> Gabriel Ramos. Last time—"palpite" [anticipation, fluttering] at Barca at 11:30. To Icarsby "precisa muito" [needs a lot]—15 or 20 $. [In margin: "X deep to hilt."] Also on Barca the young caboclo [mixed Indian and white] (thin) dark gentleman of Icarsby. Eyed constantly and wanted. Would have gone but Gabriel querido[dear] waiting at Barca Gate! "Palpite"—in *very* deep thrusts.[1]

On 28 February, apparently in Rio, Casement recorded: "Deep screw and to hilt. X 'poquino' [pouquinho: a little bit]. Mario in

---

[a] (1) The jotted diary just mentioned, held in the Public Record Office in London (HO 161); (2) the same diary printed (with many errors) not from the manuscript but from a "Scotland Yard" typewritten transcription, in *The Black Diaries: An account of Roger Casement's Life and Times with a Collection of His Diaries and Public Writings*, by Peter Singleton-Gates and Maurice Girodias; (3) a much fuller diary of the period from 23 September to 6 December, handwritten on 128 duofold foolscap sheets (i.e., 512 pages), held in the National Library of Ireland (13085–86); (4) a typewritten copy of this diary, in two folio volumes totaling 408 pages, each volume signed "George Gavan Duffy" (in Irish script) by Casement's last solicitor, also in the National Library of Ireland (1622–3); (5) Casement's formal report to the British Foreign Office, eventually printed in a government Blue Book (Cmd. 6266).

Rio—8½ + (plus) 6 40$. Hospedaria, Rua do Hospicio. 3$ only fine room shut window lovely, young 18 and glorious. Biggest since Lisbon 1904 and as big. Perfectly huge." [In margin: " 'Nunca veio maios!' " (He never came any more.)] On 1 March he left for São Paulo and similar experience: "Antonio 10$ Rua Direita. Dark followed and hard. Teatro Municipal. Breathed and quick, enormous push. Loved *mightily*." In five days in Buenos Aires he saw a great deal of a lover named Ramon whose principal haunt was the public zoo.

On 25 January, with the temperature at 100 degrees in the "shade" of his office, Casement was writing to Gertrude and resuming his railing at John Redmond's Irish "Party," noting that whereas they now held the balance of power in Parliament they still showed no signs of "Irish" statesmanship: "They are merely a tail of the Liberal party".[2] Between 16 March and 4 April when he sailed for home, Casement divided his time between Buenos Aires and Mar del Plata 300 miles to the south, " 'the Brighton of the Argentine' . . . a very fashionable place indeed," where he found many Irishmen who seemed to be among the most successful immigrants, "most of them *very* rich indeed."[3] He was scheming to take the long way home via South Africa to visit Tom Casement in the Orange Free State. Tom was now trying to promote his farm, "Rydal Mount," at Witzies Hoek at the foot of the Drakensberg, as a sort of rough-hewn country resort for jaded city dwellers. Roger Casement, naturally, was paying his annual rent of £100[4] but Tom had written on 27 January anticipating better times as both the Railroad and Thomas Cook and Son were showing interest. Meanwhile the signs were typically bad. On a recent pack trip his pony had broken a leg in a fall over a cliff and had to be despatched with a revolver. The execution required four shots and after the second, Tom said, the pony "got up & looked at me with an awful look."[5] The pathetic image haunted Roger Casement for a long time. Brother Charlie had been trying to reason with Tom's estranged wife Blanche in Melbourne, but she was both "very bitter" against him and unwilling to divorce him. In the upshot Roger Casement failed to find satisfactory passage to Cape Town and so he sailed for home on 4 April on the Lamport and Holt *Veronese*, passing several days in the Canary Islands before reaching Liverpool and London on 1 May. His absence of fourteen months had been the longest since early Africa days.

The next two weeks in London were easy and cheerful with

Casement in his old rooms with Miss Cox in Earls Court and picking up his old social, official, and amorous life. A "Greek" cost him £1 on 3 May. At the Foreign Office on 6 May Billy Tyrrell prophesied the death of Edward VII and it occurred that night. Casement spent three days with Dick Morten whom he now for some reason referred to as "poor old chap," and visited Gertrude at her girls' school in Caversham where she was now second in command and took her back to London for the theatre. He saw much of friends, particularly E. D. Morel, the journalist Robert Lynd, and Mrs. Green and her brother Colonel Stopford. With Nina or alone he went again and again to the Earls Court Exhibition, being especially taken with the Japanese and Formosan offerings.

On 18 May Casement crossed to Dublin, taking little pleasure in the company of John Redmond, chief of the Irish Party. Until the twenty-sixth he stayed at the Gresham in Sackville Street, "very comfortable." These were easy desultory days. He saw old friends, including a big party with Douglas Hyde and Agnes O'Farrelly and a generally Anglo-Irish crowd, and attended the "rotten" Irish opera *Eithne*. On 20 May instead of attending the funeral service for the King, he went to the zoo in Phoenix Park, a postcard of which he sent to his zoo-haunting friend Ramon of Buenos Aires. On 26 May in Belfast, Casement improved a chance encounter with one John McGonegal whom he found "awfully keen" and whose member was "huge and curved" so that one could "see it coming!" Next day at Richhill Castle he talked "art" with C.W.R. Gordon of the Belfast Royal Academic Institute.[b] On 28 May an old friend named Millar came to lunch at the Grand Central Hotel and they went to Warrenpoint in the afternoon and turned in together after an evening watching billiards: "Not a word said till—'Wait I'll untie it' and then 'Grand.' Told many tales and pulled it off on top grandly. First time after so many years and so deep mutual longing. Rode gloriously— splendid steed—Huge—told of many—'Grand.' "[c] The incident was essentially repeated next night after a day spent in Warrenpoint and Rostrevor: "Millar again! Back. First time he turned his back. 'Grand.' " The ensuing five days in Belfast included visits with F.J. Bigger and Bulmer Hobson and an exploration with Millar of the

[b]Identified from Casement's fragmentary diary note by Mrs. Florence H. Patterson.
[c]This seems to be one of the cases in which Casement went back and amplified a sketchy note. For Millar see pp. 184, 485–86.

Giant's Ring, a prehistoric earthwork near the city. Most of the first three weeks in June were spent in the Antrim glens and the towns at their feet on the coast. At Cushendun on 11 June Casement made a pilgrimage to the ancient cairn of Shane O'Neill with his old girl friend Ada or Ide MacNeill, whom he cited formally in his diary as "Miss MacNeill." On the ninteenth he spent a "lovely day" on Rathlin Island and left £10 for the school fund and another £2 for a prize for a scholar of Irish. His Ulster circuit was rounded on 20 June when he met Millar for dinner and the evening at the Northern Counties Hotel in Belfast: "Gave Millar pin for tie. Stayed till 9.30 and in Room XX. Then to his mother's by foot and by tram. In deep and warm."[d] Next day Bulmer Hobson saw Casement off on the night boat for Liverpool.

In Ballycastle Casement had had a letter from his old friend John H. Harris of the Anti-Slavery and Aborigines Protection Society saying that he had suggested to Sir Edward Grey that Casement was the right man to send to Peru to investigate shocking reports of atrocities in the Putumayo operations of the Peruvian Amazon Rubber Company. Casement had wired and written back the same day expressing interest and willingness. In London on 23 June he shared in "splendid talk" at the office of the society and at the House of Commons with Charles Dilke, Noel Buxton, Josiah Wedgwood, and other M.P.'s, exploring the Putumayo situation which seemed to show grim likenesses to Leopold's Congo system. Next day Casement joined E. D. Morel for dinner with Sir Arthur Conan Doyle and a performance of Doyle's play *The Speckled Band*. "I liked him greatly," he wrote Gertrude of Doyle.[6] Before retiring he managed two sexual encounters, at 1:00 and 1:45 A.M., at a cost of 16/6. In London and in a visit to Carlton Park he saw a great deal of a group of titled ladies of the family of the Earl of Norbury who were old friends of Casement's. He also saw Mrs. Green, his cousin Lizzie, and an old German crony from Africa, Count Gebhard Blücher and his English wife, the former Evelyn Stapleton-Bretherton. But most of Casement's time was going to two major undertakings: plans for a "testimonial" for Morel and for the new investigation in the Putumayo.

The Morel affair had formed the motive, for example, of the evening with Conan Doyle who was heading the national committee.

---

[d]I take it that the time-sequence of the last two sentences is reversed as often happens in Casement's jotted diaries.

Morel had been troubled for years, and Casement troubled for him, because he was making no provision for his later years or for his family. His only steady income was £400 a year as editor of the weekly *West African Mail*. His hard unselfish work for the Congo Reform Association was entirely unpaid. Casement regarded Morel as a kind of national or international resource to be prized and preserved. In 1908, he had helped the Quaker William A. Cadbury, who shared his admiration, collect a fund of £1,000, with Cadbury as major donor, to enable Morel to transfer "the fight" to London.[e] The new Testimonial scheme was Casement's own, though once again he counted heavily on Cadbury's money and his influence. "My hope now," he wrote Cadbury from Denham on 4 July, "is that we may raise from £10,000 to £15,000 possibly & with this sum . . . invested for the wife and children the besetting fear and dread that weighs on his mind may be removed forever, & his whole personality released for greater good and more work for Africa, or elsewhere where such a fearless soul as his is needed."[7] Early signs were good: Lord Cromer and Lord Listowel joined Doyle's committee and both the *Times* and the *Morning Post* carried favorable letters and leaders.

At the same time the Putumayo issue was coming quickly to a head. Rumors had been circulating since the turn of the century of gross cruelties perpetrated against the native Indians of the rubber producing regions in the Putumayo basin, a remote frontier area where border lines were vague and under dispute between Peru and Colombia. The most shocking of these charges were being pointed at the Peruvian firm of J. C. Arana y Hermanos, based in Iquitos, whose moving spirits were Julio Cesare Arana, his brother Lizardo, and their two brothers-in-law Pablo Zumaeta and Abel Alarco. The British Foreign Office found a lever for an investigation in Peru in the fact that in 1904 Abel Alarco had enrolled a number of black Barbadians, British subjects, under contract to work in the Putumayo, and the fact that in 1907 the Arana firm had registered itself in Lon-

---

[e]In an undated letter written just before Casement went to Rio in February 1909 Morel said: "Cadbury and his wife are as near being saints as any people I have ever met." Preparing for the move Morel was sorting out an accumulation of 22,000 letters. NLI 13073. Cadbury was born in 1867 and lived to be ninety years old. He entered the family chocolate business in Bournville near Birmingham in 1887 and eventually became its guiding spirit. He was a pioneer in the production of chocolate in Trinidad and in British West Africa. His book *Labour in Portuguese West Africa* denounced the near-slavery conditions in the cocoa plantations of the islands of Principe and San Thomé. A modest, passionate, stubborn man, he was a classic example of Quaker charity and good works, a "concerned Friend."

don as the Peruvian Amazon Company, Ltd., installed four British directors, and collected £135,000 of new British capital.

Priests' and travelers' stories of atrocities in the Putumayo had appeared in South American papers and had been loftily dismissed as fabrications by Arana and by Peruvian officials. In England, however, with the Congo cruelties a spectre still stirring, public outrage was quickly aroused by a series of denunciatory articles in the weekly *Truth* in the fall of 1909. The *Truth* articles, signed "Scrutator" and appearing on 22 and 29 September and 6 and 13 October, were based largely on a horrifying report compiled by an American engineer, W. E. Hardenburg, of his own and others' direct observations in the Putumayo. It was the Congo all over again, perhaps magnified, a tale of cynical inhumanity in the pursuit of rubber: forced enslavement, senseless brutality—flogging, mutilation, rape, murder.

In addition to Hardenburg's testimony and the swarm of depositions of witnesses he supplied, the Foreign Office had at hand the report of Captain T.W. Whiffen, an Englishman, who had passed through the Putumayo twice, in the summers of 1908 and 1909, on his way to explore the Central Japura watershed. Captain Whiffen had seen a great deal to enrage him, and sent in numbered statements from the *Truth* articles as confirmed and indeed amplified by his own experience; for example: "Aguero of Abyssinia [a rubber post] not only had a number of concubines, but bragged that no female—child or woman—was ever allowed to pass his door."[8] Whiffen himself had freed and returned to her tribe a little Indian girl of eight or nine whom Aguero had violated. In a letter to Casement on 22 July, Leslie of the Foreign Office apologized for the delay in sending him copies of portions of Captain Whiffen's letter of 21 October 1909: "they were of too indecent a nature to send to our female typewriters, so I had to copy them myself."[9]

Evidence at hand, then, was fresh but not savory and the Foreign Office had good grounds for a stiff letter of inquiry to the Peruvian Amazon Company's London office on 8 February 1910. The reply from H. L. Gielgud, Secretary and Manager of the company, that reached Sir Edward Grey a month later was merely a blanket endorsement, unsupported by evidence or even by argument, of Julio Arana's earlier disclaimer:

> . . . my Directors place absolute reliance on the statement made by their Co-Director, Senor Julio C. Arana, in his letter to

the Shareholders of the Peruvian Amazon Company, dated 28th December 1909. . . : "The alleged atrocities related in 'Truth' are entirely unfounded, our employees being incapable of committing such cruelties, which, if perpetrated, the Peruvian authorities would certainly not allow to go unpunished."[10]

An investigation being obviously called for, the Foreign Office pointer swung to Casement, a natural choice in view of his Congo report, his experience in South America, and the confidence in which he was held by humanitarian societies in England. His appointment was confirmed in meetings with Tyrrell and Grey on 13 July and Casement spent several days studying the available papers.

In June Casement had been planning firmly to attend the Irish summer school at Cloghaneely, but he had been held in London by the Morel Testimonial and the ripening of the Putumayo affair. By 16 July he was "very tired of London"[11] and his outing in Ireland had to be limited to three quite empty days in Dublin. On 20 July he noted in his diary: "Returned to *Sasana* [England]—beastly hole. At F.O." His formal appointment as Putumayo investigator came in a letter of that day from F.A. Campbell.[12] Casement's position was potentially embarrassing in that he would be accompanying, as observer and public investigator, an "independent" commission of inquiry[f] which the directors of the Peruvian Amazon Company had now decided to send in their own interest "to report on the possibilities of commercial development of the Company's properties and to inquire into the present relations between the native employees and the agents of the Company."[13] Casement's formal brief was limited, naturally, to the latter clause and further limited to the state of welfare of the Barbadians in the company's service. But it was understood that his look at the Barbadians would be taken with peripheral vision, as in the Congo, and Casement foresaw conflict between his own motives and those of the company's commission—presumably bent on exculpation and augmented profits.

At lunch on 21 July Conan Doyle rendered up a gloomy report: only £350 had come in for Morel. Disappointed and angry, Casement reacted in character by going to work harder than ever. He spent the next days in visits to the *Morning Post* and three calls at the

[f]Composed of Colonel the Honourable R. H. Bertie, L. H. Barnes, a tropical agriculturalist, Walter Fox, a botanist and expert on rubber, E. S. Bell, a "merchant," and H. L. Gielgud, Secretary and Manager of the Company.

House of Commons buttonholing Alfred Emmott, Hugh Law, and others. Then he sat up till 2:00 A.M. and "wrote E.D.M. letters." Among his letters was one accompanied by his own check for £50 to Liverpool newspapers, the *Courier* and the *Daily Post*, urging that a local committee be formed to honor Morel's association with the city of which he was a citizen and where he began his work for the cause of the Congo natives.[14] On the twenty-third before taking the train for Southampton to begin his long journey, he "wrote more letters" and from Southampton he sent off a formal eulogy of Morel to the *Morning Post*. In transit to Madeira on the *Edinburgh Castle* he was still "writing many letters about E.D.M. Testimonial."

It was all the kind of behavior, prodigally energetic and lavish of time and money, both in short supply, that made Casement an admirable and even lovable person; and makes impertinence of any fatally censorious judgment one might be tempted to form of the man based (for example) on his sexual habits. But the habits existed and they must matter to the spectator trying to understand Casement if only because they obviously mattered a great deal to him. In Madeira from 27 July to 31 July he spent much of his time in hotels with one João, described as "big," and particularly with Carlos Augusto Costa: "Splendid testeminhos. Soft as silk and big and full—no bush to speak of. Good wine needs no bush. . . . Very fine one, big, long, thick—wants *awfully* and likes very much. 7/6."[15]

At sea on the *Hilary* Casement beguiled his days dully with bridge and shipboard sweepstakes or lounged in his bunk reading, feeling tired and seedy.[g] In Pará for five days from 8 August he slept on board the *Hilary* and idled away the hot days visiting with friends and bathing in the forest streams. He patrolled the squares and even the cemetery, a favorite old haunt, in late evenings in search of comrades but with poor success. From Pará, he wrote Gertrude, he would be "going on to the uttermost parts of the Earth."[16]

When the party reached Manaos on the Amazon on 16 August Colonel Bertie of the commission, who had collapsed with illness, was

---

[g]On the blotter facing his diary entries for 7–10 August he doodled:

> Errinn
> Eran
> Dublin
> London
> Erie Era
> Eire Eire   [PRO HO 161]

forced to give up the enterprise and return to England. For the long slow journey on to Iquitos Casement boarded the *Huayna*, a "beastly ship . . . old & smelling," with only one bath and toilet for the twenty-seven male passengers. The great sluggish tropical river was several miles broad at some points. The air was heavy and hot and Casement for relief often slept on deck, only to be plagued by swarms of mosquitoes and sandflies. He kept his usual careful records of the state of the river and of their tiresomely slow progress. On the twenty-second they were still only halfway to Iquitos. Casement gave careful study to the documents provided by the Foreign Office including a typewritten copy of the manuscript of Hardenburg's *The Devil's Paradise: a Catalogue of Crime*, which he would check and annotate carefully as he made his own investigation. Hardenburg's colorful prose described another Heart of Darkness; his first reference to Julio Cesare Arana, for example: "This vile criminal, a veritable human hyena, is the fiend responsible for all the stupendous crimes we are about to reveal."[17]

On 29 August Casement joined the launch carrying the four remaining members of the commission and the party reached Iquitos at last on the thirty-first. He thought Iquitos "very well situated but horribly neglected and dirty," hot and full of mosquitoes. He took a room at the "dreadful" Hotel Cosmopolite, then lunched with David Cazes, proprietor of the Inquitos Trading Company who acted, with his left hand and for a tiny salary, as British Consul in the town. In the afternoon Casement spent nearly two hours with the Prefect, Dr. Paz Soldan, going over the ground of the investigation to come. The Prefect was cordial and apparently candid within his limits. He called the atrocity stories "fables" but to Casement's mind many of his incidental remarks tended to confirm them. Looking at the many Indian soldiers in blue dungarees about the streets Casement was ready to sentimentalize: "They are finer men than the 'blancos' and with gentle faces, soft black eyes, with a far off look of the Incas."

Next day he met Lizardo Arana who spoke expansively of the commercial prospects of the Putumayo with its fertility and its plentiful supply of Indian labor: he hoped the result of the investigation would be a large stock of "fresh capital." But in the afternoon Cazes brought to Casement M. Vatan, a French trader who had been an Acting Consular Agent for the French and had spent fourteen years in the neighborhood of the Putumayo. Vatan told him that the atrocity stories were plain truth and the Arana "system" was "slavery pure and simple." Vatan despaired of any amelioration within the disheveled Peruvian political system: "The evil inheritance of an evil past—a conquered race outside the constitution and the law with no rights—the Indians had to be civilized and this is the way it is done"—civilization by beating, rape, and murder. Later Juan Tizon, the Peruvian Amazon Company's overseer, was to tell Casement that Peru had "many inhabitants, but very few citizens," and "plenty of law and little justice."[18]

On the same day, 1 September, Casement, Cazes, and L. H. Barnes of the commission got a first taste of direct testimony from the Putomayo when they were visited by Frederick Bishop and Nellis Walker, two Barbadian employees of the company who happened to be in Iquitos. Walker gave a largely favorable account of conditions at El Encanto under Senor Loayza who was generally liked.[h] But Bishop told a different story. He himself had often flogged Indian "laborers" under orders. All of Whiffen's stories were true, he said; but the facts were even worse than Whiffen was allowed to see: prisoners and instruments of "punishment" were usually hidden when he was on the scene. The same techniques of concealment had been used to hoodwink Gielgud when he made a tour of the stations in 1909 as an inspector for a firm of auditors. Bishop said the abuses were continuing at the present moment.

Over the next week Casement was intermittently unwell, dosing with quinine against fever and suffering one of his old attacks of rectal bleeding. Yet he managed to interview several more of the men from Barbados, some of whom were suspicious and reluctant to testify. On 13 September Casement got off a preliminary report to the Foreign Office containing the depositions he had collected to date. On the same day the steam launch *Argentina*, which he had hired and sent off 200 miles to Copa Urco on the River Napo to fetch back an Indian interpreter, returned to Iquitos without its man: the queer flourish cost the Foreign Office £95.2.0, to their great chagrin.[19] Finally on the fourteenth Casement and the commission got off for the Putumayo on the *Liberal* with the cook drunk and the captain furious because two Barbadian crew members had deserted after taking an advance of pay.

[h]El Encanto and La Chorrera were the two "chief" stations.

Nearing La Chorrera on the Igaraparana River on 21 September the party saw its first symptoms of the Arana system at Indostan: the young Indian workers famished and sick, the concubine "sleek and fat," a young Indian boy, "Bolivar," in heavy chains, the blanco overseer with revolver on hip who explains that Bolivar had "tried to escape to Brazil." "(*Escape* to Brazil!)" parenthesized Casement who had been there. He gave food and quinine to the sick boys and girls and photographed Bolivar in his bonds. They then released him and took him along to La Chorrera in new pants and cap. None of this kept Casement from sleeping soundly that night on the ship and his diary records that he "dreamed and planned a great Irish romance of the future."

En route to La Chorrera next day Casement interviewed two more Barbadians, James Clark and Stanley Lewis, the *Liberal's* steward, and Lewis gave him an account of life at Ultimo Retiro under J. I. Fonseca of a kind that took on a grisly conventionality as they saw more of the Putumayo: "murders of girls, beheading of Indians and shooting of them after they had rotted from flogging." At the big station, pleasantly situated on high ground, Juan Tizon the company's chief overseer and Macedo the notorious head of the station came aboard and welcomed the party with smiles. Seven Boras Indians carried off their luggage and five Barbadians stood by "to drive them." The Indians were naked except for a bark-cloth *fono* and Casement saw that three[i] of them bore broad scars of old beatings on their buttocks, "weals for life" two inches wide. The odd conjunctions at the end of the day's account: "Played bridge with Tizon. Macedo looks a scoundrel. The whole place a Penitentiary," would also become typical.

---

[i] In his printed report this figure became "five."

8 A Fine Beastly Morality for a Christian Co.

WITH his arrival at La Chorrera Casement conceived his investigation as officially open and he now began to keep not only his jotted diary but the conflated (and inflated) fuller journal that survives in manuscript and typescript in the National Library of Ireland.[1] Perhaps recalling attacks upon the quality of his evidence in the Congo report, Casement set himself careful rules for the Putumayo interrogations: when possible, to use not one but two interpreters of native testimony and see that they were not compatriots; to invite members of the commission to be present at testimony; to keep careful notes and write them up while fresh; to check the stories of witnesses against each other wherever they intersected; to admit errors and exaggerations frankly when they were discovered.[2] His entry for 23 September in the short diary shows in compressed form his way of working:

> Got in the five Barbadians in the station this afternoon before Sr. Tizon and Mr. Barnes and interrogated them. Three had seen nothing, two, Stanley Sealy and James Chase, spoke out like men and told of dreadful things—they had flogged men and seen them flogged and killed too often, and said so and maintained it. Tizon did not like it at all but bore it and in evening began flattering me after dinner and saying nice things about me and how glad he was my Govt. had sent a man like me.

Over the next two days the dirty business gathered to an early head. In the morning of the twenty-fourth, in the presence of Barnes, Casement again interviewed Joshua Dyall, one of the three

104

men who had "seen nothing." Dyall now confessed to five murders of Indians, two of them for Fonseca at Ultimo Retiro and three for Armando Normand at Matanzas. One he had flogged to death, two he had shot, and two he had beaten to death with Normand's help, concentrating on their sexual organs. Dyall offered to face both Fonseca and Normand with his accusations and offered as well to lead the commission to a shambles of Indian skeletons. The merchant Bell had been maintaining all along that things were satisfactory in the company's operations, so Casement assembled the whole commission with Tizon in the afternoon. Dyall's account was read aloud and confirmed by him. Bishop and Lewis were called in and confirmed Dyall's statement and their own. The group "thrashed the matter out." Tizon "practically chucked up the sponge" and admitted that "things were very bad and must be changed." Shaken by the stories they had heard, the commission members resolved to take Sealy, Chase, and Dyall with them to face their chiefs on the scenes of the crimes.

After midnight Tizon came to Casement and begged him to try to prevent these confrontations: he vowed to carry out "sweeping reforms," to dismiss all the criminals, and to abolish flogging and the even more heinous brutalities. Next day the general discussion continued and Casement finally carried his point that if the accusers were not to be allowed to confront their masters then their testimony must be accepted as proven as it stood. Packing up on the twenty-sixth to resume the trip upcountry Casement was exhausted and heartsick: "Very tired—*very* tired—very sick of everything. God help all."

At Naimenes on the twenty-seventh Casement found "the *very* girl" Bishop had told of flogging on orders of Elias Martinengui and on whom Martinengui had inflicted "the nameless crime" as the short diary puts it.[a] Tizon refused even to question the girl and said: "he accepted, he accepted." That night he told Casement that he and Gielgud had issued a circular warning that any employee guilty of flogging would be discharged and handed over to civil authorities. That was well and good, Casement said, but the company must go further and prosecute the offender actively: "give the evidence and *press* the charge."

At Occidente, Fidel Velarde, by reputation one of the worst of the

---

[a]Forcing burning sticks into her vulva.

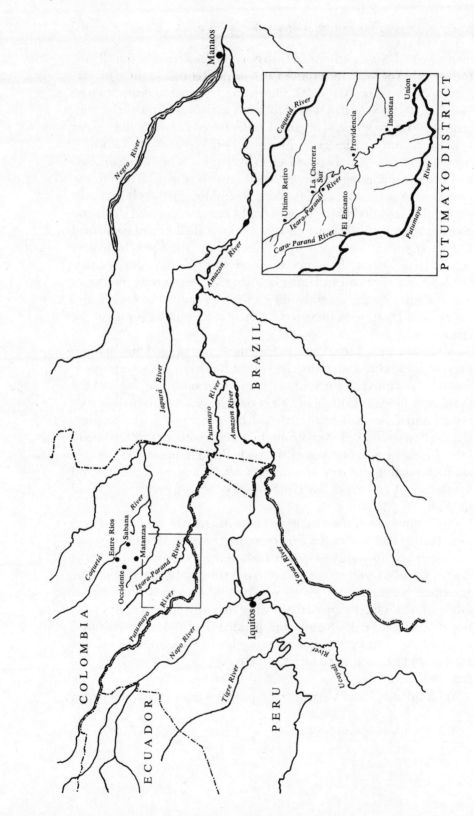

Map 3. The Putumayo area in 1910

chiefs of sections, had laid on in honor of the visitors a big Indian dance to which some 1,000 natives of the district trooped in. Most of the women were quite naked, most of the men in bark *fonos* only, and Casement saw clear signs of flogging on many exposed hindquarters, some of them unhealed and obviously recent, and common on women, girls, and small boys as well as on mature men. On the whole Casement thought the dance was a good idea and a "success": "These poor gentle creatures have few occasions like this." He took many photographs. Throughout the Putumayo journey he was touched and cast down by the sweetness and passivity of the Indians under suffering that must have seemed not only cruel but hopeless to explain. He wrote on 29 September: "I never saw anything more pathetic than these people. They move one to profound pity."

In his fuller diary Casement expanded his account of the dance and ranged out from it. The tallness of several of the visiting party has excited comment and collected crowds of gazers. One old Indian measured Barnes with a wand and carried it off as evidence of having seen the tallest man ever on the Putumayo; he also measured Gielgud and Casement who stood a couple of inches short of Barnes's 6′ 4″. Looking on with them Frederick Bishop remarked that he had seen dances that drunken blancos turned into sexual orgies, even raping women held helpless in the *cepo*, the massive stocks that were standard equipment of the rubber stations. Casement thought the black man blushed as he spoke and he knew Bishop had cried during a recent account of crimes—as Casement had wept as he listened to Joshua Dyall's grisly accusations of himself.[3] Now he was outraged to think of the cynical effrontery of Arana, collecting "an association of vagabonds—the scum of Peru and Colombia," licensing them to prey upon a powerless native population, and marketing the murderous contraption as an honorable enterprise to careless English capitalists. He recalled "the charming Lizardo Arana" in Inquitos rubbing his hands at the prospect of still more English capital. "I swear to God I'd hang every one of the band of wretches with my own hands if I had the power and do it with the greatest pleasure."[4]

Casement was deeply touched again when an Indian *capitan* at Occidente embraced him and Barnes, laying his head against their breasts: "Poor soul, he felt we were their friends." Francisco, another *capitan*, was brought in with a tale of beatings not only with the usual sharp heavy thongs of dried tapir hide that cut like a knife, but with machetes laid flat across the flesh so that they left no scars;

and of a new refinement of torture: men held under water as they washed the crude rubber, sometimes till they drowned. Sealy told "awful and hellish" new stories of Jiminez "with a simple truthfulness, and even grace of simplicity, that would have convinced anyone in the English-speaking world of the man's . . . good faith and scrupulous exactitude, and . . . all with appropriate gesture and restraint of gesture too."[5]

It was hard to find privacy in the open tropical station structures, with the "pirates" at hand to overhear. Casement talked as little as possible indoors and tried to do most of his private writing late at night when others had gone to bed. But the heat made the long day exhausting. Barnes was looking haggard and ill and taking forty grains of quinine daily. Sometimes Casement took his party out pretending to catch butterflies so as to hear the newest sorry evidence in privacy. Tizon, Barnes, and Bell all professed themselves convinced, the case of "slavery from top to bottom" against the Arana gang already wholly proven. But young Gielgud seemed uninstructable and still argued that this was a reasonable business enterprise.[b] Fox, too, was inclined to hang back and to view the criminal acts as "exceptional and unavoidable." "Here are two kindly Englishmen," Casement marveled, "seeking to excuse it . . . and actually unable to see its full enormity." Casement fell back on the comfort of factitious classification: "The world I am beginning to think—that is the white man's world—is made up of two categories of men—compromisers and—Irishmen. Thank God I am an Irishman." But he was immediately embarrassed in his system by being forced to recognize that if any relief was to reach the oppressed Indians it would come by agency of certain Saxons. So he simply naturalized them at once among "the Irishmen of the Earth": "the Edward Greys, the Harris', the Tyrrells—and even the Hardenburgs and the Whiffens."[6]

While the party was still at Occidente, the locally famous Aquileo Torres, the man whose history seemed to Casement "really like a story from medieval fiction,"[7] made a Conradian progress through the station. Torres and others of a party of Colombians had been taken prisoner by Armando Normand in a raid on a remote upper river station early in 1906. He had been kept for many months with a chain round his neck and ankles and passed from station to station, "beaten, reviled, & spat upon," until May 1908 when he had passed

---

[b]He had offended Casement also by the "infernal cheek" of calling him familiarly by his last name only. 30 September 1910. PRO HO 161.

into the employment of the company where he soon became undistinguishable from the other "murderers and ruffians," flogging and killing with the best. In the evening of 3 October, as Casement was lounging over the railing of the high verandah at Occidente, "a dirty 'blanco' " emerged from the forest with a puppy and several Indians carrying his gear. "That is Aquileo Torres," said Sealy, "and he passed on under the house to Velarde's house, where he slept the night. Next morning early he was gone."

The exigencies of the Putumayo journey involved Casement in sexual dilemmas of several kinds. With so many spies at hand he could not indulge his own inclinations and he was limited to wistful looking and occasional presents, usually of cigarettes.[c] And when he came upon a group of Indian boys "playing with each other" in a hammock outside the bathroom at Occidente he reacted with a surprising conventional censoriousness: "A fine beastly morality for a Christian Co."[9] Perhaps the boys' crime lay in their carrying on "without concealment." But Casement's reaction to the scene presents one with the same problem as his response to the suicide of Sir Hector Macdonald and can only be explained in the same way as illogical and self-deceiving, in fact schizoid.[10] The sexual cruelties and enslavement inflicted by the blancos upon the Indian women of course aroused his contempt and anger. He kept meeting little symptomatic situations such as that at Occidente when he tried to pay for his laundry and found his clothes had been washed by "one of Velarde's *four or five wives!*"[11] No charge, of course.

Casement was tense and tired, sleeping badly, often writing late at night and rising in a few hours to write again, grumbling because his coffee was "cold and late—rarely before 7 and often nearer 8." In the night before leaving Occidente for Ultimo Retiro on 6 October, in a "dreadful" nightmare he called so loudly for help that he wakened everyone in the house. The first day's passage on the river produced nothing of interest except clouds of beautiful blue Emperor butterflies and Casement's own reflections, "if these could be called interesting, which I doubt,' as he put it. His gorge was rising at the prospect of "feeding with Jiminez—the thrice-accused murderer."[12] There was some consolation in being converted to Tizon's character and good will. "I like Tizon," he wrote simply.[13]

"Butterfly day" Casement headed the entry in his amplified diary for 7 October at Ultimo Retiro. "The greatest set of villains" yet en-

---

[c]These episodes appear only in the short diary.

countered, he judged Jiminez and his crew in the shorter diary. "The redoubtable hero of the headless boy and burnt woman and burnt man" met the investigating party cordially on the beach in the afternoon: Casement was recalling a story told by Sealy of a raid on the Caquetá in 1908. "A burly young ruffian," he appeared, "—looks 26 or so. Sturdy, well-knit with that far-off look of the nigger you see in some of these Peruvian lower grade men." Tizon presented the members of the party and the scene that then ensued was pure Chekhov:

> . . . to relieve our feelings we began an elaborate butterfly chase there & then on the sandy bank of the river. They were certainly magnificent specimens & the soil was aflame with glowing wings—black & yellow of extraordinary size—the glorious blue & white, and swarms of reddish orange, yellow-ochre, gamboge & sulphur. Fox got one of the splendid big black & green & yellow.[14]

The station itself seemed a setting for another kind of drama:

> Concubines everywhere—the stocks in place of honor amidships, and the houses built like a ship—a pirate ship—and each room named after the Captain "M office" etc. I am in [blank]. The bows front river. The thick stockade basement walls (16') rise two feet above verandah and make the bulwark.[15]

Casement warned the three Barbadians to sleep together and again commanded "no girls!" All night he heard what sounded like a sentry pacing outside: "Someone certainly shaking the ship," and he vowed to himself: "Please God I'll shake this ship of state to its bilge."[16]

Next day seeing the station "filled with women, concubines of all ages," Casement concluded that the "vile, squalid place" was a mere "den of vice and degradation." The *cepo* was demonstrated. Sealy modeled it first but his legs would not fit into the ankle holes, and a thin Huitoto *capitan* named Waiteka took his place with better results.[d] Both Waiteka and the Indian lad who stood near him showed

[d]The name Huitoto (Weetoto) signified "mosquito" and was thought to describe the characteristically slender arms and legs of members of this most numerous of the Putumayo tribes. Casement measured Waiteka with the following results: "weight 120 pounds; height 5' 6"; chest 35"; thigh 17"; calf 11¼"; biceps 9½"; forearm 8"." A woman, "La Cernana," showed these measurements: weight 104 pounds; height 4' 7"; chest below breast 31"; stomach 33"; thigh 19"; calf 12¼"; biceps 9½"; forearm 8"." 8 October 1910. PRO HO 161.

"incontrovertible bottoms" bearing "the sign manual of 'Casa Arana.' "[17] And now Casement thrilled with satisfaction as the "fearless skeleton" Waiteka, understanding his unique opportunity to make a useful protest, suddenly launched into a passionate denunciation of the *cepo*, the whips, the whole catalogue of standard cruelties. "All were laughing," Casement recorded, "but in different ways." When he suggested that the commission might mark its visit to Ultimo Retiro by a ceremonial burning of the *cepo* "all looked grave."

Casement himself hardly left the station. He was catching up on his writing though he felt generally unwell and his infected left eye was covered with a bandage of boracic lotion. When Jiminez saw them off on 11 October, waving his cap, Casement wished it were possible to wave his head: "the scoundrelly murderer." The fifteen miles from the river post of Puerto Peruano to Entre Rios had to be covered on foot over a wretched forest road hacked out by enslaved Indians, "these poor patient beings."[18] The forest Indians were simply impressed for whatever labor was needed, given no pay, usually not even food. Casement thought the Indians "the most dreadfully willing" beasts of burden he had ever encountered. His own insistence on paying his carriers was considered eccentric and impolitic, as was his action in sending back to La Chorrera for more food to give the hungry Indians they met everywhere on their route.

Entre Rios was "O'Donnell Country"[19]—a station presided over by a young man of Irish descent. It was a dismaying circumstance for a man who had recently divided the white race into "compromisers and Irishmen."[e] He recorded his chagrin even before he met Andres O'Donnell: "To think that a name so great should be dragged so low! That an Irish name of valour, truth, courage and high mindedness should be borne by a Peruvian bandit."[20] He took some comfort in the fact that O'Donnell was generally considered the best of a bad lot: he was not known to "kill Indians with his own hand," managing most of the necessary cruelties by agency of a bullyboy lieutenant, a "white executioner" named Barbarini. And Casement was glad to find O'Donnell prepossessing on first appearance: "far the best looking agent of the Co. we've met yet. Honest even and certainly heal-

[e]The Indians loved cigarettes and Casement distributed them freely on his trip. To thank a donor the Indians would stroke his hand or shoulder and say "Bigara, bigara" (Good, good). It sounded to Casement like the traditional stage-Irish "Begorrah" and he began calling the Indians "the Begorrahs," a trick picked up by the commissioners. 9 October 1910. NLI 13085–86.

thy."[21] Before the day was over Casement was trying to solve his problem semantically: O'Donnell was "not an Irishman, in spite of his name."[f]

Next day Bishop described Fonseca at Ultimo Retiro for "mere sport" on several successive mornings at 6:00 A.M. ordering an Indian to be taken out of the *cepo* and shot, "like ordering morning coffee." Casement was disgusted anew with the members of the commission, with "the lack of character & humanity of these shifting, vacillating men," especially Fox and Gielgud who kept finding grounds for forgiving unforgivable brutalities. Gielgud seemed "singularly obtuse" not to have noticed even the evidences of flogging when he had passed through the Putumayo a year earlier "with the pleasing impression that this was a garden of Eden." When Gielgud palliated extreme measures on the gound that some of the Indians were mere cannibals, Casement assured him that "some of the nicest people I knew on the Congo were cannibals." Tribal cannibalism took on a kind of innocence in the context of civilized savagery that he heard on every hand. How was one to understand the civilization of Carlos Miranda who cut off an old woman's head and held it up by the hair as "an example" because she had given "bad advice" to the men of her tribe—not to work rubber?[22]

For the most part South American slavery did not follow the classic African form of a trade in able bodies—though that too did occur: persons did speak of "my Indians," they did buy and sell land on which Indians were an agreed fixture of the property, there were open markets in Peru (and not there alone) where one could "buy an Indian" and take him or her home to work, and in "civilized" places such as Lima plenty of Indians lived out their days as household slaves. In a lawless region such as the Putumayo the system was simpler and more sweetly economical. A person or a "company" who might be little more than filibustering pirates simply occupied a promising area and called it "my estate" and took possession of the local Indians along with the rubber trees. The Indians were not hired as laborers but impressed as slaves and commanded on pain of death to "work caucho." Basically they were not paid or even fed—though they might get an occasional "gift" of jimcrackery or clothing or scraps of food.

[f]In the next few days he learned that O'Donnell was twenty-seven years old and had spent seven years in the Putumayo. His grandfather had emigrated from Ireland to Spain and his father from Spain to Peru: but Casement was sure the pure Irish blood must lie deeper in the past than his grandfather. 12 October 1910. NLI 13085–86.

The blanco overseers who were installed were given no salary but in effect "licensed" to plunder—each paid according to the quantity of rubber he could press out of the land and the people of his station. Some of these "hammock warriors" as Casement called them in hatred and revulsion were sweating more than a thousand pounds a year out of their stations. Their duty was to see that the rubber was collected, washed, squeezed into barely portable bundles, and carried to a collection point where it could be hauled by river to market and traded for cash. The Indians were the blanco's useful beasts and he was free to treat them as forest laborers or household servants or whores, or to hunt them as animals if he felt savage or bored.

As one heard the stories the catalogue of cruelty grew stupefying with repetition. For Casement, of course, the Putumayo essentially recreated the Congo, though with subtle differences; and it was somehow more horrible to meet it again, recurring like a genetic corruption in the race. The Putumayo version lacked style altogether, it had none of the Congo gloss or panache. It was stupid, pointless, unimaginative: cruelty as a way of passing time, a way for gross and empty minds to fill their days. Only Arana and his closest cronies, with a fake Europeanism and taking the world for fools, gave the system a film of serpent slickness.

On 16 October, Casement and Barnes and Bell left Entre Rios for Andokes with a party of forty Indians, traveling on foot over the "atrocious" forest roads. Next day they passed a house that Normand had burned and whose people he had killed. Their own Indians had been allowed by the station a bit of beans to start the day and at mealtimes a pot of rice that gave each of them a few ounces. They "scoffed it in a brace of shakes."[23] The Indians begged constantly for food and hung about the white men's table picking up crumbs with great dexterity, "tiny scraps of biscuit like birds." At Matanzas the party found its agent Armando Normand, most monstrous of the Putumayo monsters, off "on a correria [raid] after Indians." At 5:30 a rifle shot was heard in the woods to the south, there were murmurs of "Normand, Normand," and he emerged into the clearing. Casement met him at dinner time: "a little being, slim, thin and quite short—say 5' 7"—and with a face truly the most repulsive I have ever seen . . . . perfectly devilish in its cruelty and evil."[24] That night Barnes and Bell preempted Normand's customary room and Casement slept nearby. In the small hours of the morning they were awakened by bare feet pattering on the verandah and voices saying "Normand, Normand." Casement got up and saw a man with a lantern and a rifle and five or six little red women with bundles: Normand's "harem" outpaced by their master on the road and now seeking him in his usual quarters.

All day on the eighteenth Boras Indians, a sturdier race than the Huitotos, staggered in under great loads of rubber. Trying one of these bundles on his own shoulders Casement found his knees buckling: he did not believe he could have carried the thing fifty yards. Yet these men—and women and little children in proportion—were forced to carry loads of fifty to eighty pounds over as much as seventy-five miles of rough forest tracks and that with no food supplied by the agents of the company.

Casement set out for Entre Rios with three of his Barbadians early on 19 October intending to walk the thirty miles before dark. But they were delayed first by finding an Indian youth, without food for twelve days, lying in the path, and then by a sick woman. Casement sent Sealy to get bearers for the boy and helped the woman on to Muinanes where he slept the night with a loaded revolver to make sure she was not disturbed. Next day they marched on to Entre Rios, overtaking on the way "the beast Negretti," Normand's lieutenant, and a *fabrico* or rubber caravan of forty-two Boras Indians—men, women, little boys and girls all under heavy loads. After twelve hours of struggling through the forest the *fabrico* reached the clearing late in the afternoon with Negretti behind them: "He drove them on. Hiti! Hiti! without pause."[25] Instead of stopping at the station for rest and food they were driven on into the forest beyond—in order, Casement supposed, to be out of range of prying eyes. Late at night and on into the morning stragglers reached the station in a state of collapse. Again "not a scrap" of food. Casement weighed one of the loads and it came to fifty kilos. Finally Normand himself appeared preceded by a "wonderful fright" across the compound. He sought talk with Casement, told of his gentle treatment of the Indians, and demanded that he abandon the "assertions" he was making. Casement said, "I make no assertions," and left the man to talk with Fox while he went back to his own writing.[26] Among the confirmed tales about Normand was that of his frying two Indian boys on top of a stove at Andokes; Juan Guerrido had finally shot them to end their agony.

Casement had arranged with Tizon for the eight Barbadians he had not yet seen to be collected for interrogation at La Chorrera before the end of October. He now foresaw a plot by Normand to bribe and threaten Westerman Leavine, who went in fear of him, to retract his testimony and then to join Normand and Macedo in corrupting the waiting Barbadians. Casement set going his own counterplot, first persuading Tizon to order Leavine not to go to La Chorrera but to return to Casement at Entre Rios. Normand hearing this appeared "green with rage."[27] Casement further decided to take Bishop into his confidence and send him on to La Chorrera as a spy and lobbyist, under cover of fetching supplies. Heavy rains continued, bringing some relief from the tormenting sandflies, but Casement's right eye was now infected and swelling. In the afternoon of the twenty-third came a letter from Bishop: Leavine was at La Chorrera and he and Normand were closely huddled. Normand wrote that he could not send Leavine back because he had a bad leg.

Casement gave out tins of meat to the hungry Boras rubber carriers who passed through the station[g] and took photographs including one of a boy of twelve: "terribly *flogged*, all over his backside and thighs enormous weals—a beautiful boy." Tizon announced that he would shoot anyone caught in the act of flogging and Casement vowed the same. In Africa, he recalled, he had never felt a need to carry a revolver against the "savages." At Entre Rios perforce he was much in the company of O'Donnell and he noted the irony of his actual liking for "this man of Irish name, whose record in any civilized land would consign him a hundred times to the gallows." In company with O'Donnell in the course of a day's walk of twenty-five miles he met at Atenas another of the more notorious Arana thugs, Alfredo Montt, who turned out to be an "insignificant little wretch" with only one leg. Meeting the commissioners on the way to Puerto Peruano on the twenty-seventh to catch a launch back to La Chorrera, Casement noted that their Atenas carriers were "absolute skeletons." He photographed "four skins of bones" and gave them all the tins of meat he had left.[28]

In the next days Casement saw a good deal of tantalizing sexual activity in which he could take no part. At Puerto Peruano early on the twenty-eighth "the beautiful muchacho showed it, a big stiff one, and another muchacho grasped it like a truncheon. Black and thick and stiff as poker." On the boat to La Chorrera two other muchachos were "doing same." Next day one of the boat boys was "pretending

---

[g]He sometimes traded tinned food or gunpowder for necklaces or "collars" made of jaguar and puma teeth.

to do it to small boy with huge *thrusts*."[h] Casement swam frequently in the rivers and admired the beauty of the young Indian swimmers: "The Indian boys are swimming all afternoon, lovely bodies out in the stream, and the girls too, paddling logs across to the island and lying there awash by the hour."[29]

Casement had been stirred from the outset by the beauty of the Indians, their elegance of shape and movement and color, and outraged to think of such beings in bondage to a pirate crew of degenerate blancos. He put these feelings together in a long emotional passage in his fuller diary for 30 October:

> . . . he is hunted and hounded and guarded and flogged and his womenfolk ravished until he brings in from 200 to perhaps 300 times the value of the goods he has been forced to accept.
>
> . . . .
>
> All that was once his has been taken from him—his forest home, his domestic affections even—nothing that God and nature gave him is indeed left to him, save his fine, healthy body capable of supporting heavy fatigue, his shapely limbs and fair clear skin—marred by the lash and scarred by execrable blows.
>
> His manhood has been lashed and branded out of him. I look at the big, soft-eyed faces, averted and downcast and I wonder where that Heavenly Power can be that has for so long allowed these beautiful images of Himself to be thus defaced and shamed. One looks then at the oppressors—vile, cut-throat faces; grim, cruel lips and sensual mouths, bulging eyes and lustful—men incapable of good, more useless than the sloth for all the work they do—and it is this handful of murderers who, in the name of civilization and of a great association of English gentlemen, are the possessors of so much gentler and better flesh and blood.

When Casement phrased such feelings to Barnes, this most sympathetic of his associates could only say glumly that the whole situation was hopeless: the Peruvian Amazon Company would have to be wiped out by law, and the Indians were bound to perish whatever was done.

---

[h]Such entries appear only in the short diary, being thought unsuitable for the fuller, more formal and official journal. On the blotter opposite his entry for 28 October in the short diary Casement noticed another anniversary: "This day last year 'Vaseline' at dear old Icarsby! To think of it!" PRO HO 161.

For some time Casement had played with the notion of taking one of these appealing beings into his own keeping, in a relationship he did not make clear, perhaps not even to himself. In fact he had arranged earlier to "take" Doi, a Boras Indian lad of Matanzas, but the boy had never been sent out to join him. Now at La Chorrera on 31 October he suddenly found himself taking title to not one but two young Indians. His motives were complexly and perhaps comically mixed. He was moved by the general melodramatic polarities of the Putumayo situation, by a kind of confused sentimental aesthetics, by pure kindness of heart, by vanity, by unconfessed sexual attraction, and by a sudden far-fetched idea of taking the Indians to Herbert Ward as models for a piece of propagandist sculpture: "to enlist Ward (and France) on the side of these poor Indians, and to do it through their artistic sense."[30]

The episode began with the arrival of a big *fabrico* from the station of Sur with "fine handsome types" of Naimenes Indians as porters. Casement decided to weigh some of the little boys of the party in comparison to the loads they carried.[i] Then he sent to the station storeroom for a case of tinned salmon and "distributed galore to men, women, boys and mites."[31] Then he picked out "a dear wee thing named Omarino," who had weighed in at twenty-four kilos "in fono" and his load at twenty-nine kilos, and asked him if he would come away with him. When the boy clasped both his hands, backed up to him, cuddled between his legs, and said "Yes," Casement's heart melted. The Indians crowded round and told the child's story: both his parents had been "killed by this rubber curse" and his older brother had been shot by Alfredo Montt. The boy's *capitan* suggested that a "present" of a shirt and a pair of trousers to himself would be appropriate to confirm "the agreement" and Casement gave them. Macedo then "with great unction" made him "a present" of the boy. Casement's short diary put the case succinctly: "Bought Omarino."

Then when he was swimming in the afternoon Casement saw that he was being closely watched by a youth sitting on the bank, a young muchacho of Sur whom he had noticed looking "with a sort of steadfast shyness" during the salmon episode. The lad now followed him back to the house and asked to be taken away also. He turned out to be about nineteen and married, but his wife was with her parents and

---

[i]One boy of 25 kilos carried 22 kilos; another of 29½ carried 30½.

was represented as no issue in the case. His name was given first as Aredomi, but he was also called Pedro, and it was finally settled that his true name was Ricudo. He had "the fine, long strong hair of the Indians, the cartilage of the nose and the nostrils bored for twigs and a handsome face and shapely body." Casement thought at once how well he would look in the Herbert Ward bronze of "the group I have in mind for South America." When he gave Ricudo a new pair of pantaloons he "stripped the old ones off, and stood in his fono—a splendid shape" and Casement thought how Ward would enjoy "the moulding of those shapely limbs."[32] The short diary put the matter briefly and intimately: "His beautiful coffee limbs were lovely."

Casement had foreseen critical phases to come in the Arana affair at La Chorrera and particularly later on return to Iquitos. But on the whole he felt confident, believing he had made a firm ally in Tizon, and believing that the thickening testimony of the Barbadians would make an unanswerable case. When he had reached La Chorrera on 28 October, Frederick Bishop had brought to him "a sort of written Diary," a log of what he had observed at La Chorrera since the twenty-second. Casement thought it useful, "not bad for a black man," and read it to Tizon after dinner. "Here it is," Casement says in his own formal journal—but the document itself has disappeared.[j] Normand was very much present, visibly sulking and scheming, but Casement with Tizon's support found him less alarming now. Tizon

---

[j]The matter may be important. A number of those who believe that Casement's diaries have been adulterated to create false evidence of his homosexuality have argued that the "forger" interpolated bits of a scandalous diary kept by Armando Normand of his own exploits. This theory rests on a story Casement was said to have told P.S. O'Hegarty and Bulmer Hobson: of such a diary of Normand's having fallen into Casement's hands and presumably turned over by him to the Foreign Office along with other papers contributing to his eventual Putumayo report. I find this story impossible to believe on present evidence. What Casement shows elsewhere of Normand's sexual habits suggests sadism and satyriasis but certainly not homosexuality, rather a violent heterosexuality. And he never refers to any diary of Normand's—not in his jotted diary, nor in his longer diary, nor in his formal report, nor anywhere else in his letters or papers so far as I can see. Had he possessed such a document it would have been in character to mention it in writing, probably often, rather than to keep silent about it. The only diary not his own that he does mention, and that in forms of his Putumayo journal (in the entry of 28 October in each case), is this little "Diary" of Frederick Bishop's of a week at La Chorrera. Normand was on the scene and he was probably the commonest subject of conversation among Casement, Bishop, and Tizon. My supposition is that Casement described the situation to O'Hegarty and Hobson, speaking of Bishop's diary in which Normand and his villainy would be a prime object of attention, and that his friends in recalling the occasion much later may have mistakenly identified Normand as the author. Neither Hobson nor O'Hegarty would have invented the story but they may well have confused it, and the weight of evidence seems to me to point that way.

assured him that he would "settle Normand's little game very soon . . . & it may be a hanging game for him!"[33] When Normand announced that he was going to Iquitos on the *Liberal*, presumably to carry his plot to headquarters, Tizon put a peremptory stop to the move.

On the thirtieth Normand returned tamely to Andokes. That same day the Barbados men from Sabana arrived and Casement spent most of the next three days in systematic interrogation of the group now collected at La Chorrera—black men, descendants of African slaves, now endowed with classic English names: Evelyn Batson, Sidney Morris, Preston Johnson, Augustus Walcott, James Mapp, Clifford Quintyne, Alfred Hoyte, Reuben Phillips, Allen Davis. The new testimony provided few surprises, only multiplication of incidents of barbarity of a kind now familiar: "Further infamous acts of cruelty against Normand and Aguero and the rest of these monsters" runs Casement's summary at the end of a long day on 2 November. The case he was collecting seemed to him impregnable now as he ruminated the situation in his fuller journal:

> The list of horrors has grown every hour today and yesterday and Monday. So completely are the Barbados men now vindicated that Tizon actually today asked me *"as a favour"*—his own words—to let him have a list of all the agents of the Company incriminated by the men. . . . now they shall be judged by the blackmen! What a change from the first days of my coming to La Chorrera. Through the faithfulness to me of these despised men, and their dependence on my power to protect them they have placed the truth full in the light—so that there is now no attempt to dispute it.[34]

Following Tizon's request Casement drew up on 3 November a formal "Black List" of the criminal agents of the company.

Ordinary affairs continued in the interval. Casement spent several days writing out fair copies of the Barbadians' final depositions and securing their signatures. At dinner on the sixth he "shuddered, positively" when he had to shake hands with Jose Innocente Fonseca, just in from Santa Catalina, shortly after taking down a statement in which James Chase told how "this awful wretch" killed a young Indian imprisoned in the *cepo* at Ultimo Retiro by "smashing his testicles and private parts."[35] On the eighth O'Donnell arrived with a pathetic letter from Edward Crichlow who feared for his life at Ul-

timo Retiro and begged Casement to take him away.[k] Next day the
Velos left with orders for Crichlow's return, but a second plea arrived
from the frightened man.[l] Three Barbadians who had gone to Santa
Catalina to fetch away their gear returned empty handed, having
been warned that Aguero planned to have them murdered on the
road as they approached the station—like Banquo. The *Liberal* arrived with "a big mail from home" for Casement, but he found in it
"nothing interesting in these surroundings"—though Mrs. Green
was "as usual good beyond measure." The big news from the
civilized world was that of the capture of the wife-slayer Crippen at
sea.[m] Casement considered the irony of the international excitement
generated by the pursuit of a single murderer when he was surrounded by murderers of whom Europe was peacefully unaware.

By 11 November it appeared that nearly all of the Barbados men
had decided to leave the Putumayo with Casement, most of them to
be repatriated according to his original promise. Only Francis
Greenidge, Lawrence the cook, and Armando King whom Casement dismissed as a lost cause, "a cut-throat scoundrel," announced
that they would stay. Aredomi (Ricudo) was to go all the way home
with Casement. Bathing with him in the river at Sur on 4 November,
Casement had liked his looks: "*No fono* on. Carbolic soap & glorious
limbs—a big one." Then a complication arrived: Aredomi's wife
and her brother. She wanted to go along but Casement said he could
not take her, and he wondered whether he should take the husband
without the wife. Aredomi-Ricudo assured him that was no problem: her mother would take care of her. Casement gave everyone
salmon and left the issue suspended for some days. Finally he deter-

[k]"Honorable Sir, Please to do me the favour of sending for me Sir I dont want to stay here in
Ultimo-Retiro any longer Sir it greeves me to see that after I had finish speaking with you to see
that I am up here among thease people in this foriest I am afraid of my life. And not only that
they dont treat me as they used to treat me before so I beg you to send for me if you dont want to
take me away with you you can give orders to let me work down in the Chorrero with the
carpenter but I dont want to stay here any more starving all the time Please to do me that
favour. Your obident servant." NLI 13086–87.

[l]"dear Sir if it please you to send and order me down I think it will be better for me, up here in
this forrest a man can shoot me up here and they can say that it is an indian. . . . Nothing More
at Present Your Obiedente Servant." NLI 13086–87.

[m]The American H. H. Crippen had been quack-doctoring in North London where he
poisoned his wife and dismembered her body and buried parts of it in his cellar. After a call
from the police, Crippen fled with his lover Ethel le Neve, first to the continent and then to
Canada, but was arrested before he could land in Canada. Alerted by wireless, Scotland Yard
had sent a faster ship after him. The affair attracted attention especially because it was the first
use of wireless in a police pursuit.

mined to take Aredomi and leave "Mrs. Aredomi" and he placed her in the care of one of the more trustworthy blancos who "pledged to see her safe."[36]

On the twelfth Casement had another long confidential talk with Tizon and again approved his tone. Tizon described himself as now "a member of the Commission" and promised that he would "do his duty and polish off Zumaeta, Arana, and all." Next day Tizon performed admirably in another incident. Sealy came in to report that Barbarini, O'Donnell's "principal footpad," had struck one of the Sur Indians over the head with a billet of firewood. Casement saw the man, with his scalp laid open and hair matted in the clotted cut and the weapon, a sharp-edged piece of hardwood a yard long. He told Gielgud to take the man in his gore to Tizon who was at breakfast. Tizon discharged Barbarini on the spot and ordered him to clear out on the steamer then in port. Casement exulted: "and for a mere cut on the head! All the 'blancos' will be thunderstruck."[37] But he was still full of doubts and fears that included Tizon. It was clear to him that the testimony he had collected inculpated the governmemt of Peru as heavily as the Peruvian Amazon Company, and he had a dark suspicion that when the whole party got back to Iquitos Tizon and the Prefect might make common cause to "nobble these witnesses"[38] and destroy his case.

In the morning of 16 November, the last day in La Chorrera, Donald Francis who had chosen to stay came and wept in Casement's room, homesick for Barbados and his old mother there. Sealy and Chase who remained with the commission came in for an "affectionate" goodbye. The Indian lads Ricudo and Omarino were installed on the upper deck along with Bishop and Brown who had charge of a "dear little" chiviclis, a present from Macedo to Casement. Poor Edward Crichlow had been got safely away from Ultimo Retiro and was among the party. Four of the Barbadians were taking their Indian wives and at the last moment there was a scene when Joshua Dyall's "9th or 10th wife," refusing to be parted from him, struggled to board the ship and had to be turned back on the gangway. The *Liberal* got away in mid-morning with Tizon, the commissioners, and four Barbadians waving from the bank.

9   Mightiest River, Meanest Shores

T HE first part of the journey lay down the Igaraparana to the Putumayo River and the first night brought a sign in the heavens that Casement took as an appropriate ceremonial for this final stage of his journey. A full moon rose after a glorious sunset and when it cleared the treetops the travelers saw that a total eclipse of the moon was in progress. By eight o'clock it was complete and then clouds came and obscured the sky. Casement played with his chiviclis a while and turned in early. But he awakened at 2:30 to another arresting vision:

> . . . a glorious moonlight, and the lovely palm-crested forest slipping past silently and softly against a pale-blue night sky. I looked long at it, and thought of the fate of the poor Indian tribes, who have been so shamefully captured and enslaved, and murdered here in these lovely regions, by this gang of infernal ruffians. I thought of Katenere, the brave Boras chief—of all the murdered Indians of these forests; of the incredible and bestial crimes of these infamous men, and wondered at the peace God sheds upon the trees.[1]

The *Liberal* reached the "Putumayo [River] of the Palms" before noon of the second day: "wondrous palms on left and right." Casement passed time in his cabin showing Ricudo exciting pictures "in Bates' book and others to his great delight"[a] and observed his reaction: "It got up I think—was thick anyhow." Next day Ricudo came to him for medicine against sandflies with his "nude torso beautiful bronze." Casement "rubbed it over his lovely body, poor boy." His

---

[a]"Bates' book" is unexplained.

aesthetic purpose seemed pretty thoroughly submerged though he struggled to keep it alive, as when he observed one of the "very handsome" Cholo sailors on board: "a young half Indian moco of 18 or 19, beautiful face and figure. A perfect dusky Antinoüs[b] and would make a fine type for H. W.'s statue of the Upper Amazon"[2]—a work that was never to exist, even as an idea, outside the mind of Casement.

Thinking out in the leisure of shipboard the whole grim picture of the Putumayo, Casement concluded that the original Hardenburg charges were certainly "in the main true." Moreover he had seen and heard enough himself to know that "hundreds of crimes" had occurred of which Hardenburg knew nothing. Talking again with Westerman Leavine on the *Liberal* he was given an estimate that Normand alone had caused the death of "over 500" Indians. At Matanzas Leavine had seen twenty Indians killed in five days, their bodies thrown out to be eaten by the station dogs and "stinking around the house" so nauseously that he could not eat. Now Casement felt sure that the "seven monsters" Normand, Aguero, Montt, Fonseca, Jiminez, and the brothers Aurelio and Aristides Rodriguez, had killed some 5,000 Indians by "shooting, flogging, beheading, burning" and starvation in seven years of Arana freebooting.[3]

When the *Liberal* docked at Iquitos on the twenty-fifth, Casement suffered the embarrassment of being happy to see an English flag and he went on to moralize the event:

> The "Athualpa" [sic] clearly in sight made fast at the Mole of Booth & Co. Hurrah! I'll welcome the sight of the English flag. I! Even so —since there is no Irish flag—yet. I am glad to think there is a flag . . . that stands today for fair dealing & some chivalry of mind & deed to weaker men.[4]

He went at once to the Cazes' and took up a bedroom at their house. Ricudo and Omarino had been installed in rented quarters with Bishop as keeper. When Mrs. Cazes "sniffed" at the presence of the Indians and suggested a bath, Casement assured her that the Indians were personally a good deal cleaner than most whites. He took the boys to a Spanish barber to have their hair and his own "mop" cut and the barber was "enchanted with their Indian hair—beautiul,

---

[b]Antinoüs was the lover and constant companion of the emperor Hadrian, who built a temple in his honor after he was drowned in the Nile.

long and strong." The Prefect's assistant called, a young mestizo who could not look him in the eye but stood rapping his knee with a riding whip as he delivered the Prefect's compliments and an invitation to call next day. Pablo Zumaeta also called but Casement was "fortunately" out. When he visited the *Atahualpa*, he found to his disgust that she was not due to sail for a full week; so he borrowed medicines from her doctor against a feared return of his Pará gastritis of 1908.

As Dr. Paz Soldan had no French and he himself very little Spanish, Casement reluctantly took Cazes along as interpreter for his crucial two-hour interview with the Prefect next morning. Casement spoke out frankly and in terms both general and specific, naming the worst of the criminals and their crimes: telling "of Aurelio Rodriguez killing hundreds in Santa Catalina. . . . of Normand killing hundreds and burning them alive, and of Jiminez killing and burning the old woman and the Boras man in June, 1908"; and the smaller sufferings of the Barbados men, such as Clifford Quintyne severely flogged by Normand and Augustus Walcott hung up by his hands drawn behind his back until he was unconscious. Dr. Paz Soldan was "profoundly impressed," called the crimes "revolting," and said again and again that "justice should be done." At that moment, he told Casement, he was waiting only for telegraphic instructions from Lima to dispatch a Peruvian government Commission of Justice that was ready to make its own investigation of the Putumayo scandals. The commission would include a judge, Dr. Valcarcel, a doctor, interpreters, and a company of soldiers and officers; they would travel in a government launch and be entirely free of Arana influence. The commission would be "a real one" bent on righting wrongs and bringing protection to the Indians, and it would "punish the wrongdoers." And now that he had seen Casement he would telegraph Lima at once to say that his investigation had "confirmed substantially the worst charges that appeared in *Truth*."[5] It all sounded promising but Casement kept his doubts: he was already forming a healthy skepticism about Peruvian good intentions.

Before they parted Dr. Paz Soldan let fall the "information" that the only reason the Peruvian government had permitted the company's commission to tour the Putumayo, and allowed Casement, "a foreign Consul, to go there in a public capacity," was that they had believed the Hardenburg and *Truth* charges to be "calumny and imposture," lies inspired by commercial rivalry. Had they believed any of it, they themselves would have investigated long since. Casement let this pass: it seemed impolitic, when there was a chance that the government meant to take real action at last, to point out that the story simply would not wash; that dreadful charges had been made in Peru for years; that witnesses had walked the streets of Iquitos unable to find anyone to take their testimony; that Arana bribery of judges and local officials was common gossip.[6] A few days later the former French Consul Vatan told Casement that the only reason he had been allowed to survive the Putumayo journey was the fact that he wore the cloak of a conspicuous public office. Casement laughed but Vatan insisted: "It is true—had you been a mere traveller & had seen these things they would have got away with you up there. Your death would have been put down to Indians. I know what I am talking about."[7]

Essentially Casement was marking time in these days until the *Atahualpa* could make up her mind to sail. For the Prefect and the Judge, Dr. Valcarcel, he wrote out a long memorandum of his views of the situation and suggestions as to where evidence had best be sought and sent a copy to Barnes of the commission to show what he had been doing and saying in Iquitos. He did a good deal of restless walking about the city, inspecting the local "types" but apparently making no strong approaches. On 30 November his developed films were returned, but the photographer had "abstracted No. 1": the photograph of "Bolivar" in chains that Casement had snapped at the beginning of his journey. Cazes told him "everybody in town" knew he had taken the picture and Casement had no doubt that "the Company" had stolen the negative. On 2 December he sent his camp bed on board the *Liberal* as a parting present for Tizon, and Cazes hearing of the gesture told him that Tizon "knew everything" and had lied to the investigators earlier to cover the atrocities. Casement considered this to be a pot and kettle remark and said as much: "I told him so at lunch—& he got pretty scarlet."[8] In the afternoon of the fifth Pablo Zumaeta, the Aranas' brother-in-law and local chief of the Company's operations, called saying he had been sent by the Prefect and asking for a list of "all the bad people on the Putumayo." Casement refused to discuss the matter. That night he wrote out for the Foreign Office a formal summary of his recent dealings with the commission and with Peruvian officials.

Casement "said farewell to Iquitos with every joy—but regrets for

Ignacio and the Indians all. God bless them."[c] As the crowded little vessel steamed down "the mightiest river on earth bathing the meanest shores" Casement took ceremonial notice of his experience: "My work is over on the Amazon. I have fought a stiff fight, and so far as one man can win it, I have won—but what remains behind no man can see. Anyhow, the party of Englishmen and myself have let daylight into those dark wastes, and scheme how they may we have broken the neck of that particular evil."[9] It was a hopeful but reasonable summary and it surely did not overpraise his own part in the enterprise. Casement had carried out a delicate and dangerous assignment with strict application, intelligence, and courage.

The optimistic assumption that he had scotched the particular evil of Arana rule still left the inclusive problem untouched: "the future of the S. American Indians and Native people generally." Casement had had a five-year wallow in the life of banana republics and he found it a dirty and hopeless affair: the mimic Europeanism of the governing and commercial classes, the greed, the dishonesty, the irresponsible cruelty that seemed to make up the whole texture of the life. He felt an airlessness, a settled malevolence of motive and manner that must be broken into somehow. The real Europe must force its way past the Monroe Doctrine and open windows in the whole southern continent. Casement was thinking again of Germany as the savior. The collective villain was what he was now calling the "Iberian" mentality: the influence of Spain and especially of Portugal—narrow, regressive, crass, cruel, a natural slaveholder's mentality.

At Esperanza Casement learned that the Barbadian party had got passage to Manaos on 24 November, two days after he had landed them. At midnight on 9 December he saw the lights of Manaos from twelve miles away across the intervening peninsula. In town next day he collected the Barbados men and paid over to them the compensation money he had collected from the company. Only five men, finally, had chosen to go home to Barbados: a few had gone to work for Booth's, the steamship line, and the others had elected to stay in Peru and try their luck as laborers on a new railway line. "Steaming well down river, splendid breeze" on 11 December, Ricudo, "poor

---

[c] "Ignacio" was Ignacio Torres, a young steward on the *Liberal* with whom Casement had been smitten and with whom he carried on a wistful little flirtation all during the ten days in Iquitos. Ignacio never seemed to get the point of his attentions. On the blotter facing his entry for 6 December in his short diary Casement wrote: "Left Iquitos—goodbye Ignacio—never to see again!" PRO HO 161.

wee chap," lay ill in sick bay with a temperature of 104 degrees. Much as he had hated the town as Consul there, Casement now looked forward to Pará as a familiar place where he could find recreation after the tensions of his mission: "I shall go to the old Hotel and have a good time of it—at last!"[10]

With his official mission completed Casement had closed his more formal journal in Iquitos a week earlier; now his daily movements may be followed only in the more intimate jotted diary. Reaching Pará in the late afternoon of the thirteenth he checked into the Hotel de Commercio and went out at once on what seems a familiar round—proceeding this time to a consummation: " 'Olympio' first at Big Square, then Polnara and followed and pulled it out and to *Marco* where in *deep*." Walking out early next morning to Baptista Campos and the cemetery, he met his old companion João who presented him with "a big bunch of flowers, very nice indeed" as was his pleasant custom. As tended to be the case when he was sexually active, Casement was feeling a bit "seedy" again. Still he spent his days visiting and seeing friends and his nights strolling the parks and streets. He heard the depressing opinion that the system on the Brazilian rubber rivers was little better than the Peruvian: they were "worked by slavery pure and simple" and "the rule of the rifle" began "right here in Pará." On the night of the sixteenth came another successful encounter: ". . . then to Theatre and met Aloes . . . and back at midnight. *Into* Aloes back door."[11]

When the *Ambrose* sailed for Lisbon next day the scene was invigorating: "Fine breeze blowing up the splendid estuary of Pará. . . . and blue sails flying before the wind." But Casement was "ill and glad to be going."[12] Ricudo was better and both the Indian boys were on board. But Casement had decided he must prepare the ground for them in England and so he had written to his friend Father Frederick Smith at the Jesuit monastery in Barbados and asked him to take them in for a time. Now the boys were dropped off in Barbados in care of Frederick Bishop to whom Casement gave some cash and an explanatory letter for the governor. The passage toward Lisbon was rough and slow through strong trade winds and heavy seas. Casement brooded on "the infamies of that hellish Peruvian region" and asked himself: "How can it be ended for good. How?"[13]

Christmas Eve was passed at sea a thousand miles from Lisbon and the ship's subsequent pauses at Lisbon, Oporto, and Vigo were too brief to be of any use. Casement left the *Ambrose* at Cherbourg on 31 December and went on to Paris by train. He took a "vile room" at the Hotel Terminus and at night looked on without pleasure at the year's end jollity in the streets: "silly songs being sung, and pretended gaiety, without heart in it." When he posted his diary that night he was "already in 1911."

Sunday and Monday in Paris were largely given over to successes and failures in what Casement's new (1911) diary calls simply "love." He evidently had an established amatory circle in Paris at least some of whom appear to have been artist's models: there is a Pierre and a Denis Hilaire. "Dick" and "Noisy Nick" were also on the scene and later evidence shows that Dick was Richard Morten. Noisy Nick is never explained: perhaps a dog? On Sunday Casement saw Denis and took Pierre to the Gare du Nord: "Enormous and fine."[d] On Monday he lunched with Herbert Ward and his family, but dinner at the Hotel Mercedes with Dick and Noisy Nick kept him so late that he missed an appointment with Pierre. That night he encountered one of the homosexual's hazards, a bully who robbed him: "met Beast at Place de l'Etoile who got £ gold & 30 fcs gold & 12 fcs silver = 92 francs!"[14]

Tuesday was more conventionally social. Casement called again on Ward at his studio and went shopping with Dick, buying haberdashery at Paquins and picking up a coat from his tailor. He lunched at the British Embassy with an elegant party: Sir Francis Bertie and wife Lady Feo, their son and his wife,[e] Sir H. Austin Lee, Lady Hardwicke, and "young Phipps," son of his old Congo enemy in Brussels. Casement liked Lady Feo whom he had not met before and he told the group "something of Putumayo." In the afternoon he went back to Ward's studio, taking along George Michell, the Paris Vice-Consul whom he had known in Africa and who would soon be heading for Iquitos, though neither of them knew it yet. The evening was passed at a gala of a kind almost unknown to Casement's simple ways: a dance in honor of the Ward daughters at the Washington Palace with nearly two hundred guests. Casement did not get to bed until after four in the morning.

[d]1 January 1911. PRO HO 161. The entry concludes: " 'Oui! Msieu, Je suis bien servi!' Took in mouth—with much groaning & struggle & moans—love."

[e]Sir Francis Bertie became British Ambassador to Paris in 1905 after a long and varied career in the Foreign Office. He was made Baron Bertie of Thame in 1915 and made a viscount on his retirement in 1918. His wife had been Feodorowna Wellesley and their son was Vere Frederick Bertie.

"Very glad to do so indeed," Casement left Paris with Dick and Noisy Nick on Wednesday the fourth and reached London at eight in the evening after a cold rough crossing. He took Dick to Marylebone Station[f] and went on to 110 Philbeach Gardens where he took rooms from Miss Cox again. Though he did not get out to dinner at Gatti's until after nine, he still managed meetings with "Ernest" ("*Enormous*") at Leicester Square and "Fred" at Euston. The two encounters with a cab between cost him £1.13.0 and closed a notably strenuous Georgian day at the beginning of which Casement had been dancing in Paris.

Reporting in at the Foreign Office on Thursday Casement found both William Tyrrell and Gerald Spicer away, but he talked long with the under-secretary Louis Mallet of what he had seen in the Putumayo and he was heartened by Mallet's quick sympathy for the Indians' cruel lot and his evident determination to do something about it. Next day he met John Harris and Travers Buxton at the Anti-Slavery Society and Robert Lynd at the *Daily News* and gave them a quick review. Mrs. Green was in Rome but due home soon. As one partly responsible for Casement's appointment to the Putumayo investigation, Harris wrote to welcome him home in form on 7 January: "With heartiest congratulations on your return and heartfelt thanks for your noble work."[15] On the same day Mallet wrote that he had been "haunted ever since" by Casement's stories and hoped they could find a way to get "the chief criminals hanged." Mallet had given Sir Edward Grey "the gist" of Casement's findings and Grey suggested that he submit a short preliminary report at once, corroborating the old charges against the agents of the company and naming those against whom he could produce proofs: this to be telegraphed to Lima with a request from the Foreign Office for quick punitive action.[16]

"Alas! No chance of that," Casement noted in his diary of Mallet's hope for a hanging, which he heartily shared. But he began drafting the short report at once and sent it off to Mallet by special messenger on 9 January with a long accompanying letter. He named Normand, Aguero, Fonseca, and Montt as the men against whom the criminal evidence was thickest. Normand seemed to him the worst of the sorry lot and he thought Peru might actually deal sternly with the man inasmuch as he was not a real Peruvian, having been born in Bolivia of a French father and educated partly in England. Casement

---

[f]That this is the station for Denham is one of the signs that "Dick" was probably Morten.

mentioned Zumaeta's call in Iquitos and a letter he had just received from Julio Arana asking when they could get together to work out a program of reform: as he had rebuffed Zumaeta he would take no notice of Arana's letter. The Commissioners had wanted the rogues punished "in their own way" short of hanging; but Casement was all for capital punishment: "if we could get one man hanged for these atrocious crimes it would be the beginning of the end in this long martyrdom and hellish persecution of the Indians." He would "make any personal sacrifice in the world" to help to see justice done, he vowed to Mallet, and if more evidence were wanted he would collect it, at his own cost if necessary.[17] Shortly came Grey's thanks and his assurance that "the substance" of Casement's findings had been tele-graphed to the British envoy at Lima with instructions "to bring the facts of the case confidentially to the notice of the Peruvian Govern-ment and express the earnest hope of His Majesty's Government that steps will be taken at once to bring the offenders to justice."[18] But it was to be a long frustrating story. On the tenth came another letter from Arana asking for a meeting. Casement ignored it and merely noted in his diary: "The swine!"

Over the next days Casement was generally housebound, collect-ing his text and his financial records of the Putumayo journey for the typist he had engaged to do his formal report. The typist from Yost's agency proved "a stupid fellow . . . an ass," with small typing and less shorthand.[19] Casement still found time to mend some of his so-cial fences. Nina was in town and he saw her every evening. On Saturday the fourteenth they were joined for a reunion by the Ban-nister sisters Gertrude and Elizabeth, or Gee and Lizzie, and Case-ment gave each of the women an Indian necklace made from teeth of the big tropical cats. He saw more of the Lynds and of old Africa friends such as Cuibono who was being "divorced by Mrs. Cui" and Moule whose daughter Katie was taking to the stage as a chorus girl in Sheffield: "Alack! Alack!" Casement lamented in his diary on 12 January. The 1911 diary that has survived breaks off after 18 January and does not resume until 13 August, when he left Dublin for Eng-land, to return to the Putumayo.

10   This Sphere of Duty

HAVING dismissed his inept typist, Casement worked away by hand at his report through January and most of February in London, with frequent calls at the Foreign Office for consultation. He slipped off for a week in Dublin, then returned to his airy back room at the Mortens' in Denham on 8 February to sit down to his final draft. His report of 120 handwritten foolscap pages was finished on 15 February and submitted on 17 February.[a] When he requested leave on 17 February, Lord Dufferin answered that he was entitled to only one month at full pay after 1 March, but as he had "another big report on the stocks" his month need not commence until the report had been submitted, studied, and printed.[1]

When Gerald Spicer sent him a proof of the first printing, he also sent along a courteous note on style: Casement must be his own judge of what he wanted to say, and if the report were going to remain a private Foreign Office document, the question of style would not even arise; but as the document might have to go to the American as well as the Peruvian government and to the Peruvian Amazon Company, Spicer suggested "with the greatest diffidence" that the report would lose no strength if some of the expressions "though abundantly justified" were "a little softened." Spicer made the overriding point: "The tale is ghastly and horrible enough whatever the language used."[2] The advice was sound and phrased about as gently as possible and Casement did revise, receiving proof of his second version on 5 April. Meanwhile on 21 March he had submitted as addenda to his report his transcriptions of the oral testimony of the thirty Barbadians which formed the hard evidence in support of his sweeping indictment.

[a]"Finis coronat opus!": Casement's note. NLI 13086–87.

131

News from the Putumayo began to drift in. Juan Tizon had written from La Chorrera on 29 December thanking Casement for his gift of the camp bed and trappings and reporting that "all your *friends* here," Normand, Aguero, Fonseca, Montt, Velarde, Jiminez, had been fired and had left the Putumayo: "I am very busy dismissing all these people."[3] That was all very well in its way: but Casement wished to see these men not dismissed but hanged. Were they merely being turned loose to roam free and unpunished or would Peruvian justice show itself more than a nullity?

In the meantime the testimonial for E. D. Morel was a major preoccupation. It seemed to have prospered little during Casement's absence. Sir Arthur Conan Doyle had written optimistically in the summer when he and his committee were preparing to send out a four-page appeal including a letter from Lord Cromer and puffs from a number of admirers including Casement. Doyle had predicted "a good harvest" by Christmas, but when Casement got home in January he found there was only £1,400 in hand, including £250 from William Cadbury, already a major benefactor of Morel's, and several gifts of £50, one of them Casement's. Much of Doyle's letter was given over to a scheme for "a sort of wild boy's book" in which a party of Englishmen were to explore an unknown plateau on an Amazon tributary where biology had stood still and where otherwise "extinct flora & fauna" still flourished. Doyle invited Casement to send along "anything weird & strange" he had turned up in the Putumayo for inclusion and he closed with a pleasant compliment: "Goodbye, my dear Casement. It has been a real pleasure & privilege to make your acquaintance. May our friendship survive all geographical separations."[4]

Casement had dreamed originally of a purse of £15,000 as an endowment to free Morel of ordinary fiscal anxieties so he could go about his public service with a mind more whole and less troubled. Now he scaled down his dream to £10,000 and he soon despaired of raising even that much. As he wrote to one of Morel's few generous supporters, John Holt of Liverpool who was one of the great pioneer African traders, he was baffled and angry at the apathy he was meeting. Holt shared his disgust: "It is all very well to have a houseful of great men to make the presentation, and to talk the truth in regard to Morel's great work," he wrote on 30 March, but what Morel needed was cash in useful amounts. "At present it can only be a pleasant thing to say of Morel, instead of a practical thing to give him a means of living." The appeals had taken up a wrong tone, Holt thought: they had been too elegant and passionless and had not really touched the heart. Holt's own heart was warm enough. He had already pledged a thousand pounds and he now resolved that he would give a second thousand if the general solicitation produced as much as nine thousand.[5] For a full four weeks in March and April Casement made headquarters with the Mortens and traveled to London and Manchester and Liverpool on the Morel affair. The Manchester situation was particularly irritating: from a subscription list that had been open since July a total of £7.10 had been collected by April. Casement was convinced that somebody high up in the "Congo movement" had spread lies to the effect that Morel's work in Africa had been motivated by private gain. Casement himself had to pay the hire of a room in the Town Hall for a meeting in April where he had unwillingly agreed to put the case for Morel. Putting himself forward was "the most distasteful thing possible to me," he wrote Cadbury.[6] The presentation to Morel was due to be made in six weeks at a luncheon at the Hotel Metropole in London, and the campaigners had less than £3,000 in hand.[b]

Traveling with Mrs. Green, Casement crossed to Belfast on 13 April and settled into rooms at 105 Antrim Road for what he planned as a stay of some length in which to do "writing in peace and quiet."[7] Just what Casement had in mind to write at this time is not certain, but he was probably meditating a book on slavery in the Putumayo as the major example of his thesis that slavery was still a thriving disease in the world. His expanded journal of the Putumayo mission really made sense only as "a book" or a potential book, and no doubt that was why he went to the labor of keeping it.

Slavery and the Putumayo troubled Casement's mind constantly in the spring of 1911 and they came together in a long letter to Cadbury on 26 May—coupled with increasing doubts of his own readiness to deal with the problem in a book. He had returned to London for the Morel occasion and he got up at 4:30 to write with a cuckoo sounding in the cherry trees at 110 Philbeach Gardens. The polite world, he wrote, had got used to making two wrong assumptions about slavery: that it had been confined almost entirely to the black race and that it had effectually ceased with the end of the American Civil War. But both he and Cadbury, a benign emperor of chocolate,

[b]Herbert Ward had donated a bronze statuette valued at £250.

knew that the condition of "thousands of labourers" on "scores & scores" of estates in Portuguese Angola was still "slavery pure and simple" in the form of both "debt bondage" and "purchased body bondage"; and the extension to the cocoa islands of San Thomé and Principe was merely an outreach of an "Iberian" pattern centuries old in Africa and not a great deal younger in Central America and South America, dating from the first European landings among primitive peoples. Casement could attest that slavery still flourished in Peru, in Colombia, in Bolivia, and Brazil. And what he had seen close up in the Putumayo surpassed "in horror—in down right ghast-liness" anything he had seen in Africa or dreamed of anywhere on earth.[8] Apart from the size, the inaccessibility, and the primitiveness of the areas involved, what made the institution of slavery in South America so hopeless to attack was its "entire lawlessness"—not its illegality but its extra-legality: "Were it legalized it could be assailed thro' law. . . . But here, in this most tragic wilderness of the Amazon rubber forests there is no law. There are plenty of lawyers! They are often 'Colonels' too and 'Magistrates'—and 'Comisarios' and all sorts of fine-sounding titles—but they are all after rubber—and all after Indians."[c]

Casement closed his letter with the hope that Cadbury would read his Putumayo report carefully, as he knew he would read it sympathetically. He was not satisfied with it and he wished for a chance to do it better. He had had to write it "hurriedly and oppressed," without the necessary calm and leisure, and his mind had been "so full of the horror of the whole thing" as to prevent the "quiet" treatment that the gravity of it all required. He had finally got at a basic problem of his style: strong feeling overriding expression and orderly thought. The Putumayo needed and deserved not only a powerful investigator but a powerful writer and Casement had evidently begun to wonder if he were the right person to give it form. He fell back at last upon the quality of his material, the case he had made: "But it is true—and I believe I could prove to any court in Christendom every single thing in it."[9]

The Morel affair (with a purse of 4,000 guineas) was over at last

[c]In a letter to Grey on 12 May Casement noted that when he first reached Iquitos and asked the Prefect of the Department of Loreto, Dr. Paz Soldan, what officials he should approach if he wished to lodge complaints about the treatment of the Barbadians, he was given the names of Arana's three principal agents, described by the Prefect as " 'all honourable men.' " NLI 13086–87. The Arana interests were synonymous with law, or with lawlessness—depending upon one's point of view.

and Mrs. Ann Barnes, wife of the head of the Peruvian Amazon Company Commission, sent a generally gratifying thank-you note on 2 June: "it does one good to come in contact with men like Mr. Morel, the type of man who sinks himself for the good of others, like you."[10] Casement went off to County Antrim for a few days to take part in the Feis of the Glens (his first real Irish gesture in about a year), but then was kept family-bound in Ballycastle when his cousin the Admiral died suddenly in the night of heart failure. On the eighth he was back in London for a "very merry" dinner party given by the Morels for Mrs. Green in which Morel in the costume of a Nigerian chief salaamed as he presented her with a rug that was a gift of the Morels, the Cadburys, Casement, and a few other close friends. She asked if the names of the donors might not be sewn on in a scrap of Irish linen.

Cadbury had given Casement £50 to help with the expenses of the two Indian boys[11] and in his letter of 6 June Casement asked permission to bring the boys for a visit when they reached England. At last Casement arranged for the two boys to sail for England on 14 June. He had been trying to make a resonable plan for their stay and had inquired of Padraic Pearse, the future hero of the Easter Rising, about placing the younger, Omarino, in Saint Enda's College, Pearse's progressive school in Rathfarnham, Dublin. On 15 June Pearse wrote that he would be pleased to have "your young Indian" during the coming year. He thought the lad would feel at home at Saint Enda's if anywhere in the Western Hemisphere and that between them they could "make a great success of this young barbarian."[12]

On 15 June, a confidential note from Sir Edward Grey reached Casement at Denham:

My dear Casement

It gives me great pleasure to inform you that the King has been pleased, on my recommendation, to confer upon you a Knighthood in recognition of your valuable services in connection with your recent Mission to the Putumayo District.

Yours sincerely
E. Grey[13]

Casement's reply was delayed for four days and preceded by a great deal of regretful soul-searching of which Richard Morten was a surprised witness; but it was finally phrased with a lush formality that returned to haunt Casement at the end of his life. As the text itself became an issue it is better to set it down here complete:

Dear Sir Edward Grey,

I find it very hard to choose the words in which to make acknowledgment of the honour done me by the King.

I am much moved at the proof of confidence and appreciation of my services on the Putumayo conveyed to me by your letter, where in you tell me that the King had been graciously pleased, upon your recommendation, to confer upon me the honour of Knighthood.

I am indeed grateful to you for this signal assurance of your personal esteem and support, and am deeply sensible of the honour done me by His Majesty.

I would beg that my humble duty might be presented to His Majesty when you may do me the honour to convey to Him my deep appreciation of the honour he has been so graciously pleased to confer upon me.

I am, dear Sir Edward,

Yours sincerely,
Roger Casement[14]

On 20 June came a notice from 10 Downing Street that he would "in due course be summoned by the Home Secretary to receive the accolade at a date to be fixed by His Majesty." On 28 June, now back in London from Southampton where he had gone to fetch Ricudo and Omarino, Casement received his copperplate letter of instructions from the Home Office; this he annotated simply: "My Knighting on 6th July 1911."[15]

Meanwhile Casement's name had appeared in the Birthday Honours List and congratulations came in from all his friends. William Cadbury set the event in a context of dignity and humane usefulness: "I know you don't care for empty honour but I am sure that this is a national expression of very sincere thanks to you for whole hearted personal & devoted service & I hope it may strengthen your hand in the future in your fight for the Right." He signed himself "Affectionately yours."[16] Replying next day Casement called Cadbury's greeting "the nicest" he had got and went on to express chagrin at the whole process: "You are right in saying I don't care for 'honours' and I wd. much have preferred that this one had not been laid upon me—but I had and have no choice in the matter."[17] Addressing Mrs. Green in one of the affectionate epithets he liked to invent for her, "My dear Woman of the Good Words," Casement wrote much more passionately and parochially. He was touched that she had seen through to "the Irish side to it all" which was the source of his most acute embarrassment. Few in Ireland, he feared, would believe that he had not labored for this honor and had indeed been "in reality, deeply desiring *not* to get it." His dilemma had repeated that of the C.M.G. award: "I couldn't help it at all—& could not possibly fling back something offered like that"—with Grey's good will and grace of manner. But many in Ireland would call him a traitor[d] and in his heart he felt the judgment true, helplessly true: "I feel always that until Ireland is safe and her outlook happy no Irishman has any right to be accepting honours or having a good time of it anywhere." He would have "rejoiced" to have rejected the knighthood "and said to the King what is really in my heart instead of the perfunctory words of thanks (cold and formal enough) I have said." Still, he had accepted and had committed himself in terms that no merely objective reader could hear as perfunctory or cold or formal: courtly, yes—but that is another matter. He begged Mrs. Green to continue addressing him in the old way as plain Roger Casement: "for oh! you don't know how I hate the thing.[18] In another letter of 13 July he quoted to her the Irish lament he had written in a boy's autograph album on the day of his knighting as a rubric for himself: "Mavrone! that son of mine should stand."[19]

A few years later, having refused a British knighthood, W. B. Yeats explained that he did not wish to empower people in Ireland to say: "only for a ribbon he left us."[20] If Yeats could do it, why not Casement? The fundamental difference was one of character or at least of personality: Yeats was a great deal more solid in himself. Was Casement lying to Grey, to Mrs. Green, or to himself? Probably the reasonable answer is: all and none. Did he want the knighthood or not? If not, why did he accept it? As in 1905 his situation was genuinely difficult, though probably not so complex, practically and psychologically, as he chose to make it in his over-dramatic way.

---

[d]A good humored version of this reading came at once in a letter of 22 July from Una Ni Fhairchiallaigh. She congratulated him but continued: "I have not dared to tell Colm yet. I fear another poem ending 'die, traitor, die.' " NLI 13073.

Casement's livelihood depended, as Yeats's did not, upon the sanction of British officials. And on Casement's rather fragile livelihood partly depended a number of persons and causes very dear to him.[e]

Half of Casement's nature did want the knighthood and no shame to him. He liked praise at least as much as most people, and he did not scorn the knighthood per se, it was not a wicked thing in itself. On the one hand it meant that he had arrived as an English gentleman, and that was a condition he at once coveted, despised, and feared. On the other hand it was a certification of professional success, a seal of public approbation upon his character and his work which he was quite naturally glad and grateful to receive.[f] His personal and professional relation to Sir Edward Grey affected the issue profoundly: Casement quite simply liked Grey and Grey had acted in a kind and courteous way. Within these limits the letter to Grey was an honest document. It grew corrupt only when he disowned it, called it false himself. There is no reason on the other hand to doubt that his partisan Irish motives were real, as they certainly were potent: they were even strong enough to silence and disown the "British" and human half of himself that wanted the knighthood. In this sense he was not lying to Cadbury and Mrs. Green but telling a half-truth he had already sold to himself as whole. In the same way he was probably quite convinced that the fawning tendencies of his letter to Grey were not so, that his tones were in fact "perfunctory . . . cold & passionless."

But the problem of the letter is not only moral and psychological but aesthetic. Casement and a pen made a dangerous combination in any crucial situation: his pen was liable to be seized by his vanities and his inner insecurities. Then one got the kind of overwriting and general bad style that came from vanity conjoined with faulty natural taste. Casement's luck in this particular case was peculiarly bad: it is not extravagant to say that the style of his letter to Grey was one of the things that hanged him at last.

Casement was now working on several intersecting lines for the

[e]One of the signs: a bill of 20 July 1911 from W. J. Allison and Co. for cabling £75 to Charlie in Melbourne on Casement's instructions. NLI 15138.

[f]Otherwise why would he write to A. W. Clarke of the Foreign Office to thank him for his good offices in the matter? Clarke wrote back on 30 July: "I fear I can lay but little claim to anything of the kind though naturally I did what I could. But indeed there was small need for me or anyone else to 'push' the matter since it was the general feeling that you deserved some small recognition at least of what you had done and what you had gone through." NLI 13073.

welfare of the Putumayo Indians: he pushed for action by Peru to apprehend and punish the criminal agents; he sought the continuance of the Peruvian Amazon Company, reorganized and purified, as an antidote to a reign of pure piracy in the rubber districts; he pressed the Foreign Office to install a new full time Consul in Iquitos as a sort of resident British conscience; and he labored to create a new device he thought particularly hopeful, a Christian Mission in the Putumayo.

On 12 June he gave Travers Buxton of the Anti-Slavery and Aborigines Protection Society three and a half pages of suggested questions to be raised in the house by Noel Buxton and J. C. Wedgwood to keep the issue warm there. [21] The Peruvian Amazon Company's four Commissioners had returned in late May and on 1 June Casement began attending meetings of the Company's directors as an invited observer and adviser. Of the first meeting he observed: "No go!" and of the second on 28 June he commented: "Nothing good or serious."[22] He had been seeing J. C. Arana at the Company board meetings and he now judged that he had cowed Arana to the point where it might be good policy to leave him in office—reduced to be the figurehead of a pure-minded English Company. "Arana is, at present, completely subdued," he wrote Cadbury. "I have him submissive, pledged and ready to give proofs of sincerity. I have not been satisfied with words.[23] It was a characteristic reversal of an emphatic judgment and it is bound to strike one as naive.

Casement had been given permission to show copies of his report during the interval of waiting, in a guarded confidential way, to persons likely to be influential in the future. His first readers were shaken and impressed. F. W. Hirst of the *Economist* called the report "masterly & horrifying" and promised the help of his paper when the time came.[24] H. W. Nevinson, now a friend and admirer of several years' standing, "supposed," surely accurately, that the report was "one of the most awful official documents ever written."[g] A year later

---

[g]29 June 1911. NLI 13073. Henry Woodd Nevinson (1856–1941) was a distinguished writer in many forms and probably the most influential crusading journalist of his day. He served as a war correspondent, chiefly for the *Daily Chronicle* and the *Manchester Guardian*, in every major conflict from 1897 to 1918. In 1904-05 he investigated slave trading in Portuguese Angola and published a report that led to the boycotting of the produce of the cocoa islands by such firms as Cadbury's. In fact he was a passionate and effective advocate of almost every good cause; and he was one of the bravest of Casement's loyal friends.

Nevinson was still horrified and angry. He wrote a sardonic piece proposing, as an alternative to African safaris to hunt "peaceful giraffes," a "sportsman's shooting party to hunt Normand & the rest." But his editor thought it "too violent."[25]

The most promising idea to emerge from the current brainwracking, Casement considered, was that of the Christian Mission which he envisioned as a permanent establishment somewhere central in the rubber country with missioners free to travel the rivers and forests as a dispersed benign monitory presence. To be accepted in Peru the Mission would have to be officially Catholic, he felt sure, but he hoped that both Catholic and Protestant branches of the Church would be willing to back the venture for Britain. His first attempts to rally support were discouraging. In these early stages of the Mission scheme Casement was staying often with the Duke and Duchess of Hamilton, whom he had met through T. H. Hoste, and who had interested themselves in his cause. The Duke himself was making an appeal to Carnegie, and Casement called on the Catholic Archbishop of Westminister and the Anglican Archbishop of Canterbury. The Catholics he found little more enthusiastic than the Protestants and he denounced "this great Official Church with its preposterous claims to be the beginning and end of all life" in a letter to Mrs. Green on 13 July. He was driven back upon an incoherent humanist affirmation of what he could only call "life": "Life is more beautiful than death, and the world we live in and should work for more lovely than all the plains of heaven. There can be no heaven if we don't find it and make it here—and I won't barter this sphere of duty for a hundred spheres and praying wheels elsewhere."[26]

Randall Davidson, Archbishop of Canterbury, was one of those to whom Casement had shown his report and he returned it at the end of July with a comment that seemed to promise action: "I think nothing could be better than your marshalling of the appalling facts. It is one of the blackest stories of cruelty that I have ever read."[27] But on the question of supporting a Catholic Mission, Davidson soon began to equivocate and continued to do so for the better part of a year: must the Mission be Catholic? Can the head of the Protestant Church of England support it? And so on. Casement finally wrote him with disgusted irony:

> I have lived so much abroad—and so much among savages—
> that I fear I have come to regard white men as a whole as Christians as a whole—and not sufficiently to realize the distinctions

that exist at home and separate them into separate schools of thought. In what I felt to be an appeal to a common pity and a common compassion that animates all kindly civilized men I was, I fear, underrating the influences that separate Christian Churches and perhaps revealing myself as something of a heathen.[28]

The Duchess of Hamilton redressed some of the balance in a highly personal way: "My husband wants me to say he will gladly contribute £100 towards the funds you are trying to raise, but indeed we would quadruple the amount if instead of peace you were getting up a punitive expedition to extirpate those vipers off the face of the Earth."[29]

For the first and last time Casement found himself in a state of embarrassingly complete approbation of the British Foreign Office. "The F.O. are doing and have done everything a great department could possibly attempt," he wrote Cadbury on 11 July: in the matter of the Putumayo they had been "splendid." They had accepted Casement's point about the need for a real Consul in Iquitos and had also accepted his recommendation of an old friend from Stanley Falls, George B. Michell, for the post. Michell had been posted to Paris but he had found himself spoiled for civilization by twenty-five years in Africa and he welcomed a chance to get back to something more primitive; Peru would give him that.[30] Aside from stubbornly maintaining a discreet pressure for action, there was little the Foreign Office could do in Peru itself. The news coming in from L. J. Jerome, Chargé d'Affaires in Lima, chiefly in the form of copies of telegrams from Dr. Paz Soldan to the Peruvian Ministry of Foreign Affairs, was vivid but confusing. In telegrams of 19, 22, and 24 July the Prefect announced that Dr. Romulo Paredes had returned to Iquitos after visiting all the twenty-six stations of the company. He had confirmed Casement's story of the "crimes and horrors committed," had issued 215 "apprehension warrants," and was giving the Prefect "the names of culprits for their immediate arrest." Prisoners were said to be "arriving in next steamboat from Putumayo," and there were "so many warrants out gaol too small." On the other hand "many" had "escaped to Brazil" and only "accessories" were said to remain in Peru. And only four men were named as actually arrested: Homero and Aurelio Rodriguez, Alapno Lopes, Pablo Zumaeta. Paredes had compiled a report of 1,300 pages and his work according to Dr. Paz Soldan was "to be commended."[31]

For the second time a controverisal report of Casement's had stood up to a second investigation and that was a personal relief and gratification. Otherwise it was hard to be sure just what was going on in Peru. Casement doubted that the Iquitos jail would prove too small or that the principal criminals would ever see the inside of it. Whereas he would have been glad enough to see Zumaeta hanged, he had no faith in that event, and neither Zumaeta nor any of the other three "arrested" had been among those marked with an asterisk, denoting "infamous criminal" or "atrocious scoundrel," in the copy of the Black List Casement had sent to Sir Edward Grey on June 20.[32] The number of warrants (it later grew to 237) was certainly impressive; but on second thought it began to seem absurd: it was too big. What one wanted was to see a half-dozen master criminals arrested, tried in detail, convicted, and signally punished. By the end of July the Foreign Office had decided to send Casement back to Iquitos—to look into things directly and to show Peru that the eye of Britain was still upon her; at the same time he could install Michell and set the new consulate on a sound course.

He would also be taking the two Indian boys back to Peru. That experiment had been trying as well as exhilarating and Casement was glad to see an end to it. He had done nothing about his first notion of presenting the boys to Herbert Ward as models for sculpture, and in London they filled no function save as a kind of mildly exotic spectacle. Casement had shown them about, to the Anti-Slavery Society, to the board of the Peruvian Amazon Company, and to a few close friends outside London such as the Cadburys.[h] But Casement's time was well filled and in the upshot much of the care of the Indians devolved upon Nina who was fortunately in London. William Rothenstein, who had painted E. D. Morel and wished to do a portrait of Casement, asked permission to paint the boys in native costume, "although there was very little of it," as Nina recalled.[33] She described the general impression they made: "They were light-mahogany colored, their skins smooth as satin, extremely clean; they would bathe, if permitted, half a dozen times in a day." Rothenstein gave an account of the first sitting in a note to Casement on 15 July: "The boys turned up happily, & put on their ornaments with

[h]In September he thankfully accepted Cadbury's offer of a second £50 toward the boys' expenses. Endorsement on Casement's letter to Cadbury, 3 September 1911. NLI 8358. Cadbury papers.

care—almost with pedantry, with the help of a comb, water & a looking glass, & then stood like rocks."[34] But as Nina remembered the matter the boys hated posing and had to be bribed with candy and ice cream. There were a half-dozen sittings between mid-July and mid-August when the boys left to sail with Casement; but Rothenstein required three times that many, and the double portrait remained unfinished.

Rothenstein and his wife came to Waterloo Station to see the party off for Southampton. The Indian boys seemed glad to be heading for home, Casement wrote in a note to Cadbury on 16 August: "look quite happy and smile at all around them."[35] The Duchess of Hamilton sent a cordial farewell: ". . . to wish you godspeed in your work of mercy. May each of those villains be brought to justice. I feel *sure* you will succeed. It is *quite* splendid your going out."[36]

II The Whole Dirty Business

CASEMENT resumed his 1911 short diary on 16 August when he left Southampton for Cherbourg and Barbados, but the entries were trivial until 28 August when he landed in Barbados and was amazed to find Andres O'Donnell in residence, happy and prosperous and about to be married to a flower of the local English colony—apparently quite unaware that a warrant was out in Iquitos for his arrest for "atrocious crimes." Casement sent word of this apparition at once to Gerald Spicer of the Foreign Office. Having failed to find any of his old Barbadians to engage as interpreter, Casement left for Pará on 5 September on the *Boniface*, a "filthy tub" carrying sixteen passengers in space designed for five.[1] On board he quickly made the acquaintance of an American medical man, Dr. Herbert Spencer Dickey, who was returning to his frontier practice on the Upper Amazon. Dickey was a man of considerable past experience in the Putumayo, having traveled overland from Colombia shortly after the dispossession and murder of a party of Colombians by Arana agents on the Caquetá in January 1908. In April 1908 he took the post of doctor at the El Encanto station and left the Aranas' service after fourteen months when his salary was cut in half. Dr. Dickey had seen little direct criminality at El Encanto, but he had heard plenty of ghastly stories from the country round, and he affirmed the probable accuracy of the figures as to the decline of the Indian population: from 45,000 in 1900 to 15,000 in 1908 and 10,000 in 1910.

In a long letter of 7 September from shipboard Casement sent Louis Mallet Dr. Dickey's more recent news and hearsay: the beast Normand had almost certainly got away to Argentina; Fonseca and Montt, along with ten Boras Indians they had impressed from the Putumayo, had gone to work for a Brazilian rubber firm on the

Javari, the river that formed a frontier between Peru and Brazil; the only major criminal known to have been arrested, Aurelio Rodriguez, who had earned as much as £4,000 a year for services that included burning thirty-five or forty Indians in one day at La Chorrera and "innumerable other crimes," had been freed on bail of £2,000 supplied by Pablo Zumaeta and had now fled Peru entirely. Zumaeta himself would not be found in jail, Dr. Dickey said, if indeed he had ever been arrested: in fact he thought no faith whatever should be placed in the honor of the Iquitos officials.[2] Dickey's "information" was a mixture of knowledge, rumor, and informed guesswork (he even named the New York hotel, the America, where a Spanish-speaking Peruvian fugitive such as Victor Macedo could be expected to appear); its general tone and tenor were all too ominously familiar, however, and probably close to the truth.

On Thursday, 7 September, Amazon water began to be visible while the *Boniface* was still at sea 700 miles from Pará. Casement's mind ran much on sexual prospects. Indeed the sexual theme is obsessive to the point of pathology in what time remains of the 1911 diary. Looking ahead to Pará in three days Casement laid plans: "Shall go on shore to Baptista Campos & look for João Anselmo at 251." Next day his fantasy was more explicit: "I'll go to Hotel de Commercio and after room & dinner will be out to Praça de *Palacio* where I hope almost at once to run across a good *big* one. Will grasp and off to Marco. It is delightful to think of Olympio & the others." On the ninth he looked back lyrically to an episode in Barbados: "Thinking much of poor young Stanley Weeks in Bridgetown and his beautiful specimen and his gladness in showing it and youth and joy. His glorious limb of Antinous!" On Sunday in Pará the reality was anti-climactic. Though he patrolled restlessly until after midnight and saw "one Huge standing on young Portuguese & girl," he found nothing really available: "None. . . . Not one."

Casement's only reason for being in Pará was to await passage upriver to Iquitos, but he was held there for two weeks, partly because the customs inspectors mysteriously refused to release his baggage. Aside from long sessions with jigsaw puzzles, sometimes with Dr. Dickey and Ricudo, and a bit of reading in *The Heart of Rome*, Casement could think of no way to spend his days except in meals and drab conversation with local English acquaintances. At night he lived another life altogether: prowling the streets for sexual adventure, sometimes tentative and only voyeuristic, sometimes violently actual and complete. His sexual obsession is almost pitiable to watch: he seems to be thinking of nothing else, really, day or night. It will be enough to show a few typical episodes.

On the evening of the thirteenth: "To Palace Square & . . . suddenly 'Whist' under trees on pavement & Tram inspector called. He entered Kiosque I followed & he put hand at once softly fingering & milking—I put hand and found, in dark, a *huge* stiff one—long & thick and firm as poker. He had near the dark caboclo." The story ends there, as presumably the event did, too. Apparently this well equipped tram inspector is the "Friend" Casement mentions several times later, possibly called "Pequeno" [Little One]. (One cannot always find the joints in Casement's jotted notes: after all he did not intend them for general reading.) Next day occurred another little unfinished movement in the odd gentle affair Casement had carried on over several years with the flower-bearer João Anselmo of whom he had dreamed on the *Boniface:* "Out to zoo—seeing many—and on way met João Anselmo de Lima & shook hands long & softly—ªgave 10$000 [ten milreis]—He wanted to give me roses but I said tomorrow morning." But that night at the Cemetery: "Friend appeared & said '*Gosto*' [I like]—& tried awfully hard—saying 'much milk'—worked like Oscar round & round & deep." Next morning, as one has learned to anticipate, Casement had a "bad headache"; he felt "too seedy" to keep his appointment with João. On Saturday by appointment at 8:00 P.M. at the Cemetery he "met Friend who entered *at once*—Huge testeminhos." They saw policemen passing behind the fence palings nearby but gusty Friend only "laughed & went on deeper."ᵇ On Sunday night at the Palace Square "a beautiful moco in white looked & entered Kiosque. Met outside & invited to passear [walk] and away we went. Felt in darkness big head—& then to B. Campos & on by . . . tram to Marco where in dark travessa he stripped almost & went in furiously—awfully hard thrusts and turns & kisses too & biting on ears & neck. Never more force shown. From Rio." Next day Casement "felt tired all day," but he was still ready at night for a full encounter with a young man from Lisbon, four years in Pará, memorable among other reasons because he was the "*first*

ªIt must be remembered that Casement lacked the language really to talk with these people.

ᵇIn all the surviving records of these risky encounters this is the only time we see Casement nearly caught in the act. At other times he speaks of interruptions after which he or his companion "fled."

since Dublin" who "*refused any present*": Casement thought the circumstance remarkable enough to justify italicizing every word.

In the early hours of Saturday, 23 September, Casement finally
got away from Pará on board the *Hilda*, a Brazilian craft which he had
favored because he had in mind to try to do something himself about
Fonseca and Montt who had slipped away to the Brazilian Javari. But
she was a "filthy pigsty." Ricudo and Omarino were also on board,
looking "very miserable"; Casement felt little sympathy for the latter, "a wee fox." Manaos was reached on 28 September, and they
remained tied up there until 3 October. Brazilian authorities had already been asked to expel Fonseca and Montt and Casement called
on the Brazilian governor and proposed a scheme whereby the "ref-
ugees" would be put across the river and arrested by the Peruvians at
Nazareth only a few hundred yards away. The governor was enthusiastic and promised to send along a police officer to oversee the
expulsion.

The five-day stay was notable chiefly as the occasion of the most
impressive, statistically, of Casement's visible homosexual episodes.
On the night of 1 October, love was made to him first by a "young
sailor apprendez" of about sixteen (a "pure Indian boy"); then by a
"darkie sailor"; then a passage with a second black sailor failed for
lack of time; then followed three consummations with "Agostinho of
Madeira" with whom he spent the rest of the night. Because he had
run out of space in Sunday's entry Casement summed up the
crowded night above his entry for Monday, 2 October: "Up at 5
stars cooling the sky. Took shower bath & Agostinho in again awfully kind. Three times he did it & three times from the two
sailors—in all six times tonight." It is the point in Casement's diaries
that one feels most acutely the possibility of forgery.

When the *Hilda* left Manaos on 3 October, Casement was carrying
a big Blue Arara Macaw in a cage, a gift from a friend in town. The
"glorious bird" slept in his cabin when she slept and during the day
sat on his shoulder emitting eldritch screeches and snapping at passersby. The weather was stifling and progress slow. The Indian boys
stayed well, but Dr. Dickey took to his bed with a bad attack of fever
and by the fifth Casement himself felt "seedy" again: "fear it is the
old complaint of Lisbon *1904* & *1909*," he noted, suspecting a recurrence of his old intestinal and rectal troubles. By the seventh he was
in a thoroughly irritated state, very sorry he had let himself be persuaded to come back to Peru. The note, "Damn Dr. Dickey—say I!"

appears, scratched out, in the entry for this day—as if a quarrel had occurred. There was still a fortnight to go to Iquitos and Casement fretted: "It is perfectly insane, the way time is wasted." The *Hilda* stopped at fifty-five mail posts between Manaos and Tebatinga, in addition to passenger and cargo ports, and she also stopped whenever the whim took her to fish, to cut grass for the cattle on board, or to trade with Indians on the banks for big turtles, eventually accumulating 200 of the creatures: she moved like a water-borne tinker's wagon. Apparently reluctant to consult Dr. Dickey, Casement was trying to treat his own ailment. Above his entry for 9 October he wrote: "Took candy—Enema broken I find—only ear syringe left. One week after event."[c] The "event" was certainly the sexual marathon in Manaos. Casement was at last visibly connecting his symptoms and his pathology.

On the eleventh Casement went over his strategy for entrapping Fonseca and Montt with the Brazilian officer on board, Jose P. de Campos. Next day the police commandant from Remate de Males, a "big degenerate German Brazilian" named Helm, came on board and joined de Campos. From this point the situation swiftly fell apart. In the afternoon the two policemen were seen drinking in the town with Serra, one of the Brazilian partners who employed the two rogues from the Putumayo. Casement could not catch sight of de Campos, but Dr. Dickey had seen both officers well drunk by five in the afternoon and assumed that Helm had been successfully bribed by Serra. De Campos told Dickey that the two renegades had " 'gone away day before yesterday.' He could not say *where* or anything more being then half drunk & an evident ass." Casement could only sit back in frustration as the *Hilda* dawdled in port for another day: "I never saw such people to waste time—All they do is spit and eat etc."[3]

When he finally reached Iquitos on 16 October, the city was in the grip of a long dry spell and the heat was so intense that Casement feared he would fall in a faint. Indeed he was probably feverish, for next day he grew ill with a severe cold and sore throat which lasted through the ensuing week. At long last Casement collected from the Prefect what sounded like a reliable account as to the actual arrests of the Putumayo criminals: only Aurelio Rodriguez and eight insig-

[c]The homely circumstantiality of such an entry, its palpable truthfulness of coloring, seems to me the kind of thing that is outside the reach of a forger unless he is a first-rate imaginative artist. I do not believe many forgers are of that class.

nificant small hoodlums were in jail and awaiting trial. (Had Dr.
Dickey been wrong in saying that Rodriguez had skipped bail? It was
impossible to know what to believe.) The Prefect explained solemnly
that border disputes with Colombia had slowed down the normally
resolute course of Peruvian justice. Casement thought the whole picture showed "apathy not to say indifference."[4]

Still suffering from his cold Casement poked about the city looking for a house for the Michells, going so far as to engage one house
and occupy it himself for a few days' trial before rejecting it as a
"pigsty" with a "cesspool" of a back yard in which the neighbors
dumped their garbage. He pursued homosexual prospects in a dilet-
tantish sort of way, rarely going beyond ogles or gifts or a bit of petting: the diary contains dozens of such passages, as the stay in
Iquitos dragged out to nearly a month, in which Casement was visibly holding himself in check, apparently on grounds of "health" but
also out of what he called simply "fear": "Nearly did it," he writes
(10 November). After dodging back from his window to avoid being
seen by a young soldier to whom he had previously made approaches, he writes: "And so I have again sacrificed love to fear" (9
November). On the morning after an abortive episode ("Tried feel it
but got match box instead") he writes: "After last night's two on the
Malecon I am tired and a bit afraid" (11 November). The "two" here,
like all these Iquitos episodes, were unfinished affairs but none the
less produced tension and "fear." He never specifies what it is he
fears. Health is a part of it: his cold lingers, he suffers from indiges-
tion and sciatic pain, and by now he must have been associating his
rectal problems with his full consummations. But surely he also
feared exposure, the danger intensified by the celebrity of his local
role: he was a person of special note in Iquitos now and peculiarly
vulnerable to scandalous attack.

On 1 November, Casement had heard from Dr. Paredes and A.
H. Harding of the John Lilly Company the disgusting news that the
Iquitos Court had not only quashed the proceedings against Pablo
Zumaeta but had ordered the dismissal of Dr. Valcarcel, the judge
who had issued the order for his arrest. Dr. Paredes struck Casement
as the only hopeful element in Iquitos, uniquely admirable and amiable among Peruvians. To encourage him to stand firm in Iquitos and
possibly to strengthen his hand in Lima, Casement sent Paredes on 7
November a formal letter of congratulation on his successful comple-
tion of a courageous mission to the Putumayo: he was pleased, he

said, to have his own findings confirmed by a Peruvian official, but more pleased that Paredes's mission suggested a Peruvian determination that "those evils must be brought to an end and a *régime* of right dealing and legality take their place."[5] But he was already sure this was whistling in the dark, and when he left Iquitos on 12 November on the Lilly Company launch *Anastasia* to return to the Javari to follow the "pursuit" of Fonseca and Montt, he was convinced that the errand would prove only ritualistic. He was right: the journey filled another eleven days and produced only new instances of evasiveness, no sight of the criminals. The trip proved another dull airing and a tiresome *causerie* and Casement came back to Iquitos on 24 November no wiser than he had set out.

In Iquitos the days passed almost as placidly as before, nearly always including a session with Jose Gonzalez, a young pilot in training on the *Liberal* with whom Casement had spent much time in October. They divided their time between heavy petting and desultory study of a Spanish-English primer. On 30 November the Michells arrived on the *Ucayali* with their two grown daughters and Casement spent much of the next days helping them settle in and taking them out to meals. Dr. Paredes brought a synopsis of his official report for Casement to study in confidence. It was a distillation of 3,000 pages of minutes and records and after three days' study he concluded that it was "very well done."[6] Paredes would be telling a story even grimmer than his own, having uncovered among other things incidents of enforced cannibalism in which agents had compelled muchachos to eat the flesh of other Indians and given starving prisoners the cooked genitals of murdered comrades. Casement set down these details in notes for November 30,[7] but he was so horrified that he could not bring himself to spell them out in his letters to the Foreign Office. Paredes told him that he went in daily fear of his life, having created by his warrants a society of 237 potential assassins. Both he and Isaac Escurra of the John Lilly Company begged Casement not to return to the Putumayo: there was nothing new for him to learn on the scene, and there were plenty of "ruffians still there" glad of a chance for a shot at him. Casement had already pretty well concluded that such a trip was pointless. Paredes, who had seemed to Casement the only immediate hope in Peru, said he was hopeless, too: "Nothing will be done."[8]

"God help the Michells," Casement wrote in his diary on 4 December, chagrined to think his recommendation had brought them to live in a place he could hardly bear. They had relieved one of his embarrassments when they agreed to take on Ricudo and his wife as well as little Omarino as household servants. He gave Michell a long circumstantial briefing on "the whole dirty business here,"[9] the Putumayo story from beginning to end as he had come to know it. At long last apparently on the evening of the fifth, the affair with Jose proceeded to a climax: "felt Jose's stiff & *really* this time. It was very big & he allowed me to do it just as I liked—*never moving all the time*."[10] That night he had a dream set in an African scene of the deep past that haunted him now by its air of purity: "I waked with vivid dream of 1887-88 going up Mozamba Hill—Oh! God—to think of it—'the fields of Heaven'—24 years ago in the heyday & glowing flush of my youth—just 23 years old—more than half my life gone since then."[11]

Next day, his last in Iquitos, came a wire in garbled cipher from the Foreign Office still clear enough to indicate that "strong representations" were being made to Lima. On 7 December he boarded the *Ucayali:* "Off at 11 A.M. with Hat waving & so to the downward path." He hoped never to see the place again. Across the top of a letter of 9 December to Gertrude Bannister he scribbled: "Left Iquitos! Hurrah!"[12] He went on to call it a "vile & pestilential hole," his mood perhaps aggravated by a big cinder in his eye from the funnel of the *Ucayali*. With Manaos reached on Monday, 11 December, Casement evidently felt he was released from the inhibitions of Iquitos, for he took two lovers on Tuesday, another on Wednesday, and two more on Thursday.[13] Sunday he sailed on the *Hubert* and reached Pará on Thursday, 21 December. Next night he sustained two encounters with a "Darkie" who worked "fiercely & hugely" and later "still more *furiously*" and inquired " 'Ebon?' [Do you like it?] when putting in with awful thrusts."[14] Next day Casement dodged across the Paz Gardens when he saw the man coming toward him again and avoided him.

Awaiting him in Pará was a letter from William Tyrrell which settled the question of what was to be his next move: he was to proceed at once to Barbados, thence to the United States to lay the British view of the Putumayo situation before American officials and try to persuade them to join Britain in united pressure upon Peru. The situation was complicated not only by the Monroe Doctrine, which Casement found so stifling, but by the fact that the United States looked upon Peru as her particular friend in South America. Tyrrell's letter also brought news that the consulate at Buenos Aires, for which he had put in a bid, had gone to another man. Casement was disappointed but evidently not crushed or angry, for he merely noted in his diary: "Alack—alack—so I am clean done out of that—what a shame."[15]

On Christmas Eve he was off for Barbados on the *Denis*, rattling about comfortably with only four other passengers, and troubled only by the fact that his big Blue Arara with gold eyes, "Polly" or "Hyacinthus," was off his feed. The companionable bird had been especially fond of milk with sugar: "When I put sugar with it his indecency knows no bounds & he wallows in it and chortles."[16] Landing in Barbados on the twenty-ninth Casement read that Andres O'Donnell had married his British bride two days earlier, with pages in white satin and bridesmaids in pink voile and picture hats and many British guests in attendance. So much for Paredes's warrants.

In Washington in early January at the British Legation, Casement made the valuable acquaintance of A. Mitchell Innes, a highly civilized and humane person. The two men were to correspond throughout the year on their common cause of the Putumayo and on English and Irish politics in general. Casement was also taken in hand by Ambassador James Bryce, the diplomat-historian, who took him to talk with President Taft and with South American specialists in the Department of State. Reports he saw indicated that American officials were being led into a false ease by their South American representatives' uncritical acceptance of Peruvian assurances: that many arrests had been made, that the criminals were being hotly prosecuted, that Pablo Zumaeta had "not been released," and so on.[d] Casement believed that he had convinced the Americans that such things were simple lies, as he had just seen for himself, and that he had led them a step or two toward active cooperation with Britain.

When he returned from the United States in mid-January 1912, Casement was ordered to stay within reach of London while the Putumayo affair continued active. He had now been absent from his post of Consul-General at Rio, to which he still held title, for nearly two years. In fact he would never return to Rio and indeed would never take up routine consular duties again. In early February he

---

[d]8 March 1912. Casement's note on Bryce telegram to Foreign Office, 29 February 1912. NLI 13086–87. Of course, Zumaeta had never been arrested. Now the Foreign Office protested to Lima when it learned that he had been made acting Mayor of Iquitos.

filed a rather empty-handed report of his second mission which had never penetrated to the Putumayo and produced only a new accumulation of rumor and evidence as to the climate of chicanery and dissembling that prevailed in Peru. In returning a corrected proof of this report of 12 February, he sent along a précis and partial translation of Paredes's synopsis, explaining to Grey the confidential circumstances in which he had come by the document.[17] Louis Barnes of the Peruvian Amazon Company Commission wrote Casement in admiration of the nerve and the integrity, unique in their experience in Peru, that Paredes had demonstrated: "Paredes I think deserves a gold medal. I could not have believed that any Peruvian would have shown things up as he has evidently done. I could certainly not advise him to continue to reside in Iquitos or to visit the Putumayo, especially when any of those blackguards are anywhere within reach."[18] Three copies of Casement's new report, printed for internal circulation, were sent to L. J. Jerome to be handed to the government in Lima. He was directed to say that His Majesty's Government could not stall critics much longer: unless Peru produced some real action, Casement's report would have to be generally circulated.[19] By now the United States had allowed her minister to join the British minister in "urgent representations" and a reply, typically evasive and disingenuous, had been issued by Peru.

Meanwhile Casement had submitted a long memorandum on 30 January suggesting various measures that might be attempted after publication and after the public outcry he felt sure would follow. The whole issue of effective punishment of the criminals was now dead, he argued, and publication was now the only feasible punitive device: "to drag into daylight and hold up to universal reprobation . . . that the civilised world should know how Peru has used her primitive, defenceless, innocent populations in this greedy rush for rubber." The welfare of the Indians needed now to be thought of as a problem for the future, and Britain could serve them best by helping to create "some civilised machinery of administration" in the Putumayo as a check upon the exploiters and a shield for the exploited. He pointed out that "government" in the Putumayo had been represented by a single "Comisario" who up to November 1911 had been a salaried agent of the Company and a single "Juez de Paz" who got no public salary and was actually a Company dependent. Paredes had laid great stress upon the basic lawlessness of the region and had proposed details of a new administration which Casement heartily approved. In fact Peru could not do better than install Paredes himself as supreme magistrate. Casement was remembering Paredes's deep anger and pity, so rare among Peruvians, at the scarred bodies of Huitotos and the walking skeletons who were the survivors of the tribesmen of Atenas.[20]

12   Pegging Turf

THROUGHOUT the winter Casement remained faithfully in London on call at the Foreign Office, his only break being a brief visit late in February to Sir Arthur Conan Doyle at Lyndhurst in the New Forest. Doyle wrote first to renew acquaintance and to say that his "wild boy's book," now called *The Lost World*, would begin running in the *Strand* in April and it would contain surprises for an Amazon expert like Casement: "It will certainly tell you some things about the hinterland of the Amazon which you have never known. I get quickly off the river into a land of my own."[1] A few days later Doyle wrote to offer horses "of a mild type" if he would come for a visit,[2] and Casement then went down to the New Forest for a weekend at the Grand Hotel. In the spring he was ready for a prolonged airing, beginning with ten days in Belfast and Larne. On 4 May he left with Dick Morten for a three-week motor tour in Germany. They picked up an old African friend[a] in Strasbourg and went on to Lake Constance, Nuremberg, Coblenz, Rottenberg, Wiesbaden, Heidelberg, and Frankfurt. On return, after another pause in Denham, Casement went on down to Falmouth in Cornwall where he spent two weeks at the Green Bank Hotel with Nina.

He wrote of his travels and other homely affairs in a long chatty letter to William Cadbury on 26 May. The Cadburys had accepted the care of Polly as a loan that might turn into a gift and now complained mildly of certain of her (she had now been classified as female) habits, particularly a tendency to nip careless passersby with her big horny beak. This was a hangover, Casement explained, from Amazon journeys when she would perch on his shoulder "assaulting

[a]Perhaps Heinrich Heyn.

all who approached me!"[3] Soon Casement was required to take her back. No cage being available she traveled in a taxi to Paddington Station on his shoulder. While he went to buy a ticket he installed her in a railway car in charge of two porters, but she "eloped thro' the window on the roof chortling & chuckling" and he returned to find her surrounded by "quite a mob" of admirers, including many porters and travelers and an old acquaintance, Sir John Simon, with two "quite lovely" ladies. Polly held audience, chattering away, as Casement climbed onto the carriage to recover her. The affair ended with Casement promising to take the bird to Fritwell Manor in Bambury to entertain Sir John Simon's children.[4]

On returning from Cornwall early in June, Casement had settled in with the Mortens again and he remained in Denham through June and most of July, frequently called upon for one or another service related to the Putumayo affair. He had been wishing to get away to Ireland for a long stay and had written the Bannister sisters in early May that he hoped to join them at Cloghaneely for the Irish summer school. But he wrote Gertrude again on 19 June to say that he was unable to lay coherent plans from week to week: he was ordered to stay near London "until the Putumayo is cleared up—and that may be months!"[5] Nor was it clear what lay beyond the Putumayo for him, unless a return to Rio—which he hoped to escape. By July it was settled that the Putumayo report was to be published and on 17 July he proclaimed to Gertrude that "the Putumayo horror" was "out at last!" He was "bombarded" by interviewers, he said, and planning to "fly" to Ireland that night with Mrs. Green. But he was still not given a clearance.

In another letter to Gertrude on the twenty-fifth he weighed his achievement: "I've blown up the Devil's Paradise in Peru! I told you I should—and I've done it. It is a good step forward in human things—the abodes of cruelty are not so secure as they were & their tenants are getting very scared."[6] He had done all one man could do to disestablish a wholesale viciousness. He had been over-optimistic about the timing of the publication, however, and the Putumayo papers, delayed by a plea from the United States, were not released for general circulation until mid-August. Casement lingered restlessly in Denham, "in attendance on F.O. almost daily."[7] At long last he got away to Ireland and he spent the remainder of August, all of September, and the first half of October, mainly at Falcarragh in

County Donegal but with stays of some length in Belfast and Dublin. Nor was he free of the old task: from Falcarragh on 12 September he wrote Gertrude that he had "pegged turf at those Devils on the Putumayo till my hand nearly drops!"[8]

Alongside his official work Casement had carried on throughout the year with his volunteer labors for a Christian Mission in the Putumayo. Partly because the sectarian issue of the sponsorship of the Mission had proved so sensitive, solicitation was being done rather quietly and privately, though an office for the fund had been set up with the banker Percy H. Browne in charge. Browne and Casement worked closely and harmoniously together in the campaign for the £15,000 needed. Catholic and Protestant rivalry over sponsorship of the Mission continued heated though neither group of communicants seemed in any great hurry to offer cash. The conflict also began to press uncomfortably upon Casement's own ambiguous religious position. Born and reared "Protestant," of a Protestant father and a Catholic mother who procured his secret Catholic baptism, orphaned, reared by Protestant relations, and educated in Protestant schools, Casement's training and habits were surely Protestant not Catholic, and he passed universally for Protestant—in the family, among friends, and at large in Ireland. Yet in adulthood he was scarcely a churchman at all and, so far as can be seen, never entered a church expect for a wedding or a funeral. If he thought deeply about the matter, the fact is not visible among his papers until the extreme crisis at the end of his life. No doubt he thought of himself as a Christian, but his philosophical position (to give it too grand a name) was really general and humanist, a sort of sentimental rationalism. He saw himself as a man of good will, an enlightened spirit, a sophisticated benign intelligence, committed to Christian principles but above any need for forms.

When Casement went off to Ireland at the end of July, his work for the Mission fund and for the Foreign Office did not cease and he had a good many other problems on his mind as well, including as always his family. Charles Casement had written a chin-up letter[9] in which he said that though he was earning only £3 a week at the Melbourne Steamship Company he was making ends meet. Still it was a poor show for a man of his years: "I am no chicken now, nearly fifty-two." His daughter Nina was old enough to be involved in a depressing love affair. Charlie noted that in the past he had been known as a snappy dresser, but he had not had a new suit in six years now. He had been getting by on Roger Casement's old clothes, altered, and he would be glad of more of those anytime. Tom Casement's problems like his ideas were larger. Blanche had finally given him a divorce and he had taken a second wife, a young woman named Katje Ackermann who was said to be both an artist and a good businesswoman. Now he was desperate again for capital for his South African mountain inn, Rydal Mount, and, of course, had appealed to Roger. Katje's father had promised £400 of the £1,200 needed. On 29 July, Casement wrote to William Cadbury to appeal, with many apologies, for £400. He was also writing to the African rubber investor Sidney Parry, who was rich and childless, and to Herbert Ward who owed him a good deal, he thought, "for old times sake & things I did for him that are not to be bought or sold, many years ago." Casement represented Rydal Mount as a promising venture, needing only a vigorous boost. Tom had told him that he had had to turn away £500 in custom the past Christmas for lack of room. Tom himself, he said, was "not a waster or ne'er do well but an extraordinarily unbusinesslike human being—much worse than I am. . . . He is everybody's friend & extraordinarily reckless and unconventional and amusing too."[10] But he wrote of the family's Micawber to Gertrude Bannister two weeks later: "I wish he would either grow up or revert to infancy. In one case you could reason with him—in the other smack him."[11] It is not clear from the correspondence whether or not Cadbury came through with cash. Partly by borrowing against his life insurance, Casement himself managed to send Tom just over £300 before the year was out.[12]

The Mission fund appeal languished through the summer and autumn then closed successfully with a rush in December. Though by October only £2,600 was in hand of the £15,000 sought, planning and recruiting for the Franciscan Mission was going on. Father Genocchi of Rome was to be in charge and was to be accompanied by four other Franciscans. A few weeks later the necessary angel had appeared: George Pauling of Victoria Mansions, London, who wrote Casement on 12 December that he had followed his "most excellent work" for the Mission, applauding especially the fact that his motives had been "purely humanitarian." As indeed they had: Casement's hard work for such causes paid him nothing but moral satisfaction. Pauling had been sad to see how slowly subscriptions had come in and he had determined to settle the matter himself: "I have great pleasure in offering you such necessary financial support as would enable the Mission to get firmly established & to carry on its . . . work."[13] Percy Browne, whose conduct of the campaign had been a model of its kind, wrote on 20 December to give Casement entire credit for their success: "The work you have done for the mission could not be counted in money. It is *you* who have done everything."[14]

Browne was thinking particularly of Casement's success in influencing British Protestants in support of a Catholic Mission. On the vexed question of Casement's definition of his own religious position a few more bits of evidence had appeared. When Casement had inserted a letter in the *Nation*[15] attacking the Monroe Doctrine and signing himself "A Catholic Reader," and when he wrote to his friends the McVeaghs: "I am more Catholic than anything else,"[16] he appeared to be cutting away more or less purposefully at his own Protestant roots. He was reacting primarily against Ulster Protestantism, a sectarianism scarcely to be matched anywhere else in the world outside Dublin Catholicism, for tunnel vision and bigoted parochialism. Writing to Gertrude from the Antrim Road on Sunday, 22 September, he gave a vivid impression of the look of Belfast Protestantism to the musing eye: "The Church parade has begun past my windows—heavens, how appalling they look, with their grim Ulster-Hall faces all going down to curse the Pope & damn Home Rule in Kirk and Meeting House & let their God out for one day in the week—poor old man with his teeth broken with the cursing."[17] Visible there, quite apart from any philosophical preference, is one of the primary motives of Casement's piecemeal rejection of Protestantism: he identified it logically enough with blind loyalty to England and with hysterical resistance to any degree of self-determination for Ireland. It was the spirit that would soon create the bitter Ulster Covenant and that still helps to tear the province today.

The point finally was that Casement's easy shifting of religious posture suggested that the issue itself was false at root: it was possible because there was no clear definition of the self in the psyche. Role-playing is probably harmless so long as one keeps hold of the knowledge that the role is histrionic, an unreality. For Casement the alternative Catholic-Protestant role-playing was a symptom of danger because it was self-deluding, a set of unrealities that he took for true, each time he spoke, on whichever side. It was another example of the tendency to factitiousness in his character, his way of organizing conduct theatrically, in roles that were seductive because they were dramatic, and false because they were empty of real content—and dangerous because he believed in them himself.

Evidently it was the appointment of a Select Committee of the House of Commons "with reference to the Putumayo atrocities" that brought Casement back to England at the beginning of October. Charles Roberts, the chairman, wrote Casement that the Committee was "not engaged in a prosecution" but merely "conducting an enquiry to obtain information for the House of Commons" and that he would be called to give evidence.[18] Casement stayed first with the Mortens, then on 1 November moved into the new rooms at 45 Ebury Street (George Moore's street) in Pimlico that were to be his last address in London. He testified before the Committee on three occasions: 12 and 27 November and 11 December. In his first appearance he charged Julio Arana and Abel Alarco with prior knowledge and complicity in the systematic atrocities; but he exonerated the English directors of the Company of anything but sloth and complacency.[19] The second occasion brought out the fact that a Peruvian deputy had accused Casement of "blackmailing" the Company, and Roberts wrote next day to say he thought the charge was dangerous enough to require formal repudiation by His Majesty's Government.[b] Further to assist the Committee Casement offered them the use of the long rather disorderly diary of his 1910 Putumayo investigation; seizing the chance for a bit of free labor he suggested that they have it typed for convenience in handling. Charles Roberts wrote on 20 December: "I think possibly I can use my statutory power to send for documents and get the typing done. As the work is only being done for our Committee I think it may be considered legitimate.[20] This maneuver probably explains the provenance of the copy of Casement's extended 1910 diary, neatly typed in two folio volumes, that came into the possession of his solicitor George Gavan Duffy and ultimately passed to the National Library of Ireland.[c]

[b]Julio Arana had apparently set this talk going as early as 1910 when he asserted in a letter to his stockholders that both Casement and the American Hardenburg had tried to blackmail him, for £1,000 and £7,000 respectively. Casement to Grey, 24 March 1910. NLI 13086–87.

[c]In view of the controversy that surrounds all of Casement's diaries it may be useful to set down what is visible of the history of the handling of this document. A letter of 1 February 1913 shows that Roberts for some reason did not accept the diary at once: "I was a fool not to have pounced on a document so valuable, before you left." Casement caused it to be sent to him while on a trip to the Canary Islands and South Africa, and it reached Roberts on the same day

At the end of the year Casement was staying in London only because the Select Committee might call him for further testimony, and he resented the constriction. He had now had two and a half years of the Putumayo issue and, with the only hopeful instrument to emerge, the Franciscan Mission, well launched, he felt there was little more he could do or say and he wished he might be spared any more of it. There were signs that the Foreign Office itself was growing bored with the question. Lucien Jerome wrote Casement from the British Legation in Lima on 18 December: "I have had a hint from the F.O. that they want no more about the Indian question in South America, and so I shall henceforth keep my peace.[21] By the end of the year, too, Casement had worked himself into an unhealthy and unhappy condition in his mind, his body, and his career that reminds one of his state at the time of the Lisbon debacle in late 1904.

---

he wrote Casement: "The Diary has arrived with your letter. It has gone to be typed by an expert. Very many thanks" (NLI 13073). The Select Committee sat until 5 June 1913 when it finished its report, to be issued within a few days. Roberts wrote on 5 June: "What shall I do with all your documents? . . . I have your diary, & the typewritten copy I have for you, & a good deal besides!" (NLI 13073) At that time Casement was in Connemara. On 3 July 1913 with Casement back in Denham Roberts wrote to invite him to lunch at his home in Palace Green on the 7th, when he would hand over the papers. Presumably this occurred. Gertrude Bannister's later charge that British officials retained the diary and used it in a forgery seems unfounded; but the case is complicated. See below, pp. 462–63, 479–80.

13   Sorry to Lose You

O NE source of Casement's tension, never to be relaxed thenceforward, was the recurrence of his Irish agitations in the spring
of 1912, set going in a powerful way by the Carsonite resistance in
Ulster to the long-awaited prospect of Home Rule for Ireland.[a] It
was a challenge to the very center of Casement's personal patriotism
and he could not possibly ignore it. He reacted first in the readiest
way, in letters to the newspapers. He alerted Gertrude on 25
March: "get tomorrow's D. News & see the 'Irishman's' letter
(D.V.). It . . . would land the Scodge [himself] in Holloway 'one
time' as the Kruboys used to say at Old Calabar. . . . Don't tell who
'Irishman' is if the letter appears."[1] Casement's letter was perhaps his
first positive step toward the gallows. The Carsonite challenge was
irresistibly infuriating, it must be admitted: to one of Casement's

[a]Sir Edward Carson (1854–1935) was not an Ulsterman but a product of the Protestant Ascendancy in southern Ireland. After being called to the Irish bar in 1877, he served ably as a
crown prosecutor and entered British politics as a protégé of Arthur Balfour in 1892 when he
became the Conservative and Unionist M.P. for Dublin University. His political rise in England was swift, and his powers as a legal advocate quickly made him a wealthy man. In 1900 he
was made Solicitor-General of England. The first Home Rule Bill had died in the House of
Commons in 1886 and the second in the Lords in 1893. With the Liberals in ascendancy after
1905 and with the Lords deprived of their power of veto in 1911, it was generally assumed that
the coalition of English Liberals and Irish Nationalists, the latter led by John Redmond, could
no longer be prevented from pushing a Home Rule Bill through Parliament. Carson had been
all his life a passionate partisan of the cause of Irish union with England, and the preservation of
the status quo in the whole of Ireland, not merely in Ulster, was the strongest motive of his
political life. In February 1910 Carson was chosen as leader of the Irish Unionists in the House
of Commons, and in July 1911 he accepted the call of the Ulster Unionist Council in Belfast to
head the movement in the North in opposition to Home Rule—not because he favored Ulster
separatism but because he hoped Ulster energies could be used as a fulcrum in a resistance
designed to forestall Home Rule altogether in a still united Ireland.

temperament it was an extremity certain to elicit an extremity. He brooded and raged about the issue all through the summer and fall, in Ireland and England. His statement to William Cadbury on 12 October was one of his more temperate: "The whole 'Ulster' business is outrageous—an impossible appeal to the bigotry of a dead age. Were England to champion those intolerant and ignorant fanatics she says goodbye to her own fair name."[2] Mitchell Innes at the British Legation in Washington received Casement's full charge and he was finally driven to pull him up short in a letter that could have saved Casement's life, if he had heeded it—and if he had felt it worth saving on such terms of compromise. "Steady on, my dear Casement," wrote Innes on 22 November, "steady on with your denunciation of poor Carson." From a barrister friend of his who was well acquainted with Carson and his work, Innes had received a very different judgment than Casement's: "He tells me of a man of the highest honour, who, though a strong fighter, is full of human feeling and sympathy, a man to be trusted in all things." Casement had been representing him, according to Innes, as "a cross between a jackal and a bloodhound, dishonest, a castle hack, a man who would dip his hand in Irish blood." Innes supposed that Carson used comparable language of Casement's nationalist party, also without altogether meaning what he said. A plague on both your houses, Innes said in effect of the general carriage of Irish political controversy: "But you lash yourselves with your own eloquence, till the pain makes you forget everything else."[3]

Mitchell Innes was counseling the kind of correction of view of the infuriating and formidable Carson that a great many persons found themselves being forced to make, and indeed it was not long before Casement himself was expressing reluctant admiration. Innes's last sentence was the salutary one, for it put a finger on a truism of Irish politics and on a sick tendency in Casement's personal psychology: the volatile and erratic relationship between his thought, his feeling, and his language. It was true in a way that he lashed himself with his own eloquence; but the habit was especially dangerous because the eloquence was artificial. Casement's eloquence was rarely genuine, rarely subjected to reflection or reason. Commonly it was close to bombast: pretentious diction, false heat and false color, a bludgeoning style that hid its loose thinking and loose feeling, its poverty of evidence and argument, under a noise of verbal forms. Unconsciously it was designed to deceive not only the reader but the writer. When the verbal trance was sufficiently gripping, content and language began to corrupt each other in a gyring sort of movement that turned a subject passionate but abstract, unreal, cut loose from its base in fact. It was Mitchell Innes's sense of that tendency that elicited his wise colloquial imperative: "Steady on, my dear Casement."

His month in Donegal in August and September of 1912 was one of the purest idylls of Casement's life, a consolation in the years remaining; but toward the end of it he began to feel painfully and mysteriously unwell. He was cramped and bent with severe pains in his back and hips and legs, and he did not know what was causing it all, or what to call it except rheumatism. In early October he went to Dublin for medical help and there he wrote Gertrude on the eighth that the rheumatism was no better: "indeed it is settling down on me like a winter cloud on Muckish."[4] The Dublin doctors could not find the source of his misery though they talked vaguely of kidney stones. Held unwillingly in London through November and December, Casement continued unwell and comprehensively unhappy. He was frightened by his illness, enraged by Ulster politics, baffled and bored by the Putumayo, revolted by the thought of going back to Rio yet unable to find a feasible alternative inside or outside the Foreign Office.

To add to his anxieties Tom Casement's new wife Katje turned up ill in London in October. Casement met her for the first time and liked her at once. On the twenty-fifth he sent her £5 to go on with as she was leaving the hospital for a few days' convalescence at Eastbourne. "Don't worry *at all* about money," he comforted her with his usual openhandedness. "I'll give you, with a heart and a half, all I have." It was of course very nearly true. He urged her to make Tom "stick to Rydal Mount" and promised to send her regular sums to be put into supplies and so to reduce current costs.[5]

In the last three weeks of the year Casement's actions in regard to his health and his career were hectic and confused.[b] On 12 December he asked the Foreign Office for two months' leave "on medical grounds" which he planned to spend "in a warmer climate" before going back to Rio—which might have been thought warm enough. Next day he wrote to Grey withdrawing his request, for no clear reason: "I find it would be more convenient for me to leave at once

---

[b]In a letter to Tyrrell of 14 January 1913 he said that "constant pain" in December had upset him "mentally as much as physically." NLI 13080.

for my post . . . at Rio de Janeiro."[6] He had hinted repeatedly that he would like an assignment elsewhere. In a note to Spicer on 15 December he called Rio "that infernal hole I am departing for."[7] But Tyrrell's note of the sixteenth was not helpful: "Many thanks for your letters of the 12th and 13th. There is no objection to your going back to Rio now as you proposed to do. I am afraid that the Secretary of State cannot offer you any change from there at present."[c]

Meanwhile Casement had been undergoing examinations and treatment from two London physicians with Gilbert and Sullivan names: Ironside Bruce and Sir Lauder Brunton. Returning to Ebury Street after a course of X-rays on the eighteenth he found not only another urgent summons from the Select Committee but a letter from Algernon Law asking him to go to Manchester before leaving for Rio to talk with the Chamber of Commerce about British business interests in Brazil. He sent off by special messenger a note to Law saying that his health was so poor that he was unlikely to return to Rio or to active service of any kind. He then went in person to Law and to Charles Roberts of the Select Committee to explain his situation. Apparently Casement was now convinced that he was suffering from something exotic and disastrous; what he thought it was remains unclear, but he evidently found a name for it and reported it to some of his closest friends in terms that alarmed them badly. Mrs. Green repeatedly sent advice and anxious inquiry. Henry Nevinson wrote on the nineteenth: "I cannot get over your sad news. I can think of nothing else. You always seemed such a model of health and completeness. I have never heard of this disease, and did not know it was possible. It sounds horribly painful and depressing. Do please let me hear at once when they know the result of the X-rays."[8] Others sent the kind of eulogy or proto-elegy that is ordinarily elicited by approaching dissolution. These impressive testimonials were faintly comic in the upshot, as expressions of feeling in excess of cause. This is by no means to call them insincere, and they came from men such as Percy Browne and Lucien Jerome who were not fools.

"Anyhow," Nevinson had written consolingly on 15 December,

---

[c]NLI 13073. On 18 December Casement drafted a sardonic reply to Algernon Law's despatch of the second informing him that the state of Goyaz was to be added to his jurisdiction at Rio. He thanked Grey for "this singular mark of His Majesty's favour," suggested that his office allowance be increased enough to allow him to locate the state geographically, described the custom of deputies' leaving Goyaz a year in advance when they had to go to the capital, the road being lined with graves of those who had perished on the way, and so on. The letter was clumsily done and in bad taste and Casement fortunately never let it go beyond a rough draft.

"every woman I meet is in love with your portrait."[9] Indeed Casement was surely still at forty-eight one of the most elegantly handsome men of his day, keeping his tall, spare, strong, graceful figure and his close-cut curly hair and beard beginning to turn a sable silvered. And however badly he felt, the somatic realities emerged as hardly dramatic. Dr. Ironside Bruce's X-rays uncovered nothing tangible and Sir Lauder Brunton's exhaustive examination also showed nothing serious: a slight cough and a "curious creak in inspiration as if from an old adhesion" and the liver "full & *very* tender"; in the appendix area an "ovoid swelling like a ¾ inch rope very tender," examination "per rectum" confirming this tenderness and showing evidence of ancient fistulae. The patient suffered pain in his hip and his sacroiliac area, he was constipated, and his appetite was poor.[10] All in all Casement sounded like a reasonably healthy middle-aged man who needed to watch his appendix. Mrs. Green continued to hover anxiously, however, and even went to Sir Lauder to elicit an opinion that Casement should not travel out of reach of a good surgeon: he might risk Cannes, but he should not go to the Canary Islands as he had been threatening.[11] But Casement's mind was made up at last: he would go to the Canary Islands for sun and rest and if he prospered he would go on to South Africa to see Tom and Katje and Rydal Mount. So he wrote once more to Grey on 23 December asking now for three months' leave to commence at Teneriffe.[12]

Making long stops in Las Palmas, Teneriffe, and St. Helena to rest and soak up the sun, Casement spent a leisurely two months en route to South Africa. It was obviously good for his nerves to be free of both England and Ireland. The malaise that had hung over him since September was now officially labeled arthritis. From a doctor in Las Palmas he drew a cautionary statement for future use: "I am quite sure it will be *most* unwise for you to return [to] Rio de Janeiro & your old life for some considerable time as you will not only undo any good you may have derived from your treatment but your condition will probably become permanent."[13] But in fact he grew rapidly better and by the end of January he was able to tell Gertrude that he was "getting furiously strong and well."[14]

Early in the month he received a shock when his account from his bankers showed that he had been placed on half-pay on 1 July 1912, apparently without notice. On 14 January Casement wrote feeling letters to both Spicer and Tyrrell to review the situation and to protest. His understanding had been that Sir Edward Grey wished him to remain indefinitely in the United Kingdom—until he was otherwise assigned or himself asked to return to Rio; and he thought he had been as busy in the public service during the past six months as at any time since he was first sent to the Putumayo. Now he suddenly found himself £264 worse off in his "spendable cash" than he had had any reason to anticipate.[d] Had he known of the cut in pay he could have chosen to go on leave or to return to Rio. Instead he had had to dangle about London where expenses were high, at a time when he was in constant physical pain, unconsciously suffering in pocket at the same time. He assumed, he told Tyrrell, that all of this must have been done without the knowledge of either Tyrrell or Grey, and he asked him to look into the matter and try to see justice done.[e]

The letter to Tyrrell was aggrieved, though temperate in tone. But he was furiously angry at the Foreign Office for trying to "force" him back to Rio against his wishes and against his and his doctors' reading of the state of his health, and the salary issue exacerbated his feeling. That it all got added into the score he was keeping against Perfidious Albion was shown by the very different tone of his letter to Gertrude from Las Palmas on 3 February. There he called the Foreign Office "those pigs" and "absolute Anglo-Britannic swine" and cited the salary matter as part of the evidence: "Aren't they beauties?"[15] His plan now was to continue taking leave until he returned to England, probably in mid-April. Then he would try once more to "get shifted from Rio"; if that still did not work he would ask for his pension and retire from the Consular Service entirely.

To Cadbury Casement spoke of better health: he now felt he would master "this horrid complaint" arthritis, "a sort of creeping paralysis of the bones."[16] He left Las Palmas on the sixth or seventh of February on the *Grantully Castle*, glad enough of her slow seventeen-day schedule to Cape Town which would provide that much more rest and sunshine. From Cape Town he would go up to Witzies Hoek, inspect Tom and the property, "report to the stockholders—myself," as he put it to Gertrude, and see what more could be done to help the "poor old chap."[17] His current leave being

---

[d]It was apparently at this time that he drew up a sort of crude balance sheet for the last six months of 1912. He listed total expenditures of £744.13.6. He had given Nina £70, Charlie £15, and Tom £314.13.9. The "Irish Cause" got £27.10.0 and the "Putumayo" £20. He summed it all up as £447.3.9. "on Tom & Co." and £297.9.9 "on Self & Nina & others." NLI 13080.

[e]NLI 13080. The record does not show what if anything his plea accomplished.

due to expire on 31 March, Casement wrote Grey from St. Helena on 17 February to ask for a further two months: after a brief stay in Cape Town, he wrote, he would be going on to "a sanitorium in the hills of the Orange Free State," as he thought it politic to describe Tom's mountain inn, where he would remain until he received Grey's reply.[18] The extension of leave was granted by Grey's telegram of 28 February. Casement had also thought it wise to inquire—describing himself as feeling very ill—as to what he could count on in the way of a pension if he chose to retire. On 17 March Lord Dufferin sent him a formula that had been worked out by the Chief Clerk's office. His service from 1 July 1895 to 30 December 1904 and from 21 September 1906 to 31 March 1913 came to sixteen years; to that would be added a credit of eight years for "unhealthy service" (service in areas so classified), making a total of twenty-four years. The formula yielded a pension of £440. As Casement would be applying for early retirement, he would have to submit a certificate of bad health; but Dufferin "gathered" that he would have no difficulty in supplying one "strong enough to satisfy the Treasury." He hoped indeed that South Africa would restore Casement's health and he would not need to retire: "We would, I need hardly say, all be sorry to lose you."[19]

Casement was by no means determined on retirement as yet, and he was still following with great interest the hearings before the Select Committee in the verbatim reports that Charles Roberts was having sent to him. It no longer appeared that the English directors of the Peruvian Amazon Company had been so ignorant or innocent as everyone had assumed. Roberts himself took time to send Casement a long personal summary of recent events on 1 February. Exasperated at the company's reluctance to produce requested papers and their habit of extracting crucial data, Roberts had "practically raided" the company's office, sending down the Clerk of the Committee in a cab with two porters and orders to seize everything useful. The action was "perfectly regular" and got results. A striking fact was the way such phrases as "conquest," "reduction of the Indians," "conquering them or rather attracting them to work and civilisation" kept turning up in letters not only of Arana, Alarco, Zumaeta, and Tizon but of Gielgud and some of the English directors. Gielgud, for example, had certainly known from his work as an auditor that more than eleven thousand pounds had been spent in 1907 and 1908 in "subjecting" the Indians in various sections. He was going to be recalled and asked for an explanation. Roberts and the Committee were sorry they were not to be treated to "the dramatic moment" of a confrontation of Arana and Casement. Meanwhile the British hand had been strengthened when the United States House of Representatives brought out a volume called *Slavery in Peru* incorporating the text of Casement's report.[20]

A report of the hearings came through with a touch of romantic coloring from "Shelagh"[f] who wrote from 30 Portland Place on 17 February. Addressing Casement as "Dear Don Roderigo," she said that she had been attending the hearings and at one of them the Ranee of Sarawak (Lady Brooke) had told her she had "*such* an admiration" for Casement. Being one of the women who had felt the same, Shelagh had felt inclined to say: "no use my friend, his eyes are on the hill tops!" She inquired now about the progress of a novel Casement had told her he was going to write with "no heroine or romance": would it not be "a little *dull*?" She went on in an obviously customary vein of kittenish teasing: "How odd that you should look so much more dangerous than you are. You know I always tell you that you look as if you ought (in slouch hat & cloak, with perhaps a guitar, & *certainly* a dagger handy) lurk in the moonlight near some balcony. (How you will hate being told this you always pretend not hear, but you will have to read it.)"[21] Unsatisfactory as all that is, it is the most intimate glimpse we ever receive of Casement in company with any woman other than his sister or his cousins.

At Rydal Mount Casement wrote Elizabeth Bannister on 21 March: "I am *so* much better I laugh arthritis to scorn! The pains have *all* gone—lock, stock & barrel & I feel I shall return in May a new man."[22] His month with Tom and Katje was marked by an epistolary silence that probably indicated peace and contentment. Tom saw him off for Durban and Cape Town on 6 April and he was back in London by the middle of May. He had told Elizabeth that he hoped to "square up things at F.O." before his leave expired at the end of the month. It seems apparent that Casement would not have retired at this point if the Foreign Office had offered him an interest-

---

[f]I have been unable to identify this lady clearly. She appears to be a member of the family of the Earl of Norbury at whose seat, Carlton Park in Market Norbury, Casement occasionally visited. In his diary for 25 June 1910 he noted: "To Carlton Park at 4.55 train. Lady S., Lady Caledon, Lady Morgan." On 28 June: "In London. Lunched at Princes with Lady Caledon and sisters. Lady Caledon, Lady Margaret, Lady Charlotte. Last time of seeing Sheelagh." The last clause is as close as Casement ever comes to expressing heterosexual feeling.

ing alternative to Rio—but equally clear that they were not inclined to humor him in his insistence. Nobody at the Foreign Office was showing great dismay at his talk of retirement and nobody tried to talk him out of it. William Tyrrell wrote kindly on 21 May, but even he displayed no passionate regret: he said that Casement himself must judge what shape to give his life. If he elected to ask for his pension, Tyrrell was sure Grey would recommend him to the Treasury for "the highest your long, valuable & distinguished services under the Crown and the Regulations allow." He concluded: "I can quite understand the wrench you feel, but I also know it will not make any difference to those happy relations which you have established with everybody you have had to deal with from my Chief downward."[23]

In a letter of 17 May Casement had put it to William Cadbury that he was "hoping" to retire from the Consular Service on grounds of its triviality and boredom: "I am very tired of it—there is no future or hope of change in it—nothing but Rio, Brazil and discomfort & no work of interest."[24] At forty-eight it was not the way he wished to think of spending the active years remaining to him. He had never stopped hankering back to Africa as the scene of his youth and freedom and the image returned to him now as a place where he could still work in a significant and independent way. Voices from his African past were still audible. Alfred Parminter, his old friend and Vice-Consul at Lourenço Marques, was in town on his first holiday in more than five years from the storekeeper's job that Casement had got him in 1907 after the Foreign Office led by the "fierce cad" Sir Eric Barrington had dismissed him in "snobbish spite."[25] He was looking for a change and Casement hoped Cadbury would give him something in Trinidad or elsewhere. Parminter, he pointed out, had been the first to denounce "Leopoldism"—in a Reuters interview in 1896 that had led the Birmingham papers and the *Daily Telegraph* to take up the cause of the Congo natives.

The Putumayo report also woke certain voices from the deep past, such as that of Hans Coudenhove whom Casement had known in Africa nearly thirty years earlier. Coudenhove wrote on 25 May from Tkombe in German East Africa to say that he had read "every single word of that lovely, jolly book of yours with the blue cover." He was sorry there was little chance of "an adequate reward" for the worst of the Putumayo blackguards and like everyone else he itched to get his hands on Armando Normand. Coudenhove had accumulated such a distaste for Caucasians that he had issued standing orders to the "boys" of his caravan never to pitch camp within reach of possible exchange with any white man.[26]

Nerved at last to cut his ties with British officialdom and not yet obsessively gripped by the fate of Ireland, Casement felt seduced by Africa. He would go back, he wrote Cadbury, "& revisit many of the spots of my youth . . . & look into things all round there *de novo* and with the eye of a natural specialist in the infinite variations of African wrongdoing." He thought he saw his way to "doing something useful" there still before he died.[27] Meanwhile he was off to Dublin on 18 May and he promised to "look the Irish painter up." Cadbury had asked leave to commission a likeness by the Dublin portraitist, wit, and *grande dame* Sarah Purser. But he would not sit until his hair which he had had "shaved to the crown" while staying with Tom had grown out a bit. "What a jolly idea," Morel commented when he heard of the portrait scheme, and he looked forward to seeing it on Cadbury's wall when he next visited Wast Hills. "Lucky artist," had been Mrs. Morel's remark.[28]

In Dublin Casement took a sitting room and a small bedroom at 55 Lower Baggot Street where all the other tenants seemed to be not only spinsters but "Unionist" spinsters: when they passed him on the stairs, they averted their eyes as from "a thing of horror."[29] On the eleventh he suggested that the Cadburys meet him at Glendalough for a motor tour to include Dunsany, Tara, and Dublin where they could see Miss Purser and the three-quarter-length portrait for which Cadbury was paying £50.[30] He gave Miss Purser ten sittings and the work was finished on 25 June. The Cadburys did come and evidently the motor tour turned into an extensive affair, for Casement noted: "2,432 miles on speedometer 20 June 1913"[31]— but perhaps not all those miles were logged in Ireland. On 2 July Casement assured the Cadburys that they had left many friends behind them.[32] Sir William Armstrong, Director of the National Gallery of Ireland, had seen the portrait and called it Miss Purser's best. If Cadbury heard that, the artist thought, he might only say, "Well, the rest can't be up to much!": she had formed the impression that Cadbury had not liked the picture, and she told Casement that she would be quite happy to keep it "for Dublin." Privately she was calling it "Colmcille in Iona." Writing to Gertrude on 26 June Casement judged it "a *great* success."[33] Cadbury, of course, did accept the painting, and years later he gave it to the National Gallery in Dublin, which also possesses a mysterious second version, very slightly different in detail. But the truth is that the Casement portrait was a disappointing work of Miss Purser's, rather clumsily drawn and muddy in coloring, lifeless in pose and expression.

As always when he was in Ireland for any length of time, Casement was soon caught up in his country's problems. Unconsciously a die was cut when he had lunch in Dublin late in May with Major John MacBride, the swashbuckling *miles gloriosus* who had stolen W. B. Yeats's beloved Maud Gonne and later been divorced from her after doing her "most bitter wrong."[34] MacBride told him how, as leader of the Irish Brigade fighting for the Boers against the British, he had received the surrender of Colonel Bullock of Colmso. In South Africa in 1900 Casement had expressed anger and scorn at this Irish treachery and presumption. Now he was intensely excited as he listened to MacBride's account of the British officer's chagrin when he had to give up his sword to an "Irish rebel"—excited, too, to learn that MacBride was an "Ulster Scot" and an old neighbor: "He comes from Ballycastle—from Glenshesk—my own glen & I know his family."[35] In the winter Casement had "dipped[his] pen in gall . . . and written a scorcher"[36] which appeared in *Irish Freedom* in March. His major Irish enterprise in the spring and summer was more charitable than political, however. It was Nina who suggested that he take up the cause of poor Irish people in Galway, particularly the Connemara islanders of Gorumna and Lettermullen where poverty was extreme and fifty people had died of typhus brought on by starvation and unsanitary dwellings. Casement took hold of the issue at once, opening a relief fund of his own and persuading the *Irish Independent* of Dublin to open a subscription. His letter on "The Irish Putumayo" attracted a great deal of sympathy. In early June he went himself to see the scene of distress and he endorsed a letter of 6 June from Charles Roberts about the winding up of the work of the Select Committee: "Recd. in Dublin, on return from Connemara, 9 June 1913 at 11 P.M. very wet cold & *tired* with today's glimpse of the Irish Putumayo. Mavrone! The 'white Indians' of Ireland are heavier on my heart than all the Indians of the rest of earth."[37]

Casement's trope was labored but honorable. As a practicing polemicist in need of emphatic images and with his range of analogy limited by a mediocre education, he tended to force elements into uneasy conjunctions, to explain one thing that he knew by the other thing that he knew. None of which kept him from doing a good job for the poor people involved in this case. To Gertrude he reported on

26 June £333 in his fund and another £40 promised.[38] On 2 July he listed for William Cadbury £2,440 in the total "Connemara fund" deriving from four separate appeals of which the *Independent's* had been the most successful with £1,800. Cadbury had given generously and anonymously as "an English friend."[39] Whereas he blessed Nina for doing "a fine thing & a mercy"[40] in turning him onto a task that had both moved and invigorated him, Casement was growing alarmed about Nina herself. "I do seriously think she is going crazy," he wrote Gertrude on 24 June. She had been sending him pell-mell letters and telegrams that sounded quite mad: exaggerated expressions of "that spirit of devilish unrest—there is no other word—that afflicts her." Always volatile and irritable she appeared to be veering entirely out of control: "She *cannot* be still, or at peace with anything."[41]

Through May and June Casement had remained in Ireland, using up his leave, his mind still divided between the wish to retire and the hope that the Foreign Office might yet offer him a palatable alternative to Rio. Africa kept drawing Casement, but he was far from sure to what she was calling him. Perhaps he would simply throw in his lot with Tom at Rydal Mount: it was that he referred to when he told Gertrude on 26 June that he thought of going "out to Africa for a long spell."[42] To E. D. Morel he wrote vaguely of possibly retiring to "a Boer farm." Morel wrote back in perplexity: "But you are a difficult man to help. You are very proud, for which I admire you, in the first place. Also, forgive me for saying so, it is a little difficult sometimes to know how exactly anything could be done that would fall in with your exact wishes."[43] With awkward delicacy Morel had put his finger on the main trouble: Casement was not sure himself which way he wished to cast his life.

By the end of June the issue seemed to be settled in favor of retirement and Casement crossed to England to see the matter through in person. He expected to stay about a week with the Mortens, but in fact he remained in Denham for nearly two months. On 29 June he wrote both a formal letter to Algernon Law and a private letter to William Tyrrell, announcing his intention to retire. It was perhaps significant that he held the letter to Tyrrell out of the post until next day, the very last of his leave. To Law he said that he had "put off from day to day from a sort of moral reluctance" making the move that meant "severing my connection with a Service with which I have been for so long connected" and taking leave of "a department from which I have received so many proofs of consideration, kindness and esteem." As he still felt "quite unfit to return to Rio de Janeiro," there was nothing to do but apply for retirement.[44] To both men he named his grounds as those of ill health, specifically prospective at Rio. That he meant to leave the door open a crack for a last-minute offer seems almost explicit in his statement to Tyrrell: he had delayed because he was hoping that he "might see a way out that would still allow me to stay in the Service while getting away from Brazil."[45]

Nevertheless, the Foreign Office chose to take Casement's application at face value and Law wrote on 7 July to say that his pension would now be asked of the Treasury. At second hand he expressed his chief's formal thanks and regret: "Sir E. Grey's high appreciation of the very valuable services which you have rendered to His Majesty's Government . . . and the regret that he feels at the cause that has induced you to tender your resignation."[46] On 8 August the Treasury duly granted a pension of £421.13.4 to commence on 1 August.

As usual it fell to E. D. Morel to pronounce the eulogy upon Casement's service to England, and as usual he overstated a truth sufficiently impressive in itself:

> Your two exploits are the bright spots in a record of foreign policy marked by some disgraceful episodes, and by great lack of moral purpose. . . . I know of no living man who deserves so much at the nation's hands as you do. But what you have done, and what you have inspired others to do, will remain in the history of this country, a page which will endure, and which one humble pen at least will consecrate later on. You have shown a noble example and . . . your name should be enshrined in posterity as one of the British heroes.[47]

Casement varied his long stay with the Mortens by visits to the Cadburys in Kings Norton and the family of the Duke of Hamilton at Studland Bay and finally by a quick trip to France. It was another old Africa hand, the former missionary T. H. Hoste, who suggested Casement invite himself to the house of Hamilton: "The Duchess takes a great deal of interest in you & appreciates very highly the way in which you have sacrificed your own career to champion the cause of the helpless. She longs for an influence like yours over the boys.

Do try to come."[g] It was Nina Hamilton's reaction to Casement's Putumayo exposures that had been so notably bloodthirsty.

Casement left Southampton for France on 26 July. Herbert Ward and Ward's brother Charlie met him at Rouen and they drove along the Seine to Rolleboise, where Casement wrote to Cadbury from the verandah of the Villa Sarita, Ward's country house named for his wife: "this lovely house on a steep hill overlooking the river." In the slow English way Casement and Cadbury had at last advanced to first names, and this letter begins "My dear William."[48] The two weeks in the valley of the Seine appear to have been easy and uneventful. By the middle of August Casement was back in Denham and by early September back in Belfast, unconsciously about to begin the definitive and final movement of his life. In Belfast he settled, much as was his custom with the Mortens, in a comfortable room of his own in F. J. Bigger's spacious bachelor establishment "Ardrigh" in the Antrim Road. A wealthy solicitor and Irish antiquarian, Bigger had been playing for several years with a complicated and expensive new toy. He had bought a fourteenth-century O'Neill castle, Castle Seán, one of the rough square-built tower structures of the Normans, overlooking the harbor of Ardglass in County Down, and he was working with love and fascination to restore the building and equip it with authentic furnishings. As the castle had stood derelict for 300 years, the task was not a light one; but eventually Bigger completed it and opened the castle to visitors, having installed as host, caretaker, and exhibition piece in period costume one whom Mrs. Florence Patterson has called "the handsomest young man I ever saw."[h] Casement heard much of all this, of course, as did Mrs. Green who followed the story with keen interest as a friend of Bigger's and a historian of Ireland.

[g]4 July 1913. NLI 13073. The Duchess of Hamilton had not read Casement's diaries.
[h]To the author, 26 June 1972. Mrs. Patterson is the sister of Bulmer Hobson.

14   Ireland Always and Only

AFTER ten years of flirting about its edges, Casement was about to be sucked into the center of the strange, ugly, and yet mysteriously beautiful maelstrom that was modern Irish history. What set the process going for him was an event he saw as singular not realizing that it was only the first in a necessary sequence: the organization of a meeting of amateur Ulster Nationalists in October 1913 in Ballymoney. The idea had originated in revulsion against the blatancies of the Carsonite Unionists in their loud refusal to accept Home Rule in Ulster, their threat to resist separation from England by force of arms if necessary. The Carsonites had drafted their Covenant, formed a provisional government, run in arms, drilled openly, and held massive "reviews" as occasions to show their muscles and make defiant orations. Nobody quite knew how far their nerve actually ran, but the whole thing had taken on an air of deadly seriousness. Carson's dark bitter face with its clenched prognathous jaw loomed everywhere backed by that of his sleek "Galloper" Frederick E. Smith and another formidable stone-face, James Craig. Though he hated everything Carson stood for, Casement was still subtly fascinated by the man himself. Attending one of the "reviews" in September he thought Carson's face was "awful." He wrote Mrs. Green: "I think the man is very unhappy—he looked wretched, gloomy dark & foreboding."[1] Unhappy or not the man was clearly dangerous: able, arrogant, and determined. Carson and his movement meant death to Casement's hope for an Ireland united and independent of England, a free-standing whole island nation. When Carson and his party spoke of Unionism, they meant a sustained union of Protestant Ulster with England; they had no thought of union with Catholic southern Ireland: that was precisely what they

176

ATLANTIC

OCEAN

Tory Island

Rathlin Island

Portrush

Ballycastle

Coleraine • Ballymoney

DONEGAL

LONDONDERRY

ANTRIM

Donegal

TYRONE

Belfast

Sligo

FERMANAGH

DOWN

ARMAGH

MONAGHAN

Warrenpoint

CAVAN

IRISH

SEA

Galway

Tawin Island

Dublin

Limerick

• Tralee

• Cork

Map 4.   Ireland in 1910

refused to stomach. They represented the hyperbole, the perfection of the Orange bigotry Casement had always despised and feared.

To persons like Casement, steeped in love of Ireland and longing to recover her ancient integrity—persons who happened by accident of birth to be Protestants and Ulstermen—the Carsonite defiance seemed to demand a challenge, something that would say forcefully that the parading Orangemen did not speak for them, or for a monolithic Unionist Ulster, or even for all of Protestant Ulster. A meeting was planned for 24 October in the Town Hall of Bal-lymoney in County Antrim. Its theme was to be one of "affection to Ireland & of faith in Ireland," as he put it to Gertrude, and the ges-ture was intended to put England and Ireland on notice of "the great fact that Protestants of Co. Antrim are standing out to fight Car-sonism & proclaim their faith in a united Ireland." And "Scodgin," he told her in delight and trepidation, was to be a principal speaker: "O! how I shiver at the thought."[2] He was to share the plat-form with his friend Alec Wilson of Belfast and Captain Jack White, a Cushendun landowner and son of Sir George White of Ladysmith. F. J. Bigger was rejected as a speaker because Captain White thought his recent gesture of kissing Cardinal Logue's ring made him look "too much of a papist," as Casement wrote in seeking to enlist Mrs. Green for the occasion. "I've almost pledged you to come," he told her, and he suggested she bring 500 copies of her *Irish Nationality* for sale. "It will be a meeting of *extraordinary* significance," he promised. "A protest from the heart of Antrim, by Antrim men, Presbyterians & Protestants & a flaming appeal to Ireland! It will breathe much of the spirit of '98 & will be definitely Irish—not of an English party at all." Casement thought of the affair as marking "the beginning of the uprising of the north"—against Carson and England, for solidarity with southern Ireland in unity and independence.[3] Mrs. Green agreed to come and to speak. It is noteworthy that in all of this politi-cal maneuvering Casement was passing as a Protestant, as he always had done in Ulster, and not only raising no objection but exploiting the position.

Most of his letters were now political in cast and excited in tone. He was writing Mrs. Green almost daily, addressing her as "Woman of Abundant Words," "Woman of the Piercing Wail," and other such affectionate epithets. In a letter to Gertrude on 15 October he did take time for a few personal and family notes. He confirmed that he was indeed "finished with F. O. for good and all" and glad of it. They had not "behaved generously in the matter of pension" but he was too busy to brood about it and in any case "freedom at any price is a blessed thing." He was worried mainly about Nina, who seemed "so lonely & miserable," and about Tom, who had branched out from Rydal Mount to a new business venture in Durban, failed, of course, and piled up a new load of debts. Now the "ungrateful bruit" was not writing at all. He called Gertrude's attention to two new articles: "Get last week's *Nation* . . . & read Scodge in it on 'Ulster.' It is a very long communication & will make you laugh. Also in next month's, November, *Fortnightly Review* read the O'Scodge on *Ulster and Ireland*. It is a fearful tirade! You will revel in it." Mrs. Green and Erskine Childers had both praised his manuscript, Mrs. Green calling it not only stirring polemic but sound history. "It will be a (minor) bombshell," Casement predicted. He confirmed the fact that the Ballymoney meeting would mark his first appearance on a political platform and he claimed to hope it would be his last. He was obviously fearful as well as pleased: "God help me!"[4]

By this time, rumors were passing that the Provisional Government that the Carsonites had arrogantly set up in Belfast would "forbid" the Ballymoney meeting. But the affair went off unhindered on 24 October and Casement described it next day to Gertrude as "a *grand* success": "Hall packed—smiling, good-faced farmers of the Route in hundreds & a magnificent table of *reporters*! I never saw so many in a small hall."[5] The audience was enthusiastic and Casement's speech was given special praise in Belfast and Dublin papers. But the *Irish Times* of Dublin, a voice of the Anglo-Irish establishment, stung him by referring to him condescendingly or indulgently as "Citizen of the World" and "the romantic Nationalist."[6]

Immediately after the meeting Casement and Mrs. Green had gone on to Ballycastle for a "rest" and while there they visited Rathlin Island to make a bit of propaganda. Rathlin was dear to Casement as one of his native places and as a place where the Irish language had found a dwindling haven, about two-thirds of the 325 islanders speaking some Irish. He urged the cause of the Irish school to the "proprietor" or landowner of Rathlin, a strident spinster, but that "Woman of the Hair and Voice" gave him and Mrs. Green a cold and derisory reception. Later he heard reports of her sneering remarks in Ballycastle about his attempts to interfere with "her island" and "her people."[7] Casement was already feeling the strain of a political life and the unpleasantness of such encounters was one of the things that made him long to get free of the partisan hurly-burly and into a situation where he could read and think and write in some peace. "I can't go on living at Ardrigh forever," he realized, and he sketched a wistful alternative: "I wish I had a wee wee cottage far from the Fetiche men of Ulster pulpits & the Hags of Ulster islands."[8] He had started dreaming about that sort of retirement when he first got caught up in the preliminary bustle of the Ballymoney meeting, which he had tried to pass off as an elaborate flourish that he would never need to repeat. "Please God," he had written Mrs. Green on 29 September, "I'll go from Ballymoney to the Glens & stay there *quiet* till the day of Judgement."[9] But he was already more fatally caught in the web of Irish political activism than he knew, and he went from Ballymoney not to the Glens but to the squabble on Rathlin, and from there not to a wee cottage but to Coleraine where he hoped to organize another Ballymoney, picking up the challenge of the Belfast papers that such a meeting could have been held nowhere else in Ulster. But the Coleraine venture failed, thwarted by the power of the local Unionists who dominated the Town Council.[10]

In fact Casement's position was probably even more difficult than he realized, even with his tendency to feel sorry for himself. He was caught in the hectic first flourishing of the apparently hopeless political conflict that crucifies Ulster today. It already looked irreconcilable. Then, more personally, he was a man not only without a home but almost without a country. The division in his mind about his religion was a primary symptom of an inclusive dilemma. The question as to whether he was Catholic or Protestant was hardly a religious question at all or a philosophical one; it was really a political question, a matter of where he wished to throw his political loyalties, not practically separable in Ireland from religious forms and affiliations. Casement's surest feeling about what he called his religion was that he did not wish to identify himself with the hate-filled countenances, stony or ranting, that passed for the public face of Protestantism in Ulster. Yet he knew he was not "really" a Catholic. He was one of those—"Protestants," "Ulstermen," "Irishmen"—who had pronounced at Ballymoney a message of "affection to Ireland & of faith in Ireland." What did all that mean, practically? One's definition of one's self is not entirely within one's own control.

Casement had to endure the scrutiny of Ulstermen, of southern Irishmen, and of Englishmen in general, as well as of a spectrum of partisan groups under each of those crude labels; and to all of them he was a baffling kind of creature. To the classical Protestant Ulster Unionist Casement was a culture-hero in his exploits in British public service, a renegade and a class-traitor in his Nationalist activism. To a classical Catholic Irishman of the South he appeared tainted as northern, Protestant, a willing veteran English official, an alien cosmopolite. To doctrinaire Englishmen he was a cranky talented outlander who had done the state some service, but had fed at the public trough without the gratitude and good taste to make one with them, to submit to naturalization: an unrepentant "Irishman." Was Ireland a country, a nation at all?—to England a dangling inflamed appendage, occasionally useful but always irritable and always irritating: a "question," a chronic "problem" that would not hold still and let itself be solved on other people's terms; to "Ulster" an inconveniently detached province of "Britain," with troublesome neighbors to the south and even in their midst: ignorant, lazy, superstitious, mendacious, sly, charming, dangerous people; to Irish Ireland an unreal present reality of bonded service to be resented and evaded, a haunted dream of a different past and a different future: "the sorrowful legend of Ireland." It was not simple for anyone to call oneself an Irishman, as Casement wished to do; and it must have been more difficult for him than for almost anyone else in his day. Even at the simplest quotidian level his situation was hard—his safe position resigned, his income reduced, his obligations continuing, his role obscure—and always silently under it all his sexual problem, the tensions of which one can only surmise.

Quite rapidly now and quite adventitiously Casement put together a new role piece by piece. Or rather time put it together for him, enwrapped the old persona in a new scenario. From now on one feels Casement as peculiarly a creature in the hand of events, helpless but unconsciously so, never quite losing his illusion of control, a decent man of moderate ability becoming notorious—turned into a saint or a fool.

On 11 October W. L. Courtney, editor of the *Fortnightly Review*, wrote agreeing to print Casement's paper "Ulster and Ireland" provided it was signed: "Of course an article of this kind gains enormously by a signature so well known as yours."[11] Casement agreed promptly in a letter of the fourteenth. He promised Gertrude that the article would "make *some* squirm."[12] It was the kind of polemical piece that he would not have dared to sign had he stayed with the

Foreign Office: that was part of the logic of leaving them. It was not his signature but his name that was well known and his name's currency was of a kind that had little to do with the present and future shape of his career. Most of his non-official writing to date had been desultory and fugitive and most of it anonymous, and this, coupled with the fact that he had spent most of his mature life abroad, meant that his name was even less familiar in Ireland than in England. For example the invitation at this time to speak at the installation of one Michael J. Ryan as Auditor of the Literary and Historical Society in University College, Dublin, was largely persiflage: "your world wide reputation in the cause of liberty and freedom for all peoples stands as high if not higher in Dublin than in any other part of the British Empire."[13] This was ingratiating but extravagant. Yet it defined Casement with some accuracy not as an Irish patriot but as a sort of world figure with a British ambiance: probably most Irishmen who were aware of him at all thought of him in that way. It was pleasant to be called famous but not to be called British, and not at all pleasant to hear Dublin called part of the British Empire without a second thought. There was enough accuracy to sting in the *Irish Times*'s reference to him as "Citizen of the World" and "romantic Nationalist."

In Cushendall on 11 November Casement wrote two letters to Mrs. Green, the longer of which was a crucial document for his future. Both letters showed his obsession with Ireland and showed that he was clearing his mind for action. In the briefer letter he wondered wistfully whether there was any hope that "the British Providence" might withdraw itself from the island for perhaps six months, leaving "Ireland and 'Ulster' to settle this question, man to man." But he supposed the British Providence would go on looking in "in the intervals of dining" and go on "doing the wrong thing at the usual intervals."[14] The longer letter began in heaviness, "despair," and worked through to resolution. Casement was revolted and depressed by the quality of the air in Ulster, "the pulpits resounding with yells for a Holy War!" But he had to admit that that kind of bigotry was Irish and was general: "It is that aspect of life is so appalling in Ireland." And the sweeter peasant kind of Irish mind was too spongy and weak to form an alternative:

> In the South & West where one finds spiritual & intellectual kinship with the gentler Irish mind, one is forced to confess, too, it is blurred by the long contact with the depression of the

penal swamp . . . out of which they are only climbing slowly.
One is conscious that one is talking to men who are not yet quite
free & still have the fears & weaknesses of slavery round them.

In the North freedom was real but fierce and jealous, not yet civilized: "it is the freedom of the wild beast. They have no spiritual,
no intellectual freedom of their own—and they will not allow others
to have it."[15]

About Home Rule Casement was now more pessimistic than ever.
He was convinced that the Bill would not be passed, or if
passed never genuinely implemented, that it would never produce a
freestanding Irish Parliament. He had felt a flicker of hope that the
very blatancies of Carsonism, "when Carson was at the height of his
Blasphemies over here," might finally stiffen John Bull's backbone
and lead to constructive action for the whole of Ireland. But
no: "The British public is actually in love with 'Rebellion in Ulster'!" Casement felt angry and sick: "when these infuriated &
selfish bigots, who have suffered no wrong, no threat, no injury to a
hair of their heads, go out in thousands to break the law, to arm &
drill against Crown & Parliament, they are taken to the bosom of that
great Constitutionalist." He felt about the English as Swift felt about
the human race as a whole: "Individually I like many—collectively I
loathe them." Institutionalized, the Englishman was "repellant to
my whole nature," and in Ireland the institution of England had been
"a curse . . . transcending all the maledictions of history. And they
are at it still—God save Ireland."[16]

Casement had begun to consider that there might be a lesson to
learn from Carson and his "Volunteers" that was not only bitter but
invigorating. Why should not "Ireland" take instruction from "Ulster"? If it was admirable, as the English said, for Ulster to "arm &
drill against those who . . . never hurt her," how much more admirable, and wise, for Ireland to "arm & drill against those who have
always hurt her." The end of his letter was mournful: "These, O!
dear Woman of the Great help, are the thoughts, the vain thoughts of
my heart. Like you, I think of Ireland always—and only." But along
the way he had mused: "I think I'll end by going to Athlone &
Tipperary, & seeing what can be done in that line."[17] The statement
was tentative, but it had the making of an action with consequences: "that line" was the Carsonite line of "Volunteer" defiance
and resolution. It was a long way to Tipperary.

A breathing space of several weeks ensued. In the middle of

November Casement passed several days with the Cadburys at Kings Norton. From there he went to the Mortens' in Denham for about two weeks. Two parts of his mysterious love life intersected at this time. Ada (Ide) MacNeill, who had long thought of herself as Casement's intended, had been pursuing him for about a year with letters of an amorous cast that had got on his nerves rather badly, as he wrote to Gertrude. If he had ever thought of her seriously in a romantic light, the feeling was long past, but he remained fond of her and wished to keep her friendship. When Miss MacNeill exhibited a number of her very good little watercolor landscapes in a show in Belfast in the fall, Casement had asked one of his genuine lovers, Millar, to pick out something of hers for him to a limit of £5. Millar wrote on 19 November that he had bought "Evening on the Moor" and "A Grey Day in the Glen" at £2.2 each, choosing those two because he thought the Irish scenes and the gilt frames would please Casement's taste. The show as a whole seemed to him "jolly nice." Millar assured him that he had bought the pictures in his own name, not mentioning Casement. He signed himself "Ever yrs affectionately."[18]

But the crucial letter of the interval arrived on 29 November from Eoin MacNeill, accompanied by a manifesto announcing the organization of the "Irish Volunteers" to rebut the Carsonite movement in the North and to speak the language of force on the side of Irish independence. MacNeill's message seemed an echo of his own impulse, and Casement lay awake until three in the morning turning it over in his mind. "It *is* right," he wrote Mrs. Green next day, "& if we love Ireland we must help this movement."[19] He sent MacNeill a promise of hearty help and enclosed the check for £3.3 he had just received for an article. His additional message to Mrs. Green was more ominously premonitory than either of them could suspect: "Oh! how I sometimes in my heart long for the thud of the German boot keeping guard outside the Mother of Parliaments!—& the Times office as the head [quarters] of the German Intelligence Division!"[20] Casement's admiration for Germany was an old story, but it was shallowly based and largely theoretical. Aside from a couple of brief tourist experiences he really knew almost nothing about Germany. In his bookish notion of the country she stood for a place where things got done quickly and cleanly without the usual "British" maundering and muddling. And she was the most promising obstacle to the perpetuation of the power of that international bully, the British Empire.

Moreover Germany figured largely in a coup Casement was planning: to persuade the Hamburg-Amerika Line to step cleanly into the vacuum created by another of John Bull's muddling insults to Ireland, the abandoning of Cork harbor as a port of call for Cunard and White Star liners.

There is no need to trace the roots of the Irish Volunteers to their long subterranean origins in the old tradition of Irish resistance to English rule. The nearer roots were traceable enough and Casement's friend Bulmer Hobson had been one of the principal gardeners. Hobson had joined the clandestine Irish Republican Brotherhood, heirs of the old Fenians, in 1904 when he was barely of age. Immediately he and his friend Denis McCullough founded the Dungannon Clubs in the North as an open and active separatist organization; then in 1909 Hobson and Countess Markiewicz, who as Constance Gore-Booth of Lissadell had been one of the beautiful sisters to be celebrated by W. B. Yeats, founded the boy-scout organization Fianna Eirann as a consciously protomilitary body in Dublin. Soon the Ulster Volunteers began to flourish, eventually enrolling nearly 100,000 men. At Hobson's suggestion secret drilling of the southern Volunteers under Fianna Eirann instructors began in Dublin in July 1913. Thus the frame of a new general organization already lay ready when Eoin MacNeill issued his personal call to arms in his paper "The North Began" in the Gaelic League organ *An Claidheamh Soluis* on 1 November 1913. MacNeill, Hobson, and the O'Rahilly thereupon agreed to join in summoning a public meeting to "found" the Irish Volunteers at the Rotunda in Dublin on 25 November. The occasion was a ringing success with immense attendance and about 4,000 first recruits. They included, as it happened, an Irish veteran of British army service in the Boer War named Robert Monteith who was to be a major performer in the last movement of the Casement scenario. What MacNeill did not know was that the I.R.B., through Hobson, Padraic Pearse, Tom Clarke, and others, intended from the outset to work its own violent purposes under the mantle of the movement: they never meant for it to be merely defensive.

Eoin MacNeill's invitation of 29 November found Casement a brand for the burning and he took fire at once. It was a sense of the gravity of the issue for him personally that kept him awake till 3:00 A.M. He could not know the grand and awful thing history would make of it for him and for Ireland, but he could see that it meant a

major new direction in his life. Within a fortnight he was moving
about Ireland helping to organize local cadres of the Volunteers. On
12 December, for example, he described for Gertrude "a *grand* Volunteer meeting" in Galway. Young men filled the Town Hall to the
roof, "clinging like limbs of ivy to the rafters & wings," and they
"stormed" the platform in eagerness to sign the lists. A Galway "regiment" now waited only organization and equipment.[21] Three days
later he and MacNeill led a Volunteer meeting in Cork and this one,
too, Casement called "a *great success.*" The description needed some
insisting on, for the meeting had nearly degenerated into a riot, possibly dangerous and certainly embarrassing. With naive bravery the
two speakers had called for cheers for Sir Edward Carson, thinking
their view of Carson as a man of Irish nerve and activism and a
champion of the independent spirit would be self-evident. But the
crowd saw Orange and reacted in simple southern spirit. Chairs
were thrown and the crowd swarmed toward the platform. Next day
the press reported that Casement and MacNeill had fled through a
rear door, abandoning the field. Not so, Casement said, it was all
"lies": it was the reporters who had fled when the row began and so
failed to see the gratifying peripeteia: "we held our place & then
when the tumult died the O'Scodge called the sea back to its bed."
The Cork men had heard him out enthusiastically and he had received "a hurricane of cheers & embraces too from workmen." Seven
hundred had joined up and "it all ended splendidly."[22]

A less tumultuous patriotic note was sounded at the end of the year
when Jane Lubridy, teacher of St. MacDara's Infant School at Carraroe, County Galway, wrote to thank Casement for the difference
worked in the daily lives of her pupils by the hot meals provided by
the generosity of Casement and his friends, especially Mrs. Green
and the Cadburys. "It is touching in the extreme," she wrote, "to see
them now coming in in crowds many of them half naked to partake of
the daily meal. I assure you Sir Roger in order to enable many of
them to atten[d] school the fathers and mothers' clothes are called
into requisition." Miss Lubridy wished the Cadburys to have special
thanks for cocoa, biscuits, and cash. Mrs. Green, who had proposed
the gift of Cadbury's stock in trade, had been told that nobody in
Ireland would drink the stuff; but cocoa was an instant success when
tried out on the hungry children. In conveying the gifts Casement
had stipulated that Irish was to be used in prayers, grace, a hymn,
and conversation. Miss Ludbridy recalled that when she took charge

of the kindergarten twenty-five years earlier, fresh from a training college, she had been instructed to make "Happy English Children" of her "little Celts." Instead she had begun on her first day "what is *now* recognized as Bilingual Programme."[23]

Casement had gone to Cork in the middle of December with the double purpose of organizing Volunteers and promoting his Hamburg-Amerika scheme. He then believed that the first German ship, the *Hamburg,* would be arriving from Boston on 6 January and he was anxious to celebrate the day as resonantly as possible. By the beginning of January he had sketched out a plan that was to center upon F. J. Bigger's presentation of a portrait of O'Sullivan Beare to the University of Cork, [a] the event to be timed to coincide with the arrival of the first liner. Casement imagined the picture's being drawn through the streets of Cork in triumphal procession by a "vast multitude" including marching Volunteers and "guarded" by Gaelic athletes. After the presentation the multitude would proceed to Cobh harbor "to welcome the Germans!"[24] Then it was learned that the *Hamburg* would not be coming after all; but the *Rhaetia* was promised for 20 January. Casement now amplified his scheme: he would charter a tug to meet the ship on the water and would convey Bigger and Mrs. Green, contingents of Volunteers and students, and a band—"all who want to give the ship the proper welcome." The party would display two flags, Irish and German.[25] But in a second letter to Mrs. Green on the same day Casement said he had just heard from the London office of the German line that they preferred that no large welcome be given their vessel: they were tender about British feelings in the tense European situation. Two days later they asked that no notice whatever be taken. And by the sixteenth the call of the *Rhaetia* at Cork had been canceled altogether. From Belfast where he had been laying his plans, Casement left for Dublin in a deflated and vengeful mood. "I know the agency that moved," he wrote darkly to Mrs. Green, [b] "I know its power; its 'bribes'; its

[a]Presumably the subject was not D. R. O'Sullivan Beare who succeeded Casement as Consul at Rio but Donall O'Sullivan Beare (1560–1618), a native of Cork who adhered to Philip III of Spain. He received a Spanish garrison in his castle of Dunboy in 1601 and was besieged there. He escaped with 1,000 men and tried to fight his way to Ulster under constant attack, arriving with thirty-five survivors. He settled in Spain and was killed in Madrid by another refugee.

[b]Referring presumably to the British Foreign Office. 16 January 1914 to Alice Stopford Green. NLI 10464. Green papers.

diplomacy—& it has again locked the door & shut us off from that friendly people coming to our shores. . . . Sean Buide [John Bull] has won!" Hope revived briefly a week later when it appeared that the *Furst Bismarck* might be calling at Cork on 11 February. But by the end of January it was clear that the whole scheme had collapsed: Casement called his final letter from the Hamburg-Amerika Line a "Nunc dimittis."[26]

Casement interpreted the debacle as a classic example of Britain's habitual interdiction of Ireland's efforts to hold up an independent head and touch hands with Europe. Perhaps he had a fairly clear case both for anger and for a new resolution, although his response sounds ranting and canting and grandiose: "I shall certainly go to U.S.A. *now* & burn all boats and compromise & raise this issue thro' all the land. We'll wreck the 'Anglo-Saxon' Alliance anyhow."[27] The statement shows that his appearance in America in the summer of 1914, surprising and improbable to a casual view, had actually been conceived a half-year earlier. Casement's headlong passionate polemical nature, simplistic withal, required both an object of defense and an object of attack, positive and negative shibboleths, and his objects of veneration regularly produced his objects of disgust and vituperation. Tensions in the great world had thrown up in the Anglo-Saxon Alliance the same sort of tangible *bête noire* he had found in Leopoldism and the Monroe Doctrine. Loving "Ireland," hating "England," admiring "Germany," all as absolutes and at least one of them virtually unexamined, Casement saw the Alliance as a new creature of a cynical organ of Empire, the British Foreign Office, intended not only to quarantine Germany in Europe but to quarantine Ireland in insular dependence by cutting her links with America, her big awkward friend across the Atlantic. It was all a "damnable conspiracy," he wrote Mrs. Green at the end of January and it was really aimed at the whole principle of freedom in the world. If the Saxons brought it off, it would be "all up with Ireland for a century or more." Hence it was vital to "hold up the head of Ireland"[28] in the United States itself. Apparently Casement had already begun to cast himself as Ireland's volunteer minister of that portfolio.

Meanwhile Casement did not relent in attacks upon his established negative causes: John Redmond, the Parliamentary Party, and Home Rule in the form now bruited in Westminster. The bill now apparently approaching the statute books after nearly fifty years of agitation, Casement dismissed as a shrunken and lifeless shadow of the Home Rule ideal: "mean in spirit; mean in intention; and con-temptuous in scope," he scoffed in one of the letters that went almost daily to Mrs. Green in this tense interval. He was certain of her sym-pathy. England's notion was to keep all powers that mattered in Westminster and placate the Irish with a sham local Parliament little better than a debating club. If England supposed that would pur-chase Irish loyalty, Casement promised her flatly: "It will not."[29] He had abandoned all faith in politics conducted on party lines. He, and Ireland, must work henceforward in terms of absolute princi-ples. Ulster had shown how to do it.[30]

Early in February Casement accompanied by Bigger crossed to London to discuss campaign plans with Mrs. Green; their talk prob-ably included preliminary forms of the April meeting that would lead to the gun-running at Howth in the late summer. After they left her at Euston Station to begin the journey home, they came upon Jack Johnson, the black American heavyweight champion, and by Casement's account "walked round him in extended admiration," marveling at the breadth of his brawn and of his smile, and "glad to be out of reach." Johnson himself was "the Isle of Man," Casement mused.[31] Mrs. Green's Irish politics resembled Casement's closely in outline and emphasis but not in intensity, and her very affection for him made her deplore his obsession with the issue and the nearly hysterical negativism of his view of England. From Malahide he wrote back to defend himself against her gentle chiding. His "con-suming hatred for Sean Bwee [John Bull]," he protested, was as "wholly impersonal" as a hatred of sin. The rule of Britain in Ireland was "an iniquity" and he felt compelled to resist it in the same spirit in which he had fought Leopold and Arana: "If it remains it cor-rupts, destroys, and debauches this people." The refusal to surren-der to anything other than superior force was a truism of English history and English character. Hence the impending triumph of Ul-ster and the continuing helplessness of the South: "Ireland is Catholic, moral & blood-shunning—& so the immoral & blood-delighting win the day." Casement did not repent of his Irish radicalism. His only regret was that he was nearly fifty years old and not thirty.[32]

Recruits to the Irish Volunteers now numbered at least 100,000 men, but the organization was essentially a holding operation, a way of accumulating strength in readiness for an opportunity. Spirit was united and optimistic, but there was little money and no arms, and policy and conduct at the executive level were flexible and fortuitous. Casement seems to have acted largely on his own inspiration, for example, when, having resolved to do something personally about the lack of arms, he took Eoin MacNeill along to confer again with Mrs. Green in London. Joining them at lunch was Darrell Figgis, an adventurous English writer and yachtsman who lived much in the west of Ireland and became a convert to Sinn Fein. Figgis was much moved by Casement and came to regard him as the man of most "single and selfless" mind and of the most "natural and noble gesture of soul" he had ever known. In his *Recollections of the Irish War* Figgis left a dramatic impression of Casement's aspect during the discussion of ways and means of procuring arms for the needy Volunteers:

> Looking outward before the window curtains, stood Roger Casement, a figure of perplexity, and the apparent dejection which he always wore so proudly, as though he had assumed the sorrows of the world. His face was in profile to me, his handsome head and noble outline cut out against the lattice-work of the curtain and the grey sky. His height seemed more than usually commanding, his black hair and beard longer than usual. His left leg was thrown forward, and the boot was torn in a great hole—for he gave his substance away always, and left himself thus in need.

By Figgis's account, when he himself offered to go to the Continent and buy arms with whatever money could be collected, Casement crossed the room toward him, "his face alight with battle. 'That's talking,' he said, throwing his hand on the table between us."[33] A sum of £1,500 was pledged by the English "sympathizers," about half of it by Mrs. Green, the money to be recovered eventually by the sale of the rifles to individual Volunteers. It was agreed that Figgis and Erskine Childers would buy the rifles in Europe and that Childers and Conor O'Brien would deliver them to Ireland on their yachts by a plan to be perfected.[34] The £1,500 would buy only a token quantity of arms, but at this stage the token was important as such. The Volunteers needed a sign.

It was again on his own initiative that Casement resolved to go to America to seek support in arms and money for the movement. He would be a self-appointed envoy and very few people even knew of his scheme: Mrs. Green, Bigger, Hobson, Childers. He wrote Mrs. Green on 26 March from Malahide: "I shall go by a German ship

about Mid-April—just skip without a word when the time comes &
be no more seen."[35] But in fact he lingered on in Dublin and Belfast
through April, May, and most of June, busy with recruiting and fe-
vered journalism. Another motive for delay was provided by an invitation in late April from Lord MacConnell to testify as to desirable
reforms before his Royal Commission on the Civil Service. Casement relished the thought of venting his mind on the untidy logic and
the ramified inequities of the British Consular Service, and he did so
on 8 May. The preceding day he and Eoin MacNeill had gone to the
House of Commons on John Redmond's invitation to discuss the
Constitution of the Volunteers with Irish M.P.'s. When Joseph Devlin offered to show them about while waiting for Redmond, Casement said, "I know the place very well"; and MacNeill, "grim, dour,
loyal Sinn Feiner of the Glens of Antrim," said, "Thank you, Mr.
Devlin, it does not interest me." Devlin mentioned that there was a
statue of Henry Grattan to be seen; Casement observed that when
Home Rule came they must get the ashes of Grattan moved from
Westminster Abbey to Dublin. Devlin had not known that Grattan
was in the Abbey, and Casement scorned his ignorance and scorned
his English clothes; he and MacNeill were clothed in "Irish." Mac-
Neill went off to lunch with a group and Redmond asked Casement
to stay behind to hear his objections to the Constitution and to some
of the leaders, especially Bulmer Hobson and Padraic Pearse. Casement never forgot Redmond's revealing words on parting: "Well,
Sir Roger, I don't mind you getting an Irish Republic if you can."[36]
From London he wrote to introduce himself to Wilfrid Scawen
Blunt, a fine poet and a humane person much concerned for the fate
of Ireland, and on Blunt's invitation went down to see him in Sussex.
He reminded Blunt of Michael Davitt, the hero of the Irish land
wars: "only much bigger and better looking. . . .He is well-bred,
well-educated, altogether vigorous, and a good talker."[37]

The situation of the Volunteers was growing more and more tense
and complex. Casement had lost none of his admiration, mixed with
something very like fear, for Sir Edward Carson as the most
courageous and resolute man in the island and he tried to persuade
himself that his feeling was shared by most men in southern Ireland.
The problem with Carson was simple but apparently insoluble: the
parochialism of his politics, his adamant narrowing of his vision to
the welfare of the Unionist North. But Carson alone in Ireland was
speaking to John Bull with efficient defiance, and Casement believed

he could lead the whole island to freedom if only he could be brought to choose the broader course. "If he would *only* appeal to Ireland & not to Tory England," he wrote to his Belfast friend Alec Wilson, "if he would only hold out a hand of good will & kinship for the Fenian spirit of self-reliance & belief in Irish manhood, he would be amazed at the response." He asked Wilson to carry that message to Carson. In fact Casement had tried and failed to carry it himself when he went to Belfast in mid-April to beg Carson to bring his Ulster Volunteers to Clontarf on the twenty-third to join in parade with the Irish Volunteers. He had found Carson at Craigavon, "ringed around with bayonets & 'war' correspondents," and had drawn back, in disgust and in fear of a rebuff, without even speaking to the Ulster leader. But he was still convinced that Carson was the necessary great man and that he was missing "the greatest chance ever came to an Irishman": the opportunity to "raise Ireland from mendicancy to manhood."[38]

The letter to Alec Wilson in the midddle of June was written in the sore and sick frame of mind brought on by illness and by a dangerous crisis forced upon the Volunteers of the South by John Redmond. Redmond had watched the quick growth of the movement with a baleful and suspicious eye: it was a potentially powerful creature not of his begetting, a big popular movement not identified with his principles and not responsive to his control. He was doubtless right in his argument that the great majority of rank and file Volunteers like most of the ordinary folk of southern Ireland were content with his goal of Home Rule and approved his tactic of angling in parliamentary channels by conciliation and political trade; and right in his charge that the thirty-member Provisional Committee, generally radical and separatist in temper, was neither responsive to his national leadership nor representative of the quietist politics of the Volunteer membership as a class. Redmond had been rumbling in this tone for some time and threatening more and more frequently to "take action."

While organizing in the northern counties of Derry and Tyrone in the latter half of May, Casement had picked up a bad cold that turned into influenza and finally put him to bed in Bigger's house in Belfast. Sensing that Redmond was about to move, Casement roused himself and went to Dublin, on 9 June, a Tuesday. At Volunteer headquarters he put down a resolution calling for the election of delegates in all the thirty-two counties and summoning a special meeting for Friday,

ulmer Hobson in later life. Oil portrait by Sean
'Sullivan. Courtesy of the National Gallery
f Ireland.

ohn Devoy. Drawing by Sean Keating. Cour-
esy of the National Gallery of Ireland.

Joseph McGarrity. Courtesy of the Natio[nal]
Library of Ireland.

Robert Monteith. Courtesy of Mr. and M[rs.]
Liam Redmond.

12 June, to discuss the question. He then wrote to Redmond begging him to "exercise good will and dismiss mistrust,"[39] posted his letter at 1:00 A.M. in time to catch the morning boat, and went to bed at Buswell's Hotel in Molesworth Street hoping that he had "saved the situation." But in the morning papers appeared a "truculent" letter from Redmond demanding the right to appoint twenty-five of his supporters to the Provisional Committee: otherwise he would start his own Volunteers, splintering the movement. Redmond must have released his ultimatum before receiving Casement's plea, which he would probably have ignored in any case. Casement wired Redmond begging patience again and the special meeting of the committee was hurriedly moved forward to the same evening, Wednesday, 10 June, when the resolution was voted. Next day he wrote Redmond again, assuring him of the good will of the Provisional Committee and arguing that his resolution would guarantee due representation of the Irish Party in the leadership of the movement.

Casement then returned to Belfast and to his sick bed at Ardrigh and it was there that he received Redmond's curt reply: "of course" he adhered to his published ultimatum.[40] On Sunday, 14 June, Casement went back to Dublin "to try & help a settlement," as he wrote to Gertrude Bannister the same day, in "this hellish row raised by 'the Party' to capture the Volunteers" which he feared meant the death of the movement.[41] That night Casement, MacNeill, and Colonel Moore, all staggering with influenza, resolved to resign in a body rather than to protract a quarrel that would split the South, and to announce that the Irish Volunteers as orginally conceived had "ceased to exist."[42] They seemed to assume that they had the power to make such a determination. But on Monday morning Bulmer Hobson appeared at Buswell's Hotel where Casement lay glooming and astonished him by arguing that the Volunteers must be preserved at any cost including that of capitulation to Redmond. Hobson then collected MacNeill and Moore and brought them back to Casement's room where in an extraordinary scene he again pressed his case upon the three sick men and this time carried the day. The four of them drafted what Casement called a document of "surrender" acceding to all of Redmond's demands. Their resolution was placed before the Provisional Committee the following night and passed by eighteen votes to nine after bitter debate. Along the way Casement had resisted the heady suggestion that he present himself as "the new Parnell"[43] to lead a movement "on principle" in opposition to both John Redmond and John Bull. "The 'principle' might have been saved—but nothing else!" he wrote to Mrs. Green a week later. "Out of the raging faction fight wd. have emerged a disgraced Ireland with no Home Rule & no Volunteers. . . . It was for the sake of this poor distracted country & *to* this poor distracted country on what I knew to be its wish I surrendered."[44]

The hectic week had left Casement exhausted and wretched yet convinced that Hobson had led the Volunteer executive committee to the wisest of the inglorious courses open. Hobson was persuaded that the Redmond invasion of the Volunteers could be contained and sterilized, that by minding their business and playing a quiet hand the old executive body, and particularly the hard-core I.R.B. members among them, could go on controlling both the purse and the politics of the movement. Events proved him right, even after September 1914 when the Redmondite Volunteers were disowned and became the National Volunteers following Redmond's unauthorized public promise at Woodenbridge that the Irish Volunteers would fight on the side of Britain in the War. In the short term, however, the immediate consequences to Hobson of his peacemaking in the June crisis were ironic and disastrous. Led by Tom Clarke the I.R.B. men in Dublin made the controversy an occasion for picking a quarrel with Hobson, charged him with taking a bribe from Redmond for "selling the Volunteers,"[c] and forced him to resign from the Supreme Council of the I.R.B. and from the editorship of *Irish Freedom*. Along the way Clarke let Hobson know that he was convinced that Roger Casement was a British spy.[45] Very shortly thereafter Hobson also found himself dismissed as "home" correspondent of John Devoy's New York *Gaelic American* which had been paying him his only regular income of ten dollars a month for a weekly article.[d] Tom Clarke's eyes were fixed on armed revolt and he intended to trust very few men on his route to Easter 1916.

In the midst of the hullabaloo, plans for the gun-running scheme had been going quietly forward. Darrell Figgis would carry the arms

[c]Hobson, *Ireland Yesterday and Tomorrow*, p. 53. Tom Clarke was a hard-bitten old Fenian jailbird who had returned to Dublin in 1907 after years of exile in America. He maintained close liaison with John Devoy and the Clan-na-Gael, and his little tobacconist's shop in Dublin became the nerve center of the radical militarist faction within the Irish Volunteers. He was executed in 1916 as a leader of the Easter Rising.

[d]Later, amused and persuaded by Hobson's spirited defense of his action Devoy reappointed him. O'Brien and Ryan, eds., *Devoy's Post Bag*. ii; 456.

in a hired tug from Hamburg to a rendezvous in the North Sea where the yachts of Childers and O'Brien would take them aboard for Ireland. Childers and Casement had put Hobson in charge of arranging the actual landing and he recalls 23 June as the date when he met the other two men in Buswell's Hotel to concert a final plan: Childers would bring his yacht into Howth harbor at noon on 26 July and Hobson would meet him with a contingent of Volunteers to take off the rifles and ammunition.[46]

Among the consequences of the Dublin crisis for Casement was another postponement of his trip to the United States. Apparently that had been most recently planned for June: in the brusque letter of 3 July in which he dismissed Hobson as his Irish correspondent, John Devoy mentioned that he had gone down to meet Casement "at the steamer on which he was to have arrived" but found him not on board. Devoy advised that it was now pointless for "your friend" to come at all, owing to "the very general irritation here" over the Volunteers' capitulation to Redmond's demands.[47] From Dublin in the last week in June Casement retreated again to Ardrigh with a plan to go thence to the north coast of Antrim to visit with Nina and other relations and find a bit of "peace and quiet & *retrenchments*," being "ruined financially" as he put the case to Mrs. Green.[48] But the northern trip must have come down to a matter of only a day or two, for Casement was still in Belfast, still feeling ill, on 29 June when he wrote to Richard Morten, "My dear old Dick," in a veiled farewell. He reported that he had addressed a Volunteer meeting in the Glens of Antrim "on the tomb of Shane O'Neill" on the preceding day. Now he was about to "go away": "I will write from abroad & tell you more," he promised.[49]

15 R. D. Casement, Emigrant

C ASEMENT left Ireland on 2 July for Glasgow whence as
"R. D. Casement, emigrant," an identity designed to foil the
presumably feeble-minded British spies who had been so "maladroit-
ly pursuing" him (he believed) about Ireland, he sailed second-class
on the S. S. *Cassandra* for Montreal on the fourth. The same day, not
having received John Devoy's interdiction, Bulmer Hobson wrote
him that Casement was on his way.[1] Early on Sunday, the fifth,
Casement saw in the distance the outline of Tory Island off Donegal
and inland "the blue . . . hills of my heart," and remembered that
two years earlier he had rowed out to Tory with a party that included
a fiddler and a piper. The Atlantic voyage was peaceful and undisturbed. A passenger asked Casement if he was related to "that well-
known Irish baronet" and Casement answered that he "knew him
well." Off Newfoundland they sighted seventeen icebergs at one
time, "great Arctic palaces, green and gold." From Montreal Casement traveled by train to New York, arriving in the evening of 18
July and taking a room at the Belmont Hotel opposite the station. In a
stroll down Broadway the same evening with a notion of revisiting
"old points of view, like Pond's and the Hotel I lived in in 1890,"[a] he
was accosted by a burly blond young man who was to play a large
and equivocal part in the hectic courses of Casement's final two
years. Eivind Adler Christensen represented himself as a Norwegian
of twenty-four who had run away from home at twelve, stowed away
on a collier to Glasgow where he was picked up by Norwegian

---

[a]This bare note in Casement's diary of 1914–15, with its reference to J. B. Pond's lecture
bureau, is probably the source of the story that he "lectured" in America about 1890. In fact he
was simply accompanying Herbert Ward. See above, p. 16.

sailors, and lived a knockabout existence for a dozen years as fireman on a succession of Norwegian vessels. Now he was "out of work, starving almost and homeless."[2] Casement listened sympathetically, told him to call at his hotel next day, and eventually made himself the young man's patron and guarantor.[b]

John Devoy's reception of Casement must have been reluctant, but it was none the less courteous: he took him to lunch at Moquin's. At some point in these first days Casement also made himself known to Bourke Cockran, an Irish-American politician and professional silvertongue, friend and rhetorical model of Winston Churchill, and to John Quinn, a successful corporation lawyer and a bold collector of books, manuscripts, and contemporary art. Quinn and Cockran were friends and strong in their Irish sympathies though far more conservative than Casement or Devoy.[c] Both were established ports of call for Irishmen on what Quinn always called (derisively) "missions": persons seeking entree to sources of American cash. In his openhanded way Quinn now invited Casement to make his New York headquarters at his big top-floor apartment at 58 Central Park West, already bursting with books and the strange new pictures of the School of Paris, and Casement moved in. He must have struck the New York Irish, even hard-headed John Devoy, with effective *panache*—with his elegance and good looks, his English knighthood, his traveled air, his reputation as a champion of the helpless in exotic parts, his evident unselfish embodiment of the aspirations of Ireland at a critical point in her melancholy history.

In a conversation of the evening of 20 July Devoy evidently vented his anger at Bulmer Hobson's "deception" in moving to submit to the Redmondite invasion. Casement was "pained and startled" at Devoy's angry reading of the matter but reserved his defense of his friend until the next day when he sent Devoy a long letter reviewing systematically the chain of events in Dublin as well as the defensive logic that had led to the capitulation: "to save the Volunteers from

[b]Among the Casement papers in the National Library of Ireland is an "autobiographical" fragment (NLI 17023) in Christensen's primitive hand which seems to be telling a story of meeting Casement much earlier, during his consulship at a South American port. Perhaps he was one of the "wonders of the deep" at Santos or Pará. There is no way to tell whether there is any truth in the baffling little piece. It sounds like something that might have been dictated by Casement for some obfuscatory purpose; but Christensen himself was a great fabricator.

[c]Devoy described Quinn and Cockran as "both honorable men but neither of them in agreement with our policy." *Recollections of an Irish Rebel*, pp. 404–06.

disruption and Ireland from a disgraceful faction fight in which all original issues would have gone by the board."[3] Casement also quoted two paragraphs from his own last message from Hobson, sent from Dublin on 30 June, in which Hobson had advised him to trust Devoy and Joe McGarrity of Philadelphia but to beware of other factionists who might try to "capture" him as a political prize. Casement pointed out that it was not the letter of "a man conscious of having broken faith": he invited Devoy to "amend" his judgment of Hobson. But Devoy was a man not easily charmed or placated, an old campaigner with a skeptical mind of his own. He never recovered his whole faith in Hobson; and whereas he cooperated energetically with Casement once he convinced himself of his genuine revolutionary motives, he remained suspicious of his tactical wisdom and his psychological soundness.

On 22 July Casement went down to Philadelphia for an overnight stay with Joe McGarrity and laid the foundation for the closest of his American friendships. In the warm American way they settled that Casement was to be "Rory." McGarrity urged him to go down to Norfolk, Virginia, to address the national convention of the Ancient Order of Hibernians as spokesman of the Irish Volunteers. Though he was still shy of speaking in public, Casement agreed to go if he were formally invited. Back at Quinn's in New York he received a wire from the Hibernians asking him to come to Norfolk and to bring Bourke Cockran along. Shortage of time created the kind of bustle that Quinn enjoyed: he hired a Packard and a driver as he liked to do when he had to travel quickly or elegantly, and he and Casement motored out to Port Washington, gathered in Cockran "by assault," and dashed back to Manhattan in bare time for the nine o'clock night train to Norfolk. Next morning, 24 July, both Casement and Cockran addressed the shirt-sleeved and fan-waving Hibernians in the sweltering convention theatre. Casement spoke briefly of the general situation of Ireland and of the Volunteers and made his customary point in praise of the Ulstermen "to the evident content of the great majority."[4] To Mrs. Green on the twenty-ninth he wrote that the Hibernians had "cheered repeatedly" when he referred to himself as a Protestant. He concluded that the American Irish were "mad for a Protestant leader."[5]

Casement dropped off the train at Philadelphia on the return journey to pass the anxious interval until Sunday night with McGarrity in whom, along with Devoy, he had confided the story of what he called in his diary "my prearranged coup": the landing of the

German rifles at Howth. A letter had arrived from Mrs. Green: all was well so far and "our friends are on the sea."[6] But the crucial news must come by cable, and in the hot evening of a day of restless waiting Casement and his host walked down the fields in front of McGarrity's house and lay in the grass, watch in hand, talking of Ireland. About nine o'clock McGarrity received a telephone message from a friend on a Philadelphia paper: the guns had been landed, but British troops had seized them and killed several Volunteers. McGarrity rushed down to the Hibernia Club to wait for further news. Soon he telephoned a corrected message: the guns had not been captured after all; the Volunteers had been able to carry them off into hiding. Nobody slept much at McGarrity's that night.

In Dublin over the past few weeks Hobson had set the scene for the gun-running by ordering a series of Sunday route marches to accustom the army authorities to look upon such outings as harmless exercises. Hence on the crucial Sunday, 26 July, the 800 Volunteers who marched to Howth harbor to meet Erskine Childers's yacht were at first not interfered with at all.[d] They had time to disembark the 900 rifles, which were then distributed without cartridges among the men, and the 26,000 cartridges, which were sent separately into the city in taxis. On the march back into the city there was a brief scuffle with a contingent of soldiers and policemen, confused and without orders, but the men carrying the rifles were able to break free and scatter across the fields toward their houses. Marching back into Dublin following the episode the British soldiers fired into a crowd of hostile civilians at Bachelor's Walk along the Liffey, killing and wounding a number of people: it was this that confused the first accounts to America. The event had no real connection with the gun running, but it provided the future rebels with a rich slogan: "Remember Bachelor's Walk." A week later the remaining 600 rifles were successfully landed at Kilcoole, County Limerick, by Conor O'Brien's yacht and hauled up to Dublin. The total of 1,500 rifles were hardly grand, but the gesture had been one of heartening bravado for a hitherto powerless organization and it was an earnest of capacity. It was something *done* after years of grumbling and fumbling. Hobson noted that $5,000 came from Irish-Americans by cable on the day after Howth and that thenceforward the Volunteers

[d]Childers had sailed straight through a great naval review at Spithead where King George V was reviewing his ships on the eve of the great war. Hobson, *Ireland Yesterday and Tomorrow*, p. 67.

received, from Ireland and the United States, enough money to carry them along.

Addressing her as "Dear Woman of the Ships!" Casement sent Mrs. Green his paean in celebration: "How can I tell you all I have felt since Sunday! I can never tell you. I was in anguish first—then filled with joy—& now with a resolute pride in you all. We have done what we set out to do! And done it well."[7] "Old J. D.," he said, was moving about in "a glow of joy" murmuring: "The greatest deed done in Ireland for 100 years." It was a "grief" to Casement not to have been at Howth on Sunday. Signing himself "Yours devotedly and always, The Fugitive Knight" he closed with a prayer and a prophecy dense with sentiment: "may the god of Erin put rifles into the arms of Irishmen & teach them to shoot straight. . . . May this bring a new day to Ireland—I see it coming—new hope, new courage on the old, old manhood."

Following the confused but generally triumphant news of Sunday, Casement was interviewed and photographed by reporters from the Philadelphia evening papers on the twenty-seventh. He denounced the "murder of women and-children" in Bachelor's Walk and "put the blame fair and square on the shoulders of Mr. Asquith" the Liberal Prime Minister.[8] When McGarrity had returned from the Hibernia Club at 2:00 A.M. on Monday, he told Casement that he had made all the arrangements for a big protest meeting in the city on 2 August and had already committed him to be the chief speaker. Casement was shaken by a mixture of pride and agitation at the forms his American mission seemed to be taking. The enthusiastic McGarrity was urging him to tour the whole country, seeing him as the man to "unify" the contentious sects of transplanted Irishmen, no less divided than the Irish at home, and he kept assuring Casement that the people would rally to him as if he were "another Parnell."[9] John Redmond's claim to general support from the Irish-Americans Casement dismissed as "absurd": "They are sick of talk & Parliamentarianism & will give their strength & hearts only to some leader who will fight." Everywhere, he said, people kept telling him: "You are the man we want."[10] A Philadelphia deputation informed him that he had been rechristened "Robert Emmet."[11] Everywhere he felt a yearning for a leader who would reincarnate the heroes of the past and keep alive the extraordinary succession of Protestant leaders of Irish nationalism.

Casement and the leaders of the Clan-na-Gael, the lively American reincarnation of the Fenian movement of the 1860s, had evidently been so preoccupied with their own Irish politics that they had hardly noticed the omens gathering for war in Europe. Now Casement noted resentfully that the grand crisis had crowded the Howth exploit out of the American newspapers: it struck him as bad luck and bad taste. For the American press as a whole he felt only contempt: "They are a bad press . . . . uninstructed, fumbling, stupid & unenlightened on everything but baseball, American finance & politics. Their 'interviews' are ineptitude condensed."[12] But the visible imminence of war no doubt lent urgency to a new scheme of Casement's, apparently conceived with remarkable casualness: to travel from America to Germany as an envoy of Irish nationalism, again self-appointed. It appears that he broached this idea to John Devoy, to his total surprise, at the Philadelphia meeting on 2 August, on the very eve of world war.[13] Casement was uneasy to notice photographs being taken of himself and the old Fenian at the meeting. He had begun to need anonymity now rather than publicity and he felt sure there were "spies everywhere," hirelings of the British Legation as well as "recreant Irishmen." He warned Mrs. Green that her letters to Devoy were being opened in transit.[14]

The idea of a rapprochement with Germany had occurred to other revolutionary Irishmen as well as to Casement, and it was not a new thought in his mind: he had been playing with the idea in a literary and theoretical sort of way for nearly ten years. It was implicit and at times almost explicit in the series of articles he wrote in 1912 and 1913 under such titles as "Ireland, Germany and the Freedom of the Seas" where he took the position that Ireland was vital to England's baneful dominance of the oceans and hence a card of strength potentially to herself or to an enemy of England, a card to be played by the Irish in such a way as to wrest independence from England and to achieve recognition as a nation among other nations. Once one had resolved to define England not merely as the proprietor but as the enemy of the real Ireland, it was logical enough to see England's enemy as Ireland's friend. Casement and the Clanna-Gael executive were certainly thinking that way with all candor. But turning the idea into program of personal action was something else, and Casement suspended it in his mind as he went on about his American errand for the Volunteers. By 30 July when he wrote to John Quinn from Philadelphia to beg letters from him and from Bourke Cockran endorsing his mission in America, it had dawned on him that war was almost certainly coming. But he chose for the moment only to look at the world crisis as adding practicality to his enterprise in the form of the old general Irish principle: "England's difficulty is Ireland's opportunity." In writing to Quinn he wisely said nothing of friendship for Germany, he spoke only of the logic of adding power to the powerless at a time when the powerful were in trouble:

> Everything looks like war, with John Bull pulled in; and, if so, I think we should lose no chance to arm the Volunteers so that we may be able to repeat 1782 over again. Bull will want our help, and it should be given *only* on terms that we get freedom at home, and if we have the men armed we can ensure a greater measure of respect for our claims.[15]

Quinn sent a "fine letter" and a check for $250.[16] But collections in general were disappointing. Casement had hoped for at least $50,000 from his mission, but when he wrote Mrs. Green on 15 August he could report "only $6,000 or $7,000" for his three weeks' work to date. He blamed the poor showing on "the war."[e]

McGarrity arranged a meeting in Baltimore on 6 August and Devoy another in Buffalo on 9 August with Casement as principal speaker at both, and he was receiving more invitations than he could accept. The American Irish still seemed inclined to turn him into "a demigod,"[17] but Casement though flattered was disinclined. By mid-August he was beginning to feel exhausted by American heat and American hurry and more conscious of age and fatigue than of heroism: "I would I were young," he wrote Mrs. Green on the fifteenth; "I should know what to do: but I feel broken & old & I see the Evil powers are again winning."[18] He was enraged and depressed to read of John Redmond's promise at Westminster that Irishmen would adhere loyally to Britain in the war. In an interview arranged by Quinn, Casement warned former President Theodore Roosevelt that England would "swell to bigger things yet, and in the end inoculate *you* with the virus of her own disease. You will become Imperialists, and join her in the plunder of the earth."[19] Roosevelt only flashed his chronic grin; on 12 August he wrote Bainbridge Colby: "Sir Roger Casement was charming."[20]

---

[e]He had cabled Mrs. Green on 29 July to ask her to see that Nina, who was alone in London, was got over to Ireland where she could be near friends and family; and in his letter of 15 August he asked her to send Bulmer Hobson £20 for personal needs, promising to repay her when it was safe to send a check. NLI 10464. Green papers.

About to board a train for Chicago on 24 August Casement wrote Quinn about a new scheme. With Ireland closed to German trade by the war he proposed an open business arrangement with America: rifles to be bought in the United States in the name of an Irish "company" and shipped openly to an agent in Cork. "The argument is clear," he wrote. "A market for rifles is open in Ireland. U.S.A. *only* country can supply them. Why not begin a trade and take advantage of closure of other sources of supply? Can the Washington Administration object?. . . A new development of American commerce! To capture the Irish rifle market!" He wanted Quinn to act as American legal agent for the scheme and "put it up to Bryan & Co. in Washington" as the entering wedge for a new general market in Ireland: "A grape-juice Secretary of State" ought to see the advantages.[21]

On board the train on the same day, suffering violently in a hot crowded carriage with a journey of twenty-seven hours ahead of him,[f] Casement wrote Quinn a second letter to enclose "an interesting document" to be treated as "strictly confidential." He wanted Quinn to join other Irish-American leaders in signing a letter he had drafted to the German Emperor, to be sent from the German Embassy "by a special Imperial messenger." The letter expressed "sympathy and admiration for the heroic people of Germany" and went on to exonerate Germany of any aggressive intention:

> We recognize that Germany did not seek this war, but that it was forced upon her by those jealous of her military security, envious of her industrial and commercial capacity and aiming at her integrity as a great World power that was capable, if peace were maintained, of outdistancing the competition of all her rivals.

Far from being the bully of Europe, Germany was "fighting the battle of European civilization at its best against European civilization at its worst"—the worst of course being England. The salute concluded with a plea to Germany to recognize the importance of Ireland to England's power at sea and to the eventual freedom of the seas, and to do all in her power when the war should end to secure the political independence of Ireland.[22]

---

[f]More than half the letter was given over to a nearly hysterical protest at being cramped into a seat with "a d---d Italian knife grinder. . . . with a knife-grinding wheel on a high stand, with *five* umbrellas and a lot of spokes, too. . . . Well, I'm damned!"

This letter, probably Casement's first legally treasonable act, was approved by the Clan-na-Gael leaders and sent forward under a date of 25 August 1914. But it did not carry Quinn's signature. Casement was pushing him too hard and from the wrong direction; for Quinn's hatred of Germany was nearly as rabid as Casement's hatred of England. Though Casement was slow to realize the fact, once he had determined to "go to bed with the Germans" (in Quinn's phrase) he could expect no more sympathy or help from his New York host.

As Casement was setting the first torch to his boats, his brother Tom, thinking Roger was still in Ireland, was sending him homely caution from South Africa: "I suppose one has to be careful at home in what one says. You can't lash out at John Bull now. It would not be wise. People lose their heads when the Flag waves & become so d - - - patriotic."[23] But Roger Casement was in Germany when Tom's pathetic note of 19 August finally reached him. Ten days after Tom wrote, Mrs. Green addressed Casement as "My dear Watchman of the Night" in attempting to comfort him in one of the depressed phases of his veering moods: "You write in great sorrow, and indeed I wish you were not so far away. . . . Some day you will come to stay with me in Ireland & see a country in which good men & a great spirit will still be left. . . . Do not let hope fail you. We will keep a flame alight to warm your heart when you come back."[24]

Approaching his fiftieth birthday far from anything he could call home, Casement stood badly in need of comfort: his mission was floundering indecisively in a big disorderly country, the Volunteers and the national movement in Ireland were neutralized by the power of Britain and an acquiescent Irish Party, the whole Irish issue was dwarfed and obscured within the colossal motives of World War. Casement was again seeking identity and direction and again confused by his own chronic rootlessness. He was not happy with America or within it. When he wrote to Gertrude on 1 September, his actual birthday (and hers), he conceded, confusedly, that America was "a great country," but his own response to it was still flatly negative: "I don't like U.S.A. The more I see of it the less I like it." Americans were "ignorant and unthinking" and easily credulous of whatever they read in their "rotten papers": the press was simply "the worst in the world."[25] He was thinking mainly of the pro-British tendency of most American papers, amazed that they could not see the perfidy of Britain, the purity of Germany. Writing to Mrs. Green two weeks later he was already gloomily certain that "the

Miracle won't operate": Germany would "go down for 40 to 50 years" and England would be left still supreme in the tyranny of empire. So he had told Roosevelt. He was afraid to come "home" to Ireland because he knew he could not keep quiet, a passive loyal British subject in time of war: he would be "in jail within a week, or in a Concentration Camp or in flight to the hills."[26] Three days later he showed her a sample of his bloody thoughts: "If Asquith & his ally [Redmond] come to Dublin they should be shot—were I at home I'd do it. I trust someone will."[27] And poor Tom, still picturing his brother as going about his sufficiently radical course in Ireland, was writing plaintively: "I am getting a bit anxious about you old man. I have not heard from you for ages & I have been wondering if they have laid you by the heels for 'Treason' or shot you. They when in a d - - - funk are up to any villiany [sic]."[28]

Seeking in his obsessive phrase to "give a lead" to American and Irish opinion, Casement kept writing and talking in ways that for a British subject approached ever closer to treason and "villiany." In the middle of September, enraged at the spectacle of Redmond's outriders addressing American Irishmen "on the lines of the British Imperial claim to flesh and blood," Casement struggled to draft a manifesto of one who stood for "a worthier ideal of Irish responsibility."[29] His document of about a thousand words emerged as one of the most satisfactory examples of his polemical prose. As usual the rhetoric was lush and to a degree conventional, but it was controlled for once by structure and grammar, unified by a clear principle, and enriched by genuine feeling. As "one of those who helped to found the Irish Volunteers" and speaking in their name, Casement protested against the British assumption that Irishmen owed her military service for any reason, more especially in return for a Home Rule Bill of limited scope and subject to amendment and still suspended after thirty years of public promises by the Liberal Party: what he denounced as a "promissory note (payable after death)" for which the Irish people were expected to "contribute their blood, their honour, and their manhood in a war that in no wise concerns them." Irishmen, he contended, had no reason to quarrel with the German people, and a nation whose own commerce "was long since swept from land and sea" could hardly share British enthusiasm for destroying the German navy and her role in international trade. It was not Germany who had destroyed Irish liberties, and Casement knew who had done the deed. By deliberate English policy drained of wealth, of men, and of energy, "bled to the verge of death," Ireland must scorn England's call for the sacrifice of the remnants of her vitality. If this war was indeed conducted, as its "planners" asserted, for the survival of "small nationalities," Casement thought he could name one small nationality for whom it had better begin at home.

Casement dated his manifesto 17 September, and when he sent a copy to Quinn next day to ask his advice about circulating it in the United States, at least among "Irishmen," he had already sent it to Ireland where it was printed in the *Irish Independent* on 5 October.[g] When Devoy and McGarrity saw the document, they were nonplussed to learn that Casement had already shown it to Quinn and Cockran, "both honourable men but neither in agreement with our policy."[30] But indeed all four men advised against publishing the piece in America: the situation was too touchy, tempers too uncertain for such inflamed language. In his note to Quinn Casement had spoken scornfully of American pusillanimity: "There is too much 'Anglo-Saxon' here, too much 'Evening Post' (a weak imitation of the 'Westminster Gazette').[h] But three days later he wrote Quinn again from Philadelphia to apologize for his "cranky letter" and to explain its tone: "I am so distressed at Redmond's treachery, and the deplorable state of things in Ireland . . . that I am raging, like a caged animal, at the impotence enforced upon me here."[31]

It is noteworthy that in both the letters to Quinn, written less than a month before he left for Germany, Casement spoke as if he intended to return to Ireland very shortly. On the eighteenth, for example, he said that his "words" (his anti-enlistment "manifesto") were already en route for Ireland and he would, "thank God, follow them soon." He thought it was high time for him to go home and try to keep "some of the poor boys from this abominable sacrifice of Irish manhood to English mammon." But by this time Devoy had already

---

[g]Perhaps by agency of Mrs. Green to whom he sent a copy on 17 September with a request to procure its publication in Ireland. NLI 10464. Green papers.

[h]18 September 1914. NYPL. Quinn collection. That caution was good policy was suggested by the reaction of an old American friend: the journalist Poultney Bigelow who had met Casement twenty years earlier at Delagoa Bay. After many years of beating about the world, Bigelow was now living in his old family home at Malden on Hudson. He had been pressing Casement to come for a visit and to occupy the room Bigelow's father had been born in in 1817. He wrote on 7 October: "have just devoured your eloquent—passionate—treasonable document! Were you a German this would mean your end—but thank God you are a British subject." He suggested that Casement had better come up in any case and "spend a month or two incognito—unless you are courting the dungeons of martyrdom." NLI 14100.

arranged for him to meet Count von Bernstorff, the German Ambassador, to explore plans for a mission to Germany the purposes of which remained rather vague and grand but included a scheme for forming an "Irish Brigade" on the John MacBride model from among prisoners of war: Casement had already suggested to the Germans that they collect prisoners of Irish extraction in a common place for handy proselytizing. In spreading the impression that he was about to return to Ireland Casement many well have been trying to confuse his trail against potential pursuers; equally it would have been quite in character, and natural in his equivocal situation, for him to have been still unsettled as to his own course. In fact he was writing to Mrs. Green as late as 11 October, four days before his departure for Germany, that he had been offered an American editorship and he thought he might accept it and "live out my days" in the United States.[32] At this point Casement was probably thinking of a more distant future; but he did not say so, and the note may have indicated honest indecision, or may have been another bit of calculated obscurantism. There were good grounds for caution: Casement's movements were undoubtedly being watched by British agents, and more suspiciously than ever after the publication of his "manifesto" in Ireland on 5 October. Furthermore a cable of 1 October from von Bernstorff to the Foreign Office in Berlin, announcing that Casement was going to Germany "to visit the Irish prisoners," had now been intercepted by the Admiralty.[33]

Poultney Bigelow was later to publish letters he received from Casement at this time as evidence of what he thought was real unbalance of mind—in an effort, for which Casement did not thank him, to secure his reprieve on grounds of insanity.[34] His letters, especially those to Mrs. Green whose entire sympathy he counted on, were showing signs of almost incoherent disturbance, growing more and more impassioned and rambling. On 11 October, for example, he raged against his old chief Sir Edward Grey as a "wicked, stupid, obstinate fool," the worst specimen yet of the "villainous fools" cast up by "British greed of Empire" and a tool of a "gang of unscrupulous anti-Germans" among whom he listed his old friend Sir William Tyrrell. At the same time he was enthusiastic over the rapprochement of "German" and "Irish" national groups in the United States and the pro-German, anti-British energy he expected their union to generate. He described in ecstatic terms the "electrical" atmosphere of a recent Irish-German rally in New York, attended by four thousand people with another thousand turned away: "on *every*

German lip 'By God if Germany wins this war, we are going to free Ireland.' It is said everywhere—in their papers, by their public speakers, on the streets, in the cafes—& Oh! how the Anglo-Saxons squirm." In a postscript he sent his love to the Quakers William and Emmeline Cadbury and asked Mrs. Green to assure them how little his excitement was motivated by approval of the war itself: "how strongly I disapprove the war, how great an iniquity I believe it to be, how great a *moral wrong*—for it has been wrought from a lie."[35] Even his condemnation of war as such was helplessly partisan.

It was well for what remained of Casement's peace of mind that he did not need to read as yet certain letters that were going forward to him: an invitation, for example, from the Patriotic League of Britons Overseas to join "an influential Central Committee" in London to solicit funds toward "the gift of a warship which it is proposed to present to the nation from our fellow subjects abroad," a project approved by the Admiralty and "viewed sympathetically by the Foreign Office;"[36] or the cold call for an accounting sent by Arthur Nicolson of the Foreign Office that followed the publication of his manifesto against enlistment of Irish soldiers:

> Sir:—
>
> The attention of the Secretary of State has been called to a letter dated New York, September 16th which appeared in the *Irish Independent* of October 5th over your signature. The letter urges that Irish sympathies should be with Germany rather than with Great Britain and that Irishmen should not join the British Army.
>
> As you are still liable, in certain circumstances, to be called upon to serve under the Crown I am to ask you to state whether you are the author of the letter in question.[37]

But when those letters finally reached him Casement had been in Germany for many weeks and was deep in a different disenchantment.

Meeting with a group of American Irishmen at their club in New York Casement was revolted by their timidity; they were all "tame Nationalists." "I have tumbled into a party of English Liberals," he told them. One of the men offered to help organize a subscription for arms to go to the Volunteers after the war; Casement said: "If you are not good enough Irishmen to help to arm your countrymen at home I will go to Germany and get arms there."[38] The Clan-na-Gael leaders, especially Devoy, had had mixed feelings about Casement's proposal of a mission to Germany, but they had agreed to give him their formal and practical support: to accredit him as their representative and to cover his costs beginning with an outlay of about a thousand dollars while he was still in New York and an initial stake for the journey of $2,500 in gold. An elaborate smoke screen was thrown up to shield his departure for the voyage which was to be managed via Norway on the Norwegian steamer *Oskar II*. Casement had demanded that he be allowed to take along the young Norwegian sailor, Adler Christensen, much against the better judgment of Devoy who mistrusted the man and was suspicious of Casement's apparent infatuation with him. But Casement wanted him along as guide, guard, courier, and interpreter (at least), so Christensen booked a second-class passage on the *Oskar II*, ostensibly to visit his parents at Moss in Norway after a twelve-years' absence, and went aboard carrying Casement's papers. Devoy had procured for Casement a passport in the name of a real person, the Clan-na-Gael member James E. Landy of Orange County, New York; John Quinn would have been nonplussed to learn that Casement carried a card in Landy's name and bearing Quinn's own business address: 31 Nassau Street, New York City. An official in the Austrian Embassy booked a first-class ticket for Landy for the sailing on 15 October. Two days before the sailing Casement went to earth in a Manhattan hotel as "Mr. R. Smythe of London," at the same time telegraphing to reserve rooms in the name of Smythe at the La Salle Hotel in Chicago.

From the New York hotel on the morning of departure Casement sent John Devoy a brief but ceremonious "farewell word and grip of the heart," phrasing his admiration of Devoy's long devotion "to the most unselfish cause on earth" and his hope that they might meet next in a free Ireland.[39] He was leaving in an hour's time and he had still to shave off his distinctive black beard now streaked with white and to wash his face in buttermilk in pursuit of a fair complexion—an expedient that was a good index of the amateurishness of this essay into international conspiracy. Having paid his bill and given out that he was leaving for his reservations in Chicago, Mr. Smythe left the hotel by a rear stairway and went on board the *Oskar II* at noon as a visitor accompanying the real James Landy. At sailing time the real Landy left the vessel and Smythe-Casement remained snugly on board occupying Landy's identity.

16   A Regular Spy Fever

THE ship was bound for Copenhagen with stops at Christiansand and Christiania (Oslo) in Norway and the passengers were a mixed and edgy lot, including several Americans and a variety of European nationals, Germans among them, with grounds almost as good as Casement's for uneasiness. Of Casement's several accounts of the voyage the most circumstantial was a mock letter to "My dear Sister," written as by an American girl in obviously bogus "American" vernacular, and begun, according to his endorsement, at daylight on Wednesday, 28 October, as the vessel lay in sight of shore off Christiansand. [1] Leaving New York harbor they had witnessed a collision between two steamers and watched the *Matapan* sinking with her propellors in the air as the British cruiser *Lancaster* hurried to the rescue. After that the voyage passed peacefully for some days; Casement and Christensen soon got together and consorted comparatively freely as shipboard acquaintances. Casement's American persona fooled no one, particularly not the several real Americans on board, though he explained his odd accent by a tale of years in Europe and English schooling. By the same irony that would bedevil him in Germany (and even in Ireland) he was generally taken for an English spy—as he learned at the end of the voyage and "laughed to split my sides." In fact there was "a regular spy fever" on board.

On Thursday the twenty-second Casement noticed that the ship was changing course, and the "dear, kind Captain, *such* a nice Dane with a beard just like Cousin Roger's," told him that he intended to go more northerly in hope of avoiding British cruisers lurking about the Shetlands and Orkneys. But Saturday afternoon the *Oskar II* was stopped by a British cruiser that fired a gun across her bows. Casement hurried below to his cabin where he and Christensen secreted his papers and his gold, returning to the deck to find the big warship alongside "like a great granite battery" in the swells of the sea. To complete the poetry of the occasion their captor proved to be the H.M.S. *Hibernia*. The first action of the prize crew was to "cut the Marconi connection—slick," after which the *Oskar II* was pointed south for Stornoway in the Isle of Lewis in the Outer Hebrides, there to await orders from London. Casement was up at sunrise on Sunday to witness the arrival at Stornoway and, though his later account of it was gay, his feelings must have been shaky enough at the time. He had no way of knowing what or whom the British were seeking, whether he was a part of their quarry, and he thought the cliffs and islands jutting up gave the harbor a distinct look of shark's jaws.

But he was not molested and when the British officer returned from shore on Monday morning, he carried orders only for the internment of six German nationals on board: two young men who had stowed away at Hoboken, two sailors of the crew, the second cook, and the bandmaster. Casement organized a sympathetic collection that yielded about $65 for the six prisoners. In the afternoon the *Oskar II* was set free and she proceeded again toward Christiansand, her first port of call in Norway. That night she was stopped again by a torpedo boat who satisfied herself with merely taking the name of the vessel. It seems fairly clear that no general alarm was out for Casement. Casement had not been traveling well, feeling seasick and generally nervous, and he would have preferred to go on by train from Christiansand, but none being available he stayed on board perforce until the ship docked at Christiania at midnight on 28 October. He took rooms with Christensen at the Grand Hotel and at once wired James Landy in New York of his safe arrival.

Now ensued the first motions of the comic melodrama that Casement referred to thereafter as "the Findlay Affair." According to Casement's version, which was largely supplied to him by Adler Christensen, the action began on the first morning in Norway, 29 October: the long arm of British power, terminating in the British Minister M. de C. Findlay,[a] was lifted ready to strike him when he arrived in Christiania and it sought to reach him by first entrapping his servant. According to his own version Findlay, far from waiting

[a]Mansfeldt de Cardonnel Findlay (1861–1932) was a Scot and a career diplomat who had served under Lord Cromer in Egypt. He became Minister to Norway in 1911 and remained there until he retired in 1923. He was knighted in 1916.

to entrap Casement, had hardly known his name and supposed he was still vaguely active somewhere in the Consular Service; he had known nothing of his trip to the United States or of his "mission" to Germany or even of his presence in Norway; far from seducing Christensen he had been approached by Christensen with an offer to sell Casement to the British.[2]

Indeed the Findlay and the Christensen-Casement accounts of the events of 29–30 October agree in general outline, but they differ profoundly in detail and on such crucial questions as who set the whole plot moving and whether or not Findlay proposed causing actual bodily injury or death to Casement. The differences begin with the matter of what occurred in the first hours of 29 October in the Grand Hotel. Christensen's later deposition, sworn to in the American Consulate on 9 April 1915, says that they simply "slept and breakfasted."[3] But months later Findlay sent Sir Arthur Nicolson of the Foreign Office a much more colorful account of the scene, supplied by a Norwegian of "private interests" who was willing to put himself forward only "if *absolutely necessary*."[b]

Casement carried with him a letter of introduction from von Bernstorff in Washington to Count-von Oberndorff, the German Minister, and a request that his entry into Germany be expedited, and he and Christensen set out in the morning to present these credentials at the German Legation. As they left a draper's shop where they had stopped along the way, Casement pointed out a man who looked as if he might be following them. At the Legation von Oberndorff received Casement politely but asked him to return next morning: he needed time to "decipher" von Bernstorff's message.

[b]The Norwegian informant's story was that, for two days before Casement arrived in Christiania, a "German Secretary" who had been staying in the Grand Hotel (possibly Richard Meyer: see below, p. 217) had inquired repeatedly for "Mr. James Landy." After Christensen and Casement had taken their rooms at the hotel, the German turned up at 2:00 A.M. and insisted that he must see Landy at once. Findlay's informant had been asked to inquire at Landy's room, and there he found the two men "sitting on Casement's bed with their arms around each other." They were "not undressed," Findlay conceded, "but the nature of their relations was evident." When admitted, the "German Secretary" had remained until 6:30 A.M. A hotel waiter had later told the informant that Casement and Christensen were "evidently spies." Casement's several accounts make no mention of the "German Secretary" or of the nocturnal episode in any way, and Findlay's story seems strange in several respects, though he apparently believed it himself. Would one not knock before entering a private hotel room at two in the morning? (I suppose one might possibly try the knob and peep in quietly.) If the story should happen to be true, it represents the only occasion in which we actually find Casement observed in a homosexual posture. Findlay to Sir Arthur Nicolson. 13 March 1915. PRO FO 95.776.

Casement supposed that he merely wanted to check out his *bona fides* with Berlin: he thought the man a good deal of a fool. Back in the hotel in the afternoon Casement sent Christensen off on an errand and settled down to write letters.

In his first account of these events, sent to Eir Edward Grey on 31 October 1914, Findlay wrote that Christensen had simply presented himself at the door of the British Legation at 79 Drammensvein in the late afternoon of the twenty-ninth. He had talked with Francis Lindley, First Secretary of the Embassy, and had intimated that he possessed information implicating a well-known "Englishman" in an "Irish-American-German conspiracy."[4] Lindley had expressed a guarded general interest and a willingness to hear details if the man cared to return next day. When Christensen returned to the hotel, he told Casement a much gaudier and more circumstantial tale. He had been picked up in the afternoon by a stranger, with whom he had played along because he knew of Casement's anxiety about spies on his trail, and had been taken in a "large touring car with a chauffeur in livery" to a large house at 79 Drammensvein. There he had been conducted to an upper room by a gentleman who locked the door and then put probing questions about his shipboard acquaintance, "a tall dark gentleman, an Englishman." Adler had given generally evasive answers. His interlocutor had shown him out after suggesting that there would be money in it if he would render reports on the movements of the tall dark gentleman.[5]

Having looked up 79 Drammensvein in a directory and found it was the address of the British Legation, Casement hurriedly sent Christensen off with a note to von Oberndorff begging for an early meeting, which was appointed for seven o'clock that evening at the German Consulate. When the two men left the hotel that evening, their taxi appeared to be followed by another carrying three men, one of whom Christensen said he "recognized" as his conductor of the afternoon. Casement ordered his driver to make a sharp turn into a side street where he jumped out and sent the taxi on with Adler alone, then went on to the Consulate in another taxi. Count von Oberndorff gave no satisfaction; he had telegraphed to Berlin and could do nothing until he got a reply. Casement pointed out the exigency of his situation and the disaster he feared for "the cause he represented" if the British laid him by the heels while he was detained in Christiania. But von Oberndorff would only promise to send word the moment he got a clearance.[6]

Casement slept little that night. From his window at dawn on Friday, 30 October, he could see men who appeared to be watching the hotel. At seven he was greatly relieved when a German messenger arrived: a wire had come from Berlin and von Oberndorff would come at noon to arrange his departure for Germany. The watchers were still there. Casement sent Christensen down to breakfast with instructions to circulate and "keep his eyes open."

According to Findlay's report to Grey, Christensen appeared at the Legation at eleven o'clock and asked to see the Minister alone. He revealed the name of the conspiratorial "Englishman": he was "Sir Roger Casement C.M.G." For a fee, he said, he would reveal the alias under which the Englishman was traveling. Findlay gave him twenty-five kroner (about thirty shillings), "the traditional price in such transactions," for the name: James Landy. The informer now showed certain papers that he said Casement had given him for safe keeping when the *Oskar II* was stopped by the *Hibernia:* a pamphlet annotated in Casement's hand and a typewritten sketch of a plan for an incursion into Ireland by a body of Irish-Americans in German ships and bringing a load of German arms, to be met by Irish sympathizers, and preparing the way for an eventual German invasion. Christensen asked if he would be well paid if he kept Findlay informed of Casement's actions in Germany. Findlay said yes, if he supplied information of value. Before they parted in this second session, Christensen had "implied" that his relations with Casement "were of an unnatural nature and that consequently he had great power over this man who trusted him absolutely."[7]

Again Christensen's account to Casement was much more detailed and melodramatic. He had been approached in the hotel after breakfast by a man who gave him a telephone number to call, and the call produced instructions to go by taxi to 79 Drammensvein. There he was received in the same locked room by "a very tall man, clean shaven except for a short greyish moustache, with his hair brushed back straight, and dressed in a tweed suit," who announced himself as the British Minister, Mr. Findlay. Findlay assured him that he "knew all about" Adler Christensen and his companion who was Sir Roger Casement. He had copies of Christensen's telegram to his parents in Moss and Casement's cable to James Landy in New York. Casement was on his way to set up a conspiracy with the Germans to make trouble for England over the issue of Ireland. But the Irish were chronic rebels who always failed and they would fail this time, too.

The Germans would make a fool of Sir Roger for their own purposes: they cared nothing for Ireland, only for England's embarrassment.

Findlay came to his point. Casement's Irish cause was hopeless, but he could make a great deal of trouble for England. As a British official in a neutral country Findlay had no legal means of preventing him from going to Germany, but England would like very much to see him stopped. Christensen showed interest but pretended mystification. "Nobody but you and I know that this gentleman is Sir Roger Casement," Findlay pointed out. "He is here under an assumed name. Sir Roger Casement is supposed to be in America. Now, if the gentleman down at the Grand Hotel under the assumed name should disappear, no one will know because there is nobody to make any inquiries—it is only an assumed name that disappears." Christensen again acted puzzled. It would be "worth a good deal," said Findlay, to the man who "caused him to disappear." There would be money in the enterprise if he were "knocked on the head." Christensen now admitted that he liked the sound of the money, but Sir Roger had trusted him and been kind to him. Findlay told him to think over the proposition and come back at three o'clock if he felt inclined to "go further," and gave him twenty-five kroner for his cab fare. Christensen returned to the hotel with what Casement called an "absolutely incredible" story of Findlay's "outrageous suggestions."[8] Casement instructed him to keep the afternoon appointment to see what further chicanery was intended.

Of this third session Findlay says only that he gave Christensen an address for future communications and that his informer produced as a sample of Casement's handwriting a James Landy business card with a message written on the back, signed "Cousin Jimmie," that Casement had given Christensen to cable to New York when they reached Christiania. Findlay enclosed a photographic copy of the message in his 31 October report to Grey, to be compared with specimens of Casement's hand in Foreign Office files.[9]

Christensen's late-afternoon report to Casement mentioned these matters and a good many others. Findlay had said of Sir Roger: "If you get him any place on the Skaggerack or North Sea we shall have men-of-war ready and will take good care of him." When the talk turned to cash, Adler put on a show of insolent blackguardism: "smoked a cigarette in his face" and "used bad language several times and swore that I was not going to do anything against Sir Roger for a small sum."[10] After a show of temper of his own, Findlay finally named the sum of £5,000 in gold as the reward to be paid on delivery of the quarry—dead or alive, as Christensen represented the deal. Christensen demanded guarantees, but Findlay said he must accept his "word of honour." After more bluster and rudeness, Christensen gave his agreement. On parting Findlay gave him 100 kroner: Christensen had told him nothing of value as yet and in any case that was all he had. At the hotel Adler again told his story and handed over his bribe to Casement, who had been deeply troubled to think of the temptations to which his innocent young friend was being exposed by his loyalty—but was amused by his resourcefulness and his bravado, and newly outraged at British unscrupulousness.

Looking back over the two parallel yet divergent versions of the "Findlay Affair," particularly its inception, one finds Christensen's story of his waylaying and seduction inherently less probable than Findlay's story that Christensen was "selling Casement from the beginning,"[11] that he "came to the legation and informed me of Casement's presence and object of his journey of his own accord," and "having first pretended British sympathies he offered documents for money."[12] In fact Christensen's story, which is set down above in barest outline, reads like the awkward invention of a sly, disingenuous, ignorant mind steeped in pulp fiction: hence an expression of his actual character. Christensen was a mean little adventurer who loved to line his pockets by petty intrigue and the truth was not in him: he was a liar by instinct and by habit. Shrewd old John Devoy who had spent a lifetime in conspiracy smelt the crook in him from the beginning. It appears that Christensen was playing a double game from the outset, shaded in favor of Casement as long as that suited him: he set the plot running by revealing Casement's presence, then lay in watch to see where his greater profit lay, taking a keen pleasure meanwhile in his role as go-between and fulcrum and in the knowledge that he held both the principals, more honorable and more innocent men, in his power. This is not to say that Christensen did not admire Casement and even tell himself that he loved him, and by his murky lights continue to serve him for the time. But the whole process was basically egoistic and self-serving.

Findlay and Christensen differ entirely not only as to the instigation of the plot but on the question of whether any physical attack upon Casement was a part of the proposition. It was this feature of the affair, as retailed by Christensen, that seemed so cynical and "outrageous" to Casement and kept him turning the whole thing with a morbid obsessiveness in his own mind for many months to come. But Findlay always denied categorically in his despatches to the Foreign Office that he had ever proposed or even contemplated direct harm to Casement's person.

The other matter on which the two accounts differ markedly is, of course, that of Christensen's "revelation" of his "unnatural" liaison with Casement. It is hardly surprising that neither Christensen's deposition nor any of Casement's several accounts refers to such a relationship. But Findlay referred to it several times in his messages to London and it may have been the detail that caused the gravest injury to Casement in the whole affair. The homosexual inference formed part of Findlay's first report to Grey on 31 October, and in a wire of 24 February 1915, Findlay said that Christensen had spoken of it both to him and to Francis Lindley.[13] In his letter to Sir Arthur Nicolson on 21 February, at a time when he was trying to collect material to defend himself against an anticipated attack from Casement, Findlay asked for "information as to circumstances under which he left Consular Service. *Was it sodomy?*" and inquired whether Casement was "generally known to be addicted to sodomy."[14] These references and inquiries may have been particularly consequential, as they may have inspired the opening of a file in the Foreign Office on the "unnatural" side of Casement's life that was later held ready to damage him.[15]

The hectic two days in Christiania neared an end at last. Adler had told Findlay that he and Casement would be taking the 5:38 P.M. train to Copenhagen so that Casement could leave him in Moss to visit his parents whom he had not seen for twelve years, but that he planned to persuade Casement to take him on to Germany so that he could commence his spy work at once. Richard Meyer, an agent of the German Foreign Office and a brother of the great Celtic scholar Kuno Meyer, was to travel with them to Berlin, and the German Legation had arranged for a group of "sturdy friends" to see Meyer off at the station and to make sure that no harm came to the other two travelers. In line with the story told to Findlay, Casement and Christensen boarded the Copenhagen section of the train, but at the Engelholm junction they shifted quickly to the Sassnitz section, leaving the British agent Casement thought he had spotted to travel on bemused to Copehagen. Findlay's report of 31 October to Grey reveals that in fact he had sent his Naval Attaché, Captain Consett, to the station to observe the departure. Consett had seen Casement and Christensen board a sleeping car that was also occupied by the King's Messenger, Park Goff, on his way to Copenhagen, and had warned Goff that his fellow passengers were two "dangerous rascals."[c]

After the tense two days in Christiania, Casement found himself tired out but unable to rest and he got only an hour's sleep before waking at seven in the morning at Malmö, where "the glimpse of the beautifully clean streets, fine stone buildings and pleasant-faced Swedes was a charming awakening."[16] With a good breakfast, a sense of relief at having escaped Findlay, and generally improved prospects, Casement's mood lightened on the peaceful journey to Traelleborg. He caught a bit more sleep on the five-hour journey over the "stormy, white-capped" Baltic to Sassnitz. There he was thankful for his telegram from Berlin and for the presence of Meyer when the inspectors, "stupid peasant reservists," looked very hard at James Landy's passport with its red American seal and forced all of them, even Meyer, to turn out their pockets. Higher officials finally cleared them onto the train for Berlin.

Casement took note of fertile fields, good harvests, and numbers of young men evidently still available for civilian tasks. Beyond Strelsund a pair of "Junker landlords," one with an "excessive Prussian" beard, began to glare at him with an air of fury. Meyer explained that they were talking of the "extraordinary insolence" of an Englishman's being there and were planning to call the guard and have him put off. Meyer interposed and vouched for his companions as Americans on their way to Berlin and soon he had to intervene again to settle a man who had seized Christensen's seat. The trouble in both cases, Meyer said, was that they had spoken in English, "the tongue of treachery." He tried to explain the distribution of German feelings in these first weeks of the war. Whereas the Germans felt "only pity for Belgium, respect for France, frank enmity for Russia," for England, "the cousin, the good friend who had betrayed Germany & tried to stab her in the back & to incite the whole world against her," they felt a hatred surpassing anything they had ever felt toward an enemy.[17] Yet Casement had a friendly talk in excellent English with a German woman in the carriage who spoke of her

---

[c]Consett watched the "alleged Casement" for fifteen minutes and brought back the following description: "tall, spare, very dark, clean-shaven with heavy jaw, rather distinguished looking, but does not hold himself well and has a somewhat flat-footed gait." PRO FO 95.776.

English aunt, now a virtual prisoner in Germany, and who eagerly accepted the copies of the *Times* and the *Daily News* which he reluctantly but courteously offered her: he had bought them in Christiania as a stay against the "dreary night" he saw ahead of him in Berlin. Certain things in England obviously still composed a part of Casement's homesickness.

His arrival in Berlin at 7:30 in the evening of 31 October was treated very quietly in Casement's diary. He noted without comment the presence of wounded soldiers and a waiting ambulance. At the Continental Hotel he registered as "Mr. Hammond of New York": having decided to "bury" the useful Landy "on the shores of the Baltic." The hotel officials seemed a good deal impressed by Meyer who told them that they would be responsible to the Foreign Office if "anything unpleasant" occurred to trouble Mr. Hammond. Christensen was put into No. 240 and Casement into No. 219, a few doors away, a "by no means magnificent" room with a bath. He saw with dismay that the rate of eighteen marks was three times the $1.50 he had paid for a better room at the St. George's in Brooklyn. The financial anxiety that would help to keep him wretched in Germany had begun. Meyer warned the two men to remain in the hotel until their presence could be explained to the police: two English speakers without German papers were sure to land in trouble. He then went off to the Foreign Office to announce Casement's arrival and to seek appointments for the next day. So Casement ate a quiet and lonely dinner, had a talk with Adler, and went to bed. "At last in Berlin!" he mused in his diary. "The journey done—the effort perhaps only begun! Shall I succeed?—Will they see the great cause aright and understand all it may mean to them, no less than to Ireland? Tomorrow will show the beginnings—"[18]

17   The Irishman Who Acts

ON Sunday, 1 November, Casement spent the whole day in the hotel, finding it quiet, uncrowded, and comfortable but a dreary place to pass an unrelieved Sunday. After he had given his order in English at luncheon, he saw one of his neighbors slip out to make inquiries; then the man returned placated and led Casement about the lobbies to point out portraits of the Emperor and other worthies. But as Casement had no German and his guide almost no English, they soon "bowed and parted." Mr. Hammond, Christensen told him, was passing in the hotel as an American millionaire, and Adler had improved his image by describing his "fine steam yacht." Meyer called twice during the day. He had found the Chancellor, von Bethmann-Hollweg, and the Secretary of State, von Jagow, both away with the Emperor at Charleville on the French front; but later he had found Zimmermann, the Under-Secretary of State, and he had agreed to receive Casement the following morning. He had been interested in Meyer's story of the Findlay incidents and wanted to hear more of that matter. Meyer left Casement feeling that he was "a welcome guest" and "as easy in mind, as it is possible to be in so strange a position." But that was not altogether easy: "Here I am in the heart of the enemy's country," he reflected again that night, "a State guest and almost a State prisoner."[1]

Sitting in his pajamas in his room on Monday morning Casement composed a memorandum to submit to the German Foreign Office; it included an outline of a declaration of friendly intentions toward Ireland that he hoped to persuade the government to issue as a state proclamation. Meyer called for him at eleven and they walked down Unter den Linden to the Wilhelmstrasse and to the Foreign Office at No. 76—passing along the way the closed embassies of Great Britain and Russia. No. 76 turned out to be a large, plain, old-fashioned

220

white house "of the time of Frederick the Great or earlier." Upstairs a male servant took their wraps and sticks, Meyer left him for a moment, and Casement sat down to await a summons, absorbing the atmosphere of the place which he found "so different" from that of the British Foreign Office. In his diary he did not explain his vague phrase; but apparently he was referring to a general air of quiet courtesy and confidence. In the large handsome waiting room Casement sat "on a big sofa in this centre of policy of the German Empire."[2] He felt acutely the tension of the moment, the strangeness of his situation, the importance of the errand with which he had charged himself. Doubtless his feelings were more tremulous than they appeared when he recollected them in posting his diary twelve days later. Then at last he began to put words to the strange fatality of his case, yet still with a curiously "literary" and theoretical air that did not express reality faced as a body of potentially deadly fact.

"No regrets," he mused, "no fears." Then he corrected that: "Well—yes—some regrets, but no fears." He thought of Ireland that he would "almost fatally" never see again. Only a German victory could carry him home again and that was "a miracle" for which he saw little hope. He was acting "all for Ireland" and he believed that Ireland could not possibly lose by the strange thing he was doing. "I may, I must suffer," he foresaw, "but my country can only gain from my treason." At last he had begun to use the deadly word; yet one feels that it is still only a word in his mind, not a reality ending with a man hanged by the neck until he is dead. If he succeeded with his proposals, it would mean, he thought, nothing less than "a national resurrection—a free Ireland, a world nation after centuries of slavery. A people lost in the Middle Ages refound and restored to Europe." Yet even his failure, consequent on the defeat of Germany, must work a basic change in British policy toward Ireland: "Things will never be again quite the same. The 'Irish Question' will have been lifted from the mire and mud and petty, false strife of British domestic politics and into an international atmosphere." England would have to deal with Ireland thenceforward under the scrutiny of the whole world. At the very least, "by one bold deed of open treason," he would have accomplished more for real Home Rule than "Redmond & Co." had gained by years of talk. England had long ago taken the measure of the talking Irish patriot: "She only fears the Irishman who *acts*." He was about to hit England with his "clenched hand . . . a blow of sincere enmity, based on a wholly impersonal disregard of consequences to myself." The grosser treason would be not to act, not to strike the "blow for Ireland" that he had long promised to deliver when he got the chance.[3] The war had made the chance.

But the true crime in any case, he reasoned, was not his but England's: "Grey and Asquith are the real traitors." In the service of "the greedy jealousy of the British commercial mind," its jealous fears of German "efficiency," they had betrayed the true interests of their country. For the Liberal administration and for the "governing classes . . . of the pirate realm" Casement professed only "unmeasured contempt," a scorn too deep for expression; whereas for "the people themselves, and for many individual Englishmen" he felt "deep sorrow, regret, pity and affection." He recalled lunching in May in Sussex with Wilfrid Blunt and "that lovely girl," a great-granddaughter of Lord Edward Fitzgerald. Blunt had said that the time had come for the breakup of the British Empire and he hoped to live to see it happen. Casement's fervent hope was "to *do* something" to bring down that "monstrosity." The world could only be "the better, the more sincere, the less hypocritical" for a triumph of German arms.[4]

When Casement was admitted to Zimmermann, he immediately liked the fair-haired man with a beaming cordial face and a warm handclasp: "He was warm-*hearted* as well as warm-handed." Zimmermann asked for details of the Christiania episode and Casement told the whole story again. "Dastardly," Zimmermann called it, and they agreed that it was representative British behavior: "They stick at nothing." Casement brought out the memorandum he had composed that morning, containing his proposed German declaration. Germany, he suggested, could counter the British pose of defender of Belgium and champion of small nations by issuing a state declaration of support for Ireland and Irish independence. When Casement read through his draft, Zimmermann assured him that he "agreed with every paragraph and sentence." "I accept it entirely," he said as he took possession of the paper. Casement's first German reception, all in all, had been warmer, more affirmative and respectful than he had dared to hope.[a]

When he was taken in to see Count Georg von Wedel, chief of the

---

[a]Next day Zimmermann wired his Embassy in Washington: "Sir Roger Casement has arrived. His proposals are being carefully gone into." 3 November 1914. *Documents Relative to the Sinn Fein Movement*, Cmd. 1108 (1921).

English Department of the Foreign Office, Casement again found himself charmed. Von Wedel was an erect brown-eyed man with an air of candor and good will and he spoke perfect English. Their "long and friendly" talk turned mainly on Casement's scheme to organize Irish prisoners in Germany into a "Brigade" or "Legion"—defined as specifically Irish and functioning for specifically Irish not German purposes. Vague as his conception had always been, Casement came to feel that it was chiefly this scheme that interested the Germans in his mission. "If you do that," von Wedel exclaimed, "it is worth ten *army corps* to us!" Casement was anxious to keep the tone of the thing positively pro-Irish and not merely negatively anti-British. He analyzed the character they could expect to find in the Irish soldier: "he would not do anything mean or treacherous. He would put his neck in the noose, as I had done, for love of Ireland; he would not desert to an enemy or forsake his old colours merely to assail England." Hence the importance of the German declaration again: to provide a positive and Irish motive for adherence. Casement was confident that with that clear lead "scores, perhaps hundreds of the Irish prisoners would follow me."[5] Follow him where? To do what? Casement did not know. In the expansive vagueness of his view of the practical situation and in his large optimism he was behaving in character.

Addressing himself to the problem of Casement's immediate comfort and safety in the city, von Wedel pointed out that he needed protection not only from the English but from the Germans; he thought he had better go himself to the head of the Secret Police to explain what Casement was doing in Germany. In the afternoon Meyer brought round to the hotel a general pass signed by von Jagow for the Political Police stipulating: "Mr. Hammond aus New York, hier zur Zeit im Continental Hotel wohnhaft, ist polizeilich nicht zu behelligen."[b] As a Norwegian and so not an "offensive personage" Christensen did not require such a credential; but he and Casement agreed that they would both wear little American flags in their buttonholes to forestall mystification and casual harassment. Feeling free to move about at last, they took a long walk after dinner; Berlin struck Casement as solid, clean, and orderly but not really an imposing capital. The River Spree and Unter den Linden and the lindens themselves

---

[b]"Mr. Hammond of New York, presently living in the Continental Hotel, is not to be troubled by the police."

he judged "frankly, disappointing." Thinking over the situation at the end of the day he considered himself "fairly launched" in Germany: he had made his major points promptly and emphatically and in the right quarters and had set going such machinery as he could hope to move.[6]

At the Foreign Office von Wedel was preparing a cautiously favorable report of his impressions of Casement and his arguments to go to Chancellor von Bethmann-Hollweg. He enclosed Casement's memoranda proposing the formation of an "Irish Legion" and the issuing of a state proclamation of benign intentions toward Ireland, and summed up Casement's reasoning which he was inclined to support: the two measures should help to slow recruiting in Ireland and should influence opinion in America powerfully in favor of Germany. As a first step von Wedel urged that all Irish prisoners of Catholic faith be collected in a single camp where Casement, with the help of Irish priests, could undertake a concentrated appeal to Irish patriotism.[7] Obviously nothing had been done as yet on this measure that Casement had suggested soon after war broke out in August; but the Germans had a big war on their hands.

Until he could begin "recruiting" among the prisoners, there was little more for Casement to do as self-appointed envoy of Ireland, a non-existent state. He decided to improve the interval by making some capital of the Findlay Affair. It evidently never occurred to him to suspect that Christensen might have betrayed him to the British, and having accepted Adler's version of events in Christiania entirely, he was outraged by a British insult to himself and to Ireland and by a representative bit of British unscrupulousness: employing "the Black Lie and the Silver Bullet," their usual weapons, to do away with anyone who looked dangerous or even embarrassing. The issue swelled in his mind to an obsession that soon approached hysteria. He ached to punish Findlay and to spread this dramatic example of British cynicism before the eyes of the world. But he needed tangible evidence to show and in seeking it he thought he might as well have the pleasure of making as much incidental mischief as possible for England and particularly for Findlay.

Casement now decided to send Adler back to Norway for his deferred visit to his parents, under cover of which he could carry to Findlay "Casement" papers fabricated to be as confusing and trepidating as possible. One of these documents took the form of a letter addressed to Joe McGarrity and dated 1 November. In it Casement told a straight story of his "somewhat trying journey" to Berlin with special reference to the detention of the *Oskar II* and the spy activity in Christiania, included pointed asides jibing at the British and praising the Germans, designed to irritate Findlay, and then settled down to "business" using a bogus conspiratorial vocabulary calculated to be both easily translated and exasperatingly vague. He found "our friends here . . . *very* well disposed," he wrote, and he was confident they meant to "go the whole road with us." Then details of the plot:

> The *sanitary pipes* will be furnished and on a big scale, with a plenty stock of *disinfectants*.
>
> Enough for 50,000 health officers at least. . . . The difficulty of shipment is . . . very great, and I fear nothing in that direction is possible until next month. . . . meantime the other effort can be well considered and pushed forward. . . . When project No. 1 is ripe and all arrangements complete I shall wire by the arranged code from the Scandinavian firm.
>
> You must be ready to leave by end of this month or early in December with the four friends selected already. At home Pat and the Galway men and our head agent in the South have been advised—you know how. I know the message got through.
>
> We shall be fully prepared here by Christmas and before that I hope to be ready.
>
> I will send full details in ten days—or less. Have Michael and C and the Boston men ready. Fifty will be enough. [8]

The second letter was a Chinese-box affair, dated 14 November and written to "Patrick" but enclosed in envelopes addressed to a Philadelphia hotel manager and a Philadelphia priest. Patrick was told of the happy progress of complex vague schemes and enjoined to do his part. Preparations in Germany would be ready by the end of December and "the campaign on your side" should plan to move in January: "By that time the Canadians will have sent over their best men . . . and the allied invasion should go far. The German-Irish alliance will beat the Entente yet." The mysterious signer, "R," indulged in a bit of gloating:

> It was fine when John Bull thought that all the work would be done by the Russians and the French and he would come in at the end to divide the spoils and keep the Lion's share for his own belly. But it is getting plainer every day that our friends will and can dispose of the Russian bear and the French tiger-cat, and then have their strong hands free to tackle the sea-serpent.

"R" promised that he would "go across" by late December, as he and his friends had found a way to turn even the closed North Sea into an advantage: "two can play at laying mines!" he hinted. "There are other seas can be sealed up as well as the North Sea!" He claimed to have in hand "60,000 here and ample stocks for them and a picked band of trained men to go over." He would be traveling to Denmark in two weeks "to arrange with the shippers." Patrick was to "keep all ready to sail at the word." All signs were good: "The charts are excellent, and we have all the localities clearly marked—and the clearing out can be done in a few hours with the right men on the spot." When John Redmond had told him in May, "Get an Irish Republic if you can," he had not imagined, "R" supposed, that he was talking of a near reality. Now it looked as if they would "certainly have the flag up by Patrick's day."[9]

It was arranged that Adler would leave for Norway on Saturday, 21 November, after some necessary dental work had been completed,[c] carrying the two faked letters and a few pages of Casement's diary that he would pretend to have stolen: all calculated, quite accurately as it turned out, to raise the hair on the head of Findlay and of as many other British officials as possible. On the seventeenth Richard Meyer arranged to have Christensen's passport "visé" so as to prevent trouble with his papers at Sassnitz on the German frontier.

The previous day Casement had suddenly been summoned to the General Staff headquarters in Berlin and told that he must go to military headquarters at Charleville, on the French front, to discuss ways of handling the Irish prisoners. He would travel as Mr. Hammond, an American, and the officer accompanying him would know nothing of his errand. Moving about Berlin that day he was deeply impressed by the air of simple confidence and well-being of troops he saw going off for training or for the front. Some were in uniform, others in plain clothes; many carried paper-wrapped packages and wore flowers in belts or bosoms. Women and friends walked companionably alongside the men who looked young and happy: "marching sedately to the trenches of death," Casement reflected. "A quiet, patient, obedient and sure-hearted people this, if ever Europe had one. There is an entire absence of jingoism."[10]

On Tuesday, 17 November, while he was waiting to see von

---

[c] "When his teeth are finished, poor boy!" Casement's account. NLI 13082–4.

Wedel at the Foreign Office, he heard from Professor Theodor Schiemann[d] that the sister of Richard and Kuno Meyer had had a letter from Kuno saying that he was sailing to New York from Rotterdam without a certain "coffre" that had failed to appear. The news agitated Casement because he knew that Meyer was really going to America as a German spy and that he carried papers not only incriminating himself but dangerous to Casement and to some of his friends. He warned Schiemann that if the British had laid hold of Meyer's secret papers they would arrest him at sea anywhere short of New York harbor. Probably the letter of his own that troubled him was that of thirty-five pages dated 12 November from the Continental Hotel in Berlin, surviving in a draft or copy in Casement's hand in the National Library of Ireland. The name of the addressee is not given but internal evidence (such as references to eminence as a Celtic scholar and status as honorary "citizen" of Dublin and Cork) makes it clear that the letter was written to Kuno Meyer. Casement advised him to call first on Justice Daniel Cohalan in New York; Cohalan would introduce him to John Quinn "who will very likely ask you to stay with him as he did me in his charming flat."[11] Quinn would put him in touch with persons who would organize his proposed lecture tour. Clearly Casement had still not understood the politics of Quinn who was soon to break an old friendship with Cohalan on the issue of Irishmen "going to bed with the Germans."[e] Next Meyer should meet John Devoy and Joe McGarrity, the latter identified as "my trusted friend—for whom I feel the affection of a brother," a student of Irish history and a collector of Irish texts, and a warm if exhausting personality: "always on the rush and has 2 motor cars and a heart big enough to fill both."[12]

Casement also directed Meyer to tell the Clan-na-Gael leaders of his arrival in Berlin and the work he was doing there and to give them

---

[d]German diary, 1 December 1914. NLI 1689-90. Schiemann (1847–1921) was Professor of History at the University of Berlin, an authority on Eastern European history. During the war he functioned as a propagandist and political agent. He had gone to Britain just before the war broke out and taken instruction in Irish politics from his friend Kuno Meyer. He studied the Ulster controversy carefully and it is generally believed that his report of imminent civil war in Ireland had much to do with Germany's urging Austria to proceed against Serbia, on the assumption that England would be immobilized by internal troubles. In Berlin in 1915 Schiemann published a pamphlet on Ireland as "the Achilles heel" of England in which he exhorted the Irish to arm and revolt.

[e]In fact Quinn did receive Meyer, though not as a house guest, and liked him until he realized that his lectures were only a screen for German propaganda and subtler spycraft.

the story of the Christiania episode as far as it had developed: then when Casement had his proofs against Findlay in hand he would wire America via von Bernstorff, "publish *Christiania story*." That story of "the plot against my life of the Br. Govt.," when joined with the proclamation of the Irish Brigade as a fact in being, would form a case to "sway American opinion profoundly." Another fact that emerges from this letter of 12 November to Meyer is that Casement had had in mind from the beginning the possibility of using the Irish Brigade as an outright auxiliary of German troops. This appears in his reference here to even earlier discussions with the Germans of what he grandly and pathetically described as a "march on Egypt." If, when the Brigade was formed, Ireland should be still "ringed round with ships, mines—and spies," then the men should be sent to fight in another theater: "Until there is a clear stretch of seaway to enable me and my men etc. to make a descent on Ireland itself, we might best help the Irish cause, *morally, spiritually*, & materially by aiding physically in driving the British out of Egypt."[13] When John Devoy heard that notion, it struck him as purest nonsense, a bit of the exasperating Casement moonshine. If there should ever be an Irish Brigade, Devoy wanted it to fight in Ireland—if not in England. The fact that Meyer did deliver Casement's message implies that his missing "coffre" turned up or that if it remained missing it had not contained the dangerous papers.

On joining von Wedel Casement was first shown his own declaration of German good will to Ireland, back from the German Home Office where it had been edited and affirmed. His text had been cut down a bit, but it had also been given "a more emphatic character" that he liked and his basic points remained intact. He was jarred slightly to see that the Germans had attached a reference to him as "the distinguished Irish Nationalist"; he felt the phrase had a vaunting air, and in any case he would have preferred not to call such general attention to his presence in Germany. But the Germans insisted on the identification. The proclamation was going out immediately to the world's press, von Wedel promised, and Casement felt that here was at least one solid piece of work accomplished by his mission.

En route to Charleville, where he was to try to see both von Jagow and von Bethmann-Hollweg, Casement was to be escorted by Richard Meyer and "a baldish headed young Prussian nobleman" Graf von Lutterich whom von Wedel introduced. The three travelers now adjourned to the Continental Hotel where they confirmed arrangements for the decoy papers for Findlay, and Casement said goodbye to Adler who "nearly wept!"[14] Then Mr. Hammond and his impressive escort were "bowed out of the hall by the manager and staff" and went off to take a sleeper for Cologne. On the station platform Casement noticed with little comment soldiers of a different aspect than those of the day before: wounded men back from the front, some borne on stretchers, some walking painfully.

At Cologne early next morning, Wednesday, Casement recalled that he had last seen the Rhine at Coblenz on his motor tour with Richard Morten in May 1912: "What changes!—to all the world—and to me," he reflected. A big military staff car met them at the station and took them off after breakfast on the journey of 270 kilometers. Casement noticed two loaded Mauser rifles clipped on the back of the partition behind the chauffeur. They drove fast over frozen roads in weather so cold that Casement sat on his gloved hands to keep them bearable; he noticed that he was the only man in the car without a fur-lined coat. They traversed the arid Eiffel region, then passed through northern Luxemburg and into northern Belgium via Bastogne. Save for an occasional shattered house Casement saw few signs of war or conquest. At Neufchateau boys were playing marbles in the square. In Sedan most of the fine houses appeared abandoned, closed and shuttered, but generally undisturbed; people too poor to flee seemed to be going about their business as usual. But as the six-hour journey lengthened, they passed scenes of worse and worse destruction.

In the German offices in the former Préfecture of Charleville, Casement had a long interview with Baron Kurt von Lersner whom he had last seen at the Ritz-Carlton Hotel in New York. They talked of the only subject that seemed to interest the military men: how to manage the formation of an Irish Brigade. The Germans were having trouble collecting the right kind of Irishmen, finding it hard to distinguish Catholic from Protestant and Irishmen from English, Welsh, and Scottish prisoners. Casement tried to "explain things." Von Lersner promised to notify him as soon as enough prisoners had been assembled for him to commence recruiting.

The Berlin party had been billeted ingloriously in the Hotel du Commerce where a few candles were the only amenity—no heat, no electricity, no hot water, no food. All the staff had fled except for a single Luxemburger named Joseph. Supper had been arranged at an officer's mess, but when they had eaten only a little bread and cold sausage Casement was called out and required to "explain himself" to an old officer wearing general's straps on a frock coat. Meyer then hustled him out of the building: he feared that Casement, speaking no German and with his papers held at military headquarters, might even be picked up and shot by a casual army patrol. At the hotel he wrapped himself in a woolen comforter and an Irish rug against the damp sheets and slept "on & off" till morning. Irish diplomacy at the French front was turning out an uncomfortable affair.

Meyer had arranged an interview for Thursday morning with Baron von Stumm, head of the political department of the General Staff; his fellow travelers had begged Casement to limit the session to one hour so that they could use their official car to advantage by taking a long way back to Cologne through some of the famous scenes of early stages of the war such as Dinant, Namur, and Liège. Facing von Stumm with only a cup of "truly abominable" coffee under his belt, Casement found him another forthright German with perfect English, and the two men talked with concentration about practical politics. In times of peace von Stumm had met Sir Edward Grey on several occasions, and he wondered now why the English thought so highly of that "mediocre intelligence."[15] Casement agreed as to Grey's brain power but said he still considered Grey an honest man and von Stumm accepted that. On the German's invitation Casement went through his Christiania story once more, and von Stumm agreed that it would be worth the effort to try to trap Findlay and to publish proof of his plots. They talked of Ireland, of Home Rule, of Redmond's recruiting for the British. Casement spoke of his "larger hope—a dream if you will—of an independent Ireland emerging from this war." When von Stumm allowed that that would be to Germany's interest, Casement insisted that it would be good for Europe as a whole; he was still trying to think in terms of large statesmanship.

Why had the Irish Volunteers not already armed themselves? von Stumm wanted to know. Because England had closed Irish ports to arms a year ago, Casement answered; and asked his own question: Why did Germany not make friends before the war with those who had reason to oppose England? "Why did you not *think* of Ireland?" Von Stumm's reply, Casement thought, showed again the fundamental "innocence" and "sincerity" that he had attributed to Germany all along: Germany had believed that England would remain neutral in a European quarrel; otherwise she would have had agents in Ireland as well as in Egypt and India. Germany "must win" the present war as an affair of land frontiers and land forces, von Stumm thought, but he was not at all sure that she could beat England with her navy controlling the seas—"this time." Germany would handle France and Russia but could hardly hope to reduce England to the point of imposing conditions of peace such as that of Irish independence—Casement's "larger hope." Meanwhile, with the British navy riding high, it was nonsense to talk of Germany's sending men and arms to Ireland—Casement's urgent present dream. Finally they talked of the German "friendship" proclamation which Casement described as good enough as an opening statement: he hoped later to elicit something grander—more explicit and farther reaching. Von Stumm seemed still interested and disposed to continue, but Casement remembering his promise pulled out his watch and made courteous adieux to "the Baron & the travelling Foreign Office."

With the frost still sharp they left Charleville at noon on Thursday and followed the valley of the Meuse toward Rocroi. Meyer pointed out the gangs of French and Belgian laborers repairing shattered bridges: all scrupulously paid by the conquerers. Casement comforted himself with "the clearest evidence of law and order" erected on the "base" of destruction in the countryside. Near Anserem they burst two tires almost simultaneously and pulled up for repairs near a "perfect little chateau" occupied by a troop of Uhlans: the Baron was off at the front in France, Mme. la Baronne kept house for the Germans, and chrysanthemums bloomed in a heated greenhouse. At Andennes Casement was shown a wall against which 350 civilians had been shot in reprisal for ambushing an ammunition column after the town had surrendered and the soldiers had been withdrawn. At the sight of the long common graves strewn with flowers and lime, he "nearly wept." His feelings about the whole scene in Belgium were deep but confused; his thoughts were confused but perhaps not deep. Seeing the Belgian people skulking away at sight of the German uniforms in his party, he thought of the strangeness of his own presence there: "How little these poor folk could have guessed that one man of that group was no German—but was the very British Consul who had indicted their sovereign and his abominable Congolese system only ten years before." Could it be that this war was "a *repayment* for Africa"? Certainly it was an "awful lesson" for the Belgians. In consequence of what general guilt? Casement could not have said. As was his habit he forced an illogical association upon two hardly related facts because the two were what he happened to know at the moment. And as usual he laid the real criminality at the door of England who "*knew* she could not help the Belgians" and deliberately exposed her to German attack.

He kept hearing again von Stumm's adamantine phrase: "What we hold we will keep." And he pictured the European landscape at the moment: "A ring of iron, trenched in blood and bones of a million dead and wounded Germans, stretches now from the Channel to almost in sight of Paris, and holds in a band of steel what France will die rather than give up. How will it end?" Now he forced the Irish Question into his prepared stereotype: England was funking the land war in order to keep her hold on the world's trade; she intended to dupe Ireland into supplying the bulk of her foot soldiers by offering the bribe of Home Rule to come, a vague bill on a mysterious statute book, "a promissory note payable after death." His rhetoric swelled with his reflections:

> I rejoice mightily in my "treason" when I read these things— and think of those oleagenous scoundrels, like Haldane— quivering masses of blubber—who are so busy killing the Kaiser with their mouth while trying to seduce my brave-hearted countrymen to do the real killing—or be killed themselves.

> If my treason does nothing else but save Ireland from this, I shall have deserved well of my country. To keep our young men at home, for the future of our own country & for all her needs— that is the counsel every true Irishman should give today. Thank God I came to Germany—and God be praised for the aid these people and their government are giving Ireland today.

These were still early days, of course, but the German aid Casement was celebrating remained almost as vague and promissory as Home Rule and it remained to be seen whether it would be paid before or after death, or ever. Casement had a long hard way yet to travel, as Irish envoy, as English traitor, and as ordinary suffering mortal.

Outside Liège, traveling in mist and bitter cold, the party passed acres of barbed wire strung "like grape vines on low trellises," the wires lit by hoarfrost, "the white and clear lacework of death." Arriving at Cologne in mid-evening they took a hurried dinner and boarded their sleepers and reached Berlin next morning, Friday, 20

November. Looking back over the elaborate little junket it was hard to see what it was all about. Nothing had been required of Casement that he could not have performed equally well in Berlin, and the Germans had not delivered their promised interviews with the great men, von Jagow and von Bethmann-Hollweg. Possibly the military men of the General Staff at the front had simply demanded to have a look at Casement for themselves before going ahead with the onerous business of sorting out the Irish prisoners and shuffling them about Germany.

18   A Gang of Poor Devils

O N his return to Berlin, Casement found the German "friend-ship" statement in gratifying prominence in the *Midday Gazette*, inset in bold-face type in the middle of the front page; it had appeared first in the morning issue of the *North German Gazette* and all the German afternoon papers were to give it full play. He asked the Foreign Office to order 3,000 copies of the item as printed in Mrs. White's *Continental Times*, the pro-German paper appearing three times a week in English, as part of his propaganda material for the Irish prisoners. The article was cabled to papers about the world and also printed as a leaflet for circulation in Ireland and the United States. It was dated Berlin, 20 November 1914, and began by an-nouncing that "the well-known Irish Nationalist, Sir Roger Case-ment," had arrived in Germany and "been received at the Foreign Office." Sir Roger had sought "a convincing statement of German intentions" in regard to Ireland as a counterweight to British-inspired propaganda warning the Irish people that German victory would mean invasion of Ireland "whose homes, churches, priests, and lands would be at the mercy of an invading army actuated only by motives of pillage and conquest." At Sir Roger's request and on orders of the Chancellor, the Acting Secretary of State made the fol-lowing "official declaration":

> The German Government repudiates the evil intentions attri-buted to it in the statements referred to by Sir Roger Casement, and takes this opportunity to give a categoric assurance that the German Government desires only the welfare of the Irish people, their country, and their institutions.
>
> The Imperial Government formally declares that under no cir-

cumstances would Germany invade Ireland with a view to its conquest or the overthrow of any native institutions in that country.

Should the fortune of this great war, that was not of Germany's seeking, ever bring in its course German troops to the shores of Ireland, they would land there, not as an army of invaders to pillage and destroy, but as the forces of a Government that is inspired by good-will towards a country and a people for whom Germany desires only NATIONAL PROSPERITY AND NATIONAL FREEDOM.[1]

Such a document was perhaps not worth a great deal as diplomatic currency or as an earnest of history to be made. But though it was a scrap of paper, it caught the eye in an interesting and emphatic way. Its publication particularly in England, Ireland, and the United States turned Casement into a more formidable nuisance to England than he had been supposed there. It also proclaimed him a British subject who was treating formally with the enemy in time of war.

That evening von Wedel called Casement to the Foreign Office and read him a message from the German Ambassador at the Vatican: through the Irish College in Rome two "nationalist" priests, Crotty and O'Gorman, had been found to work among the prisoners. The names at least sounded promising and Casement was pleased to sense some forward movement. Von Wedel also told him that the American Ambassador, Gerard, presumably coached by the British, had been making pressing inquiries as to Casement's whereabouts; the Germans had claimed total ignorance. But von Wedel thought he ought to give up his "James Landy" passport and other credentials to be returned to the United States, and Casement shortly made up a package containing these documents as well as a long account of his actions to date with emphasis on the Christiania episode and the "friendship" declaration, to go via Rotterdam by special messenger to Justice Daniel Cohalan in New York.[2] Earlier in the month (6 November) Casement had asked Cohalan, in one of the cable messages to von Bernstorff that were evidently decoded and read by the British in transit, to send a "fully informed" messenger to Ireland to procure a priest for the Irish Brigade and incidentally to "tell Bigger, solicitor, Belfast" to "conceal everything" that Casement had left in his keeping.[3]

On Sunday morning, tardy by yet another day, Casement at last saw Adler Christensen off for Norway with the bogus "Casement" papers for Findlay's eyes. Late that afternoon when he was entertaining the Baroness von Nordenflycht and her daughter Gussie, old German friends from Africa and Brazil, he received a frantic wire from Adler in Sassnitz: he had been detained by border guards and enthusiastically searched and interrogated, and he professed to have "lost" a portion of his papers. Casement left his guests and hurried to the Foreign Office to beg von Wedel to telegraph to Sassnitz and try to straighten things out.

By telephone on Tuesday Casement heard with "great joy" from another old African friend, Count Gebhard Blücher, and "hurried off" to lunch with him at the Esplanade Hotel, haven of assorted displaced nationals in Berlin. Count Blücher was the great-great-grandson of Marshal Blücher, savior of the British at Waterloo, and was heir to a higher title and to very large landholdings in Germany.[a] His wife had been born Evelyn Stapleton-Bretherton, daughter of an old Lancashire family. The couple had lived in England from their marriage in 1907 until the war forced the Count's return to Germany, and Casement had met them often and cordially in those calmer days. Blücher now promised to arrange lunch for Casement with von Jagow whom he knew well and who had returned to Berlin for the Reichstag sessions. Countess Blücher was grieving for her young brother, captured with both legs broken in a trench overrun by the Germans; but she allowed herself to approve Casement's announced intention of raising "a real good rebellion" in Ireland as a means of "terrifying" Britain and so hastening the coming of peace.[4]

Casement had counted Thursday, 26 November, as the beginning of Adler's campaign in Christiania but there was no news of that as yet. In his diary that evening Casement set down two opposing readings of the "German" character as he had seen it to date, official and popular, negative and positive, both interpretations reflecting conventional views of the day. "If only these people were less machine-made," he fretted unreasonably, "they could get every Irish regiment in the Br. Army to join my Brigade! But they will proceed only by machinery and not by individual intelligence." Presumably he meant that the Germans needed, or he needed the Germans, to approach the Irish soldiers in a warmer, more intuitive fashion. Against this complaint he set the sentimental, *gemütlich* image of

[a]He became Prince on the death of his father in 1916.

convalescent wounded men about the city, accompanied by "kind-faced" nurses and "guides": "Crowds of kind-eyed people go with them often—& press things on them & all are so full of courtesy, real *affection* and love for the soldiers, that every day I feel more & more in love with German manhood and womanhood. A great people—a *good* people."[5]

It was apparently on Saturday, 28 November, that Casement saw Father O'Gorman and Father Crotty for the first time. He thought O'Gorman a "loyalist nationalist" and Crotty "a raging Fenian!" and his fears that they might have been seduced by the recent *rapprochement* between England and the Vatican were set at rest. Their instructions from Rome were to remain "non-political." Casement accepted that idea apparently peaceably at the time, telling himself that he would be content to have them attend only to "their holy business."[6] But in fact he was disappointed: he had counted on at least one Irish Catholic priest as an active ally in his recruiting. Subconsciously he was preparing to blame German stiffness and Catholic professionalism for an anticipated failure with the Brigade.

Richard Meyer called on the thirtieth to deliver the news for which Casement and the priests had been waiting. In a quick sweep of captives from Irish regiments only, about 2,300 Irish Catholics had been identified and of these nearly 400 had been collected at Limburg near Frankfurt. Casement determined to go to Limburg as soon as possible and to go in advance of the priests: "will sow seeds first—& leave them papers & pamphlets & words of love."[7] As a way of viewing a proposition inviting men to put their necks in a noose, it seemed remarkably soft and disembodied. Casement resolved as well to abandon "Mr. Hammond of New York" and come back from Limburg in his own identity, honoring the event also by changing to the Eden Hotel from the Continental which he had never liked.

An entertaining document in Christensen's straggling hand, his account of his meeting with Findlay on 26 November, reached Casement on 1 December just before he left for Limburg. Findlay had been "pretty keen" and Adler judged that he had "got him going now all right." He had handed over the letters to McGarrity and "Pat" and had embroidered freely on their contents in an interview of nearly two hours. Adler had scorned the promised £5,000 as too little for delivering up an agent as dangerous as Casement; Findlay had given him 500 kroner "to keep me going" till their next meeting when he would "lett me know for sure how mutch the Gov. are willing to pay." Most of Christensen's letter was composed of instructions as to the form of a new letter he commanded Casement to write him, developing the hints Adler had "trowed" and summoning him back to Berlin for new orders. The flavor of Christensen's present letter is best conveyed by its postscript:

> P.S. Dear Sir Roger! Please be quick about this And this Bastard I will get. I got a good plan and I will tell you all when I see you. And do it good. your
>
> > Adler
>
> I almost forgot he said he knew you and a very clever. And he used a bad word And that you was very dangerous and that they must get you. your Adler.[8]

Casement wrote the requested letter at once and took it to von Wedel to look over and send on. Von Wedel approved it and promised to send it, but Casement later learned to his disgust that he had held it back. So Christensen remained in Norway without instructions and without the new leverage he had hoped for. But his invention was equal to the situation and when he returned to Berlin on 15 December he was able to report on two complete sessions with Findlay.

On 26 November the two amateur spies had met in a room with drawn blinds and Findlay had "betrayed great agitation, walked up and down the room excitedly, pale and with perspiration on his forehead": so Casement stylized Adler's stylized account in a long summary of 17 December.[9] Adler had told him "a whole tissue of lies": Casement was fomenting rebellion not only in Ireland but in India; German admirals called on him in Berlin and they exchanged maps of the route for German arms going to Ireland; he had dealt with very high men in the United States and had unlimited funds from Irish-American sources; a party of powerful Americans were about to set out to join in Casement's expedition; he would rendezvous with them off the coast of Schleswig with two sailing vessels and crews that Christensen was authorized to hire in Norway. Findlay grew more and more agitated. Was that yacht the one Armour of Chicago was building? They knew about that one. This Casement was "a very clever, a very dangerous son of a b . . . " but he was "a gentleman." Findlay ordered Christensen to get hold of as many details of the coming expedition as he could, particularly the names of Irish and American conspirators and the latitude and longitude of the rendezvous with the yacht. Again he insisted that the

Germans would sacrifice Ireland and make a dupe of Casement for their own ends. Adler had agreed with him; and by 17 December Casement himself had come to the same conclusion, at least for the moment: "(So do I!)" he parenthesized.[10]

Christensen's account as paraphrased by Casement and Findlay's reception of the "information" can be checked against Findlay's dispatches to the Foreign Office in London. The two accounts agree in the main and it is clear that the British Minister was taking the matter with absolute solemn seriousness. In a "Most Private and Secret" telegram to Sir Arthur Nicolson on 26 November he reported on the meeting of that day. "Informer" had just arrived from Berlin with letters to Joe McGarrity and "Pat." Findlay had taken copies and he gave their ominous purport in careful detail[11] and added a few details that Adler had forgotten to report: Casement had been received by the German Emperor and was about to join him at the front; 600 men were working incommunicado on a "secret job" at the Krupp munition works; Casement possessed charts of British and German minefields at sea; a "picked band of German officers" would accompany him to Ireland and the rendezvous with the American "conspirators" would occur somewhere off the Irish coast. Findlay and Christensen told slightly different stories of their dickering over a price for "information leading to capture of Casement and his accomplices and of shipments of arms" (as Findlay phrased the prescription). According to Findlay, Christensen demanded £5,000; he offered £1,000; Christensen "insisted on his own price." Findlay made no mention of the figure of £10,000 that Christensen said he had finally promised, but he did now ask official authorization to offer "informer his price": £5,000. And he showed his faith in Christensen and his mistaken estimate of his rascality: "I believe information he has given to be genuine. He is not clever enough to invent it."[12]

When Casement received the first scrawled note from Christensen and drafted the reply that von Wedel decided not to transmit, he was of course still in Berlin. But his actual deeds, so tentative as yet, his bogus conspiratorial messages ("50,000 health officers"!), and Findlay's sober and alarmed communication of those to London had created a more satisfactory sensation than he had any means of knowing. Britons around the globe lay in watch for him now, and that same day, 1 December, Sir A. Hardinge in Madrid telegraphed the Foreign Office that Casement was believed to be sailing that day from Cadiz to New York under the name of Phillips. The wire went the rounds of the London office and one commentator remarked that whereas Casement's conduct had been placed in the hands of the Director of Public Prosecutions, no warrant had been issued, and England could not in any case arrest him on the high seas; he suggested a humbler retaliation: "I suppose the question of stopping Casement's pension is being considered, though this is a minor one in comparison with the question of his treasonable performance." Sir Edward Grey's plaintive note on the document runs: "I gave instructions some time ago that his pension was to be stopped. I assume this has been done. We cannot take him on a neutral ship outside territorial waters or get him extradited."[13] In fact Britain's highest security officers were looking for Casement from now on, and Basil Thomson, head of Scotland Yard's C.I.D., and Captain Reginald Hall, Chief of Naval Intelligence, concocted a nearly incredible scheme to have the waters off the west of Ireland patrolled by a chartered yacht, the *Sayonara*, with a German-American master and owner, who was to poke about the coast watching for strange ocean-going apparitions and try to pick up information on shore. Ironically one of the persons to whom they played their charade was Darrell Figgis, a major figure in the Howth gun-running.[14]

On that same busy day, 1 December, Casement got off a long letter to Eoin MacNeill to travel by a route of excessive deviousness: it was enclosed in a letter to Mrs. Green, which was enclosed in a letter to Wamberzin and Sons in Rotterdam, who would send it to Herr Ballin in Hamburg, who could "get it through to England unopened."[15] He left the complex missive to be mailed by the Blüchers, who had heard of the route from the Princess of Pless who used it "regularly." But the letter was intercepted by British authorities, was shown to Casement in Scotland Yard in April 1916, and duly appeared among the *Documents Relative to the Sinn Fein Rebellion* in 1921. "You know who writes this," he wrote darkly to MacNeill. "I am in Berlin, and if Ireland will do her duty, rest assured Germany will do hers towards us, our cause, and our whole future." Much of the letter repeated such assurances of German friendship and exhortations to Irish nerve and steadfastness. He invited MacNeill to make their needs known—"rifles, officers, men"—and assured him of things of which he had had no assurance himself: "Rifles and ammunition can be found and good officers, too." Again he pleaded for "one or two thoroughly patriotic Irish priests," placing great emphasis on this point. He enclosed a copy of the German declaration of 20 November and ordered MacNeill to give it the widest possible circulation in Ireland. "Tell all to trust the Germans," he urged, "—and to trust me. . . . We may win everything by this war if we are true to Germany; and if we do not win today we ensure international recognition of Irish nationality and hand on an uplifted cause for our sons."[16]

A deeper revelation of Casement's spiritual condition, his accumulating loneliness and lostness and confusion of mind, was suggested by a letter, also of 1 December, to Adler Christensen at home with his parents in Norway. "I wish I had a father & a mother to go to now," he wrote wretchedly. "I am very lonely often—& get most miserable." He had spent all the preceding day alone in the hotel, even taking his meals in his room, feeling "broken hearted" as he brooded on "friends I shall never see again—and of Ireland I have looked my last on." "Come back soon to me dearest Adler," he begged, "and then you and I will go away together to the country to *work*."[17] The final image pointed to no visible reality, of course, and almost certainly it corresponded to nothing in Christensen's own dream of the future. Casement signed himself "Your affectionate Master and Friend, R.C."

In a call late the same night Professor Theodor Schiemann upset Casement badly by reporting unfavorable opinions of Christensen in official German quarters. Casement did not specify the charges; in his phrase Schiemann retailed "disquieting statements about Adler that were unwarranted and malicious."[18] Casement felt "annoyed beyond words—and disgusted"—at Schiemann whom he came to despise as an officious person and a general trouble maker. His sympathy and loyalty adhered to his embarrassing friend. "Poor Adler!" he mused. "God knows he is bad enough without these professional inquests on him." In his diary for 3 December Casement revealed that Adler had come to him on the eve of his departure for Norway and made a "confession" and this he chose to regard as "the truth" in preference to Schiemann's "remark." Yet Schiemann was a political agent of the Foreign Office and his warning had to be taken seriously as reflecting upon Casement's own good name and that of his mission.

The actual contents of both Schiemann's charges and Adler's confession remain mysterious. Casement's hushed tone suggests something shameful, and René MacColl deduces generally homosexual behavior, apparently on the basis of a conversation in March 1954 with the elderly Princess Blücher who told him that "Christensen's appearance and mannerisms were very feminine, and he habitually made up."[19] The Princess was always an unreliable witness, however, and she had an ancient grievance against Casement; but she could have been right in this instance. Findlay also found Christensen in the flesh a distasteful person and a blackguard but evidently not an effeminate blackguard—even though he professed to know of an "unnatural" relationship between Casement and his "follower." On 3 January 1915, by which date he had seen Christensen a half-dozen times, Findlay sent to the Foreign Office the following description which he recommended circulating through the Admiralty:

> ADLER CHRISTENSEN, age 24, height about 6 feet, strongly made, clean-shaven, fair hair, blue or grey eyes very small and close together, gap in front teeth. Wears thick double-breasted great-coat and soft dark hat. Speaks English fluently, but with Norwegian-American accent. . . . Has a fleshy, dissipated appearance, has been wanted by the police in New York as a dangerous type of Norwegian-American criminal.[b]

But again a letter of February 1915 from Casement to "dear, faithful old Adler" seems to bring real weight to bear upon Princess Blücher's side of the question: "Now *don't* go & be foolish with the money—you will soon have not a cent! . . . You are fearfully wasteful of money, my dear, faithful old Adler—much more than I am even—because you buy things you don't need at all—like that Rain coat & the gloves etc. I have *no* gloves & you have about 6 pairs!—& face and complexion 'blooms'! & God knows what."[20]

Whatever the facts of Casement's bedroom deportment with Christensen, he understood his fundamental relationship with the man as proprietary and paternal: his tone was patient, monitory, sentimental, often grieved, but always fatherly. His personal letter to Christensen of 2 December, covering the new decoy letter for Findlay that von Wedel did not let go through, shows this characteristic tone and also shows that his sense of himself as gentleman was suffering affront in the devious necessities of his office as Irish patriot. Casement wrote:

[b]PRO FO 95.776. The final detail appears to be one of Christensen's gaudy inventions accepted as fact by Findlay.

> I do not want you to get into trouble for me or to do anything wrong (beyond the wrong we are both doing in meeting deception with deception). I want you to become an honest good man, dear Adler, and to help you to this—and so I am really unhappy when I think of you telling lies for me.[21]

He asked Christensen not to touch Findlay's dirty money but to come to him for cash when he needed it. "I am always sorry to think of you with that rascal!" he continued. "I want to fight him—not to intrigue against him and tell lies." He wished to confront Findlay as a gentleman and "tell him to his face what a ruffian I think him." It was confused, beleaguered, and perhaps pathetic high-mindedness, and surely wasted upon the ruffian Christensen.

Casement got away from Berlin at last on the night of 2 December, traveling on the same train as the Crown Princess whom he saw arrive at the station with no ceremony except that everyone stood with his hat off. He carried a special Imperial passport for general travel in Germany as well as a letter from the Minister of War to the commandant in the Frankfurt region identifying him as "Sir Roger Casement, an Irishman"[c] and granting him free movement in the prisoners' camp and in the Limburg area. He supposed he must be the only male or unmarried "British subject" freely at large in Germany. When he registered at the Hessischer Hof in Frankfurt in the early morning of 3 December, he was amused to see that it had recently been the Englischer Hof. He showed his passport and for the first time in Germany signed his own name, birthplace, and date of birth. He carried with him "plenty of literature" for the soldiers, including copies of Devoy's *Gaelic American* and of his own little book of seven ranting essays now entitled "The Crime Against Ireland—and How the War May End It." The German Foreign Office had printed two thousand copies at his request in a style he thought sturdy and tasteful.

General de Graaff received Casement before noon, and again he saw a charming German, speaking good English, a former friend of Edward VII of England. Arrangements were settled in a few minutes: the General would take him out to the camp next day, leave him free to stay as long as he wished, and place a car and two orderlies at his disposal. In the afternoon Casement walked about the city, admiring its handsome spaciousness and "the general air of extreme

---

[c]Casement noted that the document represented the first such recognition of an Irish *national* by any state. Notes to Counsel, 7 June 1916. NLI 13088.

well doing." But what particularly caught his eye were the young men: "the fine, strong, well shaped bodies I notice all thro' Germany—soldiers & sailors—very strong, wellbuilt young men . . . I met enough for a division in the streets! No lack of fine, strong handsome boys & young men."[22]

On the morning of 4 December Casement motored out to Limburg with de Graaff; their big staff car bearing the spread eagle of the War Ministry attracted salutes from all sides. At the Prussischer Hof in Limburg they met General Exner, the camp commandant, and Prince zu Leiningen, who identified himself as a native of Osborne and "an old Harrovian." The camp turned out to be unfinished, with about 400 French prisoners still at work on the construction. The two generals quickly attracted a score of satellite officers, so that the progress on foot to the compound of the "Irish" prisoners (Casement put them in inverted commas) turned into a small parade. The first view of the prisoners was the first of several shocks in the next days for Casement. They looked a sorry lot, for reasons that were not altogether their own fault, and Casement showed himself unbecomingly shamed to be viewing them in company with the natty German officers, who made disparaging remarks. Dirty and miserable and shivering in their thin khakis, the " 'Irish' " looked "a *very* wretched lot" especially alongside the sturdy neat French prisoners.[23]

Happily the Germans left Casement to his task and he spoke first for about ten minutes to a group of about twenty NCO's, most of them quite young. He told them who he was, briefly denounced the "Home Rule fake," described the loyal work of patriot Irishmen in America, and announced his general aim of sending aid to the Volunteers in Ireland in the form of men and arms. He told them bluntly: "I don't think any of you are brave enough to do what I've done." They still seemed "a poor lot" with "*horrid beards.*" (His own handsome beard had grown out again.) One of the NCO's, "more English than the English themselves," said that the main thing he wanted was to find a way to get even with the Germans. Casement then spoke briefly with the main body of the prisoners. One private asked him if he was an Irishman; when Casement answered yes, the man exclaimed: "God bless you, you look Irish too." This little incident appears to have been the only point of light in the whole occasion. Casement passed out his newspapers and pamphlets and left with the men a picture of the Pope he had brought all the way from New York.

Inspecting the kitchens and tasting the food on his way out, Casement found his eye caught again by the well set up French cooks, one of whom was especially comely: "a splendid young fellow—about 6 feet, fair, strong—in blue puttees showing splendid calves & with the figure of a young Hercules." But he reasoned that the French soldiers were "the men of a nation—a national army, citizens under arms" fighting for their own country; the Irish by contrast were "mercenaries" with no national cause "to fire the eye." Perhaps, indeed, the very seediness of the Irish prisoners, "the scum of Ireland—literally," was grounds for comfort of a sort: a sign of the success of the campaign against recruiting in which he had tried to play a major part. But Casement completed his first visit to Limburg "with a sense of despair" and went to bed after a quiet dinner in a gloomy and foreboding mood and with a sore throat threatening.[24]

The following morning he was escorted through the camp by two English speakers, Major Grunert and "Professor" Brezien, an elderly school teacher and a "pest." Again he was left alone to talk with the prisoners and his impressions were mixed, or confused. He heard a good many anti-British sentiments. Men said that the Irish regiments had been pushed to the front and sacrificed first, and some said they had surrendered "on purpose." A young soldier of the 18th Royal Regiment said: "We threw down our rifles at Lille—400 of us!" But the Irish soldiers had nothing good to say of the Germans, whom they blamed for the "wanton" destruction they had seen, especially of churches. One young man shook Casement's heart when he said: "I paraded in front of you, Sir Roger, at Six Mile Cross."[d] Casement did not remember the man, but he recalled the occasion with a wrench: a dreary Sunday in June 1913 when he, Eoin MacNeill, and Patrick MacCartan had stood on the wall outside the Catholic church and addressed the local Volunteers before driving back to Dundalk in MacCartan's car late at night. But what was one of those Volunteers doing here now as a British soldier? The prisoners gave varying views, optimistic and pessimistic, of his prospects for recruiting a "Brigade," a body which he had as yet explained only hazily: its form and function were still far from clear in his own mind.

Casement left two exercise books, to be filled up with the names and regiments of the men, in charge of two men who showed signs of

[d]Near Dublin.

eagerness for his cause: Corporal Quinlisk from Wexford, a mere lad of eighteen or so, and Sergeant MacMurrough, a man of thirty-two, a former Belfast postal clerk who said he had enlisted because he had got into "financial trouble." As on the preceding afternoon Casement was treated to an outing in the big staff car with two chauffeurs, this time to Coblenz with the pesky Brezien for company. It was a strange sensation for an already disoriented Irishman to ride about in state receiving the salutes of German civilians. Small boys down to four or five years, he noticed, "playing at soldiers" saluted their car "with a haughty Prussian pride"; and the sixteen-year-old waiter who brought him cognac and hot water that night in the hotel walked with a systematic "military strut." Casement's cold had matured and he lay awake most of the night with a rasping cough shaking his bed, his mind full of pessimistic thoughts.[25]

But on Sunday he was back at the camp a few minutes after eight o'clock. Quinlisk and MacMurrough had ready for him a list of 383 Irish prisoners, some of them actually of English birth but of Irish parents. Casement had them all assembled in one big room and then read out to them the conditions for the Irish Brigade as he intended to propose them to the Germans. He "pointed out all the risks & dangers" and told them he wanted them to think the proposal through carefully: he would return in about a week and ask for their "answers." It was a gentlemanly kind of recruiting. The room was wary and silent: the men "said nothing—all kept quiet."[26] Casement then took his car back to town, picked up Father Crotty and Father O'Gorman at the hotel where they had now arrived, and returned to the camp to introduce the priests to the prisoners. It turned out that several of the men had known Father Crotty or his brother, a priest at Kilkenny.

In the afternoon Casement was off again to Frankfurt on a new route over the Taunus Range—a sick, lonely, depressed figure in his elegant equipage with two drivers. He found zu Leiningen at tea and took him off for a long talk with General de Graaff, a handsome gray-haired man, lively and bright in humor. Casement asked for a few amenities for the men, soap and shaving tackle and tobacco; de Graaff at once wrote out an order for such items for Casement to carry back with him on the train to Limburg. Casement broached his "Egyptian idea": his notion of using the Irish Brigade as German partisans against the British in Egypt. De Graaff approved the idea but hoped that when the time came Casement would be able to get the men off secretly. He was afraid of "a hell of a row" in the German press over "special treatment" for the Irish prisoners.

In parting, zu Leiningen invited Casement to visit him in Heidelberg when the war was over. He addressed the idea in his diary in an Irish lament: "Mavrone!—for me there is no after the war—or hereafter at all. All I am & have & shall be is here now. It is all for Ireland—& I refuse to think of anything else or of any personal consequences."[27] It is one of the few occasions when one feels Casement is actually confronting the probable fatality of the course he was following: even to "refuse to think" of it was to think of it, to emerge from the dream of his days. He was entering an interval of deepest gloom. Of course he had good reason to feel tense and depressed. He was in an excessively bizarre situation, in difficulties so ramified that they could hardly be analyzed, much less surmounted. That the maze was of his own making was no comfort—and he blamed the whole situation on John Bull anyhow. But he felt that at least he had earned better treatment from the Germans, who were acting stupid and unsympathetic, and from the American Irish who did not seem to be acting at all: apparently he had heard nothing from the United States in his five weeks in Germany. And the image of the seedy, querulous, dispirited Irish prisoners preyed on his mind and left him depressed and offended. Still coughing and sleepless, Casement drew up his gloomy accounts in the Frankfurt hotel on the night of 6 December. Want of money was one problem that was growing acute: "I shall soon be penniless." Expenses had been much heavier than he expected and he had found Germany a place where one's hand was always in one's pocket, especially for servants in the hotels who drew no salary and who delivered service that he sourly thought inferior to that in English hotels. His stake of $2,500 was almost exhausted and the Americans had sent him no more money.[e]

Against the Germans Casement had already found plentiful grounds for complaint. He was aggrieved in the first place because they had not acted promptly on his suggestion from America in Au-

[e]German diary, 3 December 1914. NLI 1689-90. The Clan-na-Gael leaders certainly intended to rally round. John T. Keating of the Clan executive wrote Devoy from Chicago on 9 November: "By all means pay bills of Rory. While he was indiscreet [unexplained: perhaps the Adler Christensen association, or Casement's discussion of private Clan matters with men like Quinn and Cockran] he has rendered service *money could not buy*. Joe [McGarrity] is enthusiastic and his zeal should not be chilled by criticism. . . . I will get money from St. Louis and here." *Devoy's Post Bag*, ii; 470.

gust that Irish prisoners be held separate and waiting—not considering that the Germans had other things on their minds and that in fact the Irish prisoners and Casement and his mission might strike most Germans as a nuisance and a bore. As he saw it, the men should have been softened up and made receptive to his message; his own image should have been planted in their minds; "the only Irishman at large in Germany, the open foe of England."[28] Instead of finding a prepared situation, he had had to introduce himself out of nowhere to "a gang of poor devils; distribute the literature; point out my speeches etc., etc.— & generally stand out from the first moment as an agent provocateur trying to stir up pro-German sympathies." Instead of appearing as an established patriot Irishman, he became a mysterious traitor to the British crown to which the soldiers, the poor devils, had sworn allegiance. It must have been something of a shock to Casement, also, to find only one among several hundred ordinary Irishmen who appeared to have heard his name.

Casement was further aggrieved at the Germans' suspicions of Christensen and at their indisposition to take the Findlay Affair with the seriousness he saw in it or to make capital of it in any way. Even from a point of view merely personal, Casement felt himself bound in simple self-defense to persevere in that, and energetically. For in loosing his decoy letters into Findlay's possession he had put his head in a British noose, and if he were to withdraw from the contest at this point he would be leaving it there. Those letters, he was rightly convinced, would go to the Foreign Office in London and they would rest there as permanent documentary evidence of his treasonous courses: "To now retire from the affair, merely because Wilhelmstrasse does not like it, would be to make the British Government a present of my character indeed and enable them to poison the ears of everyone in Ireland and U.S.A. against me and to prove their charges from my own writings." Therefore he must not only persevere but attack: "I must be first in the field with the accusation." He would push the case against Findlay to the limits of his powers and at the same time he would labor "to help poor Adler to live a better life."[29]

During the long restless night Casement's thoughts "hardened." He would now demand an interview with von Jagow or von Bethmann-Hollweg and it would have to produce evidence of serious good faith in highest quarters: "I will not accept the responsibility for putting a couple of thousand Irish soldiers into the high treason pot, unless I get very precise and sure promises both in their regard and for the political future of Ireland."[30] If the Chancellor and the Secretary of State went on evading him, for any reason at all, he would take that as evidence of bad faith and a sign that his mission was hopeless and he would then ask for a passport to Norway or Sweden. In his diary he did not speculate as to what he would do there, or thereafter.

But walking through the dark next morning with "a band of red hot iron" round his throat Casement's mood by some weird chemistry had soared again. In his diary written on the train to Limburg he imagined how "English pride and prestige must be sinking" and what a "serious blow to their pride" he had delivered by his own "defection." He even found cheering, as evidence of British stupidity and trepidation, the news in the morning papers that additional Irish newspapers had been suppressed under the Defense of the Realm Act. He faced the next scene with considerable gaiety: "Now to the Hotel & back to my Treason felony!" As a first gesture he called his disciples Quinlisk and MacMurrough into the city to "fit them out & give them a good feed."

Quinlisk and MacMurrough brought no comfort from the camp. They now doubted whether anybody at all would volunteer for the Brigade. Most of the prisoners were violently anti-German and inclined to see the proposal as merely "a German trick to get them to fight for Germany." Casement considered them bitterly: "No— these are not Irishmen but English soldiers." He bought some items of clothing for his two lonely converts and sent them off "after many smokes & tea & cakes" with the list of 383 prisoners to mark each man's name with his response to the proposition of the Brigade. He could feel no optimism about the human material available, even his two recruiters: "Both look rogues." He thought it significant that Quinlisk's family had for three generations furnished men for the Royal Irish Constabulary—Irish tools of England; and he did not doubt that it had been "some serious defalcation" that had driven MacMurrough to take the King's shilling.

When the soldiers had gone, Father Crotty and Father O'Gorman paid a call and Casement laid out for them (apparently for the first time) his scheme for an Irish Brigade. After a day in bed and a visit from an army doctor, Casement straggled out to the camp in the afternoon of Wednesday, 9 December, with the two priests who were to hear confessions. He made no attempt at formal propaganda, but many of the men crowded round—to say that "all they wanted was tobacco!"[31] They would have some for Christmas, Casement told them wearily: he had given Father Crotty twenty marks to buy it. MacMurrough had pleaded illness and did not appear, and Casement suspected that he merely wished to avoid having to point out the "English" soldiers on the list whom Casement wanted to have removed from the camp. "I despair of any patriotic act coming from such men," he reflected bitterly in his diary. "My proposal brings individual responsibility to each man & the last thing a real Irish 'nationalist' ['Catholic' scratched out] wants is to be compelled to think straight & act straight."[32] When Father O'Gorman left the room for a moment after supper, Father Crotty told Casement that he was "in full sympathy" with his purposes. "So far so good," mused Casement cautiously. Father O'Gorman was to return to Rome late in January and then Father Crotty would "have the men to himself." Casement would be glad enough now to see the priest abandon his "non-political" role. He had lowered his own sights radically as a recruiter but still felt skeptical of even limited success: "But if *I* can't get get 200 or 400 . . . out of 2,400 I'm not much use—or rather the men are not much Irishmen."[33] Blame, even in advance of failure, had to fall somewhere.

19   This Bastard I Will Get

O N the train back to Berlin on 10 December Casement was depressed by a sense of failure in his week's work at Limburg but
relieved to be free of the scene itself. His moods rose and fell and took
grand forms. Reading von Bethmann-Hollweg's speech at the opening of the Reichstag, he judged it "a fine speech—but too late." The
Chancellor appeared to have discovered only now what he,
Casement, had written three years earlier on his way to the
Putumayo: that when war came it would be England's crea-
tion,"England's war."[1] He exulted at a jibe in a Swiss paper at England, the champion of free speech and a free press, for suppressing
the Irish papers. "Bravo!" he applauded. "My passage through
Christiania has borne plenty of fruit already!" His logic (apparently)
was that the scare he had thrown into the British Foreign Office (by
his presence and by his tales of a pending invasion) had driven "these
scoundrels" to repressive measures in Ireland which in turn had laid
them open to denunciation in the world's press as the "consummate
tricksters and hypocrites" he had been calling them for years. Again
he called up that contrasting image of the German people which even
in his own eyes was beginning to look mainly ritualistic: "their manliness of brow and bearing, their calm front and resolute strong chest
turned to a world of enemies." These juxtapositions, Casement
wrote, made him regret that he was not a German. But such excite-
ments lit his gloom only briefly. Certainly he was finding little present satisfaction in his Irishness: "I used to be proud to be Irish. Since
I saw the Irish 'soldiers' & read Redmond's speeches I feel
ashamed to belong to so contemptible a race." He reached Berlin in
the evening hoping for letters from America or at least from "poor
Adler," but there was nothing and he went to bed in his new room in

the Eden Hotel "wholly undecided" where to turn his hand next. On the whole he thought it had better be the Findlay Affair.

When he called on von Wedel the following afternoon, the two agreed that Casement might proceed in the Findlay matter according to his own best lights. Von Wedel then read to Casement what amounted to his first direct word from America, a telegram of 5 December from von Bernstorff in Washington—another of the messages which had been intercepted and read by British authorities unbeknown to Casement or the Germans. The message covered several subjects: the German friendship declaration had "made an excellent impression"—in the United States, presumably; a "confidential agent" had gone from the United States and reached Ireland in late November; a priest (for Limburg) would be coming as soon as leave could be arranged; money would be coming for Casement; Judge Cohalan advised against publishing the Findlay story (expressed as the "attempt on Casement's life") without firm proof.[2] Here was some comfort, badly needed: he had not been abandoned by his friends and his work had not been ignored.

Count Blücher came to lunch on Saturday and the meeting turned into an unpleasant two hours. Blücher showed none of his former eager interest in the Christiania affair and Casement guessed that he had been advised by his Foreign Office friends to drop it. On the other hand he was full of curiosity about the Irish Brigade and when Casement was reticent, feeling not free to talk of it, Blücher turned truculent and rude. Then "an angry cat escaped from the bag of wounded vanity": von Jagow had called him in, Blücher said, to discuss Casement and the whole Irish question, and the upshot, Blücher announced with evident satisfaction, was a pronouncement that the Germans did not intend to "make themselves ridiculous" by promising actions they had no intention of performing and so they would issue no full and formal declaration of state policy in regard to Ireland. "I knew this all along—or guessed it," Casement told his diary. But it was a major hope dashed and it was a shock to hear it spelled out even at second-hand—and in a spiteful way by one he had counted a friend. Casement countered in stately tones that he meant to lay his case in person before the highest German officials; if he were to be refused a hearing "I should seriously reconsider my whole position and attitude towards Germany and might find it my duty to leave the country." Blücher in his turn dismissed that threat, not without reason, as "all vanity" and the two men parted in a huff—though due to meet again in the evening for a session with the Minister of Colonies arranged by Blücher. Casement concluded that his old friend had no real interest in Ireland and none in Casement himself aside from his "exploitative" value as feeding for Blücher's ego.

Dr. Wilhelm Solf, the Colonial Minister, was yet another German official engaging at first glance: "Very charming, great big, strong, good man."[a] Solf had been Governor of Samoa and knew Nigeria well and so the two men found much common ground and talked warmly for well over two hours. Solf showed as well a flattering familiarity with Casement's essay, "Ireland, Germany and Freedom of the Seas," and so Casement confidently pressed his usual case for the crucial function of Ireland in the balance of power at sea. Germany must "knock England out," he told Solf, and to do so would require all the brains she could muster. Solf allowed that English diplomats had been too clever for the Germans in the past. Casement said they were "very charming men, hereditary pirates of long descent." "Yes, I see," said Solf, "pirates in evening dress," and the two men chuckled companionably. Solf called the friendship declaration of 20 November "an entirely new departure in German foreign policy," her first attempt to take a hand in another country's internal affairs, and said that it had cut the die for his own declaration in regard to South Africa. The two parted excellent friends and Casement went off with a superior air to dine with "poor old Blücher" at the Esplanade Hotel. He finished the evening somewhat cheered from the wretchedness of the afternoon when he had got down to admitting to himself: "In my heart I am very sorry I came!"[b]

Meanwhile confirmation in the papers of the fact that England was sending a Minister to the Vatican brought on another attack of grandiloquent excitement. Casement saw the move as a direct result of his mission to Germany: "really the most convincing proof of the far reaching character of my coup." He had "actually forced" England to take a step "hateful to every good Englishman," driven her, in grand historical terms, "to reverse the Reformation!" When he read that his friend J. D. Gregory, who had helped promote the Franciscan Mission for the Putumayo and had praised Casement's humane work emphatically in London and Rome, would be going to the Vatican as

[a]German diary, 13 December 1914. NLI 1689-90. Solf was to be Prime Minister in the last stages of the war.

[b]German diary, 12 December 1914. NLI 1689-90. He turned gloomy again when Richard Meyer called to say that the "Irish badges," the harp insignia that Casement had requested for the uniforms of the Brigade were " 'too dear' "; they would cost 1,500 marks (about £60) for a Brigade with a projected strength of 2,000 men: "If this is the measure of their good intentions towards the Irish question the sooner I end with them the better."

secretary to the new Minister, Casement again interpreted the detail in paranoiac personal terms: Gregory would be going to Rome "to aid in belaboring me and enslaving Ireland!"[3]

Now that publication of the German "friendship" declaration had shown the world what he was up to, Casement professed to await "with amusement" the comments his "treason" would draw forth in England. In his diary on 13 December he noted the *Spectator's* remark that it felt "confident Sir Roger can give an explanation that will satisfy his friends." His own comment was brief and sardonic: "Does it?" The first extended response to reach his ear was peculiarly irritating and deflating: a letter of 30 November to the *Daily Chronicle* in which Sir Arthur Conan Doyle praised Casement's character and attempted to exculpate his alleged treason on grounds of temporary aberration, induced probably by illness and strain that were a consequence of long public service in tropical climates. Were the English, even his "friends" among them, going to diminish his dramatic action as the vagary of a madman, a sick crank? Was he not to be allowed even to possess nerve and clear purpose? "What strange people the English are!" Casement wrote sulkily and with considerable justice. "When I served them I was a 'hero'—the 'most chivalrous public servant in the service of the Empire' etc. etc. Now that I dare to cut myself off from them and to do a far braver thing and surely a more chivalrous one I am at 'the most charitable view' a lunatic."[4]

In Whitehall, however, the Casement-Christensen tall tale was creating a turmoil that would have been more exhilarating had Casement known of it. (Adler had walked into the Continental Hotel in the evening of 15 December, back from Norway with a story of a new "delightful web of lies!")[5] By 8 December in London the affair had acquired the dignity of "the Irish plot."[6] Previously on 25 November Sir Arthur Nicolson had sent a "Private and Secret" telegram to British representatives in Christiania, Stockholm, Copenhagen, the Hague, Berne, Rome, Madrid, and Lisbon:

> Sir Roger Casement against whom there is strong evidence of high treason is believed to be at present in Germany whence he may any moment leave for America. Please telegraph at once if he enters country in which you reside, giving earliest possible warning of departure with details as to route, destination, etc. He may be travelling under his own name or that of James Landy.[7]

In opening the eyes of Empire to the danger posed by Casement, Nicolson was acting on the suggestion of Basil Thomson of the C.I.D. at New Scotland Yard in a letter of the preceding day: if Casement's ship were known, Thomson hinted darkly, "the Admiralty might be able to deal with the situation."[8]

On 26 November Findlay had filed a four-page telegram describing his second set of meetings with Christensen and asking authorization to pay "informer" up to £5,000 if he led them to the capture of Casement. Nicolson judged the matter important enough to send copies of the wire both to the Home Office and to Scotland Yard, and on the twenty-seventh in a note to Grey he suggested a copy be sent to Augustine Birrell in Ireland and urged approval of the reward offer. In endorsing Nicolson's note Grey ordered that the full report of the case should go to Kitchener and Churchill, commanders on land and sea: "It discloses plans for a German landing in Ireland and must not be treated merely as a personal matter affecting Casement."[9] Kitchener approved the idea of the reward in a letter to Grey on the twenty-eighth and the same day Nicolson telegraphed the official permission to Findlay: "You may promise informer £5,000 in the event of his supplying information leading to the capture of C. and his accomplices."[10]

Findlay had telegraphed London not only on the twenty-sixth but on 27 and 28 November and 2 December. On 4 December he wrote Sir Arthur Nicolson again "Most Private and Secret," chiefly to enclose full copies of Casement's earlier decoy letters (which he had already reported in summary). Findlay and everybody else had to take the letters at face value, of course, and as yet no one was showing any skepticism about the "threat." Findlay had no really fresh "information" but hoped for a new supply by the middle of the month. He warned that meanwhile constant close watch must be kept for the "Jagt" that was to "convey Casement and his companions to Ireland" and for the "American millionnaire's yacht" supposed to carry the American "advance party" to a rendezvous preparatory to a landing in Ireland. He would try to find out the point of meeting of Jagt and yacht in which event "the whole lot might be captured together." Findlay hoped London was taking the kind of measures the gravity of the threat called for: "Everything points to the truth of the information we have received," he wrote soberly.[11] There is, of course, something comic (as well as pitiful) about these three amateur conspirators (Christensen was at least a semi-professional rogue) winding each other up in a tangled spy-plot that had no real content whatsoever.

The accounts of Findlay and Christensen of their next meeting differ in so many respects that they almost appear to be describing different occasions. Indeed that is possibly the case, though I am inclined to attribute most of the discrepancy to Christensen's fabrications. According to Findlay they met in the afternoon of 7 December and the talk turned mainly on the subject of the "Jagts" (now plural) that Christensen was hiring. When Findlay pursued the question of the rendezvous at sea with the "American yacht," Christensen said that he did not know that Casement and his "companions" intended to sail on the small chartered vessels. "This modifies his previous statement," commented Findlay in all solemnity.[12] Perhaps, Findlay suggested to "informer," the little Norwegian vessels would be used to put arms aboard the American yacht or another steamship. Yes, perhaps so, Christensen agreed. He promised to try to get copies of sea charts being used, names of Irish comspirators, copies of codes and so on, and send them to Findlay by their "secret channel" by 20 December. Findlay gave his formal promise of the reward of £5,000.

According to Christensen's story, set down by Casement in his diary and in a separate summary of 17 December after Adler returned to Berlin on the fifteenth, the date of this meeting with Findlay was 12 December rather than 7 December. (Perhaps Adler altered the date to cover the fact that he had dawdled a good many days in Norway after being ordered back to Berlin.) He had gone from Moss to Christiania, again taken a room at the Grand Hotel, and telephoned the British Legation to ask for an interview. He was told to come after dark to the back entrance by the stables, and he was admitted and talked with Findlay for more than two hours. The Minister was pale, perspiring, and agitated: he "walked up and down the room in a state of wild excitement." In his report to Casement Adler reviewed the conversation about the "jagts" and the coming rendezvous at sea, and he went on to add numerous subjects of which Findlay made no mention in his report: a large and powerful pro-Irish "Secret Society" in the United States; Casement's superb intelligence system that brought him news of any event in Ireland within three hours; his spies even within the British navy; two great bankers, American and Norwegian, underwriting the "plot" to land men and arms in Ireland. "A very clever and a very dangerous son of a b----!" Findlay grated, pacing and sweating. The figure of the reward—still according to Christensen—had gone up to "at least" £10,000. "I am mounting up in value!" Casement exclaimed in his diary, in his own excitement.[13] Finally Findlay gave Christensen a key, which he displayed to Casement, that would admit him to the Legation "at any time." [c] Adler reported that again the British seemed to be trying to search his hotel room: a strange man knocked at the door, received no answer, entered, then backed out with apologies when he found Christensen watching him.

The Findlay affair was receiving Casement's passionate attention, but it was not taking all of his time. In a cordial talk at the Foreign Office on the morning of the eighteenth von Wedel told Casement that the Germans were accepting all of his proposed formal conditions for the forming of an Irish Brigade. And at noon von Wedel took him next door to the Chancellor's residence, "a fine Palace," for his long desired personal interview with von Bethmann-Hollweg. They talked "warmly" for half an hour, Casement speaking English and the Chancellor French. Casement described his "hopes or dreams" for a free Ireland, allowing that the thought was "fantastic" now with the British fleet "keeping all Ireland in jail," but begging Germany to form, with the "next war" in mind, a firm and clear Irish policy that would recognize the freedom of Ireland as necessary to the freedom of the seas. He spoke again of the blow he meant to strike against recruiting in Ireland by forming his Irish Brigade. The Christiania story was rehearsed yet once more and von Bethmann-Hollweg was dumbfounded particularly by the details of Findlay's entrusting the Legation key to "my rascal Adler!" "It is incredible," the Chancellor exclaimed, "a man in Findlay's position to so act with an unknown, with your servant." No, said Casement, for an Englishman dealing with an Irishman it was all perfectly in character. "To get me, to crush an Irish national movement, they would commit any crime today, as in the past."[14] The talk had been cordial in manner but more or less ceremonial in matter, not cutting into useful practicalities, and Casement had done most of the talking; still he felt the Chancellor had been genuinely interested and sincere in his approbation, his good wishes, his inclination to help.

The preceding day Casement and Christensen had plotted a new

[c]Findlay later denied that he had ever given Christensen any key: if he had such a key he must have stolen it. Casement never doubted the authenticity of the key, though, of course, it could have belonged to any lock. See below pp. 283, 301–02.

twist for their web in Christiania: supply Findlay with a made-up rendezvous point at sea to lure British cruisers hoping to trap the conspirators, then send German vessels to ambush the British. "I'll see if the Foreign Office here and Co. will be men enough to follow it up," Casement wrote in his diary.[15] He now explained the scheme to von Wedel who liked the sound of it and went off at once to lay it before the Admiralty.[d] He telephoned later in the day to say that the Admiralty officers had been surprised by Casement's "bombshell" but were favorably disposed; they wanted time to consider the matter.

By now Casement had begun to feel uneasy about the scheme to ambush the ambushers. It had begun to seem a bit dirty. "It is too British!" he thought. He was also seriously worried by an evident change in Christensen's deportment. The man seemed to be turning sullen and evasive: "His face is changed," he noted in his diary. "The old, boyish eyes and smile are gone and he does not look me openly in the face."[16] Christensen seemed to be taking a turn against the Germans and by association almost against Casement himself. The trouble had commenced in the crude treatment given him by the German border guards during his two days' detention at Sassnitz in November: they had stripped and searched him, split open his gloves, given him paper money for his gold, forced him to pay high prices for meals, and worst of all had read Casement's letters aloud before a crowd of onlookers. In Berlin he had heard of Schiemann's and Blücher's talk against him and of an unfavorable report sent by the police to the Foreign Office. Both master and man admitted that Adler's earlier mysterious "confession" to Casement had contained shameful passages, but Adler resented Casement's listening to the German stories and his refusal to take him along when he went to Limburg. The Germans were playing Casement and Ireland for fools, Adler said: they would take what profit they could from the Irish cause and give nothing in return. The idea was close enough to Casement's own suspicions to shake him severely.

Most astonishing of all, Adler had begun to express admiration for Findlay. Findlay, he said, was "a man—he sticks at nothing—he would roll these God d---d Germans up."[17] By the pragmatic standards that Adler had confessed himself, in which "extreme rascal-

---

[d]Before they parted von Wedel turned over to Casement a mass of clippings of references to himself in English papers. One paper had called his treating with the Germans "an act of monstrous baseness, at first thought incredible"; another had called it "an act of treason to England and of double-dyed treason to Ireland."

dom" was the highest virtue, Findlay looked an operator with a strong promise of success, a "bolder, more uncompromising and reckless rascal" than his master. Casement had won Adler's loyalty, as he said himself, by his kindness and his trust; but those motives appeared to be fading now, on both sides. Considering the "extraordinary complexity" of Christensen's character, Casement thought that perhaps the time had come to send him back to Norway and thence back to America, where he would try to get him honest work to do.

The next days were quiet in Berlin. Casement read the newspapers eagerly for signs of old perfidy and new panic in England. New disturbances in Ireland and the strengthening of British garrisons there must, he supposed, be owing to "some magnificent tale" spun by Findlay of the menace of Casement's "plot"; and he did not doubt that in England the bombardment of Yorkshire coast towns (Scarborough, Whitby, Hartlepool) would be laid to his "malign influence" in Berlin.[18] On 21 December he finally received a letter direct from Kuno Meyer who wrote that Devoy, McGarrity, Cohalan, and Quinn had all advised against publishing the Christiania story, and all had disapproved as well his notion of using the Brigade against the British in Egypt. The Findlay Affair was suspended for the moment in any case; but about the "march on Egypt," Casement told his diary, "I am right and they were wrong."[19]

On Casement's plea the young Dubliner Bryan Kelly, of whom he had heard from Antonie Meyer, had been quickly released from the camp for civilian internees at Ruhleben[e] and he called twice at the hotel on the twenty-first. He professed to be willing to cooperate in any way that would get him out of Germany and back to Ireland. On the twenty-third Kelly left for Limburg where von Wedel had arranged for him to pass as a "prisoner of war," helplessly interned. His understanding with Casement was that he would first work "to convert the soldiers" and later he would go to Ireland with "messages of good cheer to Eoin & others."[20] On Christmas Eve Richard Meyer appeared at the hotel with a sample uniform of an officer of the Irish Brigade that Casement had ordered from a Berlin tailor. He tried it on: "It fit me well—& I shall wear it!"[21]

Toward the scheme for an ambush at sea Casement remained cool, but he did not try to put obstacles in its way. In a discussion at the Admiralty on the twenty-third he was given bogus charts showing

---

[e]A former race course near Berlin where the stables had been adapted as barracks.

minefields to be laid closing the Irish Sea north and south—these to be turned over to Christensen for copying before going to Findlay. A tale was also prepared that "Mr. Hammond," Casement's first German persona, would be embarking on 8 January on the small Danish steamer *Mjölnir* at Gothenburg for Christiansand. At the hotel that night a messenger from New York, Dr. Ewald, called with what Casement in his diary described only as "good news"—probably including cash.[22]

Perhaps the loneliest man in Europe, Casement spent a sad quiet Christmas little cheered by an evening as guest of Countess Hahn. Much of the day he gave to letter writing, putting the best face he could on a dire situation. A long letter to John Quinn is important as an attempt at a systematic summing up of the whole state of affairs as he saw them at this time, or as he wished to present them to a certain kind of witness; his account mingled self-sorrow with confident assertion and the kind of praise of the Germans that Quinn did not wish to hear. Casement headed his letter "Christmas Day! All white with snow," and he did not sign it though Quinn would "know the writer and whence it comes"; he was sending it by a "bearer," perhaps the mysterious Dr. Ewald, whom Quinn would find "a good guide to the truth of things here." The truth in Germany was "a fortress of soul, a unanimity of patriotism, an unkillable courage in this land and people that not all the world in arms against them could overthrow. *They* are the true battlers for European freedom, and please God they will win right thro'." From the Germans, on behalf of Ireland, he had won "convincing assurances."[23]

Of that "certain incident" of which Quinn would have heard from Kuno Meyer, "the plot thickens. My price has risen! I am now worth ₤10,000. . . . The developments may be striking." But he promised Quinn that he would not try to publish the story without full proof and he would make sure that the name of "a certain friend near you" (James Landy whose business address was the same as Quinn's) would not be drawn in. The British tactic was the familiar one: "The Black Lie runs the Silver Bullet hard in their armory of empire." Of the exigency of his personal situation Casement spoke with ostensible candor that was still clouded by sentiment and bravado:

I am a refugee, an outcast with no place to lay my head when this present war is over. The enemy would hang me, that I know, and he dominates so much of the earth that I shall not be very safe in many parts of the world—even could I get there. But it is all in the day's work, and *had* to be done. I knew that long ago, and I never look back, only forward. Here, at any rate, I have made a strong, brave friend for our poor, defrauded little country.

Casement went on to a vision of the future that seems addressed to himself almost as much as to Quinn: "I go to Ireland, please God, if all goes well here, and *many* with me." He suggests no approximate date for the event. The statement is puzzling on several grounds, as it puts forward an old dramatic image already effectually abandoned in Casement's own sober thinking. Why did he say this to Quinn? Partly, perhaps, because Quinn was a man of a kind he wished to continue to impress: a person of wealth and force and sophistication, of more than provincial eminence; partly, too, in all likelihood, because he wished to assert the radical Devoy-McGarrity kind of grass roots Irish nationalism against the cooler, more conservative, cultural Irish loyalty of Quinn and Bourke Cockran and their like.

When Casement resumed his diary at Limburg on 8 January 1915 he noted that he had made no entry in nearly two weeks: "I have been ill and greatly upset at failure of my hopes," he explained.[24] The interval had been busy. Adler Christensen had reached Christiania on 27 December and had seen Findlay that night, delivering the bogus charts of minefields as well as a concocted letter to John Devoy in care of Bourke Cockran, saying farewell to Devoy on the eve of "the great adventure" about to begin. Findlay kept the charts, according to Christensen, and copied the letter and returned it.[f] Findlay's "Very Urgent" telegram of 27 December to the Foreign Office described the charts in detail and in a supplementary telegram of the same day he quoted portions of the letter to Devoy. "Informer," he said, was waiting word as to where he should join Casement who was supposed to be going to Sweden about 1 January, thence to Norway to "start for west coast of Ireland between January 3rd and January 5th."[25] Christensen reported the day's events in a letter that reached Casement in Limburg on 5 January, adding the detail that he had encouraged Findlay's suspicion that a body of German troops was being held ready for an invasion, their passage to

---

[f] Casement's undated statement. NLI 13082-4. He says that Adler burned the letter later at home in Moss.

be smoothed by possession of charts of the English minefields that Casement had received from his spies in the navy. "Probely," Adler had told Findlay, "3 or 4 Transports or Battleships would make a rush for Ireland" with the troops.[26]

On 3 January Findlay telegraphed details of a new meeting with Christensen the preceding evening. "Informer" had shown him his new instructions: to meet Casement on the *Mjölnir* at Christiansand on 9 January. Casement was said to be carrying a "strong-box" full of vital papers, and Findlay had instructed Christensen to lay hold of that, hide it, and make sure it did not get thrown overboard in any melee that might develop. Findlay also gave him an address to which to telegraph information about the sailing of Casement's "party" from the continent, now thought to be planned for a Danish vessel aiming to reach the west coast of Ireland on 15 January. At that point the session had turned rough. Christensen had "made impossible demands" for cash on the spot and had "left saying he would warn Casement." He had just telephoned, however, to say that he would come in again that afternoon.[27]

Casement gave a far more colorful and circumstantial account supplied by Christensen, of the episode of the cash demand. Adler's basic object was to trap Findlay into giving him a written guarantee that Casement could publish as evidence in an eventual disclosure of the English "plot," and so his rude demands were calculated to goad Findlay into a useful indiscretion. He must have £2,500 at once, Adler announced. Impossible, Findlay said: he did not have it, could not get it, and could only pay on delivery in any case. All right, then, Adler encountered, if he could not have cash he must have a written guarantee. Findlay offered his "word of honour." Adler organized a tantrum, cursed Findlay, and flung out of the room after shouting that he could lay his hands on $100,000 that Casement carried with him. A footman followed and brought him back to the room and the quarrel ran the same course again. Findlay was "pale with rage & clenched his fists"; Adler stormed out again with "the most filthy expression—'You go and ----['fuck' scratched out] yourself.' "[28] Again the footman pursued, but Adler shrugged him off and retired to the Grand Hotel for the night.

Next day, Sunday, 3 January, Christensen returned to the Legation after being importuned by a messenger at the hotel. And this time, after Christensen had scoffed at every other argument, Findlay sat down and wrote out and signed a formal guarantee in the name of

Britain: £5,000 for Casement's capture, immunity and a passage to America for Christensen. Adler left rejoicing for Moss and thence for Berlin, wiring Casement en route: "Good news." Findlay at once telegraphed to Nicolson that he had given the guarantee, supplied a formal description of Christensen for circulation,[29] and suggested that Christensen be told that he could retain any of Casement's £20,000 of Irish-American money he could get his hands on, as a means of ensuring that he did not merely "rob Casement and bolt" without betraying him to the English. "He is a dangerous criminal and should be closely watched," Findlay said, evidently still not considering that he might also be a liar. Findlay had told him to report from Christiansand and he planned to send along a Norwegian agent of his own to keep an eye on events. Apparently any thought of capturing Casement alone on his way from Gothenburg to Christiansand had been abandoned.[30]

News of Findlay's incautiousness, or stupidity, created immediate agitation in London. Sir Arthur Nicolson fired back a monitory telegram "Most Secret" on 4 January, its text carefully edited in the hand of Sir Edward Grey himself:

> Nothing should ever be given to informer in writing and all communications with or promises to him should be verbal [i.e., "oral"] only. Pray be careful as to this most important point.

> You may tell informer that he will be given any money found in the possession of Casement if he is captured by British authorities but you should make it perfectly clear that he is on no account to have any harm or injury caused to Casement's person, otherwise if he is the sort of person you describe he may do something abominable such as assassinating or injuring Casement to secure capture of him or his papers.[31]

Most of the phrasing of the second paragraph of this draft telegram, surely extraordinarily feeling and flurried for an official communication, is in the hand of Grey. It is one of a number of signs that Grey did not find it easy to subscribe to the blanket condemnation of Casement, the official vengefulness that was the pattern of reaction in Whitehall to his strange behavior. Hard as it must have been to sustain professional respect, Grey seems to have kept to the end a degree of affection and pity for his old subordinate who had lent lustre to their service.

Findlay replied to the Foreign Office reprimand in tones aggrieved and defensive in a wire of 6 January: "I regret that you should disapprove of my action in giving informer a written promise. I would never have done so in time of peace." He justified himself by the exigency of the situation—a situation that simply did not exist:

> Informer was quite determined to break off relations unless he received a written assurance respecting payment and immunity. As it was a question of rebellion in Ireland combined with extensive mining operations against the fleet and possibly military and naval attack on Ireland or elsewhere, it appeared to me imperative to run no risk of losing supplementary information.

He assured Nicolson that he had already warned "informer" emphatically against personal violence to Casement. And he predicted, hopefully and falsely, that as the guarantee mentioned Christensen by name he would "never dare to show it" except in the appropriate situation, when he should claim his reward for the capture of Casement as an accomplished fact.[32] Grèy and Nicolson had suspected at once what had not yet begun to dawn on Findlay: that publicity and supporting documents might be exactly what Casement and Christensen were after.

20   Eating My Heart Out

IN Berlin Casement had not been idle. On 23 December he had
filed with the German Foreign Office his formal proposal in ten
"articles" of the conditions to govern "the formation of an Irish
Brigade, pledged to fight in the cause of Irish nationality alone." By
special messenger on 28 December he received from Count Zimmermann, Under Secretary of State for Foreign Affairs, his government's unqualified acceptance of Casement's conditions: "I have
the honour to inform you that the Imperial German Government
agrees to your proposal."[1] It must have been one of the moments
when Casement recovered some of the sense of authentic diplomatic
function.

The matter of the civilian internees at Ruhleben had grown in size
and taken much of Casement's time in the days after Christmas.
Bryan Kelly had been freed and sent off to Limburg. Now a total of
163 prisoners had been identified as "Irish" and "Catholic" and
Casement visited them in Ruhleben on 29 December. He met a
number of young merchant seamen from Rush and other towns, including "one charming youth of 17 Paul O'Brien." He determined to
press for the release of all the prisoners as an expression of German
good will to Ireland and singled out for first favor a Professor Macran
of Trinity College, Dublin. He was able to get Macran and his wife
out quickly and talked with the man several times in Berlin. Macran
sounded "very rebel" and promised "to be a true & faithful witness to
the truth about Germany" when he got home, to call upon Gertrude
Bannister, Mrs. Green, and Eoin MacNeill and possibly F. J. Bigger, and to "communicate" with Ada MacNeill.[2] To feel that at last
he could send a direct and civilized message to his dearest friends relieved a little of the pressure of his excruciating loneliness. On 2

January Richard Meyer sent Casement, then in Frankfurt on his way to Limburg, a list of the Irish civilian internees, inviting him to "make your choice and indicate those men who you consider ought to be released"[3] —not quite *carte blanche* but none the less gratifying.

With a bad cold "on" him, in the Irish idiom, Casement had taken a train for Frankfurt and Limburg on 30 December. At Frankfurt he went to bed and stayed there until Sunday, 3 January, when he took the early morning train to Limburg, still unwell. That day and the next he passed in the town, mainly with Father Crotty and Father O'Gorman and their friend Father Berkessel of Baldinstein, a lively, chatty old priest who had spent years at Cashel in the 1880's and was full of reminiscences of Ireland and England. Father Crotty told Casement that he (Crotty) had been much impressed by Casement's pamphlet and was a full convert to his "plans for an independent Ireland through German help."[4]

In the afternoon of 5 January Casement at last made his way out to the camp to talk with the prisoners. Their attitude in general was vulgarly hostile and it left him crushed and angry. "I *very* soon saw, from the manner of the men," he wrote in his diary that night, "that all hope for an Irish Brigade from such a contemptible crew . . . must be entirely abandoned." Some of them "insulted" him, he noted without further specification. The men's main line of talk was still complaint: of bad treatment and want of food and tobacco. It had been the fate of his high purposes, he reflected bitterly, to be offered only the worst kind of Irish material, the "type of debauched Irishman" full of "utter slothful indifference" to any question not greedily personal, and politically infantile: "more English than the English themselves." He left the camp in a black muddy evening that matched his mood, despondent at "the revelation of Irish depravity I had witnessed among those 2,200 so-called Irishmen." [a]

At the hotel Casement was given Christensen's letter of 27 December describing his meeting with Findlay that day and also a wire from the Foreign Office quoting Adler's message of "good news" of 5 January and his request to be met at the train in Berlin that evening. A moment later Meyer telephoned from Berlin to confer and they

---

[a]German diary, 5 January 1915. He had not seen Bryan Kelly at the camp and had thought it better not to inquire for him. Now, judging Kelly's function as an agent hopeless in the climate of Limburg, he telegraphed army headquarters at Frankfurt recommending that he be released at once to return to Ireland.

arranged that Meyer would meet the train and keep Casement informed of developments. On arrival Adler handed over the Findlay guarantee "to give to Sir Roger" and Meyer promised to deliver it. After a night's sleep Adler was given a purse of 400 marks and sent back to Norway to carry out his supposed "instructions" to meet Casement ("Mr. Hammond") on the *Mjölnir* at Christiansand on 9 January. Casement was informed by wire. Of course he had never intended to go to Christiansand: "I must possess myself in patience and wait for developments," he wrote in his diary in Limburg on 8 January. Being now committed to the rather distasteful enterprise, he hoped that several British "pirate craft" might be "caught in their own net laid for the one Irishman today they are really afraid of! God! they are afraid of me." He still believed on the basis of Christensen's expansive talk that the British price on his head had been set at £10,000—though Findlay's promise had never gone higher than half that amount. Casement's interpretation of Adler's attitude to the actual cash in question ought to be set alongside Findlay's reading of his "informer's" motive. "Poor Adler," Casement wrote, "is anxious to get their money to give me (poor soul!), so that I may fight them with their own purse." Casement had "laughed" at this notion and told him that they must hold themselves too high to touch any of the British blood money.[5]

On 8 January Findlay wired Sir Arthur Nicolson that he had seen Christensen the preceding night "I hope for last time." He had promised the man again that he could keep any money with which Casement might be captured and had warned him again that Casement must not be "attacked or injured." Christensen had "professed horror" at the thought. Since their last meeting, Christensen told him, he had been "summoned"[b] to the Foreign Office in Berlin where he saw many naval officers including Captain Mongelas who "looked at him very hard," asked whether he had talked with anyone, warned him sternly not to do so, and sent him away with orders to keep his appointment with the *Mjölnir*. When he had asked to see Casement, he was told he was not in Berlin—as was true. Findlay was sending an agent of his own to meet Christensen at Christiansand and to receive and send on messages from him. Findlay was baffled and troubled by the Berlin episode as described by Christensen but apparently did not yet allow himself to suspect a double game. Not so Sir

[b]He had gone on his own volition.

Arthur Nicolson who annotated the telegram in a remark also initialed by Sir Edward Grey: "I expect the informer has been watched if he be not himself a spy. However he has had *very* little money."[6]

Casement's own undated account picks up the story, as told him by Adler, of the remainder of the queer charade which seems, beyond this point, to have been calculated to serve little purpose for any of the parties involved. Christensen had spent the night of January 8 in a hotel in Christiansand and watched all the next day for the *Mjölnir* which did not dock till 6:00 P.M. Meanwhile, using recognition signals involving a green necktie and a form of words in Norwegian, he had met Findlay's man, one Everson, and had chatted with him off and on throughout the day. When the *Mjölnir* pulled in, Christensen boarded her "to keep up appearances" but "of course found no 'Mr. Hammond.' " Everson observed the failure and saw Christensen telegraph to the Foreign Office in Berlin to ask for new instructions. Findlay had apparently stayed on duty awaiting news, for he telegraphed London after midnight that he had just heard by telephone Christensen's report, confirmed by his own agent, that the *Mjölnir* had arrived with "none of Casement's party" on board. She was said to have waited in Gothenburg for a party of six who never appeared. Findlay further reported, however, that two German submarines, the first in six weeks, had appeared off the Norwegian coast that day and that one of them had signaled unsuccessfully for a pilot at Christiansand. He thought it "evident" that the submarines were somehow involved in Casement's "expedition." Perhaps he had intended to get away on one of the vessels, or they might have been scouting for danger, or watching a chance to attack a "British Man-of-War attempting to intercept him."[7] What was really going on? It sounds as if the German Admiralty had laid their trap, but the British had failed to oblige, perhaps preferring to approach "Casement's vessel" on the open sea once his presence was confirmed. Beyond this point, in any case, the double "plot" collapses into confusion on both sides.

With Everson still at his elbow Christensen remained in Christiansand until the morning of 12 January, ostensibly awaiting new orders from Berlin which, of course, did not arrive. He then returned to Moss, passing through Christiania but taking care to avoid seeing Findlay. Everson traveled with him to Christiania and promised to deliver a letter Christensen had composed for Findlay on 9 January in which he "confessed" that incensed by Findlay's refusal to meet his demand for "$1,000 down" and fearing arrest, he had used his last visit to Berlin to report that his letter of instructions had been stolen in Norway; that as a consequence, all plans had been changed, Casement's "party" was withheld from the *Mjölnir* which had been chartered for them, and he had since allowed himself to be used to work a systematic deception of Findlay and the British.[8] Whether by way of gloating or to leave a chink open for still possible negotiation, Christensen now also claimed to have what he had always denied possessing: "copies of many other papers and full information as to Casement's plans." All of this Findlay reported in a shamefaced and defensive telegram of 13 January: "I deeply regret failure but have done my best." At long last Findlay was ready—almost ready—to give up on Christensen, but he remained stubbornly convinced that the man had told the truth until suborned on the fatal trip to Berlin. On Casement's present whereabouts and activities he had to report a complete blank: it was even possible that he had been on the *Mjölnir* after all.[9]

Next day Findlay resumed the whole embarrassing story in a long letter to Sir Arthur Nicolson. He confessed himself utterly baffled as to Christensen's motives and by the turn things had taken: "Conjecture is useless." He was inclined to blame Christensen's inscrutability on his low nature, and to take some comfort in the thought that at least he had not been victimized by a gentleman, whom he might have been expected to understand: "It is impossible to follow the workings of a mind absolutely unregulated by any rules of morality or intelligence, but subject to intense suspiciousness and guided by low cunning." He returned to that point later: "He is a most loathsome beast." And once more he insisted that British authorities would be wise to continue to take seriously the original threat of "expeditions" to lay mines, to run arms, and to land men in Ireland from Germany and America.[10] His credulity died very hard.

Casement had remained in Limburg, waiting news of the *Mjölnir* episode and generally out of touch. Since his "insulting" reception by the prisoners on 5 January, he had not gone back to the camp but stayed in two pleasant inexpensive rooms in the Nassauer Hof looking out on the main square of the town, a lonely man, tense and miserable. On 7 January he took young Bryan Kelly to Frankfurt, procured him a pass to Berlin, and sent him off with a letter to Richard Meyer asking that he be cleared at once for Ireland. Kelly described the Irish prisoners as a hopeless lot: they stole from each other and were despised by both the German guards and the French prisoners, who would have nothing to do with them. Next day Casement's recruiter Timothy Quinlisk confirmed Kelly's version in a session in Limburg. The other prisoners had threatened to inform on him as Casement's agent and have him hanged as a traitor on "return to England."[11] How could he expect the Germans to declare support for Ireland, Casement asked himself, "when the only *Irishmen* in Germany boast that they are English and repudiate with scorn the idea that they should fight for Ireland?" He felt "very despondent": "How lift up & unify a land that has such cowards as these to represent it?" For the exigency of the prisoners' position, soldiers under oath to Britain, prisoners of war, offered the nebulous alternative of the Irish Brigade, Casement seemed to show little sympathy and indeed little comprehension.

By the middle of January Casement had grown additionally nervous and aggrieved because he had heard nothing from Christiania or from Berlin. The Foreign Office has not even sent him word of Christensen's appearance on 5 January with Findlay's signed guarantee, the "proof" to be offered in public exposure of a criminal British "conspiracy" against him. He took the general silence to mean that there had been no attack upon the *Mjölnir* between Gothenburg and Christiansand and hence no chance to ambush the British cruisers and that Findlay had probably "at last!" penetrated Adler's role as a catspaw. He watched the papers for reference to himself. In the House of Lords Curzon had asked what was to be done about Sir Roger Casement; Lord Crewe had replied that "very sensible punishment" was due. Casement commented grimly in his diary on 13 January: "Yes." He was working now with excitement and anxiety on drafts of a document he had "long contemplated," an "open letter" to Sir Edward Grey in which he meant to review his whole case since leaving British service in June 1913. He would denounce the systematic repression of nationalist sentiment in Ireland and would bluntly charge Grey and "his despicable colleagues" with plotting his "attempted murder" or "waylaying" or "kidnapping." He would send the letter to Grey, to the embassies of other major powers, to the Pope, and to the press as a dramatization of the contemptible "moral standing" of Britain in its treatment of Irish patriots.[12] Casement was never good at easy idleness and, aside from the letter to Grey, there was little to occupy his mind now except general anxiety. "My own course is not at all clear," he understated the case in his diary on 15 January. He saw himself as having already "practically abandoned" the idea of an Irish Brigade, and that being the case he was sure the Germans would be glad to see the last of him. Count Blücher had just sent on to him an account of a question in Parliament as to whether Casement's pension had been stopped and Lord Crewe's answer that he "was not now and probably would never be in a position to draw it."[13] That case was certain, Casement judged, and he had pretty well determined to try for United States citizenship.

The tempo of life picked up at once when he returned to Berlin on 23 January. He took a room at the Esplanade Hotel to be near Blücher and the American Consul-General Lay, whom he wished to consult about the letter to Grey and about his citizenship notion. Some immediate comfort he found in a handwritten letter of twenty-five pages, dated 1 January, from "dear old John Devoy."[14] Among Devoy's cheering notes was the fact that he had recently sent on a further thousand dollars through the German Embassy. He congratulated Casement on "the splendid way in which you have done your work"—though he saluted the German "friendship" declaration rather flaccidly as "all that could be expected in the present military and naval situation."[15] Devoy divined that Casement must be lonely in Berlin not knowing the language, "but you may have time to learn it before you leave." The clear-headed old Fenian commanded Casement not to send the Irish Brigade ("if you get one," he noted cautiously) to Egypt: "*Fighting for the Turks* would be a fatal cry in Ireland. The proper place for an Irish Brigade is *in front of* the English." Finally Devoy assured him that his cranky sister Nina was being "advised and supplied" in his absence, and Casement thought of her with gratitude and compassion: "poor, desolate, lonely old girl, surrounded by sneers, jibes and hatred".[c]

It must have been about this time that Casement heard also from his closest friend in America, Joe McGarrity: a long letter put together over five weeks between 30 November and 6 January, full of strong feeling phrased with engaging illiteracy. McGarrity saluted him as "my *brave brave* man," told of the cheers that sounded at a local

---

[c]It is not clear whether she had yet reached the United States where she came to settle about this time, though Casement's diary comment sounds as if she were still in England or Ireland. German diary, 24 January 1915. NLI 1689–90.

Irish gathering when his arrival in Germany was first announced, and described the iconography of a mass meeting in celebration of Irish-German amity:

> It was a wonderful meeting every seat in the Academy filled and hundreds turned away when the first speaker finished the curtan was drawn aside and a company of German Uhlans and a company of Volunteers were revealed to the audience in a Tablo the two officers in charge clasping hands beneath the entwined flags of Germany and Ireland.

"The house," of course, "went wild."[16]

In Berlin Casement learned that Bryan Kelly and Professor Macran had got off for Ireland and presumably they would deliver his personal messages. Von Wedel also gave him the list of Irish internees and invited him to choose about a score of them to be freed. But the major development during his absence had been Adler's delivery of the Findlay guarantee, and Casement was at once exhilarated by the coup and outraged at the way the Germans had handled it—taking over the document and holding it for nearly three weeks without saying a word of the matter to Casement who had been waiting tensely for just this news. He described the action, "very discreditable" to the German Foreign Office, in his diary entry of 24 January: "They have wilfully kept me in ignorance of a fact of supreme importance to myself and the cause of Ireland and have taken possession of a document they have no more right to than to my purse!" It was a high-handedness he never forgave. Richard Meyer had called on him at noon on Saturday, 23 January, giving him the story in outline, and promised to "show" him the document—as Casement noted with an ironical exclamation mark. At 5:30 he had gone to von Wedel and they were joined by Meyer who brought three bound volumes of official papers which Casement saw all had to do with himself and his mission to Germany. The critical paper, numbered and sealed with a Foreign Office escutcheon, lay in a compartment of its own. It was an undated note in Findlay's hand on stationery of the British Legation:

> On behalf of the British Government I promise that if through information given by Adler Christensen, Sir Roger Casement be captured either with or without his companions, the said Adler Christensen is to receive from the British Government the sum of £5,000 to be paid as he may desire.

Adler Christensen is also to enjoy personal immunity & to be given a passage to the United States should he desire it.

(Signed)   M. de C. Findlay

H. B. M. Minister

Casement immediately judged the paper to be "the most damning piece of evidence, I suppose, ever voluntarily given by a Government against itself!"[17]

He was particularly exasperated by the Germans' withholding his "proof" because he had been in a passion to enter the field with his public charge of a "dastardly criminal conspiracy" before the British Parliament met in February and took "the inevitable action" against him. What action he imagined is not clear: presumably a public denunciation as a traitor, at the least. In any case he told von Wedel at once that the Findlay document was his own property, that he intended to use it promptly in a public charge against Grey, and that he planned to go to Norway to lay his story in person before Norwegian authorities. Von Wedel agreed but not enthusiastically, "in a perfunctory sort of way." When von Wedel suggested that the Germans pay the expenses involved in Adler's capture of the guarantee, Casement stoutly refused, insisting that "the matter was one between me and the British Government and that Adler was my servant and I could not allow him to accept money from the German Government." He left the room excited and angry but without having demanded the paper outright. The same evening he found Christensen himself at the Continental Hotel, struggling to compose an account of the events of the past three weeks. He had been back from Norway for four days—and that, too, the Germans had not told Casement. He accepted Adler's unfinished story and added it to his Findlay "dossier."

Adler argued that it would still be possible to devise a scheme to "catch Findlay's ships." Casement only commented: "Nous verrons." He had never cared much for that part of the plot, and he had already got what he wanted most: "I have caught the British Government in flagrante delicto"; and he had done so in spite of the fumbling of "this stupid, pig-headed German Government" who now had "the bare-faced audacity to seize my proof and regard it as a 'State paper' of their wretchedly run Foreign Office!" What was their offer to pay Adler's expenses but a clumsy way of veiling an attempt to "buy" his prize exhibit against Findlay? Perhaps the German officials deserved the insults Billy Tyrrell had heaped upon them. Casement thought back to a day in November 1912 when Tyrrell was "discharging his soul in my ears" not knowing that Prince Lichnowsky, the German Ambassador, stood outside the door waiting to be announced.

The fact that Casement now left his diary unposted for nearly three weeks was an indication not only of his anger at the Germans but of his extreme nervous tension during the interval: "full of anxiety, grave disquiet, and overwhelming doubt," as he put it himself when he wrote out a long summary of the intervening events on 11 February.[18] He had worked himself into a state of nervous crisis over the maturing of the Findlay affair, which he interpreted as coming down to a direct confrontation between himself and the British Empire. He had not dared to force the issue with the German Foreign Office by demanding that they hand over the Findlay pledge, but he now had von Wedel's promise that it would be delivered when he asked for it. He was inclined to trust von Wedel: "He is a gentleman and a friend." Exactly what use he could make of the document no longer seemed so clear. But he decided to go ahead and put into final form the "open letter" to Sir Edward Grey that he had begun drafting at Limburg, and he struggled with that for four days, finding great difficulty in striking a balance between convincing particularity and incautious disclosure.

He now told Meyer and von Wedel of his plan to go to Norway with Christensen on Sunday, 31 January, and Meyer promised to send along three good German detectives to protect him; he also proposed a "silly scheme": Casement to offer himself as bait for a kidnapping attempt by Findlay's agents, who would then be ambushed by Meyer's detectives and delivered over to the Norwegian police. Casement rejected this land version of the *Mjölnir* scheme out of hand: he intended simply to go openly to Christiania under his own name and there to "challenge Findlay and invite the Norwegian Government to investigate the whole affair"—to force a general airing on the grounds of British violation of neutrality. This gesture, along with his open letter, he trusted to open the world's press to his account of the treachery of Britain and the suffering of Ireland.

On Sunday morning he walked alone in the snow and cold across the Tiergarten to join Adler and the detectives for the 10:33 train to Sassnitz, only to find that that train no longer connected with the mail boat to Traelleborg—which had changed its schedule owing to the presence of British submarines in the Baltic. It was now necessary to travel by a night train and sleep over at Strelsund. Casement returned to the Continental Hotel with Adler and passed the day "in grave doubt." At 6:45 Meyer hustled the party back to the station: "everything in confusion." Meyer brought a message from the Admiralty: they feared that a British submarine alerted by spies in Sassnitz might stop the mail boat in the Baltic and demand Casement's surrender. "What did I propose? I said I should go on and if this happened I'd resist and not be taken alive." Christensen and the three detectives sounded a brave echo: they, too, would "fight to the death." The party of five men reached Strelsund at midnight and Casement went to bed in his clothes at the Bahnhof, "greatly upset and wondering how best to proceed." It was not the submarines in the Baltic that he feared but the sheer size of the adversary, the British Empire, that he was about to challenge to single combat: "their power and gold and my own penniless and defenseless position." He had little money and no friends and no government to appeal to except "the one bent on destroying me." He turned restlessly till dawn contemplating "this desperate act." In the condition of melodramatic imaginings to which he had been brought by circumstances and temperament Casement saw all the eyes of Empire focused upon himself. And he felt little faith now in the motives of the Germans. Those three detectives, for example, creatures of Richard Meyer: had they come to "protect" him or would they betray him into captivity and scurry back to Berlin with his papers?

On Monday, 1 February, the party reached Sassnitz at 9:00 A.M. and Casement went to the Monopol Hotel to await the two o'clock boat. There he and Adler brooded and talked over the whole feverish situation at length. Casement burned certain papers he "feared the enemy might seize" if he were arrested. At last, seconded by Adler who had been negative from the beginning, Casement determined to abandon the assault upon England via Norway and return to Berlin. He informed the three detectives, who looked disgusted, and wired the Foreign Office of his decision. "Spent a miserable day," he summed up.

In Berlin next afternoon he went at once to explain himself to von Wedel who deprecated his fears but acquiesced peaceably enough in his quieter plan to post his letter to Grey via Holland and to issue copies to the governments represented in Berlin. He took a room again at the Continental Hotel and that evening received two calls from Meyer bearing two bits of interesting news: a German cruiser had been ready, Meyer said, to escort the mail boat from Sassnitz to Traelleborg to guard against submarine attack; and only that afternoon a pro-Irish society, Die Deutsche-Irische Gesellschaft, had been formed in Berlin with a purse of 50,000 marks "as a first contribution" to the cause of Ireland, the money to be spent as Casement thought best in the interest of his country. "Generous indeed," Casement thought; but he felt he could not accept it and still retain the independence, the Irish independence, of movement on which he had insisted throughout his mission. On reflection he concluded, however, that this was a decision that ought to be made by his friends in the United States who had, after all, paid all of the very considerable expenses of his mission thus far and were committed to underwrite him indefinitely.

Casement then returned to work on his letter to Grey. It was dated Berlin, 1 February 1915, and covered eleven folio pages. Most of it was given over to a summary in terms heavily sardonic of the course of the Findlay "plot" as supplied to him by Christensen. Casement referred first to the discussion in the House of Lords of his action, its punishment, and his pension: he would consider those questions, he promised, but he wished especially to consider "the actual punishment you sought in secret to inflict upon me," the "final proof" of which he now held.[19] He had been aware for three months of the conspiracy against him, but it had taken some time to "compel your agent" to commit himself in writing. Grey would recognize, Casement wrote, that the issue between himself and England had never been "a matter of a pension, of a reward, a decoration." As long as conscience allowed, he had "served the British Government faithfully and loyally." When he could no longer do so, he had resigned, just as he had "voluntarily resigned" his pension [d] and as he now proposed to "divest" himself of "the honours and distinctions that at various times have been conferred upon me by His Majesty's Government."

Briefly and formally Casement explained his motives in committing the "act of technical treason" which he wished to contrast with the British way of responding to his action. His general views of England, Ireland, and the war in Europe were still those he had set down on 17 September 1914 and sent to Ireland for publication; he enclosed a printed copy of that open letter. [e] Fully aware of the risks

---

[d]I.e., he had ceased to claim it after September 1914. See below pp. 395–97.

[e]The anti-recruitment "manifesto" from America. Casement misdated it here as "17 September 1915."

and sacrifices and of the potential legal consequences involved, he had come to Europe in the autumn to "make sure" that Ireland should "suffer the minimum of harm" whatever the course of the war. He had been prepared to lose "income, position and reputation" and to face charges in a legitimate court of law. He had not been prepared, however, for what Great Britain, in the person of Findlay, had offered him: "waylaying, kidnapping, suborning of dependents or knocking on the head." (Here and elsewhere Casement emphasized the threat of killing or bodily injury, an item which seems to have been an invention of Christensen's.) He now attributed directly to Grey the object that Findlay (according to Adler) had "frankly avowed": "to take my life with public indignity." His own counterplot had been designed entirely to secure evidence of the conspiracy and expose it. And Findlay with his "appetite for the incredible" had been taken in by stories "that should not have deceived a school boy." The apparatus of "bogus letters, fictitious maps and charts" he had swallowed whole.

Casement enclosed a photographic copy of Findlay's pledge to Christensen. He looked forward, he said, to returning to Findlay, in person, the money he had given Christensen—along with the key to the back door of the Legation in Christiania. In due course he would lay before Norwegian authorities his assorted evidences of Britain's criminal conspiracy carried out in a neutral country. Finally and ceremonially, he "renounced" all his British honors:

> To that Government, through you, Sir, I now beg to return the insignia of the Most Distinguished Order of St. Michael and St. George, the Coronation Medal of His Majesty King George V, and any other medal, honour or distinction conferred upon me by His Majesty's Government, of which it is possible to divest myself.

With irony that doubtless mingled triumph and trepidation he signed himself: "Your most obedient, humble servant"—plain Roger Casement.

Feeling like one who had "indeed burned his boats!"[20] Casement remained at the Continental Hotel most of the day. He was having the "splendid" typist of the Esplanade make twenty-five additional copies of his letter for circulation to embassies and newspapers. Meyer thought the letter would be in the German papers by Saturday and Casement, who anticipated a large sensation, was anxious to put himself out of reach of reporters. At the Nordenflychts' he stayed to supper and asked them to take him in until the crisis had passed. They promised him a room. On Friday he remained in the hotel again, "busy and very anxious."[21] Meyer now said that publication of the letter in Germany would be held up until after it had appeared in Rome or elsewhere and Casement agreed that this was wise. He got off three copies to correspondents in Rome, urging Father O'Gorman, for example, to give the letter all possible publicity and to try to call it to the attention of the Pope.[f] "I would love to be with you in Rome," he wrote, "but alas! I am safe no where now save where the long arm of 'Prussian despotism' is strong to shield and protect."[22] He was seeing the whole situation in intensely dramatic terms and continued very agitated. In the evening papers appeared a telegraphic account of Grey's answer to another question in the House of Commons: Casement's pension had been suspended "pending investigation into his actions against Great Britain."[23] Casement judged that his own letter should have reached Grey a few hours after he spoke. Grey had also said in the House that he did not know whether or not Casement was in Germany. "The public liar!" Casement exclaimed in his diary. He found no comfort in the recurrent attempts to explain him away as Conan Doyle had done, on grounds of decayed health; a telegraph dispatch that appeared in various papers about 5 February was an example: "It has been intimated openly since [November] that long residence in the tropics where Sir Roger has done valiant service for the British Empire, has undermined his health, mentally as well as physically."[24]

On Saturday he enclosed a copy of the Grey letter in a long letter to John Devoy and sent another copy by registered mail to Secretary Bryan of the United States Department of State. He then put the head porter of the Continental into a taxi with orders to deliver a copy by hand to each of twelve embassies in Berlin.[g] With each copy he enclosed a covering letter inviting the recipient to treat the letter to Grey as "in no sense a confidential communication." What he could have meant by another statement in these covering letters—that his action in coming to Germany had been "taken openly"—is not easy to say: he had surely tried very hard for secrecy.[25] By 8 February Casement had received courteously neutral responses from the American and Swedish Ministers promising merely to forward his

[f]O'Gorman had now returned to the Irish College.

[g]Austria-Hungary, Denmark, Greece, Italy, the Netherlands, Norway, Portugal, Roumania, Spain, Sweden, Switzerland, the United States.

long letter to their governments. But the Portuguese Minister returned his letter with a rather rude note to the effect that he had no legal right to transmit it.

Still bent on escaping the expected "press row," and the Nordenflychts having given their promised room to a friend back sick from the front, Casement wrote Mrs. Behrens to ask her to receive him in Hamburg; but she wired back asking him to wait a bit. So Casement took Christensen out to Potsdam intending to hole up in the Palast Hotel; but the manager treated him so rudely on learning that he spoke only English that he came straight back to Berlin "in despair." His mood was taut and excessive and he kept telling his troubles to his friends: Blücher, Countess Hahn, Mrs. White of the *Continental Times*. On the ninth he took Mrs. White's advice to make a temporary retreat to a "sanitorium" in the Grunewald and Meyer's advice to resume his old alias as "Mr. Hammond." Meyer promised to explain the situation to the police, but Casement feared he would "make a mess of everything" and quite possibly get him arrested. Adler went with him out to the Grunewald but then returned to stay with his friend the headwaiter at the Continental Hotel, leaving Casement to spend a "wretched evening" all alone, "a semi-prisoner . . . under a false name," expecting arrest at any moment: "I feel so lonely & abandoned," he wrote miserably, "& want only to get away from police spies & military & all the rest of it." Exactly why he was so acutely fearful of arrest (evidently by the Germans) is not at all clear. News that England had forbidden all cables from the Continent threw him into a rage that was itself a kind of relief: "My God! How much more will the world have to stand from that Bitch and Harlot of the North Sea!" The action was explained as a shield for the movement of Kitchener's army to the Continent; but Casement in his paranoiac inflation felt that he knew better: "It is much more likely that the measure is a part of their d—d conspiracy against me." The English obviously intended to prevent his charges against them from coming out, particularly in the United States, until after they had managed to stigmatise him publicly and generally as a traitor.[26]

Thursday, 11 February, found Casement in his room, "writing up my diary" (covering the period from 24 January) "and eating my heart out." He had indeed sustained a visit from an agent of the secret police who had demanded to see his "military pass." Casement possessed nothing of the kind, but luckily he still had his old police identity card for "Mr. Hammond"; he produced that and referred the agent to the Foreign Office for clarification of his status—indeed sufficiently strange. At this point he broke off his systematic German diary. More than a year later, on 17 March 1916, sick and disenchanted, he explained his reasons for doing so: "I stopped that diary when it became clear that I was being played with, fooled and used by a most selfish and unscrupulous government [the German] for its own sole petty interests. I did not wish to record the misery I felt or to say the things my heart prompted."[27]

Casement must have abandoned the Grunewald retreat as well at this time, for on 12 February he was in Berlin presiding over a gathering of foreign correspondents he had summoned to the Continental Hotel to hear the detailed story of the Findlay affair and his letter to Grey. By the twentieth he had at last made his escape to Mrs. Behrens's house in Hamburg to wait out the public furor—which proved, after all, tame and anticlimactic. The world simply refused to see how dramatic and dirty had been his treatment. "The Exposé," as Joe McGarrity put it pungently later, "has fell flat."[28]

21   An Enormous Sensation

C ASEMENT had no means of witnessing the somewhat more satisfactory agitation his letter to Grey aroused in Whitehall. It attracted annotation in four hands, including those of Nicolson and R. H. Campbell in addition to Grey's. "It is as we feared," Campbell wrote after seeing the evidence of Christensen's "double game"; but he went on reassuringly: "I doubt if any great harm can come of it. The money was promised for information leading to Casement's capture, nothing more, and is surely a perfectly legitimate thing to do."[1] The major anxiety arose over Casement's insistence that he had been directly threatened with injury or death. This the British officials simply denied as fact. Nicolson's note ran: "We most certainly never suggested or contemplated any personal harm or injury to Sir R. Casement. All we wanted was to capture him and bring him home for trial."[2] Any thought of personal attack was clearly horrifying to Grey. It was determined to send a copy of Casement's letter to Findlay with instructions that, if it became necessary to discuss the matter at all with the Norwegian Minister for Foreign Affairs, he should assure him that no move of any kind on Norwegian land or water had been contemplated against Casement. By and large the Foreign Office decided to lie low for the time and see if the issue might not flutter and die of its own accord.

Sir Arthur Nicolson drafted a covering letter of instructions to Findlay which included the following reproving paragraph:

> You will see that Christensen was playing a double game, and that his reluctance to go on at the last was, as we feared at the time, merely a ruse to obtain something from you in writing. You made a great mistake in giving it and, although there is

281

nothing really compromising in the document itself, I have no doubt that Casement and his German friends will make the most of it.[3]

But as a new telegram of 13 February had reached the Foreign Office from Findlay (who had not seen Casement's letter to Grey), Nicolson's letter was not sent and Findlay never received his reprimand. Findlay's wire said that three major papers in Christiania had received a press telegram from "the notorious [Einar] Björnson" stating "in sensational language" that Casement had issued an open letter charging Sir Edward Grey with plotting with Findlay to bribe his "faithful Norwegian servant" to murder or kidnap him and accusing Findlay of a breach of neutrality in planning to carry out the operation in Norwegian territory. Björnson's dispatch (evidently a result of Casement's press conference in Berlin) included a generally accurate translation of Findlay's guarantee to Christensen. "We have nothing to fear from publication of facts," Findlay argued, "but lies woven round them if given time to spread might be unpleasant." He asked permission to lay an outline of the case before the Norwegian Minister for Foreign Affairs, "proving" that Christensen had been "selling Casement from the beginning," that Casement was planning a "filibustering expedition to Ireland from Norway," and showing his documents in proof. (It *still* had not dawned on Findlay that the "documents" supplied by Christensen were fabrications.) Meanwhile he would try to prevent actual publication of Björnson's dispatch.[4]

Nicolson telegraphed approval next day of Findlay's making representations to the Norwegian Minister: he was to emphasize the "fact" that Casement planned to start "from *Norway*" with a group of German officers to carry out a "German landing in the United Kingdom as well as extensive mining operations against the British fleet," that no injury to Casement was ever contemplated or countenanced, that no operation against him or his "expedition" would have been conducted in Norwegian territory, and that if arrested elsewhere he would have been brought to trial in England and treated "by the ordinary course of justice."[5]

Findlay's troubled calm broke up when the full text of Casement's letter appeared in Norwegian newspapers. Seeing the letter itself for the first time he described it in his telegram of 17 February as "an extraordinary mixture of truth and falsehood." The situation called for decisive action, he felt, as the charge that he had "bribed an innocent Norwegian to betray his master" could do a great deal of harm. He asked leave to issue a formal rebuttal to the letter, covering the familiar ground under eight headings which he listed, beginning with the fundamental point that Christensen, not British officials, initiated the whole tangled double plot: "That informer came to the Legation and informed me of Casement's presence and object of his journey of his own accord." In Casement's letter Findlay heard for the first time the peculiarly rankling charge that he had given Christensen a key to the back entrance to the Legation, and he repudiated the item absolutely: "If he has key informer must have stolen it."[6]

By the twentieth Findlay had at last made an effort to verify a part of his "information" and of course had drawn a total blank: the Legation's legal adviser had interviewed the lawyer named by Christensen as having drawn up the contract for the chartered Norwegian vessels and found that the man had never heard of the matter. That night Findlay received a letter in Swedish signed on behalf of "ninety Irishmen in Scandinavia" promising to "blow me up if anything happens to Casement when he comes here."[7] The same day Nicolson had telegraphed to say it would be preferable if the whole affair could be quietly dropped, but if Findlay decided he must issue a statement then he must clear his text with the office in London.[8]

Casement's threat to come to Christiania to accuse him Findlay thought, in a letter to Nicolson, "probably bluff"; but then one could not be sure: "all these people are more or less mad." The same with the threat of bombing from the ninety "Scandinavian" Irishmen: "One never can tell with *bad* Irish," and there was no lack of dynamite "in this country of granite." If Casement did come to Norway, the local police were quite stupid enough to let him pass unnoticed, Findlay thought. To aid in case of a confrontation he asked for certain items and bits of information: photographs of Casement "(asked for in Nov.)"; information as to why he left the Consular Service ("Was it *sodomy*?"); news of his habits: "Is he generally known to be addicted to sodomy?"; any information that could be got by wire from the New York police about Adler Christensen, who had once told him that he had eluded "four of the sharpest police officers in New York." Findlay himself did not know Casement and indeed had never seen him. The ingenuousness of his statement to Nicolson seems to dispose of Casement's assumption that the British had lain in watch for him in Christiania: "I only knew him by name, & knew nothing of his politics. In fact I thought he was still Consul General somewhere." [a] Findlay was still pressing for some sort of official and public statement on the case by himself or, preferably, by Sir Edward Grey. If Grey were to speak and were to admit the reality of the written guarantee, then Findlay wanted it made clear that he had given it "deliberately with my eyes open" as his only means of "securing information of vital interest to H. M. Govt.,"and well knowing that he was "taking some risk of being thought a fool." Fool or no, he was unrepentant: "I still think it was my duty to do so.[9]

After a few days of comparative peace Findlay received on 24 February Casement's own telegram from Hamburg: he intended to come to Christiania as soon as he received promise of protection from the Norwegians and he invited Findlay to meet him face to face in the courts.[10] "The whole thing" was "an impudent attempt" to discredit him, Findlay supposed, and Casement would not have dared even to threaten it had he known that Christensen had told Findlay about "the unnatural character" of his relations with his master. [b] Findlay had not replied to Casement's wire and having turned a bit sullen toward his superiors in London he left them to decide whether any public response should be made. He thought that no one who mattered believed Casement's accusations and that in effect the whole issue was peacefully dead. Nicolson telegraphed a curt reply next day: "It is best to leave the matter quite alone."[11] On the twenty-seventh he replied to Findlay's long letter of the twenty-first which had been slower to reach him. If the Casement issue was dying a natural death, then Britain should certainly do nothing to revive it.

[a]The fact that the authorities had shown no interest in him immediately before he reached Christiania, during the several days when the *Oskar II* was detained at sea and in Stornoway harbor, seems even more conclusive. If they had been actively seeking him, that was the time for an easy arrest, and they could hardly have overlooked him on the vessel. Christensen must have spilled the beans in Christiania.

[b]Telegram to Sir Arthur Nicolson, 24 February 1915. PRO FO 95.776. Ten days earlier Casement himself had been struggling to define his relationship to Adler in quite different terms. In a letter of 14 February to Mrs. White he protested at references in the German papers and in the *Continental Times* to Christensen as his *diener* or "valet" in their texts accompanying publication of his letter to Grey. His proposed alternatives were awkward enough: "my faithful companion, follower and friend"; "follower"; "dependent"; "agent." But to call him a valet was an embarrassment not only to Adler but to his "decent, respectable Norwegian family of well educated people." NLI 13082–4.

"No notice" had been taken of the matter in England "by press or public." [c]

Still waiting to see whether his letter to Grey was to be a bombshell or a damp squib, Casement was in Berlin on 17 February when Professor Schiemann arrived with three long lost letters that had been addressed to him in America months earlier. Only now did he receive Sir Arthur Nicolson's peremptory note of 26 October 1914 inviting him to explain his anti-British open letter to Ireland of 17 September.[12] Ironically Gertrude Bannister's letter had been written on the same day as Nicolson's. It was addressed to "My dearest Scodge" and continued:

> Above all, Alanna, keep well & a brave heart—Ireland needs you & your work for her is bound to live in the long run. Never despair—you are the salt of the earth, a righteous man, & it is to you that all of us over here look for inspiration & uplifting. The mere thought of you brings a sense of greater hope & energy to many a one who is working for the good of Ireland. When you talk of dying it fills me with such dread & misery that I can't bear it.[13]

She had had a letter from Richard Morten asking for news of Casement: his good friend did not even know where he was in the world. Alice Stopford Green's letter of 3 December was also written in evident ignorance of his whereabouts. She presented herself as comprehensively prepared to serve the common cause: "Remember that if you need *anything* I am ready. It doesn't matter what you want done or where or how, I only want to be in with you. . . . I am ready anytime to do anything or go anywhere & keep my mouth shut & all I want to do is to help." She signed herself "Gougane Barra" and added a functional postscript: "I have funds in hand in case of need."[14] The effect of the three notes (even Nicolson's), speaking of

[c] 27 February 1915. PRO FO 95.776. In Dublin an Anglo-Irishwoman, Mrs. Augustine Henry, an acquaintance of Casement's, pasted in her diary a cutting of six column inches from the *Irish Times* (the voice of the Anglo-Irish establishment) of Sunday, 14 February, under the headline: "Sir Roger Casement's Story/Alleged British Plot to Murder Him." The article referred to the *Weekly Dispatch* report of that day: "Sir Roger Casement went to Berlin to treat with the Foreign Office concerning plans for the 'liberation' of Ireland, and the wild statements he had made from time to time have caused some of his friends to say that his mind has become unhinged. A sensational and impossible allegation is made against Mr. Findlay, the British Minister at Christiania." The article then summarized Casement's charges. Henry diaries. NLI 7982.

loyalties and affections so old and now so far away, must have been nearly unbearable to the homeless and loveless man in Berlin. A day later came a different but still welcome letter from Richard Meyer, enclosing a check book and a record of 8,000 marks deposited to his credit,[15] apparently the first contribution from the German-Irish Society of Berlin.

By Saturday, 20 February, Casement had reached Hamburg and was gracefully situated with several rooms to himself in Mrs. Behrens's big house overlooking the Alster. Her brother showed him about the city and in the evening the whole party attended the opera of *The Huguenots*. Hamburg appealed to Casement far more than Berlin: it was "much more picturesque and old fashioned."[16] After living in hotels for the better part of a year, he found it an acute pleasure to be in a private house. Casement slept well—except for a frightening dream that Findlay's guarantee had been lost forever. He wrote Christensen on the twenty-first to make sure that the paper was safely stowed at the Foreign Office.[17] Casement's plan now was to send Adler back to the United States as soon as his function in the Findlay affair was definitely completed and as soon as a safe passage could be found. It appears from the correspondence of these days that Casement had already either paid or promised Christensen a considerable sum of money, in the neighborhood of 5,000 marks, as a general reward for services rendered. In his letter of 21 February he instructed him to write out a receipt for 4,200 marks received from Casement between 30 October and 20 February, and in that letter and in one apparently written two days later he also mentioned the sum of 5,000 marks. The large payment to Adler also makes it pretty clear that Casement did now dip into the available "German" money, on the other hand he paid it back again out of later American funds.[18]

If the Findlay affair can be said ever to have lived, it was now effectually dead; but it did not pass without anticlimactic flutters. [d] An American paper of anti-Irish temper, the *New York World*, had published as early as 10 February a report, represented as coming from a

---

[d]The Norwegian Government had taken no notice of his letter of 4 February transmitting a copy of the letter to Grey. Equally his telegrams of 24 February to Findlay and to the Norwegian Minister of Foreign Affairs, stating his intention to carry his case to Norway as soon as he received a promise of protection, elicited no response. On 4 March, Casement sent a final stately letter to the Norwegian Minister. He took the general silence to mean that "neither the Norwegian Government nor the British Government is in a position to disprove the charge I have formally preferred against the British Minister in Norway and those he represents." He concluded in terms portentous but vague: "I, therefore, hold myself free to take such further

Noncommissioned officers of the Irish Brigade in Germany. Courtesy of the National Library of Ireland.

Luncheon party in Munich, photograph printed in the *New York Times* of 7 November 1915; T. St. John Gaffney is second from left; Roger Casement is at far right. Courtesy of the National Library of Ireland.

Berlin correspondent, charging Casement with having accepted
large sums from the German Government to foment rebellion in Ireland, hence with being simply a tool of the Germans. Having acted
independently throughout, as an Irishman, backed by American
Irish money, Casement was very properly enraged. Through von
Wedel's office he tried to identify the Berlin representative of the
World and found there was no such person. Judging that his open letter would have been delivered to Sir Edward Grey about 8 February
he leapt to the reasonable conviction that the story in the *World* was
simply a new movement in the "Findlay" plot: it was a British plant,
made in England out of guilt and fear, a typical product of the British
mills of Black Lies and Silver Bullets. On 15 March he cabled John
Quinn in New York authorizing him to "take all legal steps possible
in my behalf against *New York World* or any American paper publishing the slanders circulated from London as to my alleged financial
relations with German Government"—statements which were
"wholly false."[19] Casement had also taken counsel with his new
friend T. St. John Gaffney, the American Consul-General in
Munich. Gaffney, who was Irish-born and trained in the law, took
up the cause enthusiastically, urging him to "push the case to the bitter end" to lay bare in the United States the "rottenness" of the
British Foreign Office.[21] Gaffney wanted him to sue the *World* for
slander and demand damages of $100,000. On the twentieth Case-
ment sent Quinn a letter amplifying his cable and reviewing the
whole case: when Grey read his letter the British Foreign Office
"saw at once the dreadful hole they were in":

> They could not meet my charge. They had no defence to lay
> before the Norwegian Government. They had no explanation
> of Findlay's "guarantee" to my man, and were reduced to the
> elemental weapons of British warfare against an Irishman—the
> Black Lie and the Silver Bullet.

The story in the *World* was "an absolute lie." He had never accepted

---

steps as may be desirable to deal with this matter." The threat could hardly have been emptier.
He could not strike an enemy he could not reach, and his threat fell dead when the world refused to share his feeling of melodrama and outrage. Next day Casement wrote again to each of
the twelve embassies in Berlin to which he had sent his original letter to Grey, now enclosing
copies of his two telegrams of 24 February, and announced that in default of any answer to his
representations to Norway he "held himself free" to take his own measures—unnamed and
unnameable. NLI 13082–4.

"one cent" from the German Government, though they had offered, for example, to pay all the expenses of the Findlay affair, some six thousand marks.[e]

For Quinn Casement went on to picture his life in Germany in rather glorified terms, making an image of elegance and fame very different from his private estimates of his situation. He had never been "in hiding" in Germany but had stayed openly in major hotels, "visited by scores." He wrote his present letter, for example, as the house guest in Berlin of the Baron von Nordenflycht, German Minister to Montevideo and his "former colleague" at Rio. His own name was "a household word" throughout Germany and he was "*persona gratissima*" to every German. He was fighting off offers from "publishers, lecture agents, cinematograph companies, and so forth," and a big tobacco firm wanted to bring out a cigar bearing his name and his picture. All of these seductions he had resisted as a lone patriot Irishman, his eye fixed on his country's cause. Casement asked Quinn now to help him "flog these scoundrels" in London. Then after the war he would return to America and be a citizen of "the only land where I shall be safe!"

Within the week he wrote Quinn again, to say that he would be sending over a power of attorney to be used in his behalf against the *World*, by Quinn himself or by another American lawyer of Quinn's choice: "I should prefer you to another," Casement wrote hopefully, "as I know you and value your friendship, and I am confident of your loyal belief in the purity of my motives and honesty of my actions." He recognized that Quinn might "judge" the matter differently, however. Again he mentioned his hope of returning soon to the United States, but the case was difficult "with the Pirate Empire controlling the seas."[21] On the twenty-ninth Casement received Quinn's message cabled by agency of John Devoy: "Quinn considers legal proceedings hopeless"; but he wrote once more next day begging Quinn at least to file a notice in legal form of his intention to sue the *World* as soon as he was in a position to do so in person.[22]

Quinn still declined to take any action whatever; a month later

---

[e]NYPL. Quinn collection. Casement said nothing of the fact that he had interpreted that offer as a ruse to "buy" the original of the Findlay pledge. And whereas Casement had apparently dipped deep recently into the 8,000 marks given him by Meyer, that was private Germany money and it was still technically true that he had accepted nothing from the German government. Furthermore most of the money had gone not to himself but to Adler; and in any case Casement meant to replace the money and did so later. Still his statement to Quinn moved on rather thin ice.

Casement received in Germany a copy of Quinn's letter of 22 March to von Bernstorff which showed that his refusal to act was based not only on tactical judgment but on philosophical rejection of Casement's whole course and perhaps on some honest misunderstanding of his motives. Quinn had written: "I naturally sympathize with Sir Roger's indignation at such a statement, but it is only natural it should be made, particularly when one considers the bitterness that must have been caused in England by what they regard as his treason." (Quinn was clearly taking pleasure in affronting the German Ambassador.) That statement, Casement remarked when next he wrote to Quinn on 29 May, would have struck him as "only natural" had it been an English comment on an English libel in an English newspaper; from an American lawyer on a British libel in an American paper it struck him as far from natural. He forebore to notice at this point that the American lawyer was also a nominal "Irishman"; but he noticed that case emphatically in commenting upon Quinn's remark, "it would be no crime for Sir Roger to be paid by Germany. . . . He is acting for Germany":

> I should have thought it was abundantly clear that I was acting, not "for Germany", but for Ireland. No action of mine since I arrived in Europe has been an act for Germany—any more than, say, to cite a very notable case, Wolfe Tone acted "for France" when he tried to get French help for Ireland in a previous great Continental war. However different the circumstances may be in many respects, my action and the motives inspiring it have been the same.

"I had thought," Casement went on with anger and scorn swelling under his pen, "that every Irishman would understand, at least, that much, even if a restricted political development might not permit him to sympathize with the end in view."[23] This was Casement's lofty final word to Quinn and Quinn with his face set against everything "German" chose not to reply. His political development was certainly differently restricted than Casement's and as far as he was concerned Casement was giving aid and comfort to the enemy. He never tried again to communicate with Casement until he stood condemned to death.[f]

---

[f]After Quinn refused to act against the *World*, Casement put a friend of Gaffney's, a Philadelphia lawyer named Michael Francis Doyle, onto the case. Doyle secured a retraction of the story but no damages from the paper.

During this same interval one of Casement's intended good deeds had come to the surface at home and rebounded against him in a way of which he was luckily unaware. On 11 February Sir Matthew Nathan, Under Secretary for Ireland, filed from Dublin Castle a report enclosing a thirteen-page statement of 8 February in which Bryan A. Kelly gave a detailed account of his experiences as an internee in Germany, centering upon his association with Sir Roger Casement. Kelly had volunteered his statement at the Castle, acting presumably out of his own interpretation of political duty. He acknowledged that he owed his freedom to Casement and he had requested that his account not be used at any time as evidence against Casement. That assurance had been given him by Nathan and Augustine Birrell. "It is a pity that they promised not to use this as evidence. It might be useful one day," noted one commentator in the Foreign Office. But the scrupulous Grey, before sending the report on to be read by Lloyd George, Lord Kitchener, and the Prime Minister, marked it: "The promise must be kept & the information treated as confidential."[24]

The young man's long statement is worth reviewing with some care because it is the only circumstantial account of Casement in Germany to be found outside Casement's own writings and Robert Monteith's almost equally subjective later memoir. Kelly explained that he had studied for a year at the Sorbonne before moving on in April 1914 to Marburg where he had completed a term when war broke out in August and he was interned. He was held for short periods in Marburg, Cassel, and Berlin before being sent to the big lager for English civil prisoners at Ruhleben. There he wrote to Kuno Meyer whom he had known in Dublin and believed to be teaching in Berlin. Meyer did not reply, but on 18 December 1914 Kelly was summoned before the prison commander, confirmed his identity as Bryan A. Kelly "an Irish Nationalist," and was told that an order for release had come through. He was told to speak to nobody and to report at once to Count Georg von Wedel at the Foreign Office. Von Wedel gave him orders to confer with Sir Roger Casement, who had asked to see him.

Kelly saw Casement at the Eden Hotel at eleven o'clock next morning (19 December). "He seemed in an extreme fidget" and struck Kelly as "a very impulsive excitable man." He gave Kelly "his book" (*The Crime Against Europe*) to read while he dressed and then they talked at large: of Kerry, of the Irish language, of the Gaelic

League. Casement said he believed he could get the young man out of Germany. Then he launched into "a long invective" against England and the Empire: "England was the enemy of Europe; the ruthless betrayer of peace: Germany was the nation of the future; she was Ireland's natural friend. For himself, he had burnt his boats behind him: he was trying to save Ireland from falling with the ruins of the British Empire." The German Government, he went on, had publicly affirmed its friendship for Ireland. He himself had procured favorable treatment for the Irish prisoners, "the poor Irish fellows who had been sent to the shambles in Flanders." Now he was forming them into an Irish Brigade, to have its own uniforms, to be led by American officers, and to fight in Ireland to free their country from "the octopus grasp of England." Casement told of his visit to the front at Charleville, of his recent interview with the Imperial Chancellor, of the cordial approval of the German leaders and their resolution "to strike a blow in Ireland." Meanwhile the British lay on watch for him, knowing the menace he represented. He told of his detention and escape at Stornoway, of the British minister who had offered his man £5,000 "to do away with him." British methods, Casement said, remained "the same as in the days of the good Queen Bess." It occurred to Kelly that this man was "unhinged."

He needed help, Casement told him, Irish help. "Irish jockeys and such people" had written him from Ruhleben but he "did not care to have much to do with people of that class." He put the case to Kelly abruptly: "Will you help me?" Kelly protested that he really did not feel "cut out" for that kind of work. Casement looked disappointed but said at once that he did not intend to force the young man to do anything against his will. But at least he could see persons in Ireland whom Casement would name and assure them of Germany's greatness, her friendliness to Ireland, her certainty of success. Kelly, who had thought himself virtually freed already, was dashed to hear that Casement expected him to go to Limburg for ten days or so; but Casement assured him that he need not fear he would be forgotten while he was again behind barbed wires.

It was the evening of 5 January 1915 when Casement himself appeared in the camp and talked with the men. This was the occasion on which Casement (in his diary) said he was "insulted" and which in later accounts of some of the repatriated prisoners was amplified into a scene of general patriotic revolt and manhandling of the traitor. Kelly's account was brief and bare and tends to corroborate Casement rather than his hostile witnesses: "A crowd gathered about, and there were cheers for Redmond. One man asked: 'How much are the Germans paying you?' Sir Roger called the man a scoundrel and left the Camp." Two days later when Kelly was told to call on Casement at his hotel in Limburg, he found him despondent over the hopelessness of his "Irish" material at the camp: if he were raising a Brigade in Ireland such men were "the last he would think of." Perhaps he might yet "send for one hundred youngsters" out of the crew, but he despaired of doing anything with "the whole lot." He showed Kelly a big green flag that he had brought down from Berlin but now thought he would not give to the prisoners. On the train trip to Frankfurt where Casement was to procure him a pass back to Berlin, Casement rambled on about his career under the Foreign Office and his warnings to Grey and Tyrrell that a belligerent attitude toward Germany was "bringing England to the brink of ruin." Kelly could not believe that Casement cared much for the fate of England, and he thought that his tendency to contradict himself, to say "things which seemed strangely at variance with other utterances of his," suggested actual mental imbalance, "some nervous affection." From Frankfurt Casement turned glumly back toward Limburg and Kelly saw him no more.

In reading Bryan Kelly's narrative one is struck again by the strange air of amateurishness, of ingenuousness or even innocence, that hangs about the story of Casement in Germany—and not alone on Casement's part. Indeed young Kelly seems the most sophisticated person, Irish or German, involved in these episodes. Casement's own program is an affair of whim and happenstance: he is a captive of his own moods and he makes policy out of what falls at his feet. And the high-placed Germans—Meyer, von Wedel—also seem curiously acquiescent and naive. Why on earth should they humor Casement in this way and trust so willingly in his judgment in a case so transparently ill-considered?

But unaware of Kelly's report and British knowledge of his actions, Casement, down with influenza, used his illness as one reason for refusing the request of the American priest Father John T. Nicholson that he come back to Limburg and make another try at recruiting. The profounder reason for his reluctance he made equally clear: "I will not return to Limburg to be insulted by a handful of recreant Irishmen. I cannot meet insults from cads and cowards with insults. I can only avoid the cads and cowards." He would go to Limburg only if the men themselves demonstrated that they were eager to see him.[25]

In writing to Gertrude Bannister two weeks later, a letter that had to follow a tortuous route to England by way of Kuno Meyer in California,[g] Casement tried to strike a more affirmative note. "I am well still," he wrote, "and busy for the Poor Old Woman—I have made friends for *her* here and all are devoted to me." In fact he was "guarded and cared for like a National Treasure!" He said he had managed to send two sums of money to Nina: "100 tokens" and "10 tokens."[h] Casement's deep sadness showed through when he spoke of how often he thought of Nina and Gertrude and Elizabeth "and all the old times—like a dream now"; but he blamed his sadness not on his personal dislocation but on the general madness of war: "Some day peace will come again to the world & men's minds will be restored to sanity & they will see things aright." Finally he enclosed a copy of his bulky letter to Sir Edward Grey, asking Gertrude to send it on to Ireland. In Germany and on the Continent, he assured her untruthfully, the letter had raised an "enormous sensation."[26]

---

[g]Meyer had written on January 10 that he had been visiting Joe McGarrity in Philadelphia and had slept in Casement's old bed. He said that McGarrity's oldest child prayed for Casement every night. NLI 13073.

[h]Pounds, presumably.

22 The Long Dreary Wait

MOST of the letters between Casement and his friends in America traveled by German couriers following routes through neutral countries. Though such letters got through eventually, the process was complex and slow and delays left Casement aggrieved at what he tended to interpret as neglect. [a] Telegrams from the United States were subject to greater perils. For example the wire of 30 March 1915 from "John, New York," to "Roger Casement, Berlin" carrying the message "All letters received publications approved new york man dishonest," was intercepted in Ottawa and copies sent to the British Foreign Office and Basil Thomson of the Metropolitan Police.[b] Joe McGarrity's "bracing" letter of 2 April 1915 was one of those that reached Casement during his deep despondency of the spring. "My dear Rory," McGarrity addressed him:

> Now about your self you seem to be despondent and down cast brace up you owe it to yourself to be proof against the vile attacks of your enemies the more they attack you the more we will love and admire you. . . . do not give the dogs the satisfaction of saying the [sic] were fit to hound you down.

[a]In his *Recollections* Devoy noted the awkwardness of Casement's habit of writing at great length "in the plainest terms on large sheets of foolscap" which he sent in very large envelopes usually further swelled out with masses of paper—clippings, pamphlets, and documents of all kinds—making packages that were not easy to carry discreetly. P. 431.

[b]PRO FO 371.2557. Devoy was probably approving publication of the Findlay-Grey documents, and he was warning Casement to beware of a New York Irish journalist named Brogan who had made his way to Germany as a self-elected representative of the "cause" in which he had no real standing—one of the "butters-in," as Devoy called them, the troublesome volunteers by whom the movement was harassed. *Recollections*, pp. 442–48.

Take comfort, McGarrity advised him, in the thought that you have "written a new page of love and self sacrifice in Irish history." And he reassured Casement as to Nina's welfare in terms that indicated that she had now made her way to the United States (where she was to live out her life): "Your sister is looked after and will be so let your mind be easy on that score."[1]

Casement always tended to go to pieces when he did not have an active regimen forced upon him from without. His sick fretfulness and depression, intensifying often to a point very near hysteria during the year he had still to endure in Germany, must be attributed mainly to his loss of true function, the lack of any genuine role to play. In fact he was doing little work of any kind now. The tattered prospect of an Irish Brigade offered a bare excuse for being, but Casement's work to that end came to little more than a set of verbal flourishes. In mid-April he composed another formal "state" document: a proposal, contingent upon the establishment of the Brigade, for a new public statement to be issued by Germany, more forceful and circumstantial than that of 20 November 1914, of her official intentions toward Ireland, her concrete "Irish Policy," her support of an independent government, to take effect in the event of German supremacy at the end of the war. This memorandum he handed personally to von Wedel on 13 April and subsequently he met with Under Secretary of State Zimmerman to discuss "possible peace terms for Ireland."[2] Upon both officials he pressed the argument that such a proclamation would win friends for Germany at once and would add long-term strength to the Nationalist cause in Ireland. His document was a ragbag construction in which Casement apparently saw no incongruity in appending to large matters of state obscure provisions about an insignificant entity (the Brigade) that did not exist and showed no signs of doing so, and in which he tried to legislate a hopeful immunity from the consequences of any conceivable action by the non-existent body: legalized irresponsibility for everyone save himself—who would insist on taking his medicine like a gentleman.

Though he was doing nothing himself about the Brigade, Casement kept pressing the German Foreign Office for "support" of that cause. In a memorandum of 7 May he chided the Germans for taking the position that they would be satisfied to enroll two or three hundred men out of the 2,200 at Limburg and would thereupon announce to the world that an Irish Brigade had been "formed." That, he wrote grandly, would not "secure to the German cause that sweeping effect on public opinion, or permanent moral result hoped for." He wanted the agreement of 23–28 December published at once, the lists kept open at Limburg, and recruitment actively encouraged—having enrolled a total of two men himself.[3] Not surprisingly, von Wedel returned Casement's memorandum without comment. It seemed the thinking of a man far gone in unreality. Meanwhile from Limburg Father Nicholson reported better results than Casement's. Having never let himself be hampered by any nonsense about a priest's non-political position, he had enrolled seventeen recruits in his first sixty personal interviews, "amongst them the champion four mile runner of Ireland."[4]

Sometime about 20 April, evidently to Casement's complete surprise, a notable visitor had appeared in Berlin bringing him his first direct contact with affairs in Ireland in nearly a year. He was Joseph Mary Plunkett, the tubercular young poet and intellectual who would be a prominent and pitiable figure in the Rising to come. The I.R.B. element in the Irish Volunteers, committed to an armed insurrection, wanted their own man in Germany and Plunkett was their emissary. Knowing no German he had traveled by way of Italy where he bought a German phrase-book in Florence, through Switzerland where he procured a German passport at the Embassy in Berne, and into Germany via Basle. He traveled as "Mr. John Peters" but also used the alias of "James Malcolm" and he took the passport in his own name.[5] Plunkett had his own job to do and he carried it out apparently without asking much help from Casement. He conferred with von Wedel and with von Bethmann-Hollweg, who promised to send a shipment of arms and ammunition timed to coincide with the Rising already set for Easter 1916. Plunkett evidently did not show his whole hand to Casement (not the date of the Rising for example), but he did share a good many confidences. Only Plunkett could have told him of matters about which Casement wrote Captain Nadolny of the German General Staff on 24 August 1915: of the division in Volunteer ranks of which he rightly suspected Eoin MacNeill was ignorant; of the radical I.R.B. group—he named Plunkett, Pearse, and Thomas MacDonagh—and their revolutionary intentions; of the password, "Aisling" (pronounced "ashling"), and the secret sign, a stylized Irish cross.[6]

It was enough, surely, to suggest no utter abandonment of Casement in radical Irish councils. But his head whirled a bit with the evidence of all this mysteriousness and violence impending, and he felt hurt and dismayed to see how much real action was being planned without his advice or even his cognizance. For the time he felt more lost than ever. But he liked Plunkett, was grateful for his confidence and ignorant of his reticence, and heartened to find himself in company once more with a real Irishman. Sometimes he had felt he was the only one on earth, that the race was a deluded dream from his past.

On Casement's urging, and also in response no doubt to the Volunteers' curiosity as to the real state of the Brigade scheme, Plunkett agreed to go to Limburg and even to try his luck as an advocate. The report he sent back to Casement on 15 May was generally pessimistic. About thirty-six men now appeared to be committed to the Brigade. Casement had thought that Father Crotty should turn into a more overt recruiter, but Plunkett now agreed with the priest that to do so would bring a complete loss of the men's faith in him as a spiritual adviser. Father Nicholson had had some early successes but the downrightness of his proselytizing had cost him influence in the long run: "His arguments are taken as merely his brief and his statements of fact are frankly discredited."[7] As far as Plunkett could see the men showed little susceptibility to patriotic pleas and were moved only by self-interest. He thought the situation was hopeless unless the motives of the men could be lifted, and he and Captain H. W. Boehm,[c] the German officer in charge, joined in urging Casement to come back again and try a new appeal on grounds more emotional and idealistic.

At the same time Joe McGarrity was writing of a banquet of 110 plates, held in honor of Kuno Meyer at the Irish-American Club of Philadelphia on 7 May at which the sinking of the *Lusitania* was celebrated as an Irish victory: "The news of the sinking of the Lusitania was recd the same day so the banquet was timely the health of the captain of the submarine was the first toast drank."[8] Roger Casement was also named and cheered. The perils of the war at sea were obviously acute and McGarrity warned Casement emphatically against trying to make his way back to America as he was threatening periodically to do: "Dont dare attempt a trip here it would be suicide. Dont do it!" It happened that Raimund Weisbach,

---

[c]Boehm was used as a political agent, dealing with separatist groups in India as well as Ireland. Early in 1917 he was arrested in British waters off Falmouth and interned. Cmd. 1108.

the young German torpedo officer who slew the great liner, was the same man who was to captain the submarine that carried Casement to Ireland at Easter 1916. Fifty years later he told Dr. John de Courcy Ireland how he was ordered to fire at an unnamed target, then called aloft to view the result, seeing with amazement the huge shape going down.[d]

A week later John Devoy was also writing about the *Lusitania*, uneasy with good reason over the effect of the sinking upon American opinion, but persevering and resolute as always. He described the reaction of John Quinn, grieving and enraged: "Your friend J. Q. has gone completely wrong over the Lusitania. He says he would give his whole fortune 'to bring the miscreants to Justice.' Sir Hugh Lane was one of the victims, which probably explains that." [e] Devoy noted that "poor O'Brien Butler" who had come to New York to put on an Irish opera had likewise perished: "He was all right,[f] but he went on that vessel in spite of personal warnings." It was off Kinsale in Ireland that she went down with 1,200 lives. As to Quinn himself Devoy issued a peremptory warning: *"Don't write to him again."*

That warning was doubtless the main function of this brief letter of 21 May, for a week later Devoy was writing again at great length: thirty-nine pages.[g] This time Devoy intended to review the whole situation and to consider especially the querulous tendency of Casement's recent letters. He asked Casement to recognize the inevitability in the slowness of their communication, the awkward syncopations and time-lags that were bound to occur. Casement's letters were taking about six weeks to reach him, and whereas Devoy always answered promptly, "your next letter is always written before you receive my answer, while you are ignorant of things which would relieve your uneasiness if you knew them." Devoy had long been irritated by Casement's habit of referring to Ireland as "the Poor Old Woman" nor did he like his shorthand phrase for the Irish prisoners, "the poor friends": such piteous terms clashed with Devoy's

---

[d]Information from Dr. Ireland, who chose to withhold the story from his valuable little book *The Sea and the Easter Rising*.

[e]21 May 1915. NLI 13073. Lane was the beloved nephew of Quinn's dear friend Lady Augusta Gregory, playwright and officer of the Abbey Theatre. Like Quinn, Lane was a collector of modern paintings though less advanced in taste. He had been Quinn's guest in New York and had dined with him the evening before the sailing.

[f]That is, a loyal Irishman.

[g]The eight surviving letters from Devoy to Casement range from seven to thirty-nine pages in length and total 156 pages of handwriting.

instinctive and professional optimism in regard to the cause of Irish independence to which he had already devoted more than fifty years. Now he noted Casement's recent expressions of hopelessness and his tendency to blame his troubles on the Americans: "There are some things you seem to think easy which are entirely beyond our reach. . . . Now you seem to find fault because we have not sent more men to help you and officers to take charge. We had no idea that you wanted more men." Devoy had always been skeptical about the Brigade scheme and he reminded Casement that he had advised him not to make that his major object in Germany but to devote himself to more formal diplomacy, "the higher task for which you are eminently fitted and in which you have achieved splendid success—a success which will go down in history as a great achievement."[9] By heavily overstating his real valuation of Casement's accomplishment to date, Devoy was trying to keep him from falling into a morbidity in which he might do something silly and dangerous to the cause.[10]

As far as Devoy was concerned the movement of which he was an important officer—the heirs of the old Fenianism of the 1860s, the Clan-na-Gael in America, and the hard core of I.R.B. men within the Volunteers in Ireland—amounted quite simply to a *de facto* government, unhappily but only temporarily clandestine: in fact the only authentic Irish polity. He put the case to his desponding envoy:

> We have a system of government that has stood the test of many years and outlived many crises. It is the skeleton of an Irish Government and in the present emergency must take the place of a Provisional Government. There is no other body of men to deal with and it is able to deliver the goods. There is perfect coordination between the body at home—which is now steadily growing—and the one here. *They* control all action in Ireland: *we* control it here and you represent both in Germany.[11]

With quiet pride Devoy noted the way the American Irish had sustained the nerve that had marked their first approaches to Germany, refusing German money, insisting that they "wanted nothing but military help when the military situation should justify it." The Clan-na-Gael had more than met its financial obligations and in fact had sent "home" (as they always referred to Ireland—Devoy after forty-five years of exile) twice as much money as had been asked. He summed up Casement's own subvention to date: he had had $1,000 in his last days in New York; $2,500 as he left for Germany in October; three lots of $1,000 each in December, April, and May; a further $240 had gone to Christensen's wife in Philadelphia. Devoy refrained from remarking that Casement's mission was costing the Clan far more than they had bargained for. His letter was by no means unsympathetic and it carried its meed of praise, carefully overstated; but its unstated suggestion was that Casement needed to brace up and count his blessings and find himself less abused.

During this period it was settled that the recruits to the Brigade should be moved out of Limburg and given a more distinctive status, and on 20 May fifty men arrived at their new billet at Zossen near Berlin.[12] It was a pitiful harvest from a field of about 2,200 Irishmen and faint hopes of improving the yield were kept alive. But in fact the situation was a stalemate and depressing one. Three corporals were left behind to keep the lists open at Limburg and eventually they recruited two other men one of whom soon had a leg broken "by treachery."[13] By 9 June Father Nicholson had given up the cause and was ready to return home via Holland or Denmark. He wrote Casement in despair: "I feel that our wrestling here was not so much against present conditions as against the disintegration of the last twenty years. If it goes on there will soon be no Ireland left."[14]

The time had come when Joseph Plunkett had to return to Ireland and he and Casement went to the German General Staff to make a new appeal for arms: they asked for fifty thousand rifles. But they were told that the Germans could send nothing, "not even a pistol" at this point.[15] Casement gave Plunkett a copy of the "Treaty" of 23–28 December and a generally pessimistic message to carry home: the Volunteers should not dream of rising without the help of a German army, and the landing of an army and probably even of arms was a hopeless prospect; they should hold onto the guns they had and wait for a better day. When they parted in Berlin about 20 June, Casement said: "We shall never meet again." But Plunkett responded: "No, we *shall* meet again. I tell you I know."[16] The exchange showed clearly enough why the I.R.B. leaders were reluctant to trust Casement with their revolutionary affairs.

Casement remained wretchedly functionless and lonely in his big hotel in the big alien capital, fortunately unaware that he had the better part of a year still to wear away in Germany. From time to time in the spring and summer he stirred himnself to send an anti-British letter or article, sometimes under his own name, sometimes as "Justinian" or "an American," to Mrs. White's *Continental Times* which called itself "the only newspaper published in all Europe which tells the truth in English." He hardly dared to try to make his way back to America, and anyway Devoy had ordered him to stay in Germany as "representative" of Irish "Government." Yet he was given no work to do and the coming of Joseph Plunkett, though it had been a comfort of sorts, still suggested that the Irish leaders did not intend to manage any crucial enterprise through Casement's representation. He felt, too, a bitter kind of obligation to the pathetic little band of "Brigadiers" at Zossen whom he had led into a condition of technical treason for no purpose presently visible.

For the moment Casement found little to do but fret and maunder over trivial issues related to the Brigade. He seems to have felt that if he could generate enough words about the poor thing it would take on a kind of reality. It is hard to see how the Germans by now could have seen him as anything other than a chronic nuisance. Yet Count von Wedel, who was the man most badgered, remained apparently patient and at least outwardly gracious. As late as June Casement was still pressing the German Foreign Office to make a ceremonial announcement of the "establishment" of the Irish Brigade, preferably to be accompanied by the manifesto of a German "Irish policy." On 15 June von Wedel informed him that that matter would have to wait until the Brigade was more than a joke, or as he politely put the matter: "until the number of the Irish Brigade has increased to a point at which the Brigade before the eyes of the world will be considered as of some account, which, I hope, will be the case in the near future."[17] Casement was not silenced. Next day he filed a formal memorandum headed "Irish Brigade: Points for consideration and Steps to be now taken."

It had been settled at last that Adler Christensen was to return to the United States early in July, traveling as "Olsen." On 24 June Casement took dinner with Christensen, Captain Boehm, and another friend at his hotel. Still hoping that he might find a way to create international excitement over the Findlay affair, he had carefully kept as eventual "evidence" the 1,125 kroner (about £60) given to Adler by Findlay on 30 October, 26 November, and 7 December, together with the "Legation" key that Findlay denied having given. In dressing to go down to dinner Casement had left the envelopes containing the money and the key on a table in his room. After dinner he returned to his room and fell asleep, and he did not realize until the next morning that the two items had been stolen. He told the story only to Christensen and T. St. John Gaffney—reluctant to make an issue of the matter because he feared that Findlay and Grey would learn that he had lost part of the evidence against them. [h]

Gaffney, the American Consul-General at Munich, was turning into Casement's closest confidant in Germany. He was a lantern-jawed Limerick Irishman of Casement's own age, a loudmouth and a bore but a loyal and warmhearted friend, completely sympathetic personally and politically. [i] Gaffney and his wife were Irish Catholics and both qualified lawyers. His early schooling had been at James Joyce's Clongowes Wood College. After settling in America, Gaffney had become a friend of Theodore Roosevelt who had made him Consul at Berne in 1905. Mrs. Gaffney was a Suffragist and in her husband's consular affairs she was aggressive and officious, something of a Mrs. Proudie. Now, with the Brigade stalemated and with Adler's departure creating an end-of-an-era mood, Casement resolved to escape from Berlin for a while and go off to Munich as a guest of the Gaffneys. Newly arrived in Munich and finding a rare bit of "true, warm friendship," Casement sent Adler a sentimental farewell on 3 July:

> I cannot get your face out of my head—I thought of you all the
> time—I know what you felt—and I love you for it, you faithful,
> loving soul. I did not want to add to your grief by any show of

[h]NLI 13089. This folder contains an empty envelope marked "Key of the Back Door of the British Legation at Christiania. Handed by Mr. Findlay to Adler Christensen 6 Decr. 1914."

[i]Evelyn Grant-Duff, the Argus of Berne, thinking that British police should keep an eye out for Gaffney, supplied the Foreign Office with a colorful description in a dispatch of 1 October 1915:

Height	5 feet 10 inches
Forehead	high
Eyes	blue
Nose	medium, rather broad
Mouth	large; moustache
Chin	squarish and clean-shaven; tendency to double-chin
Colour of hair	dark brown, turning to iron grey
Complexion	fair, usual puffy subcutaneous redish type of hard drinkers
Face	fat and round; bloated
Hands	large and puffy; wears several rings with jewels
General remarks	Usually speaks in a loud voice and gesticulates a great deal with his hands. Wears pince-nez. PRO FO 371.2367.

mine. But one thing be sure of, in life and death I will never forget you and your devotion, affection and fidelity to me. Whatever comes to you in this world I pray God to bless you and help you to a good, honest, strong and manly life.

. . . .

I thought of you all the journey from Berlin yesterday—and this morning I have been thinking of you all the time. God bless you, dear faithful friend of my heart—you who are true to the death—Rest assured we meet once more—of that I feel sure.[18]

Casement's check stubs show him paying sizable sums to "A.C." during the remainder of the year—some of the money apparently intended, at least hopefully, for the relief of Nina.[19]

By letters from Munich Casement continued to agitate small questions of the Brigade—uniforms, for example. On 10 August Captain Boehm reassured him comprehensively: the grey-green uniforms with green facings and harp and shamrock insignia were arriving that day; new barracks were being provided; Brigadier Josef Zerhusen had joined the unit as interpreter.[j] The physical situation of the men seemed comfortable enough, but Casement brooded heavily over their spiritual hardship: the men must feel that he had "deceived them," he wrote von Wedel.[20] He blamed himself and blamed the American Irish for the fact that the Brigade was amounting to so little. He had repeatedly asked John Devoy to send him an American "commander" for the little troop, believing that such a person would swell enrollments and would convince the Germans that the Irish were serious about the enterprise. As usual he phrased his idea in grand terms, asking for a "man of high rank who could meet the Germans as an equal," a Colonel at least. Devoy could not make him understand that such men, West Pointers in particular, held high notions of their own dignity and would be insulted to be asked to lead (lead where?) a little group of fifty-odd "deserters."[21]

At Munich Casement found his load of guilt and frustration temporarily lightened. The Gaffneys led him to other friends. In a previous visit at the end of May an Egyptian acquaintance, Mouhamed Ali Hassan, had introduced him to an American medical man resident in Munich, Dr. Charles E. Curry, and Curry soon became a friend as intimate and even more trusted than Gaffney. It was

---

[j]NLI 13085. Zerhusen's wife was Irish.

Curry's habit to spend summers at Riederau on the Ammersee, and now in August when he saw the peace and beauty of the scene Casement engaged through Curry two comfortable rooms in a country inn at Riederau. For the first time since leaving Ireland he felt physically at peace. A visit at Riederau with the Pacha "and his wives!" whom he found "very charming" rekindled Casement's exotic scheme of "taking" the Brigade to fight in "the East,"[22] which Devoy had still not persuaded him to abandon, and for which in his general idleness and frustration he began to agitate again with much passion and little point.

But none of this basically altered Casement's sense of the hopelessness of his general situation and he kept seeking ineffectually for a way out. "I feel . . . that I cannot stay longer in Germany, idle and useless," he wrote von Wedel on 8 August. "I shall, therefore, seek to leave this country at an early date."[23] He asked for a passport that would get him into Sweden or Switzerland, thence probably to the United States. But when Richard Meyer wrote on 12 August that the passport was ready for him in Berlin, Casement wrote that the document must also allow travel to Constantinople where he expected to go at the end of September—presumably in the course of his *Drang nach osten*.[24] Quite apart from the danger and difficulty of traveling, Casement could not return to Ireland without facing certain arrest; and again apart from the danger of traveling, the Clanna-Gael did not really want him back on their hands in America. He was doing no harm in Germany and a situation might still arise in which he could do some good. Something of the tone of Clan-na-Gael feeling is suggested by a letter of this period from McGarrity to Devoy. "Let there be no room for complaint later that we handicapped him in any way," McGarrity wrote. He went on:

> Of course, he is an idealist and it is well that he is one, even if we cannot live up to his ideals. You must take into consideration his situation away from friends and getting such a keen disappointment with the "Poor Brothers" [the Brigade] . . . Don't write anything that would hurt his feelings, as of course the enemy [England] would be delighted to see a break. My feeling is that he should be allowed sufficient to move in certain circles necessary to carry on the work to which he is assigned.[25]

Perhaps fortunately, this condescending kindness was inaudible to Casement, and it did not provide him with what he needed: a function in Germany, a genuine role to play to fill his vacuum and relieve his essential disorientation. In a despondent letter of 2 September to Captain Boehm he claimed that he had had no direct word from his American friends since May: he did not even know whether Father Nicholson had got home safely.[26] A week earlier he had been startled to hear from Boehm that a mysterious messenger, "a lady," named "Miss B.," was being sent from Berlin to Ireland to carry and collect information: Casement was asked to come to Berlin to confer, or to send Captain Nadolny a list of persons to see and points to be explored.[27] He was furious at this evidence of important plans being made without consulting him and presented to him at the last moment as a virtual *fait accompli*, and when he wrote to Nadolny next day, he vowed that he would not come to Berlin unless officially invited by the German General Staff. But then he went right ahead and listed some of the arcane matters he had apparently picked up from Joseph Plunkett in the spring.[28]

"As for myself," Casement told Boehm, "I am only anxious to get away somewhere and try to do something to end this intolerable strain of waiting in idleness." He could not bear the thought of going back to Berlin, with no plan and no prospect, merely to wait about in more pretentious and expensive circumstances. It was the strain of his empty life that kept his mind running on his mad scheme to take the Brigade to fight in the East; to have faced the absurdity of the idea would have been to confront the fact that really nothing at all was visible ahead: "If I could go to Turkey I should go and take the handful of men with me if they were willing. If not I should (and probably shall) go alone; because I cannot bear any longer the life I have been forced to live now for so many months."[29] Stories had begun to circulate of surliness and general rowdiness among the men at Zossen and Casement blamed that behavior on the same idleness that was driving him distracted. So he kept writing to urge that the soldiers be used in "Turkey" or "Egypt" or elsewhere in "the East." He had gone so far as to offer "the command" of "the Brigade" in "the Dardanelles" to the only American military man who had come under his eye, a correspondent of the *Chicago Tribune* named Henry J. Reilly who was said to have been a Captain in the United States Army. But on 5 September Reilly wrote with many flourishes to decline the honor: he had decided to go back home to head a new National Defense Department of his paper; that way he could do more good in the world—his only aim.[30] Casement went on dully hoping for at least one "commanding officer" from the United States.

By 24 September Casement had returned to Berlin and was setting down a financial accounting for Devoy and McGarrity. His record accorded with Devoy's except that it appeared to him that one of the lots of $1,000 that had been handed to von Papen in cash to be tele-graphed to Germany had failed to arrive or at least to be credited to his account by the time he wrote. He acknowledged as personal obli-gations the $240 paid to Christensen's wife and the £100 paid to his own sister Nina.[k] He promised to supply a detailed accounting of all his expenditures since reaching Germany, and indeed he undertook to repay "so far as it lies or may hereafter lie in my power to do" all of his personal expenditures and in fact the entire sum his mission had cost the Clan-na-Gael.[31] He made similar promises in other letters to Devoy and McGarrity both of whom told him to forget such scruples. McGarrity wrote on 25 September, bearing in mind that Casement had reported as long ago as 6 April that he had reluctantly dipped into the fund of 8,000 marks supplied by Meyer and other German friends in February (the money going principally to Adler): "I trust the money necessary for your wants has been recd by you J.D. tells me he has sent two thousand since July 15 or there-abouts." On the notion of eventual refunding McGarrity was em-phatic: "you indeed make all concerned feel bad to talk of such a thing the money you received was for doing Irelands work."[32] No-body who knew Casement well ever charged him with personal in-dulgence; his life was austere and self-denying and his extravagances took the form of generosity to others. The Clan men recognized this, but it remained a hard fact that Casement's mission was costing heav-ily and producing little at a time when they were straining every nerve to raise money for the cause "at home"—in Ireland. McGarrity had put the case to Devoy on August 1: "There is only one test of sincerity now 'SPOT'."[33] To Casement he expressed the harried quality of his life: "I should be as all men engaged in this work should be a Batchelor." A bachelor could marry Ireland, as Devoy had done.

McGarrity's letter of 25 September brought the first definite news of Adler Christensen's arrival:

> Your friend got here safely and delivered to me some of

---

[k]This must have been the "100 tokens" mentioned in his letter to Gertrude. See above, p. 293.

Findlay's souvenirs. Brave boy but fool hardy we have placed him in a good job and he likes it and is grateful he would as he says die for you. His personal troubles I will not mention as he made a confident of me and the matter rests there.

Christensen's "personal troubles" were murky and complex like everything about the man and they usually turned into trouble for other people. He was married to a woman named Sadie whom McGarrity described elsewhere both as "Indian" and "half-breed." Now he had brought back with him from Germany a girl named Margaretta or Greta whom he "married" without divorcing Sadie. He had children by both women.[1] Casement almost never referred to Christensen's "family" and it is not clear whether or not he had been privy to the ripening of the affair with Greta in Berlin.

Acting on the theory that "I shall not write much again—if ever," Casement began in late September to keep a "Diary for John Devoy." The impulse lasted only a few days but the document is valuable, in its privacy, as a record of the confusions and despondency of his mind: his melancholia, sentimentality, and dislocations of scale and judgment. When he went to Munich in early July he had thought himself determined to leave Germany, to go on from Bavaria probably to Switzerland and from there somehow, back to the United States. But then he had received a letter from the men at Zossen begging him not to desert them and he "determined," as he put it later in his notes to counsel at his trial, "to stand by them & see the long dreary wait through till the end of the war." The long dreary wait was his present situation as he saw it. He was caught in Berlin again and newly appalled at the cost, "certainly not less than £2 a day,"[34] of maintaining the pose required of him in the capital: "I have to stay in a good hotel, go about, be entertained & entertain, dress well etc. etc. etc. in order to keep up the character attributed to me." Accompanying the Germans' refusal to send arms to Ireland in June had come their refusal on 15 July to declare the Brigade or to announce an "Irish Policy" and that had seemed to Casement to mark a point of "final failure" and a point at which he had had to consider his mission essentially "at an end." Devoy would hear something of these matters directly from Christensen ("Olsen"). Now it behooved him, he thought, as long as he was only marking time anyway, to

[1]Greta, who was the daughter of a banker in Berlin, left Christensen and went back to her parents about 1920. McGarrity kept in touch with Sadie and helped her with gifts from time to time. NLI. McGarrity papers.

mark it in Riederau where he could live for a few pennies a day. His gloom was very nearly absolute: "I am sick at heart—sick to death at heart." He felt that he did not "wish to live beyond this war," for he foresaw only "personal shame, degradation & scorn from those whose opinion I value much." For his failure he did not blame Devoy or anyone else (for the moment) but himself: "I simply tried too much—flew too high & fell. Still, for Ireland's sake it was worth trying—who never aspires, never dares." He took some pride in his reckoning that England had put a higher price on his head than on that of any other rebel save Prince Charles Edward of Scotland.

Casement judged his general treatment by the Germans as execrable: "again & again I got rebuffs—& so rudely administered that I got quite despondent." In the face of that rudeness he "simply withdrew." He still found the German "civil element" a tolerable breed but the military men were hostile and stupid. None of the Germans had shown a sound instinct for dealing with people, especially with Irishmen: they could not be brought to understand that Irishmen needed work and discipline but also freedom, humor, affection, and a light rein. Of course the prisoners had responded in forms that could not be allowed "in a country like this"—disobeying orders, getting drunk, breaking leave. Casement's disgust with the Germans was now as absolute as his melancholy:

> They deserve nothing at our hands but contempt—we have given a great deal, made sacrifices at home & in U.S.A. & enormously helped their public cause—while they—My God! an academic utterance of bare "goodwill" to Ireland a year ago—(*and every word of that I wrote*) and since not a single *act* of public goodwill to drive home the truth or purport of the public statement.[35]

Casement was working himself into a mood in which he was lashing at everybody—at the Americans, at Devoy himself as one of them (Devoy really thought of himself as an Irishman unavoidably detained abroad since 1871). Casement had heard somehow, perhaps from Devoy himself, that some of his gloomier confidences to McGarrity had been shown to Devoy who had then read them aloud to associates as evidence of Casement's frame of mind in Germany: in the "diary" he spoke of that action in hurt tones of personal betrayal: he was grieved to hear that his "utterances of a man writing as he believed to a near friend on things that greatly worried him &

were almost in the nature of a confessional act" had been so callously exposed. He spread his revulsion broadcast: what could one expect from a country that had "shown itself a disgrace & discredit to Humanity—harbouring under the sham of a republic an assortment of the dirtiest rascals in Christendom, headed by a loud-voiced bully Roosevelt and hypocritical prig Wilson"? He completed his boat-burning: "nothing now save the direst necessity would ever induce me to set foot in America."[36]

In the privacy of his diary Casement gave a grandiose looseness to his dream of a March on Egypt: "Were I free & had I means to equip say 500 Irishmen, I'd take them there, link the green flag of Ireland with the green flag of the Prophet & with the Germans directing drive the allies into the sea & march on Egypt—as next step." [m] By contrast his prevision of revolt in Ireland, also phrased in emotive platitudes, was despairing and lacked any ebullience: "*If* anything occurs in Ireland," he wrote on 28 September. "I'll try & go to help—but I regret it as almost a crime." The idea of an insurrection was simply "hopeless—foredoomed to abject failure"; he would join such a movement "only because having counselled always resistance & reliance on ourselves I must stand with those—& fall with them—who act on that principle however futile the effort & vain the hope." One learns to discount the resonant formulae that come out of Casement's passing passionate moods; but this one happened to hit the mark not yet visible: it defined his true attitude to the Rising and described his own melodramatic and pitiful part in it. But it was precisely the kind of talk calculated to enrage Devoy—without shaking him, for Devoy never doubted for a moment that the independence of Ireland was a historical necessity, a coming fact. It is easy to see why he wanted Casement kept away from Ireland on Easter 1916.

---

[m]"Devoy diary," 28 September 1915. NLI 13085. Devoy wrote Laurence de Lacy on 20 July 1916: "*To impress the world by sending sixty men to a place where they could do nothing. We had told him nearly a year before that we could not consent to this, but he took no notice. He was obsessed with the idea that he was a wonderful leader, and that nothing could be done without him. His letters always kept me awake on the night of the day I got them.*" *Devoy's Post Bag*, ii: 504.

23   You Among Strangers

AS Casement was putting together his brief sad diary in Berlin, doom was gathering for his good friend Gaffney in Munich. The American Consul's difficulties had been accumulating for at least a year. He had been sent to England in the fall of 1914 to report as a neutral on the treatment of German prisoners and he was said to have offended Englishmen and embarrassed Americans by loud pro-German remarks and threats to "show England up."[1] In Germany he had made himself an open critic of Woodrow Wilson's foreign policy and had been warned frequently by his service for indiscretions of various kinds. In the conduct of his consulate, where he was supposed to represent both England and America in conditions of war, both he and Mrs. Gaffney acquired a reputation for general rudeness to citizens of both countries. Or so said the *New York Herald* which was clearly out to get Gaffney. The *Herald* also charged on 25 September that Daniel A. Spellissy, a New York lawyer and treasurer of the American Committee of the Irish National Volunteers, had sent letters to Gaffney via the Austro-Hungarian Consulate in New York—apparently in order to prevent their coming under the scrutiny of the State Department in either the United States or Germany. Next day the *Herald* noted with evident satisfaction that Gaffney's dismissal was "under discussion" in Washington.

In a letter to the British Foreign Office on 28 August the vigilant Evelyn Grant-Duff of Berne had called attention to an account in the *Munich Neueste Nachrichten* of the preceding day of a dinner party given by Gaffney in honor of George B. McClellan, former mayor of New York City, with Sir Roger Casement listed among the guests. "I have already drawn attention to Mr. Gaffney's Anglophobe opinions," Grant-Duff reminded his superiors.[2] On 27 September the *Herald* made much of this occasion and turned the whole emphasis upon the association of Gaffney and Casement. "Gaffney Friend of 'Irish Traitor' Is New Charge," ran the headline: "Accused of Entertaining Sir Roger Casement, Who Went Over to the Germans." In the text Casement was identified as "the Irish Benedict Arnold, who deserted the British service" and his recent career misrepresented as follows:

> Sir Roger Casement, it will be remembered was in the United States at the outset of the war as an agent of the German government to win over Irish nationalists to the Kaiser's cause on the theory that Ireland stood the best chance to win freedom through a German victory over England. . . . In Germany Sir Roger Casement has served as the tool of the Kaiser's government to promote this German-Irish movement, which sought to stir Ireland into open revolt against England.

On 28 September the *Herald* carried another hopeful headline: "To Oust Gaffney from Consulate, Belief in Capital," and the following day announced victory: "St. John Gaffney Directed by Cable to Resign Office." On 1 October Sir Cecil Spring-Rice, the British Ambassador in Washington, telegraphed his Foreign Office of Gaffney's dismissal and of his own anxiety: "I fear he will do much mischief here."[3] On the same day Grant-Duff submitted his colorful description of Gaffney and his dark warning: "As he may possibly proceed to the United States via Great Britain I think it may be useful for the police to be in possession of his description."[4]

When Gaffney's dismissal notice arrived late in September, Casement was in Berlin and he remained there during much of October and the whole of November. He was in Munich again late in October, however, and then he must have heard most of the story and taken bitter counsel with Gaffney. But it was from Berlin that he wrote Gaffney on 1 November, after reading in an American newspaper of the part his own contaminating society had played in his friend's disaster: "you are charged . . . with having given a dinner in my honour at which anti-British speeches were made." He denounced the story as "a deliberate lie": Gaffney had given him no dinner and no speeches of any kind had been made on occasions when he had been Gaffney's guest. He had never found the Consul careless of his duty or "forgetful of the standing" of his country.

Gaffney had been guilty only of an Irishman's kind of hospitality: "An Irishman does not turn his back upon a man because he is assailed with calumny and persecuted by the strong; and in showing me courtesy and kindness you revealed yourself as an Irish gentleman. I know no higher honour than to be worthy of that designation."[5] It is not clear just when Gaffney left Germany or whether Casement was present at the scene, but he had evidently gone by the middle of November and Casement had shed real tears in his warmhearted way, for he wrote another friend on 17 November: "I wept at Gaffney's departure—a true, staunch friend—and a faithful Irishman. I shall not forget his loyalty to me."[6] Casement and Gaffney were still to see a good deal of each other, however.

Latter stages of the Gaffney affair had coincided with an event small in itself but full of consequences for Casement: the coming of "Captain" Robert Monteith to serve as executive officer of the Irish Brigade at Zossen. Monteith was a burly, able, resourceful Irishman who had fought for the British in the Boer War and been wounded twice. In 1911–13 he had been a supporter of James Larkin and James Connolly in the bitter labor strife in Dublin, and when the first Volunteer units were formed, he was elected Captain of a company in Dublin. Having been dismissed by the British from his post as an ordnance storekeeper and "deported" under the Defense of the Realm Act he moved to Limerick as a Volunteer organizer. When word came that officers were wanted for "Casement's Brigade" in Germany, he offered himself and was chosen. He traveled under cover of "emigration" to the United States and this meant that he had to cross the Atlantic twice to get to Germany. Monteith reached New York on 9 September 1915, settled his wife and two daughters in the city, and set about arranging the trip to Germany.

Monteith told his story in a careless, energetic, emotional book called *Casement's Last Adventure*,[a] in which he is so parsimonious with dates that it is hard to follow his movements with real precision. He apparently spent two to three weeks in New York during which his mentor and confidant was John Devoy, who arranged his passage to Copenhagen as a stowaway in the keeping of Adler Christensen. Hiding under Christensen's bunk and in empty cabins Monteith survived a wretchedly uncomfortable crossing that was reminiscent of Casement's own voyage. On the eighth day at sea the vessel was halted by a British cruiser, taken by a prize crew into Kirkwall in the

---

[a]Published first in Chicago in 1932 and then in Dublin in a revised edition in 1953.

Orkney Islands, searched, and detained for five days. Monteith avoided notice by moving from one empty cabin to another behind the searchers. When they finally reached Christiania, Monteith was induced to leave the ship by a scare story of Christensen's which he later found to be a lie: Adler simply wanted a chance to visit his family in Moss.[7] At last the two made their way to Copenhagen and on to Berlin. Casement's Notes to Counsel give 20 October as the approximate date of Monteith's arrival in Germany.[8]

Monteith's orders in Ireland had sounded simple: "to report to Roger Casement and follow out his instructions." But at Casement's hotel he was told that he was now "living" in Munich. Monteith's coming had been awaited by the Foreign Office, however, and Meyer and von Wedel gave him courteous treatment. It was true, von Wedel said, that Casement was in Munich and he was reported to be ill: "he was prone to take too little care of himself."[9] Monteith had already wired Casement of his arrival and in his reply Casement asked him to come to Munich: he himself was "not fit to travel." Early one morning "at the end of October, 1915"[b] Monteith got Casement out of bed in his Munich hotel. He described his meeting with "the Chief," as he liked to call him, as "the proudest moment in my life." He continued ecstatically: "Here was a man who had made, and was still making history; the man who had walked through savage Africa armed only with a walking stick, whose written word had shaken the throne of Leopold II of Belgium, a man who had saved millions of lives in the Congo and Putumayo."[10] It is not easy to go on trusting a man who has once written like that; but one discovers that Monteith does not ordinarily falsify actual events: what he distorts is color, shading.

Casement, it turned out, was not so much ill as "recuperating" from illness. Monteith recorded his first impressions: "His deeply tanned face and lithe, wiry figure seemed strangely out of place with his surroundings. I noticed his movements were sinuous and panther-like, bringing to my mind the rolling veldt and trackless forests of Africa."[c] A few pages later Monteith gave a systematic description which must be quoted at full length and read with due allowance for style:

---

[b]*Casement's Last Adventure*, p. 89. This is the first "date" supplied by Monteith since that of 9 September.

[c]Ibid. p. 80. He did after all know the rolling veldt though not much, I think, of the trackless forests.

At this time Casement was fifty-one years of age. He stood about six feet two inches high and was of striking appearance. He was straight as a ramrod, deeply tanned by tropical suns, and his black hair and beard were touched with silver. Vigorous in every fibre of his body, if ever a man looked a knight, Roger Casement did. One would unconsciously associate shining armour with this resolute, courtly champion of the oppressed. I have known no eyes more beautiful than Casement's. In his case they were truly the windows of his soul. Blazing when he spoke of man's inhumanity to man; soft and wistful when pleading the cause so dear to his heart; mournful when telling the story of Ireland's centuries old martyrdom. Eyes that seemed to search the heart and read one's very soul. At times when speaking of Irish children, particularly those of the west, whom he knew so well, his smile would transfigure his face in a manner that defied power of description. A man is indeed fortunate, who can say that he has clasped Casement's hand, and received his kindly smile of welcome.[11]

On acquaintance Monteith found Casement reserved, at times downright shy. He could hardly bear the sight of hunger or want and would give his last penny in charity. His own living was frugal and good things to eat and drink appeared on his table only when he had guests. He struck Monteith as "deeply religious, with decided leanings toward the Catholic Church": he kept Thomas à Kempis on his bedside table and he told Monteith of his secret baptism in Wales as a child. He seemed a soul out of its element in European civilization, appalled by the pettiness, greed, and unscrupulousness of men and of governments, and horrified by the terrible destructiveness of the war—sin gone systematic. His mind kept returning, in despair and love, to the grand beauty of Africa and the honorable simplicity of the black men.

In their first conversation in the hotel room Monteith found Casement cordial but deeply depressed at the course of the war and what he called the "failure" of his mission. He had "stopped recruiting" for the Brigade, he said, when he lost all hope of a German victory at sea. Monteith immediately urged a new effort and Casement agreed to let him try his hand. Casement warmed to the new man at once, both as a personality and as a sign that his enterprise had not been utterly abandoned by the Irishmen: Monteith brought him a new access to energy and a means to brighter spirits at least for a time. By lunch time it had occurred to Casement that he was well enough to take up his bed and walk: they traveled back to Berlin by the night train and the following morning Casement arranged through the War Office for Monteith to resume recruiting at Limburg. Next day the two men went down to Zossen where the fifty Irishmen formed a queer enclave in the immense training ground of a quarter of a million German troops. Casement made a little speech and introduced the new commander, sent from home. Monteith was touched by his evident "love" for the men, his air of paternal protectiveness. Monteith spoke to the men briefly and inspirationally, then inspected the Brigade's arrangements. The men appeared well fed, well housed, and quite natty in their new uniforms of a design adapted by Casement from a German infantryman's outfit.

But Monteith's first task lay with the unconverted, and after a couple of days' rest in Berlin he went on to Limburg in early November, taking along three sergeants and the interpreter Zerhusen from Zossen. Monteith showed himself a good deal more susceptible to the beauty of the little medieval cathedral city on the Lahn than Casement left any evidence of being. His party stayed at a hotel in the town but he was given free run of the camp and an office for his interviews in which he talked to as many as fifty men in a day, with no Germans in attendance. He had nothing to offer but a chance, still necessarily undefined, "to fight for Ireland in Ireland"; but he found the men willing to talk and most of them, he said, receptive. "I had no difficulty in getting men," he wrote later, but he gave no figures.[12] Perhaps he meant only men to talk to—for there is no evidence of many converts: the Brigade never numbered more than fifty-three or fifty-four men, and Casement said later that Monteith got only one recruit.[13]

Monteith wanted also to investigate the truth of rumors current in Ireland of Casement's having been hooted and "driven out of camp" by the Irish prisoners, as several exchanged prisoners had reported on return to Britain. The *New York World*, for example, under a headline of "Casement Active in German Scheme to Recruit Irish," had printed on 27 August a story told by Corporal B. Thompson of Dublin of such treatment not only of Casement but of the American priest, Father John Nicholson. On 9 October the *World* printed a cable dispatch from London: "Germans Starved Irish who Hooted Casement's Offer," in which William Dooley said that the men who "hooted, hissed, and called him all sorts of names" had been subjected to a vengeful diet so rigorous that seventy of them had died of starvation. After wide inquiry among the men at Limburg Monteith concluded that both parts of the story were entirely false. Indeed the tale of starvation, which was told and retold against Casement, seems to have been pure fabrication, classic atrocity propaganda; but there can be no question that on 5 or 6 January (he gives both dates) Casement was given treatment by a part of his audience that was "insulting" and left him angry and crushed.[14] Monteith speaking as an old soldier who had "made the same mistake they had made"[15] (in joining the British army) apparently met no such embarrassment from the men at Limburg.

The coming of Monteith had lifted Casement's spirit only briefly, and as always when he was nervy and depressed he turned comparatively small issues into major anxieties. He brooded over the Gaffney debacle and worried constantly about money. John Devoy's letter of 22 August, though kind in general intention had carried a reprimanding effect. Devoy's chiding was at once gentle and pointed: "You, among strangers, in a foreign land and perplexed by a thousand difficulties and worries, imagined that we are failing to do things easily done, but which at the time were impossible. . . . Your letters were one long series of complaints."[16]

During this same period Casement had believed he sensed a new coolness on the part of the Foreign Office in Berlin. He thought he could trace this official temper at least in part to a series of letters on stationery of the *Gaelic American* sent to the Foreign Office by a busybody named Freeman for mysterious mischief-making purposes of his own. Freeman was a mere employee of the paper, a person of no standing in the Irish movement, yet he had taken it upon himself to undermine Casement's embassy to Germany. While still at Riederau on 15 August Casement had received from Professor Schiemann letters of 12 and 17 May and 12 July in which Freeman stated that the Irish leaders in America had lost faith in Casement and all now regretted that he had ever been "sent" to Germany.[17] Casement had sent the letters back to Schiemann with an assurance that Freeman was a nobody and could not speak for the Clan-na-Gael and certainly not for Devoy. Schiemann appeared satisfied, but it still seemed to Casement that Freeman's strange attack had had a noticeable effect. What worried him more sorely, however, was the thought that perhaps after all the man *did* speak for Devoy and thereby for the general rejection of his American friends. Characteristically Casement put the matter straight up to Devoy, telling what he knew of the story and asking for an explanation. During his unhappy November in Berlin he had not yet had the comfort of Devoy's answer of 21 November in which he expressed shock and complete surprise and denied emphatically that Freeman had had any warrant to pronounce such opinions. In a scene in the office of the *Gaelic American* Devoy had taxed Freeman with his interfering assertion that "Everybody regrets that [Casement] was sent over." Freeman had shuffled and said he meant "only a limited number"; Devoy had insisted: *"It is not true* of anyone at all." And he assured Casement that he had taken steps to reaffirm to the German authorities his status as the trusted representative of the Irish movement. [18]

Monteith writes that he was called back to Berlin early in December by word that Casement was "seriously ill."[d] Casement's illness proved to be not physical but an affair of nervous prostration and it was not yet terribly "serious." Evidently Casement had wanted to get Monteith back mainly so that he could put the affairs of the Brigade in his hands—as he now did. Monteith persuaded him to move out to the Golden Lion, a quiet village inn at Zossen, for rest and recuperation; there he remained till the end of the year, seeing Monteith nearly every day. Occasionally he joined the Brigade on their route marches, enjoyed the singing of "Clare's Dragoons" and "O'Donnell Abu," and treated all hands to refreshments at one inn or another. His physical soundness at the time is attested by Monteith's description of his way of walking. He could not be held to a marching pace but would stride out at an easy five miles an hour so that the two men would soon pull out a mile ahead of the column. He told Monteith that in Africa he would sometimes walk fifty miles a day. [19]

On 1 December Casement had received from von Wedel a letter enclosing a mysterious document: a three-page letter from Joe McGarrity, with no salutation and no signature save "M," which had been handed in at the German Legation in Copenhagen with directions that it was to go to Casement "by safe messenger." Its tenor was familiar Irish Revolutionary double-talk, though of mysterious provenance:

---

[d]*Casement's Last Adventure*, p. 87. When Monteith tried to pay his bill at the Alte Post Hotel in Limburg on 1 December he was told that military authorities were covering all his expenses. He then insisted on depositing the amount of the bill to the credit of the Red Cross.

> Ask them [the Germans] to give the old woman a chance to keep
> the children home . . . .
>
> . . . .
>
> The harvest is ripe and the reapers are there but no sythes. Our
> friends have them in abundance the attempt to deliver would
> cost so little and might mean so much. *Can* nothing be done.
>
> . . . .
>
> The landlord is in a panic and will allow no friend near her least
> the [sic] would bring her messages or help![20]

The message was less interesting to Casement than the messenger
who had brought it to Berlin: a young American Irishman named
John McGoey who explained that the penciled numbers on the back
of the letter were his "control numbers" as member of the "Irish
revolutionary Union."[21] The next day, 2 December, McGoey submitted to the Foreign Office a signed statement drafted by Casement
stipulating that he had "arrived in Germany to aid the Irish cause in
any way that might be useful," that he would join the Brigade at Zossen on the terms of the agreement of 28 December 1914, and that he
was to be held free to serve Sir Roger Casement anywhere he was
required.[22] With his usual incautious (and lucky) precipitancy
Casement had determined at once to trust the man, and he was considerably heartened to think that he now controlled a messenger he
could summon quickly to send to Ireland at a point of crisis.

Two days later Casement formally returned to von Wedel the
8,000 marks he had been given by the German friends in February
when the Findlay affair was in full career. He explained that he had
given Adler Christensen 4,000 marks (nearly $1,000) as a reward for
"his fidelity and skill in upsetting the British Minister's plans against
me."[23] The other half of the money had been spent on the Findlay
enterprise and on needs of the Brigade. Now, without consulting his
American backers, Casement returned the entire sum—though he
tried to suggest, rather elliptically, that the money might be held for
other Irish needs of the future. So far as he knew the German money
had come entirely from private subscriptions, but he had never liked
using it and he was relieved to be able again to say that he had not
accepted "German gold"—though he could no longer quite say that
he had "never touched a penny" of it.

From his room in the inn at Zossen Casement worried his vague
scheme of "taking the Brigade to the East" more intensively than

ever. Monteith had said he would go anywhere "the Chief" directed and Casement had ordered him to sound out the men at Zossen on the idea. On 9 December Casement sent Captain Nadolny of the General Staff a list of thirty-six men, plus Monteith and himself, as "Volunteers for Egypt or the East."[e] Two days later he filed, under five heads on seven pages, a formal "Memorandum Stating Some of the Reasons for Active Service of the Irish Soldiers now at Zossen," urging that the Irish, possibly supplemented by Germans, be used as a fighting unit in the Ottoman army. He recognized that their value must be mainly psychological and propagandistic. He ordered copies of his memorandum to go to Captain Nadolny, to Count von Wedel, to John Devoy, and to Halil Bey—the "prominent Turk" who called on him in Berlin in late September and spoke favorably of the scheme.[24] The men at Zossen were dispirited by the uselessness of their lot and he shared their almost frantic need for action. "As for myself," he wrote Nadolny on 11 December,

> I will only say that if I do not go on this journey and make this attempt I shall be forced to attempt some other line of action that offers less prospect of useful result than this and involves far greater danger to myself.
>
> I cannot remain longer in my present position of utter uselessness and inactivity.
>
> I have been accustomed all my life to action and the strain of this long period of hopeless idleness is more than I can longer bear.[25]

In point of fact the Germans seem to have considered the odd notion with some seriousness and not to have been merely humoring Casement. Nadolny merely put him off quietly for the moment: "the matter in question is not yet quite settled."[26]

Devoy, who always regarded the eastern scheme as mad, had not yet heard of its recrudescence and wrote of other matters on 21 November. Casement had questioned the wisdom of Nina's coming to America and Devoy now assured him that the move had been necessary and right: life had been made "positively intolerable" for her in England and Ireland after her brother began to be heard from

[e]NLI 13085. To H. J. Reilly he had written on 17 August 1915: "I have no military training, altho' I have been in fights and led lots of men in my time and have one war medal." He referred apparently to his African experience in general and his largely abortive Boer War service in particular. NLI 13085.

Germany and she was not a person to take insults tamely. For her own sake as well as Casement's the New York Irishmen were treating her as a member of one of their own families: "We'd be recreant if we felt otherwise." She was living in a boarding house kept by sisters of a priest and finding plenty of Irish women friends to visit. Casement could do as he pleased after the war about the money advanced to Nina, Devoy said; he did not expect to be on the scene himself: "If you and I are not in Ireland together I'll have been either shot or hanged, and you can settle with anyone who may be left." Devoy again dismissed Casement's talk of repaying the Clan's general outlay and said he did not wish to see the kind of detailed accounting Casement had sent; he asked only to be kept informed of sums received in Germany, and he went on in terms that did damage to his own sense of the truth: "so far as we are concerned, the money has been expended with greater benefit to our work than any we have ever paid out." A further $1,000 had been sent on 15 November and another was to go soon[27]—bringing the total to date, so far as the visible record shows, to $10,740.

A month later Devoy devoted seven pages to the roguery of Christensen who after returning from delivering Monteith in Germany had been making lying attempts to extort money from Devoy, McGarrity, and others. And his German girl friend had just produced a baby.[28] McGarrity had written in veiled terms of the same situation a few days earlier.

> . . . our hero has done certain things that has made matters very unpleasant and has made uncle John loose confidence in him no break of course had occured so far but there was ample cause for a break. While ample provisions have been made for him and every kindness and courtesy shown he appears to be criminally neglectful of his duty or he has been trying to take advantage of his friends.

McGarrity hoped matters would "come right" but he had to admit that only recollection of Christensen's "splendid service and loyalty" to Casement had stood in the way of a decisive parting.[f]

[f]16 December 1915. NLI 13073. In his *Recollections* John Devoy says that he never got around to writing the full story of how Christensen "double-crossed" the Clan-na-Gael in their coming third attempt to use him as a conductor to Germany. Some fifty Volunteers, Irish-born Clan-na-Gael members in New York, stood ready to go to Germany to join the Brigade and Christensen agreed to arrange their passage via Norway. Of the event Devoy says only that "he proved himself a trickster and a fraud, with the result that we were compelled to abandon the project and summarily dismiss him." P. 441.

Nina sent sad family news on 19 December. Gertrude Bannister had written her that her brother Eddie, the Casements' first cousin, had been wounded by a shell burst in France and brought to London with parts of his jaw blown away, his teeth knocked out, and bits of shrapnel still in his head; he was expected to be in the hospital for at least three months and the prognosis was guarded. Such images added to Casement's thickening gloom at Christmas time as he thought of his homelessness and his "failure" and the general deadliness of the war in Europe. To Antonie Meyer he wrote on 20 December of Christmas evidences, of greenery and toys, signs of old German good feeling, and of the sadness of war which had "killed Christianity in the life of nations." His mood was not far from suicidal: "I do not like to think of the future—it is all dark & hopeless & forbidding—& I think the dead are best."[29] To young Max Zehndler of Augsburg, a school boy living with his aunt and uncle who were old friends of Casement's, he wrote a week later:

> I wish very much that peace would come—it is dreadful to think
> of all the world beginning a new year with nothing but
> Death—killing and murdering wholesale and destroying all that
> makes life happy. I feel very sad and it has been the most un-
> happy Christmas I have ever spent.[30]

The very quietness of his sorrow, the toneless absence of energy, was ominous in itself. His second Christmas in Germany marked the end of a year that he could only read as disastrous, a gradual sinking for himself and his cause into a state not much above degradation.

An immediate cause of Casement's agitation and despondency was the strange half-reality of the scheme for the "Turkish Expedition" as it was now called—the idea itself being a product of the general desperateness of his situation. Casement had interpreted Captain Nadolny's note of the fourteenth saying that the matter was "not yet quite settled" to mean that it was "being arranged."[31] But then on the twenty-second he was called to the General Staff where Nadolny told him that, whereas Enver Pacha had agreed to accept the Irish soldiers, the German commander-in-chief at Baghdad had absolutely refused to be bothered with them. Nadolny promised to try to "place" the unit somewhere else in the East. "So it went on!" Casement exclaimed in despair in the notebook he prepared for St. John Gaffney before he boarded a submarine for Ireland in April. From Dresden where he had gone to spend Christmas with friends he wrote pressingly to Nadolny and back in Berlin on 5 January he went in to see him again; Nadolny told him that "everything would *surely* be arranged for the men *without fail*, to go East." Casement passed the promise to Monteith and warned him to get the men ready. All resumed waiting. Monteith had been begging the Germans for weeks, without results, to allow the men weapons for training, particularly machine guns.

Casement evidently felt enough faith in Nadolny's promise to begin to put his affairs in order, for on 7 January he wrote Mrs. Gaffney in Munich (Gaffney was in Washington) that he was about to send her a trunk full of books and a great many letters and papers that he wanted "kept safe till the end of the war (It sounds like till the end of the World!)."[32] On 14 January he advised her that he had put in a "useful" summer suit as packing and he hoped she would take that out and hang it up. His papers should stay in the trunk until he claimed them, or if "for any reason" that never happened, then they should be sent to Joe McGarrity after the war: in fact he wished everything he might finally leave in Germany to go to McGarrity.[g]

According to Monteith, Casement had come back from Dresden on 5 January looking "quite cheery." As the days passed, however, he began to look ill again, restless and haggard yet refusing to see a doctor.[33] Casement's later statement for Gaffney put the matter this way: "I got very ill at this time threatened mental collapse."[34] It fell to Monteith to see him through the first stages of the crisis and he left a colorful account of it. Summoned to the golden Lion in Zossen one morning in the middle of the month Monteith "found him prostrate; his nerves had gone to pieces and his general breakdown was complete."[35] It seemed to him the saddest sight he had ever seen. Casement showed all the signs of acute depression. He lay unmoving and seemed hardly to breathe, in his dark, overheated, overfurnished room, his face thin and grey, his forehead icy and hand hot. He waved Monteith languidly to a chair and still did not speak. At last he said in a weakened voice that he had asked Monteith to come because

[g]NLI 8605. Pasted in the front of the second volume of Casement's major German diary is a sheet of Irish Brigade stationery dated 3 January 1916 from Dresden with the following note in his hand: "In the event of my death, or when the war is over, if I am absent to be sent to

Joseph McGarrity,
5412 Springfield Avenue
Pennsylvania [sic], Pa.

To whom *all* my letters, books, papers, etc. in Germany or elsewhere are committed." NLI 1690.

he expected to die within a few days. Monteith begged to call a doctor, but Casement grew so excited that he let the question pass. After a silence Casement asked him to read to him from the contents of a letter file that lay nearby. Most of the letters had come from the United States and most were critical of his work in Germany. In a broken voice Casement rambled back through the whole of his story since leaving Ireland and then he "turned to the wall and cried."[36] After a bit he got into a dressing gown and tottered about the room "in a convulsion of grief " at his wretched failure to help Ireland toward freedom.

Finally Monteith helped him to a couch and knelt before him supporting his body, while Casement leaned his head on the younger man's shoulder and sobbed like a child. "It was a tragic thing, this great man's sorrow." Monteith wrote.[37] Monteith had seen Casement in an abyss of helplessness, but he did not falter in his respect that approached idolatry. He went on placing Casement "with Finn or Cuchulain"[38] as one whose courage like his honor was absolute. That night he saw to it that a specialist took Casement in hand and between them they got him off on 18 January to the Kuranstalt, a sanitarium near Munich. Monteith had been to him "a tower of strength," Casement later wrote Dr. Curry. "Without him I think I should have died."[39]

24   The Most Hopeless
Position a Man Was Ever In

O N 24 January Monteith sent Captain Nadolny a list of thirty-eight men who had volunteered for service on "the South East front," interpreted as Egypt or "Asia," accompanying a signed agreement that they were to serve "as a fighting unit" and were to obey the regulations of whatever force they joined. The document specified "the understanding that we will be commanded by Lieutenant R. Monteith, our present commander, or, in the event of his death, by an officer of Irish Nationality appointed by Sir Roger Casement."[1] On the same day Monteith wrote cheerfully to Casement:

> As your body is fit, you may also get your mind in the same condition, and be ready to join us as we pass through Vienna on our way to the front. I am sure we will go this time, I have made the boys sign an agreement, so I will not be troubled with backsliders as heretofore.

He closed with hope "to see you soon where the sun is warm and the skies blue."[2]

On 1 February Monteith sent to the Kuranstalt certain books and papers that Casement had asked for, but he did so reluctantly, taking the request to mean that Casement intended to "start writing again" and knowing the effect of a pen on the state of his nerves. "A spade and a garden rake would be better," he advised.[3] Two days earlier that silly woman Countess Blücher had written Casement to say that she was writing her memoirs and wanted him to put style upon them for her: "if I sent some of my notes now and again you would embellish them and put a little more force and life into them."[4] It was an extraordinary proposal to make to a bad stylist in the midst of a breakdown; but Casement answered patiently on 4 February that he would do what he could for her.

Ill and reluctant, Casement left the Kuranstalt on 16 February to travel to Berlin on a summons from St. John Gaffney, just returned from the United States and carrying with him a scheme to get Casement off to America on a Norwegian ship accompanied by a Norwegian friend of Gaffney's named Schirmer. In the upshot it was decided that he should wait for a later crossing with Schirmer, but on Gaffney's urging he entrusted to Schirmer his most precious document, the original of the Findlay guarantee, along with related papers to be given to Judge Cohalan and produced at the big Irish Race Convention called for 4–5 March at the Hotel Astor in New York. He also saw Mary McFadden, a Clan-na-Gael messenger, and turned over to her 1,750 marks as expense money. She sailed with Schirmer on the *Kristianiafjord* on 23 February, but the ship was held up at Kirkwall for two days by the British and did not reach New York until 7 March—too late for the Convention.

After about ten days in Berlin Casement returned to the Kuranstalt entirely ignorant that crucial events were being planned in Dublin and New York. It was St. Patrick's Day, 17 March, when he abruptly picked up again the German diary he had abandoned in disgust more than a year earlier when he was already convinced that the Germans intended to use him and to use Ireland for their own selfish purposes alone. Now he expected to be on the high seas very soon "on the maddest and most ill-planned" undertaking in the history of Irish revolutionary enterprises. "I go," he wrote with appropriate resonance, "because honour calls."[5] He resumed his diary, which is really only a small part of the hectic verbal record of his last weeks in Germany, "in order that some day the truth may be known, to make a little daylight for the hereafter." Vanity apart, Casement knew he was involved in an episode of history, that he was playing out the strangest of roles in a notable action the climax of which was imminent. "No man was ever in a falser position," he judged. It was typical of his fate that the crisis had come upon him when he was "sick at heart and soul, with mind and nerves threatening a complete breakdown." For months he had not dared to write Ireland or the United States his true judgment of German motives: he was quite certain the Germans read his letters. Now, viewing the Rising as doomed from the start, and seeing no way in which he could come out of it with honor or even with life, Casement pictured himself as preparing a record that could be produced after the disaster to show the necessity and the purity of the course he was about to follow—not that he knew what it was to be: he was certain only that it would be fatal and honorable.

"On or about February 5, 1916,"[6] to the surprise of the Clan-na-Gael leaders who had expected no move in the current unfavorable posture of military affairs, the courier Tommy O'Connor appeared in New York with a message for Devoy in a new cipher. The Supreme Council of the I.R.B., fearing decisive suppression by the British, had determined to seize the initiative and to begin armed action in Ireland on Easter Sunday, 23 April. (The choice of Easter for a "Rising" was hardly accidental.) A "shipload of arms" was requested to be sent to Limerick Quay between 20 and 23 April, and the rebels counted on "German help immediately after beginning action." Devoy assumed at once that the men in Dublin, knowing that the Clan treasury had already been emptied in their behalf, and that in any case it was impossible to buy and ship arms in such quantity under the eyes of the American Secret Service, obviously meant the request for arms to be directed to Germany. After a hurried consultation with his Executive Committee, Devoy made a typewritten copy of the decoded message and handed it with a covering letter next morning to von Papen; he in turn notified von Bernstorff who ordered it telegraphed to Germany.[a]

A week later Philomena Plunkett, sister of Joseph, reached New York with a duplicate of the first message, along with codes and signals to be used in communications between the arms ship and men on shore. Within a few days a German answer to the original message had been received:

> It is possible to send two or three small fishing steamers, with about ten machine guns, twenty thousand rifles, ammunition and explosives, to Fenit Pier in Tralee Bay. Irish pilots should wait north of Inishtooskert Island from before dawn of April 20, displaying at intervals three green lights. Disembarkation must be effected immediately. Let us know if this can be done.[b]

[a]For some reason the telegram was dated as late as 10 February. Cmd. 1108.

[b]This is the text as given in Devoy's *Recollection*, p. 461. It differs widely in phrasing though not essentially in purport from the presumably verbatim copy of the telegram given in Cmd.

Devoy translated the wire into the new I.R.B. code and gave it to Miss Plunkett who carried it on the next ship to Liverpool and thence to Dublin, along with the stipulation that the Supreme Council should telegraph New York if it found any objection. About a week later the Germans notified Devoy that they had decided to send a single larger merchant vessel and this message was sent to Dublin by Tommy O'Connor.

Meanwhile Devoy had got off on 16 February a much longer general letter to Berlin at the end of which he took measures, as polite as possible, to insure that Casement be held in Germany out of direct involvement in the Rising: "The R.D. [Revolutionary Directory of the Clan-na-Gael] direct me to respectfully suggest that Sir Roger Casement be informed that in case an expedition should be sent to Ireland, we wish him to remain in Germany as Ireland's accredited representative until such time as the Provisional Government may decide otherwise."[7] In public utterances, his *Recollections* of 1928 for example, Devoy was careful to treat Casement with gentleness and courtesy. Therein he was no doubt influenced by the fact that Casement was by then a canonized Irish martyr; still it seems clear that in one part of his mind Devoy remembered him with affection and respect. His private utterances took a different emphasis, however, and one that was savage enough, for there he assessed Casement by his own rigid pragmatic valuation of work done or work prevented—by which Devoy would have meant, of course, the work of revolution. On 20 July 1916, when Casement was only a martyr-elect and when one could not yet see that the Rising was to succeed by failing, Devoy was holding him largely to blame for what then seemed a bitter fiasco. Devoy's long letter to Laurence de Lacy which tries to account for the failure of the revolt contains a grieved but infuriated and very efficient decaptitation of Roger Casement. The loss of the arms ship was a serious blow, but other ships could have been sent if the men had really been "in the field." The irreversible act was the message that Casement got off on Good Friday to Eoin MacNeill leading to his fatally confusing "countermand." Devoy underscored his judgment: *"Casement did the rest."* He made it per-

---

1108, which also states that it comes in reply to a telegram of 17 February. There appear to be some gaps and imprecisions in Devoy's account, though no basic inaccuracies. The Germans had changed Limerick to Fenit on the basis of their own knowledge of the Irish coast and on the basis of a map supplied earlier by Devoy naming Fenit as the best spot for a future landing of arms. *Recollections*, p. 462.

fectly plain that his letter to Berlin on 16 February was designed to
keep Casement's hands off the Rising:

> From our experience of a year of his utter impracticability—he
> had been assuring us, till we were sick, that "there was no hope
> for the poor old woman" until the next war—we
> . . . transmitted to Berlin a request that R. be *asked to remain
> there* "to take care of Irish interests." We knew he would meddle
> in his honest but visionary way to . . . spoil things, but we did
> not dream that he would ruin everything as he has done. He
> took no notice whatever of decisions or instructions, but with-
> out quarreling pursued his own dreams.

Devoy pointed to the absurd scheme to take the Brigade "to Egypt"
as an example of Casement's deafness to instructions and of his fixa-
tion on the idea that he was "a wonderful leader" of men.[8] Casement
had been incapable of keeping counsel: he "told everything to every
fellow who called on him": he bared all his own secrets and those of
the movement to Christensen, "one of the worst crooks I ever met."
Devoy flatly denied that the Germans had betrayed the Irish movement or that Casement had been responsible for the aid that was
sent:

> It is not true that the Germans treated us badly; they did every-
> thing we asked, but they were weary of his impracticable
> dreams, and told us to deal directly with them *here*. He had no
> more to do with getting that shipload than the man in the moon.
> The request was made from Dublin, and we transmitted it from
> here.

But the thought that kept Devoy grinding his teeth three months
after the Rising was that Casement's morbid pessimism, had been
able to blunder through and lay a quelling hand on the whole enterprise. "Every note he struck was one of despair" and as Devoy saw it
Casement's merely personal despair had been able to prevail over the
energy of a whole movement.[9]

It is clear that the Germans had known of a plan for definite action
in Ireland for nearly a month before they made any move to inform
Casement. That they should have choosen to speak first to Monteith
is less striking, in view of Casement's illness and his absence from
Berlin (though he spent ten days in Berlin in February after they had

heard from Devoy of the plans for Easter) and the fact that he had left Monteith "in charge," than the long silence in a situation approaching crisis in which time was of the essence. Casement might be Ireland's "accredited representative" in Germany, but obviously nobody in Ireland, America, or Germany intended to trust him with the practical management of the German end of the Rising. For the time being, however, neither Casement nor Monteith showed any perturbation over the approach to Monteith or even over the delay in communication: they were too caught up in the excitement of the event and then by its developing complexities. In fact Casement at first interpreted the matter as simply a gun-running scheme and reacted with pure delight.[10]

On 4 or 5 March[c] Monteith was suddenly called in to the General Staff and told of the plan for a Rising at Easter, little more than six weeks hence, and the request for arms from Germany. Captain Nadolny asked for suggestions; Monteith said that his first duty must be to confer with Casement.[11] Going on to the Admiralty Monteith learned that the arms ship was to be a little steamer of 1,200 tons, a captured Wilson Liner now called the *Aud*. When asked how many rifles might be needed, Monteith named one hundred thousand— estimating the enthusiasm of the Volunteers and going on the principle of one man, one gun. But the Admiralty officials said that the ship must be the *Aud* and she could not carry nearly so many guns: they would send twenty thousand. Monteith protested vehemently but without effect. That night he wrote Casement that a "move" was on and asked him to come to Berlin to discuss details. Casement answered that he was forbidden to travel and asked Monteith to come to him instead.

At the Kuranstalt on 7 March Monteith found Casement looking better though still thin and shaky; he was allowed to be out of bed four hours a day. "My news," as Monteith remembered the meeting later, "gave him great satisfaction,"[12] and Casement immediately began to show signs of his old animation and energy. Casement put it later in his Notes to Counsel: "I jumped to life—or tried to—for there was not much jump in me."[13] They discussed the scheme from all sides as far as they understood it. It appears that Casement did not

[c]The date is not certain, but time must be allowed for the exchange of letters between Casement and Monteith that preceded their meeting at the Kuranstalt on 7 March.

yet take in the fact that a full-scale rising in Ireland was planned to coincide with the landing of the arms—or perhaps Monteith simply thought it wiser to withhold that part of the scheme. After several hours' talk they drew up a proposal which Monteith carried back to Berlin: as the means of landing the arms was crucial and no clear plan for that existed, Casement and a sergeant of the Brigade would be sent to Ireland at once by submarine with a detailed plan for the landing; this would be discussed with the men in Ireland and necessary modifications, if any, brought back to Germany by the sergeant, also by submarine (Casement to remain in Ireland?); Monteith would stay in Germany to oversee the shipping of the arms and continue training the machine gunners, with a "picked battery" of whom he would make the journey on the *Aud* to act as a covering force for the landing.[14] But this scheme was quashed summarily by the Admiralty on the grounds that they could not afford to commit a submarine for such an enterprise.

When Casement staggered back to Berlin a week later, he had no better luck in persuasion. He talked with Nadolny for a long time on 16 March and he now considered him the "biggest fool" he had encountered in a nation of fools. Not much was left of Casement's early German euphoria. Nadolny had predicted that the new German "help" would enable Ireland to dictate her own terms to England and to secure *"at least autonomy!"*[15] The "war" to be mounted in Ireland would compel England "to surrender to us!!" Casement's mind reeled in amazement and disgust. Seeing the limits of German intentions he saw the cause as lost from the outset, hopeless by definition. From now on he labored only to see that it did as little harm as possible. At the same time he saw that he must do nothing to keep the men in Ireland from receiving the German arms for which after all he had been pleading for nearly a year and a half. Henceforward his notes show the hectic intensity of his double motive: stop the Rising; secure the arms.

When Casement asked to see Devoy's latest message (that of 16 February) and it was rather reluctantly produced, he saw that the Rising was set for Easter Sunday—and that Devoy had asked not only for a hundred thousand rifles but for artillery weapons and for German officers. He saw, too, and noted in his diary with triple exclamation marks, Devoy's request that he stay behind in Germany as "accredited representative." He did not leap, as one might have expected, to suspicion or anger at Devoy; he assumed at once that

Devoy had spoken in innocent good will to himself and in innocent faith in the Germans, out of ignorance of the chicanery that seemed so patent to Casement. He brushed the idea aside with hardly a second thought. Of course, he told Nadolny immediately, it was his "obvious duty" to disregard Devoy's well-meant protective instructions: he would "have to accompany the men." Nadolny agreed with suspicious readiness: "Of course—it is impossible for you to remain behind. You must be there with them. Everything forces you to go." Casement thought the German game was crystal clear: "it is to get rid of me, him [Devoy], Ireland, the Treaty, and all their commitments [that] they now send out this shipment." They had found a way of responding to the request for help that would let them wipe out their obligations to Ireland "on the cheapest possible terms to themselves."[d]

On the personal scale a major irony of the situation, or of Casement's way of reading it, was that it had brought him quite past his original uncritical admiration of everything German and back to a kind of grudging Anglophilia. In his private record he put it in these terms: "In some ways I have acquired sympathy for the English standpoint when I contrast the individual candour, truthfulness & straightforwardness of the Englishman with the absence of these qualities in the governing classes here—or indeed in almost any section of the people."[16] The general balance of his judgment had shifted markedly and the effect was to leave himself and Ireland standing yet more hopelessly lonely and beleaguered, toys of two great national powers rather than one.

At the Admiralty on St. Patrick's Day Casement argued with three naval captains on behalf of the plan he had sent on by Monteith from Munich, and met a general rebuff: no submarine could be supplied for him and his sergeant-messenger and none could accompany the arms ship. Casement and his men would simply have to go on the *Aud;* and Captain Heydell predicted that the ship would be stopped by a British cruiser and a prize crew put on board to sail her to a British port—in which event "your only chance will be to throw the prize crew overboard." The fantasizing and sentimentalizing side of Casement's imagination went to work at once and produced

[d]"A Last Page," 17 March 1916. NLI 5244. But Devoy maintained to the end, with much justice, that the German response had been honorable, generous within the limits of their own military constraints, and but for bad luck and Casement's meddling, efficacious. See *Devoy's Post Bag*, ii: 503-06, and *Recollections*, pp. 463-65.

another of his Tom Sawyer visons: "I said we would go one better. We would try & capture the prize crew and bind them, not kill them, & take their uniforms for the Irish boys who would then become the prize crew!"[17]

Casement now decided to try a small private coup. Young John McGoey who had come from McGarrity in November had been training with the men at Zossen but was ostensibly available for a call to Casement's personal service at any time. On 19 and 28 February via letters from Monteith to Major von Baerle at the Zossen camp, Casement had asked that McGoey be detailed to him to carry a message to the United States. Both letters had gone unanswered and on 18 March Casement acted on his own, bringing McGoey in to his hotel in Berlin and briefing him carefully. He was to travel to Ireland ostensibly to arrange signals for landing the arms but actually "to seek out Tom Clarke, & through him B. Hobson" and deliver a crucial message: the promised German aid was a sham and a Rising would be suicide. Next morning Casement saw him off at 7:30 with a last blessing in Irish. McGoey carried 330 marks in Danish and German money and was accompanied by a German detective who would put him over the border into Denmark to take ship from Copenhagen to Scotland and thence to Ireland. The night before McGoey had drawn up a list of twenty-one of "the surest men to take with us from the 53 at Zossen" on the eventual arms expedition.[e] On the twenty-third Casement sent a brief nonchalant note to the Minister of War: he had withdrawn McGoey from Zossen and "despatched him on service elsewhere."[18] In the afternoon Casement went back to Zossen for the funeral of Private Patrick Holohan of the Brigade, who had died on St. Patrick's Eve and was being buried in the little local cemetery under a stone inscribed in Irish and English. Marching with Casement at the head of the column and recalling funerals of other Irish patriots, Monteith muttered to himself: "How long, O Lord, how long!" and heard Casement echo: "How long!"[19]

---

[e]He had also struggled to compose a formal farewell to his mates: "Dear Comrades   The hopes of seeing you again and, on let us trust a brighter morning for Ireland and her children, cheers me now. For on that day we will have a fuller and truerer conception of the motives that imperitavely demanded my apparently cold and feelingless departure. However I full realize that dispite my". The letter breaks off there and the sheet of Hotel Saxonia stationery on which it is written is torn half across and crumpled and looks as if it had been retrieved from a waste basket. 18 March 1916. NLI 13085.

Day by day Casement grew more and more morbidly excited and miserable. He was convinced that the Germans expected the arms ship to be captured, and indeed that that was half the logic of sending it. But he saw no way out. He told himself that he must go along as the knowing scapegoat of the enterprise: perhaps the English would be content to lay all the treason on his shoulders and let the other men go unpunished. He vowed that he would "make all clear" if he lived ("for history is history")—but indeed he saw little hope of surviving. He twisted in agony: "What am I to do? Whatever way I turn misery, failure, degradation & no way out."[20]

Looking for peace for a little writing and reflection, Casement returned to his old inn at Riederau; but he was too tense and distraught to work or think or even to rest. He went to Munich and there decided he must go back to Berlin; but a feverish attack laid him in bed in the hotel. On the twenty-sixth at the Barler Hof in Munich he composed, most of it in a single day, "A Last Word for my true friend Charles Curry," running to forty-five foolscap pages of frantic recapitulation and injunction. In the evening of 28 March he reached Berlin and summoned Monteith. Monteith seemed to agree entirely with his view that the scheme was "worse than mad": Monteith's word was "dastardly."[21] He suggested that they try to stop the German end of the plan altogether, to prevent the guns or the men from going to Ireland, but Casement argued that they must not take that responsibility when they had no knowledge of what was actually being planned in Ireland or the United States. Casement had reached one major decision, however; he would spare the men of the Brigade, find some means of keeping them in Germany—though he feared the Germans would then abandon the shipment of arms and lay all the blame upon him.

The twenty-ninth was a day of verbal storms attacking Casement's tense nerves and requiring all his courage, which was obviously extraordinary. He went first to the Admiralty, having found them franker in their dealings than the General Staff or the Foreign Office. There he was introduced to the officer, Captain Karl Spindler, who was to be in command of the arms ship, and he liked his looks: "young tall & frank—a fine young fellow."[22] He presented his case in terms of German policy: he now feared it would be a mistake to take any men with him on the *Aud*, as they would probably turn "King's Evidence" if they were captured and denounce the whole enterprise as a German plot. "They saw the gravity" and sent him off with a captain in a fast car to make his point at the General Staff. Nadolny heard him out but turned rude and angry along the way, glaring and exchanging whispers with his two aides. Casement stood up to him, demanding that the whispering be stopped and the discussion be carried on in a language he understood—English or French.

What had he meant, Nadolny suddenly demanded, by sending John McGoey to Ireland? (How did he know? Casement wondered.) It was "a gross breach of faith." Not so, Casement said ("I told him he was a liar"): McGoey had been sent to him by the Clan-na-Gael for just that purpose. Nadolny then pronounced the threat that Casement had anticipated: to cable Devoy calling everything off and blaming the collapse on Casement. When Casement said he assumed that he would be allowed the same privilege Nadolny roared: "No!" Others came and went in the room as the quarrel raged, but young Captain von Haugwitz of the Admiralty stayed by his side: "a gentleman," Casement concluded. Again and again Nadolny demanded to know if he had sent McGoey to Ireland with instructions calling off the Rising. Casement merely answered that he could not give orders to the men in Ireland, only suggestions or advice. Finally at the end of a session that had lasted two hours Nadolny said that he must promise to "turn no hand or finger" to communicate with anyone in Ireland or the United States. How could he, Casement asked, when he was a virtual prisoner with all his means of communication an open book to the Germans? Nadolny dismissed him: the Germans would settle their course "tomorrow."

That afternoon Casement saw Gaffney who took him to see his friend the American political agent of the Germans, J. E. Noeggerath. Casement now told his whole story to both men, swearing them to secrecy. He asked Noeggerath to intercede for him with the Foreign Office and Noeggerath at once telephoned to secure an appointment with Zimmerman for the next day. Casement spent a sleepless night, feverish again.

Early the following morning Robert Monteith appeared at Casement's hotel to report that von Haugwitz had come to Zossen after the quarrel of the previous day to sound him out on his willingness to take the men to Ireland over Casement's veto. Monteith had told him that he held himself entirely subject to Casement's orders. Casement assumed that the failure to suborn Monteith lay behind the telephone summons just arrived from Nadolny for a meeting at 10:30: if the ploy had worked the Germans would have ignored him thenceforward—or so he felt.[f]

Casement's interview with Nadolny turned into another slanging match, more circumstantial and hardly less acrimonious than that of the preceding day. Nadolny went over the same ground again, the same charges, the same threats. Casement pointed out that Germany was not giving what Devoy had asked for—no officers, only a few poor arms. In a rage Nadolny pronounced what Casement had supposed was the true German view of the whole matter, certainly that of the General Staff: they had no ideological interest in Ireland or her freedom; they were sending rifles solely because they hoped for a useful diversion of English forces; no revolt, no rifles. Casement retorted that he himself could promise no revolution and he hoped there would be none: it was hopeless without large military support and the Germans were offering nothing of the kind—"practically three men in a boat to invade a kingdom."[g] He denounced the scheme as "an insult to my intelligence." Yet the Germans had promoted things by their promises, he told Nadolny, to a stage where the hopeless Rising must run its course, and he must see to it that the Irish at least got such arms as were to be forthcoming. The two men parted again, no better pleased with each other.

Later in the day Casement saw von Haugwitz who apologized for going behind his back, following orders. Casement "absolved" him as "the only decent man" he had met at the General Staff: "the rest are all cads, scoundrels, or cowards." (Monteith had described von Haugwitz' evident shame and reluctance.) He also saw Noeggerath who said that Zimmermann had been sympathetic and would try to find a way to help. Casement was little comforted and spent another troubled night: "I was in despair—and my fever on me worse than

<hr />

[f]"A Last Page," 30 March 1916. NLI 5244. In his "Remarks" on *The Mystery Man of Banna Strand*, by Monteith's daughter, Florence Monteith Lynch, the former Zossen interpreter Zerhusen gave a different and more colorful version of this episode (unless indeed he was recalling a second occasion of which neither Casement nor Monteith left a record): "Monteith and I had to go the General Staff. Nadolny could speak English, therefore I had to wait in the Anteroom. When M. came out of the room he was furious and quite red in the face and told me Nadolny had tried to bribe him, offered him £1,000—if he took the men with him against Casement's decision. He had thrown his sword upon the table and thereupon Nadolny had tried to appease him." NLI 15437. Monteith wrote Zerhusen on 10 April as he was about to board a submarine for Ireland: "you are one of the two men in this country to whom I say goodbye with keen regret."

[g]Ibid. An astonishing prevision of the coming submarine party.

ever." He got up at one A.M. and began drafting a long letter to Count von Wedel summarizing his whole miserable case. He returned to bed at five for a day of illness threatened with congestion of the lungs and attended by a doctor: "so sick and utterly wretched beyond expression." Yet he went on with his long letter to von Wedel. On Saturday, 1 April, he felt stronger and he finished his letter and read it to Gaffney and Monteith. Monteith then delivered it in person to von Wedel who promised "immediate attention." In the afternoon Casement was able to totter out for a walk in the sun and tea at the Esplanade Hotel.

Sunday was spent mostly in bootless circular talk with Gaffney and Monteith. Richard Meyer called to say that he and von Wedel had discussed Casement's letter and concluded that the Foreign Office could do nothing: he would simply have to try again with the General Staff. "What *shall* I do?" Casement asked his diary. His imagination drifted again into the plot and style of melodrama. Suppose he did take the men with him—and suppose they then rose up and seized the ship and gave themselves up? "That is one thought," he mused:

> Anything to punish these scoundrels and ruffians and base, dastardly cowards. . . . My God! What curs and cowards and infamous scoundrels—and *these* are the ruffians I thought might help Ireland. English rule in Ireland has indeed been a curse—but the English*man* is a truthful man and a gentleman & his word is sure—and here no one of these men is a gentleman.[23]

Still when he saw Monteith off for Zossen before midnight, they vowed to each other that they would not let the men go, come what might. Casement went back to his hotel and wrote: "I am already a dead man—but not yet a wholly dishonoured one—despite all my mistakes. God knows they were not for self. R. C." He judged the epitaph worthy of a signature.

Casement obviously needed advice but almost more acutely he needed a sympathetic audience to whom he could pour out his sorrows for the relief of his nerves; and seeing himself as dead but not yet dishonored he was obsessed with the need to leave a record, both written and oral, that would clear his name in time to come. On Monday morning, 3 April, with the Rising only three weeks away, Casement went to see a person he described in his diary as "a certain lady in whom I could trust."[24] From the story she told in her own memoirs of the strange interview in her Berlin hotel we learn that the woman must have been Countess Blücher, the English wife of his German friend, and learn that his trust was badly misjudged. Casement described his situation to her in terms that must have been veiled and baffling: "my awful doubts and the hopeless position in which I was and the use they were trying to make of 'the others'. I did not tell her who 'the others' were." He gave her copies of his letters of 30 March and 2 April to von Wedel and wrote on the cover the name of the person to whom she was to send them (probably McGarrity) after the drama was all played out. She told him, evidently with some malicious satisfaction, "some of the stories" that had been circulated against him in Germany. "She doesn't know half of them," he commented in his diary. The hectic and furtive air she noticed in his behavior was doubtless owing in part to Casement's renewed certainty that he was being followed by German spies and stood in danger of arrest at any moment.

In Countess Blücher's memoir *An English Wife in Berlin*, early portions of which she had just been sending him to edit and improve, her account of Casement was condescending, self-exculpatory, and dishonest—evidently concerned in the main to show that she and her husband had thought little of Casement, had seen him seldom, and had tried vainly from the outset to guide him away from his wrong courses. It was all untrue. The final meeting in the hotel she presents in a light that is pitiful if not contemptible, at least half mad: he burst into her room, wept and moaned and rambled incoherently, pressed letters upon her, and left—to go, he said, to his death.[25] Her version was calculated to degrade Casement and rob him of all dignity: it was a malicious distortion of a real and pitiable distraction.

In the afternoon Captain von Haugwitz called Casement to yet another meeting at the General Staff; he promised that Captain von Huelson ("a bleary-eyed pig" to whom Casement had taken a special dislike) would not be there, yet when Casement appeared he found both men and a puzzling presentation. First they showed him a December letter of Devoy's describing "Christensen's perfidy in U.S.A." Casement read it, smiled, and said he was "perfectly aware" of the story. Were they trying to shame him into throwing in his cards? They reviewed all the work that had been done in Germany to arrange the arms shipment. Silence fell, all waiting. Finally Casement said again that he was resolved not to take the men. The argument resumed politely. He could see that both the men were acquainted with the terms of his letter to von Wedel. Then at about four o'clock Nadolny entered and brought a nastier atmosphere.

Casement really had nothing to say as to the disposition of the men, he asserted, as the agreement of December 1914 had never taken on reality: "The Irish Brigade had not materialized and therefore the agreement had not come into existence!" Casement said that the agreement held as much for one man as for five hundred or five thousand. Nadolny said he could send the soldiers to Ireland himself if they agreed; he would appeal to the men directly. Casement defied him: "Try it." They would listen and then they would ask: "Where are Sir Roger Casement and Lieutenant Monteith?" Nadolny threatened to cable the Irish Committee in the United States to order the men to go; Casement said he would demand the right to cable his own views; Nadolny said it would be refused. They could never agree, Casement told him, because they had been trained in two different systems of value. Finally at six o'clock Nadolny sullenly relented: he would put the issue up to Monteith as a military problem and he promised to abide by Monteith's judgment. "The fight had been long and exhausting," Casement wrote, "but I saw I had won."[26] He had carried his point by sheer nerve and stubbornness.

Casement had summoned Father Crotty from Limburg by telegram and he met him next morning at the station, took him to the hotel for a bath and breakfast, and then told him the whole story of the planned Rising. It was obviously coming to be a badly kept secret in Germany: Casement had given more or less full versions to Gaffney, Noeggerath, Crotty, Dr. Curry, and Countess Blücher and he was soon to confide in other random civilians with that intimate loquaciousness that Devoy found so infuriating. Father Crotty at any rate was satisfactorily "horrified" at his narrative.

In the afternoon Casement joined Monteith at the General Staff to receive instructions for the journey on the *Aud* that it was now agreed they were to make alone: they were to appear at the General Staff on the evening of Friday, 7 April; Casement would go through his ritual shave, both men would change clothes, then they would travel in a reserved railway carriage to Hamburg. Von Haugwitz was to get them about £100 in gold for which Casement would pay in marks. At Casement's request he also promised to get them some poison to use in extremity.[27] Casement dined with Father Crotty in the evening and later Gaffney came to his room and talked him to sleep which was badly needed.[h]

---

[h]At some point during the day Casement wrote a brief farewell message to Alice Stopford

On Wednesday morning Father Crotty accompanied Casement out to Zossen and heard confessions. Then Casement addressed the men briefly, obscurely and disingenuously. He and Monteith had to go away for some time, he said, trying to leave the impression that they were to be arranging matters for the expedition "to the East," and he begged their good behavior in the interval. He was afraid he was going to break down and weep. "It was dreadful, I could not tell them the truth."[28] That evening before he slept, he wrote out what he called "a long Exposé" intended for German eyes, reviewing the whole doomed scheme of the Rising as he saw it, "to impress the serious character of the thing on the German Govt." He considered the question in its "military," "political," and "moral" aspects and he covered thirty-two foolscap pages. In the morning he called in Gaffney, fixed him with his glittering eye, and read him the whole long document—"with every word of which he agrees."[29]

In the afternoon of 6 April occurred a major new flurry. An urgent letter reached Casement from von Wedel enclosing another letter addressed to Casement from Berne on 5 April by a writer who signed himself "A Friend of James Malcolm" and described himself as "a delegate by the president and supreme council of the Irish Volunteers." The heart of the message was contained in four stipulations:

(1) The Rising is fixed for the evening of next Easter Sunday.
(2) The large consignment of arms to be brought into Tralee Bay [Fenit] must arrive here not later than the dawn of Easter Monday.
(3) German officers will be necessary for the Volunteer forces. This is imperative.
(4) A German submarine will be required in Dublin harbor.[30]

The signature was baffling. The letter included the code words Casement had arranged with Joseph Plunkett in June 1915 but the writing did not appear to be Plunkett's. Yet Casement thought he

---

Green on a colored postcard showing an aerial view of the Ammersee with two points on the shore marked "I spent much time here 1915": "I don't suppose dear Woman of three cows, we shall meet again—so I send you this little line of farewell & eternal remembrance. *You* know the truth—someday it will all be made clear and I shall be judged with open eyes—and a true chapter written. Alas! that life is so often too long! Remember me to Bridget and her dear old master—& so many more. R. C." The last reference is to F. J. Bigger and his housekeeper. The card shows no stamp or postmark. It must have been enclosed in a letter. NLI 15464. Green papers.

knew the hand: could it be Thomas MacDonagh? "James Malcolm" had been one of the aliases used by Plunkett; but his "friend" could be almost anyone.[i]

Though it created new problems the letter was a welcome thing to Casement: it was a relief and a diversion from the pointless headknocking with German military men of the past three weeks, and it was heartening as the first evidence that the Irish leaders were taking him seriously enough to entrust him with a critical negotiation. Later when the improbability of some of the letter's expectations dawned on him he grew enraged again at being drawn so late into an unmanageable *fait accompli*. First he simply seized the letter and rushed off with it to the Admiralty. Captain Heydell took it and returned in twenty minutes with the edict of the naval officials: no submarine could be provided. On the other points he referred Casement to the General Staff; Casement at once flew into such a tirade of denunciation of that body that he later supposed Heydell must have thought him insane. Instead of going to the General Staff he retreated with his letter to the hotel where he telephoned von Haugwitz to come to him on urgent business. When Monteith and Noeggerath happened into the lobby, Casement immediately showed them the letter. Feeling that he must not let von Haugwitz see Noeggerath, a confidential agent of the Foreign Office, he had Monteith intercept the young officer and take him straight up to his room where he showed him the letter in private. Von Haugwitz said at once that the idea of sending German officers was out of the question. Casement agreed; but in that case, he said, the Rising was doomed from the start. Apparently it had not occurred to the Irish leaders to wonder how German officers, differently trained, ignorant of the country, and speaking another language, were to command the native Volunteers. Casement predicted, accurately enough, that he himself would be blamed both for planning the revolt and for its failure. In any case, he said, he must write the man at Berne that the Germans would supply no officers and no submarine. Von Haugwitz agreed.[j]

---

[i]The writer was eventually identified as George Noble, Count Plunkett, father of Joseph and Philomena. Casement confused the two men and later referred to Joseph Plunkett several times as "Count Plunkett." John Devoy also supposed the writer to be Joseph Plunkett. See *Recollections*, p. 461.

[j]Casement continued to like von Haugwitz and spoke often in his journal of his "gentlemanliness." Heydell too he liked and he looked upon both men as victims of "this Prussian system." "A Last Page," 6 April 1916. NLI 5244.

The Dublin men had evidently imagined a submarine as entering the harbor to rise spitting like a monster from the sea in the River Liffey—which was too shallow to accommodate a submarine. Casement, however, had been thinking of a very different way to use a submarine: as a swift and quiet conveyance that might land him in Ireland in time to forestall the whole Rising with his message of disaster impending. For that sort of private and personal submarine he still held a faint hope by agency of Noeggerath, who had been so impressed after reading portions of his diary that he had gone again to Zimmermann; the Secretary in turn had authorized him to try again to persuade the Admiralty and the General Staff. (To such officials, of course, nothing would be said of calling off the Rising; he would be going to perfect a plan for landing the arms.) Now when Noeggerath came to the hotel in the afternoon of 6 April Casement kept him for dinner and another long talk. Both of them suspected that the negative on the submarine was not yet absolute, that the question was probably still under active discussion. "I said yes—" Casement recorded, "but they would not send me in her! . . . They fear my intelligence. They know how profoundly I disapprove the rising & they want it—& they fear if I get to Ireland I may be able to stop it."[31] Evidently he had taken Noeggerath very deep into his confidence. When they parted that night, Noeggerath had persuaded him to delay writing to Berne until the prospect of a submarine was positively hopeless. But Casement still expected to be leaving Berlin the following night to board the *Aud*; and he told himself that he was "praying" that the ship would be seized: "If the ship is arrested & the English govt. *publish* the fact that they have collared a ship with rifles & Sir R. C. on board, then the mere fact of the publication will stop 'the rising' in Ireland. . . . So I pray God in his mercy to have this the solution."

The state of Casement's mind was obviously hectic, deeply divided, full of fantasies. It had been settled that he would be accompanied on the steamer only by Robert Monteith and a roguish young sergeant of the Brigade, a nominee of Monteith's named Julian Beverley—whose name later turned out to be Bailey. The two soldiers were now staying in Berlin on call, Beverley wearing an old suit of Casement's. Monteith had told him only that there was "a move on," but Beverley said he was ready for anything. Casement had now formed the suspicion that "that faithful, splendid Monteith" was taking Beverley along on the *Aud* so that the two of them could "capture" him and keep him off the dangerous voyage—tie him up at Kiel or in territorial waters and put him ashore out of harm's way: Monteith was "capable of anything to save me." But Casement had told Monteith on the night of the sixth that he would be "glad to go even to death on the scaffold . . . to get away from Germany & these people I despise so much." Monteith had agreed: "Indeed I think I would too." "*What* a laugh!" Casement summed up the general irony—not having divined the true feelings of Devoy whose mind ran on revolt, not at all on diplomacy: "There in America they want me to stay here as their 'representative,' thinking there is an Irish policy here & that I can influence these people—little knowing that they insult me, lie to me, break faith—& wd. now, for their own ends, gladly see me hanged, if it served them."

His paranoiac mood had now carried him to an even more elaborate vision of German treachery: the Rising had been conceived not in Dublin but in Berlin; the General Staff had made the plan in order to free Germany of her Irish obligations and had then sent von Papen to practice upon Devoy, "a furious hater of England,"[32] to create a situation in which Casement could not abstain and in which he must go to death or degradation, sinking with all the responsibility for the Rising on his shoulders. This night (6 April) Casement composed another "final word" of ten pages for Dr. Charles Curry that showed the suicidal depths of his feeling: "I hope with all my heart, sincerely, that I may be killed in this mad attempt—for I don't want to go on bearing this wretched burden of life. . . . If only a lucky shot puts me out quickly."[33] Some of Casement's depression arose from his premonition, expressed to Dr. Curry on 26 March, that if he were taken alive the English would not grant him the dignity of a trial for High Treason that might make an Irish martyr of him; rather they would try to "*humiliate* & *degrade*" him by a charge of "something baser," would find "some dastardly means" to strike him "by a coward's blow."[34] Casement made the thought no more specific, but it seems likely that he was thinking of his vulnerability on the private side of his life. In this "most hopeless position a man was ever in" death seemed the only tolerable prospect: "To be killed at once—to perish in the attempt." His premonition was elaborate but not so elaborate as his fate: the English would accord him all three: a trial for High Treason, martyrdom, degradation.

On the morning of 7 April Casement struggled to hold himself together: "I must get ready for the ordeal of this last awful day—God keep me straight & help me to go right for Ireland's sake. That is all now I can hope to do."[35] Monteith had gone out to Zossen to pay the men their pittance and clear out the Brigade bank account.[k] At ten o'clock came another summons to the General Staff. Nadolny produced a copy of the letter from Berne and poked at it with suspicious questions, but Casement convinced him that it was genuine. Under Nadolny's eye he sent a wire asking the mysterious courier when he had left Dublin and when he could return, naming the quantity of arms forthcoming, and warning that there would be no German officers and no submarine. He also managed to give von Haugwitz separately a long private letter and asked him to send it by special courier to the man in Berne.

Late in the afternoon Casement was called to the Admiralty and left cooling his heels for more than two hours, reading back numbers of English papers. At 6:30 Heydell rushed in "in great excitement": the Admiralty had capitulated; a submarine would be provided and Casement should travel on her (not to Dublin but to the west coast of Ireland). At Casement's insistence Heydell promised that he should be landed in Ireland "in time for any fight" and Captain Stoelzel confirmed that promise. "I left feeling another victory!" Casement wrote that night.[36] All by himself he was wringing precisely what he wanted from the Germans—exotic and dangerous as it might be.

At the hotel Casement told Monteith the good news in a whisper. Noeggerath came in and was delighted with the report. The final persuasion of the Admiralty had been mainly his work: in the crucial discussion he had put the case for the submarine, but he had not been able to stay for the decision. When von Haugwitz called in the evening, he was pleased with the change in plan, but he returned Casement's letter to Berne and suggested that the Irish courier not be sent back to Dublin as yet. "I will bring the poison all the same," he promised on parting.[37] At three o'clock on Saturday, 8 April, the Admiralty telephoned a message from Heydell who had gone to Wilhelmshaven to make arrangements: a submarine would be ready for Casement and his two companions at Emden on 12 April.

Casement's frame of mind remained intensely excited and anything but cheerful. In a sense he could feel gratified that he had put himself in a fair way to accomplish his two passionate aims of the past

[k]"A Last Page," 7 April 1916. NLI 5244. He returned in the evening with Mks. 3878.30.

two months: to secure the German arms for the Volunteers and to try to forestall the Rising itself. But moving as he did always with a British noose about his neck, he was about to place himself in acute personal danger. Deeply shaken in mind and body Casement was still able to produce the courage demanded. At least he could tell himself that his devastating year and a half in Germany was coming to an end: he had told Monteith that he would rather endure hanging than more of that. He had only a few days in which to attend to the dozens of large and small concerns involved in clearing himself out of Germany and he set about those. Of course the leave taking process had begun earlier, with such gestures as the resumed journal, the farewell to the men at Zossen, the immensely long "Last Word" to Dr. Curry of 26 March.

In writing to Dr. Curry, Casement's mind had run particularly upon the safety of the "Treaty" of 23–28 December 1914. He felt sure the Germans would try to get their hands upon the original document and destroy it as evidence of the obligation they had accepted to the Brigade and to Ireland. Casement had already left at Riederau plates of a photocopy of the Treaty, but on 26 March he directed Curry to take the original out of the bank in Munich, wrap it in oiled silk and bury it at Riederau, and never give it up to anyone but Devoy or McGarrity or their messenger. If Casement himself had any future occasion to mention the Treaty, he would refer to it as "the Irish verses."[38] He had also told Curry of two trunks left with Mrs. Gaffney and one at the Barler Hof in Munich, the latter containing among other things a scarcely worn evening suit that had cost him £15 in Berlin. Remembering as usual the small along with the great Casement hoped that his clothes might be taken out and aired occasionally.

But what really mattered in the trunks was a horde of books, papers, and letters including "last letters." If he survived the Rising and the war, Casement said, he would return and claim everything; if not, he wished everything to go to Joe McGarrity of Philadelphia. For from those papers the record of his strange life in Germany could be assembled into "a memoir that . . . would make clear & . . . save my reputation after I am gone." Such a book would sell, he thought, and he wished the proceeds to be divided between his sister Nina and the Irish cause in the person of John Devoy who had "helped me nobly since I met him first July 1914." He thought first of Kuno Meyer as the man to tell his story; but then he reflected that his papers contained far too many insulting references to the Germans to put into the hands of Meyer. The best man, he considered finally, was E. D. Morel, perhaps advised by Alice Stopford Green. Those two along with William Cadbury he now listed as his truest friends. And when he wrote his "final word" on 6 April to supplement his "Last Word" of 26 March, Casement asked Dr. Curry to look up Mrs. Green and Eoin MacNeill after the war and tell them his story. "These two heads are clear and sound," he wrote.[39]

The men at Zossen were the heaviest weight on Casement's conscience. It was a satisfaction to have kept their necks out of the traitor's noose by holding them off the arms ship and out of the Rising; but what would become of them when he and Monteith were gone, perhaps to their death? Casement decided that his best course was to leave St. John Gaffney in a sort of paternal charge of the Brigade. He did not think highly of Gaffney's intelligence or his discretion, as he confided to Curry;[40] but no better person was available and so he would have to entrust the men to Gaffney's energy and good will, which were real. On 10 April he wrote out instructions for Gaffney. The men might be given work in factories until the war was over—though if things went unexpectedly well "in Erin" they could be sent home. He allowed that "some of them" were "very intelligent." Casement now planned to take about $75 in gold for himself and Monteith and Beverley to use on landing, "supposing we ever land!" What was left of his German money would be handed over to the Gaffneys for the immediate expenses of the Brigade. Gaffney should write Devoy that Casement had left him "in charge" so that he could receive future Clan payments that would be sent via Bernstorff in Washington. "They might 'accredit' you now!" he supposed. He hoped that "*later on*" Gaffney would explain to Devoy or McGarrity or Cohalan "how absolutely imperative" it had been for him to go to Ireland against their orders. Meanwhile Gaffney must tell absolutely no one that he knew where Casement was going.[41]

Next day Casement wrote von Wedel of his nomination of Gaffney and again asked that the men be given "some useful occupation" during the war; he added the suggestion that they be sent to the United States at the end: Father Nicholson was already trying to make arrangements to fit them in there. The friendly 8,000 marks that von Wedel was holding for "the Irish cause" might now be turned over to Gaffney for the Brigade, Casement proposed, to be repaid yet again out of money anticipated from America.[42] He wrote von Bethmann-Hollweg in more stately and emphatic terms, asking the Chancellor's attention to the men he was leaving behind in an apparently equivocal situation:

> Today through the channel of the Political Section of the German General Staff, I am informed that the agreement of 23–28 December 1914 is null and void and has no binding force in relation to the men; that the Irish soldiers now at Zossen, to the number of some 53 are "deserters," or "prisoners of war" and may be treated in any way that seems fitting to the military authorities.[1]

To that view Casement wished to dissent "profoundly." He recalled not only the terms of the Treaty but the engagements given by the Chancellor himself in their interview of 18 December 1914. Germany had invited and comforted these men in their act of "rebellion," he pointed out, and now they remained "a charge confided to the honour of the German Government and German People."[m]

These letters were chores of the last day in Berlin, 11 April. That evening, acting on an inspiration of Monteith's, Casement sent Julian Beverley's Brigade uniform to Gaffney to keep as a souvenir and send on to Dublin some day. Gaffney kept his bargain and the uniform hangs now in that room of the National Museum sacred to the Rising of 1916. It was the only form in which the Brigade was ever to reach Dublin. To compound the irony, it turned out to be a traitor's uniform.

---

[1]Casement to von Bethmann-Hollweg. 11 April 1916. NLI 13085. Casement was apparently postdating the language of his squabble with Nadolny on 3 April. See above, p. 338.

[m]Ibid. Scattered correspondence of the next couple of years suggests the generally untidy and unhappy future of the Brigade. The men pestered Gaffney and the Germans with a series of misdemeanors: drinking, fighting, overstaying leave, running up bills, asking for advances of pay, selling their clothing, particularly boots, begging sports and musical equipment then selling it, living with *Kriegerfrauen*, and so on. In June 1916 they were moved to Danzig to a *Gefangenlager* where they were to guard Russian prisoners. Later they were sent out in small groups to work on farms and some were placed in factories and trades. A letter of 22 August 1917 from young Timothy Quinlisk, Casement's first convert at Limburg, carries a later notation by Gaffney as follows: "This man Quinlisk was shot as a spy by the Republicans during the terror (1921–23) in Ireland." NLI 13085.

25 Three Men in a Boat to Invade a Kingdom

THE *Aud*, with the consignment of German arms, sailed from Lübeck on 9 April with Leutnant Zur See Karl Spindler in command.[a] Acting on their instructions that the arms were to be landed at Fenit Pier in Tralee Bay between 20 April and 23 April, with the Rising set for the twenty-third, the Admiralty had ordered Spindler to rendezvous with the submarine carrying Casement's little party at a mile northwest of Inishtooskert Island off the Kerry coast at midnight on Thursday, 20 April. The fact that the *Aud* possessed no wireless equipment was to prove crucial.

For Casement the last days in Berlin had been a time of talk and bustle. There were long sessions with Gaffney and Hugo Franz Krebs, another of his confidants,[b] and with von Haugwitz he worked out a simple code for sending supplementary messages to Germany in what seemed the improbable event of early success in the Rising that might make additional German help useful and possible. On the back of the code sheet Casement wrote an address given him by Noeggerath as an alternative way of cabling to Germany through Switzerland. On the eleventh Casement at last told Beverley their real destination and purpose, warned him elaborately of the hopelessness of the enterprise, and invited him to withdraw and return to Zossen. But Beverley insisted, even gaily, that he intended to

---

[a] The *Aud* was the former Wilson Liner *Castro* of Hull, captured in the first month of the war and renamed (first) the *Libau*. For the purposes of the Irish journey she had been carefully disguised as a Norwegian merchantman.

[b] Krebs was an elderly German-American newspaper man in Berlin. Casement wrote of him: "He hates the British & Germans about equally—& is a typical pre-Historic Yankee." Notes to Counsel. NLI 13088.

go along. For several days Beverley and Monteith had been receiving instructions in the use of the explosives that were part of the *Aud's* cargo. In view of his enthusiasm about the rifles and machine guns, the distaste Casement showed for the idea of the explosives was curious. Apparently he was offended by the destructive and aggressive quality of such instruments. He seems hardly to have thought of the rifles as dealing death: they were symbolic or at worst defensive; mainly they were emblems to be waved at the British in token of Irish manliness and readiness for independence. But dynamite was hard to sublimate and Casement did not like to associate it with his friends or his movement. He thought perhaps the Irish could "refuse" the explosives when they unloaded the *Aud*. [1] This was one of the details he hoped to arrange if he could manage to get himself landed in Ireland in advance of the *Aud*, perhaps on 18 or 19 April.

In the final session at General Staff headquarters in the evening of 11 April each of the three travelers was given a kit holding spare underclothing, Zeiss binoculars, a flashlight, a sheath knife, and a .37 calibre Mauser pistol in a wooden case which could be adapted as a stock converting the weapon into a short rifle. A separate tin box with 1,000 rounds of ammunition was provided and maps of the country they would be traversing, if luck held. Von Haugwitz saw the party off at the station for Wilhelmshaven and they passed the night in separate sleeping compartments, carefully paying no attention to each other. Next day they found the U.20 waiting and were soon passing the coast of Schleswig on the vessel that had sunk the *Lusitania*.

When they had been at sea for only a day and a half, the crank driving the diving fins on the U.20 broke and the vessel had to put back to Heligoland for repairs. Casement at once suspected a German plot to delay or prevent his landing in Ireland. But the damage was clearly real: in the harbor he saw the broken shaft himself. Another submarine, the U.19, was summoned from Emden by wireless and, while they waited, Monteith practiced operating the tarred canvas dinghy which was to be their actual landing craft. But in starting and stopping the outboard motor his right hand and wrist were badly bruised and strained in a backfire. The U.19 put to sea on 15 April under Captain Raimund Weisbach who as torpedo officer of the U.20 had been the actual slayer of the *Lusitania*. [c] Their course lay north round Shetland thence south along the west coast of Ireland to

---

[c] Weisbach told his story to Dr. John de Courcy Ireland in confidence in 1965 when he was preparing his book *The Sea and the Easter Rising*.

Kerry. The U.19 traveled on the surface nearly all the way, through very rough seas, stirred up by winds of gale force.

Crowded in with the officers in their small quarters on the little tossing craft the invaders' situation was uncomfortable. They could hardly stomach the tinned ham and salmon that was offered and they lived mainly on war bread and ersatz coffee. Casement cut up Monteith's food for him as his hand was almost useless. All of them suffered from seasickness, Casement acutely. He was in very bad condition, weak and restless, exhausted yet unable to sleep, wretchedly pessimistic about their prospects. They tried to make the best of things, telling stories and singing Irish songs and hanging up their "Irish flag," the flag of Gaffney's native city Limerick which he had asked them to carry in their invasion. From time to time one or more of the men would climb up to stand in the air on the conning tower, and a few snapshots were taken of them there. But Casement for the most part kept miserably to his bunk.

At 12:10 A.M. in the first minutes of Good Friday, 21 April, the U.19 lay on the surface at the point of rendezvous with the *Aud*. It was full moonlight and the sea was mirror-smooth but there was no sign of the arms ship, no signal light from shore, no life moving of any kind. Captain Spindler of the *Aud* later told the same story: he reached the rendezvous at midnight, found no submarine and no signal light, and after nosing about in the water for several hours he was forced to steam away to the south as his orders had directed. His failure to meet the U.19 has now been explained by Captain Weisbach and Dr. John de Courcy Ireland: Spindler had made an error in his navigation and had simply pulled up at the wrong place, several miles away from the point of rendezvous.[2] But why no signal lights from shore, no pilot, no Irish Volunteers reception force—visible to either ship? The answer to that question must be sought not only in Dublin but in New York and Berlin.

John Devoy recalls that in the afternoon of Friday, 14 April, to his "great surprise," Philomena Plunkett walked into the office of the *Gaelic American* in New York with a new message from the Dublin committee: "Arms must not be landed before midnight of Sunday, 23rd. This is vital."[3] By the time Devoy had the message decoded, the office of the German Embassy was closed and so next morning he delivered a copy of the message which was then sent by wireless to Berlin that evening, 15 April. By that time the *Aud* had been at sea for nearly a week and her instructions could not be corrected because she carried no wireless. But the I.R.B. leaders in Dublin, assuming

that their wishes would be followed to the letter, made no preparations whatever for any contingency prior to 23 April. In fact the Irish
pilot, Mort O'Leary, saw a ship that was probably the *Aud* off shore
on the evening of 20 April and again the following morning but paid
no attention, his mind being fixed on 23 April.[4] Other mischances
and ineptitudes occurred. On 18 April a German "advertising
agency" office in Wall Street was raided by United States Secret
Service men and among the trophies was the message from Dublin,
with Devoy's name attached, and a copy of the message in German
cypher—all sitting in plain view on the desk of Wolf von Igel. Thus
the message, the code, and the complicity of Devoy were betrayed at
a blow. But in fact the British Admiralty already knew the ship had
sailed and knew her cargo and her destination. Dr. Ireland believes
that the *Aud* was identified and allowed deliberately to pass through
the British naval blockade on 16 April.[5] Eventually she was trapped
off the southern coast of Ireland by British patrol vessels late on 21
April and sunk on Spindler's orders at the entrance to Queenstown
harbor (Cobh).

For nearly two hours the U.19 lay on the surface near Inishtooskert with the three Irishmen and the German officers scanning the
water for the *Aud* or a pilot boat and the shore for the green lights that
were the arranged signal. But there were no signs. Weisbach said he
could risk his ship no longer and he moved off toward Fenit. Casement, Monteith, and Beverley went below to make ready, crushed in
spirit by the ill omens of their reception. Did no one in Ireland care
that they were coming? Monteith tried to show Casement how to
load his Mauser pistol, but Casement finally asked him to do the
thing for him. Monteith noticed that he touched the weapon and his
cartridge belt and sheath knife only with loathing. They discussed
what they should do if they met hostile persons on the shore. Casement insisted that they must not fire upon any Irishman and eventually they provided themselves with a length of tarred rope with
which they thought they might tie up any captive they might make.
Casement and Weisbach agreed that the motor must not be used on
the dinghy for fear of attracting attention either to the submarine or
the landing party. At 2:15 A.M. the dinghy was put into the water
with three oars and the three men climbed into it. The U.19 went off
about her business and late that afternoon sighted and sank the S. S.
Feliciana, a small English cargo ship bound from Cardiff to New
York.

"So there we were," Monteith wrote later, "three men in a boat—the smallest invading party known to history."[6] In retrospect he could see elements of comedy in their situation, indeed in the whole enterprise; the immediate situation was dreary and desperate. Monteith being less exhausted than either of the others rowed most of the way in the clumsy craft, badly hampered by his injured hand. As they neared the shore, the breakers grew rougher and they were overturned and thrown out, but as all were wearing lifebelts the only damage was a thorough drenching. Clinging to the boat, they reached the beach at Curraghane or Banna Strand, cold and exhausted. Monteith steadied the dinghy and Beverley carried their kits ashore, then came back to help Casement in. Monteith tried to hole the boat to sink it but could not pierce the tough surface with his dagger and so he simply abandoned it in the waves, after it had struck him a last blow that wrenched his right ankle. When he reached the shore, he found the others stretched out in extremis on the sand. Casement appeared to be hardly conscious and lay with his body lapped by the waves. "His eyes were closed and in the dim moonlight his face resembled that of a sleeping child," as Monteith remembered it.[7] In the last letter he wrote to Nina, under sentence of death on 25 July, Casement remembered this moment and the next couple of hours in terms of a vision of beatitude erasing the terrible trials of the past two years:

> When I landed in Ireland that morning . . . swamped and swimming ashore on an unknown strand I was happy for the first time for over a year. Although I knew that this fate waited on me, I was for one brief spell happy and smiling once more. I cannot tell you what I felt. The sandhills were full of skylarks, rising in the dawn, the first I had heard for years—the first sound I heard through the surf was their song as I waded in through the breakers, and they kept rising all the time up to the old rath at Currahane . . . and all round were primroses and wild violets and the singing of the skylarks in the air, and I was back in Ireland again.[8]

Monteith got the Chief on his feet and they all struggled up to dry ground for a brief council. As they were physically unable to carry all of their modest equipment, they decided to hold onto their overcoats and bury everything else. While they labored to cover their warlike traps with sand, Monteith thought he saw a figure skulking away through the dunes. They headed inland for a half-mile or so then turned south for Tralee, dragging with cold and weighed down with their sodden overcoats, Casement's old ulster of heavy Irish frieze being particularly burdensome. Passing a farmhouse at first light they were observed by a bedraggled girl, later identified as Mary Gorman, "leaning over the half door, blinking at the morning sun."[9] In a stream of fresh water they stripped and washed themselves and their clothes of accumulated sand and slime and put the wet clothes on again. At last they reached "McKenna's Fort," an ancient earthwork or rath that they had noticed earlier on their maps. It was isolated and covered with wild undergrowth and appeared a likely place to hide. Casement was the most exhausted and the most conspicuous of the three; it was decided that he would lie up in the rath while the other two men walked on to Tralee to seek out the local Volunteers. All emptied their pockets of papers not already destroyed on the submarine and all three overcoats were left with Casement, who also managed characteristically to keep about him enough papers to hang him had such evidence been needed.

Monteith and Beverley reached Tralee at about seven o'clock on Good Friday morning and after a considerable delay got hold of Austin Stack, the commander of the Tralee Volunteers. Stack eventually accepted their bona fides, attested also by some of the local men who had known Monteith in his days as an organizer for the movement. Stack procured a motor car and set out with a friend, Con Collins, and Beverley as guide to rescue Casement. But they never reached him. Their car was stopped and searched and Stack and Collins were arrested. Beverley got away briefly but was soon caught near Abbeydorney. In the afternoon Monteith in Tralee heard of the arrest of Stack and Collins and heard also that Casement was a prisoner in Ardfert barracks nearby. Monteith that evening got a messenger off for Dublin with a warning as to the limited nature of the help coming from Germany and advising against the Rising. He directed the courier to go directly to Eoin MacNeill or Bulmer Hobson, but he learned later that his message had been carried to James Connolly, leader of the Irish Citizen Army. Monteith did not then know that MacNeill and Hobson had been turned into mere "figureheads" by the revolutionary junta within the Volunteers and knew nothing whatever of plans for a Rising. At this point Monteith went underground, hiding out briefly in Tralee, then for a half a year round Limerick, then making his way by Cork to Liverpool where in

Raimund Weisbach revisits Banna Strand in 1965. Courtesy of Gordon Standing, the *Irish Times*, Dublin.

Mary Gorman and Martin Collins on their way to testify at Bow Street. Courtesy of Radio Times Hulton Picture Library, London.

December he traveled back to his family in New York, working in disguise as a fireman and coal trimmer on a merchant vessel. Casement, whose sanity he had perhaps saved and to whom his loyalty was absolute, and who loved the man, for long feared he was dead, perhaps a suicide. Both of them carried little vials of poison, appropriately Putumayan: powdered curare procured by von Haugwitz.

Back on Banna Strand the broad trail the invaders had left behind them had been very quickly discovered. A local farmer named John McCarthy had risen before dawn on Good Friday in order, according to the story that later entertained everybody in court, to visit a holy well (the name of which he could never recall). Returning home along the shore he saw the abandoned dinghy, with a dagger lying in the bottom, beached below highwater mark; he also found a tin box partly covered with sand (the ammunition case) and saw the tracks of three men in the sand. He went off to call a neighbor, Pat Driscoll, to help move the boat and when he got back to the spot he found his little daughter, eight years old, playing with several pistols she had found. He sent Driscoll off to report these suspicious circumstances at the barracks of the Royal Irish Constabulary in the nearby village of Ardfert. The constables agreed that the matter would bear looking into and a party was sent out to scour the country round Curraghane. That the long *opéra-bouffe* of Casement's trip to America and Germany should end with the hero hiding in the weeds in Ireland and arrested by a country constable shows a dismal and bitter kind of comic symmetry.

Casement did not like the description of himself as skulking in hiding and he later said that he had shown himself fairly about the rath and had walked "across two fields."[10] But this was surely his way of hiding. When Monteith left at about 5:00 A.M. for Tralee, he had predicted that he would return with help by eight. But noon came and passed and no one had appeared. Casement tried to burn the code sheet but found his matches were watersoaked. When he looked out about one o'clock and saw a policeman coming toward him across the field, he hurriedly stuffed money and papers (chiefly copies of his recent letters to von Wedel and of the "Treaty" of 23–28 December, 1914) down a rabbit hole and covered it with a stone or two.[d] The code he could only tear across once and stuff in his pocket. He would have chewed and swallowed it, but he had had to pop the vial of cu-

---

[d] I searched for this cache in March 1972 but did not find it.

rare into his mouth to hide it. The constable, Bernard Riley, the Dogberry of the scene, had now come up and was behaving in a manner that Casement later wished not to have described in court for fear of embarrassing him: dancing about in apparent fear and agitation and waving his rifle up and down.

Riley warned him that his gun was loaded and he must not move. Casement assured him that he was unarmed and would do no harm, and wondered why an English traveler was being treated in this hostile fashion. Riley called his companion Sergeant Thomas Hearn who was searching nearby and Hearn took over the interrogation, pointing out that the suspect must answer his questions or be arrested under the Defense of the Realm Act. His name, Casement said, was Richard Morten and he lived in Denham, Buckinghamshire. Asked to name one of his works, he cited a life of St. Brendan.[e] He claimed to have come overland from Dublin and to be walking along the Kerry coast to Tralee. He could produce no passport or other identifying papers. Riley and Hearn noticed that Casement's clothes were wet and sand was caked on his trousers and boots.

Sergeant Hearn now took him formally in charge and the party walked across the field to the public road. A boy of twelve, Martin Collins, driving by in a pony trap had stopped to watch the police activity and he noticed that as the prisoner climbed over a fence he dropped some bits of paper behind his back—the torn code. Riley and Casement were sent on in young Collins's trap to the farmhouse of John Allman where Mary Gorman was a servant. She affirmed that Casement was indeed one of the three strangers she had seen hurrying past at 4:30 that morning. Martin Collins returned to the scene of the arrest and sent a still younger friend into the field to pick up the bits of paper which he then turned over to Constable Riley. "This was the *fatal* paper," Casement put it dramatically on 16 May in one of his notes for his lawyers. "This Boy has hanged me sure!— and hanged old Ireland too."[11] He wrongly blamed the capture of the *Aud* upon this finding of the code: *"Don't bring this out—but it is the chief load of one kind on my heart.* Had they not found this paper, God knows how the whole thing would have ended."[12] By the time the

---

[e]He explained later that he had given Morten's name in a spirit of obfuscation, believing he would be doing his friend no harm, while spinning a yarn that would take long enough to investigate so that Monteith and Beverley could get away to Dublin with their message. St. Brendan he named because he was the patron saint of the area in which he was arrested. Brief to Counsel. NLI 13088.

code was found and comprehended the *Aud* was already in the clutches of the *Bluebell*.

At Ardfert police barracks Casement was charged with landing arms on the coast of Ireland—presumably the hand weapons found on the beach. Casement refused to give his name and said that as he was now formally charged he would say nothing until he had the services of a lawyer. Sergeant Hearn laughed and said that he would "enjoy that privilege of the British Constitution."[13] The three overcoats and Casement's bag found at the rath were searched along with the clothes he was wearing. The yield was considerable. Beverley's overcoat pocket produced a sleeping car ticket from Berlin to Wilhelmshaven. In the black bag were maps, field glasses, a flashlight, the Limerick flag, forty rounds of ammunition, and a few articles of clothing. Casement was carrying five sovereigns and eleven shillings, in his waistcoat pocket a sort of *chronique* or itinerary or diary listing in transparent code major events since the middle of February and culminating with "12th April, left Wicklow in Willie's yacht," and in the inside pocket of a second inner leather waistcoat a bit of paper with German script that turned out to be a tailor's ticket. All of these trophies were, of course, supplementary to the items of evidence littering the beach of Curraghane.

From Ardfert Casement was taken to the Tralee police barracks for overnight detention, arriving about 6:30 in the evening. He was kindly treated and given food and a good bed though he seems to have talked much of the night, especially to District Inspector F. A. Britton who was friendly and sympathetic. Casement's account to his lawyers revealed details that he wanted suppressed in court for fear of damaging the man's career. When they were alone, Britton said: "I think I know who you are, and I pray to God it won't end the way of Wolfe Tone." Casement told him he had come to try to stop the Rising. Britton said that the authorities were already on the alert for a revolt: "traitors in Dublin" had given it away. "We would be with you to a man," Britton went on, "if there was a chance of success." He wondered why Casement had not shot the arresting constable and Casement explained his resolution not to injure any Irishman. Britton hoped Casement's name would not become known in the town for then the Volunteers would storm the barracks in a rescue and "not one of us would be left alive."[14]

The warning message to Dublin was still Casement's heaviest anxiety and with that in mind he asked to be allowed to see a priest "for spiritual counsel." In his notes he explained: "My mother was a Catholic and I am one at heart."[15] A local Dominican, Father F. M. Ryan, was brought to him. Casement told him who he was and why he had come and begged him to get a message off at once to Eoin MacNeill warning of the inadequacy of the German assistance and advising delay. Like Monteith he did not realize that MacNeill had been kept entirely in the dark as to the I.R.B. plan. Father Ryan was reluctant but finally agreed to do as he was asked. Casement further begged the priest not to reveal his identity in Tralee until after he had left, to forestall a rescue attempt, but then to "spread the news broadcast" after he was gone.[16] Father Ryan thought an attempt at rescue would have been a very likely thing if Casement's detention was known, as his picture (though with beard, of course) hung in many houses about Kerry.

Casement also asked to see a medical man, Dr. Michael Shanahan whose name he had heard in Ardfert, so Dr. Shanahan was called in ostensibly to treat "a commercial traveler" who had "got into trouble." At about 9:00 P.M. he found "a clean-shaven man of distinguished appearance" who proved nervous and worn out but not otherwise ill. He gave some simple medicine—probably aspirin, Casement thought.[17] After his examination Dr. Shanahan was shown a photograph of Roger Casement with his beard covered by a slip of paper: did it not resemble the prisoner? he was asked. He said he thought not. Then, according to Shanahan's account, he went straight to the Volunteers in the town and asked them to do something for Casement: he was sure a half-dozen men with revolvers could take him out of the barracks easily. But the townsmen refused, or professed to refuse, to believe the prisoner was Casement.[18] Of course his identity and his arrest had been known in Tralee for half a day; and it is likely that his arrival in Ireland if not his arrest was known even in Dublin by this time—by means of Monteith's messenger. It seems quite clear that Casement had been judged expendable in the interest of preserving the secrecy of the Rising.

Though he had slept little in the past two weeks, Casement lay awake most of Friday night chatting freely with Chief Constable Kearney. "We became close friends," he explained later to his lawyers. "You know what it is with Irishmen—so different from Englishmen! Whatever 'class' you may belong to at heart we are all one in Ireland."[19] As in Berlin, he seemed unable to resist an opportunity to bare his soul. Furthermore, as he explained, he was then bent on using the poison he carried at the first favorable opportunity and he "wanted this friendly man to know something to tell my friends later."[20] And so he talked at large about his hopes and his fears and his disappointments, of the arms ship, of the Rising and its probable failure, of his message to Dublin, of his private papers and where they were held in Germany—he seems to have held back very little. From the friendly man Casement learned that the local Volunteers Stack and Collins were also locked up in the barracks that night and he asked to see them but that was refused.

In the morning the Chief Constable persuaded District Inspector Britton to allow Casement to walk to the railway station without handcuffs. Before leaving he distributed cash and mementoes. He reimbursed Constable Larkin for the tea and eggs that his wife had provided and he tried to persuade Kearney to accept a pound note. He refused that but finally accepted Casement's pocket watch, not a valuable piece, as a "keepsake." (He turned it in later.) To another constable he presented his leather inner waistcoat and to Sergeant Hearn he gave his walking stick, an item of curious provenance. It was an oaken alpenstock with an iron point hiding a hollow inner tube. Casement had bought it in Berlin in June 1915 for Joseph Plunkett to use in carrying papers back to Ireland but the hole proved too small and Plunkett gave it back to him with the suggestion that he send it to him from America after the war; Casement had brought it along hoping to hand it to Plunkett ceremonially in Dublin on reunion.

At about 10:30 on Saturday morning, 22 April, Casement was marched off to the station unmanacled in the middle of a small guard party. Once or twice he slipped on the muddy paving stones. Again it occurred to him that he need only call out for help and he could raise a riot and a rescue. But he had resolved that his part was to submit. For he, too, had the welfare of the Rising on his heart and felt that he carried a specific responsibility for the arms ship and for Monteith and Beverley.

Casement traveled, then, quite across Ireland by broad daylight, in a reserved railway carriage, attended by a single R.I.C. sergeant, and utterly unnoticed by his countrymen. He could hardly have felt lonelier in Berlin. One wonders if his mind ran back to the Manchester rescue of 1867 and the lengths to which the Fenians of those days went for a comrade.[21] When the train stopped at Killarney, the head constable of the town spoke to Casement's guard through the open door of the carriage: "Did you hear what happened to the two lads at Puck? . . . They ran into the tide and were drowned." (Puck was a local name for Killorglin, twenty miles from Tralee.) The night before, two Volunteers from Dublin motoring to Kerry to take part in the landing of arms on Sunday, had blundered into the sea off a slip of land. (Nothing was going right.) The prisoner, having overheard the conversation, according to Sergeant Butler "commenced to sob and cry, and remained so for some time." Of course he had assumed that the drowned men must be Monteith and Beverley. "I am very sorry for those two men," he said after a time; "they were good Irishmen; it was on my account they came over here."[22] When they changed trains at Mallow, the seat of his mother's family, the Jephsons, Casement remarked that he "knew the Blackwater well." In the cab in Dublin on the way to Arbour Hill Military Barracks Casement said he hoped for a bed that night as he had hardly slept for twelve nights. Sergeant Butler reassured him.

But rest was not forthcoming. At Arbour Hill Casement received his first rough treatment. Sergeant-Major Frederick Whittaker was "a *brute*" and "a *cad*" who "shouted at me as if I were a dog."[23] He searched the prisoner roughly, ordering him to pull up his shirt and then dragging down his trousers himself. A person came in "dressed like a gentlemen—but *not* one" who addressed Casement familiarly as "Sir Roger" and asked him if he remembered certain "old times." Casement was still refusing to give his name. The detective showed a photograph which Casement thought was probably an enlargement of a Putumayo photograph given by Gielgud to the press in 1911. A profile sketch was made and compared with the photograph. Casement was then taken to the boat for Holyhead. He sat up all night in his cabin with four soldier guards and crossed England by train to Euston Station with Sergeant Thomas Bracken, reaching London shortly after six o'clock in the morning of Easter Sunday, 23 April: the day planned for the Rising.

At some point in this interval Casement got hold of a newspaper and read of the scuttling of the *Aud* and the loss of the arms. Though he did not know it, Beverley, too, was in custody by this time. He had been arrested along with Stack and Collins but was later let go: he had identified himself as David Mulcahy of Dublin, a casual traveler. But next day he was caught again lurking about nearby at Abbeydorney, carrying among other things four sheets of notepaper on one of which was written: "Castle near Tralee is quite a quaint old Irish structure of stone"—presumably his version of the culture-seeking hiker's notes. Within a very short time he was eagerly spilling all the beans he held, telling of Casement and the Irish Brigade and the arms ship and the submarine invasion of Banna Strand. He was not either Mulcahy or Beverley, he announced, but Daniel Julian Bailey; and he had never been a convert or an ally of Roger Casement's: his whole motive had been to find a way to get out of a German prison camp. Now he appeared delighted to offer himself as a King's Evidence.

At Euston Station Casement had been met by Inspector Joseph Sandercook of the Criminal Investigation Department (C.I.D.) and taken straight to Scotland Yard. On the way he asked if he would be allowed to see "anyone of importance" and was assured that he would see "some very important people."[24] At Scotland Yard Sandercook identified himself formally and told the prisoner that he would be detained during inquiries on a charge to be determined later. Casement asked if Sandercook knew who he was and when the inspector said that he did know, he announced himself anyway: "I am Sir Roger Casement, and the only person to whom I have disclosed my identity is a priest at Tralee in Ireland." He was about to continue, but Sandercook warned him that anything he said would be taken down and used as evidence.[25] After breakfast Casement met the important people: two of the men who had been following his activities for the better part of two years, the begetters of the *Sayonara* scheme, Basil Thomson, head of the C.I.D.,[f] and Captain Reginald Hall, Chief of Naval Intelligence; along with Major Basil Hall of Army Intelligence, Superintendent Patrick Quinn of Scotland Yard, and a young shorthand writer who was to take notes of the interrogation. Thomson noticed Casement's cadaverous look and the "mahogany" hue of his face and nervous hands which he attributed to long exposure to tropical suns. He found Casement's manner animated and "at times histrionic."[26]

There was a good deal of preliminary byplay as to the prisoner's identity. "Officially I am Sir Roger Casement," Casement said. "There may be people impersonating Sir Roger Casement," Thomson observed. "I don't think there are many people who would care to impersonate me," Casement said. He asked permission to call in his friend Sir William Tyrrell of the Foreign Office as a party to the interrogation. "He knew I would do nothing dirty or mean," he

[f]It gave supporters of Casement some pleasure when Thomson was convicted and fined for a sexual offense with a woman in a London park in 1925.

explained to his lawyers. The others demurred: they thought it unfair to Tyrrell to bring him into the case. Thomson warned Casement about the seriousness of his situation. "I do not care a rap about that," Casement retorted. "I have committed treason up to the neck, not once, but a hundred times." What he had wanted and still wanted, he tried to make plain, was to prevent a hopeless Rising: "to stop a crime." He begged them to publish at once the fact that they had captured him: that might do some good. And he begged, too, to be allowed to go back to Dublin himself, to carry his own message and "stop useless bloodshed." He promised on his "word of honour" to return to custody. Captain Hall then said, according to Casement, *"It is better a festering sore like this should be cut out."*[27] Casement later noted that though he had been in custody since 21 April his capture was not announced until 25 April, the British "having in the interval allowed the rebellion to take place."[28] He was convinced that British officials, on the Draconian principle spoken by Hall, preferred to see the revolt occur and be put down by force, rather than to prevent it entirely.[g]

Captain Hall told Casement of the capture of the *Aud*: "We have got the ship and all the survivors."[29] Furthermore, he said, they had known of the ship's sailing and even of Casement's submarine: "We were waiting for you, Sir Roger," he said smiling. Casement believed this was mere bravado. They had intercepted a message giving the date of the Rising as 23 April—the day on which they were speaking. This too Casement doubted, believing they had guessed the day from his own hectic anxiety. The rebel leaders were known, they assured him, and were about to be arrested. Again he begged to be allowed to go to Dublin and attempt a countermand. His own treasonable courses he freely admitted and said he was ready to face all consequences. But he had done "nothing dishonourable": he had acted always for Ireland, and now he wished to act again for Ireland, to prevent pointless suffering. He could tell them no more, for that would incriminate other people. The shorthand writer was then turned out of the room and in passing he whispered to Casement: "Greater love hath no man than this, that he lay down his life for his country."[30]

The interrogation continued as a "frank talk" between "gentle-

---

[g] Dr. Ireland's belief that the *Aud* was knowingly passed through the naval blockade supports the same line of argument.

men."[31] Casement discoursed at large of his bitter disenchantment with the German General Staff, making it clear that he and they had been at hopeless odds. He angrily denied that he had "seduced" the Irish prisoners to join his Brigade with promises of money: he had offered them no money, "only death" in the cause of Ireland. Nor had he accepted a penny of "German gold" for himself though it had been offered often enough. They showed him some of the documentary evidence against him: the German railway *Bettkarte*, the torn code found by Martin Collins, his articles in German newspapers, even his letter of December 1914 to Eoin MacNeill enclosed in a letter to Alice Stopford Green and intercepted in the mails. These things Casement acknowledged, as he acknowledged his treason. But he stood by his refusal to discuss the name of anyone in Ireland associated with him. Before the session ended, according to Thomson's account, the first flourishes of the crucial matter of the diaries had occurred. Casement had been asked for the keys to trunks in his old lodgings in Ebury Street but had casually advised that they simply be broken open as they contained nothing of any value. Later Superintendent Quinn brought Thomson, with a "Mephistopheles" look, two thin volumes which Thomson looked into after Casement had been taken away and judged to be matter that "could not be printed in any age or in any language."[32] Portions of the text, if genuine, showed the writer to be a habitual and record-keeping homosexual.

Before Casement had been sent off for the night to Brixton Prison, Thomson had told him that the charge against him would probably be that of high treason. That seemed to Casement appropriate: "I hope so," he said. The interrogators had also led him to think, as they then thought themselves, that he would probably be tried by court martial. That, too, suited Casement as squaring essentially with the military and political cast of his own actions. Twice on Monday, 24 April, and again on Tuesday he was questioned at length at Scotland Yard but little was added to the first day's garnering. Casement announced that he did not wish to claim any special protective rights as a British subject. "I should regard that as mean," he said, though he admitted that "in law" he was a British subject. He was a citizen of Ireland and as such preferred to think of himself as an enemy alien. In his Brief to Counsel Casement wrote that Thomson told him on Monday that both Monteith and Beverley-Bailey had been captured—"a deliberate lie." The shorthand record of the interrogation does not support this, showing only that Captain Hall told him that Bailey had been caught and had "made a full confession" and that the name of Monteith was now known. Casement was brought back from Brixton late on Monday night because Captain Hall thought "von Igell's papers"—the product of the Secret Service raid on Wall Street—showed that a second arms ship was being sent from Germany. Casement told him this was all nonsense. On both Monday and Tuesday most of the talk centered on Casement's work in Germany as preparatory to the Rising. He told them the full story of the last weeks: the surprise request for arms for a revolt now settled upon, his struggles to procure the arms and yet prevent the Brigade from being sent along, his squabbles with the General Staff, the last-minute granting of the submarine, and his hopes of preventing the Rising by that means. His interrogators stuck stubbornly to the view that the Rising was essentially a plot hatched by Casement himself and his German abettors and that they had "sent" him to Ireland to bring the arms and to lead the revolt. They were quite wrong but unpersuadable.

At noon on Monday, during Casement's interrogation, the great event itself, the Easter Rising, had commenced. It had been delayed for a full day when Eoin MacNeill, informed at the last minute of what was about to occur, issued a peremptory countermand that appeared in the Sunday morning papers calling off the Volunteer "parade" scheduled for that day. His negative order was in turn countermanded by the revolutionary junta and the original order reinstated for Monday. The effect of the contradictory orders was to throw the provincial units particularly into confusion so that when the Rising began at noon on Monday it was confined largely to the capital. The loss of the *Aud* and the arrest of Casement added both to the confusion and to the desperateness of the enterprise. Casement's questioners told him nothing of the Rising until Tuesday, though, of course, they had known of it the day before. In the House of Commons on Monday afternoon Pemberton Billings, M.P., had asked whether it was true that Sir Roger Casement had been arrested and brought to London and whether "the House and the nation" could be sure that "this traitor" would be "shot forthwith." There were loud cheers in the House, but Prime Minister Asquith fended off the question. On Tuesday Casement was taken from Brixton and lodged in the Tower of London, probably in anticipation of a trial by court martial. He now entered a sort of limbo for a time and a bitterly uncomfortable and unhappy one.

26   They Have My Body

FINALLY on 25 April, in the form of an announcement from the Secretary of the Admiralty, Casement's capture was made public in language that gave the impression (quite honestly held by the authorities) that he had come to Ireland at the head of a German arms-running expedition:

> During the period between P.M. April 20th and P.M. April 21st an attempt to land arms and ammunition in Ireland was made by a vessel under the guise of a neutral merchant ship but in reality a German auxiliary in conjunction with a German submarine. The auxiliary sank and a number of prisoners were made amongst whom was Sir Roger Casement.

In Dublin, cut off by land and sea with the central city torn by bitter fighting, news was even scantier and less accurate as can be seen from three days' entries in Elsie Henry's diary:

> April 27: There is a repeated report that a German boat has been caught off the Kerry Coast with Sir Roger Casement & German officers on board.
>
> April 28: AE (George William Russell) has returned, last night, & had to walk from Clare, with an occasional car. It took him three days. . . . Some of the soldiers [brought over from England to deal with the Rising] thought they were in France, as they had been bundled off without any word, & had had a railway journey & sea journey. . . .
>
> April 29: Mrs. Best says it is true that Sir Roger Casement was taken from a collapsible boat landing in Kerry on Wednesday & taken over to the Tower & shot.[1]

There seemed, and still seems, no doubt that if Casement were defined, as he must be, as a British subject then he was guilty of high treason. He had been applying the term himself to his actions for a year and a half. British authorities had built a careful dossier on his actions in America and Germany and they had waited only to lay hold of him. Now he was also tarred with the brush of the Rising itself, still raging in Ireland; officially and popularly assumed to be its begetter and leader. Casement was the first and only capital British traitor of the first World War and so of course he attracted the full force of patriotic public hatred and contempt. In a way that would not now be tolerated he was freely convicted of the crime for which he had not yet been tried by the epithets applied to him in the press: "traitor," "renegade," "turncoat," and so on. And the sensation he presented was intensified by the fact that he was a glamorous and well-known figure: a romantically handsome Irishman who had done big things in exotic places and been several times decorated by the Crown. Casement could not escape obloquy and he could hardly escape conviction: the only serious questions were whether he must die for his crime and whether his reputation must perish utterly in the process. British officials certainly meant to have his life. The Attorney-General, Sir Frederick E. Smith, who was to be his Prosecutor, made this clear on 25 April in his discussion with Scotland Yard officers as to whether the trial was to be civil or military. Whatever form the trial took, he said, it must be public: "lest in after years we should be reproached with having killed him secretly."[2]

In the Tower Casement was wretched in mind and body. Two soldiers stayed with him in his cell all the time and another guard looked through a pane in the door. A light burned overhead night and day. He had no clothing other than the filthy garments in which he had waded ashore and none were offered him. His necktie and braces and shoelaces had been removed for fear of a suicide attempt and so everything hung loose about him. He could not eat and did not wish to eat, taking only bits of bread and water, and soon he was threatened with forcible feeding. His room was verminous and his head was soon infested with lice and his body covered with bites. He could not sleep and he hardly dared to think. Perhaps his worst torture was his sense of total isolation and abandonment. Nothing had come of his request to see friends and to have legal assistance; he was forbidden to communicate with anyone outside the prison; and he was allowed to believe, he told Gertrude Bannister later, that no one was willing to be associated with him, that all his friends had recoiled in shame.[3]

According to the notes he made for his lawyers, Casement attempted suicide during the first week in the Tower. He still retained his "poison," a half-dozen crystals of curare in a tiny glass vial about an inch and a half long. Von Haugwitz had told him the stuff was not to be swallowed but must be applied to an open cut. About 27 April he began watching for a chance, but the close surveillance made things difficult. Finally on Sunday, 30 April, he managed to break the vial by biting it and to cut a gash in his left forefinger. Then, as well as he could manage while holding his hands under the table, he dipped a sharpened match stick again and again into the curare and rubbed it into the cut. He prayed for forgiveness and waited for death but nothing happened. Had von Haugwitz given him a placebo? The only consequence was a swollen finger that Casement said he still had as he wrote.[a]

Casement was not quite so alone as he thought and by this time help was beginning to gather, coming first from loyal women. Gertrude and Elizabeth Bannister had been spending their Easter holiday at Frinton-on-Sea near Lowestoft and Gertrude had had to take to her bed with a heavy cold. On Tuesday, 25 April, Elizabeth came back from a walk looking white and frightened. "There is bad news on the posters," she said. "They say Roger has landed in Ireland and been captured."[4] Gertrude immediately got up and dressed and the two sisters went to London and moved into a hotel. When Gertrude went to see Mrs. Green for help that night, as the most influential person she knew in London, she found her in an uncharacteristic state: appalled and exasperated by the "madness" of Casement's journey and of the Rising, angry at the "insane" Irish attempt to mimic Wolfe Tone. She seemed distraught and hopeless and could think of no useful advice to offer. She did approve a letter that Gertrude wrote out in her study to the Home Secretary asking to be allowed to see Casement.

Now began ten days of gratuitously callous and cruel treatment at the hands of British officials. The sisters trudged from department to

---

[a]Notes to Counsel. NLI 13088. One hardly knows what to make of the story. For one thing the whole passage is scored out in the manuscript, apparently by his own hand. And how had Casement managed to conceal the poison through several systematic searches? He says only that he carried it in his mouth from McKenna's Fort to Tralee. Yet he mentioned the suicide attempt at other points in his notes.

department of the government, rebuffed everywhere and often with rudeness. The Home Secretary refused to see them. They were shunted to the War Office, to Scotland Yard, to the Home Office, to the Treasury, to the Life Guards. Gertrude wrote to the Governor of the Tower enclosing a note for Casement conveying love and a promise of help; Casement told her later that the note was never given to him. They heard rumors that he might be shot at any time as was happening to the leaders of the rebellion in Dublin. They walked round and round the Tower itself, trying to will a communication. Only Major Arbuthnot of the Life Guards showed any kindness: he told them that he had seen Casement himself and that he needed fresh clothing, and he promised to write the Governor of the Tower to try to get them an interview with the prisoner. They went and bought clothing in a ready-to-wear shop.

Meanwhile Mrs. Green had rallied from her first distraction and was taking her own steps. It was on her suggestion that George Gavan Duffy of Grey's Inn was asked to undertake Casement's defense. He was the son of Charles Gavan Duffy, one of the founders of the Young Ireland Movement and of the *Nation* in the middle of the nineteenth century. He accepted the defense at once and wrote the same day, 1 May, to tell Casement that he was offering himself at the suggestion of Mrs. Green and of Gertrude Bannister; in a covering letter to the Governor of the Tower he asked to be allowed to see the prisoner promptly. None of this was communicated to Casement himself. Gavan Duffy's partners had told him he must leave the firm if he persisted in defending Casement: it was a measure of English feeling.[5] He accepted the brief and the penalty. But he was not allowed to see Casement for more than a week, not until 9 May. He had known Casement, but he hardly recognized the man he saw: cadaverous, unwashed, louse-eaten, his beard half-grown, his eyes red-rimmed, a man shuffling in his loose boots and filthy clothes, halting in speech and unable to remember names. Gavan Duffy's description wrung the heart of the Bannister sisters. A few days later they saw him themselves for the only time before his committal at Bow Street on 15 May. Casement had heard by now from one of his Welsh Guards of the executions in Dublin and he seemed to think he was being allowed to see his cousins now to say goodbye before being shot himself.[6] But better talk ensued and they were able to reassure him of help at hand and to whisper the news that Monteith was alive and in hiding in Ireland. Casement continued anxious about his friend, however, knowing he carried poison.[7]

Casement had been wishing for trial by a military court, thus to share legal pot-luck with the rebel leaders in Dublin, but Duffy was given to understand that the trial would be by civil authority. The government had apparently swung round to the view that a civil trial in a case so spectacular would make a better general impression, especially in neutral countries.[b] Duffy wrote to Sir Charles Matthews, Director of Public Prosecutions, one of those who had given Gertrude Bannister a stony stare, and asked for details of the charge in the case. He also told Mrs. Green what he had seen of Casement's condition in the Tower, throwing her into a cold rage. Affairs began to move a bit and Casement's treatment to improve. Matthews wrote Duffy on 10 May: "Sir Roger Casement is to be handed over to the Civil Authorities for trial for high treason committed within and without the realm."[8] Mrs. Green wrote directly to Prime Minister Asquith of Duffy's account and let him know that she intended to tell the story to American newspaper correspondents unless he took action. Matthews' letter to Duffy and his instructions to transfer the prisoner to Brixton Prison were the apparent results.

Mrs. Green had already set about collecting a purse for Casement's defense. She wrote out a first check of £100 herself and wrote to William Cadbury and other friends for donations. Cadbury responded with a contribution of £200 and a letter to Gavan Duffy saying that whereas he had "no sympathy whatever with his alleged actions in Germany" he wished Casement "to have every proper opportunity of stating his case." He had believed all along that Casement had turned unhinged and said now that he had observed his ill-health for two years before the war: "until sufficiently proved otherwise I shall believe that the unwisdom of recent months had been largely caused by his serious state of health." In any case, Cadbury concluded, he could not "forget the past years of his noble and unselfish life."[9] At Mrs. Green's suggestion Gertrude wrote on 17 May to the Irish-American lawyer Michael Francis Doyle of Philadelphia, a friend of Gaffney's who had succeeded in forcing a retraction and an apology out of the New York *World* for printing the story of Casement's acceptance of "German gold."[10] Doyle got to-

---

[b]Sir Wyndham Childs, *Episodes and Reflections*, p. 112. Childs had primary responsibility for custody of Casement in the Tower.

gether with Nina Casement Newman in Philadelphia and agreed to "represent" Casement and to try to collect some American cash for the defense. He put the matter up to John Devoy of New York. The Clan-na-Gael had just emptied its treasury in sending $25,000 to Dublin before the Rising, so the case was difficult. But Devoy managed to scrape together $5,000 for Casement, and this money was sent to London with Doyle by the first available ship.[11] Casement, who had been thinking himself repudiated and abandoned by his American friends, wept bitterly when Doyle appeared with his check.[c]

Gavan Duffy was collecting his staff with difficulty, finding senior counsel in London unwilling to touch the case. Eventually he enrolled a junior counsel, Artemus Jones, and J. H. Morgan, Professor of Constitutional Law of London University, who was a friend of Sidney Parry and of Richard Morten and had met Casement fairly often at their houses.[d] Duffy and Jones called together on Casement in the Tower and found that, with better treatment and with the comfort of the knowledge that friends were rallying, he was feeling, looking, and acting more like himself. They made sure he understood that it was a charge of high treason he faced and that the penalty of a finding of guilty was death. Jones recalled Casement's quiet reply: "I should be glad to die a thousand times for the name of Ireland."[12] When the commandant of the Welsh Guards on duty in the Tower asked how he was faring, Casement said that he had slept the night before "like a child," and he was enjoying instruction in the history of the Tower by his guard who had told him, among other things, that no occupant of his cell had ever escaped hanging. From what he had just heard from his lawyers, Casement remarked, he anticipated doing no damage to that record.[13]

In the meantime the government had been collecting the witnesses

---

[c]Contributions to Casement's defense eventually came to £1,750.11.4, distributed as follows: Mrs. Green, £300; Cadbury, £200; Mrs. Llewellyn Davies, £100; Anonymous, £100; Sidney Parry, £100; Gertrude Bannister, £100; Elizabeth Bannister, £50; Agnes O'Farrelly, £50; Roger Casement, £25; Margaret E. Dobbs, £10; Mrs. Fisher Unwin, £5; H. W. Nevinson, £5; Robert Lynd, £4.4.0; Mrs. Robert Lynd, £3.3.0; the American contribution, £698.4.4. Of this sum £1,086.6.0 went to fees to Counsel, £537.7.2 to Gavan Duffy "on account of costs," and a sum of £15.7.9 to "Sir Roger Casement and for his refreshments at Court (including payments at his request for Defendant Bailey)." NLI 13088.

[d]It was Morgan who had suggested that Casement try for a colonial governorship when he was leaving the consular service and offered to support his application. To Richard Morten, 8 July 1916.

for the Prosecution and bringing them to London, a colorful group consisting of exchanged prisoners who could testify to Casement's "seductions" at Limburg, the Irish and English police officers who had been involved in his arrest and detention, and the assorted citizens of the Kerry coast, from young Martin Collins on up, who had come across evidence of one kind or another. And on 10 May Arthur Nicolson sent to the Attorney-General the dossier that the Foreign Office had collected on Casement. The file was marked "Private, confidential" and has remained so: a crucial body of evidence to which all access is still denied—"closed for 100 years."[e]

The Foreign Office had received several interesting communications on Casement and the Rising from the British Ambassador in Washington, Sir Cecil Spring-Rice, a member of the same Anglo-Irish family that had produced one of the yachting gun-runners at Howth in July 1914, Mary Spring-Rice. American attitudes were a major issue, and a touchy one, throughout the Casement affair: with America legally neutral in the war and her friendship and eventual military alliance passionately coveted, the English were willing to go to any lengths within the limits of honor to avoid offense to American opinion. Spring-Rice wrote on 28 April:

> An immense amount of attention is being given to the case of Casement. His attempt [i.e., to lead the Rising] is generally condemned on the grounds that civil war would drench Ireland in blood and profit nobody but Germany. The [New York] World says that it is easy enough to understand why Irishmen must hate England but it is not easy to understand why they should hate themselves. At the same time while deploring the mad enterprise of Casement the newspaper[s] seem to be almost unanimous in pointing out that to execute Casement will be a very great error. They urge that he is generally believed in this country, where he is well known, to be insane or at least suffering from neurasthenia. It is argued that his execution would raise him to the rank of martyr and that the best thing . . . would be to put him in a madhouse.[14]

On 1 May Spring-Rice telegraphed: "Attitude of press on Irish question is favorable on the whole but execution of Casement would cause many protests. Bigelow offers to send correspondence with Casement showing what he thinks proofs of insanity."[15] Poultney

[e]I attacked it several times but was rebuffed.

Bigelow, Casement's old journalist friend from Africa and New York, shortly published Casement's letters to him in the *Philadelphia Public Ledger* and the *New York Times*.[16] His purpose was to save Casement's life, but Casement did not thank him for finding this way of doing it.[f] On the other hand he had no trouble forgiving Cadbury's gentler and more private way of advancing the same idea. On 4 May Spring-Rice telegraphed an account of an interview in which Cardinal Gibbons, generally sympathetic to England in the matter of the Rising and believing that "all respectable Irishmen" condemned the rebellion, still advised that "leniency would have an excellent effect especially in Casement's case," and warned of the danger of "manufacturing martyrs for American use." The telegram was initialed by four persons in the Foreign Office, one of whom noted: "It would require a vast amount of 'manufacturing' to turn Casement into a martyr. . . . No action."[17]

The preliminary hearing occupied three days beginning on 15 May and was held at Bow Street Police Court with the Chief Magistrate, Sir John Dickinson, presiding. The intention of the Crown at this time was to try Casement and Bailey together and so when he reached Bow Street on 15 May he saw Bailey for the first time since Good Friday when, as Julian Beverley, he had walked away from McKenna's Fort toward Tralee in the murky dawn. The charge read that the two of them, at various times between 1 November 1914 and 21 April 1916 "unlawfully, maliciously, and traitorously did commit high treason within and without the Realm of England in contempt of our Sovereign Lord the King and his laws, to the evil example of all others in the like case offending contrary to the duty and allegiance of them to our Sovereign Lord the King and against the form of the statute in such case made and provided." When the charge had been read, Casement asked permission to speak and did so after caution, pointing to Bailey: "Well, that man is innocent. I think the indictment is wrongly drawn up against him. If it is within my power to provide a defense for the man, I wish him to be in every way as well defended as myself, and if he has no means to obtain his defence I am prepared to obtain them for him."[18] When he was able to speak to Gavan Duffy, he asked him to take on the defense of Bailey, and Duffy agreed and so instructed Artemus Jones.

---

[f]Undated letter to Nina from Pentonville Prison: "I saw Poultney Bigelow's act of 'friendship'! I will not call it by the name it deserves." NLI 13077.

The small courtroom was packed tight and among the spectators were Gertrude and Elizabeth Bannister who had arrived at 1:00 A.M. and waited nine hours. Casement was wearing the neat but badly fitting tweeds they had bought for him and managed to give an impression of some elegance. In her diary over in Dublin next day Elsie Henry pasted a reporter's impression of the two prisoners in the first day's hearing. Bailey was described as "a stout young Irishman . . . with a humourous, scrubby, bearded face which contrasted extraordinarily with the striking mien of his fellow-prisoner . . . Sir Roger, huddled up on his narrow seat in the dock, made innumerable notes, sometimes leaning back to stretch his long, lithe frame, and sometimes laughing noiselessly" at something said by a witness or a lawyer.[19] Casement did make copious notes, as is shown by the number that survive, some of them shrewd and apposite, many of them trivial. And he did show himself ready to be engaged and amused, particularly by the Irish witnesses. The Kerry faces and particularly the Kerry voices entertained the whole court, in fact, and led to frequent bursts of laughter especially in the contretemps that occurred when the English and the Irish speakers failed utterly to understand each other. But what Casement really craved in the situation was a pure Irish speaker who knew no English at all, one "with only Irish on him." "What a coup," he jotted for his lawyers during his later formal trial, "in the Lord Chief Justice of England's Court a *'Subject of the Realm of England'* without a word of English. . . . Is it too late? . . . Anyone would do—just to ask him what he saw on Good Friday morning—a nice looking Irish man or woman with no English & God's blessing on his face would be the *best defence* for High Treason & the best witness in the world."[20]

In his opening statement at Bow Street before Sir John Dickinson, the Attorney-General Sir F. E. Smith summarized Casement's career, making heavy play of his courtly letter, which he read verbatim, thanking Sir Edward Grey for his knighthood in 1911, and going on to his appearance in Germany "in the character which has since become familiar to all." Smith then read Bailey's statement of about 500 words describing his joining the Irish Brigade after listening to Casement "about April 1915" in order "to see if I could possibly get out of the country," his term of nearly a year at Limburg and Zossen, his training in explosives with Monteith in Berlin, and his trip to Ireland in the submarine in general innocence and ignorance as to the purpose of the voyage. Then began the testimony of a parade of six returned prisoners (one with an arm missing, another temporarily blinded) all of whom told of hearing and resisting Casement's suasion to join an Irish Brigade to "help Germany free Ireland." The soldiers' testimony continued into the second day of the hearing and they were followed by the Kerry civilians and then by the police witnesses. The third day was largely taken up with arguments as to whether or not Bailey's statement was admissible, Artemus Jones contending unsuccessfully that it had been elicited by improper promises of immunity. Casement's counsel then suggested that Bailey should have separate representation as there was an evident conflict of interest. The Magistrate agreed.[g] The Magistrate then committed the prisoners for trial for high treason "at a place and time to be fixed hereafter." Asked if they had any statement to make, Casement said simply, "No, Sir John," and Bailey remained silent.[21]

As a civil prisoner Casement had been removed from the Tower to Brixton Prison on the first day of the hearing, 15 May, and his physical and spiritual situation improved markedly. He was well housed and well fed, could have books and newspapers and writing materials, send and receive letters (censored), see visitors in reasonable numbers, and was even allowed the extraordinary privilege of smoking, a great relief to a heavy smoker. In fact Casement seems to have been granted a kind of lightening before death: in the time that remained to him he seemed in better health and in many ways in better frame of mind than he had shown for two years. Not that he was happy: but he was full of energy. He still saw his death as foreordained, or so he told himself and told others. It is hard to know how real the thought of death was to him, or how real had been all his talk of treason and its consequence. Casement had the fantasist's protective capacity to see a thing intellectually, and even to imagine it with a good deal of practical circumstance, without taking it in as an actual impending event of the flesh: a thing could be a reality for him without ever quite becoming a fact. Yet his present situation presented him with an inexorable body of fact, a context with unalterable limits, a scenario over which he could exercise no control, and perhaps a strict finality that was not unwelcome. In a sense it was what he had been looking for all his life. The man who had never

---

[g]Gavan Duffy turned Bailey's case over to J. H. MacDonnell of Southampton Street, Strand. Note on Affidavit of MacDonnell. NLI 13088. Subsequently the charges against Bailey were dropped altogether.

been quite sure who or what or where or why he was, who had never quite inhabited his life of factitiousness and *pastiche*, so elaborately verbalized and so nearly theoretical, was supplied with a mold that imposed shape at last.

Casement's last actions were colored then by the strange relief of true helplessness, of finality; but he did not abandon himself to that, or cease to act, or cease to be himself. ("Depend upon it, Sir," said the greatest Englishman of all, Samuel Johnson, "when a man knows he is to be hanged in a fortnight, it concentrates his mind wonderfully.") Casement interested himself passionately in his case, both because it was his and because he saw it as the case of Ireland, a trust in his keeping. He saw himself quite properly as a symbolic figure: he was Ireland, the point at which her melancholy history came to a focus in the eyes of the world. Failure was traditional in the history of Irish rebellion, a part of the iconography, the agreed end of the plot line. Being anticipated it was to be prepared for and properly addressed: the address had come almost to be accepted as the most public and useful movement of the whole form. Hence the literate Irish rebel prepared his speech in the dock before he took up his arms, in bitterness made ready to apply his eloquence to the pathos of the ending. Even old John Devoy, about as tough as a patriot can be and full of contempt for the sentimental anticipation of failure, was not immune to the mystique of martyrdom and found himself treating the speech from the dock as a structural principle in his *Recollections*, the final cusp in the graph of each of his rebel heroes.

Casement, too, was a prisoner of that rhythm, and a not unwilling one. Hence it was perfectly logical for him to insist, as he did for a time, that he must conduct his own defense without professional help. He would embody Ireland graphically in her pathos and nobility, lonely, beleaguered, and proud. He would defend himself only by defiance and definition. He was not an English traitor but an Irish patriot. Indeed he was only accidentally an individual: in complete selflessness he had represented Ireland in the courts of the world. He had failed and Ireland's enemies had laid him by the heels and he would die—not as himself but as Ireland, another of the little recurrent national deaths in which Ireland bled out her history. In fact it was the right case for him to make, the only case, tactically and philosophically, that made sense. In view of the form Casement's trial eventually took, one must be sorry he was not allowed to make it. The whole thing was a play, a melodramatic charade, and he ought to have been allowed to play out his part with the right formality.

Having been forced by the kindness of his friends to accept professional counsel, Casement did his best to impose his poetical view of the case upon them. In a note written to Gavan Duffy apparently on 17 May just after the Bow Street hearing closed he put the matter this way:

> . . . the only defence . . . is complete identification of myself with the charge of High Treason & full acceptance of all its consequences. Our object should be to have *The Crime Against Ireland* [his collection of polemical essays] become the justification not only of my attitude but that of all real Irish nationalists—& the more we get it quoted the better for the Cause (& obviously the worse for me). But the *only* possible way to defend me is to let me hang myself & justify my "treason" out of the pages of Irish history. . . . Once again see *The Crime Against Ireland*—you'll see where the Sinn Fein rebellion came from, who was the inspirer & how necessary it is to get it the widest publicity—not merely the extracts the Crown will use against me—but the extracts we should use against England & English rule in Ireland.[h]

Then he seems to have come back to the reality of his situation with a little recollecting shudder: "Some of my articles in Gaelic American are terrifying." The English might even go back for evidence to his old unsigned articles of 1904 to 1907 in *Sinn Fein* and *The United Irishman*; but he thought that unlikely on the whole: "They have plenty in my recent fulminations."

The argument grew quickly more complicated as Casement saw that his own reputation was tied up not only with that of Ireland but with that of Germany as well. He was afraid with good reason that the Crown would try to tar all with the same brush. He now regretted that he had sounded off so freely at Scotland Yard about his disenchantment with Germany and he feared his own words would be

---

[h]Notes to Counsel. 16 May 1916. NLI 13088. Casement had obviously not got beyond such grandiose flights of fancy as this notion of himself as philosopher-father of the Rising. A few of the leaders, Pearse, MacDonagh, and Plunkett, would have read some of his essays, but his writings were little known generally and the leaders found similar teaching everywhere in Irish history and legend. And every one of them, John Quinn in New York wrote to James Huneker on 1 May, "probably had a speech from the dock up his sleeve." NYPL. Quinn collection.

Casement leaving the Law Courts in handcuffs after losing his appeal for clemency. Courtesy of Syndication International, London.

brought up against him in court: "The Crown will seek to represent me as 1st letting the cat out of the bag about the Rebellion—& 2nd giving my German 'Hosts' away"[22]—to make him look both a fool and a knave. Casement had now climbed down from the plane of hysterical anti-German feeling, specifically anti-General Staff, on which he had lived for a year, acutely so in March and April.[i]

He feared, too, that the Crown might "*try* to invoke scandalous rumours in Germany" to damage both himself and Germany. Casement was thinking, apparently, both about the stories that had circulated in Germany involving his relationship with Christensen and about something more recent: an item that had appeared in a Danish newspaper as he was leaving Germany to the effect that "Sir Roger Casement had been arrested in Germany on an unnamed charge." The item had been quoted in British papers in association with the delayed announcement on 25 April of Casement's capture, but his interrogators had brought it up in a jibing spirit during his first questioning on Easter Sunday, the twenty-third. Casement asserted that all of these vague scandals had been British-inspired, whereas the men of Scotland Yard had suggested that the Danish item had been planted by the Germans as a smokescreen to cover his departure. The phrasing, "scandalous rumours" and "unnamed charge," carried sexual innuendoes though Casement did not discuss the matter in those terms. He told Gavan Duffy that he had overheard the interrogators discussing uses that might be made of these items.[j] His account was vague and there is no way of knowing what he overheard. Apparently the finding of his own diaries had not been mentioned to him as yet; but the diaries may have been a part of the discussion he overheard. What he said he feared, in any case, was a general "discrediting" of himself and the Germans on the grounds of stupidity and deceit: "Ridicule both, slur both—& hold me up to contempt as too much even for the Germans to stand."[23] And indeed, the effect of that would be to discredit Ireland in his dishonored person.

So the line of his defense, Casement insisted, must be that of

---

[i]By 2 June he could speak as temperately as this: "The German Government did only what I asked them, and tried only to help us, when we sought help." NLI 13088.

[j]NLI 13088. Dr. W. J. Maloney demonstrated that the suggestive phrasing in the accounts in British papers of an "arrest" in Germany was planted propagandist distortion of a garbled item in the *Kolding Avis* of 14 April 1916: "It is rumored that the well known Irish revolutionary, Sir Roger O. [*sic*], who went to Germany at the outbreak of the war, has been arrested there for swindling." *The Forged Casement Diaries*, p. 88 ff.

defiant admission of a complex set of "responsibilities":

> This involves not only responsibility for the rising in Ireland
> which was, without question, based on my prior teaching, on
> my pro-Germanism, on my presence in Germany and on the
> hope of help from that country derived from my being there and
> the knowledge that the German Government had entered into
> an agreement with me; but it involves also my responsibility
> *vis-a-vis* the German Government and my duty to defend
> them.[24]

But in all of this the vital object was the Irish cause and that had to be
defended by proving that the Rising had not been "made in Germany" nor even in the head of Roger Casement an Irishman but in
the mind of Ireland: "that in very truth" it was a Sinn Fein (Ourselves alone) rebellion. "This I can do," Casement assured Duffy.
"For it *is* the truth." In fact, he said, the assertion that Germany had
used him and used Ireland was true in reverse: "it was I 'used' Germany and tried to drag her in a question that she knew nothing
of. . . . I succeeded in that. I did drag her in."[25] In view of what
Casement had recently been saying in Germany these were extraordinary statements—and extraordinarily sane. They were signs of the
clearing of his head.

It happened that as Casement was trying to supply his lawyers
with a line of defense, Bernard Shaw was at work on one remarkably
similar. The story is well known. Mrs. Shaw being wealthy, both
Gertrude Bannister and Mrs. Green went to the Shaws to ask for
help with the costs of Casement's defense. Shaw characteristically
refused the money but composed a defense which he offered to
Gavan Duffy. A dozen years later Shaw explained the history of the
matter in a letter to Clarence H. Norman, Jr.,[26] who had noticed a
printed version of the defense[27] listed in a sale of rare books. Shaw
never met Casement, but Gertrude Bannister "interested" him in the
issue: "I said that any attempt at a legal defence would end in pro-
fuse compliments from the Lord Chief Justice to his counsel, and
then—hanging: which, as he preferred his lawyer's advice to mine,
accordingly happened."
He summed up the advice he had given:

> I told him to plead Not Guilty; to admit all the facts and proffer
> himself as a Crown witness if necessary to save trouble; to ex-

plain his campaign for the freeing of Ireland by an alliance with Germany; to claim that he was a prisoner of war and no more a traitor than any Bulgarian captured by the Turks; and to conclude with, in effect, "You have the power to hang me; but if you do, it will be a case of hang me and be damned; for by all the laws of war it will be a murder."

And he described the upshot:

His lawyers thought that this would be quite a nice speech to make *after the verdict;* so Serjeant Sullivan, after putting up the usual pickpocket's defence—"Please, gentlemen, I didn't do it"—got his compliments, and Casement got his rope.[k]

Casement read Shaw's "defence" with gratitude and approbation and asked Gavan Duffy on 5 June to pass on his "warmest thanks." Shaw's view was essentially his own, he said, with modifications: he intended to dispute altogether the Crown's right "to try an Irish rebel under an English statute by an English court"; and he would not ask to be "let off" as a prisoner of war but tell the English, "You may hang *me* and be damned to you . . . as they have my body, they may do with it what they please, while the rest of me will remain unconvicted still."[28]

[k] As to the printing Shaw told Norman that his friend the collector Clement Shorter, whom he called "an Irish patriot by sexual selection" by virtue of having married the Dublin poet Dora Sigerson, got out a private edition of twenty-five copies with Shaw's permission after coming across his memorandum. Shaw suggested to Norman that he try to trace the purchaser of the little book in the sale and offer him the present letter (Shaw's) for "double the money." Clement Shorter wrote to Gertrude Bannister Parry on 19 March 1918: "it was first of all the shootings of Easter Week & much more the execution of your cousin which caused my dear wife's . . . death. She suffered . . . all the tortures of that execution & never recovered from it." NLI 13075.

27 Surrounded with Comforts

I N the long run all of the defenses boiled down to not much more
than verbal flourishing, though more interesting indeed than what
went on in court and more significant as an index of Casement's true
line of thought and feeling. He was in the hands of the men of law
now and they thought perforce of what might be achievable for their
client within the limits of the statutes. Having failed to find in England a lawyer to lead in presenting the defense in the trial, Gavan
Duffy had turned to Ireland and enrolled the man who would be the
most flamboyant figure of the affair, his own brother-in-law, Serjeant Alexander Martin Sullivan, "The Last Serjeant" according to
the title of his later memoirs.[1] The choice was in some ways peculiar
and it was probably unfortunate: Casement and Sullivan did not get
on. Sullivan was a man of forty-five, a King's Counsel in Ireland and
as Serjeant an officer of the Crown; but whereas he had been admitted to the English bar he had never practiced there, was unfamiliar
with English criminal law, and had only junior standing in an English court. Duffy described the case to him as "a magnificent opportunity" and Sullivan was attracted by the notoriety of the case and by
the chance to make an entry into an English career, but he was also
busy and full of doubts. Finally he agreed to take on the case if he
were "handsomely paid," and Duffy said he would see to that. Duffy
went on preparing for the trial with the help of Jones and Morgan.
The coming of the American lawyer, Michael Francis Doyle, was
also expected by Casement's counsel although it was not clear just
what good he could do as he would not be allowed to function officially in court. On 23 May Duffy was granted a writ for contempt of
court against the illustrated weekly the *Graphic* for publishing a
photograph with the caption "The Traitor Casement," pointing out

the prejudicial impression of such matter upon the minds of prospective jurors.

The last preliminary official movement occurred on 25 May: the hearing of the charge in the High Court of Justice, King's Bench Division, before the Lord Chief Justice of England, Viscount Reading, and the Grand Jury (twenty-three of them) of Middlesex and London. This was a formal affair in which the defense played no part at all. The charge was read, Viscount Reading talked for an hour about the facts and the law of treason, the jurors deliberated for an hour and returned "true bills" against Casement and Bailey. The official charge was formed under six heads, the first five listing various occasions in which Casement was described as "soliciting and inciting and endeavouring to persuade certain persons . . . to forsake their duty and allegiance to our Lord the King, and to join the armed forces of his said enemies, and to fight against our Lord the King and his subjects in the said war." On the first of these counts Casement's note read: "a Lie!"; and on each of the others he wrote: "Do."[2] Casement's point was a tricky one and probably untenable. He argued that he had not tried to persuade the Irish prisoners to "join" the armed forces of the King's enemies: he had always thought of the Irish Brigade as distinct, self-contained, somehow autonomous. How it could have been expected to remain so is far from clear and it certainly was not clear in his own head. His statement in the Brief to Counsel for the Accused at first seems plain enough: "I intended to bring the Irishmen to Ireland with a German army." But very likely when Casement said "with" he did not mean "of." The Irish Brigade would not really be part of a German army but ancillary to it, an accompanying auxiliary body, chiefly symbolic. Given his abstract and theoretical way of imagining things, it is unlikely that he thought often of the Irish soldiers as actually facing English troops in order of battle and exchanging real lead with them. In any case the argument ignored the embarrassing fact of his quixotic scheme, pursued so passionately in Berlin in the latter half of 1915, of "taking" the Brigade to the "East" to fight with a hostile army against the English. Fortunately this deadly detail was never brought up in court; but it would have made little difference: it was not needed to convict him. The last item in the Crown's charge Casement marked as "the only count that is relevant to my acts." It read: "that in April of this year he did set out from the Empire of Germany as a member of a warlike and hostile expedition equipped by the enemies of the King and having for its object the introduction and landing on the coast of Ireland of arms and ammunition intended for use in the prosecution of war by the King's enemies against the King and his subjects." Casement might very well have argued that on his *Unterseebot* he had not been a "member" of this expedition, that he had hoped to prevent the arms from being used, and that "the King's enemies" was perhaps a queer way to describe Irish citizens (though it was a definition he was glad to accept personally). But he did not wish to say any of these things: to do so would be to cast doubt upon the integrity and seriousness of himself and of the rebellion. In any case, again, the Rising and Casement's part in it were allowed to play only a surprisingly small part in the capital issue of the trial.

Notwithstanding Duffy's plea for a later date, Viscount Reading set the trial for 26 June. The subterranean drama of the Casement diaries was now well begun. The diaries were an unnamed issue in his trial and they profoundly affected the question of possible clemency after the conviction. Their authenticity and the uses to which they were put remain unresolved issues in the story of Casement's life and in any judgment of his character. It was primarily the diaries and their obscure and dirty treatment that turned Casement's spirit into the unresting spectre that W. B. Yeats heard "beating on the door" in 1937, that faced Alfred Noyes as "the accusing ghost" twenty years later, and that stirs unlaid even now.[3]

It is important to remember at the outset that the diaries were not the only documents "proving him to be a disgustingly unpleasant person," as Shaw described the diaries' supposed effect in a letter of 1934 warning against the publication of what he saw as the unproven case for their forgery prepared by Dr. W. J. M. A. Maloney.[a] The Foreign Office, in the person of Ronald Campbell, an Under-Secretary of State who had known Casement for many years, had been collecting its own dossier dealing at least in part with the "disgusting" aspects of his behavior. This was the file that Sir Arthur Nicolson sent to F. E. Smith on 10 May, the day when a civil trial was settled upon.[4] As no one is allowed even now to examine this file it is impossible to say when it was begun, or what it included, or even how big it was. But it is perfectly clear that it existed and that it dealt at least in part with Casement's "relations" with Adler Christensen—another spectre who now reentered the story, or tried

---

[a]To Gertrude Bannister Parry, 9 November 1934. NLI 5588. Maloney papers. Maloney's famous book is *The Forged Casement Diaries*.

to do so. On 10 May, Nicolson received a wire from New York: "Acting Consul General Philadelphia has received offer from a man named Adler Christensen to give evidence against Casement and if necessary to proceed to England."[5] On this message Nicolson noted: "Christensen is the man to whom Findlay gave the written promise. I am sending a copy of this, with the Casement papers, to the Attorney General"; and Sir Edward Grey wrote: "The Attorney General who has all the confidential documents relating to Christensen & his relations with Casement will not doubt what answer [*sic*] should be sent to this telegram." Similar suggestive minutes were attached to one of the communications from Berne of that veteran and vindictive Casement-watcher Evelyn Grant Duff who hoped on 3 May that this "vulgar conspirator" would soon "expiate his crimes on the scaffold."[6] On a Grant Duff message of 8 May one appended note refers to "certain secret papers kept by Mr. Campbell as to Sir R. Casement's supposed proclivities to unnatural vice"; and another: "The papers on this particular branch of Sir R. Casement's activities are at the moment with the Attorney-General."[7]

There is no evidence to indicate that British officials made any effort to bring Casement's "dear, faithful old Adler"[8] over to testify: probably the Prosecution thought its case airtight without him. John Devoy, on the other hand, wrote that Christensen's betrayal had been prevented in the United States: "Christensen was going over from here to testify against him—and incidentally to give away all our secrets that he had got from Roger—*but we kept him here*."[9] He described the man as a crook, believed he had been in the pay of the English all along, and cited Casement's loose confiding in Christensen to show how dangerous it was to trust Casement himself. And Casement began a little reluctantly to change his opinion of the man's character. "The weak point of the case for me," he wrote in one of his Notes to Counsel, "is the character of Christensen." He remembered Devoy's repeated warnings and he recalled from his own experience Christensen's failure to deliver £50 that he had sent for Nina from Germany and his failure to make any move to repay to the Clan-na-Gael, as he had promised, any part of the $3,000 that Casement estimated Christensen had extracted from him. Yes, Casement had to admit, "it is quite possible he has sold himself to the Br. Govt." Yet his view remained characteristically divided and unrealistic: "He would sell himself to them—altho' I *don't* think he would injure me."[10]

Exactly when and where the diaries themselves were found is

another crucial question that remains unresolved.[b] What is certain is
that they were in the hands of police and intelligence officers shortly
after the interrogation began at Scotland Yard on 23 April and that
by the first week in May they were beginning to be used surrepti-
tiously against him. Apparently they were not then, and in fact not
ever, shown to Casement himself. About the third of May Captain
Reginald Hall of Naval Intelligence, who had shared in the early interrogations, called into his office in the Admiralty a number of English and American press representatives and showed them what he
identified as photographic copies of portions of Casement's diaries,
describing homosexual episodes. One of the Americans told the
story to a woman named Mary Boyle Reilly who was a news agency
representative, and she later told it to Mrs. Green who asked her to
inform Gavan Duffy of what was going on. Miss Reilly wrote Gavan
Duffy on 3 June:

> About a month ago a group of important American journalists
> were called to Whitehall and there shown letters and a diary of
> Sir Roger Casement's which proved him to be a moral offender
> unworthy of public sympathy. One of these journalists, a man
> without knowledge or sympathy anent Irish affairs, but with a
> spirit of fair play, informed me that this incriminating evidence
> will be brought forward early in the trial by way of divorcing
> public sympathy from the accused.[c]

Another journalist who was shown parts of the diaries, though he
was evidently not one of the original group, was Ben S. Allen, a
member of the London bureau of the Associated Press. Allen was a
friend of Dr. Maloney's and wrote to him of his experience when
Maloney was working out his theory of the forgery of the diaries.
Allen apparently saw the material in two forms, in manuscript and
typewritten copies. On the first occasion, after Allen had already
heard gossip about the diaries, at the end of one of the regular
Wednesday briefings of American correspondents, Hall offered him
the use of the diaries as an "exclusive" for the Associated Press. He
showed a "rolled manuscript" which he "took from a pigeon hole in
his desk." Allen remembered the manuscript as "finely written in the

---

[b]I was repeatedly refused permission to examine Scotland Yard records of the process of
search and seizure.
    [c]Quoted in Hyde, *Roger Casement*, pp. 74–5. Miss Reilly's reference to "letters" is
unexplained: perhaps a confusing of the story told her.

hand writing of a person of culture and originality. The paper was not quite legal size and with sheets having ragged tops bore the appearance of having been torn from a lined composition book." Allen said that before he could accept the diary as genuine he would have to show it to Casement himself in prison for authentication and then submit it to the London chief of his bureau; and in any case he could not use excerpts out of context; he would have to have access to the whole diary. Hall was noncommittal and put the sheets back in his pigeon hole. The process was repeated for several weeks thereafter at the Wednesday briefings, with Hall always offering the prize but applying no special pressure upon Allen to accept it. At least once in a late stage "typewritten excerpts" were offered rather than a manuscript; but both forms were "evidently designed to illustrate the innuendo of perversions." Allen had relucted against the whole proposition on grounds personal as well as professional, as he wrote to Dr. Maloney: "I knew Sir Roger Casement, having interviewed him at length on one occasion and having met him again later. Frankly I do not believe the man I had met and grown to admire tremendously wrote that diary and I still hold to that belief." Hence Allen supported Maloney's supposition of forgery and was inclined to accept the Hobson-O'Hegarty hypothesis that the diary was one copied by Casement in the Putumayo.[d]

There can be no doubt that excerpts from the diaries were shown and shown early; and the matter did not stop there: they were soon being exhibited in London clubs and in the House of Commons and to individuals at the very top of the hierarchy in church and state. The story is an indelible dirty mark on the history of English justice: it was a cynical and unscrupulous action of public officials, and as a tactic it seems not only low but unnecessary and stupid, profoundly dangerous to the perpetrators—who must have realized that they stood in contempt of court. It is hard to believe that Thomson and Hall would have run these risks without encouragement in higher quarters. The actors must have counted on Casement's

---

[d] 2 December 1932. NLI 5588. Maloney papers. Allen also mentioned receiving several years after the war a wire from Bruce Bliven, managing editor of the *New York Evening Globe*, asking his advice about publishing a "manuscript" of Casement diaries that had been offered: "I replied that I doubted the authenticity of the manuscript and that furthermore I questioned the propriety of publishing it." This episode sounds like one of the early efforts of Peter Singleton-Gates to publish the "Scotland Yard Copy" of the diaries that he had somehow got hold of and eventually printed (two diaries and a cash book) as *The Black Diaries*.

helplessness: his evident guilt on the political charge, his pariah status in the climate of uncritical patriotism, the power of the universal prejudice against homosexual "perversion," and the fact that he and his counsel might prefer to let the slander pass rather than to stand convicted in the popular mind by the mere act of airing the charge.

Everyone assumed that Casement must be convicted on the charge of treason. But it was not certain that he would hang for it, or that he would die in wholly bad odor. The diaries were circulated to make sure that he would be hanged in disgrace, not only political but moral: a permanent vengeance in which his memory would be declared indefensible. The perpetrators did not have matters entirely their own way. As soon as she heard Mary Boyle Reilly's story, Mrs. Green had protested to Sir John Simon, a leading member of the English bar and one of those who had refused to defend Casement in the trial. He took action and so did Lord Haldane. But it was already too late to prevent the damage, and the sly showings did not really stop in any case: they continued during the trial and even after Casement's execution. The *Times* was finally moved to protest—a day *after* Casement was hanged. It is some small satisfaction to read that Reginald Hall's leading part in the scheme was always remembered to his discredit in London society.[11]

In her letter of 3 June to Gavan Duffy, Miss Reilly had assumed that the embarrassing evidence of the diaries would be "brought forward early in the trial" by the Crown. In fact, the Prosecution proposed a different sort of use for the diaries, as is attested by both Artemus Jones and Serjeant Sullivan. According to Jones one of the opposing junior counsels handed him "sometime before" the trial an envelope containing "the document" which he described as follows:

> . . . a number of typewritten sheets, bound within covers of smooth brown paper. The text was in the form of a diary, the entries being made on different dates & at various places, including Paris, also towns in Africa & South America [these would be the diaries of 1903 and 1910 and the cash book]. . . . Most of the entries related to trivial personal matters common to diaries. At intervals appeared passages to which the Crown attached importance. . . . In these the diarist described acts of sexual perversion he had committed with other men.[12]

If the diaries were to be used as evidence, Jones realized, the manuscript would have to be produced and the handwriting proven; he assumed that the original was at Scotland Yard—whose detectives the opposing counsel said had found the diaries in a search of Casement's old lodgings "in Pimlico" (this would be 45 Ebury Street). With "the document" came an oral message from the Attorney-General: it had occurred to him that the defense might wish to enter a plea of "guilty but insane" and in that event they might like to have the evidence of the diaries to offer in support; Smith wanted Serjeant Sullivan to read these papers with that in mind. Jones accepted the envelope but told the other counsel he thought there was no likelihood of a guilty plea. As the papers were intended for Sullivan who had not yet come to London, Jones kept them locked up in his chambers. Both Duffy and Morgan knew he had them but neither asked to read them. When Sullivan appeared, Jones gave him the Attorney-General's message and produced the envelope. But Sullivan merely waved it away impatiently: "There is no question of our pleading guilty. I don't see what on earth it has to do with us. I don't want to read it—give it them back."[13] At the trial Jones handed the envelope back to the man who had given it to him with the remark: "I am jolly glad Sullivan did not want to read it." In the noisy courtroom he was evidently misunderstood, for a day or two later he learned that Smith was angry because he thought "the document" had never been presented to Sullivan. Both Jones and Sullivan wrote notes to him explaining the facts.[e]

The episode is baffling on both sides of the case. Was the Attorney-General making a generous Christian gesture, offering the defense a genuine way out that might save Casement's life? Sullivan's reading (forty years later) was that Smith was "anxious to play down the prosecution so as to mitigate the growing hostility of Americans": prosecution could not be abandoned, but the issue might be softened by the guilty-insane plea.[14] But there is little evidence to support such an interpretation. Smith showed only a resolute, in-

---

[e]Sullivan tells the story slightly differently: in Dublin he received a letter and later a telegram saying that the diaries were at the Home Office and urging him to study them; he never went; in court, while waiting for the judges to appear, Travers Humphreys, the opposing junior counsel, handed him an envelope containing the excerpts; he had no interest in the question and passed the papers on to Jones who read them. *The Last Serjeant*, p. 270 ff. Sullivan's handling of facts in his memoir is so casual and contradictory that one is inclined to trust the Jones version.

deed vindictive, intention to convict and hang Casement; and whereas it is true that British officials were watching American opinion carefully none of them was inclined to be fundamentally swayed by it. Furthermore, nobody on either side believed that Casement was legally insane or could be proven so. Smith's maneuver may have been downright Machiavellian: to seduce the defense into a plea of insanity, which could then be disproved, but would force the spreading abroad of the repugnant matter of the diaries in open court. On the other side of the case it is easy to see why Casement's lawyers would wish to keep the diaries out of court, to see that they might feel a fastidious personal reluctance to read such matter; but one would think they bore a professional obligation to familiarize themselves with any evidence that the prosecution might conceivably bring forward: hence that Duffy and Sullivan should not only have read the excerpts but demanded to see the whole of the originals and should have put the documents in some form to Casement himself to affirm or deny. In fact Sullivan (in extreme old age) told René MacColl that he did tax Casement with the question and drew a grandiose and defiant response: Casement "gloried" in his homosexuality and told Sullivan he should read off in court a list of great names to show its inseparability from genius.[f] The style of Sullivan's memoirs is so rattling and self-celebrating that one mistrusts it automatically, and one would hardly know what to believe from such a narrator at the age of eighty-three. One need not agree with Brian Inglis, however, that Casement's "rhapsodical justification"— if such an interview ever occurred—"would have been wholly out of character."[15] Casement was capable of rhapsodizing and the personality of Sullivan was exactly the right kind to bring on a fit of it.

The diaries were brought home to Casement in any case, though in a form not quite explicitly spoken, in his first meeting with his old friend Richard Morten in Brixton Prison on 8 June. J. H. Morgan, Casement's adviser and Morten's friend, was present during part of the interview and he reported that Morten asked, "What about the other thing, Roddie?" Casement answered only: "Dick, you've upset me." When Gertrude Bannister complained to Duffy that Morten had left Casement in trepidation, Morgan assured Duffy that he himself had said nothing about the diaries and Morten had said

---

[f]MacColl, *Roger Casement*, p. 224. Mr. Montgomery Hyde tells me that Sullivan said the same thing to the late Frank MacDermot.

nothing of the notoriety they had been given. But the reference was clear both to Morten and to Casement. Later Morten had wept and exclaimed: "Oh, Roddie! To think I should see you here!"[g] Quite apart from the homosexual reference, the meeting in such circumstances of two such close friends now divided by deep political differences was bound to leave both men shaken. Casement wrote Morten on 11 June what he evidently intended at the time as a final farewell:

> I am sorry you came. It upset us both—me more than I can tell you. Please dismiss from your mind all that was said—rub it out for ever—I shall not see you again I fear—not in this life—but you are often—indeed ever—in my thoughts as one of the truest friends a man ever had—and one of the most sincere and lovable of men. . . . *Don't* worry about me—I did what I conceived to be right and my duty under the circumstances. . . . an Irishman's feeling for Ireland is a very real thing. . . . Goodbye dear old Dick. . . . It has been one of the true joys of my life to have had you for a friend so many years—and one of the bitter griefs to lose you.
>
> Your loving friend,
Roddie.[16]

On the following day Casement had his first unhappy conference with Serjeant Sullivan in Brixton Prison. Sullivan outlined the line of argument that he intended to follow: that Casement had not committed treason within the actual wording of the law—the statute of 1351 originally composed in Norman French and ambiguously translated into English, defining treason as "levying war against the King or being adherent to the King's enemies in his realm giving them aid and comfort in the realm or elsewhere." The statute has been explained as a "simple way" hit upon by Edward III to collect funds when he was hard up.[17] Sullivan was perfectly sincere in his belief that he would be basing his defense upon a valid point of law. "Neither he nor the enemy was within the realm at the time of the

---

[g]Hyde, *Roger Casement*, p. 79. In the same vein, on 25 April Mary Dunlop-Williams, an old friend from Ireland who had known Casement "since a dear enthusiastic boy of 19" and who had supposed him to be living in retirement with Tom Casement in Africa, wrote him from San Diego, California, on reading news of his capture: "I know that that dear great generous & unselfish heart of yours would prompt you only to deeds of good intent, & always I remember your beautiful love for our dear old Ireland. But, oh dear heart, has it brought you to a cell in the Tower of London!" NLI 13073.

offence," he wrote later. "Any person capable of reading the statute can see at a glance that this is the sort of charge against which Edward's Barons had protected themselves."[18] Perhaps the most irritating and inglorious of the multiple ironies of Casement's final situation was that he was to be tried at last, or at least defended, on a point of grammar, on a question of present or absent commas, at the end indeed on the distinction between a bit of ink and a fold in a piece of ancient parchment.

Casement, of course, did not like it. For what had any of this to do with the cause of Irish nationalism: were the wrongs and the passion of Ireland not to be addressed at all? On 14 June he wrote Duffy that he had spent "a wholly wretched day and night" since seeing Sullivan. To offer a London judge, prosecutor, and jury a plea on merely technical grounds was hopeless from the outset, he argued: "comparable to referring the question of the keeping of Lent to a jury of butchers."[19] But that was not the real point. The case as a whole was hopeless and the real issue was moral: how best to use the public exhibition of a lost cause to make the moral point upon which the crime had been committed. He objected to Sullivan's line "on principle," which Sullivan had called "sentiment." They stood "poles apart," he told Duffy. Sullivan's line seemed to him "dishonourable" in being "contrary to my past attitude and all my actions." Furthermore it made him look like a man without a cause, naked and stupid, undefended before "the only tribunal whose verdict I really seek": the Irish people and others in the world capable of intelligent sympathy with them. So it seemed to him he must return to his first instinct and "conduct my case myself." Then he could "at least make my position clear, leave it on record, justify the cause of Ireland before the world and leave the British Government to do what it pleased."

Again one feels that in the abstract he was right. But what he could have made of such a confrontation is another matter: was he physically, intellectually, and emotionally able to face a prosecutor as fierce and clever as F. E. Smith, for example? His friends and his lawyers thought not and in the long run they prevailed. As Sullivan planned the case, Casement would not be called to give evidence, and equally he could not be subjected to cross-examination. And so his part in the drama reduced itself to the ritual Irish speech from the dock. But Sullivan and others also held out to him the excellent prospect of reprieve after conviction, as had occurred, for example, in the case of the Irishman Colonel Arthur Lynch who had been a leader of the Irish Brigade in the Boer War, and whose defender, Sir Horace Avory, as it happened, was to be one of Casement's judges.

If Casement found frustration and irritation in the presence of Sullivan, he took real comfort in the coming of the American lawyer, Michael Francis Doyle, who reached London on 13 June. Doyle represented Nina and the Clan-na-Gael and embodied their tangible support. But Doyle had no standing in an English court and could not serve directly in the defense. He could offer legal suggestions and he could run errands, but he functioned primarily as a supporting spiritual presence.

Meanwhile other aspects of American opinion were being presented to British officials and were drawing an interesting response. On 10 May Sir Cecil Spring-Rice in Washington had telegraphed to the Foreign Office: "Executions [in Dublin] causing great excitement and may have serious effect on elections [in the United States]. Treatment of Casement most important from point of view of American politics." On this was placed the Foreign Office annotation: "I do not feel that the course of justice should be influenced by whatever the Americans may think. The man will receive a scrupulously fair trial, & feeling in this country also has to be considered." On 26 May Spring-Rice filed a three-page report on recent developments. He described a meeting held in New York to condemn the executions in Dublin and to collect money for the Irish Relief Fund. Cardinal Farley had given support, several priests were present, and Justice Daniel Cohalan, a principal speaker, had said: "if the arms going to Ireland had ever gotten there the mere sample of warfare which was shown by the handful of revolutionists would have been a real revolution."[h] Spring-Rice also sent cuttings of Poultney Bigelow's publication in the *New York Times*, 24 May, of the correspondence which he argued showed Casement's real mental imbalance. Spring-Rice thought that opinion was quite general in America: "that his brain had suffered from exposure in the tropics and that his mind did not work normally." He emphasized the nuisance that Casement had made of himself to American hosts, "one of

[h]PRO FO 95.776. This was John Devoy's conviction, too, and it was the "real revolution" that he blamed Casement for preventing. (To Laurence de Lacy, 20 July 1916. *Devoy's Post Bag*, ii: 504.) Eamon De Valera was quoted as saying after he staggered out to surrender: "If only the people had come out with knives and forks." Walter Starkie, *Scholars and Gypsies*, p. 151.

whom indeed had to break up house in order to put an end to his visit." On 25 May Michael Francis Doyle had called on Spring-Rice in Washington and they had discussed the opportuneness of the Rising in Ireland for the interests of Germany, and the further likelihood that the Germans would now welcome the execution of Casement as a demonstration of British vengefulness: the Germans would actually be "disappointed" by an act of clemency. The French Ambassador had told him the same thing. Spring-Rice had even heard the opinion that the Germans had actually organized the "expedition" and the capture of Casement precisely to provoke British savagery that would in turn hopelessly alienate the Irish, particularly those in America.[20]

Spring-Rice was a loyal public servant who recognized that British policy had to be made in the heads of British officials by their own best lights. But he was also an Irishman and a humane person, and it is clear that he wished passionately to save the life of Casement on grounds that were personal as well as political. On 30 May Spring-Rice tried again: "Situation here caused by Irish executions is serious as the whole weight of Irish party is thrown against us during elections. Irish vote is thus anti-British. . . . general feeling is that while executions in hot blood can be excused it is wiser to show clemency [i.e., to Casement] when danger is well over. Condemnation [of Casement] and subsequent commutation of death penalty is what would be expected here."[21] On this Rowland Sperling noted: "We would expect nothing but hostility from the Irish vote in any case." Sir Arthur Nicolson wrote defensively: "I do not understand what Sir C. Spring Rice means by 'executions in hot blood'— All those condemned presumably had a fair trial—We need not, in my opinion, steer our course . . . with reference to elections in a foreign country—but act simply according to the dictates of justice." Lord Cromer's minute agreed with Nicolson's.

For Casement these days were a time of waiting for the event, on the whole a peaceful and not unhappy interval. He saw much of his lawyers, and a good deal of his friends especially Mrs. Green and his Bannister cousins. He did not feel compelled to admit all visitors and on 11 June, for example, politely refused a visit from John H. Harris (now Sir John), Secretary of the Anti-Slavery and Aborigines Protection Society, explaining that his available time was taken up with family visitors and that as a warder was always present it was never possible to talk with real intimacy. Of himself he wrote: "I am, thank God, much better in bodily health than I have been for a long time, and surrounded with comforts!" He hoped that Harris and his wife were well and "full of good work and hoping always, as I am, that peace may speedily come to bring back something of kindness and good will to the world."[22] On the same day Casement sent a farewell letter to Tom's second wife Katje that assumed death was impending:

> My cousin Gertrude read me Tom's last letter to her from Kilimanjaro slopes and told me of your address so I send you this hurried line to pass on to Tommy when you see him—or when you can get at him. Tell him I often thought of him and particularly of the last look I had of him at the railway station the day he drove me across the veld to catch my train. It was a pity I ever left you both that day! It is more than three years ago now—and the world has gone to wreck and ruin since then. I hope you may soon have Tom back with you in peace and with all this dreadful nightmare gone from you and the world.
>
> Tell Tom to try and see poor old Charlie, too, some day and remember me to him—It must have been a great wrench to you and Tom to lose the farm—and for you to lose Tom going up to the East coast—and I pray for him and hope for you both to be happy together again. . . . I wish I had not left him for his sake—as well as for other things. . . . It is no use writing to me for I shall not ever get it. . . . I hope much he will see Charlie again some day—I feel much for Charlie. Goodbye dear Katje and *all* good luck to you and Tom—and so enough.
>
> Your affectionate brother
Roddie.[23]

A pure bit of macabre comedy arrived at this time in the form of a cablegram from Julio Cesare Arana in Manaos addressed to "Sir Roger Casement, C.M.G., Tower of London" on 14 June:

> On my arrival here am informed you will be tried for High Treason on 26th June. Want of time unables me to write you being obliged to wire you asking you to be fully just confessing before the human tribunal your guilts only known by Divine Justice regarding your dealings in the Putumayo business. They were all suggested by Truth Antislavery Colombian Government Agents. . . . Inventing deeds and influencing

Barbadians to confirm unconsciously facts never happened, invented by Saldana thief Hardenburg etc. etc. I hold some Barbadians declaration denying all you obliged them to declare pressing upon them as English Consul and frightening them in the King's name with prison if refusing to sign your own work and statements. You offered them good berths in Brazil to which country you brought them deceiving Peruvian authorities making yourself their accomplice as per their own information. You influenced the Judges in the Putumayo affair who by your ill influence confirmed your own statements. You tried by all means to appear a humanizer in order to obtain titles fortune, not caring for the consequences of your calumnies and defamation against Peru and myself doing me enormous damage. I pardon you, but it is necessary that you should be just and declare now fully and truly all the true facts that nobody knows better than yourself.[24]

It was entertaining to be pardoned by J. C. Arana and satisfying to hear from his own lips that one had done him enormous damage. Casement naturally took no formal notice of the message, but he wrote to Richard Morten: "Think of it!"[25] On 11 September Sir Edward Grey heard from a London Lawyer who wanted to know whether Arana's wire had been delivered to Casement and whether he had replied to it. "Mr. Arana is suffering from a keen sense of injustice," wrote the lawyer, "and it would be well to satisfy him upon the point."[26]

28   The Dock and the Woolsack

THE trial opened at the Old Bailey, the Lord Chief Justice's Court in the Royal Courts of London, on the morning of 26 June. The three judges were the Lord Chief Justice who had been Sir Rufus Isaacs and had recently become Viscount Reading, Sir Horace Avory, and Sir Thomas Horridge who has been described as having a "ferocious facial tic"[1]—a convulsive disorder of the muscles that gave the impression that he was leering sardonically upon the proceedings. There was plenty to grimace about. The ironies of Casement's situation were by now so many and so complex that it would be tiresome to list them. Perhaps the most acute was the fact that his main antagonist, the prosecuting Attorney-General F. E. ("Freddie") Smith, had defiantly committed some of the same kind of treasonable behavior for which Casement must now answer with his life. But Smith had had the good taste or good luck to carry out his performance in time of peace and with the connivance of a powerful English political party. So Casement was in the dock and Smith and his chief, Sir Edward Carson, were members of the Coalition Cabinet. In 1913 and 1914 as Carson's "Galloper," Smith had joined Carson and Craig to lead the blatant Ulster defiance of Crown and Parliament in resistance to the Home Rule Bill. They had conceived a "Covenant" of implacable resolution that was signed by many thousands of Ulster Loyalists (some in blood), formed a provisional government, collected and trained an army of nearly a hundred thousand men, traveled to Germany and bought arms for them and run them into Ireland. They had threatened civil war and they had freely applied the name of "treason" to their own defiant intentions. They had named Germany as their friend and potential ally. With the help of the Conservative Party and the extraordinary event of the

Mutiny at the Curragh in March 1914, they had got away with it all. But it had happened in time of peace. Yet they must have given a good deal of aid and comfort to the coming enemies of the King in the spectacle they afforded of a divided and weak-willed England.

It seemed a malign guiding of destiny that brought Smith and Casement together in their present relationship, though it was pure chance (not without some logic in it, on both sides). Given his office Smith could not refuse to act as prosecutor of a knight of the realm charged with high treason—the first such case in England for several hundred years. The temptation for the defense and for Casement to attack Smith on his Ulster record was irresistible and with a different strategy from Sullivan's it would have been quite legitimate and quite feasible. But on the line he had chosen, that of defense on a point of law, it was practically impossible to get at Smith himself and at the moral and political irony he embodied in relation to Casement. This situation was another of the continuous frustrations built into the structure of the trial.

The court was packed when Casement was brought in between two warders. He had recovered not only his health but much of his wonted elegance of manner and appearance. Items of his own clothing had been got from a trunk at F. J. Bigger's house in Belfast and he was wearing a dark suit with a white shirt and white collar. Artemus Jones remembered "a tall, slender, handsome man, his dark beard helping to emphasize the intellectual cast of his features," and a bearing of "dignified courtesy" and "imperturbable demeanour."[2] According to Montgomery Hyde he paid little attention to the evident interest of the spectators in himself and "affected an air of weariness" during the early stages of the trial's ritual.[3]

The King's Coroner read the charge and the prisoner was invited to plead, but Sullivan immediately moved to quash the indictment on the grounds that it did not name any offense within the phrasing of the statute: "There is not anywhere in the indictment an allegation of any act done anywhere within the King's domains."[a] The judges conferred briefly and the Lord Chief Justice advised Sullivan that the proper time for his motion was at the end of the case for the prosecution, as was the custom in cases of such significance. Sullivan

---

[a]The verbatim record of the trial is given in Montgomery Hyde's earlier volume, *The Trial of Sir Roger Casement*.

acquiesced, Casement pleaded Not Guilty, and the Attorney-General laid out his case.

Smith's opening statement was comparatively short: it covers nine printed pages. He spoke of the gravity of the charge: "The law knows no graver." He described Casement as "an able and cultivated man, versed in affairs and experienced in political matters," not at all "a life-long rebel against England" like other Irish patriots but a man who had served England for long in "a considerable career of public usefulness" until his retirement. He sketched Casement's career in the consular service and its culmination in his knighthood in 1911. Then as he had done at Bow Street he read out the whole of Casement's "fulsome" short letter of 20 June 1911 thanking Sir Edward Grey for his honor[4] and gibed at the "warmth" of its terms of gratitude and the general tenor of its "language almost of a courtier." Somehow this grateful loyal man of 1911 had transformed himself into the traitor Casement of 1914. After the war had begun, and while enjoying an English pension, he had gone to Germany and had attempted to "seduce and corrupt" loyal Irish soldiers of England to "strike a blow for Ireland by entering the service of the enemies of this country." In general the soldiers had received him with scorn and rejected him with hisses and even blows. Those who accepted his seduction were well treated, those who refused it were punished and their food reduced. He described the arms expedition and Casement's arrival at the same time "in a common adventure" ending in his arrest. "The prisoner," Smith concluded, "blinded by hatred of this country, as malignant in quality as it was sudden in origin, has played a desperate hazard. He has played it and he has lost it. Today the forfeit is claimed."

Two Whitehall officials testified as to the payment of Casement's pension, the upshot being that he had received five quarterly installments between October 1913 and October 1914 of his annual pension allowance of £421.13.4. Then again as at Bow Street a series of returned prisoners, seven of them, testified concerning Casement's representations at Limburg, the manner in which he had been received by the prisoners, and the consequences of their refusal to join the Brigade. In notes to his counsel Casement picked many flaws in their stories but none that mattered fundamentally to his case for the moment, and Serjeant Sullivan's cross-examination of the soldiers was perfunctory. He accepted their evidence as basically true. As

Montgomery Hyde has said, it added up to "a sombre and depressing narrative of the failure of a mission."[5] When court adjourned at the end of the first day, Sullivan had managed only to establish that Casement had appealed to the soldiers to join in a fight for Ireland not for Germany.

The Crown had indicated that it meant to confine its case to the prisoner's treason "without the realm," and on that Casement recorded the gloomy comment: "So much the better. I am quite content—it shortens the long tale." He did not wish to hear his whole life rehearsed in court, or even to have his achievements set off defensively against his crimes: his "early life, or Congo, or Putumayo matters" should be avoided by his counsel, he wrote them,"—no panegyrics."[6] The story that the Irish soldiers had been punished or "starved" for resisting his appeal Casement thought simply untrue; or if there were any shreds of truth in it they were not of his making: he was incapable of that kind of vengefulness. The prisoners had merely shared in the privation of the whole of Germany that was owing to the efficiency of the British naval blockade. But these were all matters by the way and Casement was more deeply irritated by two other items in the case for the prosecution: the argument that he had worked to subvert England while drawing her pay in the form of a pension; and the scornful treatment of his "courtly" letter to Grey as showing a mind not only treacherous but servile.

In Casement's directions for questioning J. A. C. Tilley, a chief clerk at the Foreign Office who had testified about details of his service there, even the handling of the tenses of the verbs carried poignancy: "Mr. Tilley should be very courteously handled—he was an old friend of mine & is a nice man."[7] The Crown had brought out testimony that Casement's pension had been "withdrawn on 30 September [1914] by order of the Treasury" and Casement called this "a fearful blunder of theirs." He recalled that Grey in the hand of Sir Arthur Nicolson had written him on 26 October 1914 after his anti-recruiting "Manifesto" had appeared in the *Irish Independent* to remind him that he was still liable to be called upon to serve the Crown, i.e., that he was still on pension at that time.[8] Casement believed his pension was not officially stopped until the winter, and he associated it with Grey's receipt of his long letter of 1 February 1915 from Berlin denouncing the "Findlay plot," and resigning his own honors. He wished his lawyers to argue that "up to 30 June 1914 I had done nothing of a treasonable kind . . . the pension in no wise deterred me from assisting in Volunteer rising in Ireland—and that until I decided to go to Germany I was quite entitled to use it—and I ceased using it in any way after 30 June."[9] He had allowed himself to be persuaded by the Clan-na-Gael men to send in the 30 September voucher to the Treasury so as to raise no suspicions of his impending trip to Germany. But he had never "drawn that £104" and he assumed it was still lying in his bank. In all he had received only about £400 of his pension, between 30 June 1913 and 30 June 1914, and "were my a/c accessible" he could show that £130 of that had gone to Nina and the rest to Irish causes. It comforted him thus to think that he had never "used" his English pension.

The "fulsome" letter to Grey on the knighthood was a still more rankling embarrassment and Casement wrote about it almost obsessively to his lawyers. Smith had made skillful play of the letter and it stuck in everyone's throat. The prison doctor, for example, told Casement that he and others found it the hardest of all his actions to forgive. Casement knew it was a side issue, but a damnably effective one against him, and he recognized it as an attempt to ruin him before they killed him: "They want to damn my character as a man first & then hang me afterwards for the breach of law." He rehearsed the whole story of his reluctant acceptance of the C.M.G. in 1905, a reluctance he had thought he had made so plain as to forestall any future offering of honors. He had never opened the package with the insignia and in fact did not know where it was at this moment; when he was knighted he had had to borrow an old C.M.G. from the chancery of the order to wear at the ceremony. Mrs. Green, Dick Morten, and F. J. Bigger could all testify as to his real feelings about English honors. And he had often told Foreign Office officials that such things should never be conferred without prior notice and consent. Then the knighthood had come out of the blue in 1911, publicly announced before he ever heard of it. He had felt that he could not refuse it "without giving *great offence* to King, Grey, the public, etc. etc.," that if he refused it he would have to resign his post and thereby "to abandon the cause of the Putumayo natives."[10] Now he suggested that his lawyers introduce his letter to Mrs. Green deploring the knighthood[11] as a riposte to Smith's tactics. But that would not have canceled out the *text* of the letter to Grey and in fact might have made it sound all the more cringing and disingenuous. The overripe language of the Grey letter expressed another of those schizoid occasions in which Casement's pen ran away with his will and said things that his mind and heart did not intend. Casement might call the language "perfunctory" and he probably even understood it as such himself. But it could not be made to sound perfunctory to any ordinary reader.

Smith's other damaging suggestion that his efflorescence of Irish nationalism was a late and sudden birth, timed unscrupulously to coincide with the desperate straits of England in the war, Casement thought could also be disproved out of the mouths of Foreign Office officials. The principle that "England's difficulty is Ireland's opportunity" was ancient and honorable in Ireland, and Casement had by a kind of accident of history acted in part in that spirit. But he did not wish to claim the fact, and the argument that he was a capricious and new-born patriot was simply untrue in any case and could have been copiously disproven on evidence in Ireland. But he wished to force his old English collegues to speak out, too, to admit the fact "that Sir Roger was a very advanced Irish nationalist" was actually "common property in the F. O.—that he was spoken of as a 'Separatist'—a 'Fenian' etc., etc." Yet they should be forced to admit that he had been "at the same time a very loyal officer who faithfully discharged his duty without fear or favour, as long as he was in the service."[12]

Perhaps the most interesting and surely the most amusing of these notes of Casement's to his counsel was that in which he urged them to find a way to work into the process of the soldiers' testimony and cross-examination a story he had heard in Germany from the Baroness Speck von Sternburg, widow of the German Ambassador to Washington. The Baroness described a meeting in August 1913 between Sir Edward Carson and the Kaiser at Hamburg, across the Taunus range from Limburg. When they met, she said, they "kissed again with tears"; and when "the Playboy of the Western World" took leave of "the imperial presence" he "bade them farewell again with tears in voice and eye—saying *You will never see me again;* I am going to be hanged!" To get that tale brought out in court, Casement said, he would almost be willing to hang himself.[13] But the trouble with all of these pleasant and instructive lines of talk was that there was no logical way to introduce them into the defense as Sullivan designed it.

The second day of the trial, 27 June, was largely taken up by testimony of the Kerry citizens, John McCarthy and Mary Gorman, and of the Irish and English police officers. The matters of the dinghy, the pistols and ammunition, the footprints, and the three strangers walking past Mary Gorman, the arrest, the overcoats, the knapsack, the "itinerary" or "diary," the code, the sleeping car ticket were all run through once more. The story of the capture and the scuttling of the *Aud* was told and a sample of her cargo, brought up by divers, was identified as a Russian rifle and ammunition of a pattern of 1905. This closed the case for the prosecution and Sullivan was now free to bring forward his motion to quash the indictment—a poor thing, but his own.

Casement had ordered his counsel not to "try & 'clear' me or cry 'Peccavi.' " They were rather "to defend and make clear an extreme Irish Nationalist's standpoint—that I wanted to put up a straight fight for Ireland, in Ireland, & if possible with some prospect of success." An Irish patriot, then, and not an English traitor—and not a dreamer, not a fool. Sullivan's defense represented his client as saying, in effect, Yes, I did all of those things, but they are not crimes within the law on which you are trying me; or, The statute doesn't say what you think it means; or, The statute doesn't mean what you think it says. Sullivan spent two hours of this day in developing his point that the unpunctuated language of the statute defining treason as "levying war against the King or being adherent to the King's enemies in his realm giving them aid or comfort in his realm or elsewhere" must not be read with the inner phrase "giving them aid or comfort in the realm" considered as parenthetical, as if set off by the commas that the scribe had never inserted, making the phrase "or elsewhere" a mere continuation of the phrase "being adherent to the King's enemies in his realm." "Or elsewhere," Sullivan submitted, was intended grammatically to be an alternative to the preceding phrase "giving them aid or comfort in his realm." Hence, he contended, Casement would have had to be within the realm when he committed his acts of treason in order to be guilty under the statute. In effect he seems to have been arguing that the statute of Edward III was simply a faulty law that did not encompass the purpose attributed to it by the Crown. He argued with learning and ingenuity, ably supported by J. H. Morgan on the third day, but it was all hopeless. They were refuted by the Attorney-General at great length, precedents were cited to show that treasons committed outside the realm by a British subject had always been held to be triable under the common law in England, the judges conferred, and the motion to quash the indictment was denied.

Sullivan had explained to Casement that he would be allowed, if he wished, to make a formal statement in the course of the proceed-ings which would not be under oath and so would not subject him to cross-examination. Casement had prepared such a statement and he read it at this point, taking about ten minutes. His protests in regard to the Crown's treatment of his pension and his knighthood were now reduced to "one word only": "The pension I had earned by ser-vices rendered, and it was assigned by law. The knighthood it was not in my power to refuse." He attacked four "misstatements" that had appeared in the evidence against him: that he had asked the Irish prisoners to fight with Turks against Russians or with Germans on the Western Front; that he had asked them to fight "for Germany" ("I have always claimed that [an Irishman] has no right to fight for any land but Ireland"); that he had got rations reduced for recalcitrant prisoners; that he had accepted "German gold." He mentioned his suit against the American newspaper that had printed this "libel" and went on to press the truth of the matter:

> I have never sold myself to any man or to any Government, and have never allowed any Government to use me. From the first moment I landed on the Continent until I came home again to Ireland I never asked for nor accepted a single penny of foreign money . . . but only the money of Irishmen. Money was of-fered to me in Germany more than once, and offered liberally and unconditionally, but I rejected every suggestion of the kind, and I left Germany a poorer man than I entered it.

For the Irish gold, on the other hand, he expressed his deep gratitude. The Attorney-General having made a "veiled reference" to the matter of the Rising itself, Casement assured the jury "that the rebellion was not made in Germany, and that not one penny of Ger-man gold went to finance it." He had touched on "these personal matters," he told them, because they had been designed to reflect upon his personal honor and thereby "to tarnish the cause I hold dear." In the process of his refutations Casement had made the point that probably lay closest to his private heart: "that a man who, in the newspapers is said to be just another Irish traitor, may be a gentle-man."[14]

Sullivan's ensuing formal address to the jury lasted nearly two hours and ended with his dramatic collapse. It was an able and eloquent performance in which, deprived of his original point of law, he now had to confront the realities of what Casement had done. His main point was that the definition of the acts as treasonable must turn upon the intention in the mind of the protagonist: "Unless he intends treachery to the King, the fact that others may use with advantage that which he does, against his intention, perhaps to the public detriment of the realm, does not make him guilty of treason." That the Germans were certainly "interested in his succeeding," as the Attorney-General had pointed out, had nothing to do with the case. German motives were their own affair: all the evidence showed that Casement's actions first and last were pointed to a fight by Irishmen, for Ireland.

After rehearsing the tenor of this evidence for an hour and a half Sullivan began to move toward Casement's real logic of action: the forming of the Ulster Volunteers, their arming and defiant gestures made with evident impunity, the forming of the Irish Volunteers in response, the need to supply them with arms to give them force. "Does not that show you in one gleam what it was that Sir Roger Casement was doing in Limburg when he recruited the Irish Brigade?" he asked, and continued:

> There was in the north of Ireland an armed body of men . . . marching about . . . deliberately originated with the avowed object of resisting the operation of an Act of Parliament which had the approval of the rest of the country. They armed, and nothing was said to them; they drilled, and nothing was said to them; they marched and countermarched; the authorities stood by and looked at them. . . . They had great forces behind them, great names and men of high position. . . .
>
> What are you to do when, after years of labour, your representatives may have won something that you yearn for, for many a long day, won it under the constitution, had it guaranteed by the King and the Commons, and you are informed that you should not possess it because those that disliked it were arming to resist the King and the Commons and to blow the statute off the book with powder? . . . You may lie down under it, but if you are men, to arms; when all else fails defend yourself.[15]

At long last Casement was hearing some of the things he had wanted said. But the trouble was that Sullivan's new line of argument had not been sufficiently prepared for by evidence as previously introduced: no "ground" had been laid for it. The judges had been showing restlessness for some time and finally the Lord Chief Justice intervened and called a halt. Smith, too, rose to object: "I am most loath to intervene, but I have heard a great many statements which are wholly uncorroborated."

Sullivan apologized, apologized again, resumed speaking, lost his thread, hesitated, appeared to sway on his feet, and said at last: "I regret, my Lord, to say that I have completely broken down." Then he dropped into his seat and held his head in his hands. Court was immediately adjourned. Sullivan later blamed his collapse on the accumulated strain of the preparation and conduct of the trial, the sleeplessness and anxious tension he had experienced over a period of days: "There was not a red corpuscle left in my body."[16]

On the fourth and final morning of the trial Artemus Jones announced that his "learned leader" was constrained from appearing by doctor's orders and asked permission to continue his discourse. He resumed and reinforced Sullivan's main arguments in a single comprehensive form: Casement had gone to Germany "not for the purpose of helping Germany to fight England, but for the purpose of forming an Irish Brigade to strive for something they had a right to strive for, the protection of their countrymen if they were coerced or tyrannized by armed forces in Ireland which were not controlled by the Executive Government." If Casement were involved in the importation of arms, as his possession of the code perhaps showed, that was not high treason but an offense under the Defense of the Realm Act and should have been so dealt with. He was pulled up often by interruptions from the bench and objections from the Attorney-General, and when he tried to discuss points of law, he was reminded that this was not matter for the jury but for the judges. The emotional appeal with which Jones closed in effect abandoned the case in law and prepared the way for the traditional Irish patriot's speech from the dock:

> The ancient and valiant race from which this man springs does not produce the type of man who shrinks from death for the sake of his country. The history of Ireland contains many melancholy and sad chapters, and not the least sad is the chapter which tells and speaks so eloquently of so many mistaken sons of that unfortunate country who have gone to the scaffold, as they think, for the sake of their native land.

This was to throw the case upon charity and to leave Casement standing in the sentimental light of a mistaken son of Shan Van Vocht, the Poor Old Woman.

It was the Attorney-General's right to have the last word with the jury and he made the most of it in the speech of a passionate and ingenious advocate. He dismissed the equivocations and "sophistries" that would make of Casement's actions anything other than treasonable behavior punishable by death, and he bore most heavily upon the "unanswered" crucial question: Why had Casement gone to Germany at all? Was not Ireland the place for Irishmen to defend Ireland? The Crown did not know and did not seek to prove how Casement had come to Ireland, but his association with the arms ship was an "irresistible inference." Reminded by one of his juniors that "the diary" ("the itinerary") bore an entry that coincided in date and implication with the sleeping card ticket, Smith made that point and induced a bit of byplay that has aroused a good deal of speculation.

> Chief Justice: "Mr. Attorney, you mentioned a passage in the diary. Is there any evidence as to whose diary it is?"
>
> Attorney-General: "It was a diary. I will give your lordship the evidence of it. It was a diary found."
>
> Chief Justice: "I know, but as far as my recollection goes there was no further evidence given beyond the fact that it was found. Whose writing it is, or whose diary it is, there is no evidence."
>
> Attorney-General: "My lord, I did not say that it was a diary of any particular person. I said 'the diary.' By 'the diary' I meant the diary which was found, and is in evidence as having been found."
>
> Chief Justice: "I thought it right to indicate that, because it might have conveyed to the jury that it was Casement's diary. There is no evidence of it."
>
> Attorney-General: "You have heard, gentlemen, what my lord has said. If there was any misunderstanding I am glad it should be removed. It was a diary found with three men as to whom I make the suggestion that they had all come from Germany. There is no evidence before you as to which of the three."[17]

This reference to "the diary" and the echolalial dwelling upon the phrase that ensued set abroad at the time a mistaken idea that Casement's private diaries, the "Black Diaries" from which the damaging extracts were taken, had been introduced and traced to him at the trial. And Alfred Noyes later made a rather persuasive case for the argument that the interchange had been planned and carried out with exactly that purpose in mind.[18] He noted that the word "diary" appeared ten times in the dialogue, and that Smith apparently made no effort to clarify things by using any of the other simple identifying phrases available to him. He assumed that F. E. Smith wrote the little play and Viscount Reading helped him recite it. Such a scheme was not an impossibly clever invention for Smith, but Noyes's theory must be finally discounted. It assumes, for one thing, the collusion not only of Smith and Reading but of the junior counsel. The impression of play-acting tends to disappear when the passage is studied carefully in context. The objection the Lord Chief Justice was raising was a legitimate one and it interrupted Smith in the midst of a long flight: in his flurry he groped for words and kept finding the same words. Smith's argument then continued in logical transition with a vague reference usefully, albeit clumsily, clarified.

The Attorney-General's address had finished off the morning. After luncheon the Lord Chief Justice reviewed the evidence and gave his charge to the jury:

> You have to determine whether the prisoner was contriving and intending to aid and assist the enemy. If what he did was calculated to aid and assist the enemy, and he knew it was so calculated, then, although he had another or ulterior purpose in view, he was contriving and intending to assist the enemy . . . if he knew or believed that the Irish Brigade was to be sent to Ireland during the war with a view to securing the national freedom of Ireland, that is, to engage in a civil war which would necessarily weaken and embarrass this country, then he was contriving and intending to assist the enemy.[19]

That reading of the law, and that construction placed upon the words "calculated," "contriving," and "intending," left the jurymen virtually no freedom of choice. They retired at 2:53 P.M. and returned at 3:48, Casement having been brought back in the meantime. He smiled and nodded to friends and shook Gavan Duffy by the hand. In answer to the question of the King's Coroner the foreman of the jury pronounced their unanimous verdict: "Guilty." The Coroner then addressed the prisoner: "Sir Roger David Casement, you stand convicted of high treason. What have you to say for yourself why the Court should not pass sentence and judgment upon you to die according to law?"

Casement's one poor moment had come and according to the impression of those present he made a fine thing of it. He read for about forty minutes from his manuscript of blue prison foolscap sheets, an address which he made clear at the outset he had prepared some three weeks earlier in the certainty of the final verdict. Casement's speech has been much praised, and probably overpraised in such judgments as Wilfrid Scawen Blunt's: "the finest document in patriotic history."[20] That is the kind of thing an otherwise sensible man says out of sentimental involvement. Certainly it is the finest thing Casement ever wrote, better formed and better controlled, but still it is marred by his old sins of wordiness, turgidity, and pretentious diction: he says "strain no strand," for example, when all he means is "draw no rope." In its own setting it must have been deeply moving, a formalizing of fatal truths for which there was no help to be found. Casement read quietly but more audibly than in his statement of the preceding day. As he proceeded his nervousness became a passion controlled by dignity and embittered resignation.

He had chosen to read his remarks, he said, because he hoped to reach "a much wider audience" than that of the courtroom: "my own countrymen." He noticed the irony of the way in which "that Constitutional phantom, 'the King' " had managed to dredge up out of the Dark Ages "a law that takes a man's life and limb for an exercise of conscience": essentially he had been tried and convicted not for "adhering to the King's enemies but for adhering to his own people." He spent a good half of his oration in an elaborate repudiation of the jurisdiction of an English court and an English jury to assess his action: "the Court I see before me now is not this High Court of Justice of England, but a far greater, a far higher, a far older assemblage of justices—that of the people of Ireland. Since . . . it was the people of Ireland I sought to serve—and them alone—I leave my judgment and my sentence in their hands." He told again the old Irish ritual story to which Artemus Jones had referred:

Ireland has seen her sons—aye, and her daughters too—suffer from generation to generation always from the same cause, meeting always the same fate, and always at the hands of the same power; and always a fresh generation has passed on to withstand the same oppression. . . . The cause that begets this indomitable persistency, the faculty of preserving through centuries of misery the remembrance of lost liberty, this surely is the noblest cause men ever strove for, ever lived for, ever died for. . . . I stand in a goodly company and a right noble succession.

The Volunteers in the South, seeking unification and independence for all Ireland, had been formed in response to the Volunteers in the North preaching apartness and civil war. He had gone to America, Casement said in his first direct reference to Attorney-General Smith, to offer an Irish answer to such assertions as that "Nationalists would neither fight for Home Rule nor pay for it." Augustine Birrell had told the Hardinge Commission inquiring into the causes of the rebellion in Ireland that the war "upset all our calculations." "It upset mine no less," Casement said: it put an end to a legal and peaceful errand and left him with a desperate choice:

> We have seen the working of the Irish constitution in the refusal of the army of occupation at the Curragh to obey the orders of the Crown. And now that we were told the first duty of an Irishman was to enter that army, in return for a promissory note, payable after death [i.e., the Home Rule Bill "on the statute book"]—a scrap of paper that might or might not be redeemed, I felt over there in America that my first duty was to keep Irishmen at home in the only army that could safeguard our national existence. . . . I saw no reason why Ireland should shed her blood in any cause but her own, and if that be treason beyond the seas I am not ashamed to avow it or to answer for it here with my life.

The difference between his course and that of "the Unionist champions" (such as Smith) was that they chose "a path they felt would lead to the woolsack; while I went a road I knew must lead to the dock." Because his treason had been played out in deadly earnest, Casement said: "I am prouder to stand here today in the traitor's dock to answer this impeachment than to fill the place of my right honourable accusers." At this point, it is said, F. E. Smith smiled sardonically and whispered audibly: "Change places with him? Nothing doing." Then he lounged out of the courtroom with his hands in his pockets.[21] Near the end Casement phrased again the basic Irish position that had inspired him all along and brought him to this pass: "Self-government is our right, a thing born in us at birth; a thing no more to be doled out to us or withheld from us by another people than the right to life itself. . . . If it be treason to fight against such an un-natural fate as this, then I am proud to be a rebel, and shall cling to my 'rebellion' with the last drop of my blood."

"My lord, I have done," he said at last. He concluded with thanks to the jury and kindly admonition not to take personally his earlier statement that "this was not a trial by my peers": he had meant only that they were unfortunately not Irishmen. When he had finished, the usher commanded silence, quite unnecessarily. A Brechtian note was lent to the final scene when the black caps were placed crookedly upon the heads of the judges and Justice Horridge continued to grimace. Lord Reading pronounced the sentence: "that you be taken hence to a lawful prison, and thence to a place of execution, and that you be there hanged by the neck until you be dead." Casement bowed, smiled once more in the direction of his friends, and passed out between the green curtains with his two warders. Gertrude Ban-nister recorded that when Lord Reading spoke his last words, "And may the Lord have mercy on your soul," she herself murmured, "And may He have mercy on yours." A reporter who had seen her lips move amplified the incident into "A woman attempted to ad-dress the court but was promptly suppressed."[22]

29 In Order That Justice Be Done

A s a prisoner under sentence of death Casement was not returned to Brixton but sent to Pentonville Prison, and thenceforward, except for the two days of the appeal proceedings in
mid-July, he wore blue convict's clothing and what Gertrude called
"a dreadful cap." When next she saw him, he quoted to her reassuringly: "A felon's cap's the brightest crown an Irish head can
wear"—the closing line of a famous patriotic song. An appeal had
been resolved upon, largely at the insistence of Sullivan who no
doubt wished to recover some of the professional ground he had lost
in his collapse in court. Gavan Duffy had little hope for a successful
appeal in the courts, but he thought there would be real hope in a
subsequent appeal—which could only be allowed by permission of
the Attorney-General— to the House of Lords, which Duffy called
"the only Court where there is even a trace of intellectual honesty left
in this country just now."[1] An appeal would have to be based on new
arguments as to the meaning of the statute and upon possible im-
proprieties in the Lord Chief Justice's directions to the Jury. Casement thought it was all pointless play-acting, as he wrote to Mrs.
Green: "I shall be a spectator this time—sitting in a reserved box and
looking on at the actors with a quite detached and even cynical
smile—especially the wigs."[2] In Pentonville he continued generally
calm and well. "Since I came here I have done nothing but sleep," he
wrote on 8 July to Morten. "I sleep day and night to make up for
much lost time in that direction. . . . I am in a cell and eat and
sleep—that is all—and read books and say prayers, in which I sometimes pray for you—that is my daily round."[3]

On 30 June, the day after the close of the trial, it was announced in
the papers that Casement had been officially de-graded or dis-

honored: "stripped" of his knighthood. He felt little pain at the loss of an English decoration and in any case he took the position that he had already stripped off his honors himself in his letter to Sir Edward Grey in February 1915. As a sample of newspaper reactions to Casement's conviction, René MacColl quotes the following headline of 30 June: "Paltry Traitor Meets His Just Deserts. Death for Sir Roger Casement. The Diaries of a Degenerate"; and the statement: "It is common knowledge that Sir Roger Casement is a man with no sense of honour or decency. His written diaries are the monuments of a foul private life. He is a moral degenerate."[4] "Common knowledge" is surely a signal statement of something extraordinary and shameful: casual public obloquy based upon documents that had never been proven or traced home to Casement. With Casement convicted, the undercover circulation of the diaries by British officials shifted in purpose to the forestalling of a clemency plea that might save his life.

In a letter to Roger McHugh in November 1956 Casement's old friend Bulmer Hobson told a highly circumstantial story in support of his conviction that "the decision to destroy Casement by using the diaries was the decision of the British Cabinet & that F. E. Smith was one of the principals in pushing it through." The story brings the guilt directly home to Smith and places his action in the actual processes of the trial. Hobson heard the account about the year 1922 from Sir James O'Connor who was Attorney-General in Ireland in 1916 and later Lord Justice of Appeal:

> O'Connor told me that he was in London on business at the time of the Casement trial & wanting to see a celebrated State trial he attended all the sittings of the court. At the end of the first day [26 June] after he had left the court F. E. Smith (whom he hardly knew) came running down the corridor after him calling out "Here O'Connor I want to show you something." He then handed O'Connor a photostat of a page of the indecent diary. O'Connor had no political sympathy with Casement but he was shocked and disgusted at the impropriety of the Attorney-General of England peddling dirty stories in this way about a man he was prosecuting on a charge of treason.[5]

A shocking story surely and one hardly knows what to make of it. Allowances must be made for the fact that the story is hearsay, that O'Connor told it six years after the event, and that Hobson was recalling it thirty-four years after he heard it. Yet it carries a strong ring of truth. On the other hand other curious documents exist that cast doubt upon the story.

On 29 June, the last day of the trial, Smith sent a note to Sir Edward Grey marked "Secret":

> I am told that the F. O. is photographing or proposes to photograph portions of Casement's diary with a view to showing them to various persons so as to influence opinion.
>
> It is I think rather a ghoulish proposal & without expressing a final opinion upon it I should be glad if you would see me before sanctioning it.[6]

Grey's reply on the same day indicates that the scheme was not of his making or knowing and that it was not to his taste:

> I had not heard of the proposal to photograph and show parts of Casement's diary nor do I approve of it. I will see that it is not proceeded with as far as the F. O. is concerned without the authority of the Cabinet, to whom I think such proceeding would not be agreeable.[7]

Apparently on the same day Grey issued a peremptory minute: "See that this plan is not proceeded with by the F. O." This was initialed by Lord Newton on the following day.[8] So far as the involvement of Smith with the diaries is concerned, the question would seem to be whether the same man would be likely to be "peddling" the "dirty stories" in court corridors on 26 June and finding their circulation by another department "rather a ghoulish proposal" three days later. It is not impossible, but the only shred of probability to be found in the conjunction is that Smith might have been afraid that the Thomson and Hall (and Smith?) game with the diaries might be thrown off course if a new department took a hand. This would make of Smith's letter to Grey a piece of nearly incredible disingenuousness. On the whole I am inclined to discount the Hobson-O'Connor story. Yet Smith was so clever and so determined to see Casement hanged that one remains in doubt.

There are other documents relating to the immediate incident that are interesting and puzzling. That the plan, against which Smith protested and of which Grey was ignorant, was a reality and was well under way on 29 June is attested by a telegram also marked "Secret" that was prepared by the Foreign Office to be sent to Captain Guy Gaunt, Naval Attaché of the British Embassy in New York:

> Photographic facsimile & transcript of Casement's diary, of which you have, no doubt, already heard is being sent to America by today's mail. Person receiving it will communicate with you when it arrives.

> In the meantime could you arrange to get Editors of Newspapers and influential Catholic and Irish circles informed indirectly that facts have transpired which throw an appalling light on Casement's past life, and which when known will make it quite impossible for any self respecting person to champion his cause.

> Diary which is a daily record of amazing unnatural vice is quite unpublishable and is the worst thing which has ever come into the hands of persons with the widest experience of cases of this sort.[a]

That seems clear enough, and deadly enough to English reputations, but the case is complicated further by a companion page in Foreign Office records. This sheet is headed "29 June 1916./Sir. R. Casement's Diary./Letter from Sir F. E. Smith to Sir E. Grey, and Sir E. Grey's reply./[b] Draft telegram to New York (not sent)." This is followed by a note in brackets: "Before Sir E. Grey's final veto had been imposed, a telegram was sent to New York (no copies were made) calling Captain Gaunt's attention to the nature of the Diary: and typed extracts from it sent to Captain Gaunt by bag [i.e. by closed Foreign Office mailbag]. The disclosures had the effect of completely alienating U.S. sympathy from Sir R. Casement" [i.e. the scheme had worked after all].[9] The whole sheet is in the hand of Stephen Gaselee of the Foreign Office and is initialed by him and dated at the bottom 3 February 1918.

This sheet appears to be an attempt by Gaselee a year and a half after the event to explain the queer combination of the Smith and Grey letters of 29 June and the drafted but unsent telegram of about that date to Gaunt. But the note creates new problems. By Grey's "final veto" does Gaselee mean that of 29 June or a subsequent veto

---

[a]PRO FO 395.43. The draft is undated but is attached to the other papers on the issue.
[b]I.e., the two letters of 29 June.

(there were several)? If the telegram to Gaunt quoted above was "not sent," what telegram "was sent" of which "no copies were made" (and when was it sent—before which veto)? Were the "typed extracts" something different from the "photographic facsimile and transcript" to which the unsent wire referred or simply a casual way of describing the same material? Before which veto were they sent? In other words, what did Gaunt receive, and when, and on whose authorization? The story was far from over on 29 June and what comes clear later is that Gaunt did at some point receive photographic copies from England and did show them in America with marked effect. It seems equally clear that F. E. Smith was not involved in this particular circulation of the diaries, that Grey opposed it, and that somebody in the Foreign Office, or working through that department, planned and succeeded in a dirty scheme to destroy effective sympathy for Casement in that foreign quarter whose opinion mattered most in England in 1916.

In reluctant deference to Sullivan who was convalescing in Dublin, the Attorney-General had consented to a date as late as 17 July for the hearing in the Court of Criminal Appeal. For a day and a half Sullivan argued his old case supported by some new authorities before a panel of five judges. At the end they thanked him, complimented him on a good show, and denied the appeal on the old grounds restated: "the subjects of the King owe him allegiance, and the allegiance follows the person of the subject. He is the King's liege wherever he may be." The matter seemed to them so clear that they had not called upon the Attorney-General for rebuttal. The next possible recourse was to the House of Lords and Gavan Duffy filed with Sir F. E. Smith on 18 July a request to grant the necessary certificate, specifying among other considerations "the need, upon the highest grounds, of demonstrating to the prisoner's fellow countrymen and to the world that the prisoner has had the advantage of every possible recourse open to him at law." Sullivan and Jones wrote supporting letters. Smith denied their petitions on 22 July, after handling the decision in a characteristically flamboyant manner. He called in his three junior colleagues as well as the Solicitor-General, Sir George Cave, and asked their opinions on the question. Each of them supported the judges' interpretation of the statute. Smith gave them leave to go and then told them that he had in fact already given his refusal to his clerk in writing. The decision was his to make and he had made it, but he could now add "that having consulted you after-

wards you were all of the same mind."[10] Smith's refusal left only the
possibility of the clemency of the King and that would probably be
guided mainly by the advice of the Home Secretary and the Cabinet
as a whole.

The Cabinet in turn would be influenced, though not necessarily
guided, by public opinion, and there was plenty of that on both sides
of the issue. It is useless to pretend that there was any great popular
groundswell of sentiment in favor of a reprieve for Casement. The
English people by and large wanted him hanged: Serjeant Sullivan
was to write later that in fact Casement was killed by "an angry public."[11] In our concentration upon Casement it is easy to forget that his
story was only a notable ripple in the tide of events and the great fact
of the day was the war—the effort, the privation, the ghastly casu-
alty lists: why bother about one traitor, and he a pretentious
Irishman and a nasty pervert, a "degenerate," when so many boys
were dying? Hang him and be done with it. Even in Ireland Casement's predicament stirred no great outcry. Mrs. Green had to admit
this when she wrote Gertrude from Ireland on 19 July: "I hear Asquith has said Ireland does not care about this case. It is true enough
at this moment. He was practically unknown here. The story that he
was an English spy has been spread everywhere, & is believed."[12] To
the Irish Casement was an anticlimax. They had been given their
epiphany by British stupidity in the serial execution of the rebel
leaders. They had their Fifteen Men and Casement was only a kind
of accidental appendage. In the enfolded ironies of his fate, he would
be the last of the leaders to be killed as he had been the first to be
taken—hanged in part for "leading" a rebellion he had tried to forestall. Yet powerful voices, individual and collective, Irish, English,
and American, did beg or advise clemency. They were not sufficiently persuasive.

On 1 July Gertrude Bannister, writing out of her passionate loyalty and grief, had sent an appeal direct to Sir Edward Grey asking
not so much clemency as justice:

> May I intrude again upon your forbearance to write once more
> about my cousin Roger Casement. Throughout this long &
> ghastly tragedy, when his deed has been painted in the blackest
> hues that journalistic power could mount, & when stealthy
> slander has been insidiously disseminated to ruin him in the
> eyes of those who might otherwise have sympathised, no voice

has been raised to point to his past great record of selfless devotion to the Cause of suffering humanity. You, Sir, know well what that record was & were able to judge absolutely truly of his purity of motive & high souled passion for justice to those who suffered. The "Honours" conferred on him by his Majesty have been recalled, the greater honour of his work & his deeds in foreign lands, lies in the hand of God & He alone can judge whether it was deserved. We can gauge that Higher Judgement when we think of these words, "Inasmuch as ye did it to the least of these my brethren ye did it unto Me."

In this wave of hate, disdain & slander, pouring over his head now that he is laid low (hatred, venom & slander, pouring from the very pens of those who lauded & courted him when he stood high in the world's honour), is mine to be the only voice raised to defend him—I, his unknown, uninfluential, absolutely unimportant relative, but proud to stand by his side & take his hand? Can you not, you who *knew*, speak a word in his defence?

His life is forfeit to the State—He would never shirk from the penalty, but must they lay his honour in the dust? There is where I appeal to you that when he is defamed you may say what he was (& still is) the Champion of those who suffered & the strengthener of the weak.

Roger Casement has injured no man, has taken no man's life, even the deed for which he is to die, brought no weakening to England no strength to Germany. He still stands as the man who helped to right those who suffered wrong & who fed the hungry.[c]

But in fact Grey needed little persuasion. His behavior to Casement in extremity was handsomer than that of any other English public official. He did remember old friendship and old service, and he even forgave the rant and invective of Casement's long letter of February 1915, thinking it simply not quite sane. He was revolted by the

---

[c]PRO FO 371.2797. On 20 July 1916 René Claparède of the Ligue Suisse pour la Défense des Indigènes sent the following letter to John H. Harris, which Mrs. Harris (her husband being absent) sent on to Gertrude Bannister: "Casement, évidemment, est assisté par un ministre de la religion. Serait-il possible de lui faire dire, par ce ministre, que M. René Claparède est certain qu'il a agi en gentilhomme dans les affaires du Congo et du Putumayo, et qu'il defendra sa reputation et sa memoire." NLI 13073.

"stealthy slander" and he would have saved Casement's life if he could have found a way.

With Casement's execution set for 3 August, and only sixteen days remaining after the loss of the appeal, the campaign of his supporters for clemency had to be intensified. William Cadbury's petition to the Home Secretary sounded a bit cool, in the Quaker style. It emphasized the value of Casement's work in Africa and South America, noted its praise in the House of Lords by Lansdowne and Fitzmaurice, and the fact that his findings on behalf of subject peoples had stood up against all shaking. Conan Doyle's petition laid stress on Casement's evident abnormal state of health of mind and body and on the unwisdom of aggravating hostile opinion in Ireland and America. The signers included such notable authors as Chesterton, Bennett, and Galsworthy and such prominent liberal journalists as C. P. Scott of the *Guardian*, Clement Shorter of the *Sphere*, and H. W. Massingham of the *Nation*. Nevinson spoke out repeatedly. Shaw declined to sign Doyle's petition, judging shrewdly that his name might do more harm than good by repelling other possible signers, but he wrote personally to Asquith and he published a brilliant long letter in the *Manchester Guardian* on 22 July. He wrote Gertrude on 12 July that both the *Times* and the *Daily News* had refused his letter: "the D. N. because it wishes to prevent the sentence being carried out, and the T. probably for the opposite reason."[13]

In his public letter Shaw said that he wished to "extricate the discussion completely from the sentimental vein," and he proceeded to do so, beginning with the impudent suggestion that "there is a great deal to be said for hanging all public men at the age of fifty-two" (Casement's age). Casement's treatment, he said, should not be made "exceptional," and he feared that was about to happen: Casement was to be hanged "not because he is a traitor, but because he is an Irishman." He contrasted the forgiving treatment of the rebel Boer leader Christian De Wet by General Louis Botha (to whom Mrs. Green had written a very long and eloquent letter on 16 June begging his support for Casement)[14] and went on to point to the "group of unconvicted, and indeed unprosecuted, traitors whose action helped very powerfully to convince Germany that she might attack France without incurring our active hostility"—the Ulster leaders of whom he did not scruple to name both Carson and Smith. Shaw went on through many telling points, culminating with the suggestion that

Casement be treated as a prisoner of war, and advising England, in mere shrewdness, not to hang him: "In Ireland he will be regarded as a national hero if he is executed, and quite possibly as a spy if he is not. . . . But Ireland has enough heroes and martyrs already, and if England has not by this time had enough of manufacturing them in fits of temper experience is thrown away on her."[d] In the morass of prose by and about Casement everything Shaw wrote on the case is a joy: clear-headed and economical, beautifully poised on the points of its argument.

Two old friends of Casement, the Volunteer leader Colonel Maurice Moore and the National University professor Agnes O'Far- relly, circulated the most notable of the petitions from Ireland. The most telling of the American ones was probably that conceived and circulated by the lawyer John Quinn, who had been Casement's host and friend but had bitterly repudiated his errand to Germany. Quinn emphasized the fact that his twenty-four signers were politi- cally opposed to Casement but wanted him saved on grounds of hu- manity and of policy: "The undersigned American citizens all of whom have been and are pro-ally in their sympathies respectfully appeal in the interests of humanity for clemency in the case of Roger Casement and are profoundly convinced that clemency would be wise policy on the part of the British Government."[15] Grey thought the telegram significant enough to be read by the entire Cabinet.

The collective pressure was powerful though in the long run not powerful enough. That so much support could be collected in favor of reprieve, even from many who were offended by one aspect or another of Casement's behavior, showed the loyalty and respect he and his achievements had inspired. Had it been possible to put the case entirely on the grounds of his political "crimes," support would undoubtedly have been a great deal more general. But the "secret slanderers" had done their work too well and the "moral" issue was bound to supervene and to put off many who would have been his advocates. And, of course, the awful presentness of the war worked hard against him. Cadbury wrote to Mrs. Green on 30 June: "The trial has ended as one can only see it must end. . . . The other side, his work for 20 years for Africa and the people of the Upper Amazon, must not be forgotten, though he was too proud to claim any credit for that. . . . Tell me if in any way I can help you. There are many

---

[d]Shaw's complete letter is given in Inglis, *Roger Casement*, Appendix II, pp. 413–16.

who cannot forget his courageous Congo report—I can't believe that *all* the Bishops wish to see him pay the ultimate penalty."[16] Mrs. Green wrote back to say that she had asked Gertrude Bannister to send him her own petition for clemency, which Mrs. Green thought an effective one. She described her own experience with Gertrude's petition: "I wrote with it to about twenty influential people, but so far all for different reasons have refused to sign. . . . We only want to create the impression of a feeling in the public. The upper classes are intensely hostile, the lower classes uninformed and silent. The clergy outdoing the laymen in 'imperialism.' . . . All effort seems to fall back from a wall of passion or of indifference. The war has formed all minds into a single groove."[17]

Herbert Ward's was a signal case. One of Casement's two or three oldest and closest friends, he refused to sign Conan Doyle's petition for clemency and he refused even to answer Casement's plea for a message in prison. When Gertrude Bannister wrote to Nina in June 1920, still bitter at his death and bitterer at his degradation, totally unable to accept any evidence of his personal "impurity," it was evidently Herbert Ward she blamed, though she refused to name him, as a traducer of Casement and one who had lent himself as an authenticator of the diaries: "That man is dead, as you know, died last year. He turned into a bitter enemy because of the political side, & wouldn't stir a finger to help us—in fact did things to hinder. They got him to look at the vile thing, & he told people the *worst* about R—I heard that from several."[18] In 1916 Ward's eldest son, a captain in the Grenadier Guards, was recently dead at Neuve Chapelle. His second son enlisted in the Royal Flying Corps from Eton, was wounded, shot down, and taken prisoner in 1915; after six months in German hospitals and prisons he escaped to Switzerland. Ward gave his fine house at Rolleboise, where Casement had stayed, to be used as a French hospital, and served himself in the British ambulance service, being given a Croix de Guerre by the French. His death in 1919 was attributed to exertion and injuries in the war. His third son had been named Roger Casement Ward. After Casement's arrest the family petitioned Parliament to change his name officially to Rodney, so that he could still be called "Roddie."[19]

The showing of the diaries went busily on. The campaign was being carried out in the spirit recommended by one of its prime movers, Sir Ernley Blackwell, Legal Adviser to the Home Office. Asked for an opinion as to grounds for using insanity in an appeal for royal clemency, Blackwell, having consulted alienists, dismissed that idea in a memorandum of 19 July and went on to propose his own program: "it would be far wiser from every point of view to allow the law to take its course, and by judicious means to use these diaries to prevent Casement attaining martyrdom. . . . I see not the slightest objection to hanging Casement and *afterwards* giving as much publicity to the contents of his diary as decency permits."[20] By "decency" Blackwell surely did not mean decent public behavior. And he must have known that what he was advising had already been going on for nearly three months. His eye at the moment, however, was fixed mainly on "weak" members of the Cabinet who needed a manly bucking up. Apparently anybody of influence could have a look. There can be no doubt that the fact or the rumor of the diaries' content alienated a great deal of sympathy for Casement. The *Weekly Dispatch*, for example, remarked on 16 July, the day preceding the appeal hearing: "Roger Casement's diary is being greatly discussed at the present time, and people are wondering whether Mr. Clement Shorter, who is raising an appeal for the reprieve of Casement has perused that remarkable document, and also whether Sir Arthur Conan Doyle is aware of its contents." The implication was that editors of the *Dispatch* had perused the remarkable document.

Two powerful clergymen, former supporters of Casement's, were silenced by the diaries. Bishop Hensley Henson of Durham was shown a copy by the King himself, according to Dean Inge.[21] Dr. Randall Davidson, Archbishop of Canterbury, who had signed a petition offered by John Harris, was invited to read the pages. Feeling that it was improper for him to do so, he asked Harris to look at them and give his opinion. Harris had had no suspicion of Casement's "perversion," but when he read the diaries he found suggestive episodes in Congo contexts that only he and Casement knew about. He told the Archbishop that those parts of the diary at least must be genuine. Davidson then withdrew his signature, though Harris persevered with his petition in other quarters.[e] Mrs. William Cadbury told René MacColl of Harris's report of the experience to her and her husband: "It was in his own dear hand-writing," Harris said. "There can be no doubt of that. It was a most terrible shock."[22] John Redmond was exposed and withdrew his personal support for

[e]Denis Gwynn, "Roger Casement's Last Weeks," *Studies*, LIV (1965): 71. Harris wrote Gwynn to tell this story soon after the publication of Gwynn's biography of Casement in 1930.

reprieve, though other Irish members of Parliament continued to work for it. The American Ambassador, Walter Hines Page, gave the diaries a salacious reception[23] and his word undoubtedly had effect in Washington.

Plaintive voices in support of Casement could still be heard from over the water. His old British friend in Washington, A. Mitchell Innes who was now serving in Montevideo, telegraphed the Foreign Office on 3 July that "exercise of mercy would be received with rejoicing in S. America where Casement was greatly respected." This and a similar wire from Spring-Rice in Washington were "not communicated to Home Office," according to the Foreign Office minute.[24] Spring-Rice telegraphed again on 4 July:

> There has been surprisingly little comment in the daily Press respecting result of Casement trial. Note is one of pity rather than sympathy and belief prevails that death sentence will not be carried out.
>
> A resolution introduced in the Senate by Senator Martine of New Jersey calling on President and State department to lodge a protest against (?execution) was referred to Committee on Foreign Affairs where it will probably remain.
>
> A large number of letters chiefly from Irish Societies are daily pouring in at White House asking President to use his influence toward securing clemency. . . .
>
> Secretary of State told me yesterday that letters would be examined and if found to express views of persons of prominence, their names etc., would be communicated to you quite unofficially by United States Ambassador.[25]

Another quiet voice came from Chicago. I. B. W. Barnett, president of the Negro Fellowship League, sent directly to King George V the unanimous resolution of his society to appeal to the British government for clemency for Casement: "We feel so deeply grateful to this man for the revelations he made while British Consul in Africa, touching the treatment of the natives of the Congo." Barnett closed by quoting *The Merchant of Venice:* "The quality of mercy is not strained."[26]

On 30 June a London correspondent of the *Brooklyn Daily Eagle,* H. W. Suydam, had attempted to send his paper a telegraphic dispatch strongly slanted toward sympathy for Casement:

casement heard sentence death hanging high treason with smile stop close impassioned forty-minute plea ireland handed manuscript warder calmly faced three red-robed judges upon white wigs black cap laid . . . casement updrew proudly gazing eyes only surviving relatives two young girl cousins smiled stop . . . readings [Reading's] charge jury appeared american standpointwards more argument prosecution than impartial summary evidence . . . striking feature behavior three judges entering court carrying black caps even before defense finished pleading casements life justice horridge placed black cap plain view in fifteen feet prisoner . . . eagle informed casements counsel condemned good spirits faces death calmly irish patriot . . . although profound conviction prevailed courtroom casements guilt open admiration expressed manner meeting fate.[27]

When Suydam's proposed dispatch was sent by the censor to Whitehall, it caused a large flurry. Hubert Montgomery of the Foreign Office said the telegram should not be passed, calling it "a deliberate attempt to supplement the already dangerous Casement propaganda in America." Moreover the detail of the advance flaunting of the black caps by the judges was "presumably untrue," an invention of Suydam's that warranted action by the Attorney-General in Montgomery's view. Lord Newton's note put the matter in the whole context of propaganda and counter-propaganda and made clear the fact that he was a leader of the Foreign Office faction that was pushing the use of the diaries:

> I certainly think that the telegram should be stopped, as it is clearly designed to be mischievous. But it is only an insignificant detail in itself. It is perfectly obvious that we shall have to face a huge pro-Casement propaganda, and unless we are prepared to make some use of the materials in our possession it will be almost impossible to combat it successfully. Apart from political considerations, it should be borne in mind that large numbers of influential persons in the States and elsewhere honestly believe Casement to be a misguided hero, and it seems only reasonable that they should be enlightened as to his real character.

Lord Hardinge agreed: the telegram should be stopped and "an effort should be made to place Casement & the Irish rebellion in their proper perspective in the U.S." Sir Edward Grey's voice still sounded quiet and lonely: "The Cabinet will have to consider the matter. The Attorney General should see this." Montgomery added a final note: "We have now learnt that the Home Secretary has decided to stop the telegram."[28]

By 20 July Sir Cecil Spring-Rice had apparently resigned himself to the likelihood of Casement's execution, or at least to the necessity of doing his part for Britain when and if that event impended, for he telegraphed Lord Newton on that day: "Could you send copy of Casement's journal to be confidentially shown here."[29] Lord Newton's note on this to Lord Hardinge ran as follows: "If this is approved, I think that we ought to act at once. Of course there is an alternative."[30] (The reference of the second sentence is unclear to me.) On 21 July Hubert Montgomery wired to Spring-Rice: "Copy of the diary will be sent by bag today, but no use should be made until authorized." The Foreign Office copy of the wire is marked "no copies" and "approved by Lord Newton."[31] A note of 22 July confirms that action was taken: "A copy went in the Admiralty bag to Captain Gaunt on July 21st."[32] Then on 25 July Sir Ernley Blackwell wrote Montgomery to enclose "two photos of specimen pages of the Diary" and urging that they, too, be sent to Spring-Rice: "They will help him to convince anyone to whom he may show the copies that the diary is not a fake or forgery." Evidently what had gone in the bag on 21 July were typewritten transcripts. This letter was one of several in which Blackwell pressed the Foreign Office to verify the Casement diaries on internal evidence, by checking references in the diary with official records of his actions: "visits to F.O. etc." If they had not yet done so, he said, "I have a copy here and it would be easy to pick out a few salient entries for verification."[f] On 28 July Montgomery wrote Spring-Rice: "Lord Newton asked me to send you the enclosed photographic reproductions of parts of Casement's diary, which may be useful to you in dispelling any doubts that may exist as to its authenticity if and when the copy of the diary which Lord Newton sent to you last week is shown to anyone."

---

[f] 22 July 1916. PRO FO 395.43. He wrote Montgomery again on the twenty-seventh: "I enclose copies of some entries from Casement's Diary & Ledger. I think it may be possible to verify many of them from your papers. If so notes might be made opposite the entries." PRO FO 371.2798.

A day later Montgomery wrote Lord Newton to sum up the state of the matter and to urge that the next step be taken:

> Lord Robert Cecil told me today that the Prime Minister had spoken to him about sending photographs of Casement's Diary out to Washington.
>
> As you know the position is that Sir C. Spring-Rice telegraphed that copies should be sent for him to show confidentially to people whom he considered useful. We sent copies on the 21st, but with instructions that he should not show them until authorized. We yesterday sent him photographs of two sample pages.
>
> Should not the necessary authority now be given to Sir C. Spring-Rice to make use of the copies confidentially.[33]

"I understand that Casement's execution is fixed for one day next week," Lord Newton wrote casually, and went on to agree to the authorization. Ronald Campbell noted: "The Prime Minister spoke to me on this subject and wished as I understood that such action should be taken. It certainly seems desirable." Newton then added: "This seems sufficient. You had better telegraph (from me) to Spring-Rice at once." The telegram signed by Newton which was accordingly prepared and evidently sent on July 30 was marked "Priority A" and "No copies whatever":

> Casement's execution is fixed for early this week, probably August 3.
>
> You may now exercise your discretion as to using confidentially copies of his Diary sent you confidentially by bag on July 21.
>
> Photographs of 2 specimen pages were sent you by bag July 28.

Perhaps the most striking feature of the whole story is that the original scheme, planned and set going a month earlier without Sir Edward Grey's knowledge or approval and flatly vetoed by him on 30 June,[34] had been persisted in and consummated against his wishes. He evidently only now got wind of the sending of the diaries and the authorization to use them, for he sent his own personal telegram to Spring-Rice on 30 July: "I think it much better that you should make no use whatever of Casement's diary. Page [the American Ambassador] has I believe taken photographic copy with him supplied by Home Office & it is obviously advisable that information with regard to it should come from him & not from British Embassy. In fact I had given instructions that F.O. was not to make use of this diary."[35] This group of messages helps to clarify, at least partially, Stephen Gaselee's puzzling memorandum of 3 February 1918 on the events of late June 1916. By Grey's "final veto" Gaselee probably meant this one of 30 July. And that probably means also that though a telegram about the succulence and usefulness of the diaries had been sent to Captain Gaunt about 29 June, no actual "typed extracts" were sent until 21 July. But Grey's telegram adds a new complicating factor: the Home Office (probably in the person of Blackwell) had taken a hand and had given W. H. Page a "photographic copy" to take home with him to America. When? one wonders; and might that copy, too, have got into the hands of Gaunt, perhaps earlier and without any Foreign Office restriction? Or had the Home Office "supplied" other copies for America? Probably not. That there was a great deal of talk about the diaries in the United States before and after Casement's execution is irrefutable, but the evidence from the experience of John Quinn, who was probably a representative case, suggests that the direct showing about of samples probably did not occur until after Casement's death. Both Spring-Rice and Gaunt in talking to Quinn laid stress upon Grey's prohibition.[36]

Spring-Rice had asked for the diaries, but what he really wanted was a reprieve, and he kept trying for that. On 28 July he sent an "Urgent" telegram to the Foreign Office only to say:

> Mrs. Newman, Casement's sister came to ask me to present her petition to the King to beg consideration of the services of her family. Her father was captain in dragoons, her granduncle General Sir William C, and her brother were in the Imperial Light Horse in Africa, invalided; four first cousins now in army and navy.
>
> Senate has refused to take up the matter [i.e., two resolutions in favor of clemency for the "Irish prisoners" that had been sent to the Committee on Foreign Relations who had reported negatively on grounds of "inexpediency" on July 27] . . . but sense of the house was strongly for clemency.[37]

On this latter point, however, he had spoken too soon on the basis of a negative recommendation of the Senate Committee on Foreign Relations. Next day he was forced to wire again, probably happily:

> Senate has passed by a large majority resolution requesting President to ask His Majesty's Government to exercise clemency in treatment of Irish political prisoners.
>
> . . . .
>
> Irish politicians are . . . anxious for execution but their opinion is not a factor which need be considered as they are hostile in any case. Main point is general public.[g]

This time Spring-Rice managed to raise a bit of a stir. Rowland Sperling noted: "Copy H. O. Immdte."; and Grey: "I suppose it has gone to the Cabinet—it should be circulated . . . at once."

The mood of the Cabinet was going to be the crucial factor, as everyone now recognized. "It now rests with the Cabinet," Mrs. Green heard from her friend Lord Haldane whom she had enlisted to work for reprieve. "What they will decide I know not."[38] "I have been to see not only the Lord Chancellor but the Judge who tried the case," he wrote again on 31 July. "The difficulty is that the case as tried out and the verdict negative the suggestion of a mission to stop the rebellion." Mrs. Green and others were at last bringing to bear the most striking aspect of the case that had never been aired in court—partly because Sullivan's line did not allow it, partly because Casement himself had scorned to urge it: namely, that he had wished to land the arms, but he had also wished to prevent the revolt. The best evidence available locally on this subject was the testimony of Father F. M. Ryan, the priest to whom Casement had given his frantic message at Tralee. Ryan's account of the episode had appeared in the *Dublin Evening Mail* on 20 May 1916 and he had now affirmed it in a letter of 12 July to Gavan Duffy:

> Sir Roger Casement saw me in Tralee on the 21st April and told me he had come to Ireland to stop the rebellion then impending.
> He asked me to conceal his identity as well as his object in com-

---

[g]29 July 1916. PRO FO 371.2797. The plural reference to "prisoners" in the resolutions involved not only Casement but prominent leaders of the Rising who had not been shot but lay under sentence of death or long imprisonment. They included such notable figures as Eoin MacNeill and Countess Constance Markiewicz.

ing until he should have left Tralee, lest any attempt should be made to rescue him. On the other hand he was very anxious that I should spread the news broadcast after he had left.[39]

Eva Gore-Booth, one of the two sisters of Lissadell near Sligo whose Pre-Raphaelite beauty W. B. Yeats was to celebrate in a famous poem,[40] now began to make concentrated use of Father Ryan's letter and of related arguments such as Casement's report (which she heard from Gertrude) of his plea in his first interrogations at Scotland Yard, to be allowed to carry a countermand to Dublin and being told that the "festering sore" had better be allowed to "come to a head." A curious friendship had sprung up between Casement and Eva Gore-Booth, who had not been acquainted before the trial and who indeed never exchanged a word at any time. Gertrude Bannister attributed the little half-affair to the fact that both were "mystics." She had asked Miss Gore-Booth to attend the trial to swell the little cluster of those who could "send him loving thoughts and try to sustain him." In her memoir Gertrude described the course of events:

> While she sat in the gallery looking down at him, Roger suddenly raised his head and turned and looked full at her and smiled. Eva smiled back, and Roger waved his hand. It was as if a flash had passed between them, and from that moment those two people . . . formed a real friendship. On several occasions when I visited him in Pentonville Roger asked, "What does Eva say, or think, about this? What is Eva doing?" Always he spoke of her thus, simply by her Christian name, and until her death she too thought and spoke of him as if he had been her intimate friend all her life.[41]

Eva Gore-Booth sent her evidence and her arguments to C. P. Scott of the *Manchester Guardian* and to members of the Cabinet. To Gladstone, for example, she wrote on 13 July:

> May I beg you to read the enclosed papers? I do not think these facts are generally known, but it seems to me a ghastly idea that Casement should be in danger of hanging because he made a frantic attempt to stop the Sinn Fein rebellion & save much misery & bloodshed in Ireland. . . . Thousands of Irish people many of them (like myself) not even Sinn Feiners are longing and praying for a reprieve not because they approve of his hos-

tile attitude during the past year but because of his personal character, and because of the much dreaded effect of another execution on what we all hope may prove a peaceful settlement in Ireland.[42]

In his notes for an answer Gladstone showed himself skeptical and unpersuaded. He had followed the trial carefully, he said, and Father Ryan's story did not seem to him to affect the case: Casement's possible wish to delay the Rising was probably based on the fact that he knew the arms ship had been lost. But Casement had not had this news when he spoke to Father Ryan, as Miss Gore-Booth pointed out in an impassioned second letter on 21 July: "The real facts did not come out at the trial because of his (to his friends) exasperatingly quixotic refusal to allow any plea to be made for him that would seem to condemn his countrymen in their failure and defeat." Casement had gone to Germany with what she supposed would seem to English people "a crazy idea—of getting Ireland into the Peace Conference through direct negotiation with Germany." When he heard of the plan for the Rising, "he was *frantic* & rushed over in that mad reckless way to try to stop it." He had had "nothing to do" with the arms ship which had been arranged for by the Americans, and he had known nothing of the sinking when he was in Tralee on Good Friday. "It was 'The Times' on Tuesday that put the two absolutely separate events together in a way calculated to make everyone think that Casement was with the ship." (The *Times* had simply printed an announcement supplied by the Admiralty, who had based it on an inference that was false but perhaps natural in the obscure circumstances. The announcement did Casement a great deal of harm.) "What I am telling you," wrote Miss Gore-Booth quite accurately, "is the absolute truth." It was known in Ireland and America and it was bound to come out some day: what "terrified" her was that it might not come out until "an irretrievable step," the hanging of Roger Casement, had been taken in England.[43]

In fact these arguments were taken to the Cabinet and discussed there, but they were talked down, particularly by Sir Ernley Blackwell: "The idea of saying that he had come with the intention and for the purpose of stopping the rising appears to have occurred to Casement only after his capture. It is at any rate entirely inconsistent with the known facts."[44] The known facts as far as Blackwell was concerned were those proved out at the trial, and he had no wish to know any others. Such voices prevailed in the Cabinet, although Casement had left behind in Germany many thousands of words, spoken and written, in the possession of such people as Curry, Gaffney, Krebs, and Count von Wedel, that proved out the precise case Eva Gore-Booth was trying to make. Robert Monteith could have attested copiously to its truth, had he been in reach and had Casement been willing to call him. So could John McGoey: it is striking and impressive that Casement apparently made no effort at all to secure testimony from the man who had carried his warning to the Volunteer leaders in March. What had happened to McGoey? Dr. Maloney says that he was "captured by the British and secretly executed at Kirkwall,"[45] but he does not say when this occurred and he cites no evidence. And Basil Thomson of Scotland Yard could have testified from his own diary that Casement had begged repeatedly to be allowed to go to Dublin and attempt a countermand.[46]

In fact on 20 July, the day before Blackwell spoke out as above, the Gore-Booth argument was pressed in a potentially embarrassing form from another quarter: Michael Francis Doyle sent from the Savoy Hotel in London to Sir Herbert Samuel, the Home Secretary, and to Sir Edward Grey, a long letter of mingled fact and assertion "in order that justice be done." Doyle's most surprising point was his first:

> . . . Casement was unable to make any defence owing to the fact that it was impossible for him to call any witnesses or produce any documents on his behalf at the trial. They would have to be brought from Germany. Before my arrival in this country on June 12th Casement made application to the Home Office for permission for me to go to Germany to have these witnesses brought over and obtain documents to establish his defence. The permission was refused and I was notified of that fact by the Home Office.[47]

Doyle went on to list fifteen "facts" that these witnesses, "numbering over 50," would have proven. Most of these points attacked the testimony of the exchanged prisoners in court and placed a more favorable construction on Casement's acts in Germany, but the others centered around the perfectly true statement: "That his intention in going to Ireland . . . was, to *prevent the rising* and inform the people that the expected assistance which they were promised would not be fulfilled." That this was his purpose, Doyle argued reasonably, "should have the greatest weight with the Government on the question of a reprieve."

The Government was already busy deciding to ignore that point. Doyle's really dangerous assertion was his first: that he had been prevented by English officials from collecting materials for the defense in Germany; he came back to that at the end of his letter and italicized his conclusion: *"Therefore his conviction is really due to the Government not permitting him to enter his defence."*[48] The Home Office answer to Doyle was a flat denial of his assertion in a letter of 24 July: "no such application was ever made to the Home Office by Casement or by anyone on his behalf nor were you informed by the Home Office that such an application had been made and had been refused."[49] On the same day that the Home Office reply went to Doyle, Blackwell sent a copy to Sir Edward Grey with the request: "be so good as to instruct Sir Cecil Spring-Rice to publish the Home Office reply if Doyle publishes his letter."[50] Instructions were accordingly telegraphed to Spring-Rice. Doyle was now back in the United States. On 1 August Spring-Rice wired to say that the two had met and agreed on a vow of silence: "I have made informal agreement with Doyle that he say nothing if I say nothing and vice versa. He has not yet made any official definite statement but I warned him if he did I must answer it."[51] That Doyle had not kept total silence, however, was attested by a telegram of the following day to the Prime Minister in Nina Casement's characteristic voice: "If you execute my brother casement it is murder home office refused doyle bring reliable witnesses from Germany who could prove his innocence have you no pity for me."[52] In his comment on this message Ernley Blackwell bracketed the middle clause and wrote: "a pure invention on the part of Mr. Doyle."

The rest was not yet silence. On 26 August Doyle replied from Philadelphia to Blackwell's letter of 24 July, "regretting" in his first paragraph that Blackwell's answer to his former letter had been delayed until he knew Doyle had left England, and going on to reassert his charges with new circumstances: Gavan Duffy had told him on 12 June that Casement had written Blackwell's office asking permission for Doyle to go to Germany to collect evidence; in a meeting in his office Blackwell had told Doyle of receiving Casement's letter, had told him his request could not be granted owing to the war, and had warned him not to discuss the matter with Casement when he saw him for the first time the next day; at Brixton Prison the Governor of the prison was present throughout the interview, and told

Doyle that he had had instructions from Blackwell to allow no discussion of a possible trip to Germany. Furthermore, Doyle said, he had submitted his letter of 20 July to the Home Secretary to both Gavan Duffy and Artemus Jones and both had approved it as a statement of the facts.[53]

Blackwell's reply to Doyle's new letter was crisp and again totally contradictory. He had not timed his earlier letter to miss Doyle, he said: Doyle had left London in the forenoon of 21 July and his letter had not reached the Home Office until that afternoon. On his other points Doyle's memory was "equally at fault":

> At the first interview with you on June 14 I shewed you the petition from Casement to which you refer. It contained no request that you be allowed to go to Germany to obtain witnesses or documents for the purpose of his defence. I have recently again shewed this petition to Mr. Gavan Duffy, and he expressed himself as satisfied that it afforded no ground whatever for the statements contained in your letter of the 20th July. . . . Neither at our interview on the 14th June nor at any other time did you propose to me that you should go to Germany on such an errand and I gave no instructions to you or to the Governor of Brixton Prison that you should not discuss this matter with Casement.

The only restriction laid upon him had been the customary one: that discussions should be confined to matters of the defense and their content not passed on to the press or to anyone else outside the prison. Blackwell concluded: "I have submitted this letter to the Secretary of State, and I am directed by him to inform you that he adheres to the terms of his letter of the 24th of July, and further that in view of the misstatements contained in your letter under reply he regrets that he must decline to continue this correspondence."[54]

Blackwell sent copies of the correspondence to the Foreign Office the same day, asking that copies be sent to Spring-Rice "with a request that he will see that my reply to Mr. Doyle is published in the event of Mr. Doyle publishing the rest of the correspondence without it." Rowland Sperling's comment began: "Mr. Doyle's letter is, I should say, certainly meant for publication. Mr. Doyle knows that he is a liar (and a very inept one at that) and must know that we know it." The text of Blackwell's reply to Doyle was accordingly telegraphed to Washington the same day.

What is the truth of the matter? *Somebody* is lying. In spite of the circumstantiality of Doyle's assertion, one is inclined to accept the Home Office refutation. After Watergate it is perhaps naive to hold on to one's wistful assumption that men in public life generally tell the truth. On the other hand it is probably statistically true that they tell more truth than lies and they tend not to lie when the untruth can be proved against them. Had Doyle been able to prove his case the Home Office would hardly have dared to deny it so categorically and to stand so ready, as they clearly were ready, to publish their denial. The unquestioning acceptance of the Home Office refutation by the Foreign Office must carry weight, too. There is other evidence that Doyle's stories were not always to be trusted. Gavan Duffy wrote on 2 January 1933 to Dr. W. J. Maloney: "I am sorry you have sent Michael Francis Doyle's story to the Dublin National Library, for I am wholly unable to corroborate it"[55]—which seems to be a polite way of saying "I do not believe it to be true." In fact it is not clear just which of Doyle's stories Duffy was referring to, and in the context of a correspondence about the diaries, it is more likely that the story in question was Doyle's account of discussing the diaries with Casement in prison.[56] But Duffy's skepticism is the point.[h]

A lone voice from Germany, at any rate, did break through to the Cabinet, though not until very late. Cardinal Frühworth, the Secretary of State of the Vatican, on 27 July asked the British Minister, Hugh Gaisford, to communicate to his government certain information that had reached him in a letter of 14 July from Dr. Charles Curry of Munich. Gaisford wired the Foreign Office the same day that the document was on its way, and his telegram was annotated: "The Sec. of State would like to see his document when it arrives."[57] Curry's letter of 14 July was quite brief, only two and a half pages. He was writing, he said, to warn the British government not to be "guided by motives that appear at present plausible but will be proven later, by history, not to have been justified." Casement, he affirmed, had opposed the Rising and would have tried to stop it early had he not been cut off from communication with Ireland.

---

[h]A curious final sentence in Spring-Rice's telegram of 1 August shows the kind of careless thing Doyle was capable of saying: "He tells me privately that Clan-na-Gael want Casement executed." What on earth does that mean? One hopes that Doyle made the point clearer than the telegram does. What part of the Clan-na-Gael? Why? Surely even Devoy, vengeful as he now felt, did not want Casement hanged. The only logic one can suppose is the cynical old principle that another martyr is always a useful thing to a cause. Probably Spring-Rice meant to convey a warning of that spirit abroad among the American Irish.

Curry went on to quote from several of Casement's letters to him to support that point and he cannily quoted also from one of his higher-minded statements about the Findlay affair. Casement had gone to Ireland at last out of a despairing sense of obligation to share the common fate, but he wished to stop the Rising altogether. His actions throughout, Curry said, were "based on his humanitarian principles and horror of futile bloodshed known to all" from his work in the Congo and the Putumayo.[58] Curry's letter did not reach the Foreign Office until 1 August and arrived at the same time as a telegram from the Cardinal Secretary of State warning against the outrage to Irish-American opinion that would follow from Casement's execution and advising a reprieve as an "act of high policy." A Foreign Office minute on the telegram remarks: "Execution will not make the slightest difference to the Irish in America; they are much too far gone already."[59] Sir Edward Grey, however, did read the crux of Dr. Curry's letter to the Cabinet, apparently on 2 August.[60]

Prayers for a reprieve also took humbler but more dramatic forms, and were addressed to other quarters presumably more sympathetic but no more effective in the kingdom of this world. Colonel Maurice Moore wrote to Mrs. Green on the last day of July to record that Mrs. Mary O'Nolan and Agnes O'Farrelly had made a penitential pilgrimage to the holy place of Lough Erne, where there were a thousand penitents at a time, to pray for Casement's life: "The hardships were fearful for 3 days—Each day 1 meal only of bread & water; 1st night watching & praying all night in chapel; each day walking barefoot on sharp stones round the island stations (result bleeding feet). Return third day but not allowed to eat till after midnight; incessant prayers."[i]

---

[i]31 July 1916. NLI 13088. Moore himself had sent a bitter letter to the *Freeman* of 27 July to protest the "libels" against Casement's character.

30 The Long Succession of the Dead

W HAT of the prisoner while all these words were whirling largely unbeknown to him? Mrs. Green wrote William Cadbury that when she went to see Casement under sentence of death she found him "calm, serene, saying that he has now no nerves and is perfect master of himself. 'All is good now,' he repeated three times. 'I know that it is all good.' "[1] Casement had heard that there was some chance that both his brothers might be coming home and he was much moved at the idea, though he thought there was virtually no chance of their arriving in time to see him alive. He had not seen Charlie, "poor old chap," since boyhood. Tom, "the African one," he wrote to Mrs. Green, "you will like beyond all other men you ever met I am quite sure. He will keep you laughing all the day and be your devoted slave into the bargain. . . . I should be *quite* heartbroken," but for friends like her he told Mrs. Green. "But between you all—and the goodness that inspires you—I have a happier mind than I had for a *very* long time."[2]

It was an artificial, self-hypnotic condition and Casement could not sustain it all the time. On 24 and 25 July he wrote two long letters to Nina, the first since his capture three months before. The first of these letters he called a "business" document, occasioned mainly by the fact that the Governor of Pentonville Prison had that day asked him to produce his C.M.G. insignia to be returned to the chancellery of the order. Casement believed he had given the unopened package to Nina to keep for him and he asked her to make a search for it in America and return it to the order in London, being careful to ask for a receipt. The demand for the insignia had opened the old wound of his unwelcome honors that had cost him such an expense of spirit, and Casement now spent a good half of his letter proving out the case of his reluctance again. His trial, he said, had been "a farce of a trial—because I was powerless, really, to defend myself." Nina would know his pure intentions, he felt sure, and "some day (very soon)" the truth would be known in America and history would do him justice. He had left "a very clear record behind to be made public after the war—in the hands of a good Executer." Curry (whom he did not name) would see her and other friends and set the record straight. Casement was facing, at least in his language, the reality of the coming end: "the days are near their end so far as my earthly days go. . . . I never had so many friends in my life as I find now when life is so nearly done."[3]

His second letter was more a cry of the heart, very difficult to write in the knowledge that what he said must pass through the hands of prison censors (in some cases through the hands of such bitter and officious enemies as Ernley Blackwell). He wished now he could see Nina and tell her in person "how in my heart I have always cared for you more than for anyone else." His heart was full of self-reproach for bitter words he had said to her in a cottage in Berkshire and had never called back: "Oh! dearest of my heart forgive me forgive me." He blamed himself for leaving her alone and for being the cause of her "flight and exile." It was her mothering he recalled and needed most acutely: "all the years roll away from me and I stand beside you as I did a little boy when you comforted me and took me by the hand. . . . My eyes are blinded with tears and I can scarcely write. . . . I bow my head in your lap, as I did when a little boy, and say Kiss me and say Goodnight." He told the misery of that last year in Germany:

> I prayed for death often and often in Germany. I was so unhappy and months before I started to return to Ireland, coming as I knew straight to death, I was fixed on it and begging for death. For I had lost all hope, something had broken in me, and I walked about as if in a dream and every day the future whispered here's but death. I was so lonely, and I could do nothing and go nowhere.

He described his various futile attempts to get out of Germany, which he represented as efforts to get back to Nina. And then he described the sensation of transfiguration that had come over him when he was "swamped and swimming" back onto the shores of Ireland.[4] Only Monteith knew the whole story and Casement hoped that he was alive to tell her the tale. In terms stubbornly veiled Casement spoke of "the strange inscrutable fate" that had come upon him: "that I am not only being put to death in the body but that I am dead before I die—and have to be silent and silent just as if I were already dead—when a few words might save my life—and would certainly change men's view of my actions." (He referred apparently to his attempt to stop the Rising, which he felt he had no right to reveal.) He asked Nina to take leave of his American friends, indicating, without naming, Devoy and McGarrity in particular. In a postscript added on the morning of the twenty-sixth, Casement spoke with deep feeling of the devotion of Elizabeth and Gertrude Bannister and of Mrs. Green and named his hope that Nina would return to live in Ireland when the war was over. He signed himself: "Roddie—or as you always called me Scodgie."[5]

During the five weeks between Casement's conviction and his execution, only Gertrude and Mrs. Green of his friends were allowed to visit him in Pentonville. Each was allowed one visit a week and Gertrude came five times. Mrs. Green was in Ireland much of the time but returned to London to claim her last two rights to call. Gertrude's final visit on 27 July was a moving and exhausting occasion when calm broke and all the collected emotion of both of them came to a head. She found Casement "for the first time broken and sorrowful," particularly depressed that day because Herbert Ward had refused him a message and because the Governor of the prison had taken it upon himself to read him a private lecture on his iniquities. "What will you do, Gee, when it is all over?" he asked her. She tried to interrupt that line of thought, but he went on: "Go back to Ireland, and don't let me lie here in this dreadful place—take my body back with you and let it lie in the old churchyard in Murlough Bay." She promised and then broke down and wept for the first time in all her visits. Casement wept too, and he said: "I don't want to die and leave you and the rest of you dear ones, but I must." She tried to persuade him that it would not happen: they were working for a reprieve, there were petitions. But he stopped her: "No, Gee, don't delude yourself—they want my death, nothing else will do. And after all, it's a glorious death, to die for Ireland—and I could not stand long years in a place like this—it would destroy my reason."

At this point the warders interrupted to take Casement out. She stretched out her hands to him; he turned in the door and said "Goodbye, God bless you." Outside in the corridor Gertrude gave way and wept without control. A warder led her across the court to the waiting room at the gate. She was sobbing and shaking, barely able to stand, but the gatekeeper said she must leave. She begged him to call a taxi but he refused: "Pull yourself together, and go now." He pushed her out and locked the gate "with a clang" behind her: "I wanted to shriek and beat on the gate with my hands. . . . I staggered down the road, crying out loud and people gazed at me." Writing it all down years later Gertrude found her eyes again blinded by tears: "I can't see now to write any more today—He was there waiting for death, such a death. I was outside and I wanted to die."[6]

Gertrude now had other consequences of her love and loyalty to bear. On 23 July her headmistress at Queen Anne's School had sent a kind and obviously reluctant letter to inform her that the governors of the school had determined to dismiss her: "The fact is that your name has come out so publicly, that disagreeable things are being said about the school—so I have been told." On the twenty-ninth she received a letter from the board enclosing a check for a half-term's salary of £40 in lieu of notice. She sent a dignified reply in which she pointed out simply that she had given seventeen years' service including terms as acting headmistress and that dismissal was supposed to occur only on grounds of "serious misconduct or other causes equally grave": what, she wondered, was her crime? She concluded: "Please understand that I do not in any way appeal against my dismissal, I accept it without any comment, but I think the Governors cannot fail to see the fairness of my request that I should be clearly told why they think I am no longer fitted to be in their service." On 31 July, J. S. Northcote replied that her letter had come and could be laid before the board at their next meeting; the governors had already decided, however, "not to state the reasons for terminating your engagement with them." He could assure her that her work for many years had given them "complete satisfaction," and they would be happy to give her a good character if she chose to apply somewhere else.[7] "What people do in war is unpredictable," Serjeant Sullivan said of the general Casement situation to René MacColl many years later. "Perfectly decent men will do perfectly shocking things in the prevailing hysteria."[8] But what is a decent man? A letter that Nina published about Gertrude's dismissal in the New York *American* came to the attention of Sir Gilbert Parker, M.P., and on 16 September 1916 he wrote to the Foreign Office to inquire if the story were true. Basil Thomson of Scotland Yard was asked to look into the matter, and on 29 September a detective who had made the traditional "discreet inquiries" reported in effect that all was well with Miss Bannister and there appeared to be nothing for anyone to worry about.[9]

Casement was now writing last letters to his closest friends. His letter of 26 July to William Cadbury was held up in the Home Office until 16 August before being sent on with a cold note from Ernley Blackwell explaining that cuts had been made of matter that was "purely propagandist in character." The surviving text is innocent enough. "Farewell, dear, gentle hearts," Casement wrote. "Please help the school children at Carraroe for my poor sake. . . . My dear love and affection to you dear, honest, faithful and affectionate friend—to you and Emmeline. . . . I have been very sad the last few days, sad with myself, but am better today. Goodbye."[10] Peace having been made with Richard Morten, Casement wrote "my dear, dear old Dick" on 28 July. His letter to "the best friend I've got" was surely one of the best of all his thousands of letters, one of the few with any real magic or charm. The tone was sometimes light, sometimes serious, but always carefully controlled, not forced or strident. He adverted to his trial but without real bitterness: "God deliver me, I say, from such antiquaries as these to hang a man's life upon a comma, and throttle him with a semi-colon." He expressed affectionate admiration for Jones and Morgan and resigned disgust with Sullivan: "I wish I had stuck with my two Welshmen, and not brought the other in at all." Someday, he said, his ghost might call upon Morten and ask for his account of the reluctance with which he had written his "fulsome" letter to Grey in thanks for his knighthood: "You'll hear me clanking up the Avenue, because I'll be in armour of course—look at the date: 1351! [the date of the Treason statute]—and I'll ask (in Norman-French) if one Dick de Morten lives there, and demand his memory or head—and it won't be the slightest use your stammering or putting it off." In the simplest possible terms he summed up his history:

> I made awful mistakes, and did heaps of things wrong, confused much and failed at much—but I *very near* came to doing some big things . . . on the Congo and elsewhere. It was only a shadow they tried on June 26; the real man was gone. The best thing was the Congo, because there was more against me there and far cleverer rascals than the Putumayo ruffians.

He had stopped short of the last chapter in his story which Morten found intolerable. Finally he recalled without bitterness their mutual friend who had denied him, and then set himself and Ward in the context of purer times, past and future:

> I am sorry Herbert had not a more understanding mind. I should not have treated him so—but I do not think of it and when I think of him it is of earlier days when the good things of life were all contained for him and me in a Huntley and Palmer biscuit tin, and we were lugging the crankshaft of the "Florida" over Mazambi Hill, down to the Bumbizi and up again, to the night camp where red ants came. Oh! so long ago (February-March 1887 it was) and Africa has since then been "opened up" (as if it were an oyster) and the Civilizers are now busy developing it with blood and slaying each other, and burning with hatred against me because I think their work is organized murder, far worse than anything the savages did before them. Hatred and Falsehood rule men's minds, and it may be the Compassionate Man of the years to come may be the Heathen Chinese or the Negro of Central Africa.[a]

A direct view of Casement on the day of this letter happens to have survived. The pacifist and socialist A. Fenner Brockway, awaiting his own release from Pentonville on 28 July, was standing on a stool in his cell looking out the window onto the exercise yard bathed in summer sunshine. He heard a door open under him and there not five yards away he saw Roger Casement standing in a doorway with two warders. He stood for some time with his hands behind his back, looking out at the sky and the sunlight. His face, Brockway thought, was "wonderfully calm." He then carried a seat outdoors and sat for a long time. At sunset he went back in, again pausing for a long time in the doorway looking back at the scene. His warders appeared kind and cooperative.[11]

Some of the calm that dominated Casement's last days, in spite of occasional breakdowns under terrific stress, must have been due to a spiritual decision he had reached: to join the Catholic Church. Though it can be made to seem so, it was not a deathbed conversion. In Germany Casement had given Monteith the clear impression that his mind was turning that way. Perhaps the strongest influence,

[a]This letter, now in the National Library of Ireland, was apparently given to J. H. Morgan by Morten. It was sold at Sotheby's in 1957. See Hyde, *Roger Casement*, p. 147.

aside from the cruel tension of his situation throughout 1915 and his general wish to identify himself more firmly still with Ireland, was the presence and example of Father Crotty. Casement had grown to love the priest and to admire the steadiness and simplicity and kindness he associated with his faith. As soon as he was imprisoned in Pentonville Casement had put down his religion as "Catholic," partly in wishfulness, partly in the hope that local priests might offer him a more efficient means of communicating with those he wished most to reach. But in fact the decision was one he had been creeping up on all his life, and his reaching it by such meandering steps and only in extremity was another symptom of the deep dividedness in Casement's nature, a sign of the long incompleteness of his definition of himself. And it was also in character that when the final step was taken it should not be simple but complex and attended by a measure of melodrama.

Casement was acquainted with Father E. F. Murnane of Holy Trinity Church, Dockhead, Bermondsey, called by Murnane in a letter to Sidney Parry, Gertrude Bannister's future husband, "the most Irish church in London,"[12] and in Pentonville he quickly became friendly with Father Thomas Carey of Clerkenwell and Father James McCarroll of Eden Grove, Holloway, priests who gave spiritual counsel to the prisoners. He began to take formal Catholic instruction as an intending convert. Then in conversation with Father Carey he mentioned that he recalled that as a child on a visit to North Wales with his mother a priest had "splashed water over him."[13] His story was checked and the baptismal record of the four Casement children was found at St. Mary's, Rhyl.[14] This meant that Casement no longer needed to be instructed as a convert but only "reconciled" as a Catholic who had not practiced his faith. But for him the matter was still not simple. He felt that the step was a tremendous one and only to be taken on absolute conviction. Now, as he explained to Gavan Duffy, his mind was in prison as well as his body, and being moved by love of his country and of his mother, he "feared to be carried away by emotion at a time when his reason was clouded."[15] On the eve of the appeal hearing he sent Father Murnane a tortuous and apparently tortured analysis of his indecisive state:

> The trouble is: *am I convinced?* or do I only *think* I am? Am I moved by love? or fear? I can only accept in my soul from love—never from fear—and part of the appeal *seems* at times to be my fear—the more I read the more confused I get. . . . And

then I don't want to jump, or rush or do anything hastily just because time is short. It must be my deliberate act, unwavering and confirmed by all my intelligence. And alas! today it is not so.[16]

After his appeal was dismissed, Casement told his advisers that he was ready for the step and they said they were ready to receive him.

But now entered a strange new element of conflict. When Gertrude Bannister visited her cousin on 13 July he said to her: "I want to be a Catholic, but they are trying to make me betray my soul."[17] She was mystified by his statement and judged it wiser not to pursue it. What had happened was that when Father Carey applied to Cardinal Bourne, Archbishop of Westminister, for permission to "reconcile" Casement to the Church, Bourne stipulated that he must first sign a recantation or apology formally "expressing sorrow for any scandal he might have caused by his acts, public or private."[18] Precisely what Bourne had in mind must remain unknown; that Casement found it an intolerable indignity is clear. Denis Gwynn argues logically that the Archbishop would be unlikely to demand a recantation of political acts: he was half-Irish himself and well acquainted with the habits of the Irish radical political mind and not inclined to condemn them out of hand. Therefore, it must have been mainly Casement's reputed private habits that were addressed in the extraordinary fiat. Gwynn's inference is that Cardinal Bourne must have been one of those to whom the diaries had been made known in some form, along with the suggestion that the Church had better be wary of appearing to condone in the person of Casement not only treason but sexual "perversion."[19] The North London priests themselves were very angry at Bourne's edict. But then it occurred to them that there was a way round it: once the date of the prisoner's execution was set, the Canon Law of *articulo mortis* could be made to apply and he could be given the sacraments. So stood spiritual matters at the end.

On 23 July an anonymous M. P. had published in the *Weekly Dispatch* a letter headed "Why Casement Must Hang. The Horrible Confessions of His Own Diary" advancing the thesis that "Roger Casement, confidant and trusty friend of the Kaiser's minions, richly merits the death to which a jury of Britons have condemned him. There is no worth in the man." He should not live "a day longer than the law allows." With "every reason to be grateful to this country which did him high honour" he had stabbed England in the back in her hour of peril. Furthermore he was a very nasty man: "Only those who have heard just the merest whisper of what is in the infamous diary that has come into the possession of the police can say whether it is right that Roger Casement should be spared. His life, as outlined by himself, has been one continuous immersion in the depths of depravity"; Casement had "warred with all the finer impulses of life." And "the Dublin dead" were mainly his work, too. This hysterical rant was labeled by Lord Newton: "Very sound for a Northcliffe organ."[20]

These were British voices and representative ones, but they did not have it all their own way. The *Manchester Guardian* spoke editorially for reprieve, pointing out that Casement dead would be worth at least an army corps to the Germans, and printing powerful letters from Henry Nevinson and Mrs. Green on 24 and 27 July. On 26 July six Irish M. P.'s presented a petition, signed by thirty-nine of their colleagues in favor of clemency, to the Prime Minister who promised "careful consideration." A general petition in Ireland had now been signed by sixteen bishops, the High Sheriff and twenty-six members of the Dublin Corporation, corporally by the Dublin National Volunteers, the Typographical Society, the Dockers, the Firemen, the Tailors and Tailoresses, and by the Irish College of Spiddall. The Ancient Order of Hibernians of America had cabled a plea for reprieve in the name of 280,000 members. Then on 1 August the Colombian Minister called on Lord Hardinge at the Foreign Office bearing two cables from his government pleading that Casement's life be spared. One of these messages came from the President of Colombia and was addressed to the King and the Minister asked, and was refused, permission to deliver it in person. Rowland Sperling's minute on the matter ran: "N. B. The Colombians have a special reason for supporting Casement. His work in the Putumayo tended to discredit their rivals in the ill-defined frontier districts of the Upper Amazon." And Sir Edward Grey's note (on 2 August) was ominous: "An interim reply should be sent tomorrow saying that it has been impossible to accede to the request [for clemency] & that a further statement will be sent."[21] The decision for death had evidently been made.

And now at long last, too little and too late, came a formal representation from at least one major branch of the United States Government in favor of clemency: Senator Pittman's resolution "that the Senate expresses the hope that the British Government may exercise clemency in the treatment of Irish political prisoners, and that the President be requested to transmit this resolution to that Government," passed by a vote of forty-six to nineteen on 29 July. The terms of the resolution were obviously designed to be bland: the sentiment expressed as "hope," the "prisoners" generalized and Casement not named, and the President "requested" merely to pass on the resolution. The vote having been taken on a Saturday and time being pressing in England, the text of the resolution was telephoned to the American State Department by the Senate Foreign Relations Committee and sent thence to the Foreign Office by telegram. Exactly what text reached London, and when, is still not absolutely clear. Rowland Sperling's note, for example, runs: "The facts [*sic*] are that the Senate Resolution of 29 July was communicated by Mr. Laughlin to Lord Grey on some date not recorded but apparently before Casement was executed (153425). It was circulated to the Cabinet & Casement was executed on 3 August."[b] Acting Secretary of State Frank Polk told President Wilson's secretary of a discussion of the Casement matter with Spring-Rice on Wednesday, 2 August, in which the Ambassador showed him a cable from his government to the effect that they had already considered the Senate resolution.[22] Senator Phelan affirmed that the Senate "action" was "in the possession of the British Foreign Office at least two days before the execution and well within the time necessary to exercise executive clemency."[23] There can be little question that the resolution was at hand in some form and was discussed in the crucial Cabinet meeting on the morning of 2 August. What mattered more fundamentally was the tepid character of the resolution and the fact that it came with no personal support from President Wilson, whose own voice was the one British officials were waiting to hear. And in fact it appears that by 3 August the resolution as an official document from the United States government had still not reached the Foreign Office.

On 2 August Sir Cecil Spring-Rice made a last gallant try at saving Casement's life. "Press announces that President has taken action on behalf of Casement," he cabled, and continued:

[b]PRO FO 371.2798. His note was a comment on newspaper reports of a letter from President Wilson's secretary J. P. Tumulty of 16 October 1916 to Michael Francis Doyle. Doyle, prompted by Nina, had written on 29 September to charge that the American government had been negligent in sending on the resolution and had thereby cost Casement a major chance of a reprieve.

442   *The Lives of Roger Casement*

If Casement is executed you must be prepared for a most serious situation here. President is very personal and his attitude toward us, already changing, will become hostile by force of circumstances and immense influence of Irish in his party. American public, which never reasons, will be inflamed against England and we may anticipate political difficulties of a serious kind. . . . On the other hand a reprieve at President's request would strengthen his hands in dealing with his own party and place him under deep obligations to us.

Publication of Casement's diary will only be looked on as an act of revenge and would only be effective if his life is spared.[24]

On this Sperling noted: "We have been informed of a resolution in the Senate requesting the President to ask H.M.G. to exercise clemency, but no communication has yet been received from the President or U.S.G." Though it might appear "grotesque" to suppose, Sperling went on, that the British Government would be influenced by such considerations, poor Spring-Rice was "only doing his duty." In any case he would have received by now a telegram that would provide him with a "defence." This must have been the telegram that Spring-Rice showed Frank Polk on 2 August. Grey now dispatched a new telegram at noon of 3 August, with Casement dead for three hours:

Your telegram No 2361 received this morning. Casement already executed when it reached me.[c]

President has taken no action here. If he had done so I should have brought it at once before the Cabinet and had our decision been that it was impossible to accede to President's request I should have proposed that you be instructed to ask for audience of President, explain the grounds on which decision of His Majesty's Government was based and leave with the President a statement of the facts now in possession of the Home Office.

This is the course I shall take now if the President moves in the matter.

My telegram of yesterday will have explained to you the reasons why the Government decided that a reprieve was impossible. A

[c]This was probably literally true, although Spring-Rice's wire of 2 August was marked "R[eceived] 8.5 A.M. August 3rd 1916" and Casement was executed exactly an hour later.

reprieve in face of the facts as known here would naturally have created the greatest resentment in public opinion at home and in the army in the field and could not have been defended or justified.[25]

In his reply of 4 August, Spring-Rice was forced to admit that reports of President Wilson's having "taken action" were nothing but rumor: The Senate resolution had "merely been transmitted without comment."[26]

Indeed Grey's drab reference to "facts now in possession of the Home Office" concealed a good deal of matter both old and new, both true and false, which was already being boiled into pap for public consumption after the execution and was being sent specially to persons (such as the Colombian Minister, for example) with a special claim to attention. This formal justification of the refusal of clemency (before it had occurred) discounted the talk of insanity; pointed out that the claim that Casement tried to stop the Rising had never been made in the trial; told as a new lie that "further evidence" proved this claim untrue; told as old lies that prisoners who had refused Casement's "seduction" were treated with "exceptional cruelty" by the Germans, some of them having returned disabled and dying, "regarding Casement as their murderer"; and made one true and telling new point: that Casement was now known to have agreed that the Irish Brigade "might be employed in Egypt against the British Crown." For that dangerous hidden matter had come to light at last in a final fling of tragi-comedy.

Casement had simply, in pure carelessness, left a package of papers behind one day in court. They were returned to him in Pentonville and he sealed them up and asked the Governor to return them to Gavan Duffy; instead that official sent the package to Ernley Blackwell for censoring. Casement had enclosed a note for Duffy that ensured careful attention to the papers in the Home Office: "There is enough in these papers to hang me ten times over. If I had been thirty-three instead of fifty-three, the arms would have been landed, the code would not have been found, and I should have freed Ireland, or died fighting at the head of my men."[27] It was a silly braggart kind of statement that would have done no harm in the hands of Duffy but could do a great deal of harm in the hands of Blackwell and the Cabinet. The second sentence made nonsense, for example, of the crucial argument for reprieve that tried to dissociate

Casement from the arms shipment and to claim that he had wished to prevent the Rising. That his remark was largely untrue made no difference in the circumstances: the Cabinet now had it in his own hand. In his queer game of hare and hounds with Britain and with fate Casement seems to have taken a positive delight in leaving a broad trail. Just when the papers reached Blackwell or how long he kept them is not clear, but he turned them over to Herbert Samuel for a Cabinet meeting as late as 28 July.[28]

There is a further puzzling aspect to this whole story. The most dangerous of these papers of Casement's was a copy of his agreement, which he liked to call "the Treaty," of 23–28 December 1914 with the Germans as to the organization and purpose of the Irish Brigade. This was the new "conclusive evidence" in the hands of the Government showing that Casement had agreed that if the naval situation made it impossible for Germany to land the Irishmen in Ireland then they could be used in another theatre of war directly against English troops. Article 7 of the Treaty specified:

> . . . it might be possible to employ the Irish Brigade to assist the Egyptian people to recover their freedom by driving the British out of Egypt. Short of directly fighting to free Ireland from British rule a blow struck at the British invaders of Egypt, to aid Egyptian national freedom, is a blow struck for a kindred cause to that of Ireland.

Article 8 went on to speak of transportation of the Brigade to Constantinople and Egypt and "recognition and acceptance of the Irish Brigade as a Volunteer corps attached to the Turkish Army." In his notes to his lawyers Casement had listed this document, along with a copy of the Findlay guarantee to Christensen, copies of his last two letters to von Wedel, and a sum of money, as the items he had hurriedly hidden as the country constables approached McKenna's Fort, stuffing them down a "rabbit hole" and covering the opening with a stone and bits of moss and trash. He later assumed that all of this matter had been found by the police in searching the fort. But no part of it was introduced against him at the trial or was otherwise referred to by the Prosecution. Had the cache simply never been found? The last search of the fort mentioned in testimony occurred on 27 April, six days after Casement's arrest, and that apparently turned up only Exhibit 15, a bit of paper that had been used to wrap the invaders' sandwiches.[29] It seems impossible to believe that had the Crown discovered the Treaty in the rabbit hole or anywhere else they would not have used it against Casement in the trial. (The two letters to von Wedel, on the other hand, would have been exculpatory and would have supported, then or later, Casement's claim that he wished to prevent the Rising, if not the landing of arms.) The possibilities seem to be: (1) that Casement's story was a fabrication; (2) that the cache was found by the police and the contents suppressed for mysterious reasons by the Prosecution; (3) that it was found by searchers instructed by Casement and Gavan Duffy; (4) that it was found by unknown persons who kept quiet about it: there was about £50 in it; (5) that it was never found and may still exist.[d]

The evidence of the Treaty undoubtedly formed part of the matter of discussion in the conclusive meeting of the Cabinet on the morning of 2 August when Casement and reprieve were considered for an hour and a half. But the new evidence merely lent support to a decision already effectually made. The thing that might have made a real difference, a strong American official representation supported by the President, had not occurred. The basic fact was that Casement was guilty as charged and English officials were resolved to express the public will by hanging him. Grey put the fundamental case in his telegram to Spring-Rice on 3 August: "A reprieve in face of the facts as known here would naturally have created the greatest resentment in public opinion at home and in the army in the field and could not have been defended or justified."[30] "The facts as known here" presumably included the evidence of Casement's private diaries. That evidence gave satisfaction neither to Grey nor to Spring-Rice, but it immensely strengthened the hands of officials dealing in justification. That the diaries were simply irrelevant to the issue seems to have troubled very few officials, journalists, or ordinary citizens. Chatting at dinner in Downing Street on the evening of 1 August, Prime Minister Asquith told the American Ambassador Walter Hines Page that the Cabinet was already virtually determined against reprieve. He asked Page if he had heard about the diary. "I should like you to see it." Asquith said. "I have," Page answered. "What is more I have been given photographs of some of it." That was "excellent," Asquith considered: "and you need not be particular about keeping it to yourself."[31] Roger Casement had become a smoking room story.

---

[d] I did search for it in March 1972, but I'll admit I was in a hurry.

Sir Herbert Samuel, the Home Secretary, summed up the logic of the Cabinet decision in a letter to his wife after the meeting had ended. "Much pressure" had been brought to bear and there had been "much doubting in the Cabinet—among a few" but the nettle had been grasped unanimously. Now he anticipated "a (somewhat artificial) row" in America, some "passion" in Ireland, and denunciations from the *Guardian* and the *Nation*. Reprieve, on the other hand, "would let loose a tornado of condemnation, would be bitterly resented by the great mass of the people in Great Britain and by the whole of the army, and would profoundly and permanently shake public confidence in the sincerity and courage of the Government." The decision had been a hard one, Samuel admitted, and it would have been a good deal harder "had Casement not been a man of atrocious moral character."[32]

It was all rebuffs for Casement's friends now. Gavan Duffy had applied to the Home Office for permission to be present at the execution and had begged that Casement's body be allowed to be buried outside the prison walls. Ernley Blackwell's answer on 2 August had returned a brusque negative on both points. Either in person or in writing, Gertrude Bannister had made a last appeal to the Prime Minister and his answer of 2 August was marked "Private":

> Dear Madam,
>   It is with sincere pain (& only in compliance with your request) that I inform you that, after very full consideration, the Cabinet today came to the conclusion that there were no sufficient grounds for a reprieve. I need not assure you that I wish it had been possible for them to arrive at a different conclusion.

Asquith closed with a postscript: "This is a *secret* communication. I am returning the documents."[33] He paid her the courtesy of writing out his disingenuous sentiments in his own hand. In this final evening before the execution a little delegation composed of Gertrude Bannister, Mrs. Green, Philip Morrell, Henry Nevinson, and Eva Gore-Booth went to Buckingham Palace hoping to ask the King in person to grant a reprieve. But they were turned back with the information that the prerogative of mercy rested by constitutional usage in the hands of the Home Secretary. "It is believed," wrote Geoffrey Parmiter, "that the King did tell the Home Secretary that an appeal had been made to him."[34]

Another message was also turned back, this one addressed to the prisoner. Spring-Rice telegraphed a message from Nina that came through as follows: "Keep up dear heart my dearest brother. Am doing everything possible. Lena." The telegram reached London at 8:35 P.M. on 2 August. Casement was asleep when the message reached Blackwell who decided "that it would have been an act of the most refined cruelty to have awakened Casement—or any other prisoner in the same position—to receive such a message" thereby "exciting hopes which could not possibly be fulfilled."[35] So the message was not delivered that night and it was withheld the following morning on the same logic. A telegram to Spring-Rice was drafted in the Foreign Office describing the circumstances to be communicated to Mrs. Newman. Then it was decided that the wire should not be sent: that it was less cruel to leave her to suppose that her message had reached her brother. But then the telegram was transmitted in error anyway on 5 August and another had to go out hurriedly on 7 August in hopeful countermand: "You should not inform Mrs. Newman unless she asks whether her message was delivered."[36] What if anything Spring-Rice actually said to Nina is not known.

It would not be true to say of Roger Casement that nothing in his life became him like the leaving it; but it can be said that he made a good end, if there is such a thing. Word of the Cabinet's final refusal of clemency was transmitted to the Governor of Pentonville Prison in the afternoon of 2 August and he told Casement that he must hang the following morning. He first wrote a postcard to Gertrude: "Tomorrow, St. Stephen's Day, I shall die the death I sought, and may God forgive the mistakes and receive the intent." He also prepared a brief general message for all friends: "My last message to everyone is *Sursum corda*, and for the rest, my good will to those who have taken my life, equally to all those who tried to save it. All are my brothers now." Casement also composed a longer more general apologia, the original of which was confiscated by prison officials as propagandist, and which has survived in a hurried and incomplete copy made by Father McCarroll. In part the document was partisan and patriotic and told again a familiar story: "My dominant thought was to keep Ireland out of the War. England has no claim on us." Then he told of his heartfelt conversion to the Catholic faith: "I accept it fully now. It tells me what my heart long sought." In joining "the long succession of the dead who have died for Ireland" he hoped he would behave in a seemly way; but if he wept it would be "not from cowardice but from sorrow." He was overcome by a dominating sense of the mysteriousness of this fate coming upon one whose main sensation was that of innocence: "one who never hurt a human being—and whose heart was always compassionate and pitiful for the grief of others. . . . It is a strange, strange fate, and now as I stand face to face with death I feel just as if they were going to kill a boy. For I feel like a boy—and my hands so free from blood. . . that I cannot comprehend how anyone wants to hang me." It was apparently the same passionate impulse that had made him wish to lay his head in Nina's lap again. Casement went on to speak of his hatred of war, his love and gratitude to his friends, and finally to claim his place in the roll of "the most glorious cause in history" along with Robert Emmet and the Manchester Martyrs. His recognition of St. Stephen's Day had not been an idle one, in his own view.

Casement was closely attended by the Catholic chaplains, Father Carey and Father McCarroll. In the evening his formal "reconciliation" to the Church took place and he made his first Confession. Afterward, according to Father Carey, he "sobbed like a child."[37] That night he slept peacefully. In the morning of 3 August he attended Mass in the Chapel at 7:30 and received "his first Holy Communion which was also his Viaticum," in Father McCarroll's words.[38] He refused breakfast in order not to contaminate the physical presence of the sacrament. Instead he passed the remaining hour in prayer with Father Carey in his cell. The Governor, the Sheriff, and the executioner appeared at his door at nine o'clock. Casement's hands were tied behind his back, and the party walked to the scaffold, Father Carey reciting the litany for the dying and Casement making the responses. His bearing was calm and resolute. In Father Carey's words: "He marched to the scaffold with the dignity of a prince and towered straight over all of us."[39] Ellis the executioner called him "the bravest man it fell to my unhappy lot to execute."[40] A crowd of about 250, neighborhood people and workers from a nearby munitions factory, had collected outside the walls in the Caledonian Road. When the bell signaling the execution tolled at a few minutes after nine there were scattered boos and cheers, but these were quickly suppressed when a group of people from Father Murnane's church fell on their knees and began to pray.[e]

[e]E. F. Murnane to Sidney Parry, 30 September 1916. NLI 13075. Sometime later the sister of Eva Gore-Booth, the "Rebel Countess" Constance de Markiewicz, sent Gertrude Bannister the crucifix that had sustained her under her own sentence of death: "I think it saved me from going mad those awful hours at daybreak when I lay in my cell at Kilmainham listening to the English murdering our leaders—during Rory's last hours before he went out to die for us, I prayed for him with it in my hand. . . . I should like to give it to you who were so near & so dear to him." Undated letter. NLI 13075.

Crowd outside Pentonville Prison awaiting announcement of Casement's execution. Courtesy of the Press Association, Ltd., London.

State funeral in Dublin, March 1965; Casement's cortège passing the General Post Office. Courtesy of the Press Association, Ltd., London.

31 Thousands Mourn and Honor

IN his letter to the Home Office on 2 August 1916, Gavan Duffy pleaded that Casement's body be given up to his cousins for burial in consecrated ground. As Legal Adviser Ernley Blackwell had refused, claiming that law required burial within the prison walls. When Duffy persisted, Blackwell referred him to the Capital Punishment Amendment Act of 1868, section 6 of which stipulated that "the body of every offender executed shall be buried within the walls of the prison within which judgment of death is executed on him." Other portions of the act, however, appeared to show that the law was meant to apply only to executed murderers. As Sullivan had argued that Casement was being tried on an inapplicable statute, so Duffy now contended that he was being buried according to an inapplicable statute. Professor Morgan supported his plea in a letter to Sir Herbert Samuel, urging that the whole question of law be set aside in favor of simple mercy.[1] But the Home Office officials were not to be swayed and Casement's body was buried in quicklime within the walls of Pentonville on the day of his execution. So the man who "never hurt a human being" was left to lie with murderers. The English seemed perversely determined to humiliate and exacerbate the feelings of Irish people. It was easier to understand why they should take Casement's life than to understand why they must also degrade him. Certainly their lack of imagination and of sympathy in the matter of Casement's burial created an unnecessary new grievance that festered sullenly thenceforward.

The effort to recover Casement's body, carried on by private persons and by the Casement Repatriation Committee, went on and on; but it took the British nearly fifty years to change their minds. It was February 1965 when Prime Minister Harold Wilson agreed to give

449

up the body to Ireland in answer to an appeal from Sean Lemass, Prime Minister of the Republic. On the night of 22 February three warders working under floodlights dug up Casement's remains where they had lain near the outer wall of Pentonville. Next day they were flown to Dublin where thousands of Irish people turned out in pouring rain to welcome him home for the state funeral of a hero. At the Garrison Church of the Sacred Heart the body lay in state for four days, visited by 165,000 people, before being moved in a military cortege, again observed by many thousands, through central Dublin to the Pro-Cathedral for the funeral ceremony. As the procession passed the General Post Office in O'Connell Street where Padraic Pearse had proclaimed a republic on Easter Monday of 1916 the coffin was tendered special military honors. Eamon de Valera, who as a young teacher on Tawin Island had known Casement sixty years earlier, defied his doctors and got out of his old man's sick bed to deliver the oration. "Casement deserves that," he said.

The state funeral on 1 March was ignored by Casement's nearest relations in Ireland, and the only members of the immediate family present were two nieces, now elderly women, daughters of his brother Charles, whom the Irish nation had brought 12,000 miles by air from Australia.[a] But representatives of fifteen nations including England joined the crowd of great and small persons of Ireland who turned out in driving snow for the Solemn Requiem Mass at St. Mary's Pro-Cathedral. Wreaths from many individuals and from every major organization in Ireland formed a great heap near the high altar. At the graveside in the plot in Glasnevin Cemetery procured by Nina Newman forty years earlier, President de Valera spoke first in Irish and then in English. He recalled 1917 when the rebel prisoners were being held briefly in Pentonville before their final release: several of the men were able to find Casement's grave near the wall, and Eoin MacNeill had knelt and plucked a few blades of grass to keep in memory. Even had there been no World War and no Eas-

[a] A letter apparently from Charlie's wife to Gertrude has survived. It is undated but seems to have been written in October 1916: "I suppose you are wondering why you have not heard from Charlie for so long, but he has been very seriously ill. On that 'Awful Day' he was brought home ill, & afterwards collapsed at the office & was for five weeks in bed & now in the second week in October is just getting about again. Severe mental strain had affected the heart & he lay for days not knowing anything, just raving day & night & calling for his brother it was just awful! I had three Drs. & they said they help heal the body but not the mind. I am not to let him speak of that dear one he loved & worshipped so much." NLI 13075. Charlie died in Australia in 1930.

ter Rising, de Valera said, Casement would have deserved to live in memory as a noble champion of the oppressed and helpless. But Irishmen were bound to revere him as an Irishman and a champion of Irish nationhood. The President emphasized Casement's Ulster origins and his love for Ulster as a province of a united Ireland; and he looked ahead to the consummation of "this great man's" noble dream.[b]

But Casement wrote the diaries and that fact must be incorporated in the legend. If the Irish are going to make a national hero or a saint of him,[c] they must bring themselves to do so without blaming the diaries on the English. The matter is less hard, or hard in a different way, than many Irishmen have apparently supposed. The diaries are true phrasing of a part of his character and as such they must interest a biographer. But they are tiresome as a fact and as a problem; the sexual side of them does not seem to me to cut very deep into what I want to call character, and I do not see why it need affect the Irish definition of Casement as hero or saint. In a sense it is nobody's business, like the sex lives of the rest of us. The Irish are right to see Casement as a national hero, though he was a singularly ineffectual one. They may also be right to see him as a saint—though to call a man a saint, even a lay saint, involves a more complex judgment. (Gertrude Stein remarked that the Catholic Church distinguishes very carefully between a hysteric and a saint.) I feel no personal objection to a homosexual saint; but I should prefer to see the matter argued on other grounds. The English laid the trap of Casement's "degeneracy," the Irish fell into it with enthusiastic truculence, and the rest of us have had to argue about it in all helplessness. But it is time to have done with that issue. Casement's homosexuality is interesting, but it is not the heart of the matter.

The truth is that his "black" diaries are more embarrassing to an admirer on other grounds: they are dull and deflating. As a body of

[b]The stone marking the grave was carved by Nuala Creagh, a distant cousin of Casement's. Mrs. Creagh also carved the relief portrait that was placed on the monument to Casement and Monteith at Banna Strand after the ceremonies marking the fiftieth anniversary of the Rising. Robert Monteith's white-haired daughter, Mrs. Florence Monteith Lynch, attended those ceremonies and carried home with her to America the first sod dug at the site to place on the grave of her father, who had died in Michigan in 1956.

[c]"Three obscure citizens of Ireland" addressed a letter to Casement in prison: "We salute you as we would salute Wolfe Tone." An Irish nun thanked a friend for sending her an account of "the holy death of our glorious martyr, the John the Baptist of our Herod-ridden 20th Century." NLI 13092.

ideas, a set of responses to challenging events, they are both narrow and shallow, limited and limiting. One thinks, if this is Casement, why bother? But that is the wrong place to stop, for it depends upon a wrong understanding of the purpose of the diaries. They were never meant to be records of reflection and judgment: they were designed to be only a quick calendar of events in order, set down with the merest suggestion of emotional coloring in order to keep them from getting away. Reflection and judgment, if they occurred, were intended to take place elsewhere. Still, having made that proper forgiving allowance, one must then go on to admit that a better mind would have made a better thing even of a diary of such limited intention. One cannot complete a study of Casement's diaries convinced that one has been in the presence of a first-rate intelligence. If he had excellence, it was not that of mind.

We remember now that Joseph Conrad called Casement "a man, properly speaking, of no mind at all." Conrad knew him briefly, but intensely, better than we can hope to know him. Casement was not a clear or penetrating or systematic or discriminating thinker. "I don't mean stupid," Conrad went on: and neither do I. It does not say much to call a man's mind better than most, as Casement's was. His thinking was always being misdirected or interrupted or dislocated by factors fatal to efficient intellectuality: by vanity or weakness, by all kinds of passion and prejudice. Casement tried to persuade himself and to persuade others that he was a thinker, but it was not so. It was related, of course, to his notion that he was a writer, which was also untrue. Accepted on his own terms these ideas had a kind of superficial impressiveness that gave him status and reputation in his own day. But they would not have stood up to close inspection even then. These notions were part of the pitiable confusion of Casement's definition of himself: a definition formed, as it were, without being arrived at, without buttressing in facts of capacity and performance, in the absence of genuine alternatives—for lack of something better.

Having called Casement a man of no mind at all, Conrad went on to refine his distinction: "I mean that he was all emotion." Again Conrad seems very nearly right. Though he observed Casement for only a month in 1890, he had seen the central truth of his nature. "A truly tragic personality," Conrad continued, then added a crucial reservation: "all but the greatness of which he had not a trace." But now Conrad's analysis has ceased to satisfy. Casement had more than a trace of greatness and it was related in a very strange way to the fact that he was all emotion. Casement lived all his life *in extremis*. He held together a personality always at the point of disintegration and made it work. There is greatness in that, so long as the work is not merely hysterical or destructive. To say that he was a man of nerves is not the same as saying that he was a man of nerve. Casement was both. At many points in his life one is overtaken by the feeling that the whole thing was an act of almost terrifying courage. His greatness is not a matter of size or accomplishment, but of intensity and endurance.

Casement also showed courage in a more conventional sense and that, too, is a part of what I am talking abour. His going to wild Africa as a boy in his teens and enduring that life for twenty years; his investigation of the Congo system as a weak and exposed solitary servant of the Empire and his subsequent standing up to Leopold and to Oxbridge officialdom; his bold and stubborn defiance of that gang of casual murderers on the Putumayo; his mad trip to Germany and enduring that semi-imprisoned life for a year and a half; his madder trip to Ireland and to what he rightly felt was certain death; his endurance of imprisonment, trial, and execution; his refusal to embarrass his country by a legitimate defense that might have saved his life: surely there are few stranger stories and few so strangely impressive. Most men would not be equal even to one of Casement's major actions. Gathered together they are staggering: a performance that the coolest and most firmly collected man could be proud of as a demonstration of mere courage. In a man who did not know who he was, so intricately divided, his nerves vibrating like harp strings, the sum of bravery almost passes belief. From the point of view of sheer nerve it does not matter much that half the total performance was in some sense absurd. Casement did fall into halves, and into far smaller fractions, but the sum made a form of greatness.

Still, greatness is not the right word to apply to Casement. There was too much in his nature, and that too central, that was petty and faulty: he was vain, he was windy, intellectually he was both arrogant and self-deceiving. These were overriding tendencies. Half the way, one can call him a bore; but the other half gives one all kinds of trouble. The right word for that half is "noble." Casement had nobility: in addition to, in spite of, and because of his manifest weaknesses. In seeing him one must try to avoid sentiment or evasion or self-indulgent paradox. He was a very complex man and his story carries exemplary functions. Consider his virtues: he was deeply kind; he was sympathetic; he was open to pity; he was generous; he was unselfish; he was loving; he was energetic; he was enduring; he was loyal; he was open to gaiety; he was brave. A formidable list. And all of those, too, were overriding tendencies—yet all of them, like his vices, in need of qualification. Casement's nobility rose out of the fact that he made a whole out of his dividedness, made it work, and carried it through to an end with a sort of dignity or serenity that was only the more impressive because it was barely controlling hysteria.

Casement's nature was divided to a depth just short of real pathology, of disastrous incoherence. Was he an Irishman or an Englishman; an Irish patriot or an English public servant; a countryman or a cityman; a man of the people or a gentleman; an Irish peasant or an Irish senator; an intellectual or an artist; an intellectual or a man of action; an idealist or a pragmatist; a sensualist or an anchorite; an African or a European; a Protestant or a Catholic; a man or a woman; a man or a boy? He did not know: he was all of them. The Irish nun called him "the John the Baptist of our Herod-ridden 20th Century." It is impressive to hear the times described so in 1916: they have not improved. And there was something of John in Casement. His head would have looked well on a charger, too, had the English chosen to guillotine him rather than hang him. But a secular analogy is better, for his dividedness represented a whole culture, a whole era; strange as he was, he represented us all: Casement was a sort of Hamlet, a lesser Hamlet. Even a lesser Hamlet may be a truly tragic personality, if he has more than a trace of greatness.

Prayer for Roger Casement at Arbour Hill Church, March 1965. Courtesy of the *Daily Mirror*, London.

The Casement diaries. Courtesy of the Public Record Office, London.

Appendix A

Inspired Innuendoes

THE Government's explanatory statement justifying Casement's execution, which had already been given to Spring-Rice and to the Colombian Minister, was published generally on 4 August 1916. The *Times* printed it and commented editorially on the wisdom of issuing the statement: "Theirs is the responsibility, and they are wise to make their position perfectly clear." The editorial continued, however, to make the point that should have been made many weeks earlier:

> . . . we cannot help protesting against certain other attempts which have been made to use the Press for the purpose of raising issues which are utterly damaging to Casement's character but which have no connexion whatever with the charges on which he was tried. These issues should either have been raised in a public or straightforward manner, or they should have been left severely alone. The colour of his proved crime is deep enough by itself. It would have been fortunate for everyone concerned, and the simplest act of justice, if he had been shot out of hand on the Kerry coast. But if there was ever any virtue in the pomp and circumstance of a great state trial, it can only be weakened by inspired innuendoes which, whatever their substance, are now irrelevant, improper, and un-English.

As chastisement this was little and late, though it was surely better than nothing. A few days later J. H. Morgan sent a personal protest to F. E. Smith which, coming from a widely respected fellow-professional, must have cut fairly sharply. Morgan reminded Smith

455

of his earlier assurances to Artemus Jones that there was "nothing in" the stories of the circulation of the diaries and pointed out that the *Times* statement had not been refuted. As "a public man who is anxious for the good name of his country" Morgan felt shamed by the evidence that "someone in authority" had been guilty of clearly dishonorable conduct.[1] Either because such reprimands took effect or simply because the diaries had done their work, they ceased to be flourished in England. Their use had been improper, as the *Times* said; but it had been carried out by Englishmen and it could not thenceforward be called un-English.

In the United States momentum carried the campaign on a bit longer. On the day after Casement's execution Spring-Rice had cabled that the event "does not excite much comment except in Hearst papers." Senators had been "warned not to make a saint of him for fear of revelations." Everything was going well and the matter had better be allowed to rest barring new developments.[2] In a letter of the same day he amplified these views. On 15 August Spring-Rice wrote that as he had previously warned Cardinal Farley of New York, he had that day talked with Monsignor Bonzano, the Apostolic Delegate, and warned him delicately that "His Majesty's Government were in possession of evidence which would make it extremely undesirable that priests of the Catholic Church should publicly ascribe to Casement the character of a Christian martyr, whose life should be held up as a model to the faithful." Spring-Rice had acted on his own initiative but at the request of "an ardent and sincere well-wisher of the Church." He had found the Apostolic Delegate agreeable and grateful for his caution.[3]

But not all of Casement's friends accepted these measures so tamely, and a day later Spring-Rice was cabling to Lord Newton: "Some friends of Sir R. Casement maintain that there were no signs of perversion here and they maintain journal is forged. I presume you have corroborative evidence if required to produce it. I decline discussion of the question at all and have merely warned people here that such evidence exists, and that they had better be careful."[4] It was a bit late to decline discussion. The Foreign Office minutes on the Ambassador's telegram are instructive in that they show no local doubt at all of the genuineness of the diaries and show surprise that the question could have arisen: the suggestion of forgery was evidently one that had not crossed their minds. Geoffrey Butler noted: "There can be no doubt. Ask Mr. Basil Thomson for further proof of the genuine nature of the diary." Another note ran: "Mr. Blackwell . . . had the question of corroborative evidence in hand about 14 days ago. Let him have a copy of this & ask him how far he has got." Lord Newton clearly assumed that the facsimile pages should have settled the matter: "He must have received the photographs by now, and the inquiry therefore seems curious." Newton cabled on 22 August: "Excellent corroborative evidence exists at the Home Office. Did you never get the photographs of two pages which were sent to you by bag on July 28?"[5] To ask Thomson and Blackwell to pass on the genuineness of the diaries might seem a bit like asking a pair of cats to judge a canary. One would like very much to know what that "excellent corroborative evidence" in the Home Office consisted of: it is what we have all been wishing to see. Presumably it rested largely upon comparison of handwriting and checking of references to dates, places, and events against Casement's known movements, in addition to the mysterious file on Casement that the Foreign Office sent to the Attorney-General on 10 May.[6] At the moment the instructive point is the confidence, the lack of perturbation shown in the Foreign Office and the Home Office on the question of forgery. On that score they did not talk to each other like men with guilty knowledge.

The "friends of Sir R. Casement" whose charge of forgery had inspired Spring-Rice's telegram of 16 August really came down to one potent figure, the New York Irish-American lawyer John Quinn. Quinn's work as a corporation lawyer often took him to Washington and he and Spring-Rice had come to know and like each other. Disapproving entirely of Casement's "mission" to Germany Quinn had still tried his best to save his life after conviction. Quinn had found him in some ways a trying guest, a man with a peculiarly Irish sort of bee in his bonnet, but he had still given Quinn the same impression of fundamental personal character that he had given to other Americans: he was "a man of the utmost austerity and purity," as Quinn had put it to Joseph Conrad, and he was "a damned fine fellow," as he put it to Ezra Pound.[7] He was especially enraged by the inspired innuendoes, the allegations of personal "impurity" that had appeared in many British and some American papers. With Casement dead, Quinn set out to purify his memory. On 13 August he published an impassioned defense in the *New York Times* Sunday Magazine where it appeared as the feature article with a portrait drawing of "Roger Casement, Martyr." The article was subtitled "Some Notes for a

Chapter of History by a Friend whose Guest He Was when the War Broke Out." Here Quinn carefully avoided any reference to stories of Casement's "perversion," not wishing to give them further currency even by attacking them. What he wrote was a eulogy and an elegy.

But the scandalous rumors and the way they had been used to undercut arguments for clemency were what chiefly preyed on Quinn's mind now. He simply could not believe them, in the first place, as he wrote to his lawyer friend Frederic R. Coudert: "Never by word or act, by tone of the voice, by a gesture or the slightest syllable or letter was there a shadow of a shade of anything of a degenerate about him."[8] He had written the same thing in slightly more temperate terms to Spring-Rice on 15 August: "I wish to say frankly, that I utterly disbelieve them. I think I knew the man and I never saw the slightest sign in act, manner or word of any such thing." Then he made his charge: "The alleged diary, if any exists, is, in my opinion, a forgery." But Quinn was assuming that the diary had been found "on" Casement: "It is absurd, on its face, that a man should carry such a self-incriminating document with him when he was going to probable arrest in what was certain to be for him the enemy's country. No; it would take more than an alleged diary to shake my faith in the purity of his life." And Quinn said that he would not be convinced by testimony of handwriting experts alone, even that of "disinterested American handwriting experts."[9]

At this time, and when he wrote to Coudert on the twenty-second, Quinn had still not seen the photographed pages, but he told Coudert that he was going to "see the Naval Attaché here in a day or two" and he would "tell him frankly how I feel about it." In fact he saw Captain Guy Gaunt at the British Embassy on 23 August and the showing took place, leaving Quinn markedly toned down. He had obviously been charmed by Gaunt, whom he now described to Coudert in a letter of the twenty-fourth as "a man of an open and lucid mind," and a man of "clean mind"—a condition Quinn attributed to his seagoing history: "I have for many years felt that there was something about the sea that made naval officers and seamen men of clean and decent minds."[a] The showing of the diary by such a clean man no longer seemed quite so dirty. At last we can observe a showing in detail. Quinn found it a quite convincing demonstration:

[a]Perhaps a heterodox view in light of other folklores.

The Captain showed me the photographic facsimilies, and, without being a handwriting expert and without having studied them under the magnifying glass (the handwriting was much smaller than Casement's usual handwriting),[b] I told him frankly that there was a great resemblance and that if I had then and there to give testimony on the subject I should be compelled to admit the genuineness of the handwriting.[10]

Quinn was also considerably mollified by hearing from both Gaunt and Spring-Rice that they had had peremptory instructions from Lord Grey against the showing of the diaries. Perhaps he had been specially favored.

But a demonstration of the genuineness of the diaries did not resolve the other sore issue, the more fundamental issue of the way they had been used to contaminate the trial for treason and the efforts for reprieve, and on this question Quinn stayed naturally unreconciled though he kept quiet thenceforward. As he had put the case to Spring-Rice: "There is no just relation between the two"—the public and the private guilt.[11] He had heard from Gaunt and Spring-Rice that the diary had been found "months ago," and he leaped to the assumption that this meant while Casement was still in Germany:

> Why did they not use it then, when it would have done some good? . . . But not until he was arrested, in their power, dead or all but dead, did they attack him, when he could not reply or fight back or defend himself or bring an action.[12]

But this was written the day before he saw the facsimiles, when he was still breathing fire, threatening to charge forgery, to rehearse the old Piggott forgeries against Parnell, to ask the English whether they had not then got their "bellyful of forgeries," and also to resurrect the story of Findlay and Christensen (which he had refused to touch when Casement was alive). The showing at the Embassy on the twenty-third reduced Quinn to sullen silence. He had been a real threat to English peace of mind, however; and as the situation has developed one must regret that he did not succeed in forcing the matter of the diaries open to a genuine airing at the time: for British offi-

---

[b]This could have been owing either to photographic reduction or to the rather cramped lineation of the diaries themselves.

cials were about to clap on a lid that no one was able to lift for forty years.

Another question on the American side of the story that must trouble one is that of why the Clan-na-Gael remained so quiet under the Casement slanders. The answer may rest in a letter from Nina to Gertrude, dated only "1 Nov." with no year given:

> Something I heard last Sunday has made me more bitter than ever against John D—A girl whose sister came out to the U.S.A. just after the dearest ones murder, went with me to see the vile old slanderer. She made the remark "How awful to make such a hideous accusation against R.C." (you know what I mean). J.D. replied "Well its all true. I know it is myself."[13]

As Nina heard Devoy's statement herself, we must assume that he made it. What lay behind it, how much of prejudice and pique, how much of real knowledge and what kind, there is no way of knowing. But if the Clan's most influential member had formed this conviction as to Casement's vulnerability the reason for the surprising silence of the organization is not far to seek.

Nina was the kind of chronically unstable person who lived in a state of emotional crisis and now, torn with grief for her brother and with rage for those she considered his traducers and murderers, her condition was acute. Her next confrontation was with Alfred Noyes. Noyes was one of those to whom samples of the diaries were shown in the summer of 1916. He was at work in the News Department of the Foreign Office when the librarian Stephen Gaselee dropped a copy of the typewritten transcripts on his desk. Noyes glanced through the papers for the few minutes allowed him and in his "first revulsion of disgust" made "the expected comment" which was then incorporated in a news article by someone else in the News Department that was sent out for propaganda purposes.[14] He did not then question the authenticity of the diaries and as a part of his work as a British propagandist he went on to publish in the *Philadelphia Ledger* of 31 August 1916 a denunciation of the Easter Rising in general and of its "chief leader" in particular:

> I cannot print his own written confessions about himself, for they are filthy beyond all description. But I have seen and read them and they touch the lowest depths that human degradation

has ever touched. Page after page of his diary would be an insult to a pig's trough to let the foul record touch it.

Such language even if true would enrage a sister far more forbearing than Nina, who was not only a hysterical personality but absolutely convinced of her brother's purity. In the winter when Noyes, then teaching at Princeton University, came to Philadelphia to deliver a public lecture on the English poets, Nina rose in the body of the hall and read him a lecture of her own, denouncing the English as murderers of Roger Casement and Noyes himself as a "blackguardly scoundrel." She was wild and weeping but impressive enough and she gave Noyes a shock he never forgot.[c]

It must have been this event that Gertrude referred to when she wrote Nina in a letter dated only "May 4th":

> I am *thankful* to hear how you set that vile brute down . . . Thank Heaven you are doing such splendid work old girl out there. It is badly needed, as lying propaganda is a deadly weapon. . . . Good luck to you, dear old girl. It must have been a great strain on you to do what you did—not an easy thing to stand up alone and denounce a liar before a lot of his admirers but your bravery has its reward and I am *sure* he [Casement] knows and will strengthen your spirit. . . . No one ever believes a word that comes from England about an Irishman. The loathsome beasts thought they would ruin his name. Never. His name stands enshrined in the hearts of his countrymen and of all decent people all over the world."[15]

Gertrude, never doubting that the diary stories were a "foul slander

[c]In *Two Worlds for Memory* Noyes described the apparition of Nina before an audience of 2,000 people: "the chairman had just finished his introduction, and I was already on my feet, when a lady of distinguished bearing rose in the audience and asked if she might say a few words. I at once made way for her and, to my horror and that of the audience, she announced that she had come for the express purpose of exposing the speaker of the evening as a 'blackguardly scoundrel'. Fortunately her next sentence clarified the matter. 'Your country-men,' she cried, 'hanged my brother, Sir Roger Casement.' Then, her tall spare figure quivering and her face white with anger, she poured out a torrent of invective against England. Chairman, audience and lecturer sat listening helplessly for some minutes. Overwrought and distraught as she was, there was a strange irrational nobility shining through all her wild charges and accusations. The men in the audience remained quite silent, but at last the women began to interrupt and hiss, and with that unhappy accompaniment (which I can honestly say I longed to silence) she left the auditorium." pp. 124–25.

on one whom we *knew* was purer and better than any man we ever met,"[d] had arrived at her own theory, which she regarded as certainty, as to how the thing was done:

> The real story of the diary is this. . . . While he was in the Putumayo he kept a diary in which he jotted down all the foul things he heard of the doings of the beauties out there whose conduct he was investigating. He used it later for his notes and report. As it contained his own movements, comments, etc. & was an ordinary private diary it was not sent in with his papers to the Putumayo Commission [i.e., the committee headed by Charles Roberts.] When he was talking things over with the head of the commission he referred to his diary & was asked to send it to them for information. He did so. Now among the papers that were handed over to me by Scotland Yard in 1916 were all the Putumayo things, but no diary. On looking through to see if I counld find any trace of it I found letters from the head of Putumayo commission of inquiry referring to the diary, saying how valuable they had found it & that typewritten copies of the useful parts had been made & the diary would be returned to R. It *never was returned*. They got the diary, cooked it & forged bits to make it seem as if it were R's own experiences & then carefully photographed odd pages here and there and sent them to U.S.A. and to Ireland and in fact everywhere. People I know were *invited* to come and look at it.

The trouble with her theory is that her facts were wrong. The diary was returned to Casement by Roberts and it exists today in the National Library of Ireland in two forms: manuscript and typescript.[16] This expanded form of Casement's Putumayo diary of 1910 is written on loose foolscap sheets, and she may have been misled by searching for a bound diary volume. It is true he also kept a bound diary for the same period, and that was not returned among his papers; but this is not the diary that was used by the Roberts Committee.

---

[d]Writing to make himself known to Casement's sister on 16 December 1916, his "executor" in Germany, Dr. Curry, gave a devout and emotional account of the impression he had left behind in that country: "I will say only: everyone, with whom your brother came in contact, loved & adored him, man, woman, and child, & when the fatal news of 3 August reached Munich & the shores of the Ammersee, which he so loved, everyone broke into tears & those tears reappear on every occasion, whenever any reference is made to him. How he was admired, adored & beloved throughout Germany." NLI 5588. Maloney papers.

Gertrude was still arguing along these lines, however, in statements of 1920 and 1926. "Don't you see this?" she wrote on 27 June 1920, trying to drive her theory into Nina's head: "They have taken, written up forged bits of, & altogether doctored the Putumayo diary to make it fit in with their own filthy stories."[e] Both in this letter and in a statement of 10 January 1926 written to accompany clippings about Sir Basil Thomson's troubles with the law for misconduct in a public park with a woman poetically named Thelma de Lava,[17] Gertrude emphasized the role of Herbert Ward (not naming him) in authenticating the diaries: "a man who for years had been an intimate friend of Roger, & who, alas, in his patriotic zeal, allowed his mind to be so poisoned against his old & true friend that he was ready to give his name as a guarantor that the diary was all in Roger's handwriting."[18] Yet "not one" of Casement's friends, she went on, "was able to point to one episode in his life that would give colour to the vile suggestions of Sir Basil Thomson." Even Ward had said that "the whole idea came as an overwhelming blow to him & he had never suspected Roger."[f]

It is obvious that Gertrude Bannister's theory—that Casement's diary was "cooked" by artful interpolation of accounts of the acts of other persons in the Putumayo recorded in his own hand—bears a family resemblance to the Hobson-O'Hegarty theory, accepted by Dr. Maloney and later by Alfred Noyes,[g] that the interpolated matter was drawn from Casement's translation and copy of the diary of the rogue Armando Normand. We must now confront the forgery theory honestly, though I hope to avoid rehearsing its long complex history in exhaustive detail. Dr. Maloney's and Noyes's arguments are in print and can be studied, as can Dr. Herbert O. Mackey's book, *Roger Casement: The Forged Diaries*. But Mackey's argument is so incoherent and so full of errors, of illogic and misprision, that it is better dismissed out of hand.[19] The most persuasive as well as the

[e]NLI 14100. By this time Nina had evidently turned against Mrs. Green, for Gertrude corrected her sharply: "And do not abuse Mrs. Green to me. It is abominable. R. wrote to me . . . 'She is the truest & noblest friend a man ever had, & as loyal as steel.' She gave up lifelong friendships (as I know for a fact) rather than abandon him . . . she spent several hundred pounds, many hundreds in fact . . . She, an old woman, was persecuted & hounded, & dragged off to Scotland Yard like a common criminal & questioned & searched & she stood it all, & wore herself out for him."

[f]10 January 1926. NLI 11488. Sir Cecil Spring-Rice had also named Ward as an authenticator of the diaries in a letter to John Quinn on 26 August 1916. NYPL. Quinn collection.

[g]In *The Forged Casement Diaries* and *The Accusing Ghost*, respectively.

most compact of the arguments for forgery appears in an essay by Professor Roger McHugh of University College, Dublin: "Casement: The Public Record Office Manuscripts." Both Montgomery Hyde and Brian Inglis offer excellent reviews of the whole course of the controversy.[20] Both Hyde and Inglis accept as fact, as I do, that Roger Casement was a practicing homosexual. To do so we must all accept the diaries as genuine, for it is there that nearly all the evidence lies.

Perhaps the most irritating feature of the issue is that it was probably unnecessary and avoidable, growing as it has out of the hugger-mugger with which English officials have handled the diaries for nearly sixty years from their first discovery to their subsequent decline into rumor and to their present guarded and reluctant exposure in the Public Record Office in London. This queer, unaccountable, probably unwise and probably reprehensible story can be followed circumstantially in the sources cited above. Had the English kept quiet about the diaries at the outset, as irrelevant to the charge of treason, they would have simply passed to Casement's legatee (Gertrude Bannister) with his other effects after his death, and would no doubt have been quietly burned or otherwise hidden. The issue of forgery and probably even the issue of homosexuality would not then have arisen. Had they, on the other hand, confronted Casement himself with the diaries, or, assuming a repudiation, submitted them to expert and impartial analysis in an early stage, charges of forgery by responsible persons could have been forestalled. Instead they circulated them slyly, then whisked them out of view, smuggled them away in a manner that looked like that of men with guilty knowledge. It is my contention that the English air of guilt does not arise from the knowledge of forgery: it arises from the shamed knowledge that Englishmen had put the diaries to a dirty use. Nothing in human nature is unforgivable, but this was a nasty business. The original tactic would have had to be called stupid—except that it had worked so well. It has surely been stupidly persisted in. And in fact the mere retention of the diaries has probably been illegal, inasmuch as they formed no part of the Crown's case against Casement. There is little in the whole affair in which "a public man who is anxious for the good name of his country," as J. H. Morgan described himself, can take any pride.

The full charge against Casement on sexual grounds may as well be spelled out bluntly. Ernley Blackwell did that for us in his memorandum to the Cabinet of 17 July 1916, "incorporating all the information I had collected," as Basil Thomson noted. Blackwell wrote:

> Casement's diary and his ledger entries covering many pages of closely typed matter [i.e., in the Scotland Yard transcript], show that he has for years been addicted to the grossest sodomitical practices. Of later years he seems to have completed the full cycle of sexual degeneracy and from a pervert has become an invert—a woman, or pathic, who derives his satisfaction from attracting men and inducing them to use him. . . . I believe the diaries are a faithful and accurate record of his acts, thoughts and feelings just as they occurred and presented themselves to him.[21]

Blackwell's statement is clinically if cruelly accurate: Casement regularly had intercourse with other men, usually younger men or youths; it was usually anal intercourse, though sometimes it was oral and sometimes only a matter of manual manipulation; more often than not he functioned primarily as the receiving or female partner. There it is, as the English say. Of course what is wrong with Blackwell's statement is its tone, its purse-lipped supercilious condemnatory delivery. It comes from the same Victorian habit of mind, puritanical, self-righteous, and wholly unimaginative, that leads a presumably more enlightened man of the generation of René MacColl still to call Casement a "degenerate," a "clandestine pervert," a "self-confessed pervert."[22] Casement was not a pervert: he was an invert; and he was not a degenerate: he was a homosexual. He was a citizen of an alternative sexual world. We may not be drawn to such habits and we may not like to observe them; but they are not in themselves degraded and nothing in the presumably happier chance of heterosexuality entitles us to call "the other love" (as Montgomery Hyde names it in his book of that title) sinful or even shameful. That more reasonable and charitable view is the one the Irish must bring themselves to face. But in fact Casement's friends were no more able than his enemies, in Georgian England and Ireland, to think charitably or even objectively about homosexuality: to all it was "the nameless vice," too revolting to name. None of which kept it from occurring pretty regularly. Perhaps it is worth noting, incidentally, that Casement was not a corrupter of helpless youths, a "vile seducer": he took his homosex with young men already that way inclined.

The charge of perversion was all the more shocking and disorienting when it was leveled against a man of Casement's quite special and long-visible purity, unselfishness, and idealism. Apparently nobody could believe that both conditions could be true—though they were true: Casement was a homosexual as well as a man of much nobility of character. It must be allowed at the outset that if Casement was a homosexual then he had fooled a great many people for a very long time: in fact, all of his friends for all of his life. Gertrude was apparently quite accurate when she said that "not one" of his friends had suspected anything of the kind: at least this is true of those who spoke audibly on the matter at the time.[h] The tide runs altogether the other way. "Never by word or act, by tone of the voice, by a gesture or the slightest syllable or letter was there a shadow of a shade of anything of a degenerate about him": John Quinn's affirmation is only a peculiarly emphatic and inclusive form of the general judgment. It was based on an acquaintance of about a month. But Bulmer Hobson judged the charge of homosexuality "completely impossible"[23] on the basis of an intimate friendship of a dozen years during which he had often passed days at a time in Casement's company, walking about the country with him and sometimes sleeping in the same tent. Hobson died convinced of Casement's "purity." John Harris was dumbfounded by the diaries; so apparently were Herbert Ward and Richard Morten who knew Casement more intimately even than Hobson did.

Herbert Spencer Dickey, the American doctor who spent most of his career in South America, was moved to write to Denis Gwynn when he came across a copy of Gwynn's biography of Casement and learned for the first time of the hurtful circulation of the diaries, in order to discount the theory of homosexuality and to advance an explanation of the blackness of the diaries out of his own experience.[24] Two years later he deposited a notarized statement of the same material in the National Library of Ireland. According to Dickey's story, he met Casement in Barbados in the bar of the Marine Hotel in Bridgetown. (This would have been in the first days of September

---

[h]A letter of 24 June 1935 from Mrs. Bernard Shaw to Gertrude Bannister (now Mrs. Sidney Parry) seems to me to suggest that by that time both women had perhaps reached a reluctant acceptance of the idea of Casement's homosexuality. Mrs. Shaw is writing of T. E. Lawrence who had a homosexual history of his own: "Yes: about Lawrence. It is as you say he 'understood' & I remember what a bound my heart gave when he said he would like to write about Roger. Perhaps he would have—who knows! But I think it was a passing inspiration. But I feel he 'understood.' Perhaps T. E. is better as he is—his life was not happy latterly. This vulgar excitement over his death is *horrible*." NLI 13075.

1911.) "At the other end of the bar stood a tall, splendidly built and black-bearded chap. The Negro barman leaned over and whispered to me, 'That's Sir Roger Casement.' "[25] Dickey introduced himself and Casement invited him to have a drink. As they talked Casement revealed that he was on the trail of certain Putumayo ruffians, notably Fonseca and Montt. Casement and Dickey traveled together to Pará, and Dickey punctually appears in Casement's diary on 5 September en route on the *Boniface*, a "filthy tub": "A Dr. Dickey on board—was the Dr. at El Encanto once—speaks Huitoto. Told me that Fonseca & Montt are at Sta. Theresa."[26] In Pará, again according to Dickey, he was amazed to see the British Consul taking a room at the Hotel de Commercio, "a very second rate house," but Casement explained that he had so many calls on his purse that he could not afford better accommodation: "His mail seemed to consist principally of appeals for aid, none of which in my experience ever remained unsatisfied." On board the sluggish *Hilda* for nine days en route to Manaos, Dickey found Casement excessively serious but otherwise likeable. At one river post mules were pulled on board by rawhide lines twisted about their lips, cutting into the flesh. Dickey looked at Casement and saw tears running down his cheeks: "It's cruel! I can't stand it," he exclaimed, and went to his cabin.

On shipboard and during four days in Manaos, Casement spent about six hours a day on his correspondence: "With amazing rapidity he turned out reams in his beautifully legible handwriting." Then one day Casement opened a letter from Conan Doyle which he said asked whether Casement knew of sexual perversions among South American primitives such as those he had told him of on the Congo. Casement asked Dickey's opinion, and Dickey responded in a "scientific spirit" out of a long acquaintance with "sexual irregularities . . . openly and unashamedly practiced among savage people." For the better part of an hour Casement copied into a notebook at Dickey's dictation details of many cases chiefly among the Huitotos. "This will be of enormous interest to Doyle," Casement said when they were finished, "but what terrible stuff to entrust to the mails!" (Casement's diary mentions Dickey often in these days but says nothing of this conversation or of the letter from Doyle.) Dickey's inference, once he had read Gwynn's account of the diaries, was that the conversation and Casement's record of it held the key to the source of the forged material: the acts attributed to Casement were only cooked versions of his notes of Dickey's "scientific" matter. And to Gwynn himself he sent his own reading of Casement's nature: "I am a physician—with thirty years of experience behind me. I have encountered many homosexuals. But, if Casement was one of those unfortunates, I am a rotten diagnostician—and I shouldn't be."[27]

Dickey's diagnosis, like those of Quinn and Hobson and Gertrude and Nina and other unpersuadable friends, is the point at the moment. About all one can say to them is that unlikely as it may seem it is indeed possible for a man to be a practicing homosexual for thirty-five years and his intimate friends to be none the wiser. It certainly requires a great deal of care and even more of luck, but it is not at all impossible. How much do we commonly know of each other's sexual lives? Surely one aspect of the folklore of homosexuality that is now exploded is the old notion that you can "tell one" by looking: that the homosexual betrays himself by his manner of walking or talking or moving his body. He may, he may not. Casement had not, though that in itself proves nothing. Dr. Dickey's diagnosis was wrong, though so confidently made. A mistaken diagnosis by a doctor is also not uncommon. It needs to be remarked, too, that Dickey never saw Casement's actual diaries. Casement was a classic instance of homosexual pathology, a textbook case, and his diaries would repay a careful psychiatric and sociological examination. If it were done in a scientific spirit, it would also be by definition done in a charitable spirit.

But, his friends' passionate conviction of his purity is an impressive part of the argument for forgery and I do not mean to dismiss it casually. I am simply convinced that the negative evidence is stronger still, finally overbearing. Most persons, including most of Casement's friends, came to accept the idea that the rumors of homosexuality were probably based on fact. But some were never convinced, and by joining passion and some logic to the furtive behavior of the English with the diaries, they have created a strong case, strong enough to be accepted by a great many persons even today, particularly in Ireland. It is a powerful point that one is hard put to find a single statement confirming the rumors out of direct experience. Gertrude Bannister's charge that Herbert Ward "told people the *worst* about R"[28] can perhaps be called an instance; but she also said that "he had never suspected Roger."[29] I suppose the statements are not necessarily mutually cancelling, but there is surely little to be made of them. In any case they seem to be based mainly on hearsay. Devoy's remark in Nina's hearing, "Well its all true. I know it myself,"[30] seems to be a clearer case. But again, not knowing Devoy's evidence, one cannot know how far to credit his statement. My suspicion is that it was probably based mainly on observation of Casement's behavior with Christensen and on Christensen's own talk. Christensen's verbal evidence would be hard to trust but not necessarily false. I do not believe that Nina would invent the story so damaging to her brother, even to strike at Devoy; and I do not believe that Devoy would merely fabricate the idea. But one must bear in mind that when he said it, Devoy was sullenly angry at Casement, blaming him for the poor military showing in the Rising, and disgusted with his naive faith in Christensen and his loose way of handling conspiratorial secrets. Still, his statement is a fact that one must weigh.

One must also weigh, according to one's own sense of probabilities, the single piece of gossip among Casement's professional colleagues that has emerged in print. Ernest Hambloch, who became Acting Consul-General at Rio when Casement was seconded for the Putumayo investigations and who had known him earlier in South America, wrote thus of Casement's reputation in the local diplomatic "community": "They felt he was not true to his cloth, and that in that unfaith he was not playing the game by them. Eccentricity would not have bothered them. But Casement was not eccentric: he was concentric. The community voted him not normal, and whispered that he was abnormal." That it was sexual abnormality of which the community whispered (according to Hambloch) is made clear in the little tale he tells in illustration:

> I was in an Englishman's office one morning at Rio when his son, a good-looking youngster, came in. This was the conversation:
>
> "I'm going out to lunch, father." "Whom are you lunching with?"
>
> "The Consul-General. I saw him at the Consulate this morning."
>
> "All right. But be careful, eh?" and father and son exchanged smiles. When the young man had gone out his father turned to me and said, "Casement is a curious chap, isn't he?" and without waiting for any reply he went on to talk of something else.[31]

What is also perfectly clear in Hambloch's general handling of Casement is that he disliked him, at least partly out of envy, and that he would take pleasure in doing Casement an injury. But this does not mean that we can dismiss his testimony, unpleasantly sly as it is.

On the other hand René MacColl's statement that Casement was a "self-confessed pervert"[32] is not far from nonsense, false in tone and dubious in fact. He based his phrase entirely on two bits of evidence, both hearsay. His main exhibit was his conversation with Serjeant Sullivan, then eighty-three, in which Sullivan told him that Casement had not only admitted his homosexuality to him but "gloried" in it as a usual concomitant of genius. When MacColl published these remarks in his book in 1958, Sullivan found his statement more starkly exposed than he liked, and he backed and filled and amended to a degree that made his original statement almost worthless. But whereas it is true that his two later letters softened and qualified and almost obliterated his first remark, I do not see that he quite "repudiated" it, as Alfred Noyes and others have put it.[33] In a letter to the *Irish Times* he wrote: "On reflection, I perceive [*sic*] that he (Casement) neither affirmed nor denied authenticity. He took up the attitude that we pigmies could not understand the conduct of great men and had no right to pass judgment on it." In a second letter he tried again:

> When the public were informed of the existence and nature of these documents, Casement was very anxious that I should enlighten the multitude on this peculiar feature of genius. . . . He told me nothing about the diaries or about himself but Mr. MacColl may well translate this peculiar communication as being a boastful confession in view of the fact that no refutation of the authorship of the diaries appeared in Casement's lifetime.[34]

This is a good example of the way "evidence" about Casement tends to turn spongy under the hand. As I read Sullivan's weasling intention, he wished to withdraw from the position of public accuser but to leave MacColl free to occupy it on the basis of an inference drawn from his (Sullivan's) general but not specific evidence. One is left with little doubt that Sullivan accepted Casement's "guilt" himself. He made that clear enough in *The Last Serjeant:* "Casement was not completely normal and one of the abnormalities of his type is addiction to lamentable practices. He had the further affliction of the craving to record erotica, and this horrible document was in the hands of the Crown."[35] According to his own statement as well as those of

Artemus Jones and Gavan Duffy, Sullivan never saw the diaries. But he did not doubt that they were genuine. Exactly what passed in his conversation with Casement about them must remain in doubt. And his report, like Devoy's, must be put down as testimony of one who had in effect become an enemy. Sullivan obviously disliked his difficult client even though his very notoriety had given him the leg-up he needed at the English bar.

Sullivan's several statements bring us face to face with Michael Francis Doyle again. Among the Maloney papers in Dublin is an undated statement from Doyle:

> When the trial was over, Gavan Duffy and I agreed we should tell Casement about this gossip. He was astounded at first and then he became bitterly indignant. . . . He referred to the reputed habits of certain individual Englishmen among his persecutors. But still he said he could not get into his mind that the British would stoop to such a forgery to destroy his character. It was clear to Gavan Duffy and me that the diary was not his; and he emphatically repudiated it. . . . he thought that they might be using some notes from his records concerning official investigations he had conducted but that there could be nothing referring to any personal acts of perversion except what was false and malicious.[36]

Doyle went on to say that he had never seen the diary or any part of it and knew no one who had. Doyle's story obviously opposes Sullivan's, though it is not even impossible that both were true (or both false): it is barely imaginable that Casement would have behaved in one way with Sullivan and in the opposite way with Doyle and Duffy. One feature of Doyle's account is hard to accept in any case: Casement's air of total astonishment. For he had heard of the diary talk before the trial from Richard Morten, if from no one else: Gertrude says that Morten had "blurted it out." Moreover she and Casement had thenceforward discussed the matter in such guarded terms as were possible with warders in the room.[37] So the "gossip" could not have been news to Casement after the trial. I am bound to say that I mistrust all of Doyle's stories. We have seen his dubious performance in the equally circumstantial story of Home Office evasions of his request to be allowed to go to Germany to collect evidence.[38] And we have Gavan Duffy's statement to Dr. Maloney: "I am sorry you have sent Michael Francis Doyle's story to the Dublin National Library, for I am wholly unable to corroborate it." Which story he meant is not entirely clear, but in the context it seems to be the story above. It is significant that Duffy told no such story himself to Maloney or to anyone else; and indeed he seems carefully to have avoided a real repudiation of the diaries. His lawyer's statement to Maloney: "I need hardly add that the attitude of Roger's defenders throughout was to treat the whole thing as an invention," was not a repudiation. Duffy's fine loyalty to Casement was a moving thing to witness, but it took other forms. He wrote Maloney that his argument for forgery was "impressive" but it was "not conclusive": he advised Maloney to remove it to an appendix rather than making it the show-piece of his book.[39]

René MacColl's second exhibit in his description of Casement as "a self-confessed pervert" looks more disheveled than his Sullivan testimony, but it may in fact be more trustworthy. It is a story told by the nephew of F. J. Bigger to "a well-known resident of Cork"[40] whom MacColl later identified as John J. Horgan.[41] The nephew said that his uncle had told him that when Casement left for America in July 1914 he left in Bigger's keeping in Belfast "a tin trunk containing his papers." Bigger opened it "after Casement's execution" and received "a staggering shock": "There lay a voluminous diary, full of homosexual notations and reminiscences; and there was also a large quantity of letters from various young men, the contents of which left no doubt as to the nature of their relations with Casement." All of this is in the language of MacColl, who goes on to finish the story: "Biggar [sic] then did what Casement ought to have done, not only with these but with the sorry records which he left behind in Ebury Street—burned them."[42] Though this story had passed through several persons, it carries a good deal of innate probability. Casement was incapable of moving without leaving a trail of paper, and he himself recorded the fact that he left a box of papers with Bigger. From Germany on 6 November 1914 he sent a message to Bigger and asked him to "conceal" the papers.[43] And he recorded the fact that he knew Bigger had done so—though the term he (Casement) used was not "burned" but "buried."[44] Again it is just possible that both things occurred: Bigger may have buried the papers on Casement's order, then exhumed them, read them, and burned them after his death. Who can say? But I believe these papers did exist and that they were somehow destroyed by Bigger. None of this makes them homosexual documents, of course: but the fact that Casement wanted them concealed when he was about to enter a phase of special vulnerability surely suggests that he considered them in some way dangerous. If the Bigger story is true, and I believe it essentially is, it may help to solve another puzzle: why were only three real diaries and a cash book produced by Scotland Yard from the years before 1914, and why no letters? For Casement was apparently a habitual diarist, and the diaries in the Public Record Office (the disputed ones) also show that he was inclined to collect and save erotic materials. Perhaps these documents perished by Bigger's cremation or interment.[1]

---

[1]Montogomery Hyde also noticed this possibility in a letter to the *Times* of 1 September 1967.

Appendix B

A Work of Art Takes Time

THE story of the Bigger papers brings us face to face with other crucial questions: when and where were the Black Diaries discovered? The record is muddled, as one has come to expect. But the question is absolutely fundamental to the argument for or against forgery. "A work of art takes time," as Alfred Noyes pleasantly remarked,[1] and forged entries of the requisite number and elaborateness, tailored into the complex fabric of existing diaries running to hundreds of pages, involved in any serious charge of forgery would not be the work of hours or days or even weeks: it would take a good many months. Whoever did the dirty work would therefore have had to possess the diaries for a very considerable time before they began to be shown within a week of Casement's arrest, in early May 1916. So far as I have been able to discover from his own remarks, Casement left caches of belongings in at least five places after June 1914: (1) at Bigger's house "Ardrigh" in Belfast; (2) at his last lodgings, 45 Ebury Street in Pimlico; (3) at his shipping agent's, W. L. Allison in Farringdon Road; (4) at Mrs. Gaffney's in Munich; (5) at Dr. Curry's on the Ammersee. It is quite likely, too, that Casement left papers in America, and there the probable custodian would have been Joe McGarrity in Philadelphia whom Casement wished to receive all of his papers in the event of his death. These deposits included books and clothing and other effects as well as papers, but all of them, except possibly Allison's, included papers of some kind. The two deposits of documents in Germany apparently had to do mostly with Casement's work there: they might have been dangerous on political grounds but probably not otherwise. In any case the

474

English had no access to them. The Bigger deposit appears to be disposed of according to the story above. This leaves the Ebury Street and the Allison consignments as the most likely sources of the Black Diaries. I went to see Mr. W. C. Allison, who was a young man in 1916, with the thought that company records might have survived to tell of search and seizure, or that he might remember the event himself, if it occurred. He remembered Casement himself perfectly well and remembered all the fuss in 1916. But company records of the period have all been destroyed, and Mr. Allison recalls no confiscation of any effects of Casement's. I tried several times to get at police records and made a special plea for an exception to the rule of "Closed for 100 years"; my request was, I believe, honorably considered, but it was denied. Very likely, facts will be revealed in 2016 that will make nonsense of many arguments, possibly including my own.

All of this brings us down to Ebury Street and to contemporary accounts, which is really to say only to Basil Thomson. Unhappily Thomson left four separate accounts of the finding of the diaries and those are as Alfred Noyes says "remarkably contradictory."[2] In the first account in the *Times* of 21 November 1921, he wrote that a policeman who had been sent to search Casement's old quarters returned at the end of the first interrogation in Scotland Yard (23 April) and asked for the key to "two or three trunks" that had been found; Casement said, "Break them open." In the second account in *Queer People* of 1922, Thomson wrote that Casement's lodgings had been searched "some months earlier, when we first had evidence of Casement's treachery" and "locked trunks" had been taken to Scotland Yard but not opened; then he repeated the story of the key at the interrogation. In the third version in *English Life* of March 1925, a detective interrupts the interrogation to ask if Casement has the keys to certain trunks that his old landlord had brought to Scotland Yard some months earlier. In the fourth account, in *The Scene Changes* of 1939, Superintendent Quinn "with the expression of Mephistopheles" lays on Thomson's table during the interrogation a manuscript volume, new to Thomson, which had been "abstracted" from Casement's luggage "which was lying in the Special Branch office"; after the interview Thomson looked into the volume and discovered its odiousness. The accounts agree in suggesting that the diary or diaries were first produced on 23 April and were new matter to Thomson. They differ most painfully on the issue of greatest moment: when did the diaries come into the possession of the police?

But they agree on the assertion that the "trunks" were not opened until 23 April in any case, whenever they came into the possession of the police.

The problem is difficult, and probably impossible to resolve until actual police records can be examined—assuming a sufficiently clear record was made and has survived. Unlike Noyes I do not find it impossible to believe that Thomson's contradictions could have been the work of a lazy or careless writer, working out of a faulty memory without consulting documents. In fact Thomson's prose feels to me more slovenly than disingenuous.[a] But again Noyes may be right in finding the four accounts not only muddled but craftily muddling, planned to lay out with an air of candor an unpursuable trail. Had the police possessed Casement's trunks for an hour or two, or for "some months," or ever since they "first had evidence of Casement's treachery"? If they had had the trunks for months, would they have been likely to leave them unopened until Casement's arrest? I share Noyes's skepticism on this point. Presumably it was illegal to search the effects of a man charged with no crime; but would that have stopped the police in wartime, especially when the man was one so eagerly sought?

Alfred Noyes accepted the Thomson story that best suited his own hypothesis of forgery: the second version, to the effect that the police had had the trunks for a period that Noyes calculated at a year and a quarter before the arrest. He went on to argue from this premise as a flat fact. But indeed the only evidence for the assumption, aside from a vague one-quarter of Thomson's accounts, is a story of Gertrude Bannister's which she recorded in 1926: "The man whose name I have not given [Herbert Ward] told a friend of mine the trunks left behind by Roger in Ebury St. were handed over to the police by the landlady at the instigation of another lodger, as soon as Roger went to Germany in 1914. Sir B. T. had the diary in his possession for at least 16 months before his trial. . . . It was shown to

---

[a]Thomson's writing shows many signs of the kind of untidiness that has no reason for being except sheer laziness. In *My Experiences at Scotland Yard* he refers repeatedly to "Lossen" when he means "Zossen"; he confuses Count Georg von Wedel with a von Wedell who was "captured by a patrol boat off the north of Scotland in 1915"; long after contrary facts were known he attributes the planning of the Rising to John Devoy: "He decided, therefore, that there must be a rising on Easter Saturday, 1916." pp. 86–93. The following two sentences from *The Scene Changes* contain at least four pointless errors of fact that could have been easily corrected: "Casement had first come into prominence when he was vice-consul in Putumayo, Colombia. . . . He was given a C.M.G. and retired very discontented." P. 259.

various people sometime during 1915, I think at the end of 1915 but am not sure.[3] It is interesting that Noyes in quoting this statement as his only support substituted the phrase "As a matter of fact" for Gertrude's vaguer datum "The man whose name I have not given told a friend of mine."[4] Polemicists have to be watched. Thomson's reference to "landlord" as compared to Gertrude's "landlady" may be significant, too: it is the kind of thing a person does when he is working from memory rather than from documents. It seems a pointless and careless variation in detail, like much of the variation in his accounts. Gertrude's vague "as soon as Roger went to Germany" presumably checks roughly with Thomson's vague "when we first had evidence of Casement's treachery." Casement left for Germany on 15 October 1914, but he did not reach Germany until 31 October, and English officials did not know of his arrival until early November when Findlay's fist cloak and dagger message reached them from Christiana. His presence in Germany was not publicly known in England (and thus available to Casement's old landlady and her lodger) until accounts of the German "Declaration" of friendship for Ireland were published on 20 November. Gertrude's story is obviously hearsay and it again makes spongy evidence, vague in details but not in its central point. There is nothing inherently improbable in it and it may well be true. Another contingency worth noting is that Findlay's first report from Christiania referred to Christensen's talk of the "unnatural nature" of his relation with Casement. It is quite possible that these rumors drifted into London gossip and that it was such speculation rather than the actual diaries that reached "various people sometime during 1915."

With so many dubieties we simply cannot know until the record is opened just when Casement's effects were first seized or when the diaries were first examined. A search and seizure at the time when Casement was actually identified and brought to London on 23 April still seems to me the more probable course of events; but I cannot begin to prove it. It is indeed possible that the English held Casement's diaries a year or more before they began showing selections a week after his interrogation: hence that there was time for a good deal of cooking. By the same token, if one adopts the tighter time-scheme for the seizure, the quick showing of the diaries argues that the right incriminating text for the English purpose was ready to hand in Casement's verbatim language.

On the evidence available the only sufficient answer to the charge of forgery resides in the text, the total text, of the diaries themselves; and that will not be sufficient to the rather numerous persons who are resolved not to believe. It is important to notice the fact that, from the beginning in 1916 until Montgomery Hyde and René MacColl were given a look in the Public Record Office on 10 August 1959,[5] of all the major early proponents of the forgery theory only John Quinn and Alfred Noyes actually saw any parts of the diaries. Quinn saw photographic copies of two pages and withdrew from the arena. Noyes saw a "typed copy" of some portion "for a few minutes" and this was his only direct knowledge of the text. The theory of forgery was formed, amplified, and copiously adopted by persons who literally did not know what they were talking about: the thing, the real object, the actual diaries. The whole elaborate structure is to that extent air-built, a superstructure without a foundation. With the publication of *The Black Diaries* by Peter Singleton-Gates and Maurice Girodias in 1959, even though their text is incomplete and littered with errors when compared to the manuscripts, and with the guarded opening of the original diaries to qualified scholars in the same year, the argument has taken on a bit more solidity, but not enough. An argument for forgery must begin with an exhaustive reading of the text. I trust Professor McHugh to have spent a good deal of time at that. Dr. Mackey wrote that he had spent "six days" in study; but that is not nearly enough for what he calls "a close and thorough scrutiny" of the diaries. And it becomes clear when one looks closely at the details he analyzes as forged that he was often working not from the manuscripts but from the *Black Diaries*, and sometimes building an elaborate analysis upon a reading that was itself inaccurate: not what Casement wrote. I spent a solid three months in study of the diaries, turning them on every side, and finished with a conviction that they were not forgeries: they are all of a piece, all the work of one man, and the man is Casement. My conclusion is based on careful reading of the diaries, cross-reference to all the other available Casement documents, and general application of what I hope is common sense. I cannot pretend to be a technical expert on handwriting[b] and I know nothing of the forger's art. I do know that English officials have at long last allowed a very careful analysis of all of the manuscript diaries by a well-qualified independent expert. But the sponsors of the study have not wished to make

---

[b]My lay experience of twenty-five years as a teacher of English during which I have read an awful lot of handwriting may be worth something.

the graphologist's findings public as yet and, of course, they have not been revealed to me. Their reluctance to publish is based evidently on a motive with which one must sympathize: the desire to do nothing to complicate the present tense political relationship between England and Ireland.

Looking at the diaries themselves, one can see that a reader who approaches them with his mind already made up that they were forged, could easily discover what he would call "evidence": bits erased or scratched out or corrected, bits cramped in at top or bottom or side of an entry, change of ink or pen, change from pen to pencil, variations in size or weight of script, oddities in sequence of events, "out of character" sentiments, and so on. But in fact there is nothing in any of that that a busy diarist might not do himself and I am sure that is what happened. The feeling of the thing is homogeneous: even the vagaries feel homogeneous within the vagaries of the character that was Casement's. The forgery theory will not wash and the reason is one not only of details but of basic size or scale in the diaries, and of their texture, the feel of the fabric. Details can be checked against the same events as visible in parallel documents certainly uncontaminated by forgery, and they do check. I have cited a number of such cases in passing out of the hundreds that are possible; and I have found no single discrepancy of detail. But the larger point is that the case for forgery grows physically and psychologically incredible in terms of scale and texture. I think it is impossible for a forger to have tailored the homosexual details into this big convincing fabric without destroying the homogeneity of it: he would have had to weave the whole fabric, and the whole fabric is not invented; it is Casement's. This matter of wholeness or homogeneity cannot be demonstrated by piecemeal analysis, it has to be felt in one's own experience of a total texture.

A final word should be said about the several forms of the theory that the diaries were falsified by interpolation of unrelated diaries or notes in Casement's hand. There are three of these hypotheses, closely related: (1) Gertrude Bannister's supposition that matter was taken from Casement's own notes of testimony of degenerate behavior by others during his Putumayo investigation; (2) the Hobson-O'Hegarty theory that Casement's copy of the diary of Armando Normand was cobbled into his own diaries: this is the chief exhibit of Dr. Maloney and of Alfred Noyes after he became a convert to the forgery thesis; (3) Dr. Dickey's suggestion that the forger had made use of the case histories Dickey had given Casement to send to Conan Doyle. Of the Bannister suggestion I argue errors of fact: the "black" Casement diaries of 1910 and 1911 are documents distinct from the much fuller "Putumayo diary" that was lent to the Select Committee; the latter diary was not retained by the Roberts committee as she thought but returned by Roberts to Casement and passed on among his papers after his death. The Hobson-O'Hegarty-Maloney-Noyes case seems to me probably to rest on misrecollection and misunderstanding. I do not think an Armando Normand diary ever existed. Had Casement possessed it or even known of it he would have mentioned it, probably often, among the hundreds of thousands of words public and private that he wrote about the Putumayo, and he did not mention it. A document of a closely related kind, Frederick Bishop's record of his week's surveillance of Normand and Leavine at La Chorrera did exist and was mentioned. Casement even says in his fuller Putumayo diary: "Here it is." But that has disappeared and I have no notion what happened to it. It can have been no more than a few scribbled pages from the half-literate Barbadian in any case. I suspect that Hobson and O'Hegarty (who were close friends and certainly discussed Casement matters often, more especially when Maloney was constructing a case) built up the Normand diary in a perfectly honest way out of their common recollection (twenty years after the event) of Casement's mention of the Bishop diary in the context of Normand's undoubted (but heterosexual) infamy. Of Dr. Dickey's theory of a corrupt use of his "dictated" notes for Conan Doyle I can say very little, except that there is again no sign of such a document among Casement's papers nor any reference to it. If it existed, I do not know what happened to it. Perhaps the "terrible stuff" was indeed "entrusted to the mails" and sent off to Doyle. Furthermore there is no sign of matter from such notes that I can discover in the diaries themselves.[c] That is the essential answer to all these theories: there is no evidence of such alien matter in Casement's texts (which, of course, treat events in the Congo and in England and Ireland and various continental cities as well as in South America). I do not believe that

[c]Dickey said that he gave Casement data on "perversions" among South American tribesmen in response to a query about such matters in a letter from Conan Doyle. The only visible letter from Doyle that vaguely fits this context is his request to Casement for Amazonian local color to go into his "wild boy's book." (See above, pp. 132, 155.) I wonder again if Dickey's story, more than twenty years after the event, is not another imaginative sexual embroidering of a hazy recollection.

such matter could be cobbled in—in hundreds of instances—without leaving traces of its falseness. The acts described seem to me Casement's acts, in Casement's situations, in Casement's language, and in Casement's hand.

A consideration that seems to have been overlooked in arguing the forgery thesis pro and con is this: if the diaries are spurious and Casement was not a homosexual, then he was a man of no sex. For he surely was not heterosexual. Nowhere in all the evidence is there any real sign of his being romantically or passionately drawn to a woman. A great many women were strongly attracted to him, quite properly and naturally; but not he to them. This is not to say that he did not respect and warmly like many women. Clearly he liked some of them very much: Ada MacNeill, his Bannister cousins, his sister Nina, Mrs. Green, Emmeline Cadbury, the Carlton Park ladies, Mrs. Morel, several women in Germany, apparently Eva Gore-Booth at the last. But they were quite simply friends and allies, comrades, good fellows: he seems never to have thought of them as sexual creatures. In fact I suspect that the closest he came to a romantic affair was his relationship with his cousin Gertrude. She seems to me to have been in love with Casement, though not he with her, really, and in their genteel unconfessed Edwardian way their feelings ran deep, hers into love. Anyone who argues that Casement was not homosexual must go on to call him passionless, and that is another notion that will not wash. He was a man of powerful sexual feeling. The problem was that he was attracted to men not to women. His passions were "abnormal" not in quantity or quality but in direction. Casement looked at men exactly as most men look at women, sizing them up as sexual prospects: measuring age and skin and bodies and ways of moving, legs and breasts and bottoms and genitalia observable or imaginable. I find nothing innately filthy-minded in any of this. My experience in working with the diaries for a long time was that I was able to work through and past my first shock and come out in a condition of tolerance. And pity: Casement's sexual life caused him acute suffering as well as occasional acute pleasure. But his mind no longer seemed to me any dirtier than my own, for example— though I suppose the two of us prove little as to the race at large. What may perhaps be more "abnormal" than his homosexuality was his fondness for writing it all down, evidently in a kind of afterglow or second experience of the event that then made it vicariously repeatable, to be savored at will. How odd or reprehensible that is as an erotic mode I am unable to judge: textbooks will tell us how odd but not how reprehensible.

I tried to make my first approach to the diaries with my mind open, willing to be persuaded either way on the issues of forgery and homosexuality. Study convinced me as I have indicated. I then turned to the question of whether any evidence was to be found in the mass of Casement documents to support the impression of homosexuality. We have seen that his impression upon his friends ran almost entirely the other way in what testimony is available. What lost diaries and letters would have shown we cannot know. In the surviving papers outside the Black Diaries there is remarkably little sexual evidence of any kind. Possibly this means only that it was successfully destroyed. But I did find odd bits of what I should call evidence that seems to me sufficient to confirm the testimony of the homosexual diaries. The reader must weigh them for himself.

The earliest occurrence is early indeed: it appears in a Smith's "Scribbling Diary" for 1881. In the book the pages are torn out down to Monday, 16 May, and thereafter, under various assigned dates in 1881–83, appear assorted notes and memoranda: titles of plays and operas, drafts of letters, drafts of poems or parts of poems, one of which is scrawled over in a very large hand, "Rubbish." Under the date of 27 June 1881, when Casement would have been sixteen years old and working as a clerk for Elder Dempster in Liverpool, the following lines are written in his already distinctive hand:

> What hand hath reft Hope of her crown
> Or ta'en her gems away
> Oh! sweet boy of Dublin
> Oft in my dreams do I see thee.[6]

The second occurrence is an incoherent note scribbled at the end of two pages of drafts of verses, also incoherent, treating of unhappy love. The whole note runs:

> Casaldo's friend—R. C.
> Naples, 3 September 1900
> Written going to lunch at Naval & Military
> on Saturday, Sept. 22
> 1900—Oh Sad! Oh! grief stricken.[7]

I take this to mean that before going to lunch on 22 September 1900 at the Naval and Military Club in London (Cambridge House, Piccadilly) Casement tried to versify his feelings about an unsuccessful amorous event of three weeks earlier in Naples. It seems to me to express homosexual feelings about a homosexual relationship. That neither the poem nor the affair came off makes no difference as evidence.[8]

The next exhibit is that of Tuesday, 22 December 1903, when Casement left London and went to Dublin. The whole diary entry runs as follows:

> Bad crossing to Dublin. At North Wall [Dublin]. Went Bray [Dublin]. Francis Naughton not there—back to Westland Row [Station]. At Harcourt Place[d]—J. B. grown greatly in all ways £1.6 /—Xmas. Dinner at Dolphin. Home to hotel—nice fire in bed and off to sleep J. B. £1.8 /—came, handled and also came.

Translated this means that Casement arrived in Dublin, went out to Bray looking for Francis Naughton, did not find him, went back to central Dublin, found an old friend named J. B. in an improved state, had a sexual episode with him that cost £1.6 in some way or ways, had dinner, and went to bed and to sleep. The entry may have been written that night or it may have been written later. The out-of-sequence final clauses are an interesting example of how Casement often added a detail late as it occurred to him, or how he apparently sometimes returned to a "completed" entry and amplified it. I cannot explain the shift from £1.6 to £1.8. It may simply represent an error; or it may refer to separate expenditures; or he may have recollected another two shillings that should have been included. "Came, handled, and also came," is sex talk, homosex talk, describing orgasms manually induced. It is impossible to say who was the subject of each verb. It is a grammatical trick common in Casement's diaries: a kind of shorthand that the intended reader (himself) would have understood without difficulty. But we are seeking evidence outside the diaries, and this is to be found on a loose notebook page (quite separate from the diaries) which is undated and which reads as follows:

> Francis Naughton
> Station Hotel
> Bray
> Co. Wicklow
> Home address Cavan House

[d]Here Dr. Mackey accepts the *Black Diaries* misreading of "Park" for "Place" and so is able to argue that the entry is forged.

Bundoran
He gets £20 a year & his keep
at the Station
Hotel in Bray
Is a Catholic
& has both parents
living at Bundoran
Has been only 9 months in Dublin.

I argued earlier[9] that this sheet is a sort of filing card reference to an actual or prospective lover. The content shows that it is a description for reference. That Casement kept at least one file of this kind, however, can only be shown from the diary: the reference to "G. B. of 6 File"—who is almost certainly the George Brown who is in New York in February 1903 and to whom Casement sent unexplained sums of some size. Equally, that Francis Naughton's ambiance was homosexual can only be inferred from his situation in the diary entry of 22 December quoted above. The file-reference to Naughton, on the other hand, never had any physical connection with the Black Diaries and so could hardly have been touched by a possible forger. Again I argue that the whole matter is evidence of homosexuality, though I should hate to take it into a court of law.

After studying the diaries and after reading Dr. Mackey's argument for forgery, I decided to make a kind of test case out of one of Mackey's prize exhibits, that involving "forged" references to a man named "Miller," as Mackey insistently misreads the name "Millar" though it appears that way clearly a dozen times in Casement's script. The case looked useful in that it involved several closely related episodes and showed Casement carrying on with an Irishman on home grounds, far removed from exotic places such as the Congo or the Putumayo. I thought I would lie on watch for Millar to see if I could establish him as real, and in what contexts. Of the several Millar entries Mackey treats, the principal ones are the following:

[20 June 1910] Gave £2 for Irish prize on Rathlin [Island] to Father McKinley. Left Ballycastle at 4 train—Millar to dinner at N. Counties hotel—splendid. Gave Millar pin for tie. Stayed till 9.30 and in Room XX. Then to his mother's on foot and by tram. In deep and warm.

[21 June 1910] At Belfast. To Castle Dobbs in afternoon and lunched there coming back with medical student in train—

Charming view and nice face. Medical student—smiling face.
Left for L'pool—Bulmer to see me off. Charming day. With A.
Dobbs at Castle Dobbs. Eden S. O.—Carrickfergus.

(Of the text it is necessary to remark first that no forger unless he
were demented would foul up sequences as they are here: this is
Casement's own careless work, jottings at several points over a day or
days, leading to unconscious repetition and to dislocations in the
time-scheme.) Mackey's mistakes in reading and logic here are so
many that it is almost impossible to straighten them out.

Mackey was convinced in the first place, after talking with Bulmer
Hobson about the period, that it was Hobson that Casement had
dinner with in Belfast on 20 June before Hobson saw him off next
day for "Larne" as Mackey misreads "L'pool." He goes on to argue
that the forger took advantage of "Bulmer's" presence in Casement's
note to invent a sinister character named "Miller" whom he then put
into various invented disreputable situations:

> The forger . . . changed the name *Bulmer* into Miller—Note
> that three letters of each name are the same (L, E. and R) and
> that they are both words of six letters each [*sic*]. At the end of this
> day's diary entry . . . the forger added a sentence in un-
> equivocal terms that the fictitious character "Miller" committed
> a criminal act with Casement in the house i.e. Bulmer Hobson's
> house. The entry for the next day reads "left for Larne; Bulmer
> to see me off." Having established by the entry the fictitious
> character "Miller," the forger then makes many entries else-
> where associating the name with Casement in similar criminal
> conduct.[10]

On this I shall note only the following considerations: (1) The name
is *Millar* not *Miller*; it is perfectly clear and shows no sign of tamper-
ing; the name of *Bulmer* is also separate and clear. (2) The "added"
sentence at the end of the entry for 20 June refers back to the experience in the hotel room and has nothing to do with the house. (3) The
house is that of Millar's mother not that of Bulmer. (4) For "Larne"
read "L'pool." (5) "The fictitious character 'Miller' " is not established here; the real character Millar is established three weeks earlier
on 28 May ("Left for Warrenpoint with Millar") and performs spec-
tacularly over several days.

But Mackey is a sitting duck and there is no point in throwing
stones at him. The real question is whether Millar existed outside the

diary and thereby out of reach of Mackey's mad forger or even of saner ones. I found him in five separate places elsewhere in the Casement papers. One is a note of £2 spent for a "writing desk for Millar," apparently a country artifact. Another is the note: "Millar £25.0.0" in an undated list of expenditures in Casement's hand.[11] I take it that both the desk and the cash were presents to Millar. Then Millar shows up three times in an undated account of expenses that fills the front end paper of Casement's 1910 diary in the Public Record Office (matter that is omitted from *The Black Diaries*): "Pin present Miss Riddell X Millar 2.0"; "Japanese Books. Millar 1/2"; "Lunch Grand Central Millar & I 7/6." The fourth appearance occurs in a complete letter of 19 November 1913 from Millar himself. He writes mainly of his choice of two paintings on Casement's commission, at a cost of £2.2.0 each, out of a show of work by Ada MacNeill, evidently water colors. He covers four pages in a neat clerkly hand and the general effect is somehow shabby-genteel. Casement is addressed as "My dear Sir Roger" and the signature goes "Ever yrs affectionately Millar." The fifth appearance seems to me the most significant. It occurs as a mere note at the top of a letter of 23 August 1907 from A. Alston of the Foreign Office to Casement who was apparently in Belfast. Casement endorsed the letter: "Recd. Saturday 24 Augt / 07 Just before Millar came!" I do not scruple to argue that that is a homosexual exclamation point. Millar did exist, he and Casement were friends over a period of at least six years, and their relationship was that of well-behaved homosexual lovers.

An unexpected sort of document also turns up among the Casement papers to testify to the reality of one of the kinds of Putumayo episodes that have been called forged. In his diary entry for 24 November 1910 Casement described a steward on the *Liberal* who "showed enormous exposure after dinner—stiff down left thigh" and who later leaned on the gunwale "with huge erection about 8"." On this evidence Casement said: "I wanted awfully." Next day he asked the boy's name which turned out to be Ignacio Torres, and he invited the boy to visit him in Iquitos. Over the next ten days the situation turns into a funny and touching little failing love affair. Ignacio never quite got the point. Casement gives him errands to do and then overpays him for doing them badly. Ignacio makes appointments and forgets them: "Looked everywhere for Ignacio. No sign anywhere. Very sad" (2 December); "Waited till 6.40; no Ignacio, or sign of him! Alack!" (3 December). Then the next day, a Sunday, "Very hot morning": "Looking out window saw *Ignacio* waiting. Joy. Off with him to Tirotero and camera. Bathed and photo'd and talked and back at 11. To meet tomorrow. Gave 4 / -." On 5 December: "Ignacio at 6.30 and off together to Tirotero and bathed . . . Gave £1—'Tanto ufano' (so much content) but no more! . . . To Store and ginger ale and on slowly, painfully dragging back toward house. At length the parting and at Factoria Calle said 'Adios'—for ever! He nearly cried I think. I gave him 2 / - more and I think he was wretched. He said 'Hasta luego.' I turned back and found him still standing at corner looking straight in front.[e] I to Fotografia and he crossed street last time saw him was then standing and looking: Poor Ignacio! Never to see again." Next day (6 December) Casement boarded the *Atahualpa* for Pará. On the blotter facing his entry for that day, like a plaintive little balloon of talk sent out to sea, appear the words: "Left Iquitos—goodbye Ignacio—never to see again." (Does such a story derive from the Normand diary or from Dr. Dickey's bad Huitotos? Surely not.) Now, quite outside any diary, on 29 April 1911 D. Brown of Booth and Co. in Iquitos writes to Casement in care of Allison's in Farringdon Road: "I have delivered the photographs to Perez on the Muelle; but up to the present I have not been able to find the boy Ignacio Torres. Some of our men are looking for him, and as the steward of the 'Liberal' informs me that the boy is somewhere in Iquitos, we should be able to find him."[12]

One final exhibit, from nearly the latest possible moment. This is a copy of *1914 and Other Poems* by Rupert Brooke. Inside the front cover is a manuscript poem with the note: "Written in Pentonville Prison by Roger Casement." The note is not in Casement's hand but the poem is, and it runs as follows:

"O Friend of my Heart!
'Tis a debt I pay in this telling
for hours of delight.
To lay my wreath of bays at
Your feet I would climb afar
to your height.
I would walk the flints with
a terrible joy, if at the
journey's end

[e]Thinking, probably: "Of all the strange blacos this is the strangest."

I would greet you O Friend!

Cathal O'Byrne

7.6.16"[13]

I do not know that that is a homosexual poem but I think it is. I also find it a moving poem. One would like to talk to Cathal O'Byrne. I know nothing of him except that he was a singer and one of the young men who made of F. J. Bigger's house in Belfast a Gaelic League enclave and a general hostel.[f] He was also the "C—" whose long letter to Casement in prison he managed to retain and on the back of which he wrote a long letter to Gertrude that was "smuggled out of the prison" as she put it.[14]

These exhibits from outside the diaries must be added to the diaries themselves and to such testimony as Devoy's and Christensen's (which may be one testimony), and perhaps Hambloch's, and to whatever was in Ronald Campbell's Foreign Office file on "Sir R. Casement's supposed proclivities to unnatural vice"[15](which may also be largely Christensen reports), to make the whole case for homosexuality. I am sure the case is decisive. The really conclusive phenomenon is the way the text of the diary stands up to every test from within or without. But I am quite sure there are persons who would not be convinced even if an aged lover of Casement's (there must be some living) come forward with photographs *in flagrante delicto*. Adler Christensen held in his grubby hand the key to this part of the Casement problem as to much else.

Finally the likelihood of forgery needs to be looked at from the point of view of the English. There is really no satisfactory answer to the question: why should they bother? And forgery would have involved a great deal of bother. To fabricate several diaries running to hundreds of pages that could be passed off as Casement's would have required the composition of an immensely detailed scenario which in turn would have required painstaking study of all the available records of Casement's movements; the scenario would then have had to be elaborated in convincing detail and written down in a hand exactly resembling his. It would be a work of years: in fact it was impossible. To invent or adapt detailed homosexual episodes by the hundreds and then to tailor those convincingly into existing innocent diaries would be easier but almost certainly too difficult for the time

[f]Information from Mrs. Florence H. Patterson.

available for the work. The whole idea involves a quantity of scheming, of invention, of labor, of skill, and of costliness that I simply
cannot believe busy government departments with a big war to fight
could have or would have invested in Roger Casement. Forgery was
being used, and by England, as an instrument of state in 1916; but
not with this kind of elaborateness and not against so small a target.
To English officials Casement was essentially only a nuisance,
though no doubt he looked a bit more dangerous, potentially, than he
actually was: could they have seen him in Germany in the winter of
1915–16 they would have been moved to mirth or pity, according to
temperament. The English case against him was one of treason. No
doubt they had begun putting together a dossier of treason at least as
soon as they learned from Findlay in November 1914 that he was
heading for Germany; more likely the collection began with the publication of his anti-recruiting "manifesto" in Ireland in October
1914—possibly even earlier, when his articles, seditious in tenor,
began to appear in Irish journals in 1912 and 1913. On the issue of
treason the English had Casement dead to rights by April 1916 and
their case needed no support from salacious documents. On the other
hand it is true that information or inference as to his private "character" had begun to be part of the treason dossier by late 1914 at least;
but this must have been small and scrappy and it was probably included because it lay to hand and looked possibly useful. By his own
actions Casement corrected any weaknesses in the government case
for convicting him as a traitor, and in the later and ancillary case for
hanging him as a degenerate and a traitor. He fattened the treason
case by traveling over to Ireland in a German submarine somehow
associated with a cargo of German arms; and he fattened the case for
perversion by offering his diaries. Casement had done the forger's
work for him.

There is something to be learned, too, by studying the handling of
the diaries by English officials at the time. What emerges in the
inter-office commentary on the matter is a clear impression of general innocence on any score of forgery. A few officials, notably Grey
and Spring-Rice, showed a humane and fastidious distaste for the
whole subject of the diaries and their use. But apparently the whole
idea of possible forgery came as a shock, to everyone in the Foreign
Office at least, as late as mid-August 1916. If there had been any
cooking of the diaries, the fact was certainly not generally known in
Whitehall and apparently not even suspected; and if there was a fact,

it was known to a very small cadre, probably only to Thomson and Hall and to their brilliantly imaginative and skillful employee (the forger). I see no evidence, for example, that even F. E. Smith and Ernley Blackwell showed any signs of possessing that kind of guilty knowledge. Note that Blackwell, for example, did not even think to raise the idea of authenticating the diaries against Foreign Office records until late June. And that action presupposes a diary or diaries in existence and complete—now to be checked in case anyone raises the question of authenticity. It also surely suggests that Blackwell is convinced that the document will bear detailed scrutiny—hence that it is authentic. Note too that a forged diary would have have had to be based on long and detailed *study* of Foreign Office records. That would have had to be carried out long since and it could not have been done without persons in the Foreign Office knowing that it was going on.

The air of secretiveness and guilt that hovers over the whole affair is not the guilt of the forgery but the guilt of the showing. Much of the atmosphere of the showing in 1916 was that of mere salaciousness: the stuff was dirty and Thomson and Hall and possibly Smith showed it with exactly the furtive and gloating air with which some men hand about "filthy pictures." But the air of the greater guilt was the air of the greater crime: the cutting down and destruction of a powerless man by powerful men using a weapon that bore no relationship to the crime that had put him in their power. It is this guilt, not that of forgery, that rests on English conscience and that in my opinion largely explains the intricate evasiveness of English handling of the diaries down to the present day. I cannot see how the showing of the diaries at the time of Casement's extremity can be called anything but shameful. On the other hand there may be a partial justification for the subsequent secrecy, that of the past sixty years, in the long tortured history of the relation of England and Ireland, grown acute: a history that has not failed to continue.

Notes

PREFACE

1 "The Chameleon & the Kilt," *Encounter*, XLI (August 1973): 74.
2 Ibid., p. 76.
3 Ibid., p. 70.

CHAPTER 1

1 To Mrs. A. W. Hutton, 26 November 1904. NLI 8602.
2 NLI 13077.
3 Agnes (Nina) Newman, "Life of Roger Casement, Martyr in Ireland's Cause," *The Irish Press*, (Philadelphia), 13 December 1918.
4 Ibid.
5 Ibid.
6 Gertrude Bannister Parry, "Early Recollections of Roger Casement." NLI 5588. Maloney papers. "Murlough" is Murlough Bay near Ballycastle.
7 Ibid.
8 N.d., ca. 1904. NLI 13080.
9 "Life of Roger Casement, Martyr in Ireland's Cause," 27 December 1918.
10 Ibid.
11 Interview in the *New York Times*, 25 April 1916; quoted in Maloney, *The Forged Casement Diaries*, pp. 126–27.
12 Rex v. Casement: Brief to Counsel for the Defense. NLI 13088.
13 NLI 13078.
14 NLI 5459.
15 London School of Economics MS.
16 NLI Microfilm P. 6830. Sanford papers.
17 Ibid.
18 *A Voice from the Congo*, p. 237.
19 *African Drums*, pp. 23 and 247.
20 24 June 1904.
21 23 October 1889. NLI 13074. Parry papers.
22 6 May 1890. NLI 13074. Parry papers.
23 Congo diary. *Last Essays*, ed. Richard Curle (London, 1926).

24 G. Jean-Aubrey, *Joseph Conrad: Life and Letters*, i: 325–26.
25 Conrad to John Quinn, 24 May 1916, NYPL. Quinn collection. Is Kurtz there, too?
26 "Early Recollections." NLI 5588.

CHAPTER 2

1   28 July 1892. NLI 13074.
2   Brief to Counsel. NLI 13088.
3   6 November 1893. NLI 13074. Parry papers.
4   4 July 1894. PRO FO 2.64.
5   Casement to MacDonald, 24 November 1894. PRO FO 2.64.
6   2 July 1894. Br. Mus. Add. MS. 46912 M.
7   Brief to Counsel. NLI 13088.
8   Brief to Counsel. NLI 13088.
9   To Gertrude Bannister, 27 July 1895. NLI 13074. Parry papers.
10 23 October 1896. NLI 13074. Parry papers.
11 12 March 1896. PRO FO 63.1316.
12 23 October 1896. NLI 13074. Parry papers.
13 PRO FO 63.1316.
14 6 June 1896. PRO FO 63.1316.
15 Telegram 16 June 1896. PRO FO 63.1617.
16 26 June 1896. PRO FO 63.1317.
17 PRO FO 63.1352. The bleeding was probably intestinal.
18 NLI MS. unclassified.
19 NLI 12116.
20 NLI MS. unclassified.
21 See below, pp. 82–83, for example.
22 Brief to Counsel. NLI 13088.
23 NLI 13089; PRO FO 2.368.
24 PRO FO 2.368.
25 Brief to Counsel. NLI 13088.
26 Telegram 24 February 1900. PRO FO 2.368.
27 5 July 1900. PRO FO 2.368.
28 3 August 1900. PRO FO 63. 1375.
29 PRO FO 63.1375.
30 Brief to Counsel. NLI 13088.
31 NLI MS. unclassified.
32 28 August 1901. NLI 13074. Parry papers.
33 21 May 1901. PRO FO 2.491.
34 28 June 1901. PRO FO 2.491.
35 19 November 1901. NLI 13073.
36 NLI 13073.

CHAPTER 3

1   15 February 1903. PRO FO 2.764.
2   *Roger Casement*, 1973. p. 63.
3   17 February 1903. PRO HO 161.

4   28 February 1903. PRO HO 161.
5   The quotations in this paragraph are from diary entries of 2-17 March 1903. PRO HO 161.
6   18 March 1903. PRO HO 161.
7   21 March 1903. PRO HO 161.
8   17 April 1903. PRO HO 161.
9   13 April 1903. PRO HO 161.
10 The quotations are from diary entries of 29 and 22 April 1903. PRO HO 161.
11 4 June 1903. PRO HO 161.
12 5 June 1903. PRO HO 161.
13 9 July 1903. PRO HO 161. The reading of the last word is dubious though surely probable.
14 The quotations in this paragraph come from diary entries for 13–16 August 1903. PRO HO 161.
15 The quotations in this paragraph come from diary entries for 25 and 26 August. PRO HO 161.
16 6 September 1903. PRO HO 161.
17 6 September 1903. PRO FO 2.764.
18 The quotations in this paragraph come from diary entries for 9 and 10 September 1903. PRO HO 161.

CHAPTER 4

1   Brief to Counsel. NLI 13088.
2   The quotations in this paragraph come from diary entries for 5–10 December 1903. PRO HO 161.
3   Quotations from diary entries for 12 and 14 December 1903. PRO HO 161.
4   13 December 1903. PRO HO 161.
5   Quotations from letter of 13 December 1903. NLI 13080.
6   1 December 1903. NLI 13073.
7   21 December 1903. NLI 13073.
8   26 December 1903. PRO HO 161.
9   Quotations from diary entries for 25 and 29 December 1903. PRO HO 161.
10 29 December 1903. NLI 13073.
11 8 January 1904. NLI 13076.
12 To Alice Stopford Green, 24 April 1904. NLI 10464. Green papers.
13 See below, pp. 75–77.
14 21 March 1904. NLI 13080.
15 27 March 1904. NLI 13073.
16 NLI MS. unclassified.
17 9 March 1904. NLI 13074. Parry papers.
18 Brief to Counsel. NLI 13088.
19 2 May 1904. NLI 13074. Parry papers.
20 27 April 1904. NLI 13073.
21 NLI 13089.
22 *Experiences of a Literary Man*, p. 258.
23 8 September 1904. NLI 13080.
24 25 August 1904. NLI 13074. Parry papers.

25 Undated note. NLI 14100.
26 8 September 1904. NLI 13080.

CHAPTER 5

1   3 December 1904. NLI 13076.
2   29 January 1905. NLI 13075.
3   20 December 1904. NLI 13076.
4   17 September 1904. NLI 14100.
5   17 September 1904. NLI 14100.
6   15 March 1905. NLI 13074. Parry papers.
7   Ibid.
8   Ibid.
9   14 April 1905. NLI 13073.
10 1 February 1905. NLI 13073.
11 12 April 1905. NLI 13080.
12 Brief to Counsel. NLI 13088.
13 20 July 1905. NLI 13080.
14 Ibid.
15 Letters cited in this paragraph are found in NLI 13073 and 13080.
16 See MacColl, pp. 50–51n.
17 10 August 1905. NLI 13158. Hobson papers.
18 5 July 1905. NLI 13073.
19 27 September 1905. NLI 13073.
20 12 December 1905. NLI 13081.
21 10 March 1906. NLI 13081.
22 10 March 1906. NLI 13074. Parry papers.
23 Ibid.
24 4 April 1906. NLI 13073.
25 26 July 1906. NLI 13073.
26 25 July 1906. NLI 13073.
27 15 August 1906. NLI 13073.
28 25 August 1906. NLI 13074. Parry papers.
29 To Gertrude Bannister, 31 May 1906. NLI 13074. Parry papers.
30 14 July 1906. NLI 13074. Parry papers.
31 8 September 1906. NLI 10464. Green papers.
32 21 September 1906. NLI 13074. Parry papers.

CHAPTER 6

1   9 October 1906. NLI 13074. Parry papers.
2   Ibid.
3   24 October 1906. NLI 8612. Hutton papers.
4   To Gertrude Bannister, 12 January 1907. NLI 13074. Parry papers.
5   To Gertrude Bannister, 26 December 1906. NLI 13074. Parry papers.
6   11 December 1906. NLI 14100.
7   To Gertrude Bannister, 26 December 1906. NLI 13074. Parry papers.
8   To Sir Edward Grey, 4 March 1907. NLI 13081.
9   20 April 1907. NLI 10464. Green papers.
10 To Gertrude Bannister, undated. NLI 13074. Parry papers.

11 20 April 1907. NLI 10464. Green papers.
12 Ibid.
13 To E.A.Stopford, 27 June 1907. NLI 10464. Green papers.
14 14 August 1907. NLI 13074. Parry papers.
15 28 August 1907. NLI 13074. Parry papers.
16 A. Alston to Casement, 23 August 1907. NLI 13073.
17 NLI 13073.
18 NLI 13080.
19 15 December 1907. NLI 13073.
20 To Gertrude Bannister, undated, ca. 1 January 1908. NLI 13074. Parry papers.
21 19 December 1907. NLI 13158.
22 4 and 6 January 1908. NLI 13074. Parry papers.
23 4 March 1908. NLI 13080.
24 Ibid.
25 6 March 1908. NLI 13074. Parry papers.
26 To Gertrude Bannister, 28 July 1908. NLI 13074. Parry papers.
27 20 August 1908. NLI 13158. Hobson papers.
28 31 March 1909. NLI 13074. Parry papers.
29 To Gertrude Bannister, 14 April 1909. NLI 13074. Parry papers.
30 To Gertrude Bannister, 31 March 1909. NLI 13074. Parry papers.
31 12 February 1908. NLI 13158. Hobson papers.
32 28 April 1909. NLI 13158. Hobson papers.
33 NLI 15138.
34 To Richard Morten, 3 August 1909. NLI MS unclassified.
35 NLI 15138.
36 2 August 1909. NLI 13074. Parry papers.
37 To Gertrude Bannister, 25 June 1909. NLI 13074. Parry papers.
38 To Bulmer Hobson, 7 September 1909. NLI 13158. Hobson papers.
39 Ibid.
40 To Gertrude Bannister, 6 July 1909. NLI 13074. Parry papers.
41 To Gertrude Bannister, 1 September 1909. NLI 13074. Parry papers.
42 Ibid.
43 Ibid.
44 To Gertrude Bannister, 17 November 1909. NLI 13074. Parry papers.

CHAPTER 7

1 13 January 1910. PRO HO 161.
2 25 January 1910. NLI 13074. Parry papers.
3 To Gertrude Bannister, 21 March 1910. NLI 13074. Parry papers.
4 NLI 15138.
5 27 January 1910. NLI 13076.
6 26 January 1910. NLI 13074. Parry papers.
7 4 July 1910. NLI 8358. Cadbury papers.
8 Leslie to Casement, 22 July 1910. 13086–87.
9 Ibid.
10 8 March 1910. NLI 13086–87.
11 16 July 1910. Diary. PRO HO 161.

12 16 July 1910. NLI 13081.
13 Ibid.
14 22 July 1910. NLI 13086–87.
15 28 July 1910. Diary. PRO HO 161.
16 8 August 1910. NLI 13074. Parry papers.
17 Hardenberg's manuscript, p. 16. NLI 13086–87.
18 Fuller version of Casement's 1910 Putumayo diary, 23 October 1910. NLI 13085–86.
19 Expense account for 1910 investigation. NLI 13086–87.

CHAPTER 8

1 NLI 13085–86.
2 NLI 13085–86.
3 29 September 1910. NLI 13085–86.
4 Ibid.
5 1 October 1910. PRO HO 161.
6 5 October 1910. NLI 13085–86
7 11 October 1910. NLI 13085–86.
8 3 October 1910. NLI 13085–86.
9 4 October 1910. PRO HO 161.
10 See above, pp. 38–40.
11 5 October 1910. PRO HO 161.
12 5 October 1910. PRO HO 161.
13 6 October 1910. PRO HO 161.
14 7 October 1910. NLI 13085–86.
15 7 October 1910. PRO HO 161.
16 8 October 1910. PRO HO 161.
17 8 October 1910. NLI 13085–86.
18 12 October 1910. PRO HO 161.
19 7 October 1910. NLI 13085–86.
20 Ibid.
21 12 October 1910. PRO HO 161.
22 Quotations in this paragraph come from diary entries for 13–15 October 1910. PRO HO 161 and NLI 13085–86.
23 17 October 1910. PRO HO 161.
24 17 October 1910. NLI 13085–86.
25 20 October 1910. PRO HO 161.
26 Ibid. (apparently in error for 21 October).
27 22 October 1910. PRO HO 161.
28 Quotations in this paragraph come from diary entries for 25 and 27 October 1910. NLI 13085–86 and PRO HO 161.
29 29 October 1910. PRO HO 161.
30 31 October 1910. NLI 13085–86.
31 Ibid.
32 Ibid.
33 28 October 1910. NLI 13085–86.
34 2 November 1910. NLI 13085–86.

35   6 November 1910. NLI 13085–86.
36   13 November 1910. PRO HO 161.
37   13 November 1910. NLI 13085–86.
38   14 November 1910. PRO HO 161.

CHAPTER 9

1   16 November 1910. NLI 13085–86
2   Quotations in this paragraph come from diary entries for 17 and 18 November 1910. PRO HO 161.
3   19 November 1910. NLI 13085–86.
4   25 November 1910. NLI 13085–86.
5   26 November 1910. NLI 13085–86.
6   26 November 1910. NLI 13085–86.
7   29 November 1910. NLI 13085–86.
8   2 December 1910. NLI 13085–86.
9   6 December 1910. NLI 13085–86.
10   10 December 1910. PRO HO 161.
11   Quotations in this paragraph come from diary entries for 13–16 December 1910. PRO HO 161.
12   16 December 1910. PRO HO 161.
13   20 December 1910. PRO HO 161.
14   2 January 1911. PRO HO 161.
15   Harris to Casement, 7 January 1911. NLI 13073.
16   Mallet to Casement, 7 January 1911. NLI 13073.
17   9 January 1911. NLI 13086–87.
18   W. Langley to Casement, 18 January 1911. NLI 13081.
19   13, 16 January 1911. PRO HO 161.

CHAPTER 10

1   2 March 1911. NLI 13086–87.
2   30 March 1911. NLI 13073.
3   29 December 1910. NLI 13073.
4   5 August 1910. NLI 13073.
5   30 March 1911. NLI 13073.
6   13 April 1911. NLI 8358. Cadbury papers.
7   To Bulmer Hobson, 19 April 1911. NLI 13158. Hobson papers.
8   26 May 1911. NLI 8358. Cadbury papers.
9   Ibid.
10   2 June 1911. NLI 13073.
11   25 May 1911. Deposit receipt from William Deacon's Bank Ltd. NLI 15138.
12   15 June 1911. NLI 13073. But nothing came of the scheme.
13   15 June 1911. NLI 13081.
14   19 June 1911. PRO FO 95.776.
15   28 June 1911. NLI 13073.
16   20 June 1911. NLI 15138.
17   21 June 1911. NLI 8358. Cadbury papers.
18   21 June 1911. NLI 10464. Green papers.

19   13 July 1911. NLI 10464. Green papers.
20   To Lily Yeats, [10 December 1915]. *The Letters of W. B. Yeats*, p. 604.
21   Travers Buxton to Casement, 13 June 1911. NLI 13073.
22   Later meetings were held on 5 July, 14 July, and 1 August. NLI 15138.
23   19 July 1911. NLI 8358. Cadbury papers.
24   19 July 1911. NLI 13073.
25   To Casement, 24 July 1912. NLI 13073.
26   13 July 1911. NLI 10464. Green papers.
27   31 July 1911. NLI 13073.
28   13 March 1912. NLI 13073.
29   25 July 1911. NLI 13073.
30   To Casement, 24 July 1911. NLI 13080.
31   NLI 13081.
32   20 June 1911. NLI 13086–87.
33   "Life of Roger Casement, Martyr in Ireland's Cause, Told by His Sister," *The Irish Press* (Philadelphia), December 1918.
34   15 July 1911. NLI 13073.
35   16 August 1911. NLI 8358. Cadbury papers.
36   15 August 1911. NLI 13073.

CHAPTER 11

1   5 September 1911. PRO HO 161.
2   7 September 1911. NLI 13080.
3   12 and 13 October 1911. PRO HO 161.
4   To Sir Edward Grey, 23 October 1911. NLI 13081.
5   7 November 1911. NLI 13086–87.
6   2 December 1911. PRO HO 161.
7   30 November 1911. NLI 13086–87.
8   Ibid.
9   4 December 1911. PRO HO 161.
10   On blotter of diary, 5 December 1911. PRO HO 161.
11   6 December 1911. PRO HO 161.
12   9 December 1911. NLI 13074. Parry papers.
13   11–14 December 1911. PRO HO 161.
14   22 December 1911. PRO HO 161.
15   21 December 1911. PRO HO 161.
16   To Gertrude Bannister, 9 December 1911. NLI 13074. Parry papers.
17   12 February 1912. NLI 13081.
18   10 March 1912. NLI 13073.
19   NLI 13086–87.
20   30 January 1912. NLI 13086–87.

CHAPTER 12

1   N.d., received 12 February 1912. NLI 13073.
2   N.d., received 16 February 1912. NLI 13073.

3 26 May 1912. NLI 8358. Cadbury papers.

4 To Cadbury, 29 July 1912. NLI 8358. Cadbury papers.

5 19 June 1912. NLI 13074. Parry papers.

6 25 June 1912. NLI 13074. Parry papers.

7 To Cadbury, 29 July 1912. NLI 8358. Cadbury papers.

8 12 September 1912. NLI 13074. Parry papers.

9 N.d., received 25 June 1912. NLI 13076.

10 29 July 1912. NLI 8358. Cadbury papers.

11 13 August 1912. NLI 13074. Parry papers.

12 Casement's note on expenditures from 1 July to 31 December 1912. NLI 13080.

13 12 December 1912. NLI 13073.

14 20 December 1912. NLI 13086–87.

15 29 July 1911.

16 20 May 1911. NLI 13080.

17 22 September 1912. NLI 13074. Parry papers.

18 24 and 29 October 1912. NLI 13073.

19 Casement to Roberts, 13 November 1912. NLI 13073.

20 20 December 1912. NLI 13073.

21 18 December 1912. NLI 13073.

CHAPTER 13

1 25 March 1912. NLI 13074. Parry papers.

2 12 October 1912. NLI 8358. Cadbury papers.

3 22 November 1912. NLI 13073.

4 8 October 1912. NLI 13074. Parry papers.

5 25 October 1912. NLI 13076.

6 13 December 1912. NLI 13081.

7 15 December 1912. NLI 13086–87.

8 19 December 1912. NLI 13073.

9 15 December 1912. NLI 13073.

10 NLI 13088.

11 Sir Lauder Brunton to Casement, 23 December 1912. NLI 13088.

12 23 December 1912. NLI 13080.

13 Dr. Francis G. Cross to Casement, 14 January 1913. NLI 13088.

14 30 January 1913. NLI 13074. Parry papers.

15 3 February 1913. NLI 13074. Parry papers.

16 2 February 1913. NLI 8358. Cadbury papers.

17 3 February 1913. NLI 13074. Parry papers.

18 17 February 1913. NLI 13088.

19 17 March 1913. NLI 13081.

20 NLI 13073.

21 17 February 1913. NLI 13073.

22 21 March 1913. NLI 13074. Parry papers.

23 21 May 1913. NLI 13073.

24 17 May 1913. NLI 8358. Cadbury papers.

25 Ibid.

26   25 May 1913. NLI 13073.
27   17 May 1913. NLI 8358. Cadbury papers.
28   Morel to Casement, 12 June 1913. NLI 13073.
29   To Cadbury, 11 June 1913, NLI 8358. Cadbury papers.
30   Ibid.
31   Note on letter of 18 June from J. H. Harris. NLI 13073.
32   2 July 1913. NLI 8358. Cadbury papers.
33   26 June 1913. NLI 13074. Parry papers.
34   W. B. Yeats, "Easter 1916."
35   To Alice Stopford Green, 30 May 1913. NLI 10464. Green papers.
36   To Gertrude Bannister, 3 February 1913. NLI 13074. Parry papers.
37   6 June 1913. NLI 13073.
38   26 June 1913. NLI 13074. Parry papers.
39   Casement to Cadbury, 2 July 1913. NLI 8358. Cadbury papers.
40   To Gertrude Bannister, 26 June 1913. NLI 13074. Parry papers.
41   24 June 1913. NLI 13074. Parry papers.
42   26 June 1913. NLI 13074. Parry papers.
43   12 June 1913. NLI 13073.
44   29 June 1913. NLI 13081.
45   29 June 1913. NLI 13080.
46   7 July 1913. NLI 13081.
47   To Casement, 9 July 1913. NLI 13073.
48   3 August 1913. NLI 8358. Cadbury papers.

CHAPTER 14

1   29 September 1913. NLI 10464. Green papers.
2   10 October 1913. NLI 13074. Parry papers.
3   N.d., [September 1913], NLI 10464. Green papers.
4   15 October 1913. NLI 13074. Parry papers.
5   24 October 1913. NLI 13074. Parry papers.
6   To Alice Stopford Green, 29 October 1913. NLI 10464. Green papers.
7   Ibid.
8   Ibid.
9   29 September 1913. NLI 10464. Green papers.
10   Public letter of Hugh Eccles and Robert Hunter, 24 November 1913. NLI
     13089.
11   11 October 1913. NLI 13073.
12   25 October 1913. NLI 13074. Parry papers.
13   1 November 1913. NLI 13073. Casement declined the invitation.
14   11 November 1913, short letter. NLI 10464. Green papers.
15   11 November 1913, long letter. NLI 10464. Green papers.
16   Ibid.
17   Ibid.
18   19 November 1913. NLI 13080.
19   30 November 1913. NLI 10464. Green papers.
20   Ibid.
21   12 December 1913. NLI 13074. Parry papers.

22 To Gertrude Bannister, 19 December 1913. NLI 13074. Parry papers.

23 13 December 1913. NLI 5463.

24 To Alice Stopford Green, 3 January 1914. NLI 10464. Green papers.

25 To Alice Stopford Green, 11 January 1914. NLI 10464. Green papers.

26 To Alice Stopford Green, 30 January 1914. NLI 10464, Green papers.

27 To Alice Stopford Green, 16 January 1914. NLI 10464. Green papers.

28 30 January 1914. NLI 10464. Green papers.

29 2 February 1914. NLI 10464. Green papers.

30 To Alice Stopford Green, 31 January 1914. NLI 10464. Green papers.

31 To Alice Stopford Green, 19 February 1914. NLI 10464. Green papers.

32 Ibid.

33 *Recollections of the Irish War*, p. 11.

34 Hobson, *Ireland Yesterday and Tomorrow*, p. 59; Inglis, *Roger Casement*, pp. 251–54.

35 26 March 1914. NLI 10464. Green papers.

36 Notes to Counsel. NLI 13088.

37 *My Diaries*, ii: 473.

38 16 June 1914. NLI 13080.

39 To Alice Stopford Green, 20 June 1914. NLI 10464. Green papers.

40 Ibid.

41 14 June 1914. NLI 13074.

42 To Alice Stopford Green, 20 June 1914. NLI 10464. Green papers.

43 To Alec Wilson, 16 June 1914. NLI 13080.

44 20 June 1914. NLI 10464. Green papers.

45 Hobson, *Ireland Yesterday and Tomorrow*, p. 52.

46 *Ireland Yesterday and Tomorrow*, p. 60.

47 O'Brien and Ryan, eds., *Devoy's Post Bag*, ii: 458.

48 20 June 1914. NLI 10464. Green papers.

49 29 June 1914. NLI 13073.

CHAPTER 15

1 O'Brien and Ryan, eds., *Devoy's Post Bag*, ii: 459.

2 Material in this paragraph comes from Casement's diary, 7 November 1914. NLI 13082–4.

3 To Devoy, 21 July 1914. *Devoy's Post Bag*, ii: 463.

4 Diary entry, 7 November 1914. NLI 13082–84.

5 29 July 1914. NLI 10464. Green papers.

6 7 November 1914. NLI 13082–84.

7 29 July 1914. NLI 10464. Green papers.

8 7 November 1914. NLI 13082–84.

9 To Alice Stopford Green, 26 July 1914. NLI 10464. Green papers.

10 Ibid.

11 To Alice Stopford Green, 29 July 1914. NLI 10464. Green papers.

12 Ibid.

13 Devoy, *Recollections*, p. 417.

14 26 July 1914. NLI 10464. Green papers.

15 30 July 1914. NYPL. Quinn collection.

16   Casement to Devoy, 31 July 1914. *Devoy's Post Bag*, ii: 465.
17   To Alice Stopford Green, 29 July 1914. NLI 10464. Green papers.
18   15 August 1914. NLI 10464. Green papers.
19   To Alice Stopford Green, 14 September 1914. NLI 10464. Green papers.
20   12 August 1914. NLI 14100.
21   24 August 1914, First letter NYPL. Quinn collection.
22   24 August 1914, Second letter NYPL. Quinn collection. NLI 13089.
23   19 August 1914. NLI 13076.
24   29 August [1914]. NLI 14100.
25   1 September 1914. NLI 13074. Parry papers.
26   14 September 1914. NLI 10464. Green papers.
27   17 September 1914. NLI 10464. Green papers.
28   23 September 1914. NLI 13076.
29   To John Quinn, 18 September 1914. NYPL. Quinn collection.
30   Devoy, *Recollections*, pp. 404–06.
31   21 September 1914. NYPL. Quinn collection.
32   11 October 1914. NLI 10464. Green papers.
33   *Documents Relative to the Sinn Fein Movement*, Cmd. 1108 (1921).
34   See below, p. 389.
35   11 October 1914. NLI 10464. Green papers.
36   29 October 1914. NLI 13073.
37   26 October 1914. NLI 13082. Copy in Casement's hand.
38   Brief to Counsel. NLI 13088.
39   *Devoy's Post Bag*, ii: 468.

CHAPTER 16

1   28 October 1914. NLI 13082–4. Successive quotations come from this account.
2   Letter of 31 October 1914, Telegram of 20 February 1915, and letter of 21 February 1915, all to Sir Arthur Nicolson. PRO FO 95.776.
3   Christensen's deposition, 9 April 1915. NLI 13082–84.
4   31 October 1914. PRO FO 95.776.
5   Christensen's deposition, 9 April 1915. NLI 13082–84.
6   Casement's account, a diary of thirty-one loose sheets. NLI 13082–84.
7   31 October 1914. PRO FO 95.776.
8   Casement's account. NLI 13082–4.
9   Findlay to Sir Edward Grey. PRO FO 95.776.
10   Christensen's deposition, 9 April 1915. NLI 13082–4.
11   Telegram to Sir Arthur Nicolson, 13 February 1915. PRO FO 95.776
12   To Sir Arthur Nicolson, 17 February 1915. PRO FO 95.776.
13   24 February 1915. PRO FO 95.776.
14   21 February 1915. PRO FO 95.776.
15   See below, pp. 380–81, 457, 488–89.
16   Casement's account, 31 October 1914. NLI 13082–4.
17   Ibid.
18   Ibid.

CHAPTER 17

1 Casement's account, 1 November 1914. NLI 13082–4.
2 Casement's account, 2 November 1914. NLI 13082–4.
3 Ibid.
4 Ibid.
5 Ibid.
6 Ibid.
7 René MacColl, *Roger Casement*, pp. 116–117.
8 Casement's account. NLI 13082–4.
9 Ibid.
10 16 November 1914. Manuscript German diary (2 Vols). NLI 1689–90.
11 12 November 1914. NLI 5459.
12 Ibid.
13 Ibid.
14 German diary, 17 November 1914. NLI 1689–90.
15 German diary, 19 November 1914. NLI 1689–90. The account of the rest of
the trip is taken from this entry.

CHAPTER 18

1 PRO FO 95.776.
2 German diary, 24 November, 1914. NLI 1689–90.
3 *Documents Relative to the Sinn Fein Movement*, Cmd. 1108. See below, pp.472–73.
4 German diary, 26 November 1914. NLI 1689–90
5 Ibid.
6 German diary, 30 November 1914, NLI 1689–90.
7 Ibid.
8 NLI 13085.
9 NLI 13082–4.
10 Ibid.
11 See above, pp. 225–26.
12 Letter to Sir Arthur Nicolson, 26 November 1914. PRO FO 95.776.
13 1 December 1914. PRO FO 95.776.
14 *Recollections of the Irish War, passim.*
15 German diary, 1 December 1914. NLI 1689–90.
16 28 November 1914. *Documents Relative to the Sinn Fein Movement*, Cmd. 1108.
17 1 December 1914. NLI 13082–4.
18 German diary, 1 December 1914. NLI 1689–90.
19 *Roger Casement*, p. 120.
20 Ca. 24 February 1915. Facsimile in *Sir Roger Casement's Diaries: His Mission to
Germany and the Findlay Affair*, ed. by Charles E. Curry, pp. 206–07.
21 Casement to Christensen, 2 December 1914. NLI 13082–4.
22 German diary, 3 December 1914. NLI 1689–90.
23 German diary, 4 December 1914. NLI 1689–90.
24 Ibid.
25 German diary, 5 December 1914. NLI 1689–90.

26 German diary, 6 December 1914. NLI 1689–90.
27 Ibid.
28 Ibid.
29 Ibid.
30 Ibid.
31 German diary, 10 December 1914. NLI 1689–90.
32 German diary, 9 December 1914. NLI 1689–90.
33 German diary, 10 December 1914. NLI 1689–90.

CHAPTER 19

1 German diary, 10 December 1914. NLI 1689–90.
2 German diary, 12 December 1914; *Documents Relative to the Sinn Fein Movement*, Cmd. 1108.
3 German diary, 13 and 14 December 1914. NLI 1689–90.
4 German diary, 17 December 1914. NLI 1689–90.
5 German diary, 16 December 1914. NLI 1689–90.
6 Nicolson to Grey, 8 December 1914. PRO FO 95.776.
7 25 November 1914. PRO FO 95.776.
8 Thomson to Nicolson letter, 24 November 1914. PRO FO 95.776.
9 Grey note on Nicolson letter, 27 November 1914. PRO FO 96.776.
10 28 November 1914. PRO FO 95.776.
11 4 December 1914. PRO FO 95.776.
12 Telegram to Sir Arthur Nicolson, 7 December 1914. PRO FO 95.776.
13 German diary, 16 December 1914. NLI 1689–90.
14 German diary, 18 December 1914. NLI 1689–90.
15 Ibid.
16 Ibid.
17 Ibid.
18 Ibid.
19 German diary, 21 December 1914. NLI 1689–90.
20 Ibid.
21 German diary, 24 December 1914. NLI 1689–90.
22 Ibid.
23 25 December 1914. NYPL. Quinn collection.
24 German diary, 8 January 1915. NLI 1689–90.
25 27 December 1914. PRO FO 95.776.
26 German diary, 8 January 1915. NLI 1689–90.
27 3 January 1915. PRO FO 95.776.
28 Casement's undated statement. 1 NLI 13082–4.
29 See above, p. 242.
30 3 January 1915. PRO FO 95.776.
31 Draft. 4 January 1915. PRO FO 95.776.
32 6 January 1915. PRO FO 95.776.

CHAPTER 20

1 28 December 1914. NLI 13085.

2 German diary, 8 January 1915. NLI 1689–90.

3 2 January 1915. NLI 13085.

4 German diary, 3 January 1915. NLI 1689–90.

5 German diary, 5 January 1915. NLI 1689–90.

6 8 January 1915. PRO FO 96.776.

7 To Sir Arthur Nicolson, 10 January 1915. PRO FO 95.776.

8 Christensen's account, 9 April 1915.

9 13 January 1915. PRO FO 95.776.

10 14 January 1915. PRO FO 95.776.

11 German diary, 8 January 1915. NLI 1689–90.

12 German diary, 14 January 1915. NLI 1689–90.

13 Blücher to Casement, 13 January 1915. NLI 13082–4.

14 German diary, 24 January 1915. NLI 1689–90.

15 Devoy to Casement, 1 January 1915. NLI 13073

16 6 January 1915. NLI 13085.

17 German diary, 24 January 1915. NLI 1689–90. The rest of the account is
taken from this entry.

18 German diary, 11 February 1915. NLI 1689–90. Casement's comments
through the end of the episode come from this entry.

19 1 February 1915. PRO FO 95.776.

20 Letter to Father O'Gorman, 5 February 1915. NLI 13082–4.

21 German diary, 11 February 1915. NLI 1689–90.

22 5 February 1915. NLI 13082–4.

23 German diary, 11 February 1915. NLI 1689–90.

24 NLI 13081.

25 Curry, *Sir Roger Casement's Diaries*, p 193.

26 German diary, 11 February 1915. NLI 1689–90.

27 German diary, 17 March 1916. NLI 1689–90.

28 To John Devoy, 20 August 1915. *Devoy's Post Bag*, ii: 474.

CHAPTER 21

1 Note on Casement to Grey, 1 February 1915. PRO FO 95.776.

2 Ibid.

3 Nicolson to Findlay, draft of letter. PRO FO 95.776.

4 13 February 1915. PRO FO 95.776.

5 Nicolson telegram to Findlay, 14 February 1915. PRO FO 95.776.

6 17 February 1915. PRO FO 95.776.

7 Findlay to Nicolson, 17 February 1915. PRO FO 95.776.

8 Nicolson to Findlay, 20 February 1915. PRO FO 95.776.

9 To Nicolson, 21 February 1915. PRO FO 95.776.

10 See Curry, *Sir Roger Casement's Diaries*, pp. 212–13.

11 25 February 1915. PRO FO 95.776.

12 26 October 1914. NLI 5463. See above, p. 000.

13 26 October 1914. NLI 13073.

14 3 December 1914. NLI 13073.

15 18 February 1915. NLI 13085.

16 To Countess Hahn, 22 February 1915. NLI 13085.
17 Curry, *Sir Roger Casement's Diaries*, p. 205.
18 See below, p. 318.
19 15 March 1915. NYPL. Quinn collection.
20 To Casement, 24 March 1915. NLI 13073.
21 26 March 1915. NYPL. Quinn collection.
22 To Quinn, 30 April 1915. Quinn collection.
23 29 May 1915. NYPL. Quinn collection.
24 11 February 1915. PRO FO 95.776.
25 To Father Nicholson, 16 March 1915. NLI 13085.
26 28 March 1915. NLI 13074.

CHAPTER 22

 1 2 April 1915. NLI 13073.
 2 Casement's memorandum book. NLI 12118.
 3 7 May 1915. NLI 13085.
 4 To Casement, 9 May 1915. NLI 13085.
 5 NLI 10999. Plunkett papers.
 6 24 August 1915. NLI 13085.
 7 15 May 1915. NLI 13085.
 8 13 May 1915. NLI 13073.
 9 28 May 1915. NLI 13073.
10 See *Recollections* and *Devoy's Post Bag*, ii, *passim*.
11 28 May 1915. NLI 13073.
12 Richard Meyer to Casement, 22 May 1915. NLI 13085.
13 Casement to Captain H. W. Boehm, 3 July 1915. NLI 13085.
14 9 June 1915. NLI 13085.
15 "A Last Word." NLI 17026. Curry papers.
16 Notes to Counsel. NLI 13088.
17 15 June 1915. NLI 13085.
18 3 July 1915. NLI 13085.
19 NLI 13085.
20 8 August 1915. NLI 13085.
21 *Recollections*, p. 458.
22 To Gaffney, 12 August 1915. NLI 8605.
23 8 August 1915. NLI 13085.
24 To von Wedel, 2 September 1915. NLI 13085.
25 1 August 1915. *Devoy's Post Bag*, ii: 473.
26 2 September 1915. NLI 13085.
27 To Casement, 23 August 1915. NLI 13085.
28 24 August 1915. NLI 13085. See above, p. 296.
29 2 September 1915. NLI 13085.
30 5 September 1915. NLI 13085.
31 *Devoy's Post Bag*, ii: 477–80.
32 25 September 1915. NLI 13073.
33 *Devoy's Post Bag*, ii: 474.
34 "Devoy diary," 28 September 1915. NLI 13085.

35 "Devoy diary," 29 September 1915. NLI 13085.
36 "Devoy diary," 28 September 1915. NLI 13085.

CHAPTER 23

1 *New York Herald*, 25 September 1915.
2 28 August 1915. PRO FO 371.2367.
3 1 October 1915. PRO FO 371.2367.
4 See above, p. 302n.
5 1 November 1915. NLI 8605.
6 To Karstensen (unidentified). 17 November 1915. NLI 8605.
7 *Casement's Last Adventure*, p. 69.
8 Notes to Counsel. NLI 13088.
9 *Casement's Last Adventure*, p. 77.
10 Ibid., p. 80.
11 Ibid., pp. 89–90.
12 Ibid., p. 83.
13 "A Last Word for my true friend Charles Curry," NLI 17026.
14 See above, pp. 000-00.
15 *Casement's Last Adventure*, p. 83.
16 22 August 1915. NLI 13073.
17 Freeman letters. NLI 13073.
18 Devoy to Casement, 21 November 1915. NLI 13073.
19 *Casement's Last Adventure*, p. 102.
20 1 December 1915. NLI 13085.
21 Ibid. Casement's note on letter.
22 2 December 1915. NLI 13085.
23 Casement to von Wedel, 4 December 1915. NLI 13085.
24 "Devoy diary," 29 September 1915. NLI 13085.
25 11 December 1915. NLI 13085.
26 To Casement, 14 December 1915. NLI 13085.
27 Devoy to Casement, 21 November 1915. NLI 13073.
28 19 December 1915. NLI 13073.
29 20 December 1915. NLI 5459.
30 27 December 1915. NLI 17033.
31 Account from notebook left for Gaffney in April 1916. NLI 13085.
32 7 January 1916. NLI 8605.
33 *Casement's Last Adventure*, p. 103.
34 Gaffney notebook. NLI 13085.
35 *Casement's Last Adventure*, p. 103.
36 Ibid., p. 105.
37 Ibid.
38 Ibid., p. 107.
39 "A Last Word for my true friend Charles Curry," 26 March 1916. NLI 17026.

CHAPTER 24

1 Monteith to Nodolny, 24 January 1916. NLI 13085.

2 Monteith to Casement, 24 January 1916. NLI 13085.

3 1 February 1916. NLI 13085.

4 30 January 1916. NLI 13091.

5 "A Last Page," 17 March 1916. NLI 5244.

6 Devoy, *Recollections*, p. 458.

7 *Devoy's Post Bag*, ii: 487. See also *Recollections*, p. 472.

8 See above, p. 309n.

9 20 July 1916. *Devoy's Post Bag*, ii: 504–05.

10 Notes to Counsel. NLI 13088.

11 *Casement's Last Adventure*, p. 134.

12 Ibid., p. 135.

13 Notes to Counsel. NLI 13088.

14 *Casement's Last Adventure*, p. 131.

15 "A Last Page," 17 March 1916. NLI 5244.

16 Ibid.

17 Ibid.

18 23 March 1916. NLI 13085.

19 *Casement's Last Adventure*, p. 131.

20 "A Last Page," 19 March 1916. NLI 5244.

21 "A Last Page," 28 March 1916. NLI 5244.

22 "A Last Page," 29 March 1916. NLI 5244.

23 "A Last Page," 2 April 1916. NLI 5244.

24 "A Last Page," 3 April 1916. NLI 5244. The rest of the account comes from this entry.

25 (New York: n.d.) pp. 130–31.

26 "A Last Page," 3 April 1916. NLI 5244.

27 "A Last Page," 4 April 1916. NLI 5244.

28 "A Last Page," 5 April 1916. NLI 5244.

29 "A Last Page," 6 April 1916. NLI 5244.

30 5 April 1916, NLI 5244; also *Casement's Last Adventure*, p. 139.

31 "A Last Page," 6–8 April 1916. NLI 5244. The rest of the account is taken from these entries.

32 "A Final Word for my True Friend Dr. Curry," 6 April 1916. NLI 17027. Curry papers.

33 Ibid.

34 "A Last Word for my True Friend Dr. Curry," 26 March 1916. NLI 17026. Curry papers.

35 "A Last Page," 7 April 1916. NLI 5244.

36 Ibid.

37 Ibid.

38 "Last Word," 26 March 1916. NLI 17026. The rest of the account comes from this entry.

39 "Final Word," 6 April 1916. NLI 17027

40 Ibid.

41 10 April 1916. NLI 13085.

42 Casement to von Wedel, 11 April 1916. NLI 13085.

CHAPTER 25

1 Brief to Counsel. NLI 13088.
2 Ireland, *The Sea and the Easter Rising*.
3 Devoy, *Recollections*, pp. 462–63.
4 Ireland, *The Sea and the Easter Rising*, p. 15.
5 Ibid., pp. 12–13.
6 Monteith, *Casement's Last Adventure*, p. 151.
7 Ibid., p. 153.
8 25 July 1916. NLI 13077.
9 Monteith, *Casement's Last Adventure*, p. 156.
10 Brief to Counsel. NLI 13088.
11 Notes to Counsel. NLI 13088.
12 Ibid. NLI 13088.
13 Notes to Counsel, 16 May 1916. NLI 13088.
14 Brief to Counsel. NLI 13088.
15 Notes to Counsel. NLI 13088.
16 Father Ryan to George Gavan Duffy, 12 July 1916. NLI 13078.
17 Notes to Counsel. NLI 13088.
18 MacColl, *Roger Casement*, pp. 164–65.
19 Notes to Counsel. NLI 13088.
20 Notes to Counsel, 16 May 1916. NLI 13088.
21 See above, p. 79.
22 Evidence for the Prosecution, 27 June 1916, in Hyde, *Trial of Sir Roger Casement*.
23 Notes to Counsel. NLI 13088.
24 Brief to Counsel. NLI 13088.
25 Evidence for the Prosecution, in Hyde, *Trial of Sir Roger Casement*.
26 Thomson, *The Scene Changes*, p. 274.
27 Brief to Counsel. NLI 13088.
28 Notes to Counsel. NLI 13088.
29 Brief to Counsel. NLI 13088.
30 Ibid.
31 Ibid.
32 Thomson, *The Scene Changes*, p. 101.

CHAPTER 26

1 NLI 7984. Henry papers.
2 Hyde, *Roger Casement*, p. 40.
3 Gertrude Bannister Parry memoir. NLI 13088.
4 Parry memoir. NLI 13088.
5 Alice Stopford Green to General Louis Botha, 16 June 1916. *Devoy's Post Bag*, ii: 501.
6 Parry memoir. NLI 13088.
7 Notes to Counsel. NLI 13088.
8 10 May 1916. NLI 13088.

9 29 May 1916. NLI 8358. Cadbury papers.
10 See above, pp. 287–89.
11 *Devoy's Post Bag*, ii: 495–98; Devoy, *Recollections*, p. 477.
12 Jones, *Without My Wig*, pp. 163–64.
13 Ibid.
14 28 April 1916. PRO FO 371.2851.
15 1 May 1916. PRO FO 371.2851.
16 21 May and 25 May 1916.
17 4 May 1916. PRO FO 371.2851.
18 Hyde, *Roger Casement*, p. 57.
19 16 May 1916. NLI 7984. Henry papers.
20 Notes to Counsel. NLI 13088.
21 Hyde, *Roger Casement*, p. 65.
22 Notes to Counsel. NLI 13088.
23 Notes to Counsel. NLI 13088.
24 Notes to Counsel, 2 June 1916. NLI 13088.
25 Ibid.
26 5 April 1928. NLI 3229.
27 *A Discarded Defence of Roger Casement*, *With an Introduction by Clement Shorter and an Appendix by Roger Casement*, privately printed in 1922 in an edition of twenty-five copies.
28 NLI 13088.

CHAPTER 27

1 London: 1952.
2 I.e., "Ditto." Brief to Counsel. NLI 13088.
3 "The Ghost of Roger Casement," in *Collected Poems* (London: 1959), p. 305; *The Accusing Ghost, or Justice for Casement*.
4 See above, p. 000.
5 10 May 1916. PRO FO 95.776.
6 3 May 1916. PRO FO 371.2844.
7 8 May 1916. PRO FO 371.2844.
8 Ca. 24 February 1915. See above, pp. 302–03.
9 To Laurence de Lacy, 20 July 1916. *Devoy's Post Bag*, ii: 505.
10 Brief to Counsel. NLI 13088.
11 Sir William James, *The Eyes of the Navy*, *passim*.
12 To Dr. William J. Maloney, 4 March 1933. NLI 5388. Maloney papers.
13 Ibid.
14 *The Last Serjeant*, p. 272.
15 Inglis, *Roger Casement*, p. 333.
16 NLI MS. unclassified.
17 Inglis, *Roger Casement*, p. 331.
18 Sullivan, *The Last Serjeant*, p. 270.
19 14 June 1916. NLI 5588.
20 26 May 1916. PRO FO 95.776.
21 30 May 1916. PRO FO 371.2797.

22 11 June 1916. Br. Mus. Add. MS. 46912 M.
23 11 June 1916. NLI 13776.
24 14 June 1916. PRO FO 371.2798.
25 28 July 1916. Quoted in Hyde, *Roger Casement*, p. 149.
26 11 September 1916. PRO FO 371.2798.

CHAPTER 28

1 Inglis, *Roger Casement*, p. 338.
2 NLI 5388. Maloney papers.
3 *Roger Casement*, pp. 87–8.
4 See above, pp. 135–38.
5 *Roger Casement*, p. 95.
6 Notes to Counsel. NLI 13088.
7 Ibid.
8 See above, p. 208.
9 Notes to Counsel. NLI 13088.
10 Ibid.
11 See above, p. 137.
12 Notes to Counsel. NLI 13088.
13 Ibid.
14 Hyde, *Trial*, pp. 133–34.
15 Ibid., p. 151.
16 Hyde, *Roger Casement*, p. 107; MacColl, *Roger Casement*, p. 205.
17 Hyde, *Trial*, pp. 175–76.
18 *The Accusing Ghost*, pp. 123–26.
19 Hyde, *Trial*, p. 185.
20 Quoted in Inglis, *Roger Casement*, p. 346.
21 Hyde, *Roger Casement*, pp. 120–21. MacColl, *Roger Casement*, pp. 210–12.
22 Parry memoir. NLI 7948.

CHAPTER 29

1 Hyde, *Roger Casement*, pp. 124–25.
2 15 July 1916. NLI 10464. Green papers.
3 Geoffrey de C. Parmiter, *Roger Casement*, p. 317.
4 MacColl, *Roger Casement*, pp. 211–12.
5 2 November 1956. NLI 8638.
6 Smith to Grey, 29 June 1916. PRO FO 395.43.
7 Grey to Smith, 29 June 1916. PRO FO 395.43.
8 Grey's minute. 29 June 1916. PRO FO 395.43.
9 Loose sheet. 29 June 1916. PRO FO 395.43.
10 Quotations in this paragraph are from Hyde, *Roger Casement*, pp. 131–33.
11 *The Last Serjeant*, p. 272.
12 19 July 1916. NLI 13075.
13 12 July 1916. NLI 13075.
14 *Devoy's Post Bag*, ii: 499–502.
15 PRO FO 371.2797
16 30 June 1916. NLI 8358. Cadbury papers.

17 Quoted in MacColl, *Roger Casement*, p. 215.
18 27 June 1920. NLI 14100.
19 Elbert Francis Baldwin, "Herbert Ward, Explorer, Sculptor, War Worker," *Outlook*, CXXX (8 February 1922): 227.
20 Hyde, *Roger Casement*, pp. 139–40; Inglis, *Roger Casement*, pp. 359–60.
21 Letter of 24 December 1953 to Alfred Noyes, quoted in MacColl, *Roger Casement*, p. 221.
22 MacColl, *Roger Casement*, p. 239
23 See below, pp. 423, 445.
24 3 July 1916. PRO FO 371.2797.
25 4 July 1916. PRO FO 371.2797.
26 PRO FO 371.2798.
27 30 June 1916. PRO FO 395.43.
28 PRO FO 395.43.
29 Spring-Rice to Newton, 20 July 1916. PRO FO 395.43.
30 *Ibid.*
31 21 July 1916. PRO FO 395.43.
32 22 July 1916. PRO FO 395.43.
33 29 July 1916. PRO FO 395.43.
34 See above, pp. 410–12.
35 30 July 1916. PRO FO 395.43.
36 See below, pp. 456–60.
37 28 July 1916. PRO FO 371.2797.
38 24 July 1916. NLI MS. unclassified.
39 Br. Mus. Ms. 46,083.
40 "In Memory of Eva Gore-Booth and Con Markiewicz," 1927.
41 Parry memoir. NLI 7948.
42 13 July 1916. Br. Mus. Add. Ms. 46,083. Gladstone papers, vol. XCIX.
43 21 July 1916. Br. Mus. Add. MS. 46,083. Gladstone papers, vol. XCIX.
44 Inglis, *Roger Casement*, p. 365.
45 *The Forged Casement Diaries*, pp. 253–54, n. 15.
46 *The Scene Changes*, p. 296 ff.
47 20 July 1916. PRO FO 371.2797.
48 Ibid.
49 24 July 1916. PRO FO 371.2797.
50 Blackwell to Grey, 24 July 1916. PRO FO 371.2797.
51 1 August 1916. PRO FO 371.2798.
52 2 August 1916. PRO FO 371.2798.
53 26 August 1916. PRO FO 371.2798.
54 Ibid.
55 2 January 1933. NLI 5588. Maloney papers.
56 See below, pp. 471–72.
57 27 July 1916. PRO FO 371.2797.
58 Draft in NLI 17028.
59 1 August 1916. PRO FO 371. 2798.
60 His note of that day. PRO FO 371.2797.

CHAPTER 30

1 MacColl, *Roger Casement*, p. 215.
2 To Alice Stopford Green, 15 July 1916, NLI 10464. Green papers.
3 24 July 1916. PRO FO 395.43.
4 See above, p. 351.
5 25–26 July 1916. NLI 13077.
6   Parry memoir. NLI 7948.
7 31 July 1916. NLI 13075.
8 MacColl, *Roger Casement*, p. 227.
9 PRO FO 395.43.
10 NLI 8358. Cadbury papers.
11 Note by Brockway, 31 July 1916. NLI 13088.
12 To Sidney Parry, 30 September 1916. NLI 13075.
13 Gwynn, "Last Weeks," pp. 67–68.
14 See above, p. 4.
15 Hyde, *Roger Casement*, p. 154.
16 Gwynn, "Last Weeks," pp. 63–65.
17 Parry memoir. NLI 7948.
18 Hyde, *Roger Casement*, p. 155.
19 Gwynn, "Last Weeks," pp. 71–72.
20 23 July 1916. PRO FO 395.43.
21 2 August 1916. PRO FO 371.2797.
22 PRO FO 371.2798.
23 Ibid.
24 2 August 1916. PRO FO 371.2798.
25 3 August 1916. PRO FO 371.2798.
26 4 August 1916. PRO FO 371.2798.
27 To Duffy, NLI 13088.
28 Hyde, *Roger Casement*, p. 146.
29 Ibid., p. 54.
30 3 August 1916. PRO FO 371.2798.
31 Jenkins, *Asquith*, p. 403.
32 Quoted in Inglis, *Roger Casement*, pp. 365–66.
33 2 August 1916. NLI 13078.
34 Parmiter, *Roger Casement*, p. 320.
35 Rowland Sperling's minutes of 3 and 5 August 1916. PRO FO 371.2798.
36 7 August 1916. PRO FO 371.2798.
37 5 August 1916. NLI 13088.
38 Noyes, *The Accusing Ghost*, p. 157.
39 5 August 1916. NLI 13088.
40 *Catholic Bulletin*, August 1928.

CHAPTER 31

1 See Hyde, *Roger Casement*, pp. 160–61.

APPENDIX A

1 Hyde, *Roger Casement*, p. 163.
2 3 August 1916. PRO FO 371.2798
3 15 August 1916. PRO FO 371.2798
4 16 August 1916. PRO FO 371.2798.
5 22 August 1916. PRO FO 395.43.
6 See above, pp. 380–81, and below, pp. 488–89.
7 29 June 1916 and 12 August 1916. NYPL. Quinn collection.
8 22 August 1916. NYPL. Quinn collection.
9 15 August 1916. NYPL. Quinn collection.
10 24 August 1916. NYPL. Quinn collection.
11 15 August 1916. NYPL. Quinn collection.
12 To Frederic R. Coudert, 22 August 1916. NYPL. Quinn collection.
13 NLI 13075.
14 Noyes, *The Accusing Ghost*, pp. 26–7.
15 NLI 14100.
16 See above, pp. 93n, 160, and below, pp. 479–80.
17 Inglis, *Roger Casement*, p. 378.
18 10 January 1926. NLI 11488.
19 See below, pp. 484–86.
20 McHugh, *Threshold* (summer 1960), pp. 28–57; Hyde, *Roger Casememt*, pp. 165–80 and Appendix 3; Inglis, *Roger Casement*, pp. 373–88.
21 Noyes, *Accusing Ghost*, pp. 17–18; Inglis, *Roger Casement*, p. 360.
22 MacColl, *Roger Casement*, pp. 225, 237.
23 1 February 1933. NLI 5588. Maloney papers.
24 4 May 1936. NLI 13078.
25 16 May 1938. NLI 5588. Maloney papers.
26 5 September 1910. PRO HO 161.
27 4 May 1936. NLI 13078.
28 To Nina, 27 June 1920. NLI 14100.
29 10 January 1926. NLI 11488.
30 See above, p. 460.
31 Hamblock, *British Consul*, p. 74.
32 *Roger Casement*, p. 225.
33 *The Accusing Ghost*, pp. 164–66.
34 Ibid.
35 See above, p. 264 ff.
36 NLI 5388. Maloney papers.
37 To Nina, 20 June 1920. NLI 14100.
38 See above, pp. 427–30.
39 2 January 1933. NLI 5588. Maloney papers.
40 *Roger Casement*, p. 224.
41 *London Times*, 16 August 1967.
42 *Roger Casement*, p. 224.
43 6 November 1914. Cmd. 1108.
44 NLI 17026.

APPENDIX B

1   *The Accusing Ghost*, p. 101.
2   Ibid., p. 96.
3   10 January 1926. NLI 11488.
4   *The Accusing Ghost*, p. 100.
5   Hyde, *Roger Casement*, p. 173.
6   MLI Ms. unclassified.
7   NLI 13082.
8   See above, p. 28n.
9   See above, pp. 51, 52n.
10   Mackey, *Roger Casement: The Forged Diaries*, p. 61.
11   NLI 15138.
12   29 April 1911. NLI 13073.
13   NLI 14220.
14   Bannister memoir. NLI 7398.
15   PRO FO 371.2844.

A SELECTED BIBLIOGRAPHY

Casement's "black" diaries are held under restricted access in the Public Record Office in London. Much additional manuscript material about him is also held there, in various Home Office and Foreign Office files. His other diaries are held in the National Library of Ireland, together with many letters and other papers. Other particularly useful collections in Dublin are those filed in the names of William A. Cadbury, Alice Stopford Green, Bulmer Hobson, W. J. Maloney, and Gertrude Bannister Parry. Casement's correspondence with John Quinn is held in the New York Public Library.

Bigelow, Poultney, *Seventy Summers*, London, 1925.

Blücher, Princess Evelyn, *An English Wife in Berlin*, New York, [n.d.].

Blunt, Wilfrid Scawen, *My Diaries*, 2 vols., New York, 1932.

Bodkin, Thomas, *Hugh Lane and His Pictures*, Dublin, 1956.

Bulfin, William, *Rambles in Eirann*, Dublin, 1907.

Cadbury, William A., *Labour in Portuguese West Africa*, London, 1910.

Carr, John Dickson, *The Life of Sir Arthur Conan Doyle*, New York, 1949.

Casement, Roger, *The Crime Against Europe: The Writings and Poetry of Roger Casement*, ed. by Herbert O. Mackey, Dublin, 1958.

Caulfield, Max, *The Easter Rebellion*, London, 1964.

Childs, Wyndham, *Episodes and Reflections*, London, 1930.

Colum, Mary, *Life and the Dream*, Garden City, New York, 1947.

Conrad, Joseph, *A Personal Record*, London, 1912.

—————, *Last Essays*, ed. by Richard Curle, London, 1926.

—————, *Heart of Darkness*, ed. by Robert Kimbrough, New York, 1963.

Curry, Charles E., ed., *Sir Roger Casement's Diaries: His Mission to Germany and the Findlay Affair*, Munich, 1922.

Curtis, Edmund, *A History of Ireland*, London, 1957.

Devoy, John, *Recollections of an Irish Rebel*, rpt, Shannon, 1969.

Dickey, Herbert Spencer, *The Misadventures of a Tropical Medico*, New York, 1929.

Figgis, Darrell, *Recollections of the Irish War*, New York, [n.d.]

Fitzgerald, Desmond, *Cry Blood, Cry Erin*, New York, 1966.

Gaffney, T. St. John, *Breaking the Silence*, New York, 1930.

Glave, E. J. G., *Six Years of Adventure in Congo-Land*, London, 1903.

Green, Alice Stopford, *The Making of Ireland and Her Undoing*, London, 1908.

——————, *Irish Nationality*, London, 1911.

Gwynn, Denis, *The Life and Death of Roger Casement*, London, 1936.

——————, "Roger Casement's Last Weeks," *Studies*, LIV (Spring 1965).

Gwynn, Stephen, *Experiences of a Literary Man*, London, 1926.

Hambloch, Ernest, *British Consul*, London, 1938.

Hardenburg, W. E., *The Putumayo*, London, 1912.

Hobson, Bulmer, *Ireland Yesterday and Tomorrow*, Tralee, 1968.

Holt, Cecil R., ed., *The Diary of John Holt with the Voyage of the "Maria,"* Liverpool, 1948.

Hyde, H. Montgomery, *The Trial of Roger Casement*, London, 1960.

——————, *Roger Casement*, London, 1964.

——————, *The Other Love*, London, 1970.

Inglis, Brian, *The Story of Ireland*, London, 1956.

——————, *Roger Casement*, London, 1973.

Ireland, John de Courcy, *The Sea and the Easter Rising*, Dublin, 1966.

James, William, *The Eyes of the Navy*, London, 1955.

Jean-Aubry, Gérard, *Joseph Conrad: Life and Letters*, 2 vols., London, 1927.

Jenkins, Roy, *Asquith*, London, 1964.

Jones, Thomas Artemus, *Without My Wig*, Liverpool, 1944.

Kain, Richard M., *Dublin in the Age of William Butler Yeats and James Joyce*, Norman, Oklahoma, 1962.

Kossuth, Ludwig, *Meine Schriften aus der Emigration*, 3 vols, Leipzig, 1882.

Leslie, Shane, *The Irish Issue in Its American Aspect*, London, 1919.

——————, *Long Shadows*, Wilkes-Barre, Pennsylvania, 1967.

Lynch, Florence Monteith, *The Mystery Man of Banna Strand*, New York, 1959.

Lynd, Robert, *Ireland a Nation*, London, 1919.

MacBride, Maud Gonne, *A Servant of the Queen*, London, 1938.

MacColl, René, *Roger Casement*, London, 1956.

MacDowell, R. B., *Alice Stopford Green: A Passionate Historian*, Dublin, 1967.

McGarrity, Joseph, *Celtic Moods and Memories*, Dublin, 1938.

McHugh, Roger, "Casement; The Public Record Office Manuscripts," *Threshold*, Summer 1960.

——————, ed., *Dublin 1916*, New York, 1966.

Mackey, Herbert O., *Roger Casement: The Forged Diaries*, Dublin, 1966.

Maloney, William J., *The Forged Casement Diaries*, Dublin, 1936.

Mansergh, Nicholas, *The Irish Question*, London, 1965.

Martin, F. X., ed., *Leaders and Men of the Easter Rising: Dublin 1916*, Ithaca, New York, 1967.

Merchant Adventure (John Holt and Company), Liverpool, [n.d.].

Monteith, Robert, *Casement's Last Adventure*, Dublin, 1953.

Morel, Edmond Dene, *King Leopold's Rule in Africa*, London, 1904.

————, *Red Rubber*, London, 1906.

Nevinson, Henry Woodd, *Last Changes, Last Chances*, London, 1958.

Noyes, Alfred, *Two Worlds for Memory*, London and New York, 1953.

————, *The Accusing Ghost, or Justice for Casement*, London, 1957.

O'Brien, William, and Desmond Ryan, eds., *Devoy's Post Bag 1871–1928*, 2 vols., Dublin, 1953.

O'Connor, Frank, ed., *A Book of Ireland*, London, 1959.

————, *My Father's Son*, London, 1968.

O'Connor, Ulick, *Oliver St. John Gogarty: A Poet and His Times*, London, 1964.

O'Faolain, Sean, *The Irish: A Character Study*, New York, 1949.

————, *Vive Moi!*, Boston, 1964.

O'Hegarty, P. S., *A Bibliography of Roger Casement*, Dublin, 1949.

Parmiter, Geoffrey de C., *Roger Casement*, London, 1936.

Pritchett, V. S., *Dublin: A Portrait*, New York, 1967.

Puleston, Fred., *African Drums*, London, 1930.

Reid, B. L., *The Man from New York: John Quinn and His Friends*, New York, 1968.

Rudkin, David, "The Chameleon & the Kilt," *Encounter*, XLI (August 1973).

Shearman, Hugh, *Anglo-Irish Relations*, London, 1948.

Sheehan, Daniel D., *Ireland Since Parnell*, London, 1921.

Singleton-Gates, Peter, and Maurice Girodias, *The Black Diaries: An Account of Roger Casement's Life and Times with a Collection of His Diaries and Public Writings*, Paris, 1959.

Spindler, Karl, *Gun Running for Casement in the Easter Rebellion, 1916*, London, 1921.

Starkie, Walter, *Scholars and Gypsies: An Autobiography*, London, 1963.

Sullivan, Alexander Martin, *The Last Serjeant*, London, 1952.

Thompson, William Irwin, *The Imagination of an Insurrection: Dublin, Easter 1916*, New York, 1967.

Thomson, Basil, *Queer People*, London, 1922.

————, *The Scene Changes*, London, 1939.

Ussher, Arland, *The Face and Mind of Ireland*, New York, 1950.

Ward, Herbert, *Five Years with the Congo Cannibals*, London, 1890.

_____, *A Voice from the Congo*, London, 1910.

Yeats, John Butler, *Letters to His Son W. B. Yeats and Others*, ed. by Joseph
    Hone, London, 1944.

Yeats, William Butler, *Collected Poems*, New York, 1951.

_____, *Letters of W. B. Yeats*, ed. by Allan Wade, New York, 1955.

Index

521